From Maubeuge to the Rhineland

A History of the 1st Division in the Great War

Simon Peaple

 Helion & Company

To Thomas and Edward of whom I am so proud …

Helion & Company Limited
Unit 8 Amherst Business Centre
Budbrooke Road
Warwick
CV34 5WE
England
Tel. 01926 499 619
Email: info@helion.co.uk
Website: www.helion.co.uk
Twitter: @helionbooks
Visit our blog at blog.helion.co.uk

Published by Helion & Company 2023
Designed and typeset by Mary Woolley (www.battlefield-design.co.uk)
Cover designed by Paul Hewitt, Battlefield Design (www.battlefield-design.co.uk)

Text © Simon Peaple 2023
Images © as individually credited
Maps drawn by George Anderson © Helion & Company Ltd 2023

Every reasonable effort has been made to trace copyright holders and to obtain their permission for the use of copyright material. The author and publisher apologize for any errors or omissions in this work, and would be grateful if notified of any corrections that should be incorporated in future reprints or editions of this book.

ISBN 978-1-912866-20-5

British Library Cataloguing-in-Publication Data.
A catalogue record for this book is available from the British Library.

All rights reserved. No part of this publication may be reproduced, stored in a retrieval system, or transmitted, in any form, or by any means, electronic, mechanical, photocopying, recording or otherwise, without the express written consent of Helion & Company Limited.

For details of other military history titles published by Helion & Company Limited contact the above address or visit our website: http://www.helion.co.uk.

We always welcome receiving book proposals from prospective authors.

Contents

List of Illustrations		v
List of Maps		vi
Glossary		vii
Acknowledgements		viii
Introduction		ix
1	Mobilisation	15
2	From Mons to Etreux	19
3	The Munsters at Etreux	21
4	From Etreux to the Ourcq	31
5	Advance to the Aisne	33
6	Aisne: Advance to Contact.	39
7	The Fateful 13th?	43
8	Battle for the Chemin Des Dames, 14 September 1914	46
9	Genesis of Trench Warfare	57
10	In Flanders Fields: An Encounter Battle	69
11	Lomax's Final Triumph	80
12	Gheluvelt, 29 October 1914	83
13	Gheluvelt: Second Day	91
14	Gheluvelt: Third Day – Morning	93
15	Gheluvelt: Third Day – Late Afternoon	100
16	First Ypres: Tested to Destruction	104
17	First Ypres: The Final Stint	128
18	1st Division in Late November 1914	131
19	Defending the La Bassée Canal	133
20	Aubers Ridge	140
21	Divisional Re-organisation and Departure of the Guards	152
22	Loos: Preparations for Battle	157
23	Loos: Battle	163
24	Christmas in the Line, 1915-16	171
25	Maintaining the Entente Cordiale	177
26	Loos Trenches	183
27	The Double Crassier	186

28	Contalmaison, Mametz Wood and Pozières	190
29	High Wood and Morval	200
30	Winter, 1916-17	210
31	The Daily Grind: January to May 1917	213
32	Operation Hush	220
33	BEF Training	230
34	Third Ypres: Second Battle of Passchendaele	233
35	Lull Before the Storm	240
36	A Successful Defence	243
37	Aggressive Defence	250
38	Training Under Maxse	259
39	Semi-Open Warfare	262
40	The Hindenburg Line	279
41	Final Push	285
42	Occupation of Germany	294
43	The Post-War British Officer Corps	299
44	A Last Hurrah	301

Appendices:
I	Planning a War	305
II	Who ordered the counter-attack that restored the British position at Gheluvelt, 31 October 1914?	310
III	BEF Divisional Command – 1st Division as a Snapshot	312
IV	Availability of Artillery Ammunition During First Ypres	314

| Select Bibliography | 317 |
| Index | 320 |

List of Illustrations

Major General S.H. Lomax (seated far right), King George V, Queen Mary and Lieutenant-General Sir Douglas Haig amongst others at Aldershot. (*The Sphere*, 30 May 1914).	I
Troyon Spur. Note the steep slope and excellent field of fire. (Sheree Peaple)	I
Chivy terrain illustrates the difficulties encountered by 1st Division. (Sheree Peaple)	II
Hooge Chateau. (Private collection)	II
Major General Sir D. Henderson. (Open source)	III
Major General Sir R.C.B. Haking. (Open source)	III
1st Black Watch headquarters, Givenchy May 1915. (Private collection)	III
Major General A.E.A Holland. (Open source)	III
The 2nd Royal Munster Fusiliers at Hulluch. (*The Sphere*, 15 July 1916)	IV
Major General E.P. Strickland. (Open source)	V
High Wood and vicinity, August 1916. (TNA WO 95/1275: 2 Brigade War Diary)	VI
Operation Hush: Assault pier and monitors. (Bacon, *The Dover Patrol*, Vol. I)	VII
Operation Hush: Assault pier interior. (Bacon, The Dover Patrol, Vol. I)	VII
Operation Strandfest: 1st Division captive officers and men marching through Brugge, July 1917. (Private collection)	VII
Vat Cottages and vicinity from the air, Passchendaele November 1917. (McMaster University)	VIII
Captain A.H.H. Batten-Pooll VC, captured at Passchendaele on 10 November 1917. (Open source)	VIII
1st Black Watch roll call, Lapugnoy, 10 April 1918. (Private collection)	IX
Duke of Connaught inspecting 1st Northamptonshire Regiment, 2nd Brigade, Bruay, 1 July 1918. (Open source)	IX
Lock No. 1, Sambre Canal. (Open source)	X
Lieutenant Colonel Johnson VC and Runner Sergeant Brown DCM, MM. (Open source)	X

List of Maps

Etreux, 27 August 1914.	22
Chemin des Dames, September 1914.	47
Gheluvelt, 31 October 1914 counterattack.	101
Aubers Ridge, 9 May 1915.	141
Loos, September--October 1915.	156
Munster Alley, July-August 1916.	195
Morval, 25-28 September 1916.	201
Nieuport, 10-11 July 1917.	221
Passchendaele, 10 November 1917.	234
Sambre--Oise, November 1918.	286

Glossary

BEF	British Expeditionary Force
BGGS	Brigadier General General Staff – senior staff officer (often a specialist)
C-in-C	Commander-in-Chief
CO	Officer commanding a unit, e.g., a lieutenant colonel in charge of a battalion.
GQG	Grand Quartier Generale or French High Command
CQMS	Company Quarter Master Sergeant
CRA	Commander Royal Artillery – senior artillery officer (usually refers to a division)
CRE	Commander Royal Engineers – senior engineer officer (usually refers to a division)
DCM	Distinguished Conduct Medal – higher gallantry award for other ranks
DSO	Distinguished Service Order – higher gallantry award for officers (occasionally reflected cumulative service)
GHQ	General Headquarters – collective term for the central command of the BEF
OC	Officer actually commanding a unit, e.g. a Lieutenant in temporary command of a battalion.
OR(s)	Other Rank(s) regularly employed in casualty summaries to denote all non-officer casualties. Also used in summarising constitution of patrols and raiding groups.
GOC	General Officer Commanding e.g. a Major General commanding a division
GSO	General Staff Officer Grade 1 – senior divisional staff officer
MID	Mentioned in Despatches – a mention by the CinC in his reports to the government.
MM	Military Medal – gallantry award for other ranks
MC	Military Cross – gallantry award for officers
MGC	Machine Gun Corps
RA	Royal Artillery
RAMC	Royal army Medical Corps
RGA	Royal Garrison Artillery
RHA	Royal Horse Artillery
RE	Royal Engineers
RFC	Royal Flying Corps
RSM	Regimental Sergeant Major
SAA	Small Arms Ammunition i.e. – bullets for rifles and machine guns.
TMB	Trench Mortar Battery
VC	Victoria Cross

Acknowledgements

Duncan Rogers, as publisher, and Dr Michael LoCicero, as editor, shared a vision that it was right that divisions without histories should have one. Divisions were the smallest all-arms units from which corps and armies were created. My first book was on the 46th North Midland Division; an unfashionable first-line Territorial division. Duncan and Michael then approached me to write a history of the 1st Division which mobilised at the start of the conflict and finished as part of the British forces occupying the Rhine. I am extremely grateful to them for their faith in me; and, their kindness to an author who was juggling, not always very successfully, numerous commitments. The friendship they have extended to me has been more than generous. Michael played a crucial role in recognising that an earlier version of the book, within the original word limit, was not up to the standard. By expanding the word limit and giving me more time, he enabled it to improve it considerably.

I am extremely grateful to Sheree. Not only has she been my wife and best friend for over 38 years, but she also undertook to read the whole book during its preparation. As a lawyer and linguist, she provided an invaluable second opinion on my overly long sentences and use of terminology. She originally trained as a solicitor and her ability to pick up on detail eliminated many errors as she proof-read the draft text and made sure my erratic style of footnotes took on an ordered appearance. Her herculean efforts are a monument to her utter selflessness. Any errors that remain are mine.

Introduction

On 23 August 1980, I was being guided around Mons by the late John Giles who went on to establish the Western Front Association. Little did I realise that four decades later I would be writing a history of 1st Division who had been present, albeit in a supporting role. Like many others, I had decided to go on a tour because my grandfather, Henry Edward Peaple, had served on the Western Front. He was a driver in the Royal Army Service Corps from 1915 to 1918. After the war he worked as a clerk at the Royal College of Music and painted in his spare time. Like many veterans, he did not talk much about the war, but he did tell me how they punched the mules in the mouth to stop them braying. He also said that at "Hell Fire Corner" you knew to wait for the signal then go as fast as you could. It was only later that I understood what he meant when he said he did not fear being wounded. If a shell had struck the ammunition boxes behind him, he would have ended up on the memorial to the missing.

Before the tour, I had read Liddell Hart's *History of the First World War*.[1] Therefore, I thought I had a picture of what had happened though few students today would be directed to his work. My own introduction to the academic study of the Great War came when I attended an Open Day at Birmingham University. My wife, noting that I still read, History books, almost exclusively, had encouraged me to undertake further study and thus I met Dr John Bourne. He introduced me to the concept of the "Learning Curve" and suggested that a study of 46th Division would both fill a gap and provide useful evidence to evaluate the theory. We agreed I would enrol for an MPhil initially, but the depth of evidence available meant that it evolved into a doctoral thesis. I probably merit the title of "most frustrating student", who graduated, as I was juggling work and local politics including taking a year off to be Mayor of Tamworth. However, with his support and guidance the thesis was completed and subsequently published by Helion as *Mud, Blood and Determination*. Delighted as I was to see the book published eventually, looking back, I would have been wiser to have followed John's advice and published some articles first. The thesis and book stand as strong evidence for the Learning Curve perspective. This view argues that after the difficulties and defeats of earlier years, the British Army of 1918 had learnt lessons and developed appropriate tactical and operational methods. Therefore, by the summer of 1918, the British Army was an effective fighting force. Thus the British imperial land forces were instrumental in bringing the German empire to the negotiating table, that resulted in the Armistice on 11 November 1918.

---

1 B. H. Liddell Hart, *History of the First World War* (London: Pan, 1970).

Historiography

Amongst the academic community, the idea that the British Army underwent a "Learning Curve" has become the new orthodoxy. The recognition that it was neither continuous nor even is also widely understood. This is reflected in Clayton's *Decisive Victory*[2] which addresses two themes. The first being the decisiveness of the attack on the Sambre in the context of the war coming to a close. The second, is the relative performance of the divisions; with a clear recognition that some performed better than others and may be judged therefore to have progressed further down the learning curve.

There remain some key areas of debate with the role of Haig as commander-in chief being one of them. John Terraine's *Douglas Haig: he Educated Soldier*[3] successfully challenged the idea that Haig was simply a Colonel Blimp-like cavalry commander throwing lives away. However, this reassessment of Haig was less convincing when it came to 1917 and especially Passchendaele. Terraine's subsequent tome *The Road to Passchendaele* succeeded in making clear that Haig's contemporary critic, Lloyd-George also shared the blame.[4] Nonetheless, it leaves Haig in a more crowded dock rather than exonerating him. Further revisions to our understanding of this iconic battle have come from Lloyd's *Passchendaele* and from Prior & Wilson's *Passchendaele: The Untold Story*.[5] The latter's earlier study on Rawlinson having done much to substantiate the idea of a learning curve. The key changes to our understanding on Passchendaele revolve around the extent to which the early stages of Plumer's time in charge saw the application of a methodology akin to the "100 Days" of 1918. These works support the thrust of Sheffield's carefully argued biography of Haig which offers a much stronger case for Haig in 1917 and 1918. However, to my mind at least, this does not exonerate Haig's two egregious errors regarding the appointment of Gough and the decision to throw away so many lives seizing Passchendaele village in the final phase.

Therefore, now the academic debates take place within the paradigm created by the learning curve thesis. Not inappropriately, one debate focuses upon when progress on the learning curve started. Excellent volumes such as *Courage Without Glory*[6] offer evidence that learning may have commenced sooner, in 1915, rather than in 1916 as argued in Sheffield's *Somme to Victory*.[7] The apparently universal derision of Sir John French's time in command means that it is unlikely that signs of learning prior to his dismissal will be identified or at least will not be seen to be linked to GHQ. The role of GHQ is also challenged in the corpus of work on the French contribution written by Elizabeth Greenhalgh. Most notably, perhaps, *Foch in Command*,[8] which challenges the British-centric view of victory.

---

2   Derek Clayton, *Decisive Victory* (Warwick: Helion, 2018), passim.
3   John Terraine, *Douglas Haig: The Educated Soldier* (London: Hutchinson, 1963), passim.
4   John Terraine, *The Road to Passchendaele* (London: Leo Cooper, 1977), passim.
5   Nick Lloyd, *Passchendaele* (London: Penguin, 2017), Robin Prior & Trevor Wilson, *Passchendaele: The Untold Story* (London: Yale University Press, 2016), passim.
6   Spencer Jones (ed.), *Courage Without Glory: The British Army on the Western Front 1915* (Warwick: Helion, 2015), passim.
7   Gary Sheffield, *Douglas Haig: From the Somme to Victory* (London: Aurum, 2016), passim.
8   Elizabeth Greenhalgh, *Foch in Command* (Cambridge: Cambridge University Press, 2013), passim.

The second area of debate relates to the extent to which the new style permeated the British Army. One of the reasons for my original study of 46th Division was that it was a first-line territorial division which pulled off a stunning assault on the Hindenburg Line. The evidence there supported the learning curve. At the Hohenzollern Redoubt in 1915, the 46th's task was conceptually flawed. In 1916 at the Somme, 46th Division underperformed versus its neighbour, and it failed again in Lens in 1917. The detailed evidence of the assault on the Hindenburg Line showed that changes had been made. Mitchinson's *Of No Earthly Use* has extended this analysis further to cover second-line Territorial formations.[9]

The gap between the academic community and public perceptions about the First World War remains considerable. Then Education Secretary, Michael Gove, accused left-wing teachers of regurgitating myths based on the *Blackadder* series. Historian Annika Mombauer recently remarked that no serious historian entertained the "Lions led by Donkeys" view portrayed in the show. Neither was addressing the real point. Time means that the First World War has become distant and so it is brought centre stage only on certain occasions; primarily on Remembrance Day. This, however, means the focus is on remembrance and therefore on those who died. Therefore, there is no attempt to contextualise death within consequent victories.

Prior to COVID, thousands of pupils per year were being taken to the Western Front. However, the visitor centres geared up for receiving coachloads of young people are situated in the Somme and Ypres, redolent of slaughter. The exception of the tunnels at Vimy Ridge demonstrates how popular success could be if appropriately supported. If the perception of the war is to be refocused on the "100 Days" then there needs to be a way of doing that whilst providing thought provoking activities for young people at those sites. Modern Britain is more diverse culturally and more work needs to be done to recognise this as well as the role of women during the Great War.

From Maubeuge to the Rhine

Writing a history of 1st Division poses a number of different challenges. As it was in action from the beginning it appears to contradict the learning curve as it was generally perceived to be excellent at the outset and very good, but perhaps not better, at the end. However, the 1st Division was effectively reduced to a cadre by the end of 1914. Therefore, it was forced to re-learn the lessons from a narrow base of experience in the bloody assaults at Aubers Ridge and Loos in 1915. It returned to the fray in the latter stages of the Somme after the New Army divisions had been blooded. Here, its experience falls within the debate about when the learning process began. In 1917 1st Division suffered a sharp reverse on the Lys and is later thrown into the final phase of Third Ypres. By late 1918, 1st Division were demonstrating that they were a successful formation. Success at the Sambre rounded off their final campaign.

The primary sources are the war diaries of the various combat units and support services. In addition, the diaries of the command staffs provide context. Whilst much of the detail relates to battles, there is also coverage of periods spent holding trenches and training. Most offer contemporaneous evidence, though the early months of some diaries had to be reconstructed. This was because some diaries were destroyed during the fighting at Ypres. The variety of

---

9 K.W. Mitchinson, *Of No Earthly Use* (Warwick: Helion, 2021), passim.

records, and their status, mean that details of officers survive more fully. I have therefore often coupled the details of dead leaders with those from the ranks who fell with them. I believe this reflects the mutual regard in which those who served held each other. My hope is that taken as a whole the book provides an overall feel for what it would have been like to serve in the 1st Division, both in combat and in the line.

Part I

The Original 1st Division – Some of the "Old Contemptibles" 1914

1

Mobilisation

In conformity with the pre-war military discussions, the British Expeditionary Force (BEF) was to be deployed to the left of what would be officially designated the French Fifth Army.[1] The British I Corps was allocated the traditional position of honour on the right of the British line and would therefore have the French to its right and the British II Corps to its left.

The process of mobilisation is designed to transfer military forces from their peacetime positions to where they are required now that war has been declared. The BEF was to be formed of infantry divisions forming the Aldershot command in peacetime. Thus, the procedures for mobilisation involved moving them from Aldershot to the designated concentration area in the vicinity of Maubeuge. Maubeuge is a town in France, close to the border with Belgium and was seen as the right place to gather (concentrate) the BEF before they advanced into action. Some units designated for inclusion in the BEF were stationed elsewhere so they too had to be moved from their bases via southern ports to France.

In the absence of conscription, the mobilisation of the BEF involved some different aspects to its continental allies and opponents. The British Army was considerably smaller than its continental counterparts and was organised to defend the Empire. The German Army had the potential to raise 3.8 million men in 1914 and mobilised just over 2 million initially. The British Army consisted of 250,000 men, of whom approximately half were stationed overseas. These men were therefore several weeks away by sea. Furthermore, the battalions in the UK were under strength as the overseas battalions had priority for the available manpower. The Army Reserve, ex-soldiers on a retainer who did 12 days training per year, numbered 145,000. The Special Reserve consisted of 64,000 men, who had done 6 months basic training and had done 3-4 weeks training per year thereafter.[2] Therefore, even the plan to send a BEF 100,000 strong was ambitious. Due to uncertainty over the situation in Ireland, the initial deployment was reduced to 80,000. It might be thought that with approximately 325,000 men available to call upon, more could have been despatched initially. However, inevitably, not everyone was fit for the rigours of overseas service. In addition, the shortage of trained staff officers to organise and command the troops, would have complicated expanding the BEF further initially. Although

---

1   For a detailed discussion of the background to this decision, see Appendix I.
2   Hutchinson, D., *Mons: An Artillery Battle* (Warwick: Helion, 2018), p.13 presents these figures and a detailed discussion of the artillery in particular.

the requisitioning of horses etcetera had been planned in detail, these plans were based upon the anticipated numbers of men and units.[3]

Following the orders for mobilisation being issued, the units of the BEF were brought to war strength before being transported to France. The 9th Battalion King's Liverpool Regiment (9th KLR) were mobilising in Woking[4], unaware that they would join 2nd Brigade in the future. Their diary reveals that "owing to rumours" all the specialists (skilled men such as signallers) and those leaving the battalion were medically inspected first and that the rest of the men were inspected by the doctors on the following day. The diary also records that as much of the day one paperwork that could be done was done; and, that the company rolls, and forms were amended to reflect all the changes. Clearly, work at the depot was a bit behind schedule as the first party of reservists, 386 out of an expected 400, arrived at 1a.m. on 6 August 1914 and so they were accommodated and distributed to companies "after Reveille".[5]

That not everything went smoothly for those in charge of the battalions designated for the 1st Division of the BEF, is exemplified by the experience of 1st Battalion of the Black Watch (1st Black Watch). On 5 August 1914, there was no civilian labour provided by the Board of Trade, except for shoesmiths, and two saddles arrived but no horses.[6] On the following day, the battalion received 302 reservists from the depot, but no horses. Two tailors and three shoemakers did appear, the former were sent away as they were "useless".[7] The following day saw another 308 reservists arrive, but apparently their documentation was in a confused state due to the need for all reservists to report on day one. Apparently, the depot enabled the men to all be received on the due date by not insisting on completing all the correct forms. That day also saw the long-awaited arrival of the horses. But it was then discovered that the head collars were the wrong size which necessitated finding new ones.[8]

The 1st Battalion South Wales Borderers (1st South Wales Borderers) received 580 reservists; this is a reconstructed diary but presumably depot records were of assistance here.[9] A similar proportion of men in the 2nd Battalion King's Royal Rifle Corps (2nd KRRC) would be drawn from reservists, as 604 other ranks were with the battalion on 5 August but six were declared medically unfit and a further 161 were unfit for active service on age grounds. Therefore when, the following day, the battalion received 563 reservists from the depot, they would have outnumbered the regulars fit for overseas service. The battalion was more fortunate than some of the others in 1st Division when it received 51 horses on 6 August to bring it up to war establishment.[10] Despite this progress, the battalion still received an order cancelling the entrainment expected for the next day as specified in the mobilisation schedule. The battalion was also ordered to send one captain, two subalterns and fifteen sergeants and corporals to

---

3   Jones, S., (ed), *Stemming the Tide* (Solihull: Helion, 2013), pp 20-21 offers a detailed discussion on the senior command issue.
4   A commuter town on the Waterloo to Portsmouth line, coincidentally where the author grew up from the age of 2.
5   The National Archives (TNA) WO 95/1269: War Diary of 9th Battalion King's Liverpool Regiment, 2-6 August 1914.
6   TNA WO 95/1263: War Diary of the 1st Battalion Black Watch, 5 August 1914.
7   TNA WO 95/1263: War Diary of the 1st Battalion Black Watch, 6 August 1914.
8   TNA WO 95/1263: War Diary of the 1st Battalion Black Watch, 7 August 1914.
9   TNA WO 95/1280: War Diary of the 1st Battalion South Wales Borderers, 5-6 August 1914.
10 TNA WO 95/1272: War Diary of the 2nd King's Royal Rifle Corps, 5-6 August 1914.

the depot at Winchester to help train a "new unit"; the places being filled by those "slightly underage". In addition, each man's basic kit was to be reduced by one pair of boots.[11] As it would take time to train the new units, removing boots from the men about to fight should have been recognised as folly *ab initio*.

The figures for reservists mean they represented approximately 60 per cent of the battalion's war strength.[12] Part of the mythology of World War One is the idea of a wonderful regular army sacrificed in 1914 whilst the wisely all-seeing Kitchener recruited a new army of volunteers who were then sacrificed at the Somme. This exaggerates the difference between 1914 battalions with 40% regulars and 1916 battalions with perhaps 75% volunteers. A distinction which is further blurred by units such as 36th Division. That division consisted of unionists, many of whom had served in the army previously or had undergone training with the Ulster Volunteers. Equally, many men in 16th Division had army experience or had trained with the Irish Citizen Army. Simkins's scholarship identified characteristics in New Army recruits, but this has gained limited traction in the popular mind.[13]

On 8 August 1914, the 2nd KRRC were addressed by their Colonel Commandant, Lieutenant General Sir Edward Hutton, who had been commissioned into the regiment in 1867, and would be recalled from retirement in 1914 to take command of 21st Division. It was clear that the battalion was unlikely to be moved for a few days so twelve officers and 363 "younger soldiers" were inoculated against enteric fever. Particular emphasis was placed upon instructing the reservists and getting them to practise their musketry.[14] In contrast, the 1st South Wales Borderers made sure that every man in the battalion was practising musketry; 100 yards (grouping) and 300 yards (slow and rapid).[15] In addition, the officers sent to the depot were not being replaced and so their total was fixed at 26, whilst the Sergeant Master Tailor was sent to the depot. On 11 August, following a brigade route march in the morning, the brigade was inspected by the King and Queen. On 12 August, the battalion was entrained in two trains at Frimley station and subsequently embarked upon its voyage to France aboard the *Galeka*, a Union Castle Line vessel. Their subsequent arrival at Le Havre was followed by a five-mile march to the rest camp, where they were joined by two French soldiers to act as interpreters. The war would see many fatigue parties created; the first fatigue parties were left to carry out the unloading.[16] The 1st South Wales Borderers, having sailed across to Le Havre in the *Braemar Castle* with the 2nd battalion of the Welsh Regiment, also marched to camp but noted that the transport had to be diverted via another route, as the route taken by the infantry was too steep.

At 10 a.m. on 14 August 1914, the 1st South Wales Borderers were paraded and, after the King's message had been read out and accorded three cheers, they were addressed by their CO. After several days of company training, the 1st Black Watch, as part of 1st Brigade, were inspected by George V.[17] The King also visited 2nd Brigade Headquarters and said goodbye to the two

---

11 TNA WO 95/1272: War Diary of the 2nd King's Royal Rifle Corps, 7 August 1914.
12 For an interesting account of the experiences of a reservist during mobilisation, see Watson, P., *Audregnies* (Warwick: Helion, 2019).
13 Simkins, P., *Kitchener's Army - The Raising of the New Armies, 1914-16* (Manchester: Manchester University Press, 1988).
14 TNA WO 95/1272: War Diary of the 2nd King's Royal Rifle Corps, 8-13 August 1914.
15 TNA WO 95/1280: War Diary of the 1st Battalion South Wales Borderers, 8 August 1914.
16 TNA WO 95/1272: War Diary of the 2nd King's Royal Rifle Corps, 8-13 August 1914.
17 TNA WO 95/1263: War Diary of the 1st Battalion Black Watch, 11 August 1914.

battalions there.[18] The sorting out of personnel, necessitated by war, was reflected a day later in the request that as Captain Robertson (2nd Battalion) had been found unfit for overseas service, 'could he be transferred to the depot so that Captain Henderson could rejoin the battalion from the depot?' On 13 August the 1st Black Watch were entrained at Farnborough, in two trains, for Southampton. At Southampton they embarked on "Italian Prince", after waiting whilst the regimental transport of two battalions of 9th Brigade were loaded first, and sailed at 9 p.m. in calm waters.[19] For others the journey had been more eventful, as on the previous day the 1st Loyal North Lancashires, (1st Loyal North Lancs) travelling on SS *Agar Penor* (which belonged to the Holt's Blue Funnel Line and was under the command of Captain Tillotson),[20] had been involved in a collision with a collier, which meant they eventually departed only at night time.[21]

The 1st battalion of the Coldstream Guards (1st Coldstreams) also embarked on 13 August at Southampton; sailing on the SS *Dunvegan Castle* to Le Havre where they disembarked on the following day.[22] The divisional cavalry formed by C Squadron of 15th (the King's) Hussars (15th Hussars) marched off at Midnight on 15th August, with the regimental headquarters and machine gun section remaining in England, the latter in particular would leave the British cavalry under - gunned compared to German cavalry with integrated Jaeger units and machine guns.[23] This judgement might seem to depend upon hindsight but Jones cites an instance of the need for cavalry to have machine guns back in 1905.[24]

The French command were highly sceptical as to whether the British would fight. On their plans, they had labelled the BEF as "Force W" in the belief that Wilson himself was committed to the concept even if his government was not. Nevertheless, the British had arrived as promised. Mobilisation had gone smoothly so the BEF were early. In case they never materialised, the French Plan XVII had allocated the British a place on the extreme left. However, Plan XVII had assumed that the Germans would only field first line Corps initially. The Germans had actually mobilised their Reserve Corps too and had therefore swung forces north of the Meuse. The Germans were therefore able to outflank the northernmost French Army but now they would discover the BEF in their path.

---

18   TNA WO 95/1267: War Diary of 2nd Infantry Brigade Headquarters, 11 August 1914.
19   TNA WO 95/1263: War Diary of the 1st Battalion Black Watch, 13 August 1914.
20   TNA WO 95/1267: War Diary of 2nd Infantry Brigade Headquarters, 12 August 1914.
21   TNA WO 95/1270: War Diary of a Second Lieutenant of 1st Battalion Loyal North Lancashire Regiment, 12 August 1914.
22   TNA WO 95/1263: War Diary of the 1st Battalion Coldstream Guards, 13 and 14 August 1914.
23   Lord Carnock, *The History of the 15th (the King's) Hussars 1914-1922* (London: Naval & Military Press, orig. 1932) p.3
24   Jones, S., *From Boer War to World War* (Norman, Oklahoma: University of Oklahoma, 2013)

2

From Mons to Etreux

Dunn records that the 1st South Wales Borderers fell in at around 2.30 a.m. on 24 August 1914 and began marching in a southerly and then easterly direction before arriving at Quievrain. They then proceeded to the brigade's concentration point at Elouges. There they were immediately told to about turn and march which led them back to Quievrain. This was the beginning of what would become the 'Retreat from Mons'.[1] The change in orders resulted from General Haig having been awakened at 2 a.m. on 24 August to be given orders from Sir John French that I Corps must retreat to Bavai.[2] The option of Maubeuge was ruled out by the French forces using that road. During the retreat, 1st Division made contact with 2nd Division at Bonnet at 11.45am.[3]

C Squadron were also part of the divisional rearguard, and they were in position by 4.30 a.m. on 24 August.[4] Also assigned to covering the withdrawal of the 3rd Brigade was the 1st Coldstreams.[5] The Hussars' regimental history records that the right hand patrols of the Hussars were "privileged" to watch the German attack on the French rearguards, and that the hussars only regained their position with the squadron with some difficulty. According to the regimental historian they were "not pressed" and C Squadron reached its billets in Feignies around 7.30 p.m.[6] According to their HQ, all 1st Division units had reached their billets by 9pm. It was noted that they had covered 14 – 18 miles and that it had been very hot. It was also noted that the men had been very tired beforehand by the time spent entrenching.

Whilst the remainder of 1st Division, as part of I Corps, continued to retreat on 24 August 1914; their divisional artillery was in action supporting 2nd Division's "powerful demonstration as if to retake Binche". Brigadier-General Horne took an active role in managing the batteries involved in the rearguard. 'They were not heavily engaged'[7] which undermines the view that it was a powerful demonstration. It would seem more appropriate conclude that the German

---

1 Dunn, *The War the Infantry Knew*, p. 20.
2 Sheffield, G. and Bourne, J. (ed.), *Douglas Haig: War Diaries and Letters 1914-1918* (London: Weidenfeld & Nicholson, 2005), p. 63.
3 TNA WO 95/1227: War Diary of 1st Division, 24 August 1914.
4 Carnock, *15th Hussars*, p.17
5 TNA WO 95/1263: War Diary of the 1st Battalion Coldstream Guards, 24 August 1914.
6 Carnock, *15th Hussars*, p.17.
7 Hutchison, *op. cit.*, p.112

infantry, having sustained significant casualties the day before, were reluctant to press ahead unsupported. It may be that they had recognised the limitations of their light field artillery.

According to the BEF's commander, 1st Division was in support of 2nd Division and this demonstration allowed II Corps to retire.[8] The 2nd Battalion the Munster Fusiliers also retreated in the hot weather, with the reservists being "galled" by carrying the pack to which they were unaccustomed.[9]

C Squadron 15th Hussars spent the day covering the rearguard formed from elements of 1st Guards Brigade, until the evening when it was ordered to bivouac (which turned out to be "horrid") in Taisnieres. On their way there, the hussars picked up a long column of divisional transport wagons. As they reached Taisnieres, they were fired upon by the divisional commander's HQ outpost, causing horses to stampede as well as considerable damage, before the mistake was discovered.[10] Amongst those keeping close to General Lomax were elements of 15th Hussars under Captain Courage who had engaged various German patrols during the day to ensure the GOC's safety.[11] Given the constant pressure from the German cavalry the jumpiness of the outposts was understandable, but the arrival of a unit at its designated billets should not have surprised the staff of the unit which had ordered them to go there.

The retreat continued on 25 August despite delays due to the French 53rd Reserve Divion using the same narrow road on several occasions. In the afternoon, Lomax was able to meet his opposite number and sort out the allocation of billets. In the early hours of 26 August, as pouring rain continued, C Squadron set off and spent the day gradually falling back on Oisy. Lord Carnock's account observes that the distribution of rations via dumps, and the issuing of orders to the rearguards to burn what was left, gave the men the clear impression that all was not well.[12] All these references to the difficulty of conducting a fighting retreat with a force consisting of 60 percent reservists are important in two ways. First, they underline the difficulties French faced in preserving his command intact as Kitchener required. Second, they are essential in understanding the famous, some would say notorious, order to dump baggage so the men could ride.

---

8   John French, *The Graphic Special No. 1: Sir John French's Despatches* (London: The Graphic, 1914), p.6.
9   H.S. Jervis, *The 2nd Munsters in France*, (London: Naval & Military Press, orig. 1922) p.1.
10   Carnock, *15th Hussars*, p.21
11   Carnock, *15th Hussars*, p.21-22
12   Carnock, *15th Hussars*, p.24.

3

The Munsters at Etreux

The retreat from Mons to, eventually, the Orque, was an extremely challenging military operation. Not only had I Corps to make an unplanned retreat over an, as yet, unspecified distance but it had to do so under pressure from a highly trained opponent. It should also be recognised that of all the major textbook scenarios it was the most challenging. The most senior British officers had significant combat experience. Haig had been a senior staff officer in the Boer War. However, whilst some might have had to conduct tactical withdrawals in the face of superior numbers; their opponents were less well armed. The Boers were well armed but less numerous. Brigadier-General Maxse, GOC 1 (Guards) Brigade, was a conscientious officer but no more equipped for the challenges he faced.

On 27 August 1914, the continuing retreat of 1st Division was to be covered by the men of 1st Guards Brigade, including 2nd Battalion the Royal Munster Fusiliers. Orders were received by1st Brigade at 2.15 a.m. that morning that they were to act as rearguard, and therefore to occupy the line north of Fesmy by 6 a.m. These orders also specified that 3rd Brigade and the trains of all three brigades were to collect south of Oisy. Those units would then open out into column and follow the main column of 2nd Division.[1] According to the subsequent report signed by Maxse, he was in the process of moving his headquarters from Fesmy to the canal bridges just north of Petit Cambresis. The latter ,which would be more central to his assigned role), when Major General Lomax arrived. Maxse then says that Lomax gave him a verbal update of the situation. According to Maxse, he was given authority over the timing of the retreat including that of 2nd Brigade at Wassigny. Lomax also told Maxse about the flank guard being provided by the Welsh Regiment.[2]

According to Jervis, Brigadier-General Maxse was determined to minimise the impact of the German ability to bring fresh troops to bear. German attacks that sought to interfere with the retreat by getting between units. Therefore Maxse planned to keep a distance of eight miles between the Germans and the main body of British troops.[3] Whilst making no mention of eight miles specifically, Maxse does record that Lomax stressed that two divisions were being routed

---

1 TNA WO 95/1261: War Diary of the 1st Infantry Brigade, Headquarters, August 1914.
2 TNA WO 95/1261: War Diary of the 1st Infantry Brigade, Headquarters, August 1914.
3 Jervis, *The 2nd Munsters in France*, p.1.

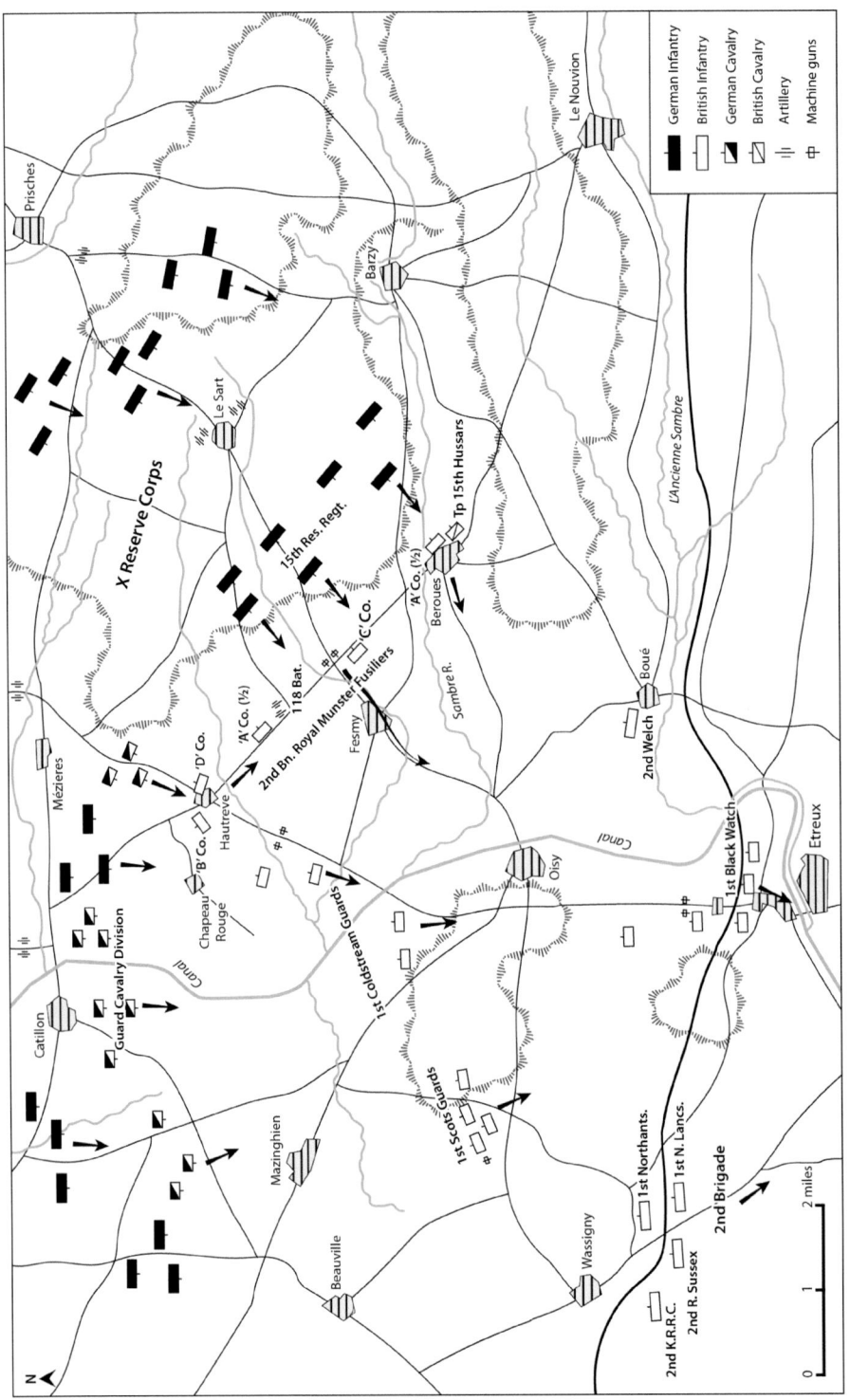

Etreux, 27 August 1914.

through Etreux. Lomax told Maxse that supplies were being issued to the troops in Etreux; and, that therefore it was vital that the line be held as long as possible.

Maxse then states that this therefore led him to conclude that the withdrawal of the 1st and 2nd Divisions through Etreux would decide the hour for the rearguard's retreat.[4] In the light of the events to follow this might be judged to be a post-hoc attempt at self-justification on Maxse's part. Maxse's account adds that he sent 1st Black Watch and 23 Field Company RE to reconnoitre an intermediate rearguard line at Feu du Gard a mile north of Etreux.[5] The distance between Fesmy and Etreux is only 4.3 miles so the distance between the Munsters' positions and the intermediate rearguard line was just over three miles from the nearest elements of the Munsters. Nevertheless, it is well short of Jervis's assertion of a planned eight mile gap. The error on Maxse's part was for these intermediate positions to be vacated too soon, but that was yet to come.

On 27 August, Major Charrier of 2nd Munster Fusiliers, with the support of a troop of C Squadron 15th Hussars and two guns of 118th Battery RFA, were therefore tasked with covering the withdrawal of the rest of 1st Infantry Brigade. Charrier was apparently fluent in French and had strong tactical ability.[6] The initial role of the 2nd Munster Fusiliers was to hold the crossroads at Chapeau Rouge as well as the villages of Bergues and Fesmy. Initially the 15th Hussars sent forward patrols, which immediately found that the Germans were pushing forward before dawn and likely to surround the rearguard. Therefore, the hussars of C squadron, with the divisional cyclists, were distributed as a screen, beyond the infantry's outposts. These outposts were being found by A company of the Munsters[7], with groups at Chapeau Rouge and Fesmy, where 1st Coldstreams had billeted on 26 August[8].

The screen in front was thinner than it might otherwise have been because of the retreat of the closest elements of the French Fifth Army. The right flank of 1st Guard Brigade was "in the air", which meant that one troop had to be deployed there.[9] According to Jervis the retreat on this flank only became known at about 9 a.m.[10], so this would seem to confirm that Charrier was having to thin the screen as the situation developed. On the left flank of 1st Guards Brigade, near Ribeauville, Corporals Appleton and Durnford led their small detachments, fighting dismounted, in stubborn resistance to the German cavalry's advance. The regimental historian says that the hussars were only dislodged when the German infantry arrived in motor lorries. The pressure from the Germans meant that all the hussars had been driven in upon the main British defensive perimeter.[11] The battle fought at Etreux, which was about to unfold, remained unmentioned in Sir John French's account of the fighting in August.[12]

---

4   TNA WO 95/1261: War Diary of the 1st Infantry Brigade, Headquarters, August 1914.
5   TNA WO 95/1261: War Diary of the 1st Infantry Brigade, Headquarters, August 1914.
6   Jervis, *The 2nd Munsters in France*, p.2.
7   TNA WO 95/1272: War Diary of the 2nd Battalion of the Royal Munster Fusiliers, Extract from Captain Gower's letter dated 14 December 1914.
8   TNA WO 95/1263: War Diary of the 1st Battalion Coldstream Guards, 26 August 1914.
9   Carnock, *15th Hussars*, pp.25-26.
10 Jervis, *The 2nd Munsters in France*, p.2.
11 Carnock, *15th Hussars*, p.26.
12 French, *The Graphic Special No 1: Sir John French's Despatches*, p. 9

According to Jervis, the *17th Brunswick Hussars*, the leading element of the approaching X Reserve Corps, only approached with caution.[13] The regiment which had fought alongside the British at Waterloo now awaited reinforcements. The fragility of the Munsters' position is underlined by Captain Gower's account of how his platoon had been detailed to protect the guns; the British commander was tasking platoons whilst the German commander was disposing brigades. At about 11a.m. the German attack opened, with the twelve battalions of the *2nd Guard Reserve Division* forcing their way into Bergues.[14] This threatened to cut off the Munster Fusiliers, as the 2nd Welsh, of 3rd Brigade, were situated much further back towards Etreux itself. The occupation of Bergues did not just turn the Munsters' flank, it also put the Germans en route to reach a point where they would be behind the 1st Coldstreams and the 1st Scots Guards. The Germans then pressed forward with artillery support and, avoiding the strong central defence, began to work around the right flank through the woods of La Queue de Boue, potentially threatening Corps headquarters.

This timing coincides with Maxse's account that the orders to retire were read out to mounted officers of each unit, sent to headquarters, including Major Day of the Munsters. The time was not filled in on the orders. The officers then went off to their units to explain the orders to their commanding officers.[15] According to Carnock, however, the strong rearguard action enabled the rest of the division to retreat intact. Therefore, at 1.30 p.m. the order was given for the rearguard to disengage from the enemy and fall back upon the rest of the division. Maxse had received a message from 1st Division staff that Etreux was now "free of impedimenta". Maxse stated that the orders to disengage were issued at 12.45 p.m., to all units in 1st Brigade and to 2nd Brigade, with the time given as "at once". Maxse too asserts that the Black Watch also took up their positions.[16] Carnock goes on to argue that the isolation of the Munster Fusiliers arose from the motorcyclist despatched with orders for them to retire being killed.

Carnock then offers the view that the Munsters were aware of the retirement of the rest of the rearguard. He explains Major Charrier's decision by arguing that he was too gallant to retire without direct orders.[17] This apparent contradiction of not receiving and yet being aware of the orders can therefore be explained by reference to Maxse having issued the orders twice. Charrier knew he was to retire but had not been told when. Much is made of FSR, and this offers a key instance. As the man on the spot Charrier had the discretion as to when to retire since he had received an order. Maxse reported to his superiors that Major Day had delivered the orders to Charrier and subsequently returned to brigade headquarters. Maxse then says that the second set of orders were given to Major Day by the motorcyclist. However, Day was only able to give the orders to Charrier after a few hours delay, as the Munsters were already engaged by the Germans.[18]

Carnock's view of Charrier's character presumably reflects the views of Major Pilkington of the 15th Hussars who operated alongside the Munsters on 27 August 1914, and who would survive the war as Lieutenant Colonel Pilkington DSO. However, if Maxse's account is

---

13   Jervis, *The 2nd Munsters in France*, p.2.
14   Jervis, *The 2nd Munsters in France*, p.2.
15   TNA WO 95/1261: War Diary of the 1st Infantry Brigade, Headquarters, August 1914.
16   TNA WO 95/1261: War Diary of the 1st Infantry Brigade, Headquarters, August 1914
17   Carnock, *15th Hussars*, p.26-27.
18   TNA WO 95/1261: War Diary of the 1st Infantry Brigade, Headquarters, August 1914

accurate, it puts more responsibility upon Charrier. Maxse supported his report with copies of the relevant message slips.

Major Pilkington's initial contribution was to gather together the various troops and form the squadron in support of the infantry, before receiving orders from Brigadier-General Maxse to assist the Munsters in extricating themselves.[19] This would appear to tie in with Maxse's account that he received verbal reports from Day and a subsequent written report from Charrier, timed at 1.30 p.m., that the Munsters were heavily engaged by two infantry regiments and artillery, and the Munsters had captured prisoners from the *15th Infantry Regiment*.[20] The patrols of Hussars then discovered that the Munsters at Fesmy had already been surrounded. So Major Pilkington focused his men on assisting the fusiliers at Bergues, where the German ring had not closed. The Hussars therefore advanced to engage the Germans around Bergues. Some of the squadron, under Major Nicholson, reached the village where there is a road coming out towards La Capelle.[21] Having dismounted and lodged the horses in a farmyard, they provided covering fire. This enabled approximately 170 Munsters to retire from the village.[22]

However, the Hussars, then came under machine gun fire from the Germans who had fallen back to a farmhouse. The Germans then emerged, driving cattle in front of them as a shield - but this failed in so far as the 15th Hussars shot both men and cattle. Having been blocked, the Germans were then surprised by the arrival of more hussars under the command of Lieutenant Hardinge, who took up a position from which they could fire into the farmyard. Hardinge's men inflicted significant casualties upon the Germans. Naturally, the Germans then brought a machine gun to bear on their tormentors. Lieutenant Hardinge was amongst the first casualties and so Sergeant Papworth took over command of the troop.[23]

The account given in the *First Seven Divisions* seems to imply that the Munsters might have given up through fatigue:

> There is always a disposition on such occasions for very tired men to throw up the sponge and surrender. In the present instance, however, any such inclination was summarily checked by the energy and determination of Mr Nicholson and Sergeant Papworth."[24]
> When the Hussars arrived, the Munsters were still resisting whilst outnumbered. It seems gratuitously insulting to suggest that once rescued they wanted to surrender.

The Munsters and Hussars then retreated, with C Squadron of the Hussars largely collected together by 3 p.m., by which time they had gained the assistance of men of 4th Hussars who, having lost their regiment, put themselves under Major Pilkington's command.[25] According to Maxse, he had delayed the retirement of the whole rearguard, whilst attempts were made to extricate the Munsters. Major Day had once again tried, without success, to reach the battalion.[26]

---

19   Hamilton, E., *The First Seven Divisions* (London: Hutchinson, 1916), passim.
20   TNA WO 95/1261: War Diary of the 1st Infantry Brigade, Headquarters, August 1914
21   Hamilton, *The First Seven Divisions*, passim.
22   Carnock, *15th Hussars*, p.27.
23   Hamilton, *The First Seven Divisions*, passim..
24   Hamilton, *The First Seven Divisions*, passim.
25   Carnock, *15th Hussars*, p.28.
26   TNA WO 95/1261: War Diary of the 1st Infantry Brigade, Headquarters, August 1914.

The retreating units were now threatened by a German movement through Villiers-les-Guise. The Germans were checked by Captain Courage leading a mixed force of 4th and 15th Hussars (1st and 2nd Troops) in a rearguard action which lasted until around 7 p.m., when they reached a ridge near La Mont Rouge to the north of Lesquelles. The squadron subsequently created bivouacs in a wet field, near Origny Ste. Benoite, at about 11.30 p.m. before emerging at 3 a.m. on 28 August 1914 to continue their retreat.[27] No wonder tiredness grew.

Whilst the Hussars had helped to effect the rescue of some of the Munsters, B and D companies of the fusiliers were strongly entrenched and defending the left flank in the village of Hautevre. Jervis details how D company's cookers arrived, and hot food was served out; to the accompaniment of witticisms by fusiliers enjoying the sight of cooks hunched up and moving at the double.[28] The fusiliers then suffered the effects of a thunderstorm including heavy rain. At around 12.30 p.m., the Germans pushed forward a strong attack and established themselves in Fesmy before being pushed out by a counterattack carried out by two platoons under the orders of C Company, commanded by Captain Rawlinson. The machine guns, under Lieutenant Chute, and the two artillery pieces worked hard to support the riflemen in an hour-long battle to keep the Germans at bay. "B" and "D" companies were able to withdraw towards their battalion headquarters once they had repelled the latest German assault and so moved to the crossroads north of Fesmy.[29] The eventual fate of the Munsters can be seen to stem from this move, as the Germans had already gained Bergues so there were now Germans on their south easterly flank.

The main thrust of the German assault was coming from the north and it would be natural for it to follow the road to Oisy and Etreux. In doing so they would come between the Munsters and Etreux. The Munsters were in fact withdrawing through Fesmy. Major Charrier had designated "B" Company under Captain Simms to act as the right flank guard (to the east) whilst "D" Company acted as the left flank guard and rearguard. Jervis states that Simms was a man with the knack of training his subordinates to think for themselves. The Munsters might still have evaded their pursuers if they had been able to move swiftly once they reached the crossroads to the east of Oisy, where they could take the road south to Etreux. However, B Company had become detached, and it took an hour for it to rejoin the main body.[30]

This extra delay probably sealed the fate of the Munsters.

To make its way through Oisy, Major Charrier reorganised the battalion and ordered "B" to proceed south, accompanied by two platoons of "A," whilst C Company under Captain Rawlinson acted as the rearguard. Elements of *6th Reserve Dragoons* were driven off by machine gun fire but as this was on the southern edge of the village it foreshadowed the events to come. "C" Company then came under sustained attack, but despite spurning Charrier's offer to reinforce them, succeeded in driving back their pursuers. Reunited, the three companies of the Munsters continued their withdrawal.[31] The aerial map (see figure 2) helps to indicate the path followed by 2nd Brigade on 27 August 1914.

---

27   Carnock, *15th Hussars*, pp.28-29.
28   Jervis, *The 2nd Munsters in France*, p.2.
29   Jervis, *The 2nd Munsters in France*, p.3.
30   Jervis, *The 2nd Munsters in France*, pp.3-4.
31   Jervis, *The 2nd Munsters in France*, p.4.

Jervis dismisses General von Barfeldt, commanding the *19th Reserve Infantry Division*, as a cautious 'dugout' who was past his prime.[32] Nevertheless, *73rd and 78th Reserve Infantry Regiments* were approaching Etreux from the east of the town[33] which would bring them to the town close to the bridge which the Munsters would want to cross.

The publication of the Official History in 1922 led Captain Addison (formally of 23rd Field Company RE) to write to Brigadier Edmonds on Valentine's Day 1923 in order to correct the published account. In particular, Addison wrote to say that he had been the last person to cross the bridge, at about 3 p.m., and that it had not been blown. He recalled having prepared to demolish the bridge but having also created a log bridge, which was out of sight, and over which the Black Watch and subsequently the Coldstreams had crossed. Addison wrote that he and a section of his men had been waiting to demolish the bridge and had prepared a plan including reconnoitring their escape. They were apparently dreaming of their picture featuring in the Daily Mail, when they received an order not to blow the bridge.[34] The timings in Addison's account contradict Maxse's report, as he says that the 1st Black Watch delayed their retirement until after 4 p.m.[35], whereas Addison's account says they had cleared the bridge by 3 p.m. This is rather more consistent with Major Day's apparent concern that the brigade were abandoning his battalion.

The concise summary of the day recorded by the Coldstreams offers no additional information, as it simply states that they initially marched from Fesmy to Etreux, where they deployed to defend the bridges over the canal. The diary then records that they subsequently retired without loss, before marching to billets at Janquese.[36] One difficulty with this source is that it is listed as part of a report on a later action, so it may have been completed after the failure to save the Munsters had aroused controversy. The record is as sparse as possible consistent with the battalion's status, i.e., they would not leave a day out. Similarly, the Black Watch's diarist has endorsed the page before that all records for August were lost in the fighting between 29 October and 2 November 1914. The interesting thing about this diary, though, is the very strong resemblance between the type of language used by both diarists - as though the Coldstreams had read the diary of the Black Watch.[37] Both battalions recorded that they retired from Etreux "without loss". Addison's description of how he and his men created a low bridge from long trees helps explain this point. He stated that, unlike the permanent bridges, this bridge was low and hid the men from view. Maxse was not providing sufficient co-ordination. This reinforces the view, implied by Addison, that both battalions withdrew, without waiting to assist a battalion known to be in contact with the enemy. Therefore, a fatal gap opened, into which an enterprising enemy could interpose themselves.

Despite the bridge apparently being intact, however, the Munsters would not be able to make good their escape. Charrier's command came under accurate artillery fire as it headed towards

---

32   Jervis, *The 2nd Munsters in France*, p.4.
33   Jon Cooksey and Jerry Murland, *The Retreat from Mons 1914: South: The Western Front by Car, by Bike and on Foot*, (Barnsley: Pen & Sword, 2014), p.40
34   TNA WO 95/1261: War Diary of the 1st Infantry Brigade, Headquarters, August 1914, Appendix A, Miscellaneous.
35   TNA WO 95/1261: War Diary of the 1st Infantry Brigade, Headquarters, August 1914, Appendix A, Miscellaneous.
36   TNA WO 95/1263: War Diary of the 1st Battalion Coldstream Guards, August 1914.
37   TNA WO 95/1263: War Diary of the 1st Battalion Black Watch, 27 August 1914.

Etreux. Jervis records that the machine guns fired north as the men marched south[38], but the artillery fire was coming from over a kilometre away and immediately damaged the Munsters' key asset, their artillery. According to the artillery commander Major Bayly:

> I gave the command 'action left' and though the enemy's fourth shell killed the sergeant, 2 men and 3 horses of the leading sub-section, both guns were got into action 70 yards apart. [Battery Sergeant Major] Strutt lifted Sergeant Perch, who was mortally wounded, from his horse, and volunteered to take command of D gun. I ordered him to open fire on a loop-holed house in Etreux, about 200 yards distant, but all attempts to bring up ammunition to that gun failed, and the detachment was shot down without exception.[39]

Jervis then describes how Major Charrier led several assaults on a house which the Germans had occupied and loop-holed.[40] The result of this gallantry was a mounting pile of Munster casualties, and its subsequent repetition by Charrier with "C" Company simply added them to the casualty list along with, eventually, Charrier himself. Jervis describes Charrier as a man who did not "give in whilst hope lasted." The successive assaults on the loop-holed house suggest he had not appreciated that hope for the Munsters to escape had already gone, once a party of Germans had got across the road ahead of them. Thus, the delay caused by waiting for "B" Company to rejoin proved fatal to the Munsters. The race was so close that the Munsters had seen the Germans, crossing the road ahead.[41] There the Germans were able to occupy a building already prepared for defence by 23 Cy. Royal Engineers and trenches dug by the 1st Black Watch.[42]

The time spent collecting B company had allowed the Germans to get between the Coldstreams and the Munsters. It does not fully explain why no British forces remained close to the bridge. The various difficulties faced by the BEF are reflected in Lieutenant Stewart-Cox being wounded whilst serving his gun, having fired all 14 shells he had.[43] it would have been better for the infantry to have been supporting the artillery by helping to load the guns. Meanwhile A company had been "pushing on" as ordered, but they were blocked and subsequently gathered in the orchard, which they defended until their ammunition was exhausted. "D" Company under Captain Jervis, came closest to breaking out as they took advantage of the terrain and extended the attack on the Germans, but ultimately failed, as *3rd battalion 78 Reserve Infantry Regiment* had lined the railway embankment and stopped the Munsters with heavy fire from strong defensive positions.[44]

It was probably the fighting here that was audible to Major Day of the Munsters, when he found Captain Addison at around 3 p.m. to say they must not abandon the Munsters. Addison says he told Day that he had been told that the Munsters were to cross by the other bridge, but

---

38 Jervis, *The 2nd Munsters in France*, p.5.
39 Cooksey and Murland, *The Retreat from Mons 1914: South*, p.41.
40 Jervis, *The 2nd Munsters in France*, p.5.
41 Jervis, *The 2nd Munsters in France*, p.5
42 Cooksey and Murland, *The Retreat from Mons 1914: South*, p.41.
43 Cooksey and Murland, *The Retreat from Mons 1914: South*, p.41.
44 Cooksey and Murland, *The Retreat from Mons 1914: South*, p.44.

that Day said they could not because of German pressure. Day and Addison then rode over the bridge and encountered a cyclist sheltering in a ditch carrying an order from Maxse to retreat at once. Addison then said that he rode on only to encounter rifle fire and that "it was late" and therefore he decided to rejoin his unit.[45] Addison recounts that his conversation with Major Day took place around 3pm so even if a whole hour had elapsed it was by now only 4pm on a summer's evening. This supports the view that the rest of 1st Guards Brigade had left the Munsters to their fate.

Jervis describes the gallantry of many individual Munster officers, such as Captain Wise and Lieutenants O'Malley and Moseley, whilst Cooksey summarises the casualties as nine officers and 112 men killed with a further 6 officers and 130 men being wounded.[46] These casualties, along with the 240 men who surrendered, would mean that the battalion would need to be reconstituted. Following his death, Major Charrier's pocketbook was passed up to 19th Reserve Division commander General von Bahrfeldt.[47]

Lord Carnock then comments that although the loss of the bulk of the Royal Munster Fusiliers appeared to be a disaster, they had probably saved the 1st Guards Brigade and therefore helped preserve the 1st Division, as the Germans had been trying to drive a wedge between the rearguard and the main body. Carnock also offered the view that the Munsters drew in many German units and thus diverted them away from pressing upon the rest of the rearguard.[48] This is echoed by Jervis in his assertion that it was unparalleled for three companies of a battalion, supported by two field guns, to stem the advance of an entire army corps.[49] Jervis states that five officers and 196 other ranks answered the roll on 29 August 1914.[50] These figures are similar to those noted by their Corps Commander, Haig; along with his verdict "By some error of judgement, this rearguard remained too long in its position north of Etreux". Haig subsequently made damning comments on Maxse's report on the events of 27 September.[51] The evidence of the surviving diaries supports Haig's view. The question whether the fault lay with Maxse or the two battalions who withdrew too soon. Maxse's distribution of two sets of orders probably means he was seriously at fault. The fact that two battalions of Guards withdrew so quickly and to such a distance was not in accordance with their fine regimental traditions.

Lord Hamilton, the author of the *First Seven Divisions* comments that the number of honours won by the 15th Hussars during the operations around Etreux was remarkable, especially given the numbers of men engaged. However, those familiar with the number of medals awarded at the Gallipoli landings in 1915 and at Rorke's Drift in 1879 might see a pattern repeated here.[52]

---

45 TNA WO 95/1261: War Diary of the 1st Infantry Brigade, Headquarters, August 1914, Appendix A, Miscellaneous.
46 Cooksey and Murland, *The Retreat from Mons 1914: South*, p.45.
47 For details on the pocketbook tale, a useful source is *Private Papers pf Major P.A. Charrier* <http://www.iwm.org.uk/collections/item/object/1030018188> (accessed 30 November 2016).
48 Carnock, *15th Hussars*, p.28.
49 Jervis, *The 2nd Munsters in France*, p.1.
50 Jervis, *The 2nd Munsters in France*, p. 8.
51 Sheffield and Bourne (eds.), *Douglas Haig*, p.67.
52 Amongst the seventeen members of 15th Hussars that were mentioned in Despatches by Sir John French in the amended list published in the London Gazette on 9 December 1914 was Sergeant Papworth, who was awarded the DCM for his part in the fighting at Bergues according to the

Nevertheless, 1st Division's retreat continued on 28 August with 1st Coldstreams reaching St Gobain, where they were allowed a day's rest.[53]

For Ivor Maxse, there was the consequence of a return to England after the loss of the Munsters attracted public attention. His brother, Leopold, was editor of the Conservative journal, *The National Review*. Leopold had been instrumental in the campaign to see Arthur Balfour removed from the Conservative Party leadership. Ivor's sister, Violet, was married to the youngest son of former Tory Prime Minister, Lord Salisbury. Ivor Maxse was soon promoted and given command of the 18th Eastern Division. A less well-connected officer might not have got a second chance. In this case, it proved beneficial to the army.

regimental historian. However, it was Sergeant W Blishen who was gazetted with the DCM on 15 December 1914 for his gallantry at Bergues.
53 TNA WO 95/1263: War Diary of the 1st Battalion Coldstream Guards, 27-28 August 1914

4

From Etreux to the Ourcq

As part of I Corps, 1st Division continued to retreat and subsequently reached the River Ourcq, close to Paris. Naturally, a great deal more attention has been focused upon II Corps and the battle of Le Cateau. This period is often passed over except for accounts relating to Sir John French and Kitchener.

The 1st Division marched approximately twenty-one miles on 28 August, and it was noted that the men were exhausted and in much need of the rest they were afforded on 29 August.[1] Modern historians may criticise French for insisting his troops needed rest, but it seems his key subordinates were in agreement with him at the time. As discussed, approximately 60% of the men were reservists.

The 31 August was a typical day for 1st Division. It can therefore be used to illustrate the pressures of a retreat conducted whilst pursued by an organised enemy. 1st Division planned to be "clear of" Soissons by 11a.m. However, the French and the Germans contrived to disrupt these plans. A column of French mechanical transport cut across the line of march and severely delayed the progress of 1st (Guards) Brigade. News then arrived that German cavalry had crossed the Oise at Ribencourt. Reportedly, this cavalry were heading for Vauxaillon. Therefore 2nd Brigade were detailed to form a rear-guard and to hold the high ground north of Crouy until nightfall. They were to be supported by an artillery brigade, two troops from 15th Hussars and two platoons of divisional cyclists under Colonel Lowther. The rear-guard was withdrawn by nightfall, despite the need to prepare the bridges over the Aisne for demolition. The bridge at Bois Roger was blown by 23 Cy. RE whilst 2nd Division were responsible for blowing the bridges below that point. The bridges over the Cree were the responsibility of the French army. As a result of all this activity, the 1st Division spent that night close bivouacked along the road to Paris, between Vauxbuin and La Ferte Feuille.[2]

The remnants of the Munsters were reassigned to be army troops. Therefore, on 5 September the 1st Division received the 1st Cameron Highlanders, initially minus one company and two platoons.[3] The evening of 5 September found the Black Watch billeted at Nesles,[4] with the rest of

---

1   TNA WO 95/1227: War Diary of the 1st Division, Headquarters, 28 August 1914.
2   TNA WO 95/1227: War Diary of the 1st Division, Headquarters, 31 August 1914.
3   Becke, A.F., *Order of Battle of Divisions – Part 1* (Uckfield: Naval & Military Press, 2007) pp.36-37.
4   TNA WO 95/1263: War Diary of the 1st Battalion Black Watch 5 September 1914

1st Brigade in the vicinity. The Coldstream Guards received their first batch of reinforcements; Lieutenant Wavell-Paxton and ninety other ranks.[5] The brigade staff recorded the arrival of the Cameron Highlanders, as well as the delight of the whole brigade in receiving orders to turn northwards again.[6]

The strategic situation, as seen by Marshal Joffre, was that a significant gap had opened up between the German *First* and *Second Armies*. Therefore, Joffre wanted to use the natural barrier of the Marne to provide a springboard from which the French could attack into that gap. Joffre had held high hopes in General Lanrezac which is why he had assigned him to the critical role of commander of the French Fifth Army. Joffre's disappointment in Lanrezac's precipitate withdrawal after the battle of Charleroi had not been offset by the latter's generally sound handling of the fighting retreat. Therefore, Lanrezac was immediately sacked once Fifth Army returned.[7]

It was in this context that Field Marshal Kitchener arrived to interview Sir John French. Kitchener, despite his position as Minister of War chose to wear his full Field Marshal's uniform. Kitchener made no allowances for having given French mutually incompatible orders, or the poor arrangements for the senior appointments. Kitchener had ordered French to take the BEF forward alongside the French. Whilst reasons of state dictated such a course of action, Kitchener's approach probably only underlined the weakness of French's position.

Ironically, General Gallieni, commanding the Paris garrison, had probably already undermined Joffre's vision. Gallieni had spotted the same situation as Joffre. However, by attacking the day before Joffre, he alerted Von Kluck's First Army to the danger they faced. The British eventually lost the race to the Aisne heights. Gallieni's ego would be partly to blame.

---

5 TNA WO 95/1263: War Diary of the 1st Battalion Coldstream Guards, 5 September 1914.
6 TNA WO 95/1261: War Diary of the 1st Brigade, 5 September 1914
7 The French used the term "Limoged" as Limoge was in central France so being posted there effectively meant the same as being sacked.

5

Advance to the Aisne

The orders to turnabout and advance reached 1st Division at 5.52 a.m. on 6 September. Naturally, they were based upon a GHQ appreciation of the German order of battle. By 8.15 a.m., XXV Brigade RFA were marching north-eastwards. At 8.45 a.m., 1st Division were told, in a British cavalry report, that large columns of cavalry preceded by motorcyclists were moving south-eastwards. It was also reported that there were German infantry moving from Vandoy. All this information suggested the German advance was continuing.

1st Brigade, in the lead role, had assigned the role of advance guard to the Coldstream Guards, who advanced towards Voinsles through Rozoy. When the Coldstreams came under artillery fire, the Black Watch were sent forward to reinforce them. 1 Brigade's view was that the Coldstreams, who had dug trenches beside the road, were opposed by dismounted cavalry and artillery.[1] The Coldstreams recorded that they took up positions after receiving a report from a sergeant of 15th Hussars but continued their advance in the afternoon.[2] According to the 15th Hussars' historian, they encountered shrapnel and machine gun fire as soon as they left Rozoy and were forced back.[3] The decision to leave the machine gun section at home on mobilisation was now making itself felt, as Carnock identified the opposition as including jaeger on bicycles. Overall, the Germans had fought a classic rearguard action, delaying the British advance.

In Carnock's estimation, the advance resumed at about 3 p.m. when the German rearguards had begun to retire.[4] The brigade then advanced and reached the line Gloise - Le Plessis – Puisseau, where it bivouacked.[5] The Coldstreams sustained losses of five other ranks killed and 35 wounded and four officers were wounded.[6] The Black Watch suffered five casualties and their advance took them to La Gloise Farm.[7] The Scots Guards noted that the Corps was advancing in a north-easterly direction and that this adjustment meant that their support line was relieved 4th Brigade (2nd Division). They recorded that the shelling of the Coldstreams by the Germans led to the Scots Guards themselves entrenching in a position which meant they were the right

1 TNA WO 95/1261: War Diary of the 1st Brigade, Headquarters, 6 September 1914.
2 TNA WO 95/1263: War Diary of the 1st Battalion Coldstream Guards, 6 September 1914.
3 Carnock, *15th Hussars*, p.40.
4 Carnock, *15th Hussars*, p.40.
5 TNA WO 95/1261: War Diary of the 1st Brigade, Headquarters, 6 September 1914.
6 TNA WO 95/1263: War Diary of the 1st Battalion Coldstream Guards, 6 September 1914.
7 TNA WO 95/1263: War Diary of the 1st Battalion Black Watch, 6 September 1914.

rear of the brigade. However, the Scots Guards did join in the general advance at 4.30 p.m. and encountered no opposition as they progressed to Le Plessis, where they bivouacked.[8] The success of the Germans in halting the British advance, even for two or three hours, would pay dividends once they reached the Aisne, by ensuring they would have time to dig in.

Meantime, the gunners of XXV Brigade RFA had waited in reserve at Pompierre until 4 p.m. before marching on to bivouac at 7 p.m. by Vaudoy.[9] With 1st Brigade now at the rear of the division, the Black Watch did not march off until 9 a.m. on 7 September, the same time as XXV Brigade RFA, though the battalion recorded reports that the Germans were retiring hastily before them.[10] That morning the Scots Guards did not march off until 10.35 a.m. and dinners were served at Amillis. The battalion then marched on to billets in La Frenois.[11] On the same day, the Coldstreams marched from Puiseau to Le Temple, two miles west of La Ferte Gauche.[12] On Haig's behalf, Gough, his chief of staff, sent an order to both divisions reminding them to draw up proper march tables. In itself, not keeping the men under arms unnecessarily was laudable. However, by emphasising march tables the implication would be that the leading units had set objectives for the day. This would encourage units to stop there rather than press on.[13] The cumulative import of this evidence is that Haig was advancing cautiously rather than conducting a pursuit.

The Black Watch demonstrated great determination on 8 September when, as the advance guard, they pushed on to the high ground north of Bellot, even though they had come under shellfire, as they breasted the heights to the south of the town. In Bellot itself they encountered the HQ of the *4th French Cavalry Division (*who had suffered from being shelled and had therefore stayed in the cover afforded by the village). The French informed the Black Watch that they were unable to break through.[14] A and D companies pushed forward and seized the ridge north of the Bellot- Sablonnieres Road, whilst B company pushed on up the Sablonnieres Road. B company, advancing in column of route[15], was met with heavy rifle fire and had to be reinforced by C company[16], and a battery from 26th Brigade RFA as well as a French horse artillery unit. The battalion suffered 28 casualties including two officers killed. Divisional HQ recorded that progress beyond Bellot was essential to allow the division to advance, and so at 10.40 a.m. the vanguard formed by the Black Watch pushed on again.

By noon the Black Watch were engaged in another battle, with German cavalry and Guard Jaegar, on the wooded northern slopes of the valley above Bellot. As they emerged from Bellot the Black Watch came under fire from German artillery located by the chateau to the east of Fourcheret.[17] To assist the Black Watch, the Cameron Highlanders were also committed to the assault. The British cavalry worked around the side and then entered the wood. This led to

8 TNA WO 95/1263: War Diary of the 1st Battalion Scots Guards, 6 September 1914.
9 TNA WO 95/1248: War Diary of the XXV Brigade RFA, 6 September 1914.
10 TNA WO 95/1263: War Diary of the 1st Battalion Black Watch, 7 September 1914.
11 TNA WO 95/1263: War Diary of the 1st Battalion Scots Guards, 7 September 1914,
12 TNA WO 95/1263: War Diary of the 1st Battalion Coldstream Guards, 7 September 1914.
13 TNA WO 95/1227: War Diary of the 1st Division, Headquarters, September 1914, Appendix VI.
14 TNA WO 95/1261: War Diary of the 1st Brigade, Headquarters, 8 September 1914.
15 TNA WO 95/1227: War Diary of the 1st Division, Headquarters, 8 September 1914.
16 TNA WO 95/1263: War Diary of the 1st Battalion Black Watch 8 September 1914.
17 TNA WO 95/1261: War Diary of the 1st Brigade, Headquarters, 8 September 1914.

the capture of 46 Germans, some identified as belonging to *8th Jaegar*,[18] as well as many of the defenders being killed.[19] The success of the two Scottish battalions allowed the French cavalry to resume their advance towards Montlacueul.[20]

Major General Lomax had also brought 3rd Brigade forward along high ground south of the valley as well as bringing his heavy artillery into position to assist 2nd Division's attack on Boitrun. During the afternoon, Lomax altered the axis of his advance to northwards towards Hondevilliers, with 1 and 3rd Brigades advancing along the eastern and western sides of the valley respectively. There was a heavy thunderstorm at about 6 p.m. but they could still hear the sound of the fighting in the battle of Montmirail.[21]

Despite these stiff engagements, which netted forty prisoners, the Black Watch pressed on a further five miles to Hondevilliers where reinforcements joined them.[22] The Scots Guards advanced to the area of Basserville and established outposts, behind a screen of cavalry. They also received reinforcements, in the guise of Lieutenant Monckton and 93 other ranks.[23]

During that day, the Coldstreams advanced under intermittent long-range artillery fire and reached a mile east of Basserville. In doing so, they noted the success of being deployed in artillery formation but did sustain significant casualties when a shrapnel shell burst close to the stretcher bearers and killed five whilst wounding seven, including the Medical Officer.[24] This suggests the German artillery had improved its hitting power since Mons. As they advanced, the XXV Brigade RFA noted signs of the German retreat were more in evidence; they had left at 11 a.m. and bivouacked at 5 p.m.[25] Early bivouacs again suggests the Germans were not being pressed too hard by all units.

On 9 September, the 1st South Wales Borderers set off and found its objective, the bridge at Nogent, not occupied by the enemy, and that some British cavalry were already across. The diarist railed against the British artillery who fired on the cavalry, wounding eighteen. The diarist's view was that the artillery officer concerned should have been shot. He also noted that they were becoming used to the sight of full ambulances as well as the destruction in the villages through which the Germans had retreated. On a lighter note, the interpreter's success in obtaining a decent meal was noted; this consisted of bacon, tea, eggs and fresh bread, which they had not seen for several days.[26]

The day had begun more positively for the Coldstreams who had received their first draft early that morning, consisting of Lieutenant Campbell and 88 other ranks. They joined the battalion in its advance due north to Lucy Le Bocage.[27] Although the Scots Guards had been ready to march at 6.45 a.m., they did not set off until later and then advanced to cross the Marne at Nogent before advancing to La Cavodiere, where they stopped for tea, before continuing on to La Maiette. Here they bivouacked and therefore were exposed to the heavy rain which fell

---

18   TNA WO 95/1261: War Diary of the 1st Brigade, Headquarters, 8 September 1914.
19   TNA WO 95/1227: War Diary of the 1st Division, Headquarters, 8 September 1914.
20   TNA WO 95/1261: War Diary of the 1st Brigade, Headquarters, 8 September 1914.
21   TNA WO 95/1227: War Diary of the 1st Division, Headquarters, 8 September 1914.
22   TNA WO 95/1263: War Diary of the 1st Battalion Black Watch 8 September 1914.
23   TNA WO 95/1263: War Diary of the 1st Battalion Scots Guards, 8 September 1914.
24   TNA WO 95/1263: War Diary of the 1st Battalion Coldstream Guards, 8 September 1914.
25   TNA WO 95/1248: War Diary of the XXV Brigade RFA, 8 September 1914.
26   TNA WO 95/1280: War Diary of the 1st Battalion South Wales Borderers, 9 September 1914.
27   TNA WO 95/1263: War Diary of the 1st Battalion Coldstream Guards, 9 September 1914.

from midnight onwards.[28] At La Croisette, XXV Brigade RFA had bivouacked at 6 p.m.; they had set off at 5 a.m. from Flagny and subsequently halted at noon before crossing the Marne unopposed.[29] None of this suggests Haig was pushing his divisions forward as fast as possible.

Five days into the offensive, on 10 September, the division lost its artillery commander, Brigadier-General Findlay.[30] The initial report that he had been wounded in the head by shrapnel was recorded by the Borderers. They also noted that the divisional cyclists had sustained approximately twenty casualties when they came under artillery fire at a range of one thousand yards. The battalion too came under enemy artillery fire at Priez and stopped, suffering three officers wounded, of whom Travers was thought to be serious enough to require treatment back in England. The battalion eventually bivouacked in Sommelans where the interpreters had again done great service by arranging a meal of bread, eggs, potatoes, and jam "with six good bottles as the French would say". The Adjutant then records that they managed to find a tub and boil water, and that he had been very dirty and was awfully glad of a bath. At the end he notes that news then arrived of Brigadier-General Findlay's death, "poor fellow".[31] Findlay's death had occurred during an artillery duel. The British were forcing the crossing of the Aisne. The Germans were holding positions along a ridge at Preuil.[32] Having marched off at 4.50 a.m., XXV Brigade RFA went into action at 10.30 a.m., when it encountered the German rearguard at Courtchamps. The ensuing engagement continued until approximately 2.30 p.m. when the British advance resumed. They noted that, 113th battery, did "great execution" on the German columns.[33] The battery itself noted that they saw the German column in Chouy but that the range from the advanced infantry line was too great. Therefore 113th battery advanced north west of Rassy and engaged the German columns at a range of 5,400 to 6000 yards, which led to retaliatory fire from the German howitzers, especially as they withdrew.[34]

According to the brigade diarist, the same shell accounted for Brigadier Finlay and Corporal Morgan of the HQ staff as well as mortally wounding the Adjutant Captain Blount.[35] Major General Lomax received the report of Brigadier Findlay's death at 10.40 a.m. and by 11.05 a.m., his headquarters were transmitting a message to Haig, asking that Horne be appointed in Findlay's place. Horne arrived to assume the role at 12.55 p.m., so that issue had been resolved speedily. Given Horne's performance at Mons, he would have been the obvious choice.

The 10 September had passed relatively quietly for 1st Queens. They had marched off at 8 a.m. from Le Thiolet along the road to Paris before turning north through Lucy, Tourcy and Courchamps where they, too, noted that 2nd Brigade (who were leading the division), had suffered heavy casualties. Having then waited until dusk, the Queens marched to Priez before bivouacking in Sommelans.[36] Similarly, the Coldstreams had marched to Latilly where they

---

28   TNA WO 95/1263: War Diary of the 1st Battalion Scots Guards, 9 September 1914.
29   TNA WO 95/1248: War Diary of the XXV Brigade RFA, 9 September 1914.
30   Becke, *Order of Battle of Divisions – Part 1*, pp. 36-37.
31   TNA WO 95/1280: War Diary of the 1st Battalion South Wales Borderers, 9 September 1914.
32   Davies, F. and Maddocks, G., *Bloody Red Tabs: General Officer Casualties of the Great War 1914-1918* (London: Leo Cooper, 1995), pp. 58-59.
33   TNA WO 95/1248: War Diary of the XXV Brigade RFA, 10 September 1914.
34   TNA WO 95/1248: War Diary of the 113th battery, RFA 10 September 1914.
35   TNA WO 95/1248: War Diary of the XXV Brigade RFA, 10 September 1914.
36   TNA WO 95/1280: War Diary of the 1st Queens Royal West Surrey, 10 September 1914.

bivouacked.[37] Although the Scots Guards had been issued breakfast at 4.30 a.m., they did not march off until 7 a.m. They then proceeded to advance through Torcy to near Courchamps where they noted that 3rd Brigade was being heavily engaged. The battalion halted for an hour and a half in the vicinity of Sommelans before marching, at 3.15 p.m., to billets at La Tilly which was "close by".[38] This seems to be further evidence of the success of the German rearguards in delaying the British advance. It also suggests that brigades were not acting in mutual support or pushing on as fast as they might.

The Borderers had been sent off at 5 a.m. when new orders had arrived as the advanced guard of the brigade. These new orders were said to arise from news that the French had defeated a German army on the day before,10 September. So, the Borderers were to be the advanced guard of the brigade (and division) and cut through to arrive on the flank of the "panic-stricken" retiring Germans. However, the diary record contradicts this explanation. The day consisted of a march to Villeneuve across wooded country before being billeted. Great pleasure was noted regarding the first lot of mail for ten days, albeit that it arrived late and so could not all be distributed immediately. Therefore, some was loaded on to the transport wagons.[39] The Coldstreams advanced to fresh billets in Bruyeres.[40] The Scots Guards had made a quicker start than on the day before; they again breakfasted at 4.30 a.m. but this time they were on the march by 5 a.m. They then advanced eastwards and halted to the north-east of Bruyeres.[41] The XXV Brigade RFA, starting at 5 a.m., marched for seven and a half hours to reach Courcy where they bivouacked.[42]

11 September was proving to be a frustrating day for Brigadier Landon's staff as they recorded that they got under way at 5.45 a.m. and reached Villeneuve but then received several different orders before going "into billets at 11.30 a.m.!!". Brigade also noted that the men had all either lost or thrown away their mess tin covers so they were all black now. The Brigadier reported seeing French guns in action at Branges and large numbers of French mounted troops and other services at Fare en Tardenois.[43] With French guns in action and the British going into billets before lunch time, it is difficult to describe the allies as pursuing the retreating Germans so much as sauntering after them.

The afternoon and evening of 11 September were described as stormy, and 3rd Brigade worked hard to get virtually every man under a roof of some kind. They also noted that with the bad weather billeting the men would be important, as the majority did not have a greatcoat. On the positive side it was noted that the abundance of oat, wheat and barley straw made the men much more comfortable. There was enough to lie on and for them to cover themselves. The benefit extended to the horses which were able to supplement their ration oats with local oats as well as green fodder.

Therefore, it is clear that individual units actively engaged the enemy on occasions. However, overall, the evidence suggests 1st Division, and therefore I Corps, were not harrying at the heels

---

37   TNA WO 95/1263: War Diary of the 1st Battalion Coldstream Guards, 6 September 1914.
38   TNA WO 95/1263: War Diary of the 1st Battalion Scots Guards, 10 September 1914.
39   TNA WO 95/1280: War Diary of the 1st Battalion South Wales Borderers,11 September 1914.
40   TNA WO 95/1263: War Diary of the 1st Battalion Coldstream Guards, 11 September 1914.
41   TNA WO 95/1263: War Diary of the 1st Battalion Scots Guards, 11 September 1914.
42   TNA WO 95/1248: War Diary of the XXV Brigade RFA, 11 September 1914.
43   TNA WO 95/1274: War Diary of the 3rd Brigade,11 September 1914.

of the Germans. Therefore, the Germans had been able to reach the Aisne with some breathing space; would it be enough to make use of the topography?

6

Aisne
Advance to Contact.

Context

Following their decision to retreat from the Marne, the Germans had decided to use the high ground overlooking the River Aisne to regain the initiative by ending their retreat. This ridge is known as the "Chemin des Dames" as the high ground was dry enough for the coaches taking ladies of the French court. This meant that the advancing British forces would now face an enemy that had turned to fight. The German "Schlieffen Plan" had failed to deliver outright victory over France with the opening blow. Therefore, what was at stake on the Aisne was whether the French, with British assistance, could convert the Marne from a defensive victory into a decisive one, in which the Germans were cleared out of occupied northern France.

Plan

The approach to the Aisne took place on the 11-13 September 1914. The plan, in so far as there was one, focused on two key challenges: the weather and the Germans, in that order. The afternoon and evening of 11 September were described as stormy. At 8.30 p.m., 3 Brigade received orders from Major General Lomax for a probable advance the next morning, and orders were issued to battalions an hour and a half later.[1] The orders from Lomax designated 3 Brigade as the advance guard and listed which units would follow behind the infantry.

The difficulties with staff work were also evident. Division had, as instructed by Gough, supplied detailed start times for all units. However, there was a caveat that if two roads were used, then the start time for the supporting brigades would be advanced by two hours. This arose from the very general nature of the initial orders from Corps; "Be prepared to continue march tomorrow at 5am in same direction as today". Not yet knowing what roads would be used created the very uncertainty Haig said he was trying to avoid. The GSO1, Fanshawe, would go on to enjoy a strong wartime career as a combat commander. He would be noted for his informal

---

1 TNA WO 95/1274: War Diary of the 3rd Brigade, 11 September 1914.

relationship with his troops. It seems he was less well suited to his initial desk role or that the fault lay with Corps who were slow to provide specific orders.

The typed orders from Corps were only timed at Midnight. The short summary regarding the routes was telegraphed over and 1st Division headquarters received it at 12.02am and acknowledged it at 12.04am. The start time was amended in pencil from the original 5am to 6am. Presumably to reflect the lateness in issuing the formal orders. Gough specifically stated the lines of march for each division. He then added that when the units reached these destinations, the troops were to be billeted under divisional arrangements. This created a built-in limit to the day's advance.

Why was Gough referring to a pursuit but planning for a procession? Gough's instructions included a very positive review of the situation. He stated that the French Ninth Army had inflicted a severe reverse on the German Imperial Guard. In addition, the French XVIII Corps was stated to be advancing against little opposition. There was also a reference to the French Sixth Army advancing south-west of Metz – this had been corrected to Soissons in the margin. A situation map retained with 1st Division's diary fairly accurately recorded where the Germans were. It also showed them in lines along the ridges ahead. However, each line was accompanied by an arrow showing it was in retreat. The map seems to reflect the dispositions described by Gough. It covers too wide an area to have been collated by 1st Division, from its own intelligence. Clearly, Gough may have been receiving inaccurate information, but Haig was not reading the ground ahead of him. As Corps commander this was a key role for him to fulfil. Advancing against a well-trained opponent, he was conceding the advantage of the ground if the Germans were professional enough to seize it. This seems to be an early example of an over optimistic view of the Germans being more damaged than they really were. The weaknesses identified in Haig during the 1912 manoeuvres resurface here.

Operations

The weather made more immediate demands upon the staff., and 3rd Brigade worked hard to get virtually every man under a roof of some kind. They had also noted that with the bad weather billeting the men would be important, as the majority did not have a greatcoat. The decision by Sir John French to offload baggage during the retreat was manifesting itself negatively now. On the positive side it was noted that the abundance of oat, wheat and barley straw made the men much more comfortable, as there was enough to lie on and for them to cover themselves. The benefit extended to the horses which were able to supplement their ration oats with local oats as well as green fodder.

Having been notified of a "probable" advance the evening before, on 12 September, 3 Brigade were advancing at the head of 1st Division with the 2nd Welsh in the vanguard and 1st Gloucesters leading the main body. The grit in the wheels of the machine could manifest itself in different ways. The Borderers were due to move off at 5.30 a.m. but were held up by Reddie's torn coverlet. Madame, with whom he had been billeted, despite the immediate offer of five Francs in payment, made three visits to the adjutant before the matter could be settled.[2] The Gloucesters advanced through Fere en Tardois, then Loupeignes, and were in close touch

---

2   TNA WO 95/1280: War Diary of the 1st Battalion South Wales Borderers,12 September 1914.

with the French on their right. The French motor-buses were seen in Mont Notre Dame. When the Gloucesters reached Bazoches, they were told that the Germans were occupying the high ground near Perles. [3]

1st South Wales Borderers recorded that they marched through Fere, Loupeignes, Bruys and Bazoches. They were following the same road as a German column which was one and a half miles ahead. According to the Borderers, the French artillery was shelling this body of Germans from both flanks. There was some delay in deploying the leading battalion of the brigade and therefore the Borderers were brought up and deployed, and the advance resumed.[4] The same comment is reproduced in the annals of the Gloucesters. According to the Gloucesters, the Welsh were sent forward to reconnoitre at 1 p.m.[5] This observation reinforces the view that Haig's Corps were not aggressively pursuing the Germans, since the Welsh were supposed to be the vanguard of the leading brigade but appear to have waited for the rest of the brigade to arrive before pushing forward.

Meantime, the Gloucesters were "ordered to deploy and advance by the S in Paars to where the word Vauxcere is written on the map".[6] The detailed knowledge of any area was limited and at least this offered clarity to the map holder. Consequently, a and b companies were deployed as an outpost line, amidst the pouring rain, with two companies of the Welsh on their left, whilst the rest of the Gloucesters went into billets in Vauxcere. Many of these men were accommodated in the caves.[7] The diarist of the Borderers recorded the observation that they had arrived too late to be able to aid 2nd Division by turning the flank of the Germans who were opposing them in a stiff fight off to their left. The Borderers eventually reached Vauxcere at 8 p.m. and billeted there. Their diarist noted the receipt of a nice mail parcel from mother containing food and tobacco. He also noted that the Headquarters mess were of the opinion that they are truly fortunate to be billeted in a house, on a night on which the weather is so dreadful. [8] The Coldstreams were less fortunate to be bivouacked at Bazoches.[9]

The Scots Guards breakfasted at 5.30 a.m. but only moved off at 9 a.m.[10] These long delays before marching would have increased the fatigue of the men and shows Haig's instructions were not being followed. However, as discussed above, Corps were late distributing the orders. So poor staff work, possibly at both levels, was leading to confusion over start times. The original Corps warning order had been for 5am, later altered to 6am but Lomax had said times for the main body might be advanced by two hours. Having breakfasted, the Scots Guards were later being given the opportunity to stop for dinners to be eaten at Soupeigne. The Guards then proceeded at 4.30 p.m. to Bazoches, where one company was fortunate to be billeted, whilst the remainder of the battalion bivouacked in the pouring rain.[11] Brigade noted that the axis of their advance had altered to a north-easterly one.[12]

---

3   TNA WO 95/1278: War Diary of the 1st Battalion Gloucestershire Regiment,12 September 1914.
4   TNA WO 95/1280: War Diary of the 1st Battalion South Wales Borderers,12 September 1914.
5   TNA WO 95/1278: War Diary of the 1st Battalion Gloucestershire Regiment,12 September 1914.
6   TNA WO 95/1278: War Diary of the 1st Battalion Gloucestershire Regiment,12 September 1914.
7   TNA WO 95/1278: War Diary of the 1st Battalion Gloucestershire Regiment,12 September 1914.
8   TNA WO95/1280: War Diary of the 1st Battalion South Wales Borderers,12 September 1914.
9   TNA WO95/1263: War Diary of the 1st Battalion Coldstream Guards, 12 September 1914.
10 TNA WO95/1263: War Diary of the 1st Battalion Scots Guards, 12 September 1914.
11 TNA WO95/1263: War Diary of the 1st Battalion Scots Guards, 12 September 1914.
12 TNA: WO95/1227: War Diary of the 1st Brigade,12 September 1914.

Edmonds notes that 1st Division stopped two miles short of the Aisne. The men of 2 Brigade went into billets at 5.30pm, though the divisional artillery were in action by then.[13] Clearly, Edmonds judged this negatively as II Corps had effected a crossing.

Commentary

In the official history, Edmonds gives a positive account of the role of 4th Division. He then adds the comment; "Had other divisions been equally enterprising – and their marches on the 12th had been shorter than those of the 4th Division,- the fighting on the 13th might have had a different result." Edmonds asserts that the objectives laid down by GHQ involved the BEF occupying the ridge known as the Chemin des Dames. The published orders do not state this explicitly but the stated roads and lines for head of Corps in Operation Order No. 23 imply this. In addition, corps and divisional commanders would have previously received Special Instruction No. 23. The latter explicitly refers to facilitating the passage of the BEF through the wooded country south-west of Laon. As noted above, 2nd Division were engaged by the Germans. Edmonds is clearly being critical of 1st Division, therefore, but his generalisation means the criticism of Haig is oblique.

---

13   TNA WO 95/2167: War Diary of 2 Brigade, 12 September 1914.

7

The Fateful 13th?

Following their advance on the Marne, the Germans had avoided envelopment by the French Sixth Army by withdrawing from the front where they faced the BEF and the French Fifth Army. As explained above, Gallieni's decision to launch his Sixth Army forward too soon had alerted the German First Army to its strategic vulnerability. As a result of the German withdrawal, the allies had been able to advance up to the Aisne.

However, as the allies advanced, the Germans then held the initiative as to where to make a stand. This is where the nature of the British pursuit becomes critical. As we have seen, I Corps was advancing into the area left by the Germans. I Corps were following the Germans rather than pursuing them. This would give the Germans time to organise a line of resistance.

Bulow, and therefore von Kluck, decided that the high ground beyond the Aisne, (known as the Chemin des Dames) would offer them the opportunity to form a new defensive "line". This is reflected particularly in the orders issued by von Kluck at 8pm on 11 September. He ordered that the divisions already on the north bank of the Aisne should cover those to the south of the river. Under this cover, the divisions south of the Aisne were to cross to the north bank. In particular, von Kluck specified that all the heavy artillery were to be on the northern side.[1] The heavy artillery were one of the slowest elements of his army; if he did not intend to stand and fight then some would have been sent further north. The presence of heavy artillery would prove crucial in frustrating British attempts at a breakthrough.

The 1st Cavalry Brigade were concerned that they had been assigned a big job in being asked to get across the Aisne. They had been told on 12 September that the bridge was blown. So on 13 September they saddled up at 4.30 a.m. and tried to find a crossing. When they reached the river, they found the canal bridge was available and used it to get across before moving on to Pargnon. They were supported by the 2nd KRRC of 2 Brigade. The 2nd KRRC moved on up to the high ground above Bourg. There they cleared away small parties of Germans. In doing so they suffered 8 men wounded. The brigade noted that the 2nd KRRC were not involved in any serious engagement. The 2nd Royal Sussex were there in immediate support. There was no sense of the need to push on. By their own account, they went into billets at 3.30pm.[2]

---

1   Kluck, Alexander, *The March on Paris* (Barnsley: Pen & Sword, 2012), p.115
2   TNA WO 95/1267: War Diary of the 2nd Brigade,13 September 1914.

The cavalry lambasted the poor staff work of the cavalry division. They were angry because when they withdraw in the evening, they find their assigned billets full of the infantry and artillery. They ended up bivouacking in the rain.³ Their withdrawal itself only emphasises how the Germans were being given every opportunity to get a firm footing on the heights ahead. When the 1st Division reached the Aisne at Bourg, the crossings were lightly held, and the Germans were observed in columns "for some hours" moving from west to east along the high ground to the north. The cavalry took the crossing and the advanced elements of 2 Brigade and the XXV Brigade RFA led the way across to the far bank.⁴ At 2.15 p.m., 3 Brigade departed for Bourg with the Queens leading, but they soon encountered considerable delays, as the cavalry division's ammunition column, train and ambulances were all using the same road. Landon blamed this on the cavalry division coming on to the road at odd moments.⁵ Landon may have been unfair to the cavalry division here, as Lieutenant General Murray's orders, issued on 12 September, assigned the route through Bourg to both I Corps and the Cavalry Division. This only emphasises that problems of poor staff work started with GHQ.

Haig's I Corps was also assigned a western road, but this would have to be shared at its western end with II Corps. In addition, Murray had added that "Cavalry transport will have precedence over that of corps."⁶ Grammatically speaking, that meant that cavalry transport had precedence over corps transport. This would have implied, cavalry, infantry, cavalry transport, infantry transport in that order. It is nonetheless easy to see the potential for confusion. Therefore, 3 Brigade reached the Aisne at 4 p.m. and had all crossed to Bourg by 5.30 p.m.⁷ The Borderers recorded that they rested in their billets all morning and only marched off at 2.30 p.m. The battalion then advanced to Bourg where they could see a portion of the aqueduct, which was effectively a bridge, had been demolished by the Germans. The Borderers proceeded to rest about five hundred yards from the Aisne until dusk, before it joined the rest of 3 Brigade in billets just north of Bourg. ⁸

The Coldstreams had also passed through Bourg but had been sent north of the Aisne and bivouacked near Moulins. The whole of 1 Brigade passed through 2 Brigade at Moulins.⁹ The Coldstreams bivouacked close to that village at about 11 p.m.¹⁰. After another 5.30 a.m. breakfast, the Scots Guards too made their way across the Aisne, at Bourg, and advanced to billets in Paissy. They crossed the Aisne as part of 1 (Guards) Brigade, which crossed at around 3.30pm. By that time, 2 Brigade, the advance guard, were going into their billets in Moulin. The division sustained some casualties from long range artillery fire. Later units were not met with the sniper fire that had greeted the cavalry. This was because the 2nd KRRC had been deployed earlier to clear them. For example, three Scots Guards were killed, by German shelling, whilst

---

3   TNA WO 95/1108: War Diary of the 1st Cavalry Division, 13 September 1914.
4   TNA WO 95/1239: War Diary of the 1st Division CRA, 13 September 1914.
5   TNA WO 95/1274: War Diary of the 3rd Brigade,13 September 1914.
6   Edmonds, *OH, 1914*, Vol. 1, Appendix 23, p.563.
7   TNA WO 95/1274: War Diary of the 3rd Brigade, 13 September 1914.
8   TNA WO 95/1280: War Diary of the 1st Battalion South Wales Borderers, 13 September 1914.
9   TNA WO 95/1263: War Diary of the 1st Battalion Scots Guards,13 September 1914.
10 TNA WO 95/1263: War Diary of the 1st Battalion Coldstream Guards, 13 September 1914.

eleven men were wounded in addition to Second Lieutenant Balfour and Second Lieutenant Monkton[11], the latter died of his wounds.[12]

The 1st Division staff had noted the stiffening German resistance encountered by the French at the Vesle in the morning. This was then partially dismissed as having stemmed from the French being caught in column of route. Brigadier Landon was in charge of the advanced guard. He was told by French troops that Germans were occupying the slopes. This had not deterred the 2nd Welsh from advancing. Initially, at least they encountered no Germans. However, infantry from 2 Brigade encountered German infantry occupying the spur east of Vendresse supported by a battery in Cerny.[13] Support for 2 Brigade arrived in the shape of the XXV Brigade RFA. They came into action at about 4.30 p.m., on high ground around Vendresse and Paissy. The gunners put down long range fire on the German positions north-west of Troyon, with French batteries coming into action on their right.[14] The 113th battery, having also crossed at Bourg, noting how stormy it was, recorded firing 167 rounds at distant infantry targets after coming into action at Pargnan,[15] with the assistance of 30th howitzer battery.[16]

Lomax's staff recorded delays in pushing on from the positions 2 Brigade had gained because it was felt necessary to throw out strong flank guards. The sound of heavy firing, presumed to be on 2nd Division's front, was noted at 3pm. No attempt was made to support 2nd Division.

Despite the fact that the divisional staff knew that most of 1 Brigade had arrived last and after dark; they asked them to be ready at 3am. At 3am they were to send a reconnaissance party to see whether the Germans were holding the western section of the Chemin des Dames. The staff had already decided at 7.50 pm to task 2 Brigade with seizing Troyon and reconnoitring it beforehand. The official, & therefore agreed, report said he received these orders at 11.30pm. That suggests that Bulfin did not know until 11.30pm. As the decision had been made four hours earlier this suggests internal communication was not a strength in the division.[17] these orders had presumably been triggered by several aerial reconnaissance reports of considerable numbers of German troops in the area of the Chemin des Dames.[18]

---

11 TNA WO 95/1263: War Diary of the 1st Battalion Scots Guards, 13 September 1914.
12 In re-compiling the diary, an error has crept in, Thus Second Lieutenant Houldsworth is recorded by the CWGC as dying of his wounds on 23 September 1914, that is, ten days later. The 23 year old son of a vicar and graduate of Magdalen College Oxford, was therefore mortally wounded rather than killed crossing the Aisne. For Houldsworth see < https://www.cwgc.org/find-records/find-war-dead/casualty-details/258389/WILLIAM%20GILBERT%20HOULDSWORTH/> (accessed 23 July 2017).
13 TNA WO 95/1239: War Diary of the 1st Division CRA,13 September 1914.
14 TNA WO 95/1248: War Diary of the XXV Brigade RFA, 13 September 1914.
15 TNA WO 95/1248: War Diary of the 113 battery RFA, 13 September 1914.
16 TNA WO 95/1239: War Diary of the 1st Division CRA,13 September 1914.
17 TNA WO 95/1227: War Diary of the 1st Division, 13 September 1914, Appendix.
18 TNA WO 95/1227: War Diary of the 1st Division,13 September 1914, Appendix

8

Battle for the Chemin Des Dames, 14 September 1914

In terms of infantry, the I Corps was on the right of the British line with I Cavalry Division and 1st Division on the right. On 14 September 1914, 1st Division, in conjunction with 2nd Division, carried out Haig's orders to attack the heights of the Chemin des Dames. Haig believed they would only be opposed by a screen of cavalry.[1] As in so many of his battles, Haig's men paid the price of his faulty appraisal of the situation facing his troops. He ignored Sir John French's orders to press forward on 13 September.[2] The delay had assisted the Germans by affording them extra time.

Corps orders were that 1st Division should continue its march to Athie via Vendresse and Chamouille. This involved advancing across the Chemin des Dames. Therefore, the advance guard was to secure the section of the road between Cerney and the crossroads south of Courecon. The advance guard, principally formed by 1 Brigade, was then to cover the advance of the rest of the division northwards.

2 Brigade

Despite the subsequent focus on 2 Brigade during the day, it had originally been planned for 1(Guards) Brigade to lead the way. The Coldstreams were ready to move at 6 a.m. The CRA, Brigadier-General Horne, had allocated 116th battery to support the advanced guard formed by 1(Guards) Brigade.[3] Horne, as CRA, had followed the original plan in allocating the artillery. Horne's understanding correlates with his notes that the allocation of artillery applied until midday. If there was only a light screen then new tasks would be assigned after the situation beyond the ridge became clear. Bulfin had received Balfour's report so he knew that there were probably more men in front of him than Haig had supposed. However, neither he nor Horne could know if they were outposts for a retreating enemy or one that was determined to make a stand.

---

1   Jones, S., (ed.), *Stemming the Tide: Officers and Leadership in the British Expeditionary Force 1914* (Solihull: Helion, 2013) p. 126.
2   Jones (ed.), *Stemming the Tide*; p. 127.
3   TNA WO 95/1239: War Diary of the 1st Division CRA, 14 September 1914.

Battle for the Chemin Des Dames, 14 September 1914   47

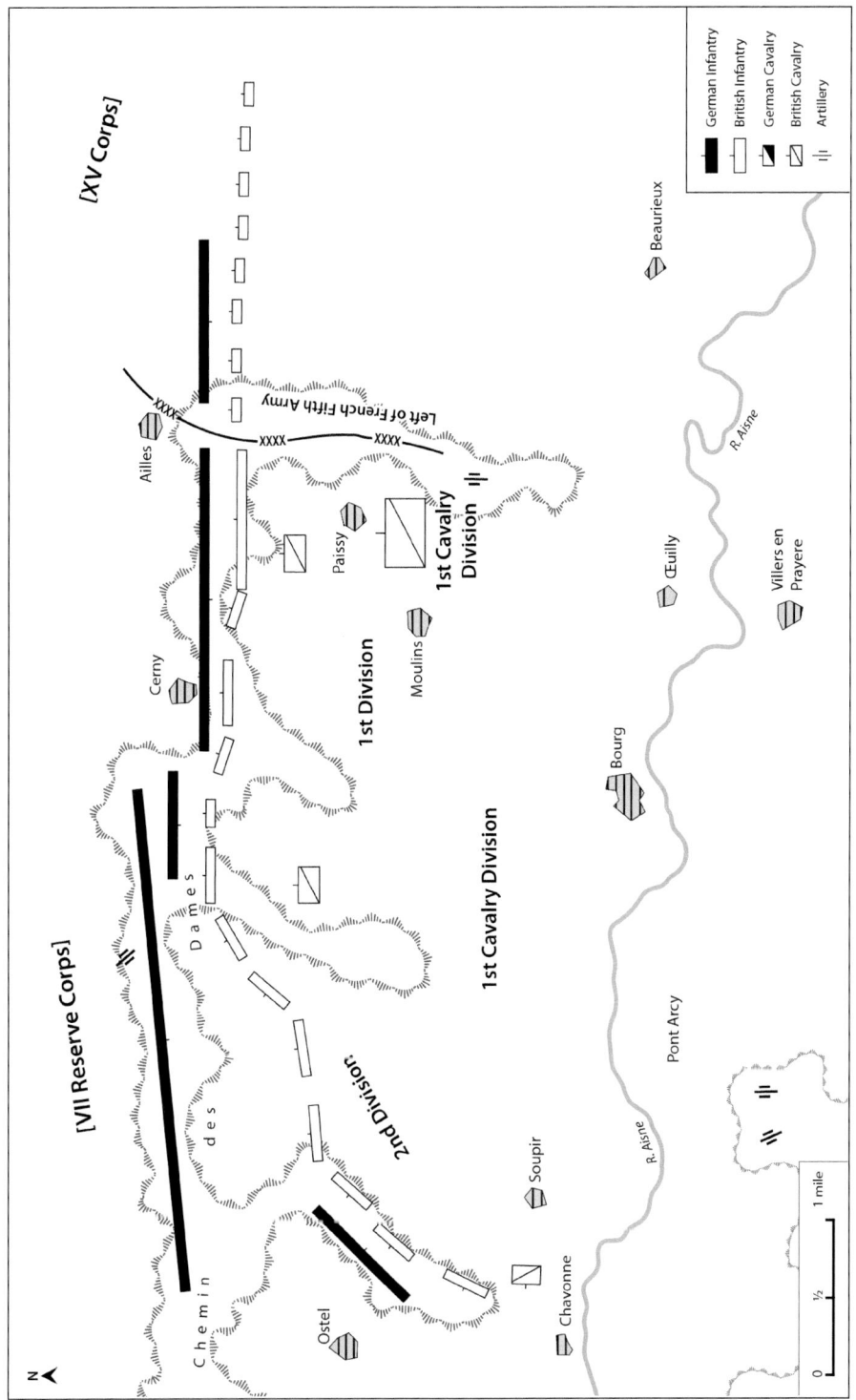

Chemin des Dames, September 1914.

During the day, the back areas of the division came under shell fire from the German heavy artillery. The casualties included Quarter-Master-Sergeant Castleton, a clerk on the CRE's staff and Sergeant Michel, a French interpreter attached to headquarters. Castleton was 35 and left a widow, Lilian, in Putney. The casualties would have been heavier, but a supply wagon had just arrived, and a company sergeant major had called the men over in order to draw rations, so they were not at the edge of the road when the shell burst. Meanwhile, the headquarters of the signal section was afforded some protection by the doors off an old motor car.[4]

At approximately 11.30 p.m. on 13 September, Bulfin received orders for 2 Brigade to seize the high ground around Troyon.[5] Horne had allocated XXV Brigade RFA, less 115th battery to support 2 Brigade. Bulfin immediately sent out a patrol of nine men to reconnoitre the ground to be assaulted and this was led by Second Lieutenant Balfour of the 2nd KRRC. Balfour's report said that there was a German picquet at the factory north of Troyon, along with other troops in the factory's vicinity.[6]

In accordance with Bulfin's orders, the 2nd KRRC, with 2nd Royal Sussex in support, set off at 3 a.m. to start to move into position. They had to go forward in a thick mist and it was raining. An hour later, Bulfin despatched the 1st Northants to take the spur to the east of Noyon. This was about the same time that the leading men of the KRRC reached the Sucerie (also referred to as the Factory) at Noyon. The hamlet is set about 80 yards below the ridge where the road runs. At 5.30 a.m., Bulfin himself went forward with his brigade reserve, the 1st Loyal North Lancs.[7] Elements of the 9th Lancers, part of 2 Cavalry brigade, had also been sent into the same area. They clashed with German troops and the KRRC moved to join them in pushing forward. However, the heavy fire received forced the cavalry to back away. So now the KRRC were engaged directly with the defenders by 5am.

Within about 45 minutes, the original three companies of the KRRC had been reinforced. Their reserve company had come up as well as elements of 2nd Royal Sussex. As the 2nd Royal Sussex came up, Lieutenant-Colonel Serocold, CO of 2nd KRRC, directed them to the left. Here the Germans were in trenches about 300 yards away. A firefight ensued. Some Germans tried to surrender but the Sussex took casualties when other Germans fired at their comrades and would be captors. The CO of the Sussex, Lieutenant-Colonel Montressor was killed in this phase of the fighting. The Sussex secure approximately 300 prisoners.

Half an hour later, at 6 a.m., Bulfin conferred with Brigadier Maxse and asked him to send a battalion to support the KRRC. Bulfin made this request because the Sussex had already been brought up on either side of the KRRC, and the officer commanding the Rifles had asked for support to be sent to his right. Maxse responded by sending the 1st Coldstream Guards.[8] They headed off in a thick mist towards Cerney.[9] They were aware that a German battery had

---

4   TNA WO 95/1255: War Diary of the 1st Division, Signals, 14 September 1914.
5   The primary source for 2nd Brigade operations is Bulfin's report which was completed after 17 September and was returned to the brigade archives by Haig in 1919.
6   TNA WO 95/1267: War Diary of the 2nd Brigade, 13 September 1914.
7   TNA WO 95/1267: War Diary of the 2nd Brigade, September 1914.
8   The official after action report says that Maxse sent the Coldstreams and the Camerons. However, the Camerons records strongly suggest they did not know they were working together though they eventually linked up. By the time the official report was completed Maxse had gone back to England to assume a divisional command.
9   TNA WO 95/1263: War Diary of the 1st Battalion Scots Guards, 14 September 1914.

been observed there on the previous afternoon. Under Bulfin's leadership the engagement had developed into an attack by both brigades.[10]

At around 7am, the Sussex had been able to overlap the flank of the German troops opposite them and some more Germans were willing to surrender. They were prevented from doing so by their own artillery. Having fired on their own men, the German artillerymen tried to get their guns away. However, the Sussex and KRRC were able to capture the guns. Amidst the continuing fighting the captured guns remained where they were and re-captured in the evening. Their neighbours, the Northamptons, lost 37-year-old Captain Gordon, whilst he was leading his company up into the advanced trenches.

Bulfin moved forward to the road junction east of the word Troyon on the map. Bulfin found that all his units had become mixed up but were forming a line north of the word Troyon on the map but south of the Chemin des Dames. Lomax himself joined his senior commanders at 8am. Lomax knew that apart from the Queen's, already deployed, the head of the column formed by 3 Brigade was about a mile to the south. Lomax was concerned that he was going to be attacked. Therefore, he sent a request to the cavalry division at Tour de Paissy to cover his right flank. At the time there was, to his knowledge, only a regiment of zouaves to his right. On his left there was 6 Brigade near Verneuil, they had been diverted to the Beaulne Spur.[11]

The fighting continued and the British eventually gained control of the factory. Due to the mist the British artillery could not risk firing but some guns were brought up in close support. They caused the Germans significant casualties and boosted the morale of the British infantry. The German artillery was less careful of its own infantry so the British were under heavy fire. Lomax then told 1 Brigade not to advance beyond its objectives until 2nd Division came into line. As we will see Lomax will show great skill in defence but he was clearly a commander who worried about his flanks. Seeing the lack of progress, Lomax ordered the rest of 3 Brigade to come into the fight at about 10am. They were to come in on the left of 1 Brigade.

Bulfin now committed his reserves, the Loyal North Lancs. They lost over half the battalion in reinforcing British control of the factory. Bulfin's appraisal was that the Loyal North Lancs held the factory, but that a line of entrenchments north and east of the factory were strongly held by the Germans.[12] Bulfin's personal courage was to be demonstrated many times but he seems to lack imagination here. He committed his reserves to hold a building that was already bleeding two battalions white. The success of the Sussex had been achieved on the flank. The FSRs (1909) stated that every officer should be ready to take the offensive at some point. Lomax was clearly thinking negatively, perhaps this did not help Bulfin who was allowing his brigade to be sucked into a deadly scrum.

Bulfin goes on to describe the very difficult conditions under which his men were fighting; heavy German shellfire and machine guns to break up any attempts by the British to advance. The British also faced hourly counterattacks, from the direction of Courtecon,[13] though Bulfin also noted that these tended to be pushed in with less vigour as time went on. Nonetheless, 2 Brigade eventually fell back to conform to the positions that 1 Brigade had withdrawn to. The

10   TNA WO 95/1239: War Diary of 1st Division CRA, 14 September 1914.
11   It is likely that he was unaware of their direction at the time. Copies of orders would make him aware of units operating on his flanks but these were not updated and distributed routinely during the day.
12   TNA WO 95/1267: War Diary of the 2nd Brigade, 13 September 1914.
13   TNA WO 95/1239: War Diary of the 1st Division CRA, 14 September 1914.

Germans then re-occupied the factory and recaptured the guns taken by the KRRC and the Sussex.

At about 3.45pm, good news began to arrive from neighbouring units. On the left, 2nd Division were reporting that the Germans in front of them were pulling back. To the right of the division, the French XVIII Corps was once again advancing after its earlier assault had been repulsed. Therefore, it was decided that 1st Division would try to advance all across its front. The divisional report states that this did not happen because; "owing to the exhaustion of the troops, the mixture of units and the lack of fresh reserves, it lacked cohesion."[14] Unsurprisingly, the Germans had re-occupied the factory and it was about to be abandoned without a fight. Holding it had not broken the German line so why try to re-occupy it?

Despite the ultimate failure to hold the factory, the commander of the KRRC, Lieutenant Colonel Serocold, was singled out by Bulfin for especial praise. Bulfin attributed to him all the success achieved on the first morning and said that the ground was held because of "his unfailing vigilance and determination". Another factor in the success of the KRRC was given as Major Philips who was "continuously in the firing line steadying the men and directing operations"[15] Bulfin also reported that Major Jelf had been wounded in the face and neck, but only went to the ambulance after nightfall when Bulfin ordered him to do so. Lieutenant Purcell, the Machine Gun Officer, was commended for the handling of the guns on both 14th and 17th. Other KRRC officers who were commended included Captain Leith, Lieutenant Currie, and 2nd-Lieutenant Balfour.

Bulfin also singled out the battalion's Adjutant, Lieutenant the Honourable Eric Edward Montague John Upton, an old Etonian freemason who was the elder son of the 4th Viscount Templetown.[16]; and the grandson of a Lieutenant General whose earlier career included commanding the Coldstream Guards in the Crimean War. Upton was another representative of the Protestant gentry, in his case from Antrim in Ulster, who formed such a key part of the pre-1914 officer corps.

The intensity of the fighting is reflected in the casualty figures for that day. The initial report on casualties was 41 officers including eleven killed and sixteen missing. In addition, no fewer than 926 other ranks had become casualties. Of whom 44 were dead and 583 were stated as missing.[17] Even if the brigade had been at full strength this would have been equivalent to losing one of its four battalions in a single day. With such high casualties, including many officers, Bulfin was keen to draw attention to the leadership shown by CSM Dean, who took charge of his company when all the officers were wounded, Bulfin also commended CSMs Walter and Reed, Sergeant Trotter and Bugler Gibson, as well as riflemen Waid and Varley.[18]

The 2nd Royal Sussex had also been heavily engaged in the fighting on the first morning, and Bulfin noted that their commanding officer Lieutenant Colonel Montresor was missing when his report was written; in fact, he had been killed. Bulfin also commended the coolness and self-sacrifice of the Sussex's Adjutant Lieutenant the Honourable H L Pelham, fourth son of the 5th

---

14　TNA WO 95/1239: War Diary of the 1st Division September 1914, Appendix.
15　TNA WO 95/1267: War Diary of the 2nd Brigade, 13 September 1914.
16　For particulars of Upton's life and later death, see *Captain The Hon Eric Edward Montague John UPTON* <http://masonicgreatwarproject.org.uk/legend.php?id=3153> (accessed 16 July 2017).
17　TNA WO 95/1267: War Diary of the 2nd Brigade, 13 September 1914.
18　TNA WO 95/1267: War Diary of the 2nd Brigade, 17 September 1914.

Earl of Chichester, who was also missing but was later known to have been killed. Bulfin later wrote to Pelham's family:

> Pelham with a handful of men of the Sussex held on to the Chemin des Dames, and it was here that he lost his life, working the machine guns, and he died one of the most brave and gallant gentlemen it has ever been my honour to know. A fine capable officer who put his duty before everything, and by his self-sacrificing devotion set a splendid example to us all. By his death the Regiment has suffered a terrible loss and the Army has lost a most capable officer, who would have gone far in his profession.[19]

1 Brigade

The Coldstreams split off, as Maxse had ordered, in support of 2 Brigade. The Coldstreams[20] moved forward in the general direction of Cerney, over the high ground between Vendresse and Paissy. This would bring them up on the left of 2 Brigade.[21] Initially, the rest of 1 (Guards) Brigade followed; the Camerons, the Black Watch and the Scots Guards, in that order. Due to the thick mist, which did not disperse until 11am, the artillery could not determine how far the British troops had advanced so they could not offer supporting fire.[22]

In the thick mist the Coldstream Guards surprised the German defenders at Cerney en Laonnais. The Germans were members of the 16th Regiment and 53rd Reserve Regiment. They had hastily dug these fire trenches after being diverted off their march the previous evening. The 16th Regiment was drawn from Westphalia and was part of VII Corps in Second Army. Given the evidence contained in the captured diary of the Adjutant it is clear that 16th Regiment were diverted southwards, at midnight, the night before.[23] This catches one of those moments when the front stabilised as there had been a gap (more properly termed an exposed flank) into which they had been inserted just hours before the British advanced. If they had not been there, 1 Brigade could have advanced past 2 Brigade's left and reached the rear of the Germans obstructing 2 Brigade.

Having been surprised by the Coldstreams, Major Bucshulz's battalion of 116th Regiment fell back in disorder. However, the trenches that they had lost were south of Cerney village. The Germans had sited machine guns to the east of Cerney, but they had been echeloned forward so they could enfilade the captured position. The Germans had also pushed forward a battery of field artillery and although one gun got away, the other five remained where they were. The Germans reacted to the initial British success by throwing in all the available companies of

---

19 For Pelham's particulars, see *Pelham, Herbert Lyttleton* <https://keymerclaytonwarmemorials.wordpress.com/herbert-lyttelton-pelham/> accessed 16 July 2016
20 The Adjutant of the Coldstreams recorded that the detailed records were lost in the subsequent fighting in October so the account in the war diary has obviously had to be reconstructed. The diary of the signals contains internal evidence suggesting it was compiled by 1 October, so it was much more contemporaneous than the reconstructed diaries.
21 TNA WO 95/1263: War Diary of the 1st Battalion Coldstream Guards, 14 September 1914.
22 TNA WO 95/1239: War Diary of the 1st Division CRA, 14 September 1914.
23 TNA WO 95/1255: War Diary of the 1st Division Signals, 15 September 1914.

53rd Reserve Regiment. Major Bucshulz's men, who were clearly being required to redeem themselves, joined the counterattack. However, the German heavy artillery fired short and hit the firing line of the 16th Regiment. So Bucshulz's men were allowed to retire whilst the village itself was shelled by the German artillery. Then the Germans noted that the British were extending to their left, so the Adjutant was sent back to Chamouille, to fetch reinforcements. This "extension" probably relates to the arrival of the Camerons on the slopes, though it could be the Coldstreams who eventually overlapped with the Camerons on their left.[24] Pending his return, initially the 53rd Regiment pulled back to the ridge, which meant they were about 500 metres from their original positions as they had also moved to the left. Although the mist had helped to create a tactical surprise, it had blinded the British artillery. Now the Coldstream Guards were in a fire fight too close to their opponents for the artillery to assist.

The Germans then sent in reinforcements; more companies of 16th and 53rd regiments with the addition of a company of 4th Jaegar and some Garde Schutzen as well as elements of 13th Regiment. Despite the weight of forces thrown against them, The Coldstreams remained there until ordered to retire at dusk.[25] The Germans were then able to re-occupy the shell that remained of Cerney. Any remaining concerns the Germans had about their left were then solved. At 8.20 p.m. Major General Fritz von Arnim arrived with 150 men from the 27th Landwehr Regiment, and the machine gun company of 16th Regiment also took station on 53rd Regiment's left. There is a parallel with the later fighting around Ypres. As at Ypres, it was easier for the defender to plug gaps in the line than it was for the attacker to achieve more than a tactical success.

The remainder of 1 (Guards) Brigade deployed at the southwest end of the spur. This was just north of Vendresse itself. The Camerons, now leading the main assault, lost Sergeant Cunningham, of C company. He was killed by long range "un-aimed" rifle fire during the early part of the ascent. The Camerons then deployed with B on the left and A company on the right. The central point was the factory at Troyon. D and C companies advanced behind A and B respectively. As they went forward the Camerons saw enemy infantry emerging from trees on the left so B company echeloned back to protect the flank.

A and D companies therefore went forward to take the factory. As they did so they entered a fire zone covered by German artillery sited on the spur north of Chivy. The Germans were firing a combination of shrapnel and high explosive. Between 7am and 7.20am, the attack by the German infantry developed into a significant one and gradually C and D were drawn into supporting B's defence. The Camerons gained touch with the Coldstreams on their right who were already heavily engaged. A critical point came around 8.15 am. One company of the Black Watch had come up on the left but the right began to fall back. This was where the Camerons overlapped with the Coldstreams. Although some men now dropped back, apparently in good order, the situation was precarious as the line regrouped below the bank of the edge of the road. At this point the situation was stabilised by some artillery fire which forced the Germans back. This had been made possible by the Black Watch They had sent two companies to assist the Camerons. In the intensity of the battle, the Camerons had only seen the company nearest them. Then B company went to assist 116th Battery into action with the remaining company protecting their flank. The German artillery turned its fire on the 116th and German infantry

---

24   See below for details.
25   TNA WO 95/1263: War Diary of the 1st Battalion Coldstream Guards, 14 September 1914.

kept the battery under fire from long range. Once the infantry started to retire the Black Watch assisted in getting the battery to safety.

Following a lull of about ten minutes, the Germans renewed their attack. The initial assault was beaten off with heavy small arms fire. However, casualties began to mount especially once the German artillery opened up again.

It is also alleged that C company, of the Camerons, lost 13 men killed when some Germans waved their rifles over their heads apparently willing to surrender. They were thought to have suddenly laid down and their colleagues behind fired the deadly volley. Obviously, no investigation was possible. Very soon afterwards, part of A company plus D company ran out of ammunition so they retreated into the wood. Many of the officers had become casualties by this point. The wood itself was being shelled. The units had become intermingled and the Brigade now began to fall back. The left fell back by stages towards Chivvy whilst the right went back into the wood northwest of Vendresse. The group in the wood included C company and the HQ detail of the Camerons.[26]

The Coldstreams finished the day holding the spurs that run northeast from Vendresse and Paissy. Such was the intensity of the fighting that whilst ten officers and 180 other ranks were wounded only eleven other ranks were noted as killed on 14 September. However, 162 other ranks and Second Lieutenant the Honourable Freeman-Thomas were recorded as missing. Amongst the wounded was their commander Lieutenant Colonel Ponsonby DSO.[27] The Coldstreams, having been relieved during the night of 14 / 15 September, spent 15 September in reserve, south of Vendresse.[28]

There was heavy shrapnel fire over the area occupied by the signallers, and they observed a constant stream of casualties, from 1st Camerons and 1st Black Watch, coming down from the firing line and into Vendresse. They noted in particular that numerous officers had become casualties, including Colonel Grant Duff. They also recorded seeing a growing number of unwounded men making their way back due, according to the signallers, to a lack of officers to guide them. In reality, after the units fell back there were few officers or NCOs left to provide guidance.

Of the 45 deaths amongst the men of 1st Black Watch on 14 – 15 September 1914 shows thirty were privates, but the others included not only their commanding officer, Lieutenant Colonel Grant Duff CB (whose widow Ursula, designed the *War Book*) but also Major Lord George Stuart Murray, son of the 7th Duke of Athol, and three junior officers. Significantly, there were ten fatalities amongst the Non-Commissioned Officers; these included three sergeants and five lance-corporals. A further 11 officers and 180 other ranks were wounded on 14 September and two officers died of their wounds during the next three days. The 1st Cameron Highlanders suffered 151 fatalities in the same period. Of these, 119 of the dead were privates and nine were officers. Amongst the 23 Non-Commissioned Officers killed were thirteen lance-corporals and four sergeants. Therefore, it would be reasonable to conclude that any unwounded men falling back from the Camerons were likely to have lost their section leaders. Given that this only refers to those killed, it is likely that many others were amongst the wounded. Other senior casualties

---

26 TNA WO 95/1264: War Diary of the 1st Cameron Highlanders, September 1914, Appendix.
27 TNA WO 95/1263: War Diary of the 1st Battalion Coldstream Guards, 14 September 1914.
28 TNA WO 95/1263: War Diary of the 1st Battalion Coldstream Guards, 15 September 1914.

included Lieutenant Colonel Cameron, 1st Division's AA & QMG, who was wounded in the foot.

3 Brigade

The Queen's had been at Moulins at 8 a.m. They had been sent north-eastwards and were aware that 2nd Brigade were already heavily engaged. Despite German shrapnel fire, they were able to reach the security of some woods. Brigadier General Landon and his staff joined the battalion officers of the Queen's in the wood. They could see the situation in the valley ahead, and the tough task it would be to seize the ridge to the west of them. The Brigade Major, Captain Jenkinson, was killed by shrapnel and Lt Johnson of A company was mortally wounded. The attack proceeded with A, C, and D companies leading and B in support. The Queens managed to reach the Chemin des Dames. They also got beyond it to La Bouvelle Farm. Unfortunately, they were not supported. As per the general pattern, this success was not reinforced whereas those who had not succeeded were. With massed Germans ahead little progress could be made. The artillery engaged the Germans at a range of 1800 yards and created piles of corpses.[29] As the mist had cleared, the artillery was able to press forward in support of the infantry. Having advanced to the Arbre de Paissy, they eventually reached the crossroads, where the Aules-Paissy road met the Chemin des Dames, in close support to the Queen's.[30] Faced by growing numbers of the enemy, Lieutenant-Colonel Warren skillfully extricated his isolated battalion.

The 2nd Welsh had set out at 7.10 a.m. to reach the right flank. They had been detached from 3 Brigade for that purpose,[31] reflecting Lomax's concerns. They reached out eastwards and were in close touch with the French on their right who had reached the Chemin des Dames. Therefore, just south of the crossroads, XXVI and XDIII Brigades RFA were in position and engaging the Germans being driven back towards Ailles and Labovelle. Whether the enemy columns seen in the distance at Chermizy and Neuville were actually retiring or not, they were also engaged.

In all this work these batteries were assisted by the heavy section positioned by Abre de Paissy. The artillerymen not only had to contend with small arms fire but also heavy field howitzer shells exploding around them. The vital role that could be played by artillery where it could get close to the action was demonstrated by this incident and underlines the benefit the French army had in defence from the practise of deploying some of the 75mm guns forward in the infantry firing line. The Queen's then advanced beyond the Chemin des Dames ridge but were forced back to the original line due to sustaining heavy casualties especially amongst their officers.[32]

The forcing back of the Queen's had then led to the guns being withdrawn for a while, but the withdrawal was covered by 30th and 118th batteries with one section of 118th battery remaining forward until darkness fell. The French troops also fell back but the Germans did not follow up the advantage and the Anglo-French line was re-stabilised and maintained until dark.[33]

---

29   TNA WO 95/1280: War Diary of the 1st Queen's Royal West Surrey, 15 September 1914.
30   TNA WO 95/1239: War Diary of the 1st Division CRA, 14 September 1914.
31   TNA WO 95/1280: War Diary of the 2nd Battalion, Royal Welsh Fusiliers, 14 September 1914.
32   TNA WO 95/1239: War Diary of the 1st Division CRA, 14 September 1914.
33   TNA WO 95/1239: War Diary of the 1st Division CRA, 14 September 1914.

Meantime, the rest of 3 Brigade had been ordered up at 10 a.m. to advance to support 1 Brigade on its left flank. 1 Brigade was by then engaged in fighting on Mount Faucon and to its right. This advance meant two companies of Gloucesters had become the divisional reserve. The Welsh and the South Wales Borderers were to attack on a front roughly from Le Mont Blanc to the wood south-west of Chivy. The attack was to be supported by XXXIX Brigade RFA and the machine guns of each battalion. The exact front for each battalion's assault was pointed out on the ground, because it was being improvised. However, at 10.30 a.m. it was seen that a German attack was developing along the Beauline Spur. This attack succeeded in driving the leading elements of 2nd Division back upon their supports. Therefore, the Welsh were ordered to deal with this German thrust. The Welsh attacked in the face of heavy artillery and rifle fire. The latter accounted for the death of Captain Jenkinson, the Brigade Major. With the co-operation of the artillery, the Welsh succeeded in pushing the Germans back, but they were unable to advance further, due to heavy enemy artillery fire. During this time, the South Wales Borderers were making slow progress through heavily wooded terrain. The battalion's machine guns, under Captain Lyttleton, managed to take a German trench in enfilade. The Borderers seized the German position and neutralised its machine gun.

Despite having been unable to maintain touch with 1 (Guards) Brigade, the Borderers were ordered to attack the Chemin des Dames Ridge at 3.30 p.m. To their left, the Welsh were ordered to advance too. The Welsh did manage to take 150 prisoners. It was in advancing forward at dusk that 3rd Brigade HQ found the Germans in possession of the Brigade objective and suffered casualties, including three signallers.

After the general advance by 1st Division around 4pm failed to materialise, one operation did take place. At Haig's request, at about 5 p.m., two battalions of 3 Brigade pushed up the Chivy Valley and advanced the line.[34] These two battalions of 3 Brigade were attempting to reach the Chemin des Dames via the Chivy Ravine. Brigadier Landon then went off to set up his headquarters in Chivy. All appeared to be going well, and visual signals suggested 3 Brigade were shifting to the crossroads at the "N in Chemin". News arrived at about the same time that the Germans had recaptured the factory which Bulfin's troops had tried to assault.

By dusk, news of the progress of 3 Brigade began to filter through, and it was not good. Overall, the attack had failed. The final attack was made by Brigadier Landon, accompanied by a platoon of the 2nd Welsh and two companies of the 1st Gloucesters. This final attack had lost its bearings in the dark and run into German resistance before falling back. Brigadier Landon corroborated this summary himself when he reported to divisional headquarters at 11 p.m. Landon reported that the Welsh, who were leading, fell back when fired on and started firing at the Germans. This left Landon and his staff in the middle of the firefight. Landon ordered his men to lie down to avoid being killed by friendly fire. However, Lieutenant Hargreaves, (commanding No.4 section of the cyclists), Sergeant Schulz, Lance-Corporal Swayne and Private Pickering were all subsequently reported missing. As their bodies were not found by a patrol sent out the next evening, it was presumed that they had been wounded and then captured. Amongst the casualties that evening were nearly all the members of the signal section with 3rd Brigade HQ. That confirms that the brigade staff were caught up in the firefight. The Divisional Signal's staff found it hard to imagine what erroneous information had led 3

---

34 Sheffield and Bourne (eds.), *Douglas Haig*, p 71

Brigade to try to move its headquarters across the enemy front in the dark across a featureless landscape.[35]

Conclusion

Nevertheless, 1st Division had performed heroically and when Haig rode over to see Lomax, he told Lomax that the conduct of his troops was "beyond all praise".[36] The commendation from Haig on 14 September, was published to all units on 15 September. Lomax himself received a gratifying despatch from Sir John French, in which the Division was highly commended, and its commander singled out by name for individual praise.[37]

The troops had fought hard and at considerable cost in casualties.

The foregoing does challenge the mutual backslapping going on at general officer level. Lomax had been given the task of advancing over the ridge. Bulfin, a courageous officer, allowed his brigade to be sucked into a fight for the key defensive feature chosen by the Germans. Knowing from his patrols that the factory was occupied, he sent his troops into a frontal assault. Then, instead of seeing his role to be pinning the enemy whilst Maxse turned their flank, he persuaded Maxse to reinforce him. Maxse agreed despite having been given his own objectives. Lomax made it on to the scene and made the situation worse by his concerns over his flanks. These were the sort of umpires who thought Gough "a bit too sharp" when he used the terrain to move his force unseen during the Annual Manoeuvres. Unlike later reports, even as early as 1915, this one restricts itself to a narrative and offers no analysis or learning points.

The day's activity concludes with a reference to 5 Brigade making contact with the 2nd Welsh in their advanced positions during the night. Haig recorded that 5 Brigade made good progress up the Beaulne Spur until it encountered opposition. However, 1st Division's battle report states that 5 Brigade was withdrawn because of the general situation on the British left. Tellingly, the diary states that the Welsh and South Wales Borderers were able to occupy their positions for six days before the Germans pushed their trenches up to a point where it was necessary to pull back. If Haking himself had not suffered a head wound, 5 Brigade might have won the battle of the Aisne by turning the flank of the Germans opposing 1st Division. Haig had asked that troops be sent there and 2nd Welsh had done well. Together with Haking's advance, it could have been a decisive intervention by Haig.

---

35 TNA WO 95/1255: War Diary of the 1st Division Signals, 15 September 1914.
36 Sheffield and Bourne (eds.), *Douglas Haig*, p.71.
37 TNA WO 95/1227: War Diary of the 1st Division, 15 September 1914.

9

Genesis of Trench Warfare

Without knowing it, 1st Division's staff were provided with a picture of the future. On 15 September they received the results of the aerial reconnaissance which had been carried out that morning. They showed that the Germans had dug sets of trenches across large sections of the front. The reconnaissance also revealed that the German artillery had also been deployed in considerable numbers. Here, albeit in a formative version, would be the set of problems that would face generals for the remainder of the war.

The Scots Guards moved into the trenches at Vendresse on 15 September and remained in that position until 19 September (inclusive).[1] The brigade occupied the positions "from tracks south of the first O in Troyon to edge of Chivy Valley" whilst 2 Brigade and one battalion of 3 Brigade were "on the right towards head of valley south of Des in Des Dames".[2] To secure the right of the Queen's, in the area between the Queen's and the French, a composite regiment, consisting of three squadrons of the Household Cavalry, was inserted. Meanwhile, the 4th Dragoon Guards were mustered and waiting in reserve but were not used. They eventually went back to their billets.[3] Haig seems to have treated this as a defensive battle and not committed his reserves. He had been cautious in August and again at the start of the battle of the Marne; it appears again that he lacked the "thruster" characteristic that his later reincarnation as C-in-C so desperately sought in Gough and others.

On 16 September, 2 Brigade only suffered a further 29 casualties, of whom only one was killed outright.[4] However, the 2nd KRRC recorded that they were in reserve but came under accurate shrapnel fire, losing two killed and 29 wounded.[5] On the flank, held by 2nd Division, there was additional help for 1st Division, as 4th Dragoon Guards were sent forward to insert themselves between the Coldstreams and Grenadiers of 4 (Guards) Brigade. They thus freed up the elements of 1(Guards) Brigade that had been fulfilling that role. The 4th Dragoon Guards had been ready to move at 4.30 a.m. but were then told to wait so that the clothing that had arrived during the night could be issued. They had received orders at 7 a.m. to go forward and had set off thirty minutes later.

1　TNA WO 95/1263: War Diary of the 1st Battalion Scots Guards, 15-19 September 1914.
2　TNA WO 95/1227: War Diary of the 1st Division, 15 September 1914.
3　TNA WO 95/1112: War Diary of the 4th Royal Irish Dragoon Guards, 15 September 1914.
4　TNA WO 95/1267: War Diary of the 2nd Brigade, 16 September 1914.
5　TNA WO 95/1263: War Diary of the 1st Battalion Northamptonshire Regiment, 16 September 1914.

At the headquarters in Chivy of 3rd Brigade, Major Frost of the Coldstream Guards reported for duty as the new Brigade Major. Brigadier Landon's staff noted that 3rd Brigade were holding the most advanced positions of 1st Division with two companies of the Royal Welsh holding the western point. The other two companies and the Gloucesters were holding the head of Chivy Valley, on their right. The vulnerability of the advanced companies is made clear in the statement that 'they are entrenched below the crestline and the trenches face in different directions according to the ground'. They were also subject to German artillery fire from batteries located on the Courtecon-Cerny Ridge constantly searching out positions by shelling the ridge.[6] When a major German assault was launched at 4.30 p.m., the guns of the cavalry division assisted the infantry in defeating it.[7] The headquarters of XXV Brigade moved to join the batteries at Moulin, and all batteries were allocated into groups which were each allocated a fire zone.[8]

On 17 September, the fighting intensified once again as the Germans brought up two or more battalions to carry out a counterattack north of the word "des" in "Chemin des Dames". The 2nd KRRC felt that initially the Germans directed their attacks against 3 Brigade before, at about mid-day, switching to focus on 2 Brigade. The attack was preceded by heavy shelling between 2 p.m. and 3 p.m. Under cover of the shelling and benefitting from dense driving rain and a rolling mist, a group of approximately 150 Germans re-occupied one of their abandoned trenches. Therefore Bulfin, who had already moved troops up behind the threatened point, ordered the officers commanding the Northamptons and the Queen's to work together to re-occupy the trench. The 2nd KRRC sent up C and D companies to the right of the Northamptons in support. They succeeded in retaking the trench, losing Captain Prialux at the head of C company. Benefiting from the same mist, a company of the Northamptons got to within a hundred yards of the trench before charging, led by Captain Parker (who was killed), and sending the Germans back in retreat.

This led to the crest of the ridge being lined by the Germans but they were partially enfiladed by the KRRC, D company having sent up reinforcements to C company, and Queen's wheeling around, aided by a squadron of the composite brigade arriving on the flank. This manoeuvre was initiated and overseen by Major Warre DSO of the KRRC and he was cited for this and other skilful leadership, on 14 September, in Bulfin's after action report. The 2nd KRRC sent up further companies and 2nd Brigade now managed to achieve an advance of 200 – 300 yards north of the Chemin des Dames, just east of Cerney. The Queen's came up on the right of the KRRC, whilst a company of the Coldstreams came up on the left. Bulfin's dwindling troops now not only faced the Germans advancing up the north slope, but also fire from a strong force of Germans in a wood. Those Germans had several machine guns, as well as the support of German artillery fire from batteries around Cerny. The Northamptons then recorded a "white flag" incident which led to the death of two of their officers as well as many other ranks.[9] The incident is described in more detail in the combat report of 2 KRRC, who say it was their C company that was targeted. The report names one dead officer, Captain Savage of the Northants, who had gone forward to meet a party of Germans proceeded by their officers,

6 TNA WO 95/1274: War Diary of the 3rd Brigade, 16 September 1914.
7 TNA WO 95/1096: War Diary of the 1st Cavalry Division, 16 September 1914.
8 TNA WO 95/1248: War Diary of the XXV Brigade RFA, 16 September 1914.
9 TNA WO 95/1263: War Diary of the 1st Battalion Northamptonshire Regiment, 17 September 1914.

who were apparently surrendering. Savage had been accompanied by Lieutenant Dimmer, of the KRRC, who became suspicious at the sound of a rifle bolt being released. Dimmer shouted a warning, but Savage's sword prevented him getting straight down and he died as the Germans opened fire. A number of riflemen also died. According to this detailed report, a similar incident then took place in front of the Northamptons, which is presumably a detailed version of the event they recorded. In this case, the officer who went forward was the Brigade Major, Captain Watson of the Queen's, who had ridden up and told the men to cease fire. He spoke to the Germans and then galloped back having become suspicious. The report notes that the 2nd KRRC machine guns, under Lieutenant Percell, then opened fire. Then, when the Germans returned fire, some of the Northants became casualties as they had stood up expecting a surrender to take place. The report particularly noted that the Queen's had been credited with the machine gun fire. However, Lieutenant Henderson of the Queen's saw Colonel Serocold of 2nd KRRC at the time and said his guns were not present. Unsurprisingly, these events initially prevented any further British advance and caused the Northamptons to fall back fifty yards.[10]

Bulfin had already asked for and received the 1st Coldstream Guards from divisional reserve; whom he had placed behind the Northants. The German counterattack was stopped by the machine gun and rifle fire of Bulfin's troops.[11] Bulfin also acknowledged the sterling work of 115th and 116th batteries which had been firing in support of the Northants during their gallant defence.[12] The latter had been attached to 1st Brigade two days earlier but were now entrenched. They had been forced to withdraw from their former position, due to a German aeroplane spotting them and bringing down heavy howitzer fire. There was pressure too on 118 Battery. It, too, had to withdraw, to a new position 300 yards north-east of the Tour de Paissy. This stemmed from a German attack that dislodged a French colonial battalion to its right.[13] Having held the line, Bulfin deployed the Gloucesters, who arrived at 9 p.m., half between the Northamptons and the Queen's and the other half as a close up reserve.[14] Given the strain on those two battalions in the line, it would have allowed them to close up their depleted ranks. The casualties for the day were put, by Bulfin, at a total of 210 of whom two officers and 38 men had been killed.[15] The growing stability of the line was reflected in the ability of the signallers to establish working lines to all three brigades including some re-laid lines, which were accorded some degree of protection from shrapnel by being laid over the edge of the bank.[16] The Coldstreams also recorded that having received three new officers on 17 September, two existing officers died of their wounds on 18 September, including Lieutenant Campbell who had joined them on 9 September.[17]

On 20 September, the Coldstreams were relieved at about 7 a.m. and joined the rest of the brigade in Corps reserve.[18] As they recovered, the Coldstreams received no fewer than

---

10   TNA WO 95/1272: War Diary of the 2nd Battalion KRRC, 15 September 1914.
11   TNA WO 95/1267: War Diary of the 2nd Brigade, 17 September 1914.
12   TNA WO 95/1248: War Diary of the XXV Brigade RFA, 17 September 1914.
13   TNA WO 95/1250: War Diary of the XLIII Brigade Royal Field Artillery, 17 September 1914.
14   TNA WO 95/1267: War Diary of the 2nd Brigade, 17 September 1914.
15   TNA WO 95/1267: War Diary of the 2nd Brigade, 17 September 1914.
16   TNA WO 95/1255: War Diary of the 1st Division, Divisional Signal Company, 17 September 1914.
17   TNA WO 95/1263: War Diary of the 1st Battalion Coldstream Guards, 17-18 September 1914.
18   TNA WO 95/1263: War Diary of the 1st Battalion Scots Guards, 20 September 1914.

218 other ranks as reinforcements as well as two more officers.[19] One of these officers was Lieutenant-Colonel Viscount Acheson. He would survive the war and would go on to succeed his father in 1922, as the 5th Earl of Gosford. Acheson had served with the regiment in South Africa before joining the reserve of Officers. He would be awarded the MC in 1915. The Black Watch benefitted from the arrival of three new officers and 254 other ranks, whilst the Camerons had the opportunity to absorb two new officers and 141 other ranks.[20] The arrival of these vital reinforcements demonstrates the effectiveness of the regimental depots during the early months of the war.

Whilst the infantry had been relieved, the artillery remained in their positions and Lieutenant Colonel Geddes's command again received thanks. This time from the GOC 18th Brigade, Brigadier Congreve VC. Their shrapnel fire had made a significant contribution to stopping a determined German assault. The assault had nearly succeeded in breaking through his right flank.[21] On the following day, unsurprisingly, the 115th and 116th batteries came under fire from German heavy howitzers but the German fire had had little effect.[22] Haig had agreed with Sir John French that he could use two brigades of 6th Division as long as Haig sent two brigades into general reserve.[23] Therefore, 1st Scots Guards relieved part of 6th Brigade in the trenches at Moussy.[24] The rest of 1 (Guards) Brigade replaced 17th Brigade in the line. Initially the brigade occupied the positions from the watercourses in the Chivy valley up to the canal, but on 22 September this line was extended to include the tracks east of Champ d' Erny. For the Camerons there was a boost from the arrival of a further officer and 89 other ranks. The brigade had two battalions in the trenches, one in support and one in Courtonne.[25] This seems to suggest the Bulfin's approach was being used as a model. Having one battalion in support and one behind refined Bulfin's approach. Meanwhile, 2 Brigade, who were out of the line, received a visit from Field Marshal Sir John French. He congratulated them on seizing the Chemin de Dames Ridge and holding it so tenaciously. In very much his own style, Sir John took the opportunity to speak to two groups of men personally.[26] More importantly perhaps, the Northamptons heard good news the following day; a consignment of boots was assigned to their battalion wagon by the divisional Quarter master's office.

As well as killing one and wounding two of the South Wales Borderers, German snipers were active in protecting German moves forward. Divisional headquarters received regular reports of significant numbers of German infantry filtering on to the slopes above the village of Chivy. Five and a half batteries of British artillery fired both at the deployments and at the likely routes that the Germans might be using to get there. Despite the assistance afforded by the artillery, the 2nd Welsh reported that the Germans had managed to get approximately 200 men into Chivy. The Germans had also been able to post twenty to thirty riflemen as outposts, in

---

19 TNA WO 95/1263: War Diary of the 1st Battalion Coldstream Guards, 20 September 1914.
20 TNA WO 95/1263: War Diary of the 1st Battalion Scots Guards, 20 September 1914.
21 TNA WO 95/1248: War Diary of the XXV Brigade RFA, 20 September 1914.
22 TNA WO 95/1248: War Diary of the XXV Brigade RFA, 21 September 1914.
23 Sheffield and Bourne, *Douglas Haig: War Diaries and Letters 1914-1918*, p.72.
24 TNA WO 95/1263: War Diary of the 1st Battalion Scots Guards, 21-23 September 1914.
25 TNA WO 95/1263: War Diary of the 1st Battalion Scots Guards, 22 September 1914.
26 TNA WO 95/1267: War Diary of the 2nd Brigade, *Headquarters*, 22 September 1914.

Chivy village. Lomax had made arrangements with 2nd Division for mutual support, as it was expected that the enemy attack would fall on the junction between 3 Brigade and 2nd Division.

Amidst heavy German shelling on the 25 September, the headquarters of the Camerons, was blown in by a shell. It was situated in a cave, and the rock collapsed. Under the debris were the Adjutant and three other officers. The Camerons, aided by men from the Scots Guards, worked through the night to try to rescue the officers. In total, the Camerons had lost five officers and 21 men in the cave. Brigadier Maxse was instructed to appoint a new commanding officer for the battalion, as they had no surviving senior officers. In the interim, Captain Brodie was left in charge of the battalion. The RAMC took charge of burying the battalion's Medical Officer, Lieutenant Micklejohn. The rest of the dead were buried by the battalion. Major Hill of the Highland Light Infantry arrived to take temporary charge of the battalion. Then on 29 September, nine new officers arrived from the UK, including Lieutenant-Colonel MacEwen.[27]

Given that the British Empire would soon be deploying troops from India, it is interesting to see the view taken of French colonial troops. Lomax's staff noted that it had been arranged for "regular white troops" to hold the head of the Vallee de Foulon at night and for regular troops to hold the flank adjoining 1st Division during the day. It was noted that this strengthened their position noticeably. The increasingly static nature of the warfare was also reflected in a lot of effort being devoted to strengthening the trenches all along the divisional line. The trenches in 2 Brigade's area were being strengthened each night with the assistance of 23 Company RE, under the direction of Major Browne.[28] At this stage of the war, wiring in front of the trenches was restricted by the amount of wire available. On the other side, too, defences were being strengthened. 6 Brigade suffered during a night attack from finding a second German trench line behind the first.[29]

The attack by the Germans on 2 Brigade on 26 September was not as strong as had been anticipated by 1st Division. Nonetheless, 2 Brigade described it as the most determined that they had yet faced. The attack principally fell upon the Sussex and 2nd KRRC. The machine guns of the latter and the Queen's took a heavy toll of the assaulting Germans, who had again advanced in close formation. Despite their success, when 3 Brigade asked for assistance, 2 Brigade responded by suggesting that three companies of the East Yorks, near Moulin, be sent forward from reserve. Bulfin reported this to 1st Division HQ. Bulfin did subsequently relent; on receiving a further request for support from 3 Brigade. He sent his reserve which consisted of two companies of the Northants.[30] Wounded prisoners indicated that 1st Division had been engaged with units of 21st and 25th Divisions of XVIII Corps.

The attack on 3rd Brigade developed into a much bigger contest in the section held by the South Wales Borderers. They came under attack in the pre-dawn darkness at 4 a.m. on 26 September. Brigadier Landon described the ground in front of their position as intricate; divisional records say the field of fire here was only one hundred yards. The Germans advanced trenches to within seventy yards of the British trenches despite fire support for 2 Brigade from 115th and 116th batteries.[31] Effectively, it allowed approximately 1200 Germans to penetrate

---

27   TNA WO 95/1264: War Diary of the 1st Battalion Cameron Highlanders, 25-29 September 1914.
28   TNA WO 95/1267: War Diary of the 2nd Brigade, Headquarters, 26 September 1914.
29   TNA WO 95/1280: War Diary of the 1st Division Headquarters, 25 September 1914.
30   TNA WO 95/1267: War Diary of the 2nd Brigade, Headquarters, 26 September 1914.
31   TNA WO 95/1248: War Diary of the XXV Brigade RFA, 26 September 1914.

the line, bringing forward machine guns, without crossing a clear field of fire until the final rush. This still took them until 7.30 a.m., approximately three and a half hours from when the attack began.

The brunt of the assault was borne by the left company of the Borderers; every officer became a casualty and Major Welby was killed. The attack was eventually repulsed, under the command of Captain Curgenven, with the aid of the supports. Brigadier Landon claimed some of the credit for this by saying that he had previously ordered the Welsh [sic] to move round from Mount Faucon and protect the flank and that they contributed to the ultimate success. He was also at pains to point out that the German bodies piled up in front of the company's position were testimony to the stout defence D company had put up. Some of the credit belongs the Camerons. Their machine got out in front of their trenches and enfiladed the assaulting Germans.[32]

Landon seems to have anticipated issues regarding the number posted as missing. So, he added that all the officers in that company had become casualties; that the brigade had been in the line for a fortnight, and that he was proud of the fight they had shown.[33] Landon's report said that heavy shelling had prevented him getting around all the trenches in the afternoon. 1st Division reported to Corps that an enquiry was being held into the number of Borderers reported missing, which had initially been reported as 110. The Borderers and the Queens were also galled by casualties arising from their own artillery firing short.[34] By the next day, revised figures had been received which were four officers and 87 other ranks killed and three officers and 95 other ranks wounded with twelve missing. These figures were regarded as much more satisfactory by I Corps, presumably because fewer missing meant there was no suggestion of poor morale.

The Germans began to prepare similar attacks in the afternoon. In total these attacks may have involved some 4000 infantry. This could have been a decisive blow. However, the gathering of these assault troops was spotted by the outposts of 2nd Division, and then the concentrated fire of 1st and 2nd Division's artillery prevented the assaults being launched. The Queen's also repulsed an assault, noting that they counted fifty German dead before their positions and that nearly all their own casualties were due to the British artillery again firing short.[35] On the 3 Brigade portion of the front, the day ended with the 2nd Welsh moving forward up the valley and making contact with the German piquets and mobile supports occupying Chivy and the neighbouring woods.

Nevertheless, the attack was successfully repulsed with rifle and machine gun fire. The German failure was partly ascribed to the Germans attacking in close formation.[36] Despite their formidable reputation, the German army was as persistent as the French in insisting upon these wasteful attacks. Anyone familiar with German military history would see parallels with Frederick the Great asking his Guards did they want to live forever. The previous generation of German soldiers had similarly been sent forward at St Privat.

---

32 TNA WO 95/1264: War Diary of the 1st Battalion Cameron Highlanders, 25-29 September 1914.
33 TNA WO 95/1280: War Diary of the 1st Division Headquarters, Report by 3rd Brigade.
34 TNA WO 95/1263: War Diary of the 1st Battalion South Wales Borderers, 25 September 1914 and WO 95/1280: War Diary of the 1st Queen's Royal West Surrey, 25 September 1914.
35 TNA WO 95/1280: War Diary of the 1st Queen's Royal West Surrey, 26 September 1914.
36 TNA WO 95/1280: War Diary of the 1st Division, Headquarters, 26 September 1914.

During 26 September, there were also strong attacks on the French troops occupying the front to the right of 1st Division. The attacks were repulsed and the French estimated that the Germans had suffered heavy losses. The predominance of trench warfare is evidenced in the recording of a report by the French liaison officer. He reported that the German trenches were similar to those of the French. Both sets afforded headcover for the men manning them. He also reported that the Germans had telephone lines between battalions and brigades. The report also stated that the Germans kept the trenches very lightly manned, with most of the men protected in dugouts.[37] Manning the trenches thinly helped the Germans sustain their war effort against the superior resources of their opponents.

The last item that the Headquarters of 1 (Guards) Brigade recorded on 26 September was that Brigadier-General Maxse was ordered home, as he had been promoted to command a division.[38] Therefore, on 27 September 1914, Brigadier-General Fitzclarence VC assumed command of 1(Guards) Brigade. He was a great-grandson of King William IV, by his mistress Mrs Jordan. Since 1898 he had been married to Violet Spencer Churchill, a niece of the 7th Duke of Marlborough. Although he had originally been commissioned into the Royal Fusiliers, he had transferred to the Irish Guards in October 1900, when they were formed. Being a member of the cadet branch of the Earls of Munster, he was using his Irish connexions to colour a socially advantageous move.[39] He had been awarded the Victoria Cross for his leadership and personal bravery during actions around Mafeking during the Boer War.[40] Having commanded 1st Irish Guards from 1909 - 1913, he was appointed as commander of 29th Brigade in August 1914.[41] That brigade was part of 10th Irish Division, and consisted of Kitchener battalions of line regiments recruited in Ireland. This transfer to command of a brigade including elements of the Guards was therefore much more prestigious.

The Scots Guards spent that day returning to the trenches north of Vendresse, which they occupied until the eve of the BEF's re-deployment in October.[42] The artillery of 115th and 116th batteries again came under German shell fire at 5 p.m. The infantry faced the problem of the Germans throwing hand grenades into their trenches.[43] This underlines the problems faced by the British troops as trench warfare began. The Germans were better equipped with entrenching tools and had hand grenades - the latter would prove to be a key weapon in these close encounters. Months would elapse before the early British grenades were reliable, and in the meantime, soldiers would have to improvise alternatives from explosive material and ready to hand containers, such as ration tins.

A more familiar problem faced 1st Division on 27th September. During the night, there was no real enemy activity, and 2nd Division reported that there had been the sound of unusual levels of movement by wheeled transport. Therefore, 1st Division received an appreciation of the situation from Corps that the Germans were about to retreat. The Corps appreciation seems to

---

37 TNA WO 95/1280: War Diary of the 1st Division Headquarters, 26 September 1914.
38 TNA WO 95/1263: War Diary of the 1st Battalion Scots Guards, 26 September 1914.
39 Edward, the son of Charles and Violet, would eventually succeed to the title as 6th Earl of Munster in 1975.
40 For the details of his citations, etc., see *Lord Ashcroft Medals* <http://www.lordashcroftmedals.com/collection/charles-fitzclarence-vc/>, accessed 15 Feb. 2017
41 Beckett, I, *Ypres: The First Battle 1914* (Harlow: Longman, 2004), p. 114.
42 TNA WO 95/1263: War Diary of the 1st Battalion Scots Guards, 27 September 1914.
43 TNA WO 95/1248: War Diary of the XXV Brigade RFA, 27 September 1914.

have allowed the wish to be father to the thought. There would be additional wheeled transport moving during any British inter-brigade relief. If the transport were moving west to east it actually implied that the Germans were strengthening their positions opposite Haig. By noon, 1st Division were busy continuing the preparations they had begun the day before, to meet a renewal of the German attacks. In the hour before dusk, the trenches occupied by 2nd Brigade were subjected to heavy shelling. This included fire from a new type of pneumatic gun. It fired shells, from a range of about 800 yards, that fragmented when they landed and generated a large amount of black smoke. The Germans then attacked, at dusk, in what was described as a more determined way than usual. Bulfin reported to Lomax that the Germans seemed to have been heavily reinforced, notably with field artillery. By 8 p.m., the 2nd Welsh had defeated a German attack down the Chivy Valley.

However, around about midnight, the pressure from the Germans eased as they put more weight into their attacks on the neighbouring French positions. The French were able to hold on to all their ground. The French units also reported that they believed the Germans were burning the bodies of the dead. It is not clear what evidence they had for making this assertion.

The South Wales Borderers and Brigadier Loudon received congratulatory messages from Lomax and Haig. They were praised for the fight they had put up in the previous engagement. That night, 1 (Guards) Brigade relieved 3 Brigade in the line, the latter being brought back into billets. 3 Brigade had been continuously under fire since September 14. The Queen's had been detached on the right flank and had suffered the most from being heavily shelled; as a battalion they were felt to have had the highest casualties in the division. The Queen's paraded on 28 September for rifle inspection and the officers censored letters. The day was then marked by the arrival of Lieutenant General Haig to congratulate them on their performance.[44] Checking the men's rifles before the Corps commander saw them was a savvy move.

The praise for the Queen's continued on 29 September when they received a visit from Major General Lomax. He said that he had noticed how high the standard of their march discipline had been during the retreat. He said and that he thought they were the best in the division – high praise considering the division included battalions of Guards. He added that he felt that such a battalion would perform very well in battle and that they had done a great job. He also said he had twice tried to give them a break but had been forced to keep them in the firing line. Lomax also told the men that had their commander survived, he would have been decorated and that Captain Watson DSO had now been given local rank as a Major.[45]

The 1 (Guards) Brigade had all its battalions in the line covering the sector from the Vendresse factory road to the watercourses in the Chivy Valley. They were disposed from left to right respectively; Scots Guards, Camerons, Black Watch, Coldstream Guards. The next few days were characterised by heavy shelling, sniping and half-hearted attacks. To strengthen the defences, the trenches were improved each night and a howitzer was brought up into the trenches of the Black Watch. The Camerons also received nine officers as reinforcements.[46]

Next to them in the line were 2 Brigade, who were operating with two battalions up and two in support. Bulfin was here anticipating what would become the norm during the static war down to early 1918, before brigades were reduced to three battalions each. During the foggy

---

44 TNA WO 95/1280: War Diary of the 1st Queen's Royal West Surrey, 28 September 1914.
45 TNA WO 95/1280: War Diary of the 1st Queens Royal West Surrey, 29 September 1914.
46 TNA WO 95/1263: War Diary of the 1st Battalion Scots Guards, 27 September 1914.

period shortly after midnight, Bulfin received a report that the Germans were attacking and had succeeded in breaking into the trenches held by the Loyal North Lancs. Bulfin felt that any breakthrough there would be very significant, and so he immediately despatched two companies of the Sussex to support the Northants. Bulfin noted that it turned out that the Sussex were not really needed and eventually returned to their original position. Help came for 2 Brigade, in the form of Brigadier-General Congreve VC. His discussion with Bulfin focused on covering the gap between 2 Brigade and the French. The Brigade also received a consignment of 75 rifle grenades; the earliest version of a weapon that would add enormously to the firepower of infantry squads in the final period of semi-open warfare in 1918.[47]

Those who were now in the line had faced another round of attacks in the early hours of the morning. Bulfin initially felt that the attacks had not been pressed very strongly, and that their main object was to deprive his men of their sleep. Though he also recognised that the Germans had pushed their line to within 70 yards of the British trenches in places. However, Bulfin revised this view during the morning once he had received detailed reports from the Loyal North Lancs, who had borne the brunt of the assault. Time was also being found to experiment with the rifle grenades.[48]

The scale of the manpower drain on the BEF is evident in 2 Brigade's summary of its casualties during September 1914. It had gone to war with a nominal establishment of four battalions, each of approximately one thousand men. The total casualties for the month were 1,591, or just under 40%. This included 77 officers of whom fifteen had been killed and sixteen were posted as missing.[49] Of the approximately 130 officers in the brigade, this represented around 60%. The casualties amongst the other ranks amounted to 1,514 or around 37.8%, although the proportion of those posted as missing is much higher. Ultimately some survived the war as prisoners. Nonetheless, they were lost to their units. The loss such a lot of experienced men from the rank and file would have two major consequences. New arrivals in 2 Brigade would have less experience to draw upon; and the pool of experienced men available to fill the role of NCOs in the New Army would be greatly diminished. On the evening of 28 September 3 Brigade relieved 2 Brigade. Before being relieved 2 Brigade had repulsed a German attack during the evening. The headquarters of 3 Brigade were established in Oeuilly Chateau. Within hours, a hundred Germans made a further attack, and this time it was 3rd Brigade's turn to repulse it.[50] The patterns of reliefs in trench warfare were rapidly becoming institutionalised.

September 1914 ended with 1 Brigade on the left of 2 Brigade, holding the line against half-hearted German attacks and suffering the constant threat of snipers and heavy artillery fire.[51]

September 1914 had begun in retreat and ended in stalemate for 1st Division; and their experience pretty much typified the experience of the BEF as a whole. During September, the BEF had gone forward effectively but probably too cautiously and therefore it had followed-up rather than pursued the retreating Germans. The evidence of the experience of 1st Division bears this out. The 1st Division's sub-units did push on in places but, on the whole, units reached agreed points and stopped each evening. This can largely be seen as a product of the higher leadership.

---

47 TNA WO 95/1267: War Diary of the 2nd Brigade, Headquarters, 28 September 1914.
48 TNA WO 95/1267: War Diary of the 2nd Brigade, Headquarters, 29 September 1914.
49 TNA WO 95/1267: War Diary of the 2nd Brigade, Headquarters, 30 September 1914.
50 TNA WO 95/1267: War Diary of the 3rd Brigade, Headquarters, 28 -30 September 1914.
51 TNA WO 95/1263: War Diary of the 1st Battalion Scots Guards,28 -30 September 1914.

The evidence drawn from 1st Division records suggests strongly that Major General Lomax was not inclined to push his men too fast. There is no evidence to suggest that Lieutenant General Haig was more than a cautious Corps commander, just as he had demonstrated after Mons. Maxse's promotion to command a division at home is an early example of promoting those who had made a serious misjudgement. From Haig's point of view, it was the best outcome, since it had absolved both Lomax and himself of any responsibility. In due course, another Brigadier, Landon, would see his career suffer when he appeared to challenge Haig's perception of his own performance. Given Haig's prejudice against Catholics reflected in his later comments on McDonagh, perhaps the establishment was silently passing comment on the unreliability of the Catholic Irish. The Munsters did not deserve that view being taken, but Maxse's promotion was a propaganda gift to those in Kerry arguing against enlistment.

When battle was subsequently joined on the Aisne, the British troops were at a significant tactical advantage; any walking of the battlefield today only reinforces that view. Nonetheless, the ridge was seized in places, which is a testament to both how narrow the race had become between the two sides and the tenacity of the British servicemen. The order given to Haking to withdraw his Brigade and to the Black Watch to await 2nd Division's arrival on their flank demonstrate the shortcomings of Haig as Corps commander. The assault by Bulfin's 2 Brigade and the less chronicled efforts of the other two brigades demonstrate the fighting qualities of the BEF. Even more than at Ypres, since they underline their abilities in both tactical offence and defence. All the battalions in the division fought very well indeed and so the accolades accorded to the Borderers and the Queen's make them outstanding, in an excellent field. Taken as a whole, the fighting on the Aisne demonstrated no difference in the performance between 1 (Guards) Brigade and the other two; the BEF shared a common standard. The stalemate of trench warfare resulted from the Germans using the terrain to maximise the advantage they held in heavier artillery and machine guns. The month of September in which it had fought so hard, and been bled so profusely, ended fairly quietly for 1st Division.

October opened as September had closed, with the units in the line suffering under heavy artillery fire. Horne, as the new CRA, was busy on 1 October as special arrangements had been made to bombard the German front line. The enemy trenches were to be targeted by the 6" howitzers. So, the units of 2 Brigade, who were holding the front line, evacuated their own front-line positions. Whilst this would create a safety zone for the infantry, it was recognised that the Germans might try to attack. Therefore, Horne had arranged for some batteries of 18-pdrs. to bombard the crest at the same time.

Whilst it was not possible for the fall of all the shot to be observed, it was felt that much of the howitzer fire was falling short. It was concluded that the danger zone for the British high explosives was greater than the German "Black Maria" and that the artillery would prefer the infantry to be 300 yards back. Given the difficulty of observation, it is unclear how they reached the additional conclusion that fragments might be thrown up to 2000 yards. In the light of this evidence, it is not surprising that both the infantry and artillery commanders felt that this exercise was not worth repeating soon.[52]

---

52   TNA WO 95/1227: War Diary of the 1st Division, Headquarters, 1 October 1914.

On 4 October 1914, Lieutenant Colonel Bent took over command of the Munsters; described by Jervis as having gimlet eyes and being "par excellence a leader of men".[53] Jervis asserts that the Munsters had meanwhile received drafts of replacements. However, Drumm's evidence suggests that few of these men were being recruited in Kerry. He argues that whilst just over 140 were recalled to the colours, only sixty more enlisted before Christmas.[54] Jervis says that Bent went to Haig to get the battalion reassigned to a brigade; he notes that there was no rest for corps troops who carried out a series of tasks as given to them by Corps.[55] Presumably, too, their performance during this period removed any concerns senior officers may have had regarding the political reliability of the Munsters, given the pre-war tensions in Ireland. From 1885 onwards, all four MPs elected to represent Kerry were members of one branch or other of the Irish Nationalists who were campaigning for Home Rule. In 1918 all four Kerry seats would be won by Sinn Fein. British officers, many of whom came from families who lived in Ireland but were part of the Protestant gentry opposed to Home Rule, would have regarded Irish Catholic soldiers with suspicion. Haig, the Corps Commander, had been a subtle, but firm, supporter of the officers at the Curragh who had opposed the army being used to intervene in north-eastern Ireland.

As Bent assumed command, the 1st Coldstream Guards were preparing to assault the German position known as "Fish Hook" Trench, just east of the Troyon factory road. This attack was to be led by Second Lieutenant Beckwith-Smith, supported by fifty men of No. 6 Platoon. Their numbers had been made up by men from No. 8 Platoon. By 7.45 p.m., the assault troops were in position in No Man's Land whilst thirty guardsmen accompanied by a corporal and two men of the Royal Engineers waited in the British trenches. They were tasked with filling in the first position once gained.

The Coldstream's assaults opened well. The first German trench was occupied and found to contain fifteen German dead who were thought to have been killed by artillery fire and sniping earlier in the day. Led by Beckwith-Smith, the Coldstreams then pressed forward the seventy yards needed to reach the next German trench. Fire was received as they crossed the last of the open ground, so the order was given to charge, and Beckwith-Smith led his men into the German trench. Here the contest was decided by the bayonet and close-range shooting and resulted in all the Germans (approximately twenty) in the trench being killed. During the fighting, the British suffered seven wounded and two who were posted missing believed killed. Amongst the wounded was Beckwith-Smith who was shot in the arm and knocked down in the struggle. Acting Corporal 8085 Russell was credited with saving Beckwith-Smith's life by bayoneting the two Germans who were attacking him. Having occupied the two trenches, the Coldstreams came under fire from a third trench and it was evident to Beckwith Smith, that it would not be possible to fill in the first trench as per the objectives. He therefore ordered the withdrawal of the force, and this was successfully accomplished.

It was noted in the battalion report that the second German trench included recesses cut into the side to afford shelter from shellfire. As well as commending Beckwith-Smith and Russell, the Coldstream's OC also reported favourably on the support given to their officer by

---

53   Jervis, *The 2nd Munsters in France*, p.8.
54   Alan Drumm, *Kerry and the Royal Munster Fusiliers*, (Dublin: The History Press, 2010) p.42.
55   Jervis, *The 2nd Munsters in France*, p.8.

two sergeants, Brown and Troke, as well as 8925 Private Paxton who had saved Brown's life.[56] Brown, holder of the Order of St George 2nd Class, would be killed 24 days later.[57] Beckwith-Smith, old Etonian and graduate of Christ Church College, Oxford University, was to go on to serve with distinction in World War One. He would go on to be awarded the DSO and MC plus the Croix de Guerre and be Mentioned in Despatches three times.[58]

Brigadier Fitzclarence supported the battalion commander's recommendations and said that he had told the battalion to sap towards the German positions, to make the life of the enemy soldiers as difficult as possible. Fitzclarence added that a supply of rifle grenades would be especially useful in achieving this aim. He added that there was also a need for iron or steel plates to reinforce loopholes, as ordinary sandbags were not of much use at short range.[59]

Other battalions than the Munster Fusiliers were also to receive reinforcements during October; on 7 October, an officer and 114 other ranks joined the Black Watch. The next day, they were joined by a further draft of an officer and 100 other ranks, whilst 45 other ranks joined the Scots Guards. On the day after, the Camerons received the largest draft, comprised of four officers and 250 other ranks. It was with their ranks stiffened by these new arrivals that the battalions would face the trials of First Ypres.

On 14 October, 1 Brigade received orders for the impending move and late on 15 October, the French troops began to relieve them. The reliefs were late and the Black Watch were not relieved until 5 a.m. on 16 October.[60] The Scots Guards subsequently entrained at Fismes on 17.[61] It took from 9 a.m. until 6 p.m. for the whole of 1 Brigade to entrain so there was a considerable amount of waiting around; this provided an opportunity for the draft of four officers and 141 other ranks, who had arrived the day before, to get to know their fellow members of 1st Coldstream Guards.[62]

---

56 TNA WO 95/1263: War Diary of the 1st Battalion Coldstream Guards, 5 October 1914.
57 Brown is commemorated amongst the missing on the Menin Gate.
58 See *Christ Church* <https://www.chch.ox.ac.uk/fallen-alumni/major-general-merton-beckwith-smith> (accessed 12 August 2019). Having transferred to the Welsh Guards in 1930, he subsequently rose to the rank of Major General during the Second World War before dying of dyptheria in a Japanese prison camp. He was subsequently given a military burial in Hong Kong and is commemorated on the war memorial at Daviot in Invernesshire.
59 TNA WO 95/1263: War Diary of the 1st Battalion Coldstream Guards, 5 October 1914
60 TNA WO 95/1263: War Diary of the 1st Battalion Scots Guards, 14-16 October 1914.
61 TNA WO 95/1263: War Diary of the 1st Battalion Scots Guards, 17 October 1914.
62 TNA WO 95/1263: War Diary of the 1st Battalion Scots Guards, 16 October 1914.

10

In Flanders Fields
An Encounter Battle

As Professor Gary Sheffield observed, having played a lesser role at Mons, I Corps was to play a central role at Ypres.[1] The battle fought in late 1914 to the north and east of Ypres arose from the attempt by the German and Allied armies to turn the flank of their opponent and win the war. In the classic era of wars of manoeuvre, in eighteenth century Europe, armies would seek to get around their opponent and surprise or relieve a strategic fortress and bring the enemy to battle in circumstances which promised victory. This continued under Napoleon, with more emphasis upon securing a decisive battle, with his brilliant campaign culminating in his victory at Austerlitz on 2 December 1805. As the nineteenth century progressed, the stopping power of defensive weaponry grew. Great victories were achieved by Moltke the Elder through the strategic use of railways to achieve his lightning success against Austria in 1866 and subsequently to defeat France, though in the latter case the failures of the French high command made a significant contribution. Victory over France had tested Moltke's skill as insubordinate royal army commanders took decisions which would, they thought, assist their reputation rather than conforming to the great plan.

However, Moltke's ability to achieve great victories with much larger armies transported by rail left his successors raising larger and larger armies, in the belief that with the assistance of great strategic railways it would still be possible to achieve a decisive outcome. By late 1914, Schlieffen's belief in a decisive "double Cannae"[2] lay in ruins, as Moltke the Younger's lack of grip on his commanders (and lower level of overall competence, which he himself acknowledged) demonstrated the failure of the Prussian / German military's attempt to bottle Moltke the Elder's genius. Joffre had defeated Schlieffen's Plan (albeit only the plan as executed by Moltke the Younger) by the very method that Schlieffen had identified himself; by switching forces to the left.[3] So now the Germans had one focus remaining, to reverse the allied advance northwards

---

1 Jones (ed.), *Stemming the Tide*, p.127
2 Hannibal had defeated the Romans at Cannae by drawing the Romans towards his centre and enveloping them with his two wings. Schlieffen's plan centred on drawing the French forward in Alsace-Lorraine and encircling them whilst encircling the more northerly French forces by sending his First Army around and behind them.
3 Bucholz, A., *Moltke, Schlieffen and Prussian War Planning* (Oxford: Berg, 1991), passim.

from the Marne, by finding the flank and rolling southwards again. At the same time, Sir John French had asked Joffre if the BEF could return to its original position on the allied left flank and this was agreed upon, so the British became the allied force moved to this strategic position. Thus, a series of encounter battles occurred as German and allied forces sought to find their opponent's open flank, and this eventually ended when the Belgians flooded the Yser area. Having failed to achieve a decisive strategic outcome, the German High Command fell back on a more unimaginative leitmotif of German military success; the frontal attack pressed home regardless of casualties. Now General von Falkenhayn would use the same basic tactics.

The strategic function of I Corps was being hotly debated even as the rank and file were moved into position. On 13 October, Sir John French had discussed the possibility of creating an armed camp at Boulogne. Sir Henry Wilson was horrified and persuaded General Foch to send a letter to Sir John French suggesting that the line to be held should be Bethune – St Omer Canal. Foch's authority derived from Joffre having made him his Adjoint in the north, but the letter was received very badly and led to a heated meeting between Foch and French on 17 October. In effect though, French accepted Foch's plan that the Belgians would hold the Yser, whilst the British and French pushed forward to the Lille – Courtrai line.[4]

Along with the rest of their brigade, the Scots Guards detrained just over 24 hours later in Hazebrouck at 6 p.m. on 18 October 1914.[5] That afternoon, after completing the care of their horses, the men of 30th (Howitzer) Battery played football.[6] Having remained in their billets on 19 October, the Scots Guards marched to fresh billets in Poperinghe,[7] with the rest of 1 (Guards) Brigade on 20 October. That day the Coldstreams received three new officers: Captain Brown, Lieutenant Murray, and Second Lieutenant the Honourable V Boscawen. Brown was a veteran of the South African War, who had been educated at Eton before passing out from Sandhurst. His service on the Western Front would extend to nine further days before his death in action. Boscawen would fall in action on the same day. Boscawen was the son of Major General Evelyn Boscawen, 7th Viscount Falmouth, who had himself formerly served as an officer in the Coldstream Guards. Brown and Boscawen would outlive Lieutenant Murray by three days. All three are commemorated on the Menin Gate.

The task faced by I Corps, along with the rest of the allied troops, was enormous. They were, as at Mons, meeting a German offensive head on. Falkenhayn, recognising the German failures to win further south, had decided once again to attempt to outflank the allies. Falkenhayn took the Duke of Wurttemberg's *Fourth Army* and added to it four new reserve corps. These corps included 25% trained reservists, as well as under- and over-age reservists. The *Fourth Army*'s ultimate goal was Calais. This army was to be supported by *III Reserve Corps* and its large allocation of heavy artillery. The artillery had been freed up by the fall of Antwerp. Further support would come from *Sixth Army* striking westwards from Lille.[8]

The 1st Division, with 2 Brigade in the van, reached a position one mile west of Poperinghe on 20 October at around 10.30 a.m. Again, the issue of poor staff work raises its head, as the division then awaited orders from Army HQ for an hour and a half. The orders were received

---

4   Greenhalgh, E., *Foch in Command* (Cambridge: Cambridge University Press, 2011) pp.61-62.
5   TNA WO 95/1263: War Diary of the 1st Battalion Scots Guards, 18 October 1914.
6   TNA WO 95/1251: War Diary of Lieutenant Price, 18 October 1914.
7   TNA WO 95/1263: War Diary of the 1st Battalion Scots Guards, 19-20 October 1914.
8   Greenhalgh, *Foch in Command*, p.58.

at Noon and the division was ordered to close up, with 2 Brigade going to Elverdinghe whilst the rest of the division, including headquarters, reached Poperinghe. Overnight, 2 Brigade were billeted in Elverdinghe whilst divisional HQ and 1st Brigade were in Poperinghe, with 3 Brigade divided between the two locations.[9]

It was only at 10 p.m. that the orders for the assault were issued. However, the orders themselves are timed at 12.50 a.m., nearly three hours later. The orders themselves are instructive of the level of staff work. There is a pencilled amendment to the orders, correcting the junction with 2nd Division from being at a crossroads south-west of Langemarck to being one south-east of the village. The task of I Corps was stated as to continue the advance in the direction of Thorout, and "driving back the enemy wherever met." The task for 1st Division was to reach Langemarck by 7 a.m., and then to attack in the direction of Poelcappelle. In contrast, the allocation of units to the advance guard and main body is detailed, including denoting the time and five minute intervals between the departure times of the units in the main body.[10] The quality of the staff-work is also questioned by 3 Brigade who note that the orders only arrived at 1.30 a.m. They say that the billeted units were very spread about and that it took longer than usual to get the orders distributed.[11]

In the early morning of 21 October, 1st Division advanced from Poperinghe to Langemarck, which had been held by French territorial troops overnight. Given the lateness with which the orders were issued, it is unsurprising to find that 1st Division's assault began at 8.30 a.m., ninety minutes later than planned. However, in a report dated 21 November 1914, this delay was attributed to French cavalry crossing the line of march, whereas 3 Brigade acknowledge that they were approximately twenty minutes late setting off. One facet of the orders proved to be accurate. It had been anticipated that the Germans might debouch from the Foret d'Houthoulst. This left flank was being protected by the French *3rd Cavalry Division*. They were supported by French territorial infantry who were covering the bridges over the Canal d'Yser.[12]

The assault was led by 3 Brigade. They, minus the 2nd Welsh, formed the advance guard. Therefore, the Queens were directed to capture Poelcappelle Station whilst the South Wales Borderers were given the task of capturing the village itself. According to the Queens' report, they were only given their objective when they reached Langemarck.[13] Lieutenant Colonel Pell, of the Queens, was tasked with reporting the answers to two questions. Whether Langemarck was held by the French, and were the Germans advancing from the Houlthulst Forest? The French were found to be holding Langemarck with territorial cavalry, infantry, and artillery. It was also clear that the Germans held the high ground near Poelcappelle.[14] At 9 a.m., the French reported, incorrectly, that the Houlthulst Forest contained no German troops. At the same time, German artillery opened fire and subsequently was joined by heavy artillery firing from Poelcappelle.

At 9.30 a.m., the divisional HQ received a report that the Germans were advancing from Koekuit, threatening the left flank of the advance. So the Gloucesters, the Brigade reserve, were

---

9   TNA WO 95/1227: War Diary of the 1st Division, Headquarters, 21 October 1914.
10   TNA WO 95/1227: War Diary of the 1st Division, Headquarters, October 1914, Appendix XXIV.
11   TNA WO 95/1274: War Diary of the 3rd Brigade, Headquarters, report dated 25 October 1914.
12   TNA WO 95/1227: War Diary of the 1st Division, Headquarters, 21 October 1914.
13   TNA WO 95/1274: War Diary of the 3rd Brigade, Headquarters, report dated 25 October 1914
14   TNA WO 95/1274: War Diary of the 3rd Brigade, Headquarters, report dated 25 October 1914.

moved to cover this threat. Initially, B company under Captain Radice was sent to occupy the Langemarck railway station.[15] Division released two companies of 2nd Welsh, who were with the main body, to become the new brigade reserve of 3 Brigade. The deployment of troops in penny packets which may have been appropriate in colonial conflicts was only going to limit further the chances of British success in such large battles.

The Gloucesters attacked Koeknit with three companies. C company, initially under Captain Temple, were sent to capture the farm. They advanced from the village and issued forth from the northwest corner, about 300 yards from the level crossing. Initially one platoon occupied the farm, but a second platoon was later sent to reinforce it. Meanwhile, D company, under Major Gardner, attacked on C's right and therefore filled the gap on the left flank of the Queens. D company sustained fifteen casualties including three dead. B company was sent to assault on C's left where they faced Germans entrenched in front of a burning windmill. B suffered twenty casualties including seventeen wounded. A company was divided, with half forming the battalion reserve and the other half, with the MG section, under Lieutenant Duncan, protecting the battalion's left flank.[16] The number of casualties looks small but these were all well-trained experienced men who would be sorely missed in the succeeding battles.

At 10 a.m., British howitzers and field guns were firing upon Poelcappelle, and the Queens had reached a farm approximately halfway to Poelcappelle station. The left flank of the Queens was becoming exposed as the French cavalry and infantry began withdrawing from Langemarck. The left of the Queens was approximately 1400 yards from Langemarck, so a significant gap was opening up. The French had heard that the Germans were pushing in on Poelcappelle from the north-west. So they were despatching cyclist companies to oppose them. The position of the Queens was improved when the Gloucesters took Koeknit by 11 a.m. The Gloucesters were in a position to fire on the defenders of Poelcappelle station. This assisted the Queens but also meant that the Gloucesters suffered casualties too, notably Lieutenant Young who was badly wounded whilst leading the Gloucesters who were nearest the Queens.[17] The Germans counter attacked the Gloucesters in the farm but, a force estimated at 150, was stopped at a range of 600 yards by enfilade fire from a platoon that was not in the farm. This positive news was reinforced by a report from the South Wales Borderers that the Germans were retiring before them, and 5 Brigade with whom they were in touch on their right.

The fact that this German retirement was not to continue was foreshadowed by the Borderers other report. They had seen French artillery, in the direction of Steenstraate, under fire from German artillery. The French troops on the left renewed their retirement. This brought the advance by 3 Brigade's right to a halt. In this context the despatch of 2nd Welsh in support of the Borderers, did not lead to the advance re-starting.[18] The French cavalry were already retiring through the same area but had said they were intending to hold Bixshoote. This would have helped anchor the left of I Corps and 1st Division, but it meant that the Queens were advancing into a salient.[19]

15 TNA WO 95/1278: War Diary of the 1st Gloucestershire Regiment, Frazebrook Diary.
16 TNA WO 95/1274: War Diary of the 3rd Brigade, Headquarters, report dated 25 October 1914.
17 TNA WO 95/1278: War Diary of the 1st Gloucestershire Regiment, Frazebrook Diary.
18 TNA WO 95/1274: War Diary of the 3rd Brigade, Headquarters, report dated 25 October 1914.
19 TNA WO 95/1227: War Diary of the 1st Division, Headquarters, 21 October 1914.

At 1 p.m., the situation worsened. The Germans counterattacked against the South Wales Borderers. Divisional HQ noted that, although the German attack had been beaten off, the fact that the Germans had delivered an attack led to the forward advance of 3rd Brigade coming to an end and increased the anxiety for the left flank. The French cyclists withdrew from the left of the Gloucesters. The cyclists reported that the Germans were closing the road southwest of Koeknit. The Gloucesters beat off a second German assault, but this time the Germans entrenched 400 yards from the British positions.

The entrenched Germans now sniped at the British positions which led to steadily mounting casualties amongst the garrison led by Lieutenant Wetherall. Wetherall sought advice from his company commander and found the gravely wounded Captain Temple in a ditch 300 yards away. Given that C company was already fully committed, he was told to seek help from the supporting troops.[20] In total C company suffered thirteen casualties; with Captain Temple amongst the three killed.

Initially help arrived in the unexpected form of a Sergeant and fifteen men of the Scots Guards. Wetherall posted them on his right flank, where they acted as a hinge as the Queens fell back.[21] The withdrawal of the French meant that the British had to conform. As noted above, the Queens and South Wales Borderers had effectively been advancing into a salient, so their position was exposed even before the French began retiring. The British units were within rifle range of each other and the Germans, so this was not a theoretical flank being turned but an actual one. The divisional record shows that the troops had been supported by naval guns mounted on an armoured train.[22] Once the Germans had got to such close quarters, however, the British heavy artillery could not fire at the German forward positions because of the risk to their own infantry.

The report submitted by the OC Queens said that they had got to within a quarter of a mile of their objective, but that the South Wales Borderers were unable to make the same progress. The Queens were therefore forced to fall back as they were suffering from enfilade fire.[23] The 1st Division's mission for 22 October was to hold its position;[24] this would prove to be a challenge.

On 21 October 1 (Guards) Brigade arrived at Boesinghe at about 10 a.m. Their leading battalion, 1st Cameron Highlanders, had been ordered to replace the 2nd Welsh as Divisional reserve. To protect the divisional left, the 1st Cameron Highlanders were despatched to the "Inn" NNW of Pilkem and were replaced by the 1st Scots Guards in divisional reserve. Therefore, for the attack to be carried out by 1 Brigade in the direction of Langemarck; it was perforce to be led by 1st Coldstream Guards on the right, and 1st Black Watch on the left. The assaulting battalions were to be supported by 1st Cameron Highlanders. The detailed records were subsequently lost in the fighting at the end of the month, so the battalion records had to be reconstructed.[25] The attack on the German positions north of Boesinghe was designed to be in support of IV Corps. The assault was to be supported by the artillery. The naval guns were on an armoured train. They could provide support up to the Pilkem – Langemarck road. The

---

20   TNA WO 95/1278: War Diary of the 1st Gloucestershire Regiment, Frazebrook Diary.
21   TNA WO 95/1278: War Diary of the 1st Gloucestershire Regiment, Frazebrook Diary.
22   TNA WO 95/1227: War Diary of the 1st Division, Headquarters, 21 October 1914.
23   TNA WO 95/1274: War Diary of the 3rd Brigade, Headquarters, report dated 25 October 1914.
24   TNA WO 95/1227: War Diary of the 1st Division, Headquarters, 21 October 1914.
25   TNA WO 95/1263: War Diary of the 1st Battalion Coldstream Guards, 19-20 October 1914.

growing German pressure on the left meant that Major General Lomax ordered two companies of the Scots Guards to go and prolong the Cameron line to the left.[26] Therefore, B company of the Scots Guards was on the left of the Camerons, with its own left flank resting on Koeknit. Despite this, the orders for the Coldstreams and the Black Watch to advance were not rescinded, so half of 1 (Guards) Brigade was advancing and the rest was forming a lengthening refused flank. The Coldstreams then pushed on into the village; in carrying out the assault they lost Captain Pollock and thirty other ranks killed, with a further 73 posted as missing. In addition, Captain Paget was wounded along with 92 men of the battalion.

The 1st Gloucesters had abandoned the farm at Koeknit when the Queens fell back but had re-occupied it by the time of the successful attack by the Scots Guards. They claimed that, without this effort on their part, the line occupied by the Scots Guards would have been untenable.[27] According to Frazebrook, the farm was abandoned by its few remaining defenders whilst Lieutenant Wetherall was absent seeking help. It was later re-occupied by Wetherall leading the thirty men that Captain Radice had given him for the purpose. Wetherall's leadership was recognised by the award of the MC. At the same time, B company occupied Grutesaelle Farm, 250 yards south-west of the village.

It was at around this point that D company under Lieutenant Caunter beat off a German assault whilst it assembled, even though it was only visible to the officer through his binoculars. The retaliatory artillery fire led to several of the wounded being killed as they lay in a ditch. Captain Radice took over command of B company that evening whilst C company came under Captain Blunt of the York and Lancaster Regiment, who had been attached to the battalion since its mobilisation. Three very young German soldiers were captured by B company.[28] These young men may have been the first indication that the German high command had brought forward units which included "the Kinder," whose sacrifice would be a feature of the folklore of First Ypres.

At 4 p.m., the remainder of the Scots Guards were sent off, under their CO, to occupy trenches at Steenstraade. C company of the Scots Guards was on the right, with its right resting on Bixschoote. The Scots Guards encountered a brigade of French territorials between the trenches and the canal, as well as several French cuirassiers regiments.[29] The French withdrawal had been followed up so closely by the Germans that the Coldstreams received orders to deploy two companies along the line of the Bixschoote – Langemarck Road. The intention was to protect the Divisional Headquarters, which had been brought three-quarters of a mile closer to Langemarck but was now potentially exposed.

Therefore, the French retirement meant that by the late afternoon of 21 October 1 (Guards) Brigade was strung out in a very thin line. Fitzclarence himself had argued with the local French commander. The latter had refused to stay and have his troops supported by the British. Fitzclarence had to get a company to spread out to gain contact with the Scots Guards. He had withdrawn the foremost men as "they were too exposed"[30] but given the terrain this would deny them of any warning of the German assault.

---

26 TNA WO 95/1261: War Diary of the 1st Brigade, Headquarters, report dated 21 October 1914.
27 TNA WO 95/1274: War Diary of the 3rd Brigade, Headquarters, report dated 25 October 1914.
28 TNA WO 95/1278: War Diary of the 1st Gloucestershire Regiment, Frazebrook Diary.
29 TNA WO 95/1263: War Diary of the 1st Battalion Scots Guards, 21 October 1914.
30 TNA WO 95/1227: War Diary of the 1st Division, Headquarters, report dated 25 October 1914.

This line became thinner and more extended by early evening, when it was decided that 3 Brigade would need to be withdrawn from the line. Haig had retained 2 Brigade as Corps Reserve, so 1 (Guards) Brigade was left holding the divisional front. The 1st Black Watch were retained as Brigade reserve and placed three-quarters of a mile north of the railway near Pilkem.[31] Here they were close to the Northamptons of 2 Brigade, who had arrived by 8 p.m. The Brigade was still in Corps reserve but had been told to send a battalion forward to Pilkem. The battalion was dispersed, with a platoon on the Pilkem – Lizerne road and another east of the canal bridge on the Langemarck road. Two platoons were positioned at the north end of the village. Every two hours, the Northamptons mounted patrols out to the positions held by the Scots Guards at Steenstraade.[32] By 10 p.m., 3 Brigade had occupied its assigned positions, with the Queens in brigade reserve at the crossroads half-a-mile east-northeast of Pilkem. That evening they received orders to strengthen the position, in readiness to fight the next day, and the assistance of OC 26 Coy RE, who was extremely helpful "as usual."

For the heavily engaged units of 3 Brigade, the days fighting had taken its toll. The South Wales Borderers had lost two officers killed and one wounded, as well as nineteen men killed and sixty-two wounded and 65 missing. The Queens had lost three officers and suffered nine dead and 68 wounded amongst the other ranks but had only six posted missing.[33]

The brigade took advantage of a quiet night to further entrench their positions. The Queens and Gloucesters were told to have one company ready to move forward to support the battalions in the line, on the orders of that battalion's commander. This was designed to get around some of the problems in communication that had been encountered.[34] The weakness of the situation on the 1st Division's left was clear early on 22 October. Brigadier Bulfin made a visit to the Steenstraade positions, about 7.30 a.m. He arranged for the 15th Hussars to be in constant touch with the left during the day. He was told that all the French cavalry had withdrawn to the west bank of the canal around Lizerne. To protect a heavy battery in action at Het Sas Ock and a battery of 25th RFA in Lizerne, a company of the Royal Sussex was ordered to go to Lizerne.[35] Bulfin was also told that the French were in touch with the Belgians at Dixmude.[36] Meanwhile, the Scots Guards remained in their trenches. The French territorials launched an unsuccessful attack on Bixschoote. Subsequently, the French infantry retired. This meant the left flank of the 1st Division was uncovered.

The Scots Guards, on the flank, were not attacked but the rest of 1 (Guards) Brigade came under very heavy attack.[37] The Scots Guards were tied to the defence of the Steenstraate bridge and could not therefore give assistance to the units on their right. The Camerons were in a position to monitor the crossings of Saint Jean Kortebeck. They could sense the enemy all around, but there was limited firing before the attack came after dark.[38] The centre of the Cameron Highlanders was broken by a superior number of Germans. Though the time given is 3.30 p.m., it may have

---

31 TNA WO 95/1261: War Diary of the 1st Brigade, Headquarters, report dated 21 October 1914.
32 TNA WO 95/1267: War Diary of the 2nd Brigade, Headquarters, 21 October 1914.
33 TNA WO 95/1274: War Diary of the 3rd Brigade, Headquarters, report dated 25 October 1914.
34 TNA WO 95/1274: War Diary of the 3rd Brigade, Headquarters, report dated 25 October 1914.
35 TNA WO 95/1267: War Diary of the 2nd Brigade, Headquarters, 22 October 1914.
36 TNA WO 95/1267: War Diary of the 2nd Brigade, Headquarters, 22 October 1914.
37 TNA WO 95/1263: War Diary of the 1st Battalion Scots Guards, 22 October 1914.
38 TNA WO 95/1264: War Diary of the 1st Battalion Cameron Highlanders, 22 October 1914.

been going dark, given the season. The divisional report commended Lieutenant Colonel Mc Ewen's control, as the Camerons fell back to just south of the Langemarck – Bixschoote Road. Part of the Coldstreams had been pushed back too.

The broken British line was initially strengthened by the arrival of half the Black Watch. Fitzclarence had ordered them forward and he felt they had stopped the Germans penetrating further. Fitzclarence gradually fed in all his reserves, except for one company, noting that the attack at the centre was much heavier than on the flanks.

By 3.55pm Lomax had put the Northamptons on standby. He also put the Queens on stand-by, to move under 1st (Guards) Brigade orders. Lomax also arranged for the KRRC to be sent to relieve the Royal Sussex and to establish posts at Lizerne, Het Sas lock and the boat bridge 600 yards from the lock. The KRRC were also to send a platoon to Boesinge, to cover the road and rail bridges there.[39] After 6pm, Fitzclarence attempted to organise a local counterattack. For this, he employed the Northamptons which had been released to him. He ordered them to advance to the left of the inn on the Pilkem Road. His conclusion was that this effort, too, played its part in stemming the German tide even though the lost trenches were not regained.[40]

The next morning Lomax focused on regaining the lost trenches. He secured the release of 2 Brigade from Corps reserve and the assistance of 2nd South Staffords from 6th Brigade.

During the ensuing fighting, the British units that were engaged not only carried out attacks but fought off several German counterattacks.[41] The Gloucesters suffered heavily from German artillery fire at 4 p.m., five being killed and ten wounded, as two companies had been put in a large barn which took a direct hit. Langemarck also came under heavy shelling and the battalion HQ of the 2nd Welsh was raised to the ground.[42]

In sending information to the historical section of the Ministry of Imperial Defence, Captain Frazebrook of the Gloucesters paid this tribute to the enemy assault troops:

> The German attack was a particularly fine feat of arms being carried out by … 46th Reserve Division. These lads, who may almost be compared to our Officer Training Corps cadets advanced with the upmost determination singing patriotic songs and though suffering appalling casualties actually succeeded in driving back their seasoned opponents.[43]

We now know that these units contained a proportion of experienced men but, nonetheless, their success against seasoned members of the BEF was an achievement.

At 4.50 p.m., the benefits of establishing the mounted link with the Scots Guards became apparent. The messenger brought news that there was a major assault developing to the right of the Scots Guards, so the Loyal North Lancs were sent forward to Saint Jean. By 5.20 p.m., Bulfin had heard that the Camerons had retired and that the Scots Guards had had to support their right. By 6.30 p.m., Bulfin knew that the Northamptons were now under Fitzclarence's

---

39   TNA WO 95/1267: War Diary of the 2nd Brigade, Headquarters, 22 October 1914.
40   TNA WO 95/1261: War Diary of the 1st Brigade, Headquarters, report dated 22 October 1914.
41   TNA WO 95/1227: War Diary of the 1st Division, Headquarters, 22 October 1914.
42   TNA WO 95/1274: War Diary of the 3rd Brigade, Headquarters, report dated 25 October 1914.
43   TNA WO 95/1278: War Diary of the 1st Gloucestershire Regiment, Frazebrook Diary.

orders; and that the rest of his brigade was to be on stand-by.[44] The Queens had also been sent forward to support 1st (Guards) Brigade.[45]

Three hours later, Bulfin would have been pleased to hear that 2nd KRRC were established in Pilkem and that all was quiet. Bulfin then sent a cake over to the Scots Guards. He said the Germans would have taken it if the Scots Guards had fallen back when their right was exposed. The Scots Guards replied that they were very grateful for the cake but that they had not retired as they had not come under attack.[46] It certainly cannot be said that the British officer class was losing its sense of humour, under the strain of the German assault.

The intensity of the German shelling led to concerns for the ambulances bringing casualties from No. 3 Dressing Station and for the safety of the dressing station too. The growing number of casualties from 1 (Guards) Brigade led to the initial assignment of five ambulances being doubled.[47] The level of casualties was such that the divisional collecting station was filling up. The flow from No. 1 dressing Station was the greatest. Therefore, the other stations were asked to help No.1 by each taking responsibility for clearing an assigned area. The ADMS had requested motor ambulance assistance from I Corps. Due to the team effort by the dressing stations, these were no longer needed when they arrived in the evening. Therefore, they were sent to clear casualties from Poperinghe.[48]

At 11.30 p.m., Bulfin and his Brigade Major went to attend a meeting at divisional headquarters. Being in support, his brigade had only suffered seven fatalities, including an officer, with two further officers amongst the thirty wounded; a further thirty men had been posted missing.[49] Brigadier Landon was also summoned to the meeting and Major General Lomax explained the situation. It was agreed that at 6 a.m., 1 (Guards) Brigade and 2 Brigade would attack with the Queens under the orders of 1 Brigade.[50] C company of the Scots Guards supported the successful assault which led to the recapture of the trenches previously lost by the Camerons. Some 250 Germans were also taken prisoner.[51]

At approximately 3.30 a.m. on 23 October, Captain Rising led half of A company of the Gloucesters to occupy some RE trenches that formed the brigade's left flank. The Gloucesters were filling a gap between the 2nd Welsh and the Coldstream Guards. This meant that the Gloucesters had observation of the Koeknit road. The road itself was occupied by Lieutenant Baxter's no. 3 Platoon, who had a low barricade and a shallow trench, with the rest of the platoon spreading out to the left. Meanwhile, No. 4 Platoon occupied a trench to the right of the road. Their view was obstructed at a range of 500 yards by the Kortebeek stream which crossed the British front, and whose banks were five feet high at this point.[52] This position had been occupied by the Queens until they were assigned to act under 1 Brigade's orders. The Gloucesters therefore had 1 (Guards) Brigade on their left and the 2nd Welsh on their right.

---

44 TNA WO 95/1267: War Diary of the 2nd Brigade, Headquarters, 22 October 1914.
45 TNA WO 95/1274: War Diary of the 3rd Brigade, Headquarters, report dated 25 October 1914.
46 TNA WO 95/1267: War Diary of the 2nd Brigade, Headquarters, 22 October 1914.
47 TNA WO 95/1242: War Diary of the 1st Division Headquarters, ADMS, 22 October 1914.
48 TNA WO 95/1242: War Diary of the 1st Division Headquarters, ADMS, 22 October 1914.
49 TNA WO 95/1267: War Diary of the 2nd Brigade, Headquarters, 22 October 1914.
50 TNA WO 95/1274: War Diary of the 3rd Brigade, Headquarters, report dated 25 October 1914.
51 TNA WO 95/1263: War Diary of the 1st Battalion Scots Guards, 23 October 1914.
52 TNA WO 95/1278: War Diary of the 1st Gloucestershire Regiment, Frazebrook Diary.

A strong German force emerged from Koeknit at about 9 a.m., and proceeded to follow the Kortebeek stream. At the same time as a large body of German infantry gathered, the German artillery opened a heavy fire. This fire fell upon both the trenches occupied by the Gloucesters and the village of Langemarck. Despite heavy British fire from the trenches, the Germans used the haystacks that they had set on fire as cover. In this way, the Germans were able to occupy some woods in front of the positions held by the Coldstream Guards, and a ridge 300 yards from the British trenches.[53]

The Germans used machine guns to cover their advance to within a hundred yards of the Gloucester's trenches. Then the Germans used a ditch running up from the Kortebeek to advance unseen, so that they could emerge suddenly from the rear and flank of the Coldstreams. At 10 a.m., the Coldstream Guards' right section fell back 200 yards, exposing the left of the Gloucesters. According to his account, The Coldstreams fell back to a turnip field, where they held firm, supported by the rest of A company of the Gloucesters under Captain McLeod. In the ensuing action, Second Lieutenant Hippisley, drawn from the reserve of officers, was killed leading his platoon in the defence of the exposed left flank, where the Germans were within fifty yards.

Captain Rising had previously gone back and diverted Lieutenant Yalland's No.15 Platoon to assist his men. D company of the Gloucesters had been sent up to assist the Welsh. Yalland was killed defending the position along with fourteen men of his regiment; a further 36 were wounded.[54] The three platoons probably only amounted to 100 men at this point, so this represents a casualty rate of approximately 60 %, including those who were wounded and remained at duty. The Germans eventually began to retire at about 1 p.m.[55] Captain Rising was awarded the DSO and Lieutenant Baxter the MC for their bravery and skill; whilst the enormous contribution made by NCOs was recognised in the award of the DCM to Sergeants Eddy, Knight, and Wilson and Private Crossman.[56]

There is no diary for the Coldstreams for that week, and the report by 1 (Guards) Brigade does not mention the battalion either. Given the bitterness of the fighting on 23 October, it is no wonder that the Coldstreams are described as under-strength on the 31st. Frazebrook quotes the German official account, which says that the failure on the 22 / 23 October was decisive and points out that the reference to "Fortress Langemarck" exaggerates the state of the defences.[57] He might have commented adversely too on the German claim, that the Germans faced superior numbers of British troops.

Amidst all the fighting, the pressures created by a war fought at a previously unimagined intensity manifested itself. Corps distributed a request to know whether all supply officers had been using a notebook to keep track of daily transactions. Commanders were to ensure that, if this was not the case already, notebooks should be issued, and daily records kept. The interesting admission contained in the order was that no records were being kept of the supplies issued in

---

53 TNA WO 95/1274: War Diary of the 3rd Brigade, Headquarters, report dated 25 October 1914.
54 TNA WO 95/1278: War Diary of the 1st Gloucestershire Regiment, Frazebrook Diary.
55 TNA WO 95/1274: War Diary of the 3rd Brigade, Headquarters, report dated 25 October 1914.
56 TNA WO 95/1278: War Diary of the 1st Gloucestershire Regiment, Frazebrook Diary.
57 TNA WO 95/1278: War Diary of the 1st Gloucestershire Regiment, Frazebrook Diary,

advance of the Base.[58] So as the Supplies Department did not know what it was issuing, and to whom, the supply officers now had to keep a record.

On 24 October, the Gloucesters were moved to the white chateau close to the level crossing where the railway to Roulers crosses the Menin road. Here they were visited by Major General Lomax. He congratulated them on their gallantry and asked for recommendations for awards.[59] For Lomax, himself, there was very positive personal news on 24 October, as he received a letter from Haig. It enclosed a telegram from the Military Secretary replying to Haig's recommendation of promotion for Brigadier-General Bulfin. Along with this news of deserved promotion for Lomax's subordinate, Haig told Lomax that Lord Kitchener had approved promotion for both Lomax and Landon. Haig added that "it will appear in an early gazette". Haig concluded by thanking Lomax for his "efforts and generous support so freely given to one at all times".[60]

Lomax noted that it seemed that the Germans had exhausted themselves in attacking 1st Division. He concluded this from the 500 prisoners taken by 1st division represented all the units of XXVI Reserve Corps. However, as XXIII Reserve Corps were engaged too, it would seem that Corps intelligence was not aware of the full picture. Lomax recorded in detail the chaotic arrangements for the relief of 1st Division by the French. Initially, all was sorted "satisfactorily" for the relief to begin at 6.30 p.m. Then a German bombardment started, and the relief was delayed. According to Lomax all the senior French officers disappeared early in the evening. Before any real progress could be made, the French Brigadier had to be wakened from his bed in the Chateau at 1 a.m.

Therefore, it was not until 8 a.m., on 25 October, that the division could be concentrated around Ypres–Hooge– Zillebeke where it formed corps reserve.[61] The fighting from 21 -24 October had cost 1st Division a total of 1708 casualties, including 56 officers.[62] This was equivalent to the loss of nearly two battalions and virtually all the officers of two battalions – so roughly one-sixth of its strength on mobilisation.

---

58 TNA WO 95/1235: War Diary of the 1st Division Headquarters, A&QMG, 24 October 1914.
59 TNA WO 95/1278: War Diary of the 1st Gloucestershire Regiment, Frazebrook Diary.
60 Sheffield and Bourne (eds.), *Douglas Haig*, p 74
61 TNA WO 95/1235: War Diary of the 1st Division Headquarters, 25 October 1914.
62 TNA WO 95/1235: War Diary of the 1st Division Headquarters, October 1914, Appendix.

11

Lomax's Final Triumph

On 25 October, 1 Guards Brigade arrived in Zillebeke by 10 a.m. and went into billets.[1] The fighting had been so heavy, that 1st Division had no further supplies of anti-tetanus serum.[2] The next day, 1st Division recorded that the plan was for their forces to assist 2nd and 7th Divisions, who had been ordered to make divergent attacks. In consequence, 1st Division's task was to gradually insert itself between the two divisions in the van of the assault.[3] This is an inherently difficult military task, and it is questionable whether it was soundly conceived given the depleted units to be employed.

1st Guards Brigade advanced to Veldhoek with the objective of assisting an attack by 2nd Division on Reutel and Poezelhoek. Lomax observed that the terrain that his troops faced was thickly wooded and very intricate. He said that the Germans had prepared positions defended by wire and involving strongpoints. He noted that these strongpoints had been secured from observation by the artillery.[4] The brigade made contact with 4th Guards Brigade near Polygon Wood.

The 1st Coldstreams and the 1st Scots Guards were sent forward to capture Poezelhoek and the nine kilometre stone on the Menin Road. The 1st Coldstream Guards managed to clear some woods on either side of the Ypres – Menin road. Only limited success was achieved in attempting to attack German trench positions west of Beclaere[5]. This was ascribed by brigade to German artillery fire emanating from Beclaere. By midnight, the brigade had entrenched on a line from east of the nine-kilometre stone on the Menin Road, one mile south of Gheluvelt, to the wood just south of Poezelhoek. Neither village had been taken. On its left was 20 Brigade, and on its right 4 Guards Brigade.[6]

On the night of 26 / 27 October 1 Guards Brigade were holding a line extending for approximately 2000 yards. They had had to assist 7th Division by taking over some of their trenches. The line was made weaker by its right forming a deep salient. 1 Guards Brigade were holding the line from west of Reutel to a point half-a-mile south of the 9-kilometre stone on the

---

1   TNA WO 95/1261: War Diary of the 1st Brigade, 25 October 1914.
2   TNA WO 95/1242: War Diary of the 1st Division Headquarters, ADMS, 25 October 1914.
3   TNA WO 95/1227: War Diary of the 1st Division, Headquarters, 26 October 1914.
4   TNA WO 95/1227: War Diary of the 1st Division, Headquarters, 26 October 1914.
5   TNA WO 95/1261: War Diary of the 1st Coldstream Guards, 25-26 October 1914.
6   TNA WO 95/1261: War Diary of the 1st Guards Brigade, 26 October 1914.

Menin road. From there, the line was held by 3 Brigade down to Zandvoorde, where they had touch with 6 Cavalry Brigade. It was noted at divisional headquarters that 1st Division held its positions, but 2nd Division gained some ground whilst successfully repelling a night attack.[7]

The 1st Coldstream Guards receive a draft of two officers and 80 other ranks, on 27 October The action two days earlier, alone, had cost them more casualties than those represented by this draft. Despite this boost they were not felt to be strong enough to relieve the company of the Queens at the crossroads. Therefore, the latter were replaced by a company of the 1st Black Watch. A further company of the 1st Black Watch was sent to reinforce the defence of the crossroads that night.[8]

Fitzclarence's judgment here may be questioned. The Coldstreams had been forced out of their positions only a few days earlier and were clearly very under-strength. It would have been more sensible to entrust the line to the 1st BW and use the Coldstreams in a support role. This would have given a greater opportunity for cohesion. The wood in front of the Coldstreams is described as being 300 yards ahead of them. By insisting on leaving the weakened Coldstreams in the line, Fitzclarence also ended up committing extra maxims where their range would be partially negated by the terrain.

Meanwhile, 3 Brigade were concentrated about a mile to the rear of the frontline. The Welsh had reported on the poor field of fire offered by the positions. It was only fifty yards in places. Therefore the positions would be difficult to hold. They had recommended that reserves should be held close to the frontline. The Welsh were deployed with nine platoons holding the line, linking the Camerons on their left with the Queens on their right. One platoon of D company acted as battalion reserve close to the point where they linked up with the Queens. The other six platoons formed a shield, approximately 300 yards in front of the remainder of the battalion; they were arranged in an arc in advance of the battalion's allocated position. In theory, No 1 Platoon of A company was at right angles to the last part of the line held by the Camerons and could enfilade any Germans advancing against the Camerons, if they were not taken in enfilade by assaulting German troops.[9]

It was also on 27 October that 1st Division took the fateful step of moving their headquarters – from the café at the five-kilometre stone on the Menin road, back one kilometre to the white chateau. The operations for the day were dependent upon 2nd Division. They were planning to advance at 9.30 a.m. in echelon from the left. In readiness for their success, 2 Brigade under Bulfin were positioned at the crossroads near Noord Westhoek. In addition to his own brigade, Bulfin had under his command a platoon of cyclists, a troop of the XVth Hussars and 25th Brigade RFA and 23 Coy RE.[10] The day passed uneventfully, despite some German shelling when the troops had to cross an open road as they moved up to the west of Polygon Wood.[11] The attack did not make much progress and so Bulfin's brigade were not committed.[12]

---

7   TNA WO 95/1227: War Diary of the 1st Division, Headquarters, 27 October 1914.
8   TNA WO 95/1227: War Diary of the 1st Division, Headquarters, Report by 1 Guards Brigade.
9   TNA WO 95/1281: War Diary of the 2nd Welsh Regiment, 27 October 1914.
10 TNA WO 95/1227: War Diary of the 1st Division, Headquarters, 28 October 1914.
11 TNA WO 95/1267: War Diary of the 2nd Brigade, Headquarters, 28 October 1914
12 TNA WO 95/1283: War Diary of the 2nd Division, Headquarters, 28 October 1914.

On 28 October, the 1st Coldstreams maintained their line.[13] They were sent significant additional reinforcements, in the shape of an additional company of the Black Watch and that battalion's maxims, as well as a company of the Gloucesters and their maxims. The contingent of the Gloucesters was led by Lieutenant Wetherall. When he reported to the 9 Kilometre stone, his men were split up to fill gaps in the line of the Coldstreams and Black Watch. One of his machine guns was posted 200 yards north of the crossroads whilst the other was placed on the road, so as to be able to fire down it.[14] It should be remembered, however, that the crossroads contained a number of buildings and that therefore there was only a limited field of fire. The Brigade report states that the position was therefore thought to be strong enough.[15] In reality, the units holding it were under – strength and in need of rest.

---

13 TNA WO 95/1261: War Diary of the 1st Coldstream Guards, 28 October 1914.
14 TNA WO 95/1278: War Diary of the 1st Gloucestershire Regiment, Frazebrook Diary.
15 TNA WO 95/1227: War Diary of the 1st Division, Headquarters, Report by 1 Guards Brigade.

12

Gheluvelt, 29 October 1914

The headquarters staff of 1st Division were now sharing the White Chateau with their counterparts of 2nd Division. At 9.50 p.m. on 28 October, 2nd Division noted the receipt of information from GHQ that the Germans would make a strong attack on the Gheluvelt crossroads at 5.30 a.m. on 29 October.[1] Exactly the same details were recorded by 1st Division headquarters, and it was noted that all the brigades were warned. It was further noted that lines of fire were agreed by 2nd, 1st, and 7th Divisions. All these divisions were under the command of Lieutenant General Sir Douglas Haig.

The impact of the warning may have been diminished by Haig's decision that the attack by 5 and 6 Brigades would go ahead as scheduled.[2] However, the 1st Gloucesters received the news of both the intention for the British attack to take place and the information on the expected German assault at 5.30 a.m., so clearly 3 Brigade had actively shared the information it had received from Lomax. The information forwarded to 2nd Welsh, at 9.20 p.m., and apparently copied to 1st Queens, and 1st South Wales Borderers, from 3 Brigade stated the expected time of the attack. However, 3 Brigade said that the battalions need not stand to at 5.30 a.m. but should be ready to move at short notice after 5.30 a.m.[3] The information seems to have been further modified, and less clear, when it reached 26th Brigade RFA. They believed that the attack was to come south of the crossroads and they understood that all artillery fire should be directed on to the German artillery as the German infantry were "to be allowed to come on".[4]

On 29 October, the right of 1st Division was formed by 1st Coldstreams who occupied positions north of the Gheluvelt crossroads. The trenches had originally been intended to form support positions; so, they were deep and narrow but not continuous. They were only protected by a stand of wire. Attached to the wire were tins containing pebbles, to act as a warning of a German attack during darkness.[5] The CRE went forward to reconnoitre around Gheluvelt at 4 a.m., only 90 minutes before the German assault on the crossroads half a mile to the east commenced. At 4.43 a.m., 1 Brigade reported all quiet, which did not add any clarity since the expected attack was timed for 5.30 a.m. Similarly, Brigadier-General Ruggles-Brise of 20th

---

1   TNA WO 95/1283: War Diary of the 2nd Division, Headquarters, 28 October 1914.
2   TNA WO 95/1227: War Diary of the 1st Division, Headquarters, 28 October 1914.
3   TNA WO 95/1281: War Diary of the 2nd Welsh Regiment, 28 October 1914.
4   TNA WO 95/ 1250: War Diary of the XXVI Brigade RFA, 29 October 1914.
5   Beckett, *Ypres,* pp. 114-15.

Brigade decided at 4 a.m., as all was quiet, to move his reserves further back to protect them from artillery fire when daylight came.[6] He too seems to have put the emphasis on "not needing to stand to".

The German assault began at 5.30 a.m., under cover of a heavy mist, and the breakthrough occurred in the area manned by B company of the Black Watch according to the post-war account supplied by Captain Krook of that regiment. B company were holding the northern side of the crossroads. According to Krook, this meant that the Germans were then able to turn the flank of the troops north of the crossroads and attack them from the side and rear as well as the front. As the Coldstream Guards had been positioned between B and C companies of the Black Watch, it was they who now bore the brunt of the German assault. In numerical order first 1, then 2 and then 3 Company of the Coldstreams were surrounded and defeated. No fewer than 140 members of the battalion are listed as falling that day; the majority, 114, appearing on the Menin Gate memorial to the missing. These casualties are not only indicative of the Coldstreams determination to fight to the last but also the extent to which their ranks had already been thinned.

It was only at 6.40 a.m. that 1st Brigade sent through an unconfirmed report that the Germans had broken through at the crossroads. The report also stated that the Gloucesters, who had been in reserve near Veldhoek, had been sent forward to the crossroads. The report does not mention that Lieutenant Duncan, the battalion MG officer, had reported back to the Gloucesters at 6.30 a.m. that the Germans had broken through the Black Watch, and that his guns had been lost.[7] It seems that Fitzclarence must have treated Duncan's evidence as unconfirmed. However, it does help explain why he had ordered the Gloucesters forward relatively quickly. Frazebrook notes that the orders were verbal and consisted only of advancing to retake the lost trenches. Lieutenant Colonel Lovett decided to send the companies forward independently as the thick fog made keeping direction extremely difficult.[8]

Lomax took the decision to order forward the 2nd Welsh, also of 3rd Brigade, from Hooge. Lomax also received 2nd Brigade's early morning report which said there had been heavy firing on the fronts of 1st Brigade and 21st Brigade at 5.45 a.m. and that the firing was ongoing.[9] On the assumption that this report was accurate, it emphasises how meaningless the 4.45 a.m. report was from 1st Brigade.

According to Captain Krook, the frontline resistance was then continued by his C company of the Black Watch and 4 Company of the Coldstreams, led by an officer he names as Gibbs. Captain Rowan Hamilton, the battalion Adjutant at that time, confirmed that survivors from B and C company said they had been taken in the flank and the rear. This determined resistance came to an end when the Germans emerged from the woods behind the British positions. Krook noted that there was a gap of approximately 160 yards between his trenches and the first detached post occupied by the Scots Guards to his left. He therefore stated that it was quite possible that the Germans had found the gap between him and the Scots Guards. He also stated that resistance ended once they were surrounded and had run out of ammunition.[10] Krook

6   TNA WO 95/1267: War Diary of the 7th Division, Headquarters, 29 October 1914.
7   TNA WO 95/1278: War Diary of the 1st Gloucestershire Regiment, Frazebrook Diary.
8   TNA WO 95/1278: War Diary of the 1st Gloucestershire Regiment, Frazebrook Diary.
9   TNA WO 95/1227: War Diary of the 1st Division, Headquarters, 29 October 1914.
10 TNA WO 95/1263: War Diary of the 1st Black Watch, October 1914, Appendices.

makes no mention of the issue of defective ammunition which is given great prominence by Edmonds.[11] Captain Hamilton said that he had no knowledge of Major Murray, OC 1st Black Watch, ordering a counter-attack as the detached companies were not under his command, and the rest of the battalion was holding their part of the line.[12] This underlines the problem created by Fitzclarence's decision to put the under-strength Coldstreams into the line and support them with detached companies rather than having the Coldstreams support other units. Ypres was to show that successful commanders should not take undue account of regimental seniority.

The fog of war still swirled around Lomax and, apparently, Fitzclarence too. It did not begin to clear when Major Peel, XXXIX Brigade RFA, telephoned divisional headquarters, to say that he could see the Germans retiring. It was noted that this probably related to prisoners being moved rearwards, but it is likely that this assessment, of Peel's report, was not made until later. Fitzclarence's own grasp of the situation must be questioned as he reported at 7.30 a.m. that he only required a further sixty men to "strengthen the position at the crossroads". Fourteen minutes later, his next report said that the enemy were massing but the Gloucesters should be enough to deal with the situation. Better news came at 8.13 a.m. when the Scots Guards reported that they were dealing successfully with the enemy on their front.[13] In reality, C company of the Gloucesters had advanced initially into the chateau grounds, but its two surviving officers then led a party forward to assist the Scots Guards and became detached from the rest of the company. The rest of the men in C company then attached themselves to whomever they found.[14]

Almost immediately, Lomax received a report that 4th (Guards) Brigade had sent two companies to reinforce the Black Watch's two companies at the crossroads.[15] Meanwhile, D company of the Gloucesters overcame the issue of the fog by following the Menin road. It reached a point approximately 300 yards from the disputed crossroads and formed a rallying point. Half of D company faced north, using the road as a breastwork, and the other half faced east. Despite artillery fire and numerous infantry attacks, they held their position Amongst their losses was Captain Burns of the East Surrey Regiment who had been attached to the battalion since mobilisation.[16]. Nevertheless, it was clear the Germans had poured men through the gap that their early morning assault had created.

Three hours after the German assault had begun, Fitzclarence reported that the Coldstreams had been pushed out of their positions and that the Gloucesters were now trying to regain the positions which had been lost.[17] Of the Gloucesters, only B company, led by Captain Blunt, had managed to force their way forward. They had proceeded behind D company and skirted north of Gheluvelt church. They had then moved forward, leaving the Guards on their left; and then crossed the Ypres – Menin road near the windmill at the eastern extremity of the village. The Gloucesters said the Guards were still fighting hard in the Chateau grounds. This suggests the Gloucesters passed the Chateau before 10.30 a.m., as after this the Scots Guards

---

11   Edmonds, *OH, 1914*, Vol. 1, p.265.
12   TNA WO 95/1263: War Diary of the 1st Black Watch, October 1914, Appendices.
13   TNA WO 95/1227: War Diary of the 1st Division, Headquarters, 29 October 1914.
14   TNA WO 95/1278: War Diary of the 1st Gloucestershire Regiment, Frazebrook Diary.
15   TNA WO 95/1227: War Diary of the 1st Division, Headquarters, 29 October 1914.
16   TNA WO 95/1278: War Diary of the 1st Gloucestershire Regiment, Frazebrook Diary.
17   TNA WO 95/1227: War Diary of the 1st Division, Headquarters, 29 October 1914.

were forced to retire. The Gloucesters managed to force their way to a point approximately 800 yards beyond the village before weight of numbers forced them to give ground. They ended up holding a line between the Menin road and a windmill 200 yards south of it. During this retreat Private Ireland, of No 7 Platoon, endeavoured to save his platoon commander, Lieutenant Harding. Harding was found to be mortally wounded when his body was brought in. Blunt, supported by Lieutenants Morris and Bush, with approximately 25 men, continued to hold their position during the attempted counterattack by the Queens and the Welsh to assist the assault. Eventually they were relieved that evening by 2nd Queens, of 22nd Brigade.[18]

Fitzclarence also reported that the Scots Guards were continuing to hold their positions. Half an hour later, Bulfin reported that the situation in front of 2nd Brigade (in Corps Reserve) was satisfactory but that the Germans may attack from the direction of Poezelhoek.[19] Lomax now left his headquarters and headed forward to confer directly with Fitzclarence. Lomax then organised a counterattack by 3rd Brigade. He declined the offer of one-and-a-half battalions from 4th (Guards) Brigade. At 9.30 a.m., the attack by 5th Brigade went ahead, in the hope that it might ease pressure on the line.[20] According to the war diary, the Queens were told at 10 a.m. that the line had been breached and that they were being sent forward to reinforce it. It then records that they went forward to Gheluvelt, and proceeded to link up with the 2nd Queens about a kilometre south-east of that village.[21] As the afternoon report from Pell, see below, demonstrates this represents a neat summary of what eventually came to pass but conveys little of the tensions involved in getting there.

The seriousness of the situation was emphasised when both RE companies were ordered forward as infantry at 10.30 a.m. However, they were halted when other reinforcements were able to take up the proposed positions. In reality, though, as we have already seen, the Gloucesters had not been committed as a body, but dispersed in companies. A company of the Gloucesters had advanced behind their C company in order to reinforce the Scots Guards. Captain Greenslade, 3rd Gloucesters attached to 1st, took a section of his platoon to the left of the Scots Guards. It appears that they were therefore part of a mixed group that was attacked from both flank and rear at about 10 a.m. The C company casualties included Lieutenant Foster who had only recently left Sandhurst, killed, and Captain Chapman who was wounded before being captured. Lieutenant Greenslade of C company was taken prisoner along with Lieutenant Fitzroy of the Scots Guards, and around 120 men of the units involved in the defence of that sector. This included a group of seven men from D company of the Gloucesters, led by Sergeant Warwick and Corporal Birley, who had joined the defence of the Menin road north of the crossroads.[22]

At 10.50 a.m., Lomax received a report from the Scots Guards that they had had to fall back due to the retreat of the troops on their right. However, the gap was still being filled by the rest of the beleaguered D company of the Gloucesters. They were able to pull back about 300 yards as a formed body, because Captain Rising had brought part of A company up to a position to the

---

18 TNA WO 95/1278: War Diary of the 1st Gloucestershire Regiment, Frazebrook Diary.
19 TNA WO 95/1227: War Diary of the 1st Division, Headquarters, 29 October 1914.
20 TNA WO 95/1227: War Diary of the 1st Division, Headquarters, 29 October 1914.
21 TNA WO 95/1280: War Diary of the 1st Queens, 29 October 1914.
22 TNA WO 95/1278: War Diary of the 1st Gloucestershire Regiment, Frazebrook Diary.

right rear of D company. The covering fire from A company enabled the survivors of D company to affect their retirement to a new line of resistance.[23]

As the Queens and the Welsh were already heavily engaged in the attempt to retake the positions lost by the Coldstreams, the final element of 3rd Brigade, the South Wales Borderers were put in to the line north of the Menin road to support the Scots Guards.[24] It is likely that the Scots Guards had actually fallen back because of their own losses described above; the report would have done little to illuminate the situation for Lomax.

The Coldstream's war diary noted "a retirement appears to have been ordered" and so a portion of the battalion reformed, covering the eastern side of Gheluvelt village and a battery of field artillery that was there.[25] The Brigade report says that the breakthrough south of the crossroads meant that the right of 1st Brigade was taken in the rear. It adds that, as no officers returned, it was difficult to get at the truth. This is as close to a statement that the Coldstreams were broken as is likely, in the understated tones of the report. Fitzclarence states that he sent the Gloucesters forward to support the Coldstreams at 6.55 a.m. and that they succeeded in stopping the further advance of the enemy north of the Menin road. However, we know that in fact this could only mean the three remaining companies, so it demonstrates just how thin the British line was at that moment. The Brigadier adds a comment that it was only at 9 a.m., that 20th Brigade reinforced the sector south of the Menin road, where the bulk of the Germans had broken through.[26] This counter-attack involved 2nd Scots Guards and 2nd Queens, the latter constituted the 7th Division reserve.[27] The detailed accounts suggest that Brigadier Fitzclarence either only had a very unclear picture of what was happening to his brigade or was economical in placing the facts before his commanding officer, or both.

Nonetheless, by 11.40 a.m., the Black Watch reported that the Germans were massing in the chateau grounds to their left; and Lomax was told that 4th (Guards) Brigade had moved one and-a-half battalions to the south-west corner of Polygon Wood. At Noon, 2nd Welsh reported to Brigadier-General Landon that the Black Watch had told them that trenches 300 yards from the small wood south-east of Gheluvelt had been occupied by the Germans. The 2nd Welsh also reported that they were in touch with 2nd Queens, on their right, so the point that needed reinforcing was on their left flank.[28] By 12.30 p.m., Lomax's staff noted that the German attack south of the Menin Road seemed to be slackening, but that localised attacks were continuing in the chateau grounds and around Poezelhoek.[29]

The uncertain situation relating to Poezelhoek also features in Lieutenant Colonel Pell's report at 1.15 p.m. Pell said that he understood no advance was to be attempted until the situation regarding the fighting around Poezelhoek was clear. Pell's report reflected the difficulties that even battalion commanders were having in analysing the battle that was taking place. Pell stated that he thought his leading company were on the road between Gheluvelt and Zandvoorde. He believed his next company was about 300 yards to the left of the first, and had the Welsh on

---

23 TNA WO 95/1278: War Diary of the 1st Gloucestershire Regiment, Frazebrook Diary.
24 TNA WO 95/1227: War Diary of the 1st Division, Headquarters, 29 October 1914.
25 TNA WO 95/1261: War Diary of the 1st Coldstream Guards, 29 October 1914.
26 TNA WO 95/1227: War Diary of the 1st Division, Headquarters, Report by 1 Guards Brigade.
27 TNA WO 95/1627: War Diary of the 7th Division, Headquarters, 29 October 1914.
28 TNA WO 95/1281: War Diary of the 2nd Welsh Regiment, 29 October 1914.
29 TNA WO 95/1227: War Diary of the 1st Division, Headquarters, 29 October 1914.

their left, who extended the line into Gheluvelt. According to Pell, his other companies were following behind his left company. Pell also reported to Major General Landon, that he had not yet made contact with any element of 7th Division on his right.[30]

The crossroads clash of forces was becoming a titanic struggle, as the Germans were now seen to be massing again and threatening to outflank the Queens and the Welsh's own counterattack. Pell's own report would have suggested this, if Lomax had been told of it. There was still a gap between 1st Division and 7th Division. Therefore, Lomax ordered Bulfin to send forward the 1st Loyal North Lancs and the 2nd KRRC to support 3rd Brigade's attack.[31]

The pressure on 3rd Brigade continued. A joint report to Landon from the 2nd Welsh and 1st South Wales Borderers, timed at 2.50 p.m., said that there had been no apparent advance on their left and that they were under intense crossfire from their right. They also reported that their furthest forward positions were just east of Gheluvelt and that they were struggling to go on.[32] At 3 p.m., A company of the Queens mounted an unsuccessful attack on the German trench in front of their C company. They were assisted by 2nd Scots Guards on their right who did succeed in silencing a maxim. The 2nd Scots Guards had been brought forward from their position as reserve for 20th Brigade, after 7th Division had been alerted to the break in the line. The advance of the Queens was credited with helping to heal the breach; their determination and the hard fighting they put in alongside their sister battalion were praised by Major General Capper.[33]

Meanwhile, Bulfin had responded to Lomax's orders by sending forward his remaining battalions. The 2nd KRRC, with B and A companies in the lead and C and D in support, succeeded in pushing the Germans back 500 yards.[34] This was the situation at 3.55 p.m., as reported by Bulfin to Lomax. Bulfin stated that the KRRC had been checked, so he had ordered his men to dig in.[35] The 2nd KRRC ended up being deployed in a thin line forming an arc from the right hand side of the main drive that connected the chateau to the main Ypres – Menin road. Therefore they were in an arc from south-east of the chateau towards the village of Gheluvelt itself.[36] The line was then held solely by B company until 3 a.m. on 30 October, when it was relieved so that it could re-join the rest of the battalion.[37] Behind the KRRC were two companies of the 1st Loyal North Lancs. Under the command of Captain Colley, D company were sent forward first followed by Captain Lucy and A company.[38] By the end of the afternoon, Bulfin recorded that A company was in immediate support to the KRRC, whilst C company and the headquarters of the Loyal North Lancs were situated more than halfway back to the Menin Road. The remaining companies were on the left-hand side of the main drive; with D company extending the line occupied by the KRRC and B company supporting them.[39] Some

---

30   TNA WO 95/1227: War Diary of the 1st Queens, 29 October 1914.
31   TNA WO 95/1227: War Diary of the 1st Division, Headquarters, 29 October 1914.
32   TNA WO 95/1281: War Diary of the 2nd Welsh Regiment, 29 October 1914.
33   TNA WO 95/1627: War Diary of the 7th Division, Headquarters, 29 October 1914.
34   TNA WO 95/1272: War Diary of the 2nd King's Royal Rifle Corps, 29 October 1914.
35   TNA WO 95/1267: War Diary of the 2nd Brigade Headquarters, 29 October 1914.
36   TNA WO 95/1267: War Diary of the 2nd Brigade Headquarters, 29 October 1914.
37   TNA WO 95/1272: War Diary of the 2nd King's Royal Rifle Corps, 29 October 1914.
38   TNA WO 95/1270: War Diary of the 1st Loyal North Lancs, 29 October 1914.
39   TNA WO 95/1267: War Diary of the 2nd Brigade Headquarters, 29 October 1914.

comfort for the men of 1st Loyal North Lancs was achieved on the very wet night of 29 October, when the first-line transport brought up tea and rum.[40]

The GOC 3rd Brigade is credited by Fitzclarence in his report for having taken the offensive with his brigade; and his men are credited with preventing the further advance of the Germans. According to Fitzclarence, initially 3rd Brigade recaptured the lost trenches, but they were unable to hold them, and so that night they entrenched a line just east of Gheluvelt. The report is at pains to point out that only the Coldstreams and one company of the Scots Guards did not hold their positions all day. In Fitzclarence's estimation, the only effect of the German attack was to blunt the end of the salient.[41] Given the account of the Gloucesters and Scots Guards, the assertion that only one company of the latter were pushed back looks to be poorly supported by the evidence. Indeed, the historian of the Scots Guards says that the Right Flank company was practically destroyed, along with the half of B company attached to it and the two sections of C company who were also on that flank. He then adds that because the Gloucesters had been broken through, the 1st Battalion Scots Guards was forced to fall back about 100 yards.[42] This is incredibly unfair, since it was the Gloucesters who were trying to plug the gap created when the Coldstreams and Black Watch were broken through.

It is also hard to argue that the supporting units regained the lost positions, albeit temporarily. The whole of Fitzclarence's report seems to be designed to minimise the reputational damage to 1st (Guards) Brigade. That night the depleted ranks of the Coldstreams were relieved and withdrawn into Brigade reserve.[43] The brutal reality of what had happened to the battalion over the opening months of the war is made clear on 30 October 1914; there were eighty men left in the battalion under the command of Lieutenant & Quartermaster Boyd.[44]

Reflecting the elite nature of the Coldstream Guards, their dead included Major the Honourable Leslie D'Henin Hamilton MVO, whose father was the 1st Baron Hamilton of Dalzell. The Major left a widow in South Eaton Place in London. His then three-year-old son would enter his late father's regiment in 1931, win the Military Cross, and inherit the barony before finishing his public career as Lord Lieutenant of Surrey. Along with Hamilton, Panel 11 on the Menin Gate bears many of the names of the 139 other members of the regiment killed that day. Alongside Hamilton, the 1st Coldstreams lost Private Frank Fish from Leicester and Lance Corporal Sydney Whatley from Norwich. Whilst the personal loss was the same for the family, the impact of the casualties amongst the other ranks was less than it would be later with the Pals battalions, because of the broad geography from which the Guards drew their recruits. In contrast, the officer casualties in these elite regiments in 1914 impacted heavily on the narrow social circle from which they were drawn. Their loss would be reflected later in the works of Vera Brittain and come to influence the narrative of a lost generation.

---

40   TNA WO 95/1270: War Diary of the 1st Loyal North Lancs, 29 October 1914.
41   TNA WO 95/1227: War Diary of the 1st Division, Headquarters, Report by 1 Guards Brigade
42   Loraine Petre, et al, *The Scots Guards in the Great War 1914-1918* (Uckfield: Naval & Military reprint of 1925 edition), p.50.
43   TNA WO 95/1261: War Diary of the 1st Coldstream Guards, 29 October 1914.
44   TNA WO 95/1261: War Diary of the 1st Coldstream Guards, 30 October 1914.

The 1st Gloucesters, from 3rd Brigade, suffered the loss of seven officers and no fewer than 219 men, significantly more than in the official account.[45] The toll taken of the officers with 1st Gloucesters is illustrated by a list that survives in the battalion's records. Thirty-one officers are listed as passing through the battalion during First Ypres, of which 27 were with the battalion before the battle commenced. Of those 27, only five had not been killed, wounded, or captured by the end of the battle. Of the four that joined after 28 October, one was captured and another wounded. Captain Chapman joined on 28 October and was captured on 29 October.[46] The battalion also suffered significant losses in experienced NCOs, with fourteen being killed and the same number wounded, as well as eight being captured.[47] Such losses as these, would damage the ability of battalions to integrate the new drafts when they arrived. The much reduced ranks of 1st Division would now have to face even more pressure as the BEF played its next part in frustrating any chance of a rapid German victory.

---

45 Edmonds, OH, *1914*, Vol. 1, p.265 and TNA WO 95/1278: War Diary of 1st Gloucestershire Regiment, October 1914.
46 TNA WO 95/1227: War Diary of the 1st Division, Headquarters, October 1914, Appendix.
47 TNA WO 95/1278: War Diary of the 1st Gloucestershire Regiment, Frazebrook Diary.

13

Gheluvelt: Second Day

Although the fighting was much less intense the next on 30 October, the hard pressed units of 1st Division enjoyed little respite. After nightfall on 29 October, 23rd Coy. RE worked on strengthening the defences of Gheluvelt in 2nd Brigade's sector. Meantime, 26th Coy. RE performed the same role in 3rd Brigade's sector south of the village.[1] Fortunately, for 1st Brigade and 3rd Brigade, 30 October was a relatively quiet day and the main German attack came further south at Zandvoorde. True to the attritional nature of the conflict, the Gloucesters still lost seven men killed and five wounded, whilst occupying the support trenches.[2] For the Black Watch, there was a new CO in the shape of Lieutenant Colonel C E Stewart. The battalion also received sixty men plus Second Lieutenant Rennie and Captain Amery. In an effort at close co-operation, Lieutenant Duncan took "E gun" forward to assist the infantry at the barrier. Lieutenant Duncan had previously placed himself in the relevant infantry fire trench when acting as the Forward Observation Officer for the brigade.[3]

Having been relieved and transferred to the right of 1st Queens; the 1st Loyal North Lancs were told to capture some German trenches in advance of their positions south of Gheluvelt but German artillery fire proved too strong. Nevertheless, the German success in breaking the line held by 3 Cavalry Brigade and 7th Division meant that 2nd Brigade were soon in action again. At 9.15 a.m., Bulfin was informed about the German attack. He then proceeded to move his headquarters and the 1st Northants and 2nd Royal Sussex to a position halfway between Veldhoek and Zandvoorde. This was because he had been told to be ready to reinforce either Kruisek or Zandvoorde as the situation became clearer.

Bulfin's demi-brigade encountered the 2nd Gordon Highlanders and 1st South Staffords, of 7th Division, who were preparing to attack the German positions around the Inn at Zandvoorde. The German rifle fire increased. Therefore, Bulfin sent a company of the Royal Sussex to clear some woods, and the Northants to occupy the road. The 2nd Royal Sussex had already lost Lieutenant Colonel Crispin to shrapnel fire on their way to the rendezvous. His horse bolted at the noise and prevented him taking cover with his men. The horse, which was not hurt by the burst which killed its rider, stopped eventually by a farm and that was where his men buried

---

1   TNA WO 95/1227: War Diary of the 1st Division, RE, 29 October 1914.
2   TNA WO 95/1278: War Diary of the 1st Gloucestershire Regiment, Frazebrook Diary.
3   TNA WO 95/1250: War Diary of the XXVI Brigade RFA, 30 October 1914.

their late CO.⁴ The Sussex, under Captain Villiers, made good progress and got within sight of the inn, though this had required B, C and D companies. However, the Northants struggled and were told to entrench where they had reached. The Gordon Highlanders' advance was also checked, so Bulfin ordered them to entrench a line extending to the right of the Northants. Bulfin directed the Sussex to withdraw their attacking company gradually and extend the line round the eastern edge of the wood to link up with the South Staffords. The Staffords occupied the ridge where the units had originally met up in their advance.⁵ The immense pressure on the British is evident from the CRE's efforts to reconnoitre a line from the south-west corner of Polygon Wood to a point east of Veldhoek on 30 October, even before the major German attacks on 31 October. The unengaged A company of the 2nd Royal Sussex worked with RE personnel to construct a defensive position to be held that night.⁶

At around 3 p.m., Lord Cavan arrived with 4th (Guards) Brigade and the 2nd Oxford and Bucks Light infantry, part of 5th Brigade. Acting with Haig's authority, Cavan ordered a line to be formed covering the Menin–Ypres railway at the bend in the canal. By 8 p.m., Lord Cavan had placed 4th (Guards) Brigade under Bulfin's orders, and a continuous line had been formed from the canal to where they linked up with 20th Brigade.

Following the withdrawal of elements of 22nd Brigade on 30 October, 1st Queens were holding trenches south of the Menin road supported, from that evening, by two companies of the 2nd KRRC, who entrenched themselves in a small farm. D company of 1st Queens were next to the Welsh on the right. However, they were therefore echeloned back from C company, which had occupied the farm buildings forward of both D and B companies. The orchard to the front left of B company was occupied by two platoons, one drawn from the 2nd KRRC. The vulnerability of B company if these advanced positions were taken was to prove critical. A company formed the left wing of the position. To the right of A company, the most southerly element of 1st Division were two companies of the Loyal North Lancs. According to Major Watson's map, submitted in early December, the Loyal North Lancs were neatly in line with the right flank of 1st Queens, but, by their own account, they had been told to occupy trenches beyond the road, further forward than A company of 1st Queens;⁷ so they would be very vulnerable if 1st Queens were forced to retire. They occupied, at the behest of 3rd Brigade, the gap between A company and a stream which ran under the Zandvoorde road. At the same time, 26th Coy. RE were entrenching a position in front of the 1st Loyal North Lancs who were holding a small wood approximately three quarters of a mile south of Gheluvelt.⁸

Tense communication, mid-afternoon, between the OC 2nd KRRC and Lieutenant Colonel Pell explicitly said that the Loyal North Lancs were uncertain of their ground and therefore would Pell please send an officer to guide them into position. It was clear that the OC 2nd KRRC had wanted to keep his units of 2nd Brigade together and asked Pell to notify III Brigade that 1st Queens had retained the use of these units. The stream therefore marked the divisional boundary.

4   TNA WO 95/1269: War Diary of the 2nd Royal Sussex, 30 October 1914.
5   TNA WO 95/1267: War Diary of the 2nd Brigade Headquarters, 30 October 1914.
6   TNA WO 95/1269: War Diary of the 2nd Royal Sussex, 30 October 1914.
7   TNA WO 95/1270: War Diary of the 1st Loyal North Lancs, 31 October 1914.
8   TNA WO 95/1227: War Diary of the 1st Division, RE, 30 October 1914.

14

Gheluvelt
Third Day – Morning

Well before daybreak Brigadier-General Landon dispatched a message to 1st Queens, saying that he understood the Loyal North Lancs were 900 yards further to the right than they were meant to be, and that Landon was endeavouring to get 7th Division to occupy the line up to the stream. Landon tersely requested Pell to confirm where his right was and whether two companies of 2nd KRRC were filling the gap.[1] Landon had the more accurate grasp of the situation as the 1st Loyal North Lancs were indeed occupying a much wider position than intended with all four companies in line. Presumably as a result of Landon's efforts, at 5 a.m., the Bedfords and Scottish Rifles took over the trenches of B and C companies of 1st Loyal North Lancs.[2] Therefore these two companies now formed the reserve behind 1st Queens, their tiredness after a night relief can only be imagined. The confusion of units within the British lines would weaken the defence but the problems would essentially stem from being outnumbered and lacking sufficient artillery to offset this.

Landon also asked Pell whether he had enough companies in his front line. The other two companies of 1st Loyal North Lancs were held back behind the left (A company 1st Queens) position as a reserve. Given the awkward configuration, battalion headquarters was sited behind the centre of the battalion. Major Watson's map of the positions on the night of 30th October shows all the units in the "correct" positions; but it was drawn up in early December. The fragility of the situation may be inferred from the order received by 1st Queens at 12.30 p.m., that a line must be established "eventually" – the attack came within 18 hours. Its imminence was foreshadowed at 7 p.m. when the Welsh messaged 1st Queens that the Germans were massing in front of their positions with fixed bayonets.[3]

The 2nd Welsh were holding a line of trenches 400 yards east of Gheluvelt village. They were north of the Menin road, except for one platoon of C company which was south of the Menin road. One machine gun had been placed on the road itself overnight but had then been withdrawn, at dawn, to an emplacement 160 yards behind B company. B company was under the command of Lieutenant Marshall and were occupying 150 yards of trench, their right resting

---

1   TNA WO 95/1280: War Diary of the 1st Queen's Royal West Surrey Regiment, 30/31 October 1914.
2   TNA WO 95/1270: War Diary of the 1st Loyal North Lancs, 31 October 1914.
3   TNA WO 95/1280: War Diary of the 1st Queen's Royal West Surrey Regiment, 30 October 1914.

on the road. On B company's left, two platoons of D company under Second Lieutenant Young were positioned facing north-east. The battalion HQ, under Lieutenant Colonel Morland, and a platoon of D company, under Captain Rees, were in support in a sunken road that connected to the Menin road. In reserve, were two platoons of A company, situated in dugouts along the Menin road between the sunken lane and the village. C company were deployed to support the junction of the Welsh and the Borderers, with two platoons in a small wood. One platoon occupied trenches from which they could offer supporting fire to B company, though only at long range.[4]

The 1st South Wales Borderers extended the line north-westwards; occupying approximately 400 yards of trench between a small clump of trees where they were in touch with the 2nd Welsh, up to the north-east corner of the Gheluvelt Chateau grounds. There they linked up with the Scots Guards. The Scots Guards noted that the Germans had withdrawn out of sight but that the woods were "full of them".[5] The Borderers held A company in close support, in the chateau grounds.[6] To the left of the Scots Guards, the line was extended by the rest of 1st (Guards) Brigade's effective battalions; 1st Camerons and 1st Black Watch. The very thin ranks of 1st Coldstream Guards were used as cover for battery positions south of the Menin road on 31 October and returned to being brigade reserve that evening.[7]

As had happened two days earlier, 1st Division suffered very badly in the opening phase of the German assault on 31 October. Those least affected initially were the detached troops from 2nd Brigade, deployed as part of Bulfin's composite command. After Bulfin had received Lomax's message that the centre of 1st Division had been broken and been told that 22nd Brigade were falling back; he organised a retirement. He sent for the OCs and made arrangements for trenches to be held lightly so that battalions could fall back in stages. Those who had retired first would be able to support those who retired later, with covering fire. In this manner, the 1st Northants and 2nd Royal Sussex were able to retire with the Germans pressing after them.[8] This was achieved despite the 2nd Royal Sussex having to send two companies and the machine guns rearwards to ward off a rumoured German outflanking manoeuvre being made by German cavalry supported by infantry.[9] The Germans were then pushed back when the two battalions of 2nd Brigade launched a counter-attack. In the attack they were supported by two dismounted squadrons of 1st Royal Dragoons. Bulfin had been assisted by Colonel Jeudwine, the Corps GSO1, who had been on hand when news of the original reverse had arrived.

When Bulfin learnt that 7th Division had stabilised their line, he initiated a series of counterattacks to regain their original positions. Bulfin himself had great courage; he himself came under fire and his orderly was killed.[10] He is rightly rated as a leader. He ordered the 2nd Royal Sussex and 1st Northants forward to re-occupy their original trenches. This attack involved each battalion advancing down a track before crossing open ground against German positions sited in woods. Although the extreme right of the 2nd Royal Sussex reached their

---

4   TNA WO 95/1281: War Diary of the 2nd Welsh Regiment, Rees's account, 31 October 1914.
5   TNA WO 95/1263: War Diary of the 1st Scots Guards, 30 October 1914.
6   TNA WO 95/1280: War Diary of the 1st South Wales Borderers, 31 October 1914.
7   TNA WO 95/1263: War Diary of the 1st Coldstream Guards, 31 October 1914.
8   TNA WO 95/1267: War Diary of the 2nd Brigade, 31 October 1914.
9   TNA WO 95/1269: War Diary of the 2nd Royal Sussex Regiment, 31 October 1914.
10   Powell, J., *Haig's Tower of Strength* (Barnsley: Pen & Sword, 2018), p.90.

objective, the battalion suffered heavy casualties especially when crossing the open ground. The German troops held their fire until the British were at close range. The operations on 30 and 31 October cost the Sussex the lives of the CO, four subalterns and a total of 394 casualties amongst the other ranks.[11] To Bulfin's credit, when it was clear that the costly attacks were not going to get his troops beyond their current positions; he consulted the OCs and decided to call-off any further attacks.[12] Having looked at the fate of the detached troops, further to the south, it is appropriate to return to the rest of 1st Division.

At dawn, the positions held by 1st Queens and the 2nd KRRC were attacked. The Germans were initially repulsed. However, the Germans dug in 300 yards in front of the Queens, in the trenches previously occupied by 2nd Queens. This is reflected in a message from D company, timed at 9 a.m., where they also asked for more ammunition and for British artillery to be targeted on the Germans. However, if the Germans were that close to D then that implies that at least some of the positions occupied by C company at the outset must have been taken, or that the two sides were so closely engaged that it would not be practicable to call down artillery fire. The Germans renewed their assault after a further artillery barrage and forced their way into an orchard which had been defended by two platoons, one each from the Queens and KRRC. This brought the Germans to within 150 yards of the Queens main line of defence. Major Watson went back to seek assistance but could not get any. Watson then returned to find that Lieutenant Colonel Pell had been wounded, mortally as it proved, and therefore he had to assume command of the battalion. The Germans managed to get machine guns forward to enfilade B company from both flanks, and therefore succeeded in capturing that section of the defences. The reserve, comprising two platoons of the KRRC, could not be found so a counterattack was not possible. Watson recorded that the Queens believed the KRRC had gone forward to support D company without orders.

At about 10.30 a.m., Captain Creek reported that the Welsh had retired, but that he was fine and would hold on. Another surviving message suggests brigade be informed. Given all the problems occurring on the left, at 11 a.m. Major Watson left the battalion headquarters and went to investigate the situation personally. He was met by another messenger from D company, who informed Major Watson that the Germans were about to occupy C company's positions. It had not been possible to get a message from C company. This news would have explained why B company had been forced out by enfilade fire. Major Watson therefore gave orders for D company to retire. Before those orders arrived, the Germans were seen to be entering the village behind D company. This demonstrates the impact of the Welsh giving way. Major Watson and Lieutenant Boyd then sought to rally the Queens at the central point of the village where the three roads met. This would mean they were on slightly higher ground than the Germans filtering in behind D company. They were rallying on a position not far in front of where the reserve of half the 2nd KRRC, comprised of A and B companies, were. This situation was not improved by the reserve half of the 2nd KRRC beginning to fall back, because they believed that the Germans were bringing up machine guns to enfilade them. This demonstrates the further ripples from the Welsh collapse, as the 2nd KRRC were reacting to having an insecure flank.[13]

---

11 TNA WO 95/1269: War Diary of the 2nd Royal Sussex Regiment, 31 October 1914.
12 TNA WO 95/1267: War Diary of the 2nd Brigade, 31 October 1914.
13 TNA WO 95/1280: War Diary of 1st Queen's Royal West Surrey Regiment, 31 October 1914.

The 2nd KRRC falling back impacted upon the reserve companies of the Loyal North Lancs who began to retire to keep touch with the 2nd KRRC on their left. More positively, 3rd Brigade noted that eventually the Welsh were able to reform behind the 2nd KRRC.[14] The 2nd KRRC, whilst retiring on the north side of the road, managed to bring up their machine guns and create a barrier from which they could hold the Germans back. Meanwhile, the detached elements of the 2nd KRRC, under Major Warre, began to fall back on their battalion. Their flanks had been exposed by the positions of 1st Queens being captured. The whole 2nd KRRC had to fall back further when some Germans reached the barrier and were able to fire directly at the defenders at point-blank range. The machine guns were saved, but the tripods had to be left behind temporarily. Lieutenant Colonel Sercold was wounded on his way to report to Brigade HQ so command devolved upon Major Philips. The battalion had lost one officer killed, another three wounded and missing, five more wounded, along with approximately 400 casualties amongst the other ranks.[15] The 1st Loyal North Lancs received orders to retire once the 1st Queens were pushed back and were able to do so in an orderly way. 1st Queens then assisted the Gordon Highlanders in a successful counter-attack. The cost was heavy; by the end of the day, they had suffered 416 casualties, including eight officers. Watson and Boyd, of 1st Queens, gathered about twenty men into trenches.[16] Given the losses sustained before Ypres, here were three more battalions of 1st Division who had suffered severely, with irreparable losses in terms of experience. Thus, the Germans were now pushing back the British who were holding the area south of Gheluvelt, meanwhile the Welsh on the Queens's left had been broken opening the way into Gheluvelt itself.

According to the Gloucester regiment account, the Welsh were devastated by the German bombardment, and it was a wonder that anyone was left. In their view, whole companies of the Welsh were annihilated and gradually, dazed individuals began to retreat through the support positions held by the Gloucesters.[17] The account submitted by Captain Rees, which effectively re-constituted the war diary, agrees that the artillery bombardment was devastating. It adds that the Germans brought up field guns to within 700 – 800 yards of the Welsh trenches, to support the infantry assault. Therefore, at around 8 a.m., Lieutenant-Colonel Morland decided that the battalion had to retire. B and D companies had suffered severe losses and the German artillery fire meant that it was not possible to support them. He had also decided that the sunken lane was not a defensible position. He then sent messages to all the neighbouring units, including the 2nd KRRC, but the Welsh account concluded that it was unlikely they reached their destinations.[18]

This account differs from Edmonds, who says that Morland withdrew both his supports and his firing line.[19] Edmonds received a very strong response to this point from Major General Sir Thomas Marden. Marden wrote from Folkstone in 1932 to point out that Morland could not have withdrawn his firing line as they had been cut off, if not annihilated by the German

---

14 TNA WO 95/1274: War Diary of 3rd Brigade, 31 October 1914.
15 TNA WO 95/1272: War Diary of 2nd King's Royal Rifle Corps, 29 October 1914.
16 TNA WO 95/1280: War Diary of the 1st Queen's Royal West Surrey Regiment, 31 October 1914.
17 TNA WO 95/1278: War Diary of the 1st Gloucestershire Regiment, Frazebrook Diary.
18 TNA WO 95/1281: War Diary of the 2nd Welsh Regiment, Rees's account, 31 October 1914.
19 Edmonds, *OH, 1914*, Vol. 1, p.315.

shellfire. Marden also pointed out that Rees's account had been drawn up immediately after the action, and subsequently written up, with extra detail, in the months following.

Marden also stated that Rees had originally over-estimated the number of officers with the battalion on 31 October and that Rees assumed command of the battalion on the evening of 31 October, being one of only two officers who had not been wounded or killed. It is clear from the tone of his letter that Marden was seeking to protect Morland's reputation. It is also clear that Marden had previously written to Edmonds about this subject. Edmonds had challenged Marden's account, since Marden could not know what happened to C company. Nonetheless, whilst Marden may be too kind in his appraisal of Morland's initial dispositions, all the available evidence for the Great War shows that few battalion commanders could communicate effectively with their dispersed companies once a heavy artillery barrage commenced. Therefore, any decisions Morland reached after 7.30 a.m. could only affect those with whom he was still in contact.

Marden was also keen to protect the regiment's honour. He had been CO of the 1st Welsh in 1914 and pointed to the fact that he had contacted those from neighbouring regiments and that no one blamed the Welsh, who happened to be in the most exposed position.[20] However, the contrast between the actions of Major Watson and Lieutenant Colonel Morland does suggest the Queens were better handled on 31 October. Nevertheless, the war diary of the Scots Guards recorded the Welsh and Queens as being broken and distinguished between them and the Borderers by noting that the latter "retired".[21]

The 1st South Wales Borderers were able to beat off the attacks by the Germans who, initially, mainly attacked on their left next to the junction with the Scots Guards.[22] The Scots Guards brought up their left-flank company to help cover the Borderers as the pressure grew on the latter.[23] However, the pressure switched to the right of the South Wales Borderers, when the Welsh gave way. The Gloucesters, in support, had been requested to support the Borderers right. Whilst they were on their way the right company of the Borderers was overwhelmed. They fell back through the chateau grounds and the company next in line began to fall back too. Initially, these men were rallied along the bank at the south-east of the grounds but then they came under enfilade fire from the German troops in the chateau gardens. Therefore, the Borderers fell back to the line of the light railway. The situation was stabilised when Captain Wood brought his A company into action on the south front of the chateau.[24]

The withdrawal of the 2nd Welsh support elements to the northern edge of the village took place under intense artillery fire, a mixture of shrapnel and high explosive. Captain Rees stated that he did not know the specific movements of the supports between 8 a.m. and 10.30 a.m. but did know that a group of men, including those carrying the wounded Lieutenant Young, lost touch with their CO. This group eventually reached the west of Gheluvelt, where they reported the situation to Major Peel, XXXIX Brigade RFA, who ordered them to man a trench covering his battery.[25] In his account of the action in 1914, Blewitt, of XXXIX Brigade RFA, describes

---

20 TNA WO 95/1281: War Diary of the 2nd Welsh Regiment, Marden correspondence.
21 TNA WO 95/1261: War Diary of the 1st Scots Guards, 31 October 1914.
22 TNA WO 95/1280: War Diary of the 1st South Wales Borderers, 31 October 1914.
23 TNA WO 95/1261: War Diary of the 1st Scots Guards, 31 October 1914.
24 TNA WO 95/1280: War Diary of the 1st South Wales Borderers, 31 October 1914.
25 TNA WO 95/1281: War Diary of the 2nd Welsh Regiment, Rees's account, 31 October 1914.

how Captain Rees and the remnants of the 2nd Welsh, which Blewitt estimated at 25, arrived at their battery position having lost touch with everyone else from the battalion. The battery commander gave Rees some tea and toast and asked Rees and his men to line a trench two hundred yards in front of the battery on the line of a crest.[26] Beckett explains that Rees had tried to withdraw the men of two of his platoons but too many were killed trying to join him, so he desisted and retired with those he had.[27]

The uncertainty of the whole situation is also evident in what happened to the 23rd Coy. RE. They were initially told to go forward to work on positions east of Veldhoek, the order was then countermanded as it was deemed that the work was impracticable.[28] By 9.30 a.m., XXXIX Brigade RFA had been informed by their FOO that the Welsh had been shelled out of their advance positions, and that two German guns on the road were doing a lot of damage. The brigade then arranged for their 51st battery to target those German guns.

At about 10.30 a.m., the Gloucesters met up with their retreating colleagues and attempted to counter-attack as ordered. B company of the Gloucesters had two platoons on each side of the road. This local counterattack was led by Lieutenant Norris on the northern side, and Lieutenant Bush was on the southern side. They succeeded in clearing the Germans out of houses in the east of Gheluvelt.[29] Captain Rees had collected about 60 stragglers of the 2nd Welsh and joined in the counterattack on the left of the Gloucesters. As he advanced towards the lane leading to C company's positions, Rees encountered Lieutenant Colonel Morland. Morland said there was no point going forward as it was just wasting men. Morland also told Rees that Captain Ferrar, the battalion Adjutant, had been killed trying to lead a bayonet charge from the barricade on the Menin road. According to Rees, the counterattack had failed by 11.30 a.m.[30]

Lieutenant Colonel Lovett and Major Ingram had attempted to organise counterattacks by gathering men from 3rd Brigade and the Scots Guards who had fallen back. These efforts benefitted from the support of the field guns firing the newly available 18 pdr. high explosive shells.[31] D company of the Gloucesters, amounting to only eighty men, were also ordered forward to retake a trench, but found it in British hands. Nonetheless, they had suffered heavy casualties due to intense shellfire during their approach. Major Gardiner, of the Gloucesters, believed that they should have been sent further south in the line; rather than await reinforcements due to the urgency of the situation. Major Gardiner tried to take his men forward again and, immediately, half became casualties. Returning to their cover in the sunken lane, they were overwhelmed in a later German assault.[32] In the account of this action given by Frazebrook, the casualties are much higher than in his own battalion summary for D company at the end of the day, so the figures for the action have been omitted.

Major Gardiner was killed, and Lieutenant Caunter was captured. At about 1.30 p.m., Moorland, Captain Moore, OC C company, Captain Rees, and Lieutenant Corder, accompanied by about 30 men, joined the others occupying the trench defending the gun battery, as they

26 Hutton, *The Gunners of August 1914* (Barnsley: Pen & Sword, 1914) pp. 172-73.
27 Beckett, *Ypres*, p.131
28 TNA WO 95/1227: War Diary of the 1st Division, RE, 31 October 1914.
29 TNA WO 95/1278: War Diary of the 1st Gloucestershire Regiment, Frazebrook Diary.
30 TNA WO 95/1281: War Diary of the 2nd Welsh Regiment, Rees's account, 31 October 1914.
31 Beckett, *Ypres*, p. 143
32 TNA WO 95/1278: War Diary of the 1st Gloucestershire Regiment, Frazebrook Diary.

regarded the village as lost. Whilst they were discussing what could be done, a shell exploded, which killed Moore and mortally wounded Morland.[33]

The desperate nature of the situation was revealed by Lomax to Bulfin, in a message sent at 12.50 p.m. In the message, not only did Lomax say that his centre had given way, but also that 1st (Guards) Brigade was refusing its right flank. Lomax also told Bulfin that he was trying to stem the German advance west of Gheluvelt, so it was clear that at this point he believed that trying to recapture the lost positions was not feasible. This conclusion echoed that of an earlier message timed at 12.28 p.m. that Lomax had also sent to Bulfin, but which reached the GOC 2nd Brigade after the second one. In the first message Lomax said that the Germans were massing for a further attack but that he was looking to counter-attack with the Worcesters. This is interesting as none of the accounts, discussed below, of the decision to launch the counterattack by the Worcesters refers to Lomax. Lomax also told Bulfin that he was planning to block the western exits to Gheluvelt with the Gloucesters and the Welsh.[34]

That afternoon, between 1.15 and 1.30 p.m., Major General Lomax was so severely wounded by German shellfire that he would die of those wounds in April 1915.[35] He was hit whilst in the Hooge Chateau, where the headquarters of 1st and 2nd Divisions were co-located to facilitate co-ordination. Lomax had returned from his battle headquarters to confer with his opposite number Monro. The 1st Division also lost its chief staff officer Colonel Kerr; he was replaced three days later as GSO1 by Colonel Jeudwine.[36] Before this happened, Lomax had reported to Haig, that 1st Division had been broken and that he was trying to reform on a line east of Hooge. As Haig's diary refers to this report coming at 2.30 p.m., Haig must be referring to when he received the message. Haig's diary states that he then went to get on his horse to go forward to 1st Division when Field Marshal French arrived. Haig updated his commander and received warm praise from French for all the work done by I Corps and Haig himself. They then parted, at about 3 p.m., as French was going to see Foch, and Haig himself planned to resume his ride up to 1st Division.[37]

Haig states that he had intended to help by organising stragglers but met General Capper, GOC 7th Division, and Brigadier Fitzclarence, and found that the situation had been restored by the Worcesters, who had retaken Gheluvelt.[38] A detailed assessment of the evidence regarding who ordered the Worcester's forward is given in Appendix II. Taking all the evidence together it seems right to conclude that the arrangements had been made by Lomax. That there was an opportunity for the Worcesters to restore the situation owed a great deal to the gritty determination of all ranks of 1st Division, most notably Bulfin's detached units.

---

33 TNA WO 95/1281: War Diary of the 2nd Welsh Regiment, Rees's account, 31 October 1914.
34 TNA WO 95/1267: War Diary of the 2nd Brigade Headquarters, October 1914, Appendix O.
35 For a brief discussion of those who followed Lomax in command of 1st Division see Appendix III
36 Becke, *Order of Battle of Divisions – Part 1*, pp. 36-37.
37 Sheffield and Bourne (eds.), *Douglas Haig*, p 75
38 Sheffield and Bourne (eds.), *Douglas Haig*, p 76

15

Gheluvelt
Third Day – Late Afternoon

With the gallant Worcesters counterattack, the greatest danger had passed. The Borderers and Scots Guards re-occupied the original positions. The Worcesters then took up a position which extended the right flank of 1st (Guards) Brigade. The battalion then supported the Scots Guards and South Wales Borderers in repelling a further attack at 2.45 p.m. A platoon of the Scots Guards was deployed to the right rear of the Borderers to protect them.[1] I Corps responded to the news of Lomax being incapacitated by appointing Bulfin to command but as he was currently detached, Landon was directed to take charge.[2] The divisional record only refers to Landon, unsurprisingly given casualties amongst the staff, and echoes Edmonds in saying that it was difficult to locate him.[3]

Brigadier-General Landon was hard to locate as between noon and 2 p.m., he was getting as many men as possible from his scattered units to form a line on the track that ran north-south just east of Hooge.[4] That afternoon, both divisional RE companies had been assigned the task of creating a defensive line on the road just east of the Hooge Chateau. However, the pressures of the battle meant that these orders were again changed an hour later, at 2 p.m., when they were re-deployed as infantry. Landon's brigade was attempting to carry out a counterattack south of the Menin road. He had been instructed to use every available company of his own brigade as well as two battalions from 2nd Brigade. The attack failed and resulted in very heavy losses, especially to 1st Queens. By 3.30 p.m., it was felt that the pressure was easing and that therefore it was not sensible to continue to try to regain the original trenches, but rather to establish a new line west of Gheluvelt.[5] There is no indication in the records as to when Landon arrived to assume divisional command. Landon's brigade had just been sacrificed on the very altar of the "necessity" to always regain lost positions. Given the extremely poor fields of fire offered by those lost positions, the logic in trying to regain them is hard to discern.

1 TNA WO 95/1280: War Diary of the 1st South Wales Borderers Regiment, 31 October 1914.
2 Edmonds, *OH 1914*, Vol. 1, p.324.
3 TNA WO 95/1261: War Diary of the 1st Division, Headquarters, 31 October 1914.
4 TNA WO 95/1274: War Diary of the 3rd Brigade, 31 October 1914.
5 TNA WO 95/1227: War Diary of the 1st Division, 31 October 1914.

Gheluvelt: Third Day – Late Afternoon 101

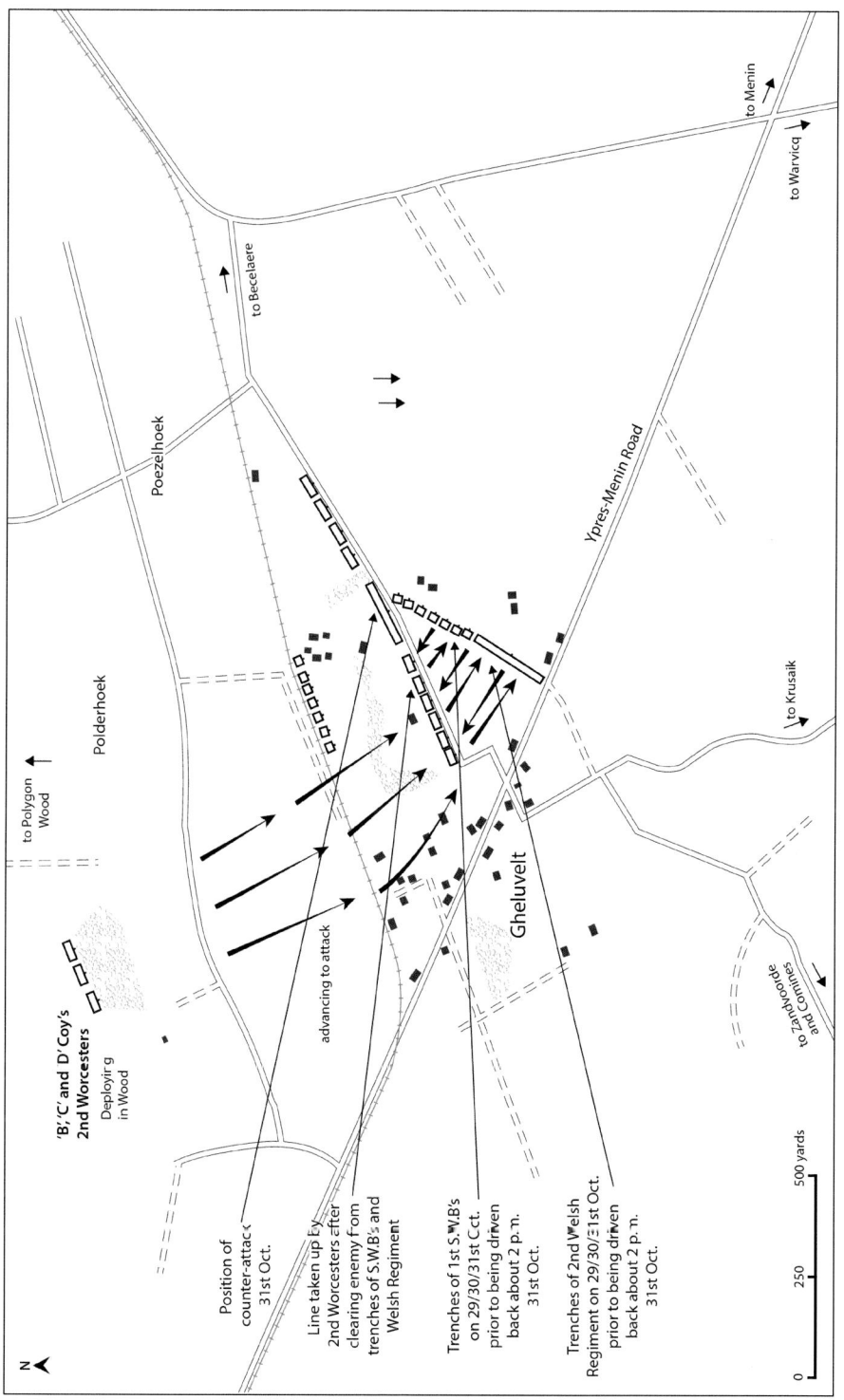

Gheluvelt, 31 October 1914 counterattack.

At around 4 p.m. on 31 October, Lieutenant Ralph Blewitt, of 54th Battery in XXXIX Brigade, RFA, obtained permission to take an 18-pdr gun forward to try to remove a gun which the Germans had placed behind a barrier in Gheluvelt. Having obtained permission, Blewitt and his men manhandled the gun out on to the road. There they succeeded in their dangerous mission. The Germans fired first but missed, so the British gunners took their opportunity and scored a direct hit.[6] Blewitt was subsequently awarded the DSO..[7] Blewitt's action enabled the Gloucesters to create a barricade across the road, from which to fire on Germans advancing towards Ypres.[8]

Their defence was aided by other operations close by. The 26th Coy. RE were ordered to advance south-eastwards and eventually came under the command of Brigadier Bulfin. Bulfin's command also included one section of 57th battery who had been detached and placed under his orders.[9] For 23 Coy. RE, as part of a scratch force including stragglers supporting 3rd Brigade, the task was to clear the Germans from a small wood south of the chateau, south-east of Veldhoek. In this they were successful, and a field gun was captured too.[10]

By 5.15 p.m., 1st Division had received a report from 3rd Brigade to say that the Worcesters' right flank rested on Gheluvelt, and that German mounted troops and artillery had been seen entering the village. These observations, also made by Lieutenant Colonel Leach, persuaded him, at 5.30 p.m., that the units defending Gheluvelt Chateau should make a tactical withdrawal.[11] His decision was then overtaken by the subsequent orders from I Corps.

The difficulties facing Haig in reaching an assessment are reflected in a further flurry of reports received by 1st Division just after 6.30 p.m. The report from 1st Brigade said that their battalions were holding on and that Gheluvelt was no longer occupied by the Germans. The OC of 2nd Welsh reported that two companies of the 1st Royal Berkshires were at the eastern edge of Gheluvelt. A further report, received from a cavalry patrol, said that General Bulfin's situation was now satisfactory and that his force had nearly re-established the original line. These positive notes were jarred by a message from 2nd Division suggesting a withdrawal west of Gheluvelt. Within a further twenty minutes, orders were received from Haig that a new line was to be established west of Gheluvelt. Haig had actually discussed a withdrawal with Sir John French and French officers before the German attacks had started and this withdrawal of about 1000 yards was the smallest of those contemplated.[12]

Cavalry would be brought into the line between 1st Division and 7th Division. Haig ordered that 1st (Guards) Brigade and the Worcesters take up a new line from the south-west corner of Polygon Wood to the junction of the Poezelhoek-Menin road west of Gheluvelt, after dark. By 11.19 p.m., 3rd Brigade were able to confirm that the Gloucesters, on their left flank, had

---

6   Hutton, *The Gunners of August 1914*, pp. 172-74 and TNA WO 95/1281: War Diary of the 2nd Welsh Regiment, Rees's account, 31 October 1914.

7   The Blewitt Papers are held by the IWM <www.iwm.org.uk/collections/item/object/1030021614> and his citation for the DSO can be found at *The London Gazette* <https://www.thegazette.co.uk/London/issue/38761/page/5419/data.pdf> (accessed 8/2/2017). He would rise to the rank of Lieutenant Colonel and be made a Sheriff of Essex in 1949.

8   TNA WO 95/1278: War Diary of the 1st Gloucestershire Regiment, Frazebrook Diary.

9   TNA WO 95/1239: War Diary of the 1st Division, Royal Artillery, 31 October 1914.

10   TNA WO 95/1227: War Diary of the 1st Division, RE, 31 October 1914.

11   TNA WO 95/1280: War Diary of the 1st South Wales Borderers Regiment, 31 October 1914.

12   Beckett, *Ypres,* pp.136ff.

touch with 1st Brigade as ordered. This link was with 1st South Wales Borderers who had suffered casualties during the day amounting to six officers and approximately 280 men.[13] Six minutes later, 1st Division recorded that Brigadier-General Fitzclarence VC had been placed in command of 3rd Brigade in addition to 1st Brigade.[14] Perhaps in recognition of the difficulties facing Brigade commanders, Lieutenant Colonel Lovell was given responsibility for 3rd Brigade and Major Ingram became OC of the Gloucesters. It was noted by brigade that he was the most senior surviving CO.[15]

The BEF had survived another stressful day. The 1st Division had been at the fulcrum of events. The men had stood the test and suffered heavy casualties due partly to due to the weight of German artillery fire. These casualties had been exacerbated by higher command wanting to see ground retaken even where it offered little tactical advantage.

---

13 TNA WO 95/1280: War Diary of the 1st South Wales Borderers Regiment, 31 October 1914.
14 TNA WO 95/1227: War Diary of the 1st Division, 31 October 1914.
15 TNA WO 95/1278: War Diary of the 1st Gloucestershire Regiment, Frazebrook Diary.

16

First Ypres
Tested to Destruction

Likely feeling it, but not knowing it, 1st Division now faced a decisive moment in the First World War. The German strategic plan called for the envelopment of the Allied left wing. The initial thrust had failed at the Marne. What was never intended as a "race to the sea" was the result of successive attempts by each side to outflank the other. Now the Germans were in the position of a rugby team 5 metres from their opponent's line. The attempt to go outside had failed. Could they now burst through the line in front of them, reach the channel to score the decisive try? Conversely, could the British line hold and deny the Germans victory. At First Ypres, the BEF's position reflected Churchill's view of Admiral Jellicoe – the BEF could not win the war but on any coming day they could lose it.

Haig noted that 1st Division's commander, Brigadier Landon of 3rd Brigade, had come to tell him that the division was so disorganised that no organised attack could really be withstood.[1] Three weeks later Landon's temporary command of 1st Division was ended by the appointment of Major General Henderson. Due to his poor health Landon was sent home to recuperate. Landon subsequently returned to duty and undertook several divisional command appointments. It might be concluded that Landon's frankness, after 31 October, had diminished him in Haig's eyes whereas Bulfin's reputation remained untarnished. Haig did recognise the strain on his men; he wrote to Leopold Rothschild that the men were tired as they have to fight by day and dig by night, getting little sleep.[2]

On 1 November, the main German thrust was further south, but the barricade manned by the Gloucesters proved to be a busy point. German infantry attacks were blunted by signallers using the houses at the crossroads as vantage points. From there, they were able to signal the British artillery, who fired very effectively. Sergeant-Major Long and CQMS Maynell proved remarkably effective snipers. They were eventually driven out of their positions when the Germans directed their machine guns onto the thin plaster of the houses. The German shrapnel shells contributed to the 75 casualties that day, which were partially offset by the arrival of a draft of fifty other ranks that evening.[3]

---

1   Sheffield and Bourne, *Douglas Haig*, p.77.
2   Sheffield and Bourne, *Douglas Haig*, p.77.
3   TNA WO 95/1278: War Diary of the 1st Gloucestershire Regiment, Frazebrook Diary.

First Ypres: Tested to Destruction   105

The fighting undertaken by 2nd Brigade led to many casualties including Brigadier Bulfin who was wounded during the late morning on 1 November.[4] Bulfin had had a more positive start when he received a congratulatory message from Field Marshal French for his leadership on 31October. At 11 a.m. on 1 November, he received a warmly congratulatory message from Haig. Haig agreed with Bulfin that his subordinate commanders deserved the praise that Bulfin had ascribed to them (One of Bulfin's attractive qualities is his apparent ability to share praise with his colleagues / subordinates).

On 1 November, the 16th Battery was part of the defensive fire supporting 1st Division. The account of the fighting by the gunners that day illustrates the strain on the British, as the Germans made their last effort at outright victory; "had shells around us as soon as we got to the guns, so I started another trench, nipping into the flooded hole when anything came along thinking that wet and mud were preferable to a bullet. This constant cannonade, screaming and whistling of shell and their burst is getting chronic. It is one continual bang, bang, weeeeeee, crack, crash, I tried to count a second without hearing one or the other, far or near, but without success...".[5]

The 26 Coy. RE was sent forward to support the 2nd Oxford &Buckinghamshire Light Infantry, who had been pushed back by a heavy German attack.[6] They suffered approximately 40 casualties including an officer.[7] At around 1.25 p.m., the 1st Northants found themselves under heavy attack. Eventually the Germans were repulsed with the aid of dismounted cavalry and 2nd Grenadier Guards.[8] Meanwhile, 23 Coy. RE were engaged in continuing to entrench the road just east of Hooge Chateau. They then had to spend the night putting out wire in front of 1st Brigade positions north of Veldhoek.[9] Their withdrawal from the line was made possible because Lord Cavan took command and shortened the line. This was achieved by withdrawing the line in the woods back thirty yards from the edge. This also afforded the men greater protection. It also made it possible for 2nd Royal Sussex to be brought out of the line that evening and placed in reserve and for 2nd Gordon Highlanders to be withdrawn preparatory to returning to 7th Division.[10]

Captain Lefroy left a detailed hand-written account of the fighting from 1st-4th November which is preserved in the divisional records.[11] Lefroy describes the positions held by 1st Division on the night of 1/2 November 1914, as follows; "from the south-west corner of Race Course Wood, through the road junction between Gheluvelt and Veldhoek , and then back into the wood 800 yards from the road in a south-westerly direction".[12] Into this defensive deployment, the 1st KRRC were inserted at a farm from 2 a.m. on 1 November. At 10 a.m. they were designated as the Divisional reserve and were located at the north-west corner of Polygon

4 Becke, *Order of Battle of Divisions – Part 1*, pp. 36-37.
5 Hutton, *The Gunners of August 1914*, p.177.
6 TNA WO 95/1267: War Diary of the 2nd Brigade, 1 November 1914.
7 TNA WO 95/1227: War Diary of the 1st Division, RE, 1 November 1914.
8 TNA WO 95/1267: War Diary of the 2nd Brigade, 1 November 1914.
9 TNA WO 95/1227: War Diary of the 1st Division, RE, 1 November 1914.
10 TNA WO 95/1267: War Diary of the 2nd Brigade, 1 November 1914.
11 Lefroy is listed on the title page as GSO1, but this could only have been in an acting capacity in the interval between the death of Lieutenant -Colonel Kerr on 31 October and the appointment of Lieutenant -Colonel Jeudwine on 3 November.
12 TNA WO 95/1227: War Diary of the 1st Division, November 1914, Appendix.

Wood, under the command of Lieutenant Colonel Westmancott. Approximately two hours later, they were moved, along with three companies of the Berkshires, up to Hooge Chateau as support to 1st Division.[13] To that end, at around 9 p.m., the 1st KRRC were ordered to take over a section of trenches running southwards from the Hooge – Gheluvelt road. In doing so they relieved men of the Gloucesters and South Wales Borderers,[14] of 3rd Brigade. These trenches were put under the command of Captain Williams who therefore not only had the 1st KRRC and three companies of the Berkshires but also 200 men of the Coldstreams. This figure for the Coldstreams reflects the battalion receiving a draft of 116 men and two officers on the evening of 1 November 1914.[15]

On 2 November, the 1st Division noted that the Germans were entrenching about 400 yards in front of the British positions. The bigger picture was that after the success of Group Fabeck in seizing Messines, the Germans were content to pin their opponents in position. General Falkenhayn was busy creating a new task force under General Linsingen. Once it was ready, this battle group would renew the assault.[16]

In the face of this threat, yet to take shape, 115th Battery, RFA, with its compliment of 4.7" guns, was attached to 1st Division. It was sited close to Halte on the north side of the Menin road.[17] The divisional reserve was formed by 3rd Brigade.[18] At 5 a.m., the 1st Loyal North Lancs moved forward from their overnight trench positions in order to be in close support. The early morning saw the Germans try to get around the right of 1st Loyal North Lancs in support, but the battalion notified the gunners. The British artillery fire was very effective in stopping this German attack.[19]

The 2nd KRRC began the morning in Corps Reserve, in the woods south of Hooge.[20] According to Lieutenant General Brockway, the state of the frontline defences was weak; and he quotes extensively from the annals of the KRRC:

> From 8.30 a.m. onwards his 30th Division, with the XXVII Reserve Corps north of it, had shown a disposition to push forward on either side of the Menin Road, where stood D Company of the 1st Royal Berkshire, three companies of the 1st K.R.R.C., and the 1st Coldstream, the last being under the establishment of a company in men and having only two officers. One company of the K.R.R.C. and two of the Berkshire were in support. These troops, it will be recalled, had only taken over from the 3rd Brigade after dark, less than twelve hours earlier, and had found but shallow disconnected lengths of trench, barely marking a front, without any wire or, of course, any dug-outs. Across the road [the Menin Road], where the 200 Coldstream stood, was a barricade. Behind this was a group of houses and a farm building which had not been prepared for defence; for, though the men in this sector worked hard during

---

13 TNA WO 95/1227: War Diary of the 1st Battalion of King's Royal Rifle Corps, 2 November 1914.
14 TNA WO 95/1227: War Diary of the 1st Battalion of King's Royal Rifle Corps, 2 November 1914.
15 TNA WO 95/1261: War Diary of the 1st Coldstream Guards, 1 November 1914
16 Boff, J., *Haig's Enemy: Crown Prince Rupprecht and Germany's War on the Western Front* (Oxford: OUP, 2018), p.47.
17 TNA WO 95/1227: War Diary of the 1st Division, 2 November 1914.
18 TNA WO 95/1274: War Diary of the 3rd Brigade, 2 November 1914.
19 TNA WO 95/1270: War Diary of the 1st Battalion of Loyal North Lancs, 2 November 1914
20 TNA WO 95/1272: War Diary of the 2nd Battalion of King's Royal Rifle Corps, 2 November 1914.

the night, they were too tired to effect much. When daylight came and they were thoroughly worn out, it was found that the field of fire, owing to a ridge on our side and a falling slope on the other, was limited to from 50 to 150 yards. This would have been sufficient if there had been a good obstacle in front of the trenches, and if the supporting artillery had had direct observation on the narrow field of fire. It was inadequate in the circumstances, particularly as hedges obstructed view along the line and interfered with mutual support. To make matters worse, less than 100 yards in front of the British line, bordering on the road, was a small house, to burn which all endeavours had been in vain.[21]

The divisional records make no mention of the attack by the Germans on the positions held by the Coldstreams, but according to Brockway's source there was intense fighting.

The barricade on the road was early blown away, and one machine gun of the K.R.R.C., which covered it, put out of action. Though held off elsewhere, the Germans managed to get up a machine gun into the small house about 9.30 a.m. Another party with another machine gun worked its way through a gap of over 60 yards between the Berkshire Company and the K.R.R.C. north of it, and now opened fire at a hundred yards range into the backs of the Rifles. This battalion had definite orders not to retire, and, with the Berkshire and the Coldstream, still kept off all attackers. Invaluable aid was rendered by the artillery, particularly by two guns of the 116th Battery, a couple of hundred yards behind the line.[22]

The Berkshires were supporting the Coldstream Guards of 1st Brigade. The Berkshires had been advised that nine French battalions would move through their positions; in order to attack towards Gheluvelt. The French had duly passed through, but the Berkshires remained unaware that they had not progressed much more than 200 yards further on. The Black Watch noted that the 120th Regiment passed through their lines but that the attack was met with heavy shrapnel fire.[23] The French attack seems to have led to the British artillery being ordered to hold their fire. According to the KRRC history, "About 11 a.m., soon after the British batteries had, according to orders, ceased to fire on the area near the Menin Road, the Germans of the 30th Division, under the covering fire of the machine gun in the small house, came on boldly down the road in parties of thirty and forty, followed on either side of it by others crawling in twos and threes. Getting up close to the British trenches they overpowered the Coldstream, taking prisoner Captain E. G. Christie-Miller, who was in command, and capturing or killing nearly one-half of their scanty number."[24]

It was noted by 1st Division that at 11.20 a.m. an orderly came from 1st KRRC to divisional headquarters and made a vague request for the support of two companies. Vague though the request might have been, within fifteen minutes the 300 strong 2nd KRRC had been ordered up from divisional reserve to support their senior battalion.[25] They advanced in columns of platoons

---

21 A detailed discussion of this topic can be found at *The Great War Forum* <https://www.greatwarforum.org/topic/134364-1st-battalion-krrc/> (accessed 15 March 2020).
22 *Great War Forum* <https://www.greatwarforum.org/topic/134364-1st-battalion-krrc/>
23 TNA WO 95/1263: War Diary of the 1st Battalion the Black Watch, 2 November 1914.
24 *Great War Forum* <https://www.greatwarforum.org/topic/134364-1st-battalion-krrc/> (accessed 15 March 2020)
25 TNA WO 95/1227: War Diary of the 1st Division, 2 November 1914.

in single file.²⁶ However, half an hour later, this order was countermanded due to the French advance relieving pressure on the British line; but there is nothing to suggest this order was received by 2nd KRRC.²⁷ For similar reasons, at about 11.45 a.m. when Major Finch received a message to send up his men to support the Coldstream Guards, he did not do so. Major Finch thought that there was no need to send his two companies forward in the midst of the French line. His decision reflected that of the divisional command, though neither was aware of the other. Finch had already, on the previous night, had to detach his D company to take over some trenches from the 1st KRRC on the Ypres-Gheluvelt road.²⁸

Then, men from the Coldstream Guards started arriving at Finch's position at Molenaar Elsthoek Veldhoek. They said their officer had been killed, and that they had been driven out of their positions. The Coldstreams had lost both their officers that had joined the day before and recorded that their casualties amounted to 50%. Finch then turned out his two companies, but he was soon wounded by shrapnel. Finch's men saw the men from the 1st KRRC surrendering at this time, 500 – 600 yards away.²⁹ According to the war diary of the Berkshires, the situation was much more confused; but they too saw the 1st KRRC surrendering.

The *Annals of the KRRC* are quoted at length by Lieutenant General Brockway to explain the detail behind the surrender of the men from the 1st KRRC:

> They then turned against the three companies of the K.R.R.C., already attacked in front, machine-gunned from the rear, and bombed by parties working up the trench from their right. Then came a final rush. There was a melee between the Germans and the two left companies, but it lasted only a few minutes. The right company held out a little longer, but in the end 9 officers and 437 men of the Battalion were killed or captured. '

The officers missing, all of whom were prisoners of war, were: Captain W. P. Lynes, Captain H. E. Ward (3rd Buffs); Lieutenants A. M. Wakefield-Saunders, G. V. H. Gough; Second Lieutenants C. H. Reynard, C. F. Schoon, R. Richards, S. Lucas, and T. Wadner.³⁰

The 2nd KRRC were in two groups with A and B companies under Captain Howard-Bury. The other group was a draft led by Captain Hawley. The use of a sub-unit in the skeletal battalions of 1st Division would recur increasingly as the fighting at Ypres continued. Both groups managed to cross the road and reach the trench held by a company of 1st KRRC.³¹ The explanation, that the Germans drove the 1st KRRC out, using machine guns and field guns brought up in close support, was also the one given by 2nd KRRC to 1st Division by mid-afternoon that day.³² Overall, it appears that Lefroy's assertion is not supported by the evidence; though the 2nd KRRC's regimental loyalties cannot be ignored.

---

26 TNA WO 95/1272: War Diary of the 2nd Battalion of King's Royal Rifle Corps, 2 November 1914.
27 TNA WO 95/1227: War Diary of the 1st Division, 2 November 1914.
28 TNA WO 95/1361: War Diary of the 1st Battalion Royal Berkshire Regiment, 2 November 1914.
29 TNA WO 95/1361: War Diary of the 1st Battalion Royal Berkshire Regiment, 2 November 1914.
30 *Great War Forum* <https://www.greatwarforum.org/topic/134364-1st-battalion-krrc/> (accessed 15 March 2020).
31 TNA WO 95/1272: War Diary of the 2nd Battalion of King's Royal Rifle Corps, 2 November 1914.
32 TNA WO 95/1227: War Diary of the 1st Division, 2 November 1914.

By 12.50 p.m., reports had reached 1st Division that troops had surrendered on both sides of the road, so the orders to the 2nd KRRC to go forward were re-issued, and it was noted that the supporting units of the Berkshires were advancing. The Berkshires had now learned that only a weakened French battalion had passed through their positions; and that it was now holding some enclosures a little distance ahead of them. Major Finch then despatched half of A Company, under Lieutenant Cruise, to assist the French. At about the same time, one platoon of B company, led by Lieutenant Vesey, was sent to the crossroads just south of Veldhoek to assist the French infantry there. Meanwhile, the rest of A company was sent forward under the command of Lieutenant Woods, with the objective of retaking the trenches north of the main road, but they were unable to advance beyond some hedges approximately 400 yards from their objective.[33]

By 1.15 p.m., 1st Division were aware that the line had been broken and therefore 3rd Brigade had been ordered forward to restore the situation. In noting their orders, 3rd Brigade referred to the Germans having "surprised" the KRRC.[34] This could be construed as supporting Captain Lefroy's suggestion that they were asleep, but it is only implicit. The divisional command was also aware that the Germans had broken through the right of Lord Cavan's positions and that 7th Division were having to commit their reserves to plug that gap, so it was clear that the overall position remained strained. The GOC had therefore sent forward 3rd Brigade through the Herenthaage wood to block the German breakthrough south of the Menin road. Whilst 3rd Brigade was moving forward, the retirement of troops ahead of them led to the loss of two 18-pdr guns of 116th battery close to the 6km stone on the Menin road. These guns had been entrenched there the night before to provide close support.[35]

Having been ordered forward at 1.30 p.m., the 1st Loyal North Lancs advanced in lines of sections on either side of the road to meet the reported German breakthrough. They believed they were fortunate, as the Germans were distracted by a British cavalry formation. According to 1st Loyal North Lancs, only the Gloucesters took part in the assault whilst they, the Welsh, and the South Wales Borderers held the wood.[36] According to the Welsh, they did attack but it was at dusk,[37] which may account for the confusion. Major Finch led his available men in assaulting the German positions. In this attack, he was assisted by 40 men of

the Gloucesters, whom he had collected. The attack succeeded in reoccupying all the trenches except the one immediately north of the road.[38]

At 3.40 p.m., Brigadier-General Fitzclarence organised the counter-attack straight down the Menin road.[39] It appears that he had done this because the advance of 3rd Brigade through Herenthaage wood had been stopped by German fire from houses on the Menin road, where they had lodged a large number of snipers. These snipers accounted for Captain Hawley of 2nd

---

33   TNA WO 95/1361: War Diary of the 1st Battalion Royal Berkshire Regiment, 2 November 1914.
34   TNA WO 95/1274: War Diary of the 3rd Brigade, 2 November 1914.
35   TNA WO 95/1239: War Diary of the 1st Division, Royal Artillery, 2 November 1914.
36   TNA WO 95/1270: War Diary of the 1st Battalion of Loyal North Lancs, 2 November.
37   TNA WO 95/1281: War Diary of the 2nd Welsh, 2 November 1914.
38   TNA WO 95/1361: War Diary of the 1st Battalion Royal Berkshire Regiment, 2 November 1914.
39   TNA WO 95/1227: War Diary of the 1st Division, 2 November 1914.

KRRC, who was killed at about 4 p.m., and Captain Blunt, OC B company of the Gloucesters, who was wounded in the shoulder.[40] The snipers were clearly very adept at spotting the officers.

The most detailed account of this British attack is contained in the records of 1st Gloucesters. It reflects very positively on Fitzclarence's personal bravery, but underlines questions about his fitness for senior command. Having advanced through Herenthaage Chateau grounds, B and C companies of the Gloucesters reached the British line where Captain McLeod, OC of C, was killed. D company then arrived under Major Ingram, having previously been left in reserve. Major Ingram tried to assess the situation but there was no clear information about where the lost trenches were. The front-line troops were of various units and there were French units there too. So there was no overall command until: - "General Fitzclarence of the 1st Brigade arrived up in the very front line. His solution to the problem was "Push on, find out the enemy, and drive him back".

Therefore. Major Ingram organized an attack against the supposed German positions on either side of an isolated building 700 yards away. As D company of the Gloucesters only had two men wounded on 2 November, it is quite likely that they did not take part in the assault. Certainly, only two companies of 1st South Wales Borderers took part.[41] The British were able to advance across the first open field but then encountered a trench occupied by a few wounded Germans. The cheering and firing there, attracted the fire of the German defenders, who had also sent men out to the right of the Gloucesters. Therefore, as the Gloucesters moved beyond the first field, they were enfiladed from the right as well as facing fierce fire from the front. They also recorded that they were fired on from behind by the French troops. The Gloucesters said the French had not advanced because their officers had not ordered them to do so. The Gloucesters' attack then broke down, and they ended up withdrawing to the trenches from which they had started.[42]

Overnight, the 2nd Welsh had numbered 148 men, but they had been joined by three subalterns and fifty men during the morning before they were called to advance.[43] The 2nd Welsh were on the left of the Gloucesters and carried out a bayonet charge. They believed they had advanced 300 to 400 yards before being beaten back by heavy frontal and enfilade fire. They noted that all the officers became "hors de combat"; for example, Captain Rees was knocked down by a spent shrapnel case. C and D companies of 2nd KRRC had reached the trenches east of Herenthaage Chateau grounds. Captain Cunningham did then succeed in leading a few men forward to the objective given by Fitzclarence.[44] The attack by 3rd Brigade was supported by a French battalion on each flank.

The Zouave battalion had suffered from some probably racially related abuse while camped at the Hooge Chateau. British troops were responsible for throwing items into the Zouave encampment. By 4.30 p.m., 1st Division knew that 7th Division had been successful in their counterattack. However, by 5.10 p.m., the only partial success of 3rd Brigade was made known to them. Later, 1st Division was informed, presumably by Brigadier-general Fitzclarence, that

---

40   TNA WO 95/1272: War Diary of the 2nd Battalion of King's Royal Rifle Corps, 2 November 1914 and TNA WO 95/1278: War Diary of the 1st Gloucestershire Regiment, 2 November 1914.
41   TNA WO 95/1280: War Diary of the 1st South Wales Borderers, 2 November 1914.
42   TNA WO 95/1278: War Diary of the 1st Gloucestershire Regiment, 2 November 1914.
43   TNA WO 95/1281: War Diary of the 2nd Welsh, 2 November 1914.
44   TNA WO 95/1272: War Diary of the 2nd Battalion of King's Royal Rifle Corps, 2 November 1914.

the counter-attack had not succeeded in regaining the trenches south of the Menin road due to the lack of officers to keep the men together.[45] The same reason for the failure is recorded by 2nd KRRC; though their diary had recorded earlier that their line was very thin so this suggests there were not enough men to accomplish the successive tasks. By 1918, leapfrogging assaulting units would be standard practice. Here, small scale assaults involved small numbers of men advancing until successive enemy actions took away their momentum. The 2nd KRRC recorded their casualties as approximately 150, including four officers, so their casualty rate on the day was approximately 50%.[46] The diary of 3rd Brigade offers no explanation for the failure, merely noting that the Brigadier had organised it.[47]

The real cause of the failure appears to have been that Fitzclarence was totally focused on regaining the positions held in the morning. The attack failed because, without appropriate reconnaissance, he had ordered under-strength units to make a frontal assault, in the growing darkness, against a well-entrenched German position. There are those who would link this blinkeredness to his impending promotion to Major General.

The Black Watch contributed three companies, A, B and C, to this counterattack, as they were the brigade reserve and were about 1500 yards from the point where the Germans had broken through. Their account says that 120 men took part in the attack and that they succeeded; but suffered as both officers who had joined the day before were wounded and Lieutenant Nolan, attached from 3rd Black Watch, died of his wounds. The five men killed, 34 wounded and 21 missing following the action[48],plus the three officers means that the effective casualty rate was just over 50%. The 1st Loyal North Lancs had a strength of only about 300 including six officers.[49]

It was only after the attack, that Lieutenant Ormaston, of 54th battery, took a gun forward to fire at a house occupied by snipers. Despite being wounded, Ormaston helped the No1 to continue firing, after the rest of the crew were wounded, before withdrawing the gun.[50]

After the assault at dusk, the 2nd Welsh were assigned to cover 100 yards of trench on each side of a company of Zouaves;[51] once again Fitzclarence was sub-dividing already weakened units in the line as he had done on 29 October. The 2nd Welsh were occupying the positions previously occupied by the 1st Gloucesters, the latter being withdrawn into Sanctuary Wood.[52] Fitzclarence may have arranged this because of the apparent bitterness towards the French reflected in the Gloucesters' diary.

The 1st Loyal North Lancs were withdrawn around 8 p.m. to their original positions but were then told at midnight to relieve the 1st Royal Berkshires, which they then accomplished by 1.30 a.m.[53] 1st Division therefore finished 2 November occupying a line from the south-west corner of Polygon Wood down via Veldhoek to the south-east corner of Herenthaage wood. The latter

---

45 TNA WO 95/1227: War Diary of the 1st Division, 2 November 1914.
46 TNA WO 95/1272: War Diary of the 2nd Battalion of King's Royal Rifle Corps, 2 November 1914.
47 TNA WO 95/1274: War Diary of the 3rd Brigade, 2 November 1914.
48 TNA WO 95/1263: War Diary of the 1st Black Watch, 2 November 1914.
49 TNA WO 95/1270: War Diary of the 1st Battalion of Loyal North Lancs, 2 November 1914.
50 TNA WO 95/1239: War Diary of the 1st Division, Royal Artillery, 2 November 1914.
51 TNA WO 95/1281: War Diary of the 2nd Welsh, 2 November 1914.
52 TNA WO 95/1278: War Diary of the 1st Gloucestershire Regiment, 2 November 1914.
53 TNA WO 95/1270: War Diary of the 1st Battalion of Loyal North Lancs, 2 November 1914.

formed the junction with 7th Division. That evening, they received orders from I Corps to say they must hold their positions on 3 November.[54]

The detached elements of 2nd Brigade were also kept busy on 2 November and were ultimately successful in their defensive role. Around 8.25 a.m., there were reports of the Germans massing in front of 2 Grenadier Guards, so D company of 2nd Royal Sussex were sent forward in close support with an officer reporting to the HQ of the Grenadiers. Two hours later, heavy German shelling forced the Northants out of a section of trench which was about eighty yards long and formed the boundary with 7th Division. Therefore, A company of 2nd Royal Sussex were sent forward ready to fire to cover the gap in the event of an infantry attack. At 11.50, following a report from the OC Northants that German infantry were now massing for an assault, C company of 2nd Royal Sussex were sent forward under Captain Waithman to Brigade HQ. Shortly after that, B company plus the battalion HQ and machine guns went forward to brigade HQ where they were assigned the dugouts used by the signallers.[55] It is interesting that, in a defensive situation, the machine guns were the last to be sent forward. Eventually at 4 p.m., the Germans renewed the heavy artillery fire before launching an infantry attack. The Northants and the supporting units successfully repulsed the assault. The Germans launched another attack at 6.15 p.m.; this time it fell to the 2nd Grenadier Guards, 2nd Royal Sussex and 2nd Oxford & Bucks Light Infantry to repel it. It was noted that the Germans gave great cheers as they advanced and that the British units held their fire until quite close range, before firing in a simultaneous burst.[56]

Despite repeated reports of the Germans massing in front of 3rd Brigade and persistent heavy shelling, the Germans did not make an assault. The local French commander, General Vidal, said he would order an attack but it did not materialise.[57] The 1st Gloucesters spent 3 November in Sanctuary Wood, the men improving the trenches and some of the officers reconnoitring a possible support line for their colleagues in the trenches held the previous night. The day was completed for the battalion by the arrival of Captain Pritchett and 200 reinforcements.[58] The rest of 3rd Brigade continued to hold their positions, and, in addition, four support points were constructed to support the front line. During the afternoon, the French decided to withdraw their troops so after dark, the South Wales Borderers took over their position.[59]

Having been reduced to a total ration strength of just 240, the 1st Coldstreams spent 3 November, and the next day, in brigade reserve. Once again, the command of the battalion had devolved upon Lieutenant & Quartermaster Boyd.[60] The 2nd KRRC, if anything fewer in number, remained in their positions and were shelled regularly. The machine guns had been dug in well and suffered no casualties. This meant the machine guns were highly effective in defence of the road. That evening, they were relieved by the 10th Hussars, and were able to return to the woods near Hooge.[61]

54 TNA WO 95/1227: War Diary of the 1st Division, 2 November 1914.
55 TNA WO 95/1269: War Diary of the 2nd Royal Sussex, 2 November 1914.
56 TNA WO 95/1267: War Diary of the 2nd Brigade, 2 November 1914.
57 TNA WO 95/1227: War Diary of the 1st Division, 3 November 1914.
58 TNA WO 95/1278: War Diary of the 1st Gloucestershire Regiment, 3 November 1914.
59 TNA WO 95/1274: War Diary of the 3rd Brigade, 3 November 1914.
60 TNA WO 95/1261: War Diary of the 1st Coldstream Guards, 3-4 November 1914.
61 TNA WO 95/1272: War Diary of the 2nd Battalion of King's Royal Rifle Corps, 3 November 1914.

The remnants of 1st Queens and 2nd Welsh were held in brigade reserve on 4 November, whilst 1st Gloucesters were held in divisional reserve. The 2nd Welsh were significantly depleted, so they were organised as two companies; one being under the command of Captain Aldworth, who had joined that day.[62] It was also agreed, with General Vidal, that the elements of his *31st Division* that were in the line were not to be moved. The need to avoid thinning the British line any further is underlined by the divisional summary of the strength of the battalions occupying the line; Berkshires 260, Scots Guards 240, Black Watch 240, Camerons 350. The Coldstream Guards which 1st Division estimated at 120 men with no officers constituted the support on the left flank whilst eighty men of 1st KRRC were creating a support post on the right flank.[63] The Scots Guards were occupied with creating a *point d' appui*. Given the numerical weakness of the British units, it would have been more useful to have had them strengthening their defences.[64] Major Warre left the 2nd KRRC, whilst they rested in the woods, to take command of 1st KRRC.[65] Still on detachment, the Northants repelled a German attack on 4 November. The Northants were then relieved in the trenches that night by the Royal Sussex.[66]

On 5 November, the still much reduced 1st Coldstreams were detached to help support 2nd Coldstreams. They remained attached to their second battalion until 12 November. The 1st Scots Guards receive a reinforcement of sixty rank and file, along with Lieutenant BW Smith,[67] the latter's service on the Western Front would only last three days. Under heavy shelling for much of the day, 1st Black Watch sustained the loss of one man killed and nine wounded, as well as 2nd-Lieutenant Graham being wounded.[68] The neighbouring 1st Cameron Highlanders lost ten dead and ten wounded, largely due to two very large shells hitting the trenches. To add to the unpleasantness, they received word that the expected relief had been cancelled.[69]

The 1st Loyal North Lancs spent the day as divisional reserve, in the woods south of Hooge. The diary recorded movingly the death, from wounds, of Captain Allen, who had taken over the role of Adjutant during the fighting on the Aisne. In the evening, the 1st Loyal North Lancs were detached to support 16 Cavalry Brigade. By this point, command of the battalion had devolved upon Captain Slade.[70] According to the Sussex's diarist, it was a typical Guy Fawkes day, as they were shelled severely. That evening the 2nd Royal Sussex were relieved by 1st Northants.[71] The sustained period of fighting had taken its toll on 2nd Brigade. The Brigade estimated that between 25 October and 5 November, it had suffered casualties amounting to 38 officers and 1652 other ranks. During that period, it was estimated that they had received drafts amounting to 200. The Brigadier's staff consisted of three officers: the Brigade Major, the Staff Captain, and a Veterinary officer, plus 47 other ranks. The figures given for the strength of the infantry battalions was as follows:

---

62 TNA WO 95/1281: War Diary of the 2nd Welsh, 2 November 1914.
63 TNA WO 95/1227: War Diary of the 1st Division, 4 November 1914.
64 TNA WO 95/1261: War Diary of the 1st Scots Guards, 4 November 1914.
65 TNA WO 95/1272: War Diary of the 2nd Battalion of King's Royal Rifle Corps, 3 November 1914.
66 TNA WO 95/1267: War Diary of the 2nd Brigade, 3-4 November 1914.
67 TNA WO 95/1261: War Diary of the 1st Scots Guards, 5 November 1914.
68 TNA WO 95/1263: War Diary of the 1st Black Watch, 5 November 1914.
69 TNA WO 95/1264: War Diary of the 1st Cameron Highlanders, 5 November 1914.
70 TNA WO 95/1270: War Diary of the 1st Loyal North Lancs, 5 November 1914.
71 TNA WO 95/1269: War Diary of the 2nd Royal Sussex, 5 November 1914.

	Officers	Other Ranks
2nd Royal Sussex	17	503
1st Loyal North Lancs	4	250
2nd KRRC	11	340
1st Northants	9	470
Total (incl. HQ)	44	1610[72]

The losses suffered in 2 Brigade, which were mirrored in the other brigades, serve to underline the way in which Corps orders were increasingly unrealistic. On 5 November, I Corps instructed 1st Division to construct *Pts d'appui*. The analogy to siege warfare might be apposite: but if Haig believed 1st Division were capable of offensive action, he was clearly out of touch. Further evidence of this came the next day, when I Corps ordered that 1st Royal Berkshires be relieved at once. 1st Division recorded that at the request of the OC of the Berkshires, the relief was delayed until after dark to avoid casualties.[73]

For the men of 3 Brigade, 5 November brought the news that the brigade was to be relieved that evening by 6 Cavalry Brigade. The close working relationship with the artillery was noted; reference being made to the artillery dealing with Germans lodged in buildings. The gunners achieved this by bringing up single guns into the firing line where necessary. There was also a positive comment about the help provided by the companies of French troops occupying part of Veldhoek village in front of 3rd Brigade's line, north of the Menin road. The usual procedure was followed, in that when an attack was made against their left, the brigade called upon the supports including the South Wales Borderers. The brigade also praised 6 Cavalry Brigade for the well organised relief which was completed between 8 p.m. and 9.30 p.m. The Brigade then marched to Bellevaarde Farm leaving the divisional reserve of 1st Loyal North Lancs and the 1st South Wales Borderers, to support the cavalry.[74] The Gloucesters noted that their total of 41 casualties, including thirteen killed, was unusually high for a day when they had only experienced shellfire, but that some of the trenches had been destroyed.[75]

There was an early boost for 1st Camerons, on 6 November, when Lieutenant Dunsterville and 106 men arrived at 2 a.m.[76] 1st Northants occupied the line, and 2nd Brigade were informed that their battalion would be relieved by the KOSB. They were also told to proceed to move their brigade HQ to the woods near Hooge.[77] Although, they had been relieved, the 2nd Royal Sussex were almost immediately called upon. After a quiet morning, on 6 November they had to send forward A company, almost immediately followed by B company, to report to the HQ of the 1st Irish Guards. The Germans had reportedly broken through the French line to their left.[78]

These reports led to 3rd Brigade being ordered forward at 3.30 p.m. After a 45-minute delay, they marched to Zwarteleen. There, acting-Brigadier Lovett met Brigadier Kavanagh of 7

72 TNA WO 95/1267: War Diary of the 2nd Brigade, 5 November 1914.
73 TNA WO 95/1227: War Diary of the 1st Division, 5-6 November 1914.
74 TNA WO 95/1274: War Diary of the 3rd Brigade, 5 November 1914.
75 TNA WO 95/1278: War Diary of the 1st Gloucestershire Regiment, Frazebrook Diary.
76 TNA WO 95/1264: War Diary of the 1st Cameron Highlanders, 6 November 1914.
77 TNA WO 95/1267: War Diary of the 2nd Brigade, 6 November 1914.
78 TNA WO 95/1269: War Diary of the 2nd Royal Sussex, 6 November 1914.

Cavalry Brigade. Lovett was told that the cavalry had been able to partially restore the line. Kavanagh also reported that there were a few Germans in the houses at the southern end of the village and some more at the crossroads. The objective of the attack was therefore to seize the village and the crossroads. The attack was to be led by the 2nd KRRC on the right and 1st Gloucesters, the latter battalion having spent the morning reorganising,[79] on the left. The Queens and Welsh would support them. The attack seemed to go well until the leading men were just about to reach the southern end of the village. Then the Germans opened very heavy fire and the British "came back instead of pushing on". The 2nd KRRC ascribed their failure to the impossibility of maintaining cohesion in the woods and villages.[80] The Gloucesters, who were attacking through the woods, recorded that they were held up by barbed wire and machine gun fire.[81]

The subsequent amplification of the record states that the Gloucesters arrived in the dark, and were immediately told to launch an attack, without specific orders. It also states that they were not in touch with the remnants of the Irish Guards who had retreated to the woods. This account also says that a section of the 2nd KRRC suddenly panicked and returned towards their own lines, exposing the right flank of the Gloucesters. The explanation given is that units at the point of exhaustion will suffer these problems.[82] Lovett was more comprehensive but echoed the reasons given by the troops; "The dark, absence of reconnaissance and the tiredness of the men are the only excuses".[83] As on other occasions, the remaining elements of 1st Division were being frittered away. The Germans did have a preponderance of heavy artillery, but pointless counter-attacks in the dark were wasting valuable trained men. In this case, they were supposed to co-ordinate an attack through a village alongside that of one through unreconnoitered woods. Neither of the attacking OCs felt their battalions were fit to try again, so they occupied a line. The Brigade Major of 4(Guards) Brigade went to Lord Cavan for orders.[84] Major Ingram and the Brigade Major of 3rd Brigade reconnoitred to the left of the Gloucesters and managed to gain touch with their neighbours.[85] That night, Major Watson of 1st Queens left to join the staff of 2nd Division.[86] The needs of higher formations for trained officers was a further drain on battalion strengths.

The Sussex heard, incorrectly as it turned out, at 5 p.m. that the cavalry had restored the line. However, at 10.30 p.m., the Sussex were told to report to the HQ of 4th (Guards) Brigade. Upon arrival they were told that the Germans had captured the line originally held by the Irish Guards They were then briefed that a counterattack was planned, and that the 2nd Sussex were to take part alongside 22nd Brigade. As 22nd Brigade would take several hours to arrive, the attack was planned for 4 a.m.[87]

In preparation for the assault, C and D companies were sent, soon after midnight, to clear the woods until they reached the south-east edge and then dig in. The plan was for the arriving

79 TNA WO 95/1278: War Diary of the 1st Gloucestershire Regiment, Frazebrook Diary.
80 TNA WO 95/1272: War Diary of the 2nd Battalion of King's Royal Rifle Corps, 6 November 1914.
81 TNA WO 95/1278: War Diary of the 1st Gloucestershire Regiment, 6 November 1914.
82 TNA WO 95/1278: War Diary of the 1st Gloucestershire Regiment, Frazebrook Diary.
83 TNA WO 95/1274: War Diary of the 3rd Brigade, 6 November 1914.
84 TNA WO 95/1274: War Diary of the 3rd Brigade, 6 November 1914.
85 TNA WO 95/1278: War Diary of the 1st Gloucestershire Regiment, Frazebrook Diary.
86 TNA WO 95/1280: War Diary of the 1st Queens, 6 November 1914.
87 TNA WO 95/1269: War Diary of the 2nd Royal Sussex, 6 November 1914.

brigade to pass through the Sussex, and seize the crossroads, as the woods extended almost to it. The Sussex reached their objectives with C in the front line and D in support by 3.30 a.m. However, the Germans began firing intensively with their rifles, so D company moved up in support. The attack had been stalled, so 22nd Brigade fell back, but the already depleted 2nd Sussex had suffered 22 more casualties. Once the evening came, D company returned to the support positions.[88] In contrast, 1st Loyal North Lancs spent the day in the woods, as divisional reserve, before being sent to relieve the 1st Royal Berkshires that evening.[89]

The early morning of 7 November saw the 2nd Brigade HQ and 1st Northants rendezvous in the woods south of Hooge. The latter's commander, Lieutenant Colonel Osbourne-Smith, found that he was the temporary OC of 2nd Brigade.[90] 1st Loyal North Lancs continued to man their trenches with A and B companies in the front line and C and D in support. That evening, the companies reversed roles.[91] The 2nd KRRC also continued trench duty; Rifleman Curzon carried out notable reconnaissance work.[92]

3rd Brigade remained engaged in combat. The 1st Gloucesters spent the day fighting in the woods and on the edge of the village. The latter followed an inaccurate report that a successful attack by 22nd Brigade had revealed that the positions opposite the Gloucesters were not occupied by the Germans. According to the Welsh's diarist, 22nd Brigade had then been driven out, but this information had not reached 3rd Brigade.[93] The Gloucesters had then gone forward in two lines, fifty yards apart. Here the possession of some houses was bitterly contested.[94] The fighting cost the battalion a further 88 casualties, including four officers.[95] Amongst the dead was Major Rising, whose leadership had proved so valuable in earlier engagements, and Lieutenant Kershaw; the whole of the latter's platoon of A company were cut off and posted as missing. That night, only 213 men answered at the roll call.[96] One of these was Lance-Corporal Royal, who was awarded the DCM for his gallantry as a stretcher bearer during the fighting. That evening, Captain Bosanquet joined the battalion and took over the duties of Adjutant. He was subsequently wounded in December; and his valise, which contained the battalion diary for November 1914, was stolen. The battalion then moved to Herenthage Wood on 8 November and remained there until 10 November, as support to 1st (Guards) Brigade.[97] Reinforcements also arrived for 1st Black Watch, 32 men plus Lieutenant Sprot;[98] the latter would not survive 11 November.

The overall situation remained unchanged. Localised attacks by the French also made no real impact, and eventually French units began entrenching with a view to taking over the line. Acting-Brigadier Lovett was unsuccessful in getting the 2nd KRRC relieved. Both field companies were sent, that evening, to help fight the fires in Ypres. They helped to prevent the

---

88   TNA WO 95/1269: War Diary of the 2nd Royal Sussex, 7 November 1914.
89   TNA WO 95/1270: War Diary of the 1st Loyal North Lancs, 6 November 1914.
90   TNA WO 95/1267: War Diary of the 2nd Brigade, 7 November 1914.
91   TNA WO 95/1270: War Diary of the 1st Loyal North Lancs, 7 November 1914.
92   TNA WO 95/1272: War Diary of the 2nd Battalion of King's Royal Rifle Corps, 7 November 1914
93   TNA WO 95/1281: War Diary of the 2nd Welsh, November 1914.
94   TNA WO 95/1278: War Diary of the 1st Gloucestershire Regiment, Frazebrook Account.
95   TNA WO 95/1274: War Diary of the 3rd Brigade, 7 November 1914.
96   TNA WO 95/1278: War Diary of the 1st Gloucestershire Regiment, 7 November 1914.
97   TNA WO 95/1278: War Diary of the 1st Gloucestershire Regiment, Frazebrook Account.
98   TNA WO 95/1263: War Diary of the 1st Black Watch, 7 November 1914.

Cloth Hall and the Cathedral being burnt down.[99] The London Scottish arrived at 11 p.m., to join 1st (Guards) Brigade, in place of 1st Coldstreams.[100]

On 8 November, temporary command of 2nd Brigade devolved upon Major Norman, as Lieutenant Colonel Osbourne-Smith was sick. In their trenches, the 2nd Royal Sussex initially suffered from British artillery fire falling short. However, this was soon rectified, and it was noted that the British artillery did significant damage to the German positions.[101] The South Wales Borderers were detailed to dig support positions in case the front line was pierced. This proved prescient as, at about 2.30 p.m., the Germans broke through into the wood north of the Menin Road.[102]

For 1st Loyal North Lancs, the day had begun quietly; but then some neighbouring Zouaves fell back accompanied by some of the Loyal North Lancs from the front line. The 1st Loyal North Lancs, with support from men of the West Riding Regiment, counter-attacked and regained the trenches. The Germans then reinforced their troops and succeeded in pushing the British back again.[103] The loss of the trenches meant that the Germans could enter the communication trench and enfilade those occupied by 1st Scots Guards.[104] The need to lead their men in facing this new threat perhaps explains why they had five officers killed that day. Lieutenant Sir John Swinnerton Dyer Bart. Survived his wounds but not the war.

He would go on to be decorated with the MC, reach the rank of Captain, and be killed on 31 July 1917, whilst holding the role of DAQMG of the Guards Division.

The divisional cyclists were ordered forward, to assist 1st (Guards) Brigade.[105] Captain Fortune led A and B companies of the 1st Black Watch in counter-attacking the Germans. At 3.10 p.m., the Northants received an order to go and retake the trenches west of Veldhoek, that had been lost by Zouaves and 1st Loyal North Lancs.[106] With the assistance of the 1st Northants, the trenches were recaptured before nightfall. The 1st Loyal North Lancs laid claim to capturing about thirty Germans and a machine gun, as well as inflicting 150 casualties; but the cost was a hundred casualties of their own, including three of the few remaining officers.[107]

By 5 p.m., 1st (Guards) Brigade had cleared the wood and the Northants had retaken the trenches. 1st Division was informed that detached units with Lord Cavan would be relieved, and the London Scottish would then be transferred to Lord Cavan's command.[108] 1st Black Watch's part in retaking the captured positions was reflected in their role in holding the line next to 1st Scots Guards.[109] It had been a torrid day, and Captain Prince was killed trying to lead a party of about 30 men to try to join up the trenches held with those of the Zouaves by capturing an intervening section of trench held by the Germans. The battalion's left rested on the Menin road and was at right angles to the trenches held by the Zouaves but not joined up to

---

99 TNA WO 95/1274: War Diary of the 3rd Brigade, 7 November 1914.
100 TNA WO 95/1227: War Diary of the 1st Division, 7 November 1914.
101 TNA WO 95/1269: War Diary of the 2nd Royal Sussex, 8 November 1914.
102 TNA WO 95/1227: War Diary of the 1st Division, 8 November 1914.
103 TNA WO 95/1270: War Diary of the 1st Loyal North Lancs, 8 November 1914.
104 TNA WO 95/1261: War Diary of the 1st Scots Guards, 8 November 1914.
105 TNA WO 95/1227: War Diary of the 1st Division, 8 November 1914.
106 TNA WO 95/1267: War Diary of the 2nd Brigade, 8 November 1914.
107 TNA WO 95/1270: War Diary of the 1st Loyal North Lancs, 8 November 1914.
108 TNA WO 95/1227: War Diary of the 1st Division, 8 November 1914.
109 TNA WO 95/1263: War Diary of the 1st Black Watch, 8 November 1914.

them.[110] The Germans proved fully alert to a possible attack, and half of the attackers became casualties.[111] As the Zouaves had not re-occupied their trenches, heavy howitzers were being brought up to force the Germans out in the morning.[112] In contrast with many of the diary entries on other days, the Camerons noted that the artillery provided little assistance during that day's fighting.[113] However, 1st Black Watch took the initiative and sent their machine guns forward to enfilade the German trench. In the morning, they found 23 dead Germans in the trench and despatched their rifles to 1st (Guards) Brigade HQ.[114]

At the end of another tough day, the London Scottish arrived to relieve the 2nd Royal Sussex, delayed by the officer sent to guide them being wounded.[115] The London Scottish had been guided to the Sussex by the Brigade Major and Staff Captain of 2nd Brigade, who reported bursts of shrapnel being fired by the Germans into the woods.[116] The 2nd KRRC found themselves in the woods, as reserve for 4th (Guards) Brigade, after they were relieved by the French troops who had initially attacked through them. They then rested and dug a support trench, which they later occupied.[117] The two officers and 170 other ranks that remained of 1st Queens, 3rd Brigade, were transferred to corps HQ, and were replaced by the reconstituted 2nd Royal Munster Fusiliers the next day.[118]

In an adjustment to the dispositions, the 2nd KRRC took over a trench from the London Scottish, deploying a company and the MG section to effect this.[119] The relief of 3rd Brigade was already underway when orders arrived from 1st Division to cancel it. Eventually, the relief was permitted, but the brigade was only allowed to bivouac in the nearby woods.[120]

After their relief, in the early hours of 9 November, the 2nd Royal Sussex were put on warning to support 1st Northants. They were not needed and were able to spend that day and 10 November resting[121] in the woods at Hooge. However, the Sussex were now designated as Corps Reserve. The Welsh and the South Wales Borderers spent the day on stand-by, to support 1st (Guards) Brigade in case of a German attempt to break their line.[122] The 1st Loyal North Lancs held their positions all day, having seven men killed by German snipers.[123] Lieutenant Kerr, and his detachment of howitzers, proved very effective in blowing the Germans out of the neighbouring former-Zouave-held trenches. Some houses opposite the Zouave trenches were destroyed, and a British machine gun joined French troops in accepting the surrender of 28

---

110 TNA WO 95/1270: War Diary of the 1st Loyal North Lancs, 8 November 1914.
111 Wylly, H.C., *The Loyal North Lancashire Regiment 1914-1919* (Uckfield: Naval & Military Press, 2007), pp.17-18
112 TNA WO 95/1227: War Diary of the 1st Division, 8 November 1914.
113 TNA WO 95/1264: War Diary of the 1st Cameron Highlanders, 8 November 1914
114 TNA WO 95/1263: War Diary of the 1st Black Watch, 8 November 1914
115 TNA WO 95/1269: War Diary of the 2nd Royal Sussex, 8 November 1914.
116 TNA WO 95/1267: War Diary of the 2nd Brigade, 8 November 1914.
117 TNA WO 95/1272: War Diary of the 2nd Battalion of King's Royal Rifle Corps, 8 November 1914
118 Becke, *Order of Battle of Divisions - Part 1*, pp. 36-37 and TNA WO 95/1280: War Diary of the 1st Queens, November 1914.
119 TNA WO 95/1272: War Diary of the 2nd Battalion of King's Royal Rifle Corps, 9 November 1914.
120 TNA WO 95/1274: War Diary of the 3rd Brigade, 8 November 1914.
121 TNA WO 95/1269: War Diary of the 2nd Royal Sussex, 9-10 November 1914.
122 TNA WO 95/1274: War Diary of the 3rd Brigade, 9 November 1914.
123 TNA WO 95/1270: War Diary of the 1st Loyal North Lancs, 9 November 1914.

Germans.[124] Divisional HQ was unaware, it seems, of the exploits of the Black Watch in creating a sense of insecurity amongst the Germans in those trenches. The 2nd KRRC were ordered forward to support the London Scottish but "nothing happened" so they returned at nightfall. The attritional nature of the war was demonstrated in that "nothing" had cost them three dead and six wounded.[125] The new acting Brigadier of 2nd Brigade was Lieutenant Colonel Cunliffe Owen RFA, who arrived at 8 p.m.[126] By 11 p.m. that evening, the 1st South Wales Borderers had relieved the 1st Irish Guards of the 4th (Guards) Brigade sector.[127] The original line-up was restored when the 1st Loyal North Lancs relieved A and B companies of 1st Black Watch. These companies then returned to being in brigade reserve. The machine guns were sent up to reinforce D company, who were holding the line next to the 1st Cameron Highlanders.[128] The Black Watch were shelled heavily all day on 10 November, with D company's positions being very heavily shelled.[129]

The artillery apparently stopped the Germans digging trenches north of the Menin Road. However, in preparing for their attack on 11 November, the Germans had benefitted from two days of misty weather, which meant that there had been no aerial reconnaissance undertaken and that therefore 1st Division's artillery had not been able to spot German batteries.[130] 3rd Brigade spent the day on stand-by to support 4th (Guards) Brigade. The 2nd Munster Fusiliers spent the day reorganising A and B companies.[131] During the early afternoon, specific orders were received for the 2nd Welsh and 2nd Munster Fusiliers to go to Lord Cavan's command and relieve 2nd Grenadier Guards, the latter arrived in the vicinity of 3rd Brigade HQ at about 4 a.m. on 11 November. This was probably due to C and D companies of the Munster Fusiliers having been completely reorganised and only joining the battalion at 2.30 a.m. on 10th November.[132] This preparation can hardly have maximised their effectiveness. The 2nd Welsh arrived at Lord Cavan's headquarters and were directed to take over the left of the line from the Grenadiers, as the latter had suffered severe casualties. They were also informed that they should dig another support line before dawn. This was made difficult by the night being particularly dark. Dawn revealed that the trees in the wood had been devastated by the high explosives fired on the trenches and had therefore created a "formidable abatis". Dawn also showed that the Welsh were too far back to support the right flank of the London Scottish. With the help of some RE personnel from 11th Field Company, some rifle pits were dug amongst the fallen trees. The preparation of these pits was aided by Private John; he managed to make his way through the German positions and provide a clear idea of them to his OC. The proximity of the enemy trenches meant there was constant sniping. The machine guns were kept in battalion reserve, as no position could be identified for their effective use.[133] They were only a hundred yards from

---

124 TNA WO 95/1227: War Diary of the 1st Division, 9 November 1914.
125 TNA WO 95/1272: War Diary of the 2nd Battalion of King's Royal Rifle Corps, 10 November 1914.
126 TNA WO 95/1267: War Diary of the 2nd Brigade, 10 -11 November 1914.
127 TNA WO 95/1280: War Diary of the 1st South Wales Borderers, 9 November 1914.
128 TNA WO 95/1263: War Diary of the 1st Black Watch, 9 November 1914.
129 TNA WO 95/1263: War Diary of the 1st Black Watch, 10 November 1914.
130 TNA WO 95/1239: War Diary of the 1st Division, Artillery, 10 November 1914.
131 TNA WO 95/1272: War Diary of the 2nd Battalion of Royal Munster Fusiliers, 9 November 1914.
132 TNA WO 95/1272: War Diary of the 2nd Battalion of Royal Munster Fusiliers, 10 November 1914.
133 TNA WO 95/1281: War Diary of the 2nd Welsh, 10 November 1914.

the Germans. Orders were also received for the Gloucesters to be designated as Corps reserve.[134] Therefore, 3rd Brigade was effectively dispersed before the fighting began on 11 November. The number of detached units, and the divisions involved, meant that 1st Division had had to seek approval of the planned trench reliefs from I Corps.[135]

The mist had also limited the ability of the Germans to carry out reconnaissance. Although the German *Fourth Army* attacked on 10 November, capturing Dixmude, held by one Belgian and three under-strength French battalions,[136] Linsingen's battle-group did not. Therefore, it was on 11 November that the German *Sixth Army*'s assault fell on the much-depleted units of 1st Division. Heavy shelling, which grew in intensity, was noted by 1st Division from 6.30 a.m. Divisional headquarters were right to anticipate bad news as this brutally frank account by the Cameron Highlanders states, that at about 9 a.m.: "the 1st Grenadier Regiment broke through our lines at more than one point. The Scots Guards, Camerons and Black Watch evacuated their trenches and fled leaving the Germans in possession."[137] Pockets of resistance did exist, but the overall result of the attack was almost as bleak as this suggests.

In the Black Watch's sector, the Germans managed to get to within fifty yards of the trenches on D company's right and were therefore able to break through *en masse* between D and the fortified post occupied by C company. D company swung round, but the advancing Germans were therefore able to pass between these two points of resistance and break through to the brigade HQ. The determined resistance of C company, led by Lieutenant Anderson, meant that passing German troops were enfiladed.[138] "The supporting point of C Company, under Lieutenant F. Anderson, held out firmly, and split the attack into small parties of twenty or thirty men, many of whom were soon lost in the woods behind. It is interesting to note that Lieutenant Anderson's post was the first instance in the war of the "strong point," or wired-in locality, which later became a salient feature of defensive warfare. This particular post was sited and constructed by a great friend of the regiment, Major C. Russell-Brown, R.E., commanding the 23rd Field Company.[139] As we have seen, Major Russell-Brown had in fact being responsible for the construction of several "strong-points" at various parts of the line.

Second Lieutenant [Neil] McNeill, commanding a portion of A Company, was last seen on the parapet of his trench, revolver in hand, fighting right gallantly to the end with all his men." The fate of the rest of A company was little different; "B Company and the two platoons of A Company, under Lieutenant Sprot, who were in reserve in the paddocks of Verbeek farm, were overwhelmed by the first onrush of the enemy; Lieutenant Sprot and most of his men were killed. A few men, amongst whom were Privates Jackson and Gardner, were taken prisoner; but when their captors took cover from a chance shell, they slipped away and escaped into the Nonne Boschen Wood.[140]

---

134 TNA WO 95/1274: War Diary of the 3rd Brigade, 10 November 1914.
135 TNA WO 95/1227: War Diary of the 1st Division, 10 November 1914.
136 Greenhalgh, E, *The French Army and the First World War* (Cambridge: CUP, 2014), p.56.
137 TNA WO 95/1264: War Diary of the 1st Cameron Highlanders, 11 November 1914.
138 TNA WO 95/1263: War Diary of the 1st Black Watch, 11 November 1914.
139 *The Courier* <https://www.thecourier.co.uk/news/130731/2014-target-for-black-watch-memorial-at-ypres/> (accessed 9April 2020).
140 *The Courier* <https://www.thecourier.co.uk/news/130731/2014-target-for-black-watch-memorial-at-ypres/>

The impact on the Scots Guards was as bad as the Camerons described. Whilst the men in the orchard were initially able to hang on, the trenches on either side were lost to the oncoming Prussian Guard. The point d'appui was destroyed by the German artillery and then stormed by their infantry. Only four guardsmen from there were able to get back to join up with battalion HQ along with the five survivors from the fire trench and thirty men from the orchard. According to the Scots Guards, the Germans reached to within 200 yards of the British guns but were driven back, having suffered severe casualties.[141] The guns are referred to as field howitzers; and of the three batteries stated as supporting 1st (Guards) Brigade that morning[142] it was 30 Battery of XXXIX Brigade who were equipped with howitzers.

The Camerons too found themselves in the thick of the fighting: "Verbeek Farm, the joint Headquarters of The Black Watch and the Cameron Highlanders, was temporarily occupied by the enemy; the actual Headquarters dug-out, a primitive brushwood lean-to against the farmhouse was, however, kept safe by the spirited defence of the two commanding officers, Lieutenant Colonels C. E. Stewart and D. McEwan, and of Sergeant D. Redpath, The Black Watch signalling sergeant. Lieutenant Colonel Stewart was wounded in the head at point-blank range by a German who was, in his turn, despatched by Sergeant Redpath."[143]

The 1st Division had initially been aware of heavy shelling from about 6.15am. Significant news arrived around 8.30am when a private from the Scots Guards reported that the Germans had penetrated to the right of his regiment. He also said that communications with the forward battalions had been broken by heavy German shelling of the communication trenches. His report tied in with the staff noting that they could now hear heavy rifle fire. It was also noted that the shelling now extended back nearly to Hooge.[144] Therefore, 2nd Brigade, less 2nd KRRC, were warned at 8.15 a.m. to be on stand-by. At the same time that 2nd Brigade were warned, the Gloucesters, along with the Grenadier Guards in Corps reserve, were put on alert to be ready to move at short notice.[145] By 10 a.m., the 1st Gloucesters and 2nd Grenadier Guards were on the move towards the wood east of Hooge chateau to support 1st (Guards) Brigade, whose line had been broken.[146] This followed hard on the heels of 1st Division being informed by 1st (Guards) Brigade that the line had been broken.[147] Brigadier Fitzclarence had received a report from Lieutenant Rowan Hamilton and Captain Brodie of the Camerons, who were the respective battalion adjutants.[148] Amongst the other casualties were all the horses of two (possibly three) ammunition wagons bringing up fresh supplies to the guns of 54 battery. Nevertheless, the guns of 46 and 54 batteries were brought to bear on the Germans who had broken into the woods. The Germans reached to within about 400 yards of the battery. The brigade ammunition column issued 1382 rounds of 18pdr ammunition and 48,000 rounds of

---

141 TNA WO 95/1261: War Diary of the 1st Scots Guards, 11 November 1914.
142 TNA WO 95/1239: War Diary of the 1st Division, Artillery, 11 November 1914.
143 *The Courier* <https://www.thecourier.co.uk/news/130731/2014-target-for-black-watch-memorial-at-ypres/> (accessed 9 April 2020).
144 TNA WO 95/1227: War Diary of the 1st Division, 11 November 1914.
145 TNA WO 95/1278: War Diary of the 1st Gloucestershire Regiment, Frazebrook Account.
146 TNA WO 95/1274: War Diary of the 3rd Brigade, 11 November 1914.
147 TNA WO 95/1227: War Diary of the 1st Division, 11 November 1914.
148 *The Courier* <https://www.thecourier.co.uk/news/130731/2014-target-for-black-watch-memorial-at-ypres/> (accessed 9th April 2020).

SAA.[149] This must have contributed significantly to helping to restrict the German advance whilst the infantry counterattacks were organised.

Even before this report had been received, the 2nd Royal Sussex had also been sent forward, at 9 a.m. They went up to Coalbox Wood and were shelled immediately after occupying the position.[150] The 2nd Royal Sussex were sent forward specifically to support the 1st Scots Guards who had been driven out of their trenches, north of Veldhoek Chateau wood.[151] Bad news was pouring in; 9th Brigade reported that they were under heavy attack and 1st (Guards) Brigade reported heavy firing in the woods. Half an hour later, reports of the German breakthrough were received in the rear echelons, and the divisional cyclists and mounted troops were ordered forward. The situation was unclear, so they eventually took up a position in a sunken road east of Veldhoek.[152] 3rd Division now reported being attacked all along their front. By shortly after 10 a.m., 1st Division knew that the Germans had taken Verbeek Farm and had entered Nonne Boschen wood. The wood contained both 1 Brigade HQ and the joint HQ of the Black Watch and the Camerons: "The 1st Brigade Headquarters was held by 1st Brigade Signal Section, The Black Watch party that had been with the North Lancashire Regiment for the past three days and had reported at 1st Brigade Headquarters during the preliminary bombardment, and a few men who had got away from the front line."[153] At the joint HQ, Captain Brodie of the Camerons was amongst those who died in this episode of the fighting. Another officer who died was Lieutenant Lawson of the Black Watch. He had recently been commissioned from the ranks; he had served for nineteen years during which he had risen to be Regimental Quartermaster Sergeant.[154]

However, the collective British response was taking shape. The corps reserve had been released to oppose the breakthrough, and 5th Brigade were sending troops south from the north-west corner of Polygon Wood. The Northamptons and Gloucesters, the Divisional and Corps reserve respectively, were put at the disposal of Brigadier Fitzclarence. They arrived under the command of acting-Brigadier Cunliffe- Owen and his Brigade Major. They had been ordered by 1st Division to make touch with Brigadier Fitzclarence. The Northamptons were tasked with clearing the southern part of Nonneboschen Wood. One company deployed on the southern edge, whilst another was placed at the south-east corner of Nonne Boschen wood. The Northamptons, supported by 80 of the Gloucesters, succeeded in their task. Unfortunately, French artillery fire, presumably directed at the advancing Germans, forced them to halt and dig in. This line faced south and was situated close to Velbeke Farm. The rest of the Gloucesters had initially been sent back. However, they were now sent forward again to cover the gap between

---

149 TNA WO 95/1239: War Diary of the 1st Division, Artillery and 46 & 54 Battery and XXXIX Brigade Ammunition Column, 11 November 1914.
150 TNA WO 95/1423: War Diary of the 2nd Royal Sussex, 11 November 1914.
151 TNA WO 95/1267: War Diary of the 2nd Brigade, 11 November 1914.
152 Carnock, *15th Hussars*, p.90
153 *The Courier* <www.thecourier.co.uk/news/130731/2014-target-for-black-watch-memorial-at-ypres/> (accessed 9th April 2020).
154 *The Courier* <https://www.thecourier.co.uk/news/130731/2014-target-for-black-watch-memorial-at-ypres/> Accessed 9th April 2020

the Northamptons and 9 Brigade on their right.[155] An hour later, the Oxford and Bucks Light Infantry were deployed on the northern and western edges of the wood to assist in clearing it.[156]

Around noon, 1st Division felt that the situation was easing.[157] The pressure was reflected in the decision to return 2nd Royal Sussex to 2nd Brigade. Technically, they were returned to 2nd Brigade's command at 12.20 p.m. Cunliffe-Owen was told to keep them at the western edge of the wood, where they could support the troops on either side as needed. He was told to only use the 2nd Royal Sussex if it was an emergency.[158] It was at about this time that C Squadron of the 15th Hussars were recalled.[159] Despite reports of Germans having broken through the line at the south-west corner of Polygon Wood, early afternoon saw 1st Gloucesters revert to being Corps reserve.[160]

For about three hours, starting at 12.45 p.m., the combined efforts of the Northamptons, supported by elements of the Camerons and the Black Watch, fought their way forward about 150 yards to reach the badly wounded Lieutenant Anderson and the other survivors of C company. Their utter devotion to duty had helped to divert *1st Guards Brigade* off course. The advance of the Northamptons beyond Veerbeek Farm was soon checked by French artillery fire falling on the British front line.[161] Given the fluidity of the fighting, it was an understandable though unfortunate error.

Whilst fighting continued in Nonne Boschen Wood, 1st Division had received a report from Lieutenant Colonel Westmancott. His force, consisting of Highland Light Infantry (HLI) and Connaughts, had reached the south-west corner of Polygon Wood, but he reported that about 1200 Germans were advancing south of the wood, and that his force had not yet been able to link up with other British units.[162] Brigadier Fitzclarence reported that he had no troops left to deploy, and that there was a gap of 400 yards between his headquarters and Herenthage Wood. Around 2.15 p.m., 1st Division learnt that 9th Brigade had not yet regained their fire trenches, so the flank of the Zouaves was in the air.[163] Therefore, the Gloucesters were sent to fill the gap.[164]

It was only at 2.30 p.m. that the 1st Loyal North Lancs were sent forward to help block any further German advance,[165] by which time, B Squadron of the 15th Hussars and the 2nd Oxford and Bucks Light Infantry were assisting 2nd Division in the clearing of Nonne Boschen Wood.[166] At about 3 p.m., the 2nd Royal Sussex sent a party off to support the 1st Royal Scots Fusiliers, temporarily attached to 8th Brigade. The Royal Scots Fusiliers were part of the force counter-attacking the Prussian Guard east of Herenthage Chateau.[167] As well as supporting

---

155 TNA WO 95/1227: War Diary of the 1st Division, 11 November 1914.
156 TNA WO 95/1227: War Diary of the 1st Division, 11 November 1914.
157 TNA WO 95/1227: War Diary of the 1st Division, 11 November 1914.
158 TNA WO 95/1267: War Diary of the 2nd Brigade, 11 November 1914.
159 Carnock, *15th Hussars*, p.91
160 TNA WO 95/1274: War Diary of the 3rd Brigade, 11 November 1914.
161 TNA WO 95/1227: War Diary of the 1st Division, 11 November 1914.
162 TNA WO 95/1227: War Diary of the 1st Division, 11 November 1914.
163 TNA WO 95/1227: War Diary of the 1st Division, 11 November 1914.
164 TNA WO 95/1274: War Diary of the 3rd Brigade, 11 November 1914.
165 TNA WO 95/1270: War Diary of the 1st Loyal North Lancs, 11 November 1914.
166 Carnock, *15th Hussars*, p.92
167 TNA WO 95/1432: War Diary of the 1st Royal Scots Fusiliers, 11 November 1914.

British troops, the 2nd Royal Sussex had sent one company to support Zouaves on their left.[168] This was in response to 1st Division orders to assist in closing the gap between the Gloucesters as they advanced, and the Zouaves.[169] The 1st Loyal North Lancs were also ordered forward on the right of the Gloucesters.[170]

By about 3 p.m., 1st Division were informed that Nonne Boschen Wood had been cleared and that the Germans had fallen back north-eastwards to the original 1st (Guards) Brigade trenches. They were also told by I Corps that 3rd Cavalry Division was at their disposal. The OBLI, assisted by the machine guns of the HLI, succeeded in regaining the trenches originally occupied by the 1st Black Watch.[171] Boff's view that the OBLI's counter-attack restored the situation is literally true, it fails to recognise how many other units were involved in restoring the British line.[172]

By 4 p.m., the darkness and German shrapnel fire led to some confusion during the operations to clear Nonne Boschen wood.[173] 1st Division noted that 1st (Guards) Brigade could not find any formed unit of its brigade. One company of the 2nd Royal Sussex were sent to assist 9th Brigade, south of the Menin road, whilst the rest were taken to join Lieutenant Colonel Lovett who was with the Grenadiers and Munsters. The 2nd Royal Sussex were given orders to carry out a counterattack and then collected to be taken to a new position so that they could carry out the attack from a different direction. However, this attack, which was to be under the command of the OC Gloucesters was subsequently abandoned. Nonetheless, the battalion had been caught on the road, marching in fours, by German artillery and was fortunate to only suffer a few casualties. That evening they received 64 reinforcements including one officer.[174] The 2nd Royal Sussex finished up, supporting 9th Brigade, in their old positions on the 5-kilometre marker on the Menin road. Meanwhile, 1st Division was drawing down the first instalment of the promised assistance; 7 Cavalry Brigade was ordered forward to Hooge.[175]

On what for them was a quiet day, 11 November, the 2nd KRRC had to dig a trench in a deluge of rain, due to events elsewhere.[176] The same heavy rain meant that 2nd Welsh struggled to make improvements to their positions; though they were afforded assistance with completing communication trenches.[177], after dark, by RE personnel drawn from the 11th and 26th Field Companies.

At 8.30 a.m., Acting-Brigadier Cunliffe-Owen was put in charge of the line from north of the chateau up to (but not including) Polygon Wood. Nevertheless, he was told that the Grenadier Guards and Irish Guards must remain in Chateau Wood. The rest of the line was made up of the 1st Gloucesters, 1st Northants and 1st Life Guards. The 1st Loyal North Lancs remained in the woods south of Hooge. Initially, Cunliffe-Owen occupied the old 1st

---

168 TNA WO 95/1267: War Diary of the 2nd Brigade, 11 November 1914
169 For a detailed discussion of the interaction between the British and French forces at First Ypres see Greenhalgh, E., *The French Army and the First World War*, pp 51-58.
170 TNA WO 95/1227: War Diary of the 1st Division, 11 November 1914
171 TNA WO 95/1227: War Diary of the 1st Division, 11 November 1914
172 Boff, J., *Haig's Enemy*, p.47
173 TNA WO 95/1274: War Diary of the 3rd Brigade, 11 November 1914
174 TNA WO 95/1269: War Diary of the 2nd Royal Sussex, 11 November 1914.
175 TNA WO 95/1227: War Diary of the 1st Division, 11 November 1914.
176 TNA WO 95/1272: War Diary of the 2nd Battalion of King's Royal Rifle Corps, 11 November 1914.
177 TNA WO 95/1281: War Diary of the 2nd Welsh, 11 November 1914.

(Guards) Brigade HQ but subsequently moved to a more central position in the line. During the afternoon, Cunliffe-Owen sent his Brigade Major to see the staff of 5th Brigade to arrange for the Northants to cover the gap between the two divisions. The thinness of the "red line" is emphasised by the evening summary. Lieutenant Thorp, the Brigade Signals Officer, had made a visit to each unit and reported to 1st Division on the revised deployment within Cunliffe-Owen's line. Starting at Chateau Wood and moving north, the line was held by: one company of 2nd Royal Sussex; one company of 1st Grenadier Guards; 180 men of 1st Gloucesters with one platoon of Grenadier Guards; 25 men and the machine guns of 1st Northants; seventy men of the Black Watch holding a key strongpoint; 120 of 1st Northants in Verbeek Farm. This position was left under the command of Major Craig-Brown of the Camerons.[178] Finally there was a post to be occupied by the Northants at night, to cover the gap, as the 2nd Oxford and Bucks Light Infantry, 2nd Division, were in a position which was echeloned back about 200 yards to the rear of the Northants.[179] Meanwhile, the 2nd Munster Fusiliers continued to fend off attacks as part of 4th (Guards) Brigade.[180] 1st Division had been requested by Lord Cavan to send him the detachment of Munsters that had been attached to the Irish Guards on 11 November. It is interesting to note that in strengthening the line, in the evening, 1st Division moved a platoon of the Grenadier Guards from the middle of the Gloucesters line, returning them to their company on the Gloucester's flank. As noted previously, Fitzclarence tended to mix units up; clearly his superiors now felt that such arrangements need not go unchallenged.[181]

Lovett's force was put under Fitzclarence's command. I Corps had ordered that the original firing line should be recaptured.[182] As a further counterattack was to take place to capture the farm, C Squadron of the 15th Hussars again moved forward at 4 p.m. This further counterattack was being organised personally by Brigadier-General Fitzclarence VC. Carnock paints a vivid picture of tired subalterns reporting to Fitzclarence upon their arrival. Each reported the strength of their units, by the light of candles stuck in bottles in the battle ravaged brigade HQ.[183] The attack on the farm itself, at the south-west corner, was led by an officer and eighty men of the 1st Loyal North Lancs. They were supported on their left by the 1st Gloucesters; and, on their right, by a combined force drawn from the divisional cyclists and the 15th Hussars. When the 1st Loyal North Lancs were withdrawn that evening, the Gloucesters occupied the position, extending from Inverness Copse to Verbeek Farm. Despite being drawn into this key action, the Gloucesters only reported fifteen casualties that day.[184]

The original local counterattack organised by Brigadier Fitzclarence for 7.30 p.m. was postponed until 1 a.m. This attack was not to be supported by the artillery unless Fitzclarence specially requested it.[185] The attack, southwards from the south-west corner of Polygon Wood, was led by Lieutenant Colonel Davis and the Oxford and Buckinghamshire Light Infantry, supported by the Highland Light infantry. This took place at 1 a.m. but failed. As planned, the

---

178 TNA WO 95/1264: War Diary of the 1st Cameron Highlanders, 12 November 1914.
179 TNA WO 95/1267: War Diary of the 2nd Brigade, 12 November 1914.
180 TNA WO 95/1272: War Diary of the 2nd Battalion of Royal Munster Fusiliers, 12 November 1914.
181 TNA WO 95/1227: War Diary of the 1st Division, 12 November 1914.
182 TNA WO 95/1227: War Diary of the 1st Division, 11 November 1914.
183 Carnock, *15th Hussars*, p.91
184 TNA WO 95/1267: War Diary of the 2nd Brigade, 11 November 1914 and WO 95/1278: War Diary of the 1st Gloucestershire Regiment, Frazebrook Diary.
185 TNA WO 95/1239: War Diary of the 1st Division, Artillery, 11 November 1914.

Irish Guards and Grenadier Guards were ready to attack from a different direction. As noted by 1st Division at 4.15 a.m., Brigadier Fitzclarence had been killed and no formed unit of his brigade could be identified.[186] The figures for the survivors of 1st (Guards) Brigade were stated on 12 November to be; one officer and 69 men of the Scots Guards, one officer and 109 men of the Black Watch as well as three officers and 140 men of the Cameron Highlanders.[187] As noted above, the remnants of 1st Coldstream Guards were currently attached to their second battalion. Reflecting their shattered state, 1st (Guards) Brigade was withdrawn into reserve.

Brigadier-General Fitzclarence VC had been killed with 1st Irish Guards, leading an attempt to re-capture a lost trench. The Germans had dug a new trench in a commanding position, behind the one that they had captured. According to Kipling, the 1st Irish Guards received fire from the front and the flank, so the attack failed.[188] According to the records of the Black Watch (who supplied the guides), Brigadier-General Fitzclarence VC fell at the rendezvous, so the attack was cancelled.[189] Major Jeffrey's account helps tie these apparently disparate accounts together as he says that the head of the column had been fired on again.[190] Jeffreys's comment that there was no chance of success once Fitzclarence was killed reflects his prejudice and disdain, rather than an objective assessment of the situation. Fitzclarence's personal bravery cannot be questioned, but this is the second occasion on which he ordered an attack in the dark, against a position which had not been reconnoitred initially. This time, after his officers had gone forward and decided not to attack, he was blundering about in the dark trying to initiate an attack despite the evidence. Several accounts refer to the column advancing in fours, a formation which was hardly designed to hide their approach. Jones may well be correct in seeing Fitzclarence VC as representing the best elements of the pre-war officer corps.[191] Nevertheless, Fitzclarence's strengths and limitations seem to underline how difficult it would be for the British officer corps to adjust to the realities of mass-mechanised warfare, pitted against a professional opponent.

It seems that, had he survived to be promoted, Fitzclarence would have been another Gough or Hunter-Weston rather than a Rawlinson or Plumer. Fitzclarence would probably have added vim to British operations away from the Western Front, where his personal impact would have had a greater opportunity to shine.

At 8.30 a.m. 12 November, Acting-Brigadier Cunliffe-Owen was put in charge of the line from north of the chateau up to (but not including) Polygon Wood. Nevertheless, he was told that the Grenadier Guards and Irish Guards must remain in Chateau Wood. The rest of the line was made up of the 1st Gloucesters, 1st Northants and 1st Life Guards. The 1st Loyal North Lancs remained in the woods south of Hooge. Initially, Cunliffe-Owen occupied the old 1st (Guards) Brigade HQ but subsequently moved to a more central position in the line. During the afternoon, Cunliffe-Owen sent his Brigade Major to see the staff of 5th Brigade to arrange for the Northants to cover the gap between the two divisions. The thinness of the "red line" is emphasised by the evening summary. Lieutenant Thorp, the Brigade Signals Officer, had made a visit to each unit and reported to 1st Division on the revised deployment within

---

186 TNA WO 95/1227: War Diary of the 1st Division, 12 November 1914.
187 TNA WO 95/1261: War Diary of the 1st Scots Guards, 12 November 1914.
188 Kipling, R., *The Irish Guards in the Great War, vol. 1* (Staplehurst: Spellmount, 1997), p.64
189 TNA WO 95/1263: War Diary of the 1st Black Watch, 11 November 1914.
190 Craster, J.M., *Fifteen Rounds a Minute* (Barnsley: Pen & Sword, 1976), p.152
191 Jones (ed.), *Stemming the Tide*, p.261.

Cunliffe-Owen's line. Starting at Chateau Wood and moving north, the line was held by: one company of 2nd Royal Sussex; one company of 1st Grenadier Guards; 180 men of 1st Gloucesters with one platoon of Grenadier Guards; 25 men and the machine guns of 1st Northants; seventy men of the Black Watch holding a key strongpoint; 120 of 1st Northants in Verbeek Farm. This position was left under the command of Major Craig-Brown of the Camerons.[192] Finally there was a post to be occupied by the Northants at night, to cover the gap, as the 2nd Oxford and Bucks Light Infantry, 2nd Division, were in a position which was echeloned back about 200 yards to the rear of the Northants.[193] Meanwhile, the 2nd Munster Fusiliers continued to fend off attacks as part of 4th (Guards) Brigade.[194] 1st Division had been requested by Lord Cavan to send him the detachment of Munsters that had been attached to the Irish Guards on 11 November. It is interesting to note that in strengthening the line, in the evening, 1st Division moved a platoon of the Grenadier Guards from the middle of the Gloucesters line, returning them to their company on the Gloucester's flank. As noted previously, Fitzclarence tended to mix units up; clearly his superiors now felt that such arrangements need not go unchallenged.[195]

The 2nd Royal Sussex recorded that 12 November was critical, and that they spent it constantly patching up bits of the line, as did 2nd KRRC; the Sussex's D company's contribution was to dig a new set of trenches.[196] For 1st South Wales Borderers, the day involved moving the battalion HQ further back behind the wood to facilitate communications with brigade. The British line remained intact, but the 1st Division now contained only shattered remnants of the proud battalions that had marched off to France after mobilisation a mere four months earlier.

---

192 TNA WO 95/1264: War Diary of the 1st Cameron Highlanders, 12 November 1914.
193 TNA WO 95/1267: War Diary of the 2nd Brigade, 12 November 1914.
194 TNA WO 95/1272: War Diary of the 2nd Battalion of Royal Munster Fusiliers, 12 November 1914.
195 TNA WO 95/1227: War Diary of the 1st Division, 12 November 1914.
196 TNA WO 95/1269: War Diary of the 2nd Royal Sussex, 12 November 1914 and TNA WO 95/1272: War Diary of the 2nd Battalion of King's Royal Rifle Corps, 12 November 1914.

17

First Ypres
The Final Stint

After the bitter fighting around Ypres, the remnants of 1st Division needed an opportunity to rest and reorganise. Until this could be arranged, they would have to continue to hold sections of the front.

Overnight, the Royal Engineers dug support trenches behind the positions held by the Gloucesters. It was during this stint in the trenches that 1st Gloucesters first came under minenwerfer fire.[1] On 13 November, the 1st Coldstreams were transferred to Zonnebeke in support of 6th Brigade and remained with that brigade until 15 November.[2] The 2nd Royal Sussex were still in Coalbox Wood, until they were moved to "Pig Sty Wood". For the 2nd KRRC, the day saw its various detached companies reunited with the main battalion and the arrival of one officer and 123 other ranks.[3] When the Germans attacked the neighbouring London Scottish, the 2nd Welsh's left most positions, under Lieutenant Gilbey, later wounded, came under attack too. The abundance of hand grenades used by the enemy was noted. The British positions were held only after a field gun was manhandled forward and delivered a few rounds into the attacking Germans. Captain Rees led the battalion reserve of 28 men to re-establish the 2nd Welsh line.[4] This underlines the thinness of the British line.

The Germans shelled 1st Division positions, including their artillery, but the main enemy activity was against the line occupied by 3rd Division, particularly 9th Brigade. 1st Division was notified by I Corps that the 2nd Munsters, 2nd Royal Sussex and 2nd Welsh were all to be relieved, but in the event the orders for the 2nd Royal Sussex were postponed and Lord Cavan was unable to release the 2nd Munsters.[5]

The remnants of the 1st Loyal North Lancs spent the day in the woods at Hooge.[6] It was on the next day that 1st Division orders officially christened the woods "Sanctuary Wood".[7] The 1st Camerons received the pleasant surprise of the return of Lieutenant Dunsterville and some of

---

1 TNA WO 95/1278: War Diary of the 1st Gloucestershire Regiment, Frazebrook Account.
2 TNA WO 95/1261: War Diary of the 1st Coldstream Guards, November 1914.
3 TNA WO 95/1272: War Diary of the 2nd Battalion of King's Royal Rifle Corps, 13 November 1914.
4 TNA WO 95/1281: War Diary of the 2nd Welsh, 13 November 1914.
5 TNA WO 95/1227: War Diary of the 1st Division, 13 November 1914.
6 TNA WO 95/1270: War Diary of the 1st Loyal North Lancs, 12 November 1914.
7 TNA WO 95/1274: War Diary of the 3rd Brigade, 14 November 1914.

the other men, who had been posted as missing after 11 November.⁸ The 1st Loyal North Lancs then went to relieve the remnants of 1st Grenadier Guards who moved into Corps reserve.⁹ The 1st South Wales Borderers received a draft of 196 men, but could not accommodate them in the trenches, so sent them back to the ammunition park. The next day Lieutenant Stewart would be sent to organise the draft.¹⁰

On 14 November, the 1st Northants mustered only two officers and approximately 300 men, having received reinforcements of one officer and 76 men the evening before.¹¹ Due to the arrival of 213 reinforcements, and the attachment of Captain Smart of the West Yorkshire Regiment, the 1st Loyal North Lancs now numbered approximately 400 men with two officers.¹² The general paucity of resources available is underlined by the note that a pivot point behind the line which had been held by seventy men of 1st Black Watch, since 11 November, was now to be relieved by 110 men of 1st Cameron Highlanders. The 1st Cameron Highlanders were relieved in turn that evening by the men who had arrived as reinforcements for the 1st Gloucesters and the 1st Northants. In the circumstances, it was decided that when his men were relieved, Major Brown, of the Camerons, would remain behind and retain command of the position. A and B companies of the 2nd Royal Sussex returned to Coalbox Wood to relieve the 1st Irish Guards.

The battalion were relieved finally of their responsibilities, in the line, by 9th Brigade in the early hours of 15 November.¹³ Senior officers in the divisional artillery began planning the movement of batteries in anticipation of 1st Division being relieved; some heavy batteries were withdrawn.¹⁴ That night, the orders from I Corps, notified 1st Division of the impending relief and made it clear that not only were positions to be held but that field companies should not be used to man trenches unless absolutely necessary.¹⁵ Given the numbers remaining in the infantry, only the impending relief was going to give them any chance of recovering and re-organising.

The day had begun with an early success after a failed assault by the infantry the night before. Lieutenant Cottrell led a team which ran up an 18pdr-gun by hand to within 60 yards of the enemy.¹⁶ It then fired five rounds into the stables, which enabled 3rd Division to storm the building and regain its old trenches. The successful assault, that morning, was led by CSM Leonard Gillborn, from Nottingham, of the 1st Northumberland Fusiliers. He was awarded the DCM but died of wounds the same day.¹⁷

---

8   TNA WO 95/1264: War Diary of the 1st Cameron Highlanders, 13 November 1914.
9   TNA WO 95/1267: War Diary of the 2nd Brigade, 13 November 1914.
10   TNA WO 95/1280: War Diary of the 1st South Wales Borderers, 13 November 1914.
11   TNA WO 95/1271: War Diary of the 1st Battalion Northamptonshire Regiment, 14 November 1914 and WO 95/1267: War Diary of the 2nd Brigade, 13 November 1914.
12   TNA WO 95/1270: War Diary of the 1st Loyal North Lancs, 14 November 1914.
13   TNA WO 95/1269: War Diary of the 2nd Royal Sussex, 14 November 1914.
14   TNA WO 95/1239: War Diary of the 1st Division, Royal Artillery, 14 November 1914.
15   TNA WO 95/1227: War Diary of the 1st Division, 14 November 1914.
16   From 54 battery XXXIX Brigade RFA
17   TNA WO 95/1227: War Diary of the 1st Division, 15 November 1914 and TNA WO 95/1376: War Diary of the 3rd Division, 15 November 1914 and TNA WO 95/1239: War Diary of 1st Division, Royal Artillery, 14 November 1914 and with credit to Nottinghamshire County Council for the effort made to remember local men of all ranks see Leonard Gillborn entry at *Nottinghamshire Roll of Honour* <https://secure.nottinghamshire.gov.uk/RollOfHonour/People/Details/32032> (accessed 28 April 2020).

In the evening, the units of 2nd Brigade and 3rd Brigade were relieved by elements of 2nd Division, except two companies of the Gloucesters. The next day, 3rd Brigade ceased to be Corps reserve and 2nd KRRC were released from the line by Lord Cavan. On 17 November, the whole of 1st Division moved into Corps reserve and concentrated in the area between Bailleul and Hazebrook.[18] On 20 November, the whole of I Corps was relieved by the French, and 1st Coldstreams returned to 1st Division.[19] From 23 to 25 November, 3rd Brigade took over some trenches in II Corp's area, suffering 27 more casualties in the process. After their return, the 1st Division began a period of rest and re-fitting.[20]

---

18 TNA WO 95/1227: War Diary of the 1st Division, 17 November 1914.
19 TNA WO 95/1261: War Diary of the 1st Coldstream Guards, November 1914.
20 TNA WO 95/1227: War Diary of the 1st Division, 23-30 November 1914.

18

1st Division in Late November 1914

It is important to reflect upon the divisional formation that Henderson, and then Haking, inherited. The staff calculated that the division, including the artillery, had suffered 7040 casualties, including 218 officers, during the period from 25 October to 20 November.[1] This is equivalent to seven infantry battalions including their officers. Added to the casualties calculated for the period from 21 October, this gives a total for the division's deployment in the Ypres sector of 8748, including 274 officers, equivalent to roughly 71 percent of its infantry strength on mobilisation. Taken together with the casualties sustained on the retreat from Mons, and the advance to the Marne, 1st Division had been reduced to a cadre of its former self, with individual units suffering even more severely.

Due to the events of the retreat, the 2nd Munster Fusiliers had been reduced to a cadre of the original unit within a month of when they had landed. The 1st Loyal North Lancs had been devastated by the fighting on the Aisne and 1st Queens had replaced the 2nd Munster Fusiliers as Corps troops after being reduced to a cadre. The original men of the 1st (Guards) Brigade had been effectively wiped out by the end of First Ypres. Even without the subsequent removal of the Guards brigade, the 1st Division would have needed a significant period of rest to restore its pre-war level of proficiency in musketry, let alone its collective military awareness. It never subsequently was regarded as an elite division until it was accorded the honour of being a part of the Occupying army in Germany after the war ended. In that sense 1st Division was a microcosm of the whole British Army of 1914; even though approximately sixty per-cent of the initial men in its ranks were reservists, they had once been trained professional soldiers. Those original men had not lacked courage or staying power under the extreme exigencies of war. However, the presence of so many reservists does help our understanding of French's orders to abandon baggage during the retreat from Mons.

That retreat had been necessitated by a several factors. The retreat of *French Fifth Army* was a key factor. However, Wilson was guilty of clinging on to a belief regarding the German deployment that encouraged French to advance to far. Wilson, in whose honour, the French dubbed the BEF "Force W" also failed as an objective link. For someone with his unrivalled connexions to the French to have served his C-in-C so ineffectively helped to expose the BEF to potential destruction. 1st Division suffered less during the opening phase due to Haig's

---

1   TNA WO 95/1227: War Diary of the 1st Division, November 1914, Appendix.

caution. This caution contributed to affording the German's just enough time to stand on the Chemin Des Dames. There, and at Ypres, the intense fighting at close quarters drained away the experienced manpower that initially constituted 1st Division.

The men sent to replace them would increasingly be men who had not previously thought of joining the army but who, influenced initially by the popular mood and subsequently under compulsion, came forward to serve their country. Therefore, this marks the point where the history of the original 1st Division ends.

19

Defending the La Bassée Canal

After the shattering events of November 1914, 1st Division was given the opportunity to reorganise and absorb the new men that arrived. During the period from 1–19 December it concentrated on route marching, training in creating field defences and the artillery practising co-operation with aircraft. On 20 December, it started to move forward in support of the Indian Corps who were holding the line. This involved concentrating the 1st Division in the area around Bethune. At this point, 2 Brigade were sent on attachment to the Meerut Division.

Headquarters 1 Brigade and 3 Brigade were put under the orders of the Lahore Division. The immediate consequence was that 1 Brigade were sent towards Gorre. The situation in front of the arriving 1 and 3 Brigades reflected the way in which units had been put in to hold key points as other units had been worn down. North of the La Bassée Canal were the 9th Bhopal and 57th Rifles. From there Givenchy was held by a mixture of French territorials and men of the Manchester Regiment. From there the line bent back and northwards along the Cambrin-Festubert road. This section was held by the Sirhind and Ferozepore Brigades. The remnants of these brigades were no longer capable of offensive action. Forming the hinge between these brigades and the Meerut Division was a unit of the Highland Light Infantry (HLI). The HLI were in fact forming a small salient as they were in advance of the troops on either side. South of the La Bassée Canal the division believed the Connaughts held the line.

The Manchesters in Givenchy were being heavily shelled and aerial reconnaissance reported that German forces were massing opposite their positions. Therefore 1 and 3 Brigades were told to be ready to attack at 2pm. Unfortunately, 1 Brigade could not get forward on schedule as the road was blocked by an Indian cavalry brigade. By 2pm, news was filtering through that the Manchesters had been forced to retire from the hill at Givenchy. The 1st Scots Guards were sent forward to retake Givenchy. By 6pm, 1 Brigade had six companies in Givenchy and it appeared that they were holding the west end along with the remnants of other battalions engaged in the fighting earlier in the afternoon.

Meantime, 3 Brigade was committed to the battle, in order to shore up the line between Givenchy and the canal which was breaking. The 2nd Munsters were put in on the left of 3 Brigade with the task of gaining touch with 1 Brigade. By 10pm, 1 Brigade had established itself in trenches on the East of Givenchy. This had been achieved with the assistance of French territorials who had charged forward on the right of the Scots Guards alongside the Cameron Highlanders. 3 Brigade was also in line but there was a 300-400 yard gap between the two brigades. Officers had been sent to guide the Munsters to cover the gap. At 7am the next morning, 3 Brigade made a further attempt to take the German trenches North and East of Givenchy. According to a wounded officer, they had charged with fixed bayonets but had been unsuccessful. Many of the trenches being contested were heavily waterlogged which complicated any attempt at movement. A further complication was that the opposing troops were so close together that it was difficult to provide artillery support. This was most graphically illustrated by the situation of the South Wales Borders and Welsh. Their trenches were not connected because the Germans still occupied a section of trench between them.

Unsurprisingly, there was a heavy cost to this close quarter fighting. In these two days the division lost 52 officers and 1889 ORs. This represented nearly the equivalent of two whole battalions at full strength. Fortunately, the pressure was eased a bit by the arrival of 2nd Division. This meant that 2 Brigade could be withdrawn along with the rest of the Meerut Division and therefore bring 1st Division the flexibility to rotate units. Major-General Haking spent the morning of Christmas Eve at Corps HQ being briefed on future plans. GHQ issued a warning that the Germans might be planning an attack on Christmas Day so 2 Brigade's relief of 6 Brigade was delayed until Boxing Day. Christmas Day itself saw the Berkshires push forward into an orchard near Givenchy and find some of the wounded from 1st Division. The Scots Guards and London Scottish also managed to recover about 20 wounded men from the fighting on 22 December. In this sector, Christmas Day was marked by a diminution in the level of sniping.

For the next few days, the focus was on strengthening defences and dealing with the impact of rain. It was noted that all units were keen to acquire rifle grenades as they had now learned to appreciate them as they knew how to use them properly. It was also noted that German sniping was increasing south of the canal. This was linked to the effective counter-sniping undertaken north of the canal. German sniping had now reduced significantly north of the canal. On 31 December the Germans turned a minenwerfer on a machine gun post of 2nd KRRC. The post was lost but the guns were saved. Reinforcements were rushed to the scene but it was not possible to retake the position.[1]

As the new year began, 1 Brigade made another attempt to push forward. The Scots guards were again in the lead, advancing north-east from Givenchy church. The attack did not succeed. After a further effort at 3am fared no better, it was decided to cease offensive operations and hold securely what was occupied already. The Scots Guards lost nearly all the officers involved in the assault. Corps ordered that 2 Brigade's positions must be held. Therefore, Haking personally went to the Brigade HQ. He then assigned command of the troops north of the canal to Brigadier Lowther. Brigadier Westmancott was given the task of defending the line south of the canal. Haking was acting very soundly by ensuring all the units, including the attached ones, knew whose command they were under. For all the genuine issues raised later, Haking's approach in 1914 certainly seems to have justified his promotion to Major-General.[2]

The normal tempo of trench holding then resumed. 1 Brigade managed to dig a fresh defensive line in front of their position. All the front line units laid white tape in front of their trenches to assist with the planned aerial photography of the area. Given the level of mud, snipers from 1 Brigade reported the Germans opposite must have been relieved as they could see men in clean

1   TNA WO 95/1228: War Diary of the 1st Division, 20-31 December 1914.
2   TNA WO 95/1227: War Diary of the 1st Division, 1-5 January 1915.

uniforms. In some trenches the water was reported to be three feet deep. Orders were received from Corps to make arrangements to get the troops out of the very wet trenches. On 10 January, the KRRC were able to take back the position they had lost on New Year's Eve. However, it was subsequently abandoned after the Germans proved able to fire on it from behind.[3]

The conditions faced by the troops were central to the visit to 1st Division on 12 January. Both the Corps Commander and Haig as Army commander consulted with Haking. It was decided to get men out of trenches where the water was over the top of their boots. The trenches would then be held by snipers and alternative positions prepared. The sense of permanence settling on the front is reflected in new arrangements. The division in corps reserve will, if the HQs are not co-located, have a brigade HQ connected by cable directly to the Corps HQ. The brigade concerned will have a battalion at 25 minutes notice to move from the time Corps notify the Brigade HQ.[4]

On 25 January the Germans attacked the positions held by 1 and 3 Brigades. They broke through 1 Brigade at the apex near the La Bassée road. On 3 Brigade front the Germans were able to get through past the barrier at Red House and enter Givenchy village. Each brigade committed its reserves and Corps made 5 Brigade available to support 3 Brigade. This reflected the importance attached to holding Givenchy. Both brigadiers were ordered to organise local counterattacks. Whilst waiting for news, Haking went and arranged for units from 8 Brigade to go forward. It was also arranged that if a second attempt was needed using elements of 4 Brigade, then Lord Cavan would take charge of it. In the meantime, a successful counterattack had been carried out by 2nd South Wales Borderers and 2nd Welsh. They had secured Givenchy village.

As there was no progress on 1 Brigade's front Haking then went in person to see Brigadier Lowther. He found that the Keep and Suez Canal positions were still being held. Haking found that the Black Watch had suffered heavily in trying to get forward and that the line now ran east of Cuinchy church and down a communication trench. The Camerons had stabilised their section by establishing a machine gun post. Near the church the lines were very close and both sides were throwing bombs at each other. Haking ordered another battalion up from 2 Brigade. They despatched 2nd Royal Sussex. That battalion joined in an attack with the Black Watch, supported by covering fire from the Coldstream Guards. The attack was successful in restoring the line except where it met the culvert road. Here another trench was dug just to the west of the old one.[5]

Despite warnings from Corps that attacks might be made on the Kaiser's birthday nothing took place. Starting at 2am on 28 January, 40 men from 2 Brigade tried three times to dislodge the Germans from the culvert road but were not successful. The GOC 2 Brigade responded to the Corps commander's request to place machine guns in the upper storeys of Cuinchy by saying that it would be inadvisable as there was constant shelling of the buildings. The Germans attacked Cuinchy on 29 January but were repulsed. The garrison of the Keep was under the command of Captain Villiers. He reported that a key contribution was made by CSM Butcher and his bombing team. A party of Northamptons were digging a trench when the attack began. Their stacked rifles were buried by a minenwerfer shell. The Germans occupied the new trench

---

3   TNA WO 95/1227: War Diary of the 1st Division, 6-10 January 1915.
4   TNA WO 95/1227: War Diary of the 1st Division, 10-24 January 1915.
5   TNA WO 95/1227: War Diary of the 1st Division, 25 January 1915.

until it was retaken by another group of Northamptons led by Sergeant Lodge. Co-operation with the neighbouring French led to French sappers assisting the Irish Guards to dig a new trench. The month closed with the further organising of the arrangements for sniping.[6]

February began with another assault on the culvert road by the Germans. An initial attempt by the Coldstream Guards and Irish Guards was unsuccessful. This created a further problem as it would make the position currently held by the Munsters (3 Brigade) untenable. Again, Haking personally went to see the GOC 4 Brigade. Subsequently the Coldstream Guards regained the first barrier. Following up, the Irish Guards took the second barrier and so the whole position was now secure. On 4 February the division was relieved (except for the Field Companies) and its artillery followed in the succeeding days. From then until 24 February, the division remained in its rest billets. A large number of replacements arrived. The time was devoted to drill, shooting practise and training. On a snowy 25 February, 3 Brigade began the process of relieving 2 Division by entering the Festubert sector. The next day, when Haking was absent, Sir John French paid a visit and each brigadier had an interview with him. By 28 February, the relief was complete with staff based in the Chateau at Hinges.[7]

March opened with more rain which added to the difficult conditions in the trenches. The Indian Corps artillery was relieved by the divisional artillery so the whole division was once again together. On 6 March, 1st Division responded positively to a French army request for fire support during an assault by their *XXI Corps* on Notre Dame de Lorette. It also faced a threat from German mining. 1 Brigade reported their belief that the Germans were mining there area. The brigadier had concentrated RE personnel there to counter-mine and the GOC ordered the CRE to assist. 1 Brigade were put on stand-by to react if an explosion occurred. Haking attended a conference at Corps HQ on 7 March where he was given secret notes on the forthcoming offensive in the area. He was told 1st Division's role would be to hold its ground but be ready to exploit an opportunity if it arose. The growing sense of staying put is reflected in the establishment of a report centre at Le Hamel with telephone cables being laid. Captain Thorne was detailed to be Liaison Officer with the Indian Corps. Lieutenant Hodge, 15th Hussars, was given the same role in relation to the 2nd Division.

The ground in front of 1 Brigade was waterlogged. The Germans had also strengthened their wire and their trenches. Haking was therefore keen to find an alternative area for potential offensive action. After careful reconnaissance, it was decided to attack East of Princes Road and East of Le Plantin. However, on 10 March the main Corps attack took place. Thanks to the report centre and his liaison officers, Haking received a constant flow of updates. 1st Division's role was restricted to sending neighbours assistance by lining trenches behind attacking troops. Effectively they were used as a backstop in case of a German counter-attack. After two days of fighting by I Corps, Haking noted that apparently gun ammunition was "not too plentiful", particularly 4.7" howitzer shells. Over the next few days, 2 Brigade were sent to be a reserve, initially to the First Army but then they were released to I Corps.[8]

On 16 March, Haking turned again to the planned local operation. Captain Boyd and Major Lewis (RE) were sent to reconnoitre to the east of Le Plantin. After they reported back it was decided to attack only part of the German position. Once captured, the position would be joined

---

6   TNA WO 95/1227: War Diary of the 1st Division, 26-31 January 1915.
7   TNA WO 95/1227: War Diary of the 1st Division, 1-28 February 1915.
8   TNA WO 95/1228: War Diary of the 1st Division, 1-15 March 1915.

up to the existing British trenches. The proposed area to be attacked was then reconnoitred by Haking himself. The continuing issue regarding shells meant that the CRA and all artillery brigade commanders had to attend a meeting with the BGGS of First Army. This meeting on 17 March was in response to the higher than expected consumption of ammunition during the recent fighting. The normal business of trench holding continued until 23 March when the division was relieved. This was a brief respite as they were scheduled to replace the Indian Corps at Neuve Chappelle, with HQ based at Locon. As soon as they arrived, it was noted that water levels in the trenches were rising. However, the weather improved quickly so the trenches were drier by the end of the month. In forwarding the War Diary for March, Captain Boyd appended a casualty return. Having not been involved in the Corps assault, these amounted to two officers killed and 13 wounded. Alongside them, 103 Other Ranks had been killed and 475 wounded.[9]

As was often the case, troops were attached for training. It was noted that they are expected to do the same work as the battalions they are attached to. Presumably this dealt with any suggestion that learning to improve your trenches did not count as training. It would have been very difficult if new units were not expected to dig. Haking established a new report centre at Locon and took an early opportunity to discuss potential projects with the Corps GOC. Even at this early stage in the war, attention had to be given to the siting of anti-aircraft guns. In the ongoing battle of the snipers, the Germans had managed to destroy a house used by British snipers. The house took a direct hit from a 6" howitzer. On a lighter note, Lieutenant-Colonel Ravenshaw surprised everyone when he arrived on 7 April to take over the AQMS role from Lieutenant-Colonel Gordon. Clarity was achieved the next day when Lieutenant-Colonel Gordon found out that he was being posted to take command of 2nd Gordon Highlanders.[10] For the platoon officers of all the battalions in 1st Division, April included their GOC's lecture on attack. Haking began his lecture by setting the context in terms of the large-scale reinforcements that would soon be arriving from England and the move by the Anglo-French armies to a vigorous offensive. He said that there was no point sending men against uncut wire. He then went on to tell them that the role of company and platoon commanders was vital. The key thing they should do was to push on, not worrying about their flanks. Haking gave them a clear picture of how guns would be needed to cut the wire. He told them that you could not get enough guns in one place to break all the wire so some of it would not be broken. Therefore, the best thing was to cut small gaps in several places. This would enable men to break into the enemy trenches and then they would spread out and overwhelm the defenders. The implication was that then those faced by uncut wire would be able to follow their colleagues into the German trench system.[11] the other obvious flaw in this logic was that if there were surviving defenders then they only had to concentrate their fire on the small gaps that had been created.

The focus of work in the trenches remained on the strengthening of key positions. Notes on reported sightings of German officers wearing red lapels were passed up to Corps. On 10 April a discussion document on a future attack was received from Corps. Haking only discussed the contents with his CRA and CRE. It has to inferred that this was the original order for the attack from Sir John French which was issued by GHQ on 5 April. Haig was to alter it significantly so it seems he sounded out his senior officers first. On the same night, the officers

---

9   TNA WO 95/1228: War Diary of the 1st Division, 16-31 March 1915.
10   TNA WO 95/1228: War Diary of the 1st Division, 1-8 April 1915.
11   TNA WO 95/1272: War Diary of the 2nd Battalion King's Royal Rifle Corps, April 1915.

of 15th Hussars held a dinner to mark the occasion of the unit leaving the division. On 13 April a secret memorandum came from Corps which said there would be a much improved allocation of ammunition for the guns. As the weather improved so did the conditions for the troops. There were numerous reports regarding the ways in which the Germans were strengthening their defences. This included one instance where they were believed to have created a double tier of firing positions.[12]

Then on 20 April, Haking attended a conference at Corps HQ, the next morning a scheme of attack, marked secret, was discussed. Immediately, 2 Brigade were set to practising signalling. Troops were also sent to practise crossing obstacles. Meanwhile, the GOCs of 2 and 3 Brigades went up to reconnoitre where they thought it would be practicable to make gaps in the wire for the assault. They were accompanied by the GOCs of 39 and 25 Brigades, who were currently attached for trench training. Even though 2 Brigade were part of the proposed operation, they were sent to relieve 3 Brigade in the line. 1 Brigade was designated as Army reserve.

The 2nd Royal Sussex had been billeted at Les Choquax from 12-14 April, and just as they were departing, they received a draft of twenty men. A further draft of 25 men arrived on 21 April during the period that they were billeted at Pont Hinges. At both Les Choquax and Pont Hinges, the focus was on company training and musketry practice.[13] On 23 April, the men of 1st Northamptons enjoyed a football match on their last afternoon at Les Harisoires, before marching to Riche Bourg St Vaast. The following day, Major Cautley DSO, rejoined the battalion from hospital. Having been assigned their billets, most of the men were assigned to working parties during the next three nights, one man was wounded on each night.[14]

The men of the Sussex marched directly to the line at 5.15 p.m. on 24 April, where they relieved the Munster Fusiliers of 3rd Brigade. The guides met them at Windy Corner and B company went into the front line accompanied by a company of 9th King's Liverpool who were allotted to them. A and C companies went into the support trenches whilst D, in reserve, was dispersed in platoons, two platoons were in the dug outs northwest of Rue du Bois, and two went to into trenches and billets 200 yards south of Windy Corner. The Sussex were also accompanied by two artillery officers, one from 114th Battery and one from 39th Brigade RFA, who spent the day observing the German lines. The Sussex also recorded that the firing line they took over was 250 yards ahead of the breastworks that they had occupied when they were last there.[15]

The 1/5 Sussex took over the trenches at Cherbourg L'Avoue, on 28 April. The battalion, as has already been noted for the assault battalions, suffered from heavy shelling by the Germans. April had begun with a move into the trenches at Neuve Chappelle, where they recorded that the enemy were approximately 450 yards away except at a point opposite C company where the positions were only 250 yards apart. On 8 April, Captain Hawthorn had been wounded whilst assisting a wounded man under fire. They also noted, three days later, that in the interval they had succeeded in dominating the Germans and had caused the enemy around thirty casualties. Subsequently, the battalion spent two weeks in a variety of billets and recorded that on 25 and

---

12 TNA WO 95/1228: War Diary of the 1st Division, 9-19 April 1915.
13 TNA WO 95/1269: War Diary of the 2nd Battalion Royal Sussex Regiment, 12 -23 April 1915.
14 TNA WO 95/1271: War Diary of the 1st Battalion Northamptonshire Regiment, 23-26 April 1915.
15 TNA WO 95/1269: War Diary of the 2nd Battalion Royal Sussex Regiment, 24 April 1915.

26 April the whole battalion was involved in working parties on the Rue du Bois so they were tired when they entered the trenches. [16]

Having entertained General Rawlinson for tea on 21 April, Haking received a visit from Haig himself at 3pm on 22 April. A further visit from Haig was arranged for four days later but did not take place.[17] On 25 April, the men of the Sussex recorded that they came under high explosive and shrapnel fire and that about ten per-cent of the high explosive shells failed to explode. They also noted that the German working parties had been continually active and that the focus seemed to have been upon strengthening the wire entanglements. The Germans repeated this on the night of 25/26 April but this time B company of the Sussex decided to open fire with their rifles.[18] As we have seen, this was only the latest report on the work done by the Germans to strengthen their defences. This activity by the Germans reflects the assessment made by Edmonds that they employed the time before the attack to strengthen barbed wire defences in breadth and thickness.[19]

Since December, 1st Division under Haking's energetic leadership held its sector of line successfully. It had had to improvise to regain sections of lost trench but with only minor exceptions this had been achieved. Minor gains at different locations offset minor losses. Even at this stage in the war it was clear that the Germans, with artillery superiority, could always hope to effect an entrance into the British lines. Therefore 1st Division was a good formation and it had now been selected for a forthcoming assault. Haig must have been reassured, following his earlier disagreements with acting GOC Landon, that Haking had restored the fighting edge of the division.

---

16   TNA WO 95/1269/3: War Diary of the 1/5 Battalion Royal Sussex Regiment, 1-27 April 1915.
17   TNA WO 95/1228: War Diary of the 1st Division, 20-26 April 1915.
18   TNA WO 95/1269: War Diary of the 2nd Battalion Royal Sussex Regiment, 26 April 1915.
19   Edmonds, *OH, 1915*, Vol. 2, p.15

20

Aubers Ridge

The 1st Division's part in the battle of Aubers Ridge reflected the Allied decision to mount a joint Anglo-French offensive to put pressure upon the Germans. Cynics have argued that it also meant that the French felt assured that the British would now take an offensive part in operations. The original BEF had suffered the equivalent of 80 percent casualties: in the Official History the overall estimate of the British casualties, from the commencement of hostilities to the end of November, is given as 86,237 other ranks and 3,627 officers, against an original strength of 84,000 in the first seven divisions deployed to Western Europe.[1] In the opening months of the war the French had suffered very heavily. This resulted from the *offensive a l'outrance* legacy. Sending infantry into the assault without artillery support; as Joffre wrote, "In less than 5 months of war, the permanent losses for the active and reserve armies (killed, prisoners and wounded so severely as not to be available in future) is 420,000 men."[2] With their losses running at five times those of the British, the French were naturally keen to involve the British in their next set of offensives.

Joffre's strategic conception was to attack the German defences along the high ground they occupied on Vimy Ridge and Notre Dame de Lorette, in order to open up the opportunity for the French armies to advance across the Douai Plain.[3] Such a strategic breakthrough would have restored the war of movement. However, such a French offensive needed the British to relieve French forces, and the arguments between French and Joffre, exacerbated by Kitchener, did not help to move plans forward. In order to improve critical relations, Foch decided to visit Haig, who would be in charge of the British assault, on 19 April 1915. The meeting went well, and Haig was flattered by Foch being so interested in and complimentary about the success at Neuve Chapelle.[4]

As the Northants rested after two nights of hard work, Haig had a meeting with his corps and divisional commanders on 26 April to explain his plans to them. Haig had decided to attack both north and south of Neuve Chapelle; instead of the main operation being to the south of the village as directed by Sir John on 5 April.[5] This meant that 1st Division would be called upon to

---

1 Edmonds, *OH, 1914*, Vol. 2, p.467.
2 Joffre, J., *Memoires Du Marechal Joffre* (Paris: Librarie Plon, 1932), Vol. 1, p.484.
3 Edmonds, *OH, 1915, vol 2*, p.429.
4 Greenhalgh, *Foch in Command*, p. 110.
5 Edmonds, *OH, 1915*, Vol. 2, p.7.

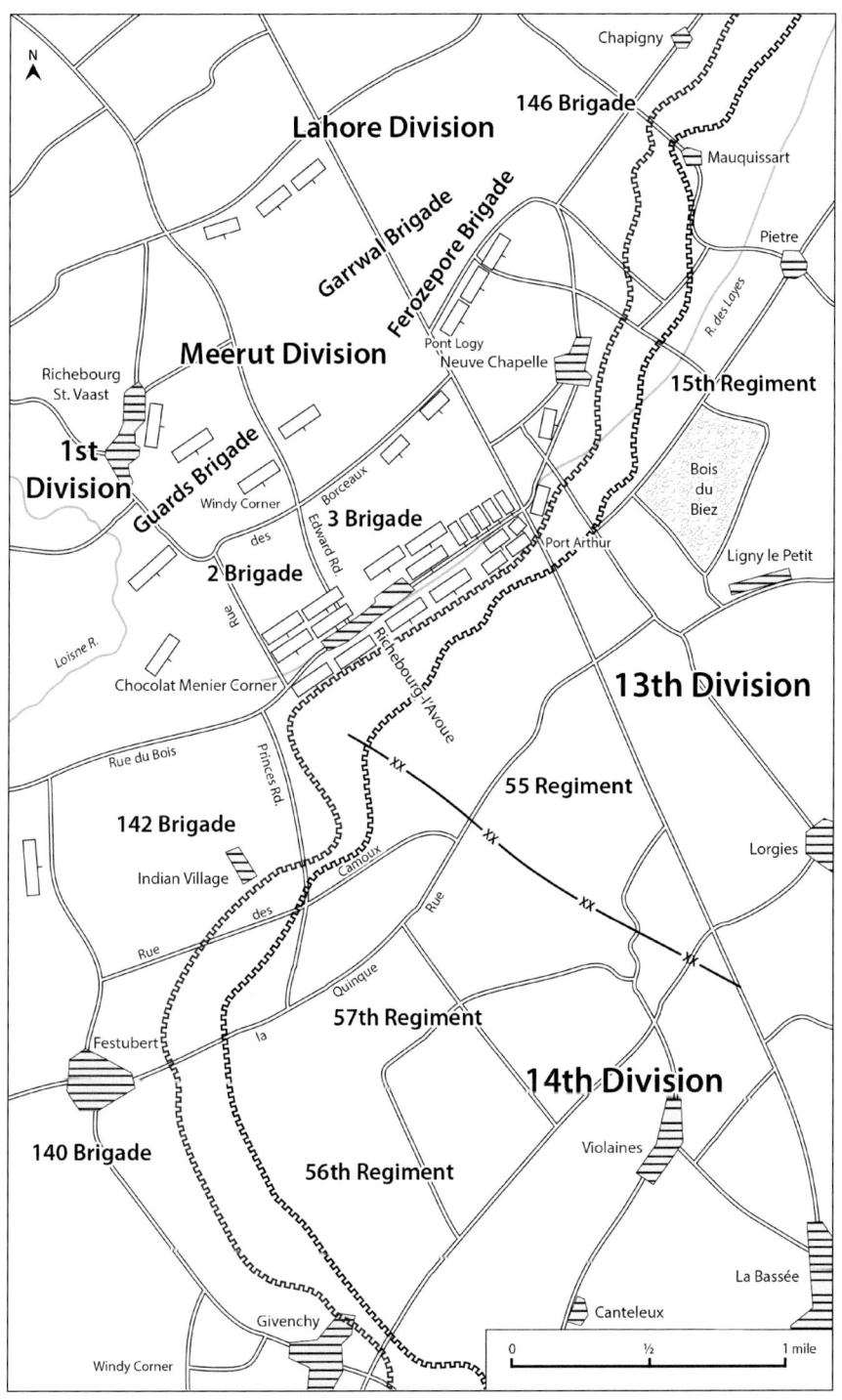

Aubers Ridge, 9 May 1915.

attack south of the village; with 2 Brigade and 3 Brigade carrying out the assault and 1 (Guards) Brigade brought up in support.

On the left would be 3 Brigade with their right resting on the cinder track. Haking's official sketch has markings showing a 200 yard gap between the brigades. This may apply only to the supporting battalions but it appears to apply to the assault too. If so, this would not be inconsistent with his stated view that the breakthrough would be in small sections based on the concentration of the guns. The left leading battalion on this side was 2nd Welsh and 2nd Munsters formed the link to 2 Brigade. Each battalion was to advance in two waves with 2 companies in each. Supporting the 2nd Welsh were the South Wales Borderers with one company leading and three in the second wave. This was copied by the units behind the Munsters. Here, a company of 5th Royal Welsh Fusiliers were in immediate support, They were then to be followed by the Gloucesters with 3 companies behind the 5th Royal Welsh Fusiliers. The final company of the Gloucesters created an extra wave in this section. The attached 60th Rifles and 9th Liverpools had a similar support role for 2 Brigade. As noted above, it had been made official policy that attached units did the same work as their parent. Presumably, it was felt it would be damaging for morale if attached units were excused combat. Being involved in a support role did offer those units an introduction to the stress of combat, for example, the tension as the bombardment began and ended.

The right flank of the attack was to be carried out by 2 Brigade with its right flank resting on Chocolate Menier Corner; whilst on its left 3rd Brigade were responsible for the assault from the cinder track at its junction with 2nd Brigade up to Ferme du Bois at the edge of Orchard Redoubt. The additional responsibility of clearing the enemy trenches to the south of Chocolate Menier Corner was given to a battalion of 2nd Brigade.

The operational orders issued to the assaulting brigades anticipated the future use of leapfrogging. Each brigade, with two battalions in the lead, were given specific lines to entrench upon. Whilst it was the role of the battalion in brigade reserve, with any additional troops that might be "collected", to advance beyond that line.[6] To assist the infantry in destroying strongpoints that could not easily be targeted by the artillery, each assault brigade was assigned a section of 4-inch mortars and a section of 1½-inch mortars in addition to a section of No 7 Mountain Battery, Royal Artillery. To assist with the entrenching of the captured positions, each brigade had the assistance of a field company of the Royal Engineers, minus one section.[7] Each assaulting battalion would be issued with six three-foot square flags to mark their positions to aerial observers; they were additionally enjoined to screen the markers from observation by the enemy.[8]

During the afternoon of 26 April, the Germans appeared to have put three dead over the parapet, which the Sussex linked to their rifle fire. The Sussex then concentrated upon strengthening their own wire after dark by creating "knife rests," at the cost of three men wounded.[9]

On the day after the conference, the Northants were ordered to move into the support trenches which they did at 7.30 p.m., having received seven men back from hospital as well as

---

6 Edmonds, *OH, 1915*, Vol, 2, p.434.
7 Edmonds, *OH, 1915*, Vol, 2, p.435.
8 Edmonds, *OH, 1915*, Vol. 2, p.436.
9 TNA WO 95/1269: War Diary of the 2nd Battalion Royal Sussex Regiment, 26 April 1915

Second Lieutenant Davison who rejoined the battalion as it held the line at Windy Corner.[10] The next day they moved forward into close support to the Sussex[11] in the trenches. The Northants recorded that they were in the front trenches, but this confusion arises from C company of the Sussex having been sent forward to the fire trench, so the Northants were asked to occupy the breastworks which had previously constituted the front line. Nevertheless, the Northants were still employed each night on trench repairs and improvements. The Sussex received a draft of 93 men which were distributed to companies but suffered four other ranks being wounded during the day. Then they found a working party from the men of D company, including Lieutenant Downes who was subsequently wounded, to work on the left communication trench.[12]

The 28 April saw the Sussex relieved by their own first line territorials of 1/5 Sussex at 8 p.m. and the regular battalion reached its billets in Pont Avelette at 3 a.m., having had one man killed. The following day was therefore spent in company training and giving the men a chance to have a bath.[13] The perils of dealing with live ammunition were underlined on 29 April when Lieutenant Wauchope, of the Northants, was wounded when a grenade, being loaded into a catapult, exploded prematurely.[14] On the next day the Sussex practised bomb throwing as well as more men getting a bath. Brigadier Westmacott went on leave to England and so Lieutenant Colonel Green DSO of the Sussex became the temporary officer commanding 2 Brigade, leaving Captain Cameron in temporary charge of the Sussex.[15]

May Day saw the Northants back in the support trenches and undergoing an hour's bombardment, which forced them to stand to in case of an attack. [16] The bombardment also caused the Sussex to be aroused at 5 a.m. They were initially told to be at readiness to move. Therefore, the battalion was allowed to breakfast and then waited but no further orders were received and so, later in the day, training was carried out within companies. The diary noted the opinion that the Germans had anticipated an attack and so had tried to disrupt it; and that the Camerons at Lacoutre had suffered casualties in the bombardment.[17] If the troops had known that the actual planned hour for the bombardment to herald the real attack was also scheduled for 5 a.m. it would have been very disquieting that the Germans had bombarded them at that hour.

The next day, the 2nd Sussex, having lost Captain Dashwood (who was evacuated as a measles case) marched to Allouange.[18] whilst The Northamptons were relieved by the Coldstream Guards at 9 p.m. Having been relieved, they marched out to billets at Oblingham, where they were technically in Army Reserve. They reached their billets at 1 a.m., having stopped for tea at Essairs after two hours. A draft of 81 men arrived which put their strength at approximately 1000, with a trench strength of around 800. 3 May was spent cleaning up the billets, whilst the following day was spent in drill and cleaning kit etcetera.

10   TNA WO 95/1271: War Diary of the 1st Battalion Northamptonshire Regiment, 26 April 1915.
11   TNA WO 95/1269: War Diary of the 2nd Battalion Royal Sussex Regiment, 26 April 1915.
12   TNA WO 95/1269: War Diary of the 2nd Battalion Royal Sussex Regiment, 27 April 1915.
13   TNA WO 95/1269: War Diary of the 2nd Battalion Royal Sussex Regiment, 28 April 1915.
14   TNA WO 95/1271: War Diary of the 1st Battalion Northamptonshire Regiment, 29 April 1915.
15   TNA WO 95/1269: War Diary of the 2nd Battalion Royal Sussex Regiment, 30 April 1915.
16   TNA WO 95/1271: War Diary of the 1st Battalion Northamptonshire Regiment, 29 April-1 May 1915.
17   TNA WO 95/1269: War Diary of the 2nd Battalion Royal Sussex Regiment, 1 May 1915.
18   TNA WO 95/1269: War Diary of the 2nd Battalion Royal Sussex Regiment, 2 May 1915.

On 4 May, Haking attended a conference at Corps HQ. The Conference was presided over by Haig. Haking's staff noted that the Germans were continuing to build up their defences and that everything was a lot stronger than two weeks ago. The next day a conference was held by Haking at his HQ. It was attended by the brigadiers, the CRA and CRE. Operational orders were issued and a presentation was given about the obstacles the troops were likely to face. The staff again noted further strengthening of the German defences.

The 1/5 Sussex had placed A company and Headquarters in the front trenches and were accompanied by a company of 1/9 King's Liverpool "for trench instruction". The German minenwerfer fire they experienced on 28 April and the artillery bombardments on subsequent days would therefore have been a true baptism of fire for the King's. The Sussex claimed to have supressed the minenwerfers by using rifle grenades, but they could not prevail against the artillery.[19]

On 7 May it was reported to Haking that all the guns were now in position and had registered. When Corps postponed the attack for 24 hours, the staff moved to get all the men under cover. At 6.40 pm on 8 May, Corps confirmed that the attack was to go in on 9 May. Therefore at 1am, Haking departed for his battle station 200 yards north of Chocolate Meunier Corner. The observation point was under the roof of the house and the command centre was in the basement. The Royal Engineers had specially strengthened the room. One aspect of the successful formula to be followed in the "100 Days of 1918" was present on 9 May 1915, and that was the placing together in the Rue de Bois, approximately 300 yards behind the front line, of Haking's battle headquarters and the HQs of both assault brigades. Therefore, Major-General Haking had Brigadier-General Thesiger[20] (2 Brigade) and Brigadier-General Davies (3 Brigade) close at hand, with each commander occupying a house reinforced with sandbags. In addition, Brigadier-General Fanshawe, BGRA of 1st Division, was in the same house as Major General Haking.[21] The divisional report said this battle station had a clear view of the German trenches which were 650 yards away. Haking had been wounded in 1914 and would be again, his personal courage cannot be questioned.

2 Brigade prepared to carry out the assault and was disposed as follows; the assault battalions were the 1st Northamptons and 2nd Royal Sussex led by Lieutenant Colonels Dobbin and Green respectively. The Northamptons were informed that they were to carry out an assault with artillery support at 5 a.m. the next morning.[22] In support therefore were 2nd KRRC, under the command of Major Philips and 1/5th Royal Sussex, whose commanding officer was Lieutenant Colonel Langham. To their rear, and behind the Rue de Bois, were 1st Loyal North Lancs under Lieutenant Colonel Sanderson alongside Major Bolland and 1/9th Kings. Each of the assaulting battalions was assigned a front of 350 yards.[23]

The Northamptons entered the trenches just south of the Rue de Bois and recorded that they and the 2nd Sussex had been "given the honour of making the initial assault" and had a trench strength of 26 officers and approximately 750 other ranks. The diarist also recorded that all

19 TNA WO 95/1269/3: War Diary of the 1/5 Battalion Royal Sussex Regiment, 28 -30 April 1915.
20 Thesiger had just replaced Westmancott, the latter had not been able to return from leave due to medical grounds.
21 Edmonds, *OH, 1915*, Vol. 2, p.20.
22 TNA WO 95/1271: War Diary of the 1st Battalion Northamptonshire Regiment, 7 May 1915.
23 Edmonds, *OH, 1915*, Vol. 2, p.20.

ranks were "keen and eager for the coming fight". This spirit is reflected in the early entry for 9 May, as the diary notes that everyone was up early carrying out last minute preparations, dealing with stores such as wire cutters, bombs, and flags for various purposes.

The battalion had the company of two officers of the Royal Engineers who were mining experts and were there to cut the wires to any mines in the captured trenches.[24]

Ahead of the men of 1st Division, as they waited in their trenches as the sun rose at 4.06 a.m. on 9 May 1915, were passages made in their wire. These were the ones selected by their brigadiers. There were also ladders to assist leaving the trench, and 64 light bridges had been built to help carry them across any dykes. RE personnel had laid these out during the night. The divisional report says they were laid out without hindrance. No one seems to have considered whether they were a massive giveaway to the Germans as to where the attack was coming and that it must be on 9 May. Forty-four minutes later, the artillery bombardment opened with Brigadier-General Fanshawe, BGRA of 1st Division, in charge of the Corps artillery.[25] Edmonds estimates that the Corps had the support of 96 field guns assigned to wire cutting, situated 1600 yards from the German wire, whilst 46 howitzers were in position a thousand yards to the rear with the objective of destroying the German parapets. However, it should be noted that of the 96 guns assigned to cutting the wire, twelve were 15-pdrs. belonging to the territorials of V London Brigade RFA and a further eighteen were 13-pdrs. belonging to the N, V and X batteries of the RHA.[26] None of these smaller guns would have had much effect so the division was only supported by 66 field guns plus the howitzers. In Point 9 of his report, Haking stated that the front was too wide for effective wire cutting unless more time was devoted to it.[27]

The plan involved the artillery opening fire at 5am to cut wire and moving from a "deliberate" to an "intense" bombardment at 5.30 a.m. This change of tempo was intended to allow the infantry to move forward from their trenches and deploy within eighty yards of the German trenches. The infantry assault itself was due to take place at 5.40 a.m. when the artillery would lift to targets beyond the German front line and to create a barrage on the right flank. At this point 1 (Guards) Brigade was due to occupy some of the British front-line positions and the 47th Division were tasked with occupying some of the original first-line positions behind them. The artillery was then scheduled to carry out a further lift and barrage the second line objectives from 6.15 to 6.45 a.m.[28]

Counter-battery work was hampered by some topographical features. The possibility of using sound ranging was also ruled out. The French had adopted the technique and recommended it to the BEF. Two artillery experts were sent by GHQ but did not consider it worth pursuing. Therefore, the request to the War Office for the appropriate equipment was only submitted in August 1915.[29]

As the opening bombardment intensified at 5.30 a.m., the men of 2 Brigade endeavoured to carry out their plan of leaving the trenches and forming up eighty yards from the enemy

---

24   TNA WO 95/1269: War Diary of the 2nd Battalion Royal Sussex Regiment, 7-8 May 1915.
25   Brigadier-General Montgomery, BGRA of I Corps had no executive authority, in common with his contemporaries in that role. This was subsequently changed.
26   Edmonds, *OH, 1915*, Vol. 2, p.17.
27   TNA WO 95/1228: War Diary of the 1st Division Headquarters, May 1915, Appendix 36.
28   Edmonds, *OH, 1915*, Vol. 2, p.436.
29   Edmonds, *OH, 1915*, Vol. 2, p.19.

trenches. However, Edmonds comments that it had been hoped to carry out this manoeuvre undisturbed but that the Germans opened fire, having been able to look over their parapet during the bombardment. Haking's divisional diary noted that the Sussex were out of their trenches first but that the Germans manned their trenches with bayonets fixed and started firing. The leading waves suffered heavily from rifle and machine gun fire. Haking only saw the Munsters break into the trenches and it was noted that this is where Major Rickard was killed.[30]

Edmonds commented that no provision had been made for covering rifle fire "in accordance with pre-war teaching".[31] Part of the solution to this problem would ultimately come in the form of barrages by heavy machine guns, but in 1915 the guns themselves were too scarce to be brigaded separately. This would only be possible when the Lewis gun had been designed and produced in sufficient quantities. By the later stages, each infantry battalion would have 32 Lewis guns, sixteen times the number of Vickers guns issued to a battalion in 1914. The assault by the Northamptons was led by company D under Captain Farrar and company B led by Captain Dickinson. It was these two companies that went forward under cover of the bombardment to within a hundred yards of the German positions[32], not the whole battalion as Edmonds implies. Headquarters and C and A companies did move beyond the British line but were in support of the other companies so they cannot have been as close.

Edmonds then summarises the attempts of the Northamptons to break into the German line and gives their casualties as amounting to seventeen officers and 543 other ranks. These figures which would easily compare to those more famously suffered on the first day of the Somme in 1916.[33] Captain Dickinson and about twenty men found a gap in the wire cut by the British guns. Captain Dickinson was killed almost immediately as was Captain Farrar. The diary bears out Edmonds' summary by stating that the men were mown down by rifle and machine gun fire, and that the British artillery had not done much damage to the German breastwork, wire, or their trenches. The Northamptons reported that they were under heavy fire from the distillery. Haking felt that the fire was probably coming from Point V6 which was an objective of the Meerut Division. He therefore checked on the progress of that attack. Once Haking knew the Meerut were held up too, he ordered an artillery bombardment on V6. He also tried to co-ordinate with the Indian Corps so that bombardment and renewed assault were co-ordinated.[34] Many of the Northamptons were then forced to lie out in No man's Land during the day, though a few who had not got far were able to get back to the British line. The German artillery then bombarded the British line and the Rue du Bois. Once darkness fell, those who could crawled back to their own lines, and those wounded who could be retrieved were; the medical officer was kept busy.[35]

Alongside them, 2nd Sussex lost fourteen officers and 537 men.[36] Their day had begun at 3.30 a.m. with the issue of tea and rum. The battalion was to be led forward by C and D companies, left and right respectively, supported by A and B, though No 8 platoon was detached

---

30 TNA WO 95/1228: War Diary of the 1st Division Headquarters, 9 May 1915.
31 Edmonds, *OH, 1915*, Vol. 2, p.20.
32 TNA WO 95/1271: War Diary of the 1st Battalion Northamptonshire Regiment, 9 May 1915.
33 Edmonds, *OH, 1915*, Vol. 2, pp.22-23.
34 TNA WO 95/1228: War Diary of the 1st Division Headquarters, May 1915, Appendix 36.
35 TNA WO 95/1271: War Diary of the 1st Battalion Northamptonshire Regiment, 9 May 1915.
36 Edmonds, *OH, 1915*, Vol. 2, p.22-23.

and occupied the breastworks to the rear of the Rue du Bois. The battalion decided to locate two of its four machine guns on its left flank whilst the other two were placed approximately one hundred yards from its right flank, which means they were roughly in the centre of the assault, as the battalion frontage was approximately 350 yards. Like the Northamptons, the Sussex moved forward at 5.30 a.m. with B and D companies going over the parapet. The platoons advanced in line, except for fifteen platoon under Second Lieutenant Roberts and thirteen platoon under Second Lieutenant Child, who crossed at a particular spot where there was cover. They were followed by A company whose platoons advanced in pairs,[37] so again a significant part of the assaulting battalion could not have been as close to the German positions as Edmonds believed based upon issued orders.

The supporting battalions also suffered significant casualties, with 2nd KRRC losing eleven officers and 240 other ranks, whilst 1/5 Sussex lost the same number of officers and 191 men.[38] For 1/5 Sussex, the orders were to follow immediately behind the assaulting battalions and act as the moppers-up to clear the enemy left as the assault progressed, including securing prisoners and sending them to the rear. The battalion was to support the assault, which had the primary objective of consolidating the farm at Q10 as a strong point. They were then to proceed to the second objective which involved securing all the buildings which comprised Ferme Cour d'Avoue. The final brigade objective line would prove to be as irrelevant as these initial goals. The battalion was to attack with A and C company leading on the right and left respectively, with each company forming the first two lines. B company was tasked with going forward behind A and then helping to support the 1st Northants.[39] This too helps to explain the problems that would occur; if the initial assault were to fail, the supporting troops were being spread thinly and could therefore only provide limited additional impetus.

As the support battalion, 1/5 Sussex initially had to advance across 250 yards of open ground before they would reach the British advanced trench. Both B and C companies went forward minus one platoon each. Their records state that they came under heavy rifle, machine gun and shell fire during this first part of the advance and that C company suffered approximately 30 casualties including Second Lieutenant Haigh who was wounded. As the leading companies were pinned down in No Man's Land, Lieutenant Colonel Langham ordered the platoons that had been left behind not to advance. In particular, the Germans were able to take advantage of a salient in their line, to the battalion's left, to pour machine gun fire on to the area in front of the British advanced trench. In the case of C company, another platoon had also been told not to advance by their own company commander, but casualties still occurred in the advanced trench with the lieutenant being wounded. The attack had gone so badly that by 7 a.m. they had received an order to retire; three times. Sergeant Roberts took orders up to the firing line despite the heavy enemy fire.

However, these orders were subsequently modified in line with the evolving plans of the generals to launch another attack. Langham received orders to gather his men together in D5 Line and to be ready to resume the attack. Amongst the fatalities suffered by this stage was twenty-three-year-old Second Lieutenant Fazan from Bexhill-on Sea. In addition, Major Langham had been wounded along with three subalterns: Dodd, Perry, and Hobart. The usual

---

37 TNA WO 95/1269: War Diary of the 2nd Battalion Royal Sussex Regiment, 9 May 1915.
38 Edmonds, *OH, 1915*, Vol. 2, pp.22-23.
39 TNA WO 95/1269/3: War Diary of the 1/5 Battalion Royal Sussex Regiment, 9 May 1915.

toll of company officers in such actions was completed by captains Stewart and Grant being posted missing along with 2nd-Lieutenants Powell and Dennison. Alongside these individuals a further 230 other ranks were killed, wounded, and missing.[40] So, the battalion had lost almost a quarter of its nominal strength, equal to a third of its effective trench strength, as a support battalion in an attack which had barely reached the enemy trenches in a few scattered places. If the CO had not acted to hold some platoons back the casualty roll would have been even longer.

Meanwhile the support brigade had been moving forward into the back lines. Brigadier Lowther reported to the battle HQ at 6am. Within an hour, the two assaulting corps and divisions had compared notes. Both now knew the other had failed. After the renewed assault by 2 Brigade, their GOC reported that his men could not get forward. He stated that the Germans were using low loopholes in their breastwork through which to fire machine guns at his men. Haking states that at 7.30pm he informed I Corps that he did not propose to use 1 (Guards) Brigade because it would be pointless. At 8am, Haking spoke by telephone to the BGGS at I Corps. He was asked if his guns were anchored for wire cutting. He said they were. He was therefore ordered to the start of deliberate wire cutting once his troops were clear. He said he told Corps that he thought there was no point using 2nd Division. He stated that he was told to await orders regarding whether to use 1 (Guards) Brigade . Haking received another call 45 minutes later from the BGGS to say Haig wanted 2 and 3 Brigades to make a further effort. Haking's account of the conversation says he told the BGGS that he had just spoken to the GOC 3 Brigade who felt that a further assault was not possible due to the machine gun fire. Nonetheless, he was ordered to go ahead. A further call an hour later confirmed that Haig had set the assault for Noon. Haking again explained the losses suffered. Haking was then told he could attack on a one battalion front if necessary.[41]

It is clear that Haking's next meeting was a difficult one. Haking met with the GOC 2 Brigade who said he did not think his brigade would attack again. Haking told him they had too. However, Haking's doubts about the attack seemed to be further revealed in the next exchange. Haking gave the GOC the option to attack on a one battalion front. Theissiger thought that two battalions would be better but agreed with Haking that there was no need to pile up men in the assault trenches. They agreed that there was no need to put out more men at first than was necessary. It seems there was an unspoken agreement to limit the number of lives wasted on fulfilling an order neither agreed made sense.

Haking received a further call to say that the new assault would be put back to 2pm as the Indian Corps would not be ready until then. Haking was also told to be sparing with ammunition. Given that cutting the wire was key to the success of the renewed attack this did not augur well. Haking noted that up till then 1st Division had used 12,500 18pdr shells. It is notable that they had used almost twice as many shells for the smaller calibre field guns. Therefore, only about one-third of the shells fired were likely to have done any real damage. Haking then met with the brigadiers of 2 and 3 Brigades. They discussed the situation and the heavy casualties. Haking amended the objectives to reaching the German second line. It was noted that although the 9th Liverpools had not been engaged in the battle they had become scattered. Both their CO and Adjutant were known to be casualties by this time. It is likely

---

40 TNA WO 95/1269/3: War Diary of the 1/5 Battalion Royal Sussex Regiment, 9 May 1915.
41 TNA WO 95/1228: War Diary of the 1st Division Headquarters, May 1915, Appendix 36.

that the unit had taken a battering from the German guns firing on the Rue des Bois. In their assembly positions they were close to the road.

Corps then telephoned Haking again to delay the infantry assault until 4.20pm. Haking had been in further discussions with GOC 2 Brigade. Haking had queried how 1st Loyal North Lancs had also suffered heavy casualties as they had not been engaged. Nonetheless, Haking sent the figures on available men to Corps and said that he would have to put in 1 (Guards) Brigade instead unless Corps objected. The brigade was Corps Reserve so this was a real decision for Corps to make. At 12.40pm, Corps telephoned Haking to say he should put 1 (Guards) Brigade into the attack. He was also told that IV Corps and the French attacks had been successful. Corps also informed him that if the next attack failed then Corps intended to make a further attack with 2nd Division at dusk. Haking therefore saw the relevant brigadiers and gave them their orders. Haking gave each brigadier full authority over their half of the assault. 2 Brigade were assigned the role of defending the British trenches in case of a German attack. GOC 2 Brigade was told that he could rely on the support of 1 and a hal battalions from 1(Guards) Brigade but ONLY if the Germans captured his trenches and a counter-attack was necessary.

At 3.15pm, Major-General Horne, GOC 2nd Division arrived to assess the situation. He and Haking then conferred with Corps. It was felt it would take six hours for 2nd Division to be ready to assault given that their officers would need time for reconnaissance. Haking said he had two brigades ready to field two battalions each so 1st Division would try again. It was also agreed that if this attack were successful 2nd Division would then push troops forward as Haking's troops were unlikely to push very deep without support.

The attack opened at 4pm. Initially Haking was informed some Black Watch platoons had entered the German trenches. At 2.30 p.m., 1/5 Sussex had been ordered to occupy the D Line in readiness to support 1(Guards) Brigade who were to attack at 4.30 p.m. Their diary records that the subsequent attack of the Black Watch, supported by men from 2 Sussex and 1/5 Sussex who got up too, "failed as it did in the morning". [42] Ten minutes after the first report, Haking was told 510 men had got in. He therefore ordered 1Brigade to throw in everything they had got. He also told 2 Brigade to throw in all the support they could. Whilst there would have been a lot of smoke, if the HQ had a clear view, then the 510 men of the Black Watch would have been visible and the report could have been checked. In his after action report, the GOC 1 (Guards) Brigade estimated that about 50 to 60 of his men were able to climb the parapet, mostly on the right. He put the failure of the Loyal North Lancs to get forward in support down to the order being countermanded as 3 Brigade's attack had failed. By 4.30 the reports were much bleaker. 1 Brigade had by now revised its estimate down to the original two platoons and confirmed the Cameron Highlanders had not reached the trenches. 3 Brigade also said they had made no entry. At 4.40pm, Haking told his brigadiers to withdraw their men under cover of the artillery fire.

Many of the critics of First World War British generals are accused of abusing the power of hindsight, but the casualties sustained in the renewed assault could be seen to be pointless at the time against unsuppressed defences. It was possible to over-estimate the effect the artillery

---

42   TNA WO 95/1269/3: War Diary of the 1/5 Battalion Royal Sussex Regiment, 9 May 1915.

had before the morning assault but not afterwards. Haking's own account says his advice not to renew the assault was ignored.

The 1/5 Sussex were then relieved and gathered at Chocolate Menier Corner, from where they set off in fours through "a considerably disorganised mob of men from other regiments."[43] However, the damage done to the battalion itself was evident just under three weeks later when both the Adjutant and Captain Dawes were sent to hospital with nervous breakdowns. They recorded that by the end of May the battalion had six company officers and "360 effective rifles for the firing line" with a total battalion strength of 566.[44]

The 1st Division estimated its total casualties on 9 May as 3968. This included 160 officers of whom 49 were killed, 79 wounded and 32 missing. The cost in Other Ranks was 3808, of whom 595 had been killed, 2255 wounded and 958 posted missing. The equivalent of an entire brigade had been lost for no gain at all. A key reason why the whole division suffered so badly for is hinted at in Edmond's account, where he says that whilst Haig was kept very well informed, the reports he received did not make clear the extent of the failures or the heaviness of the losses. Unless Haking's account was a complete fabrication then this is clearly incorrect. He advised Corps that he would not be inclined to use 1 Brigade and sent details of the remaining strengths of battalions in 2 Brigade. The latter was sent to justify the view that it was not fit for renewing the assault. Haig had to be aware therefore of the level of casualties. The dichotomy in their views is evident from Point 33 of Haking's report; "Unless the first assaulting line gets in, it is useless to push other troops in on top of it."

Therefore, it is clear Haig wanted to renew the assault against the advice of a trusted combat commander. The response from Major General Haking was that if the wire was cut by deliberate artillery fire and a few more machine guns knocked out, then it would be possible to attack again after mid-day, and so it was agreed that zero hour for the second assault would be at Noon. In order to carry out these orders to which he had agreed, Haking told 2 and 3rd Brigades to ready their supporting battalions for the renewed assault and obtained permission from Corps to utilise the Black Watch and Camerons of 1st Guards Brigade too.[45]

Despite the steady shelling of the German positions, including the communication trenches, during the interval between the two assaults, the German *55th Regiment* received more reinforcements than the casualties it had suffered because of the first assault.[46] The failure to damage the German positions in the initial assault helps to explain why so many machine guns were able to fire at the assaulting troops. Lowther said there was heavy machine gun fire from the left, which explains why his right companies of the Black Watch were more successful. They were on the right of 1 Brigade, furthest from these machine guns. Haking too had machine guns as key; he had spoken to his DMO who said many of the wounds were consistent with machine gun bullets rather than rifle fire.[47]

Haking submitted long and detailed observations at the end of his after action narrative. These dealt with key issues such as the way in which deliberate wire cutting removed the

---

43 TNA WO 95/1269/3: War Diary of the 1/5 Battalion Royal Sussex Regiment, 9 May 1915.
44 TNA WO 95/1269/3: War Diary of the 1/5 Battalion Royal Sussex Regiment, 24-31 May 1915.
45 Edmonds, *OH, 1915*, Vol. 2, pp.24-25.
46 Edmonds, *OH, 1915*, Vol. 2, p.25.
47 The DMO based this analysis on cleaned wounds whereas at short range it was common for German riflemen to reverse the bullet or manually blunt it.

element of surprise. He also made the point that each of the German trench lines had obstacles between. He pointed out that this would have diminished the effect of the bombardment as there was twice as much to destroy. Haking also drew attention to his decision to reduce the lift by the artillery to 50 yards for the final assault. He felt this should be the rule to help the men get into the parapet. He also said that he observed Germans with fixed bayonets during the bombardment. He felt the German positions were strong enough that many of them had not needed to wait in their dugouts.

In short, the attack by 1st Division on Aubers Ridge failed because the artillery preparation was inadequate to destroy the strong defensive position that the Germans had built up. Many of the guns were of inadequate calibre and too short a time was allocated to wire cutting. Even as preparations for the assault were underway, the senior staff were noting the increasing strength of the German position. The level of supply of gun ammunition was a concern throughout this period. On the day itself, Haking was told to economise on gun ammunition at the time he was told to prepare for the afternoon assault. All these factors contributed to the scale of casualties but there was another one. The documentary evidence is clear that Haig insisted on a further attack even though he was aware of the scale of casualties suffered in the morning. That the official historian could argue otherwise seems to rest upon a belief that Haking would not go public in his own defence. On that correct assessment, Edmonds was able fudge the issue of Haig's culpability.

After the action was called off, 2nd Division moved up to relieve 1st Division. By 3am on 10 May, the relief was complete and 1st Division moved into Corps reserve. It is possible to believe that the senior officers believed the men were cheerful and keen on the way to the front line. It begs belief that the staff could record on 12 May "the troops were not disheartened". The 1st Division then returned to the line covering Givenchy and Cuinchy, 2 Brigade entering divisional reserve. [48]

---

48   TNA WO 95/1228: War Diary of the 1st Division Headquarters, 9 May 1915.

21

Divisional Re-organisation and Departure of the Guards

The 1st Division remained in the line for several days following the Aubers Ridge assault. On 13 May Sir Douglas Haig arrived and told Haking that his division was to move south and relieve the French *58th Division*. The GOC London Division would command both his own and 1st Division in order to form a solid defensive front. On 15 May when they entered the trenches, the division found they were good ones "clean and strong". It was also arranged that the French would leave behind three batteries of 75mm guns for four days. The staff made notes of the successes of the I Corps and Indian Corps.[1]

On 20 May, the division continued to assist the Corps offensive by taking over line from 47th Division. This meant 1st Division now had all three brigades in the line. This seems to mark a key point where the division was not seen as one to call upon for offensive operations. The needs of the fighting divisions were causing further supply issues; it was noted on 21 May that the issuance of 13pdr ammunition should take place only under exceptional circumstances. The rest of the month was spent improving the trenches, rotating units and following the news from other fronts.[2]

June opened with a busy day of engagements for the GOC. First, he welcomed General Arendrop and his staff from the Danish Army. They were on an official visit to see the trenches. Then he went to meet Generals Franks and Fanshaw. During this latter meeting it was agreed on the support 1st Division would provide for forthcoming operations. In addition, it was confirmed that the GOC 47th Division would take over the responsibility for the line at 6pm on 2 June. Even though future operations were being prepared it was noted that ammunition supply was not adequate. Before the men were relieved the Germans exploded a mine in front of Hanover Street and Seymour Street. The Germans made no move to attack. Therefore, their motive seems to have been related to British mining. The explosion destroyed No 9 Sap. Seven tunnellers were killed along with 8 men of the 1st Loyal North Lancs who were manning the thirty yards of trench that were destroyed. At a meeting at 4pm the brigadiers of 1 and 3 Brigades received details of the planned attack on the Haisnes-Douvrin Ridge. The CRE and CRA were also present. It was noted that preparations had to be complete by 7 June but that it was unlikely that operations would take place that soon. It was also noted that ammunition was

1   TNA WO 95/1228: War Diary of the 1st Division Headquarters, 11-15 May 1915.
2   TNA WO 95/1228: War Diary of the 1st Division Headquarters, 16-31 May 1915.

being conserved again as it seemed useless to start operations without a fortnight's supply for all guns. Repington's story in *The Times* about the shortage of shells had caused a furore on 14 May. These notes by a senior commander a fortnight later offer an interesting insight into operational constraints and offer support to the argument that there was a genuine shortage. The following day the divisional commanders met with General Haig at First Army HQ where it was noted that almost all the guns were in position, but that registration had not started yet.[3]

When 1st Division re-entered the line on 5 June, a further problem manifested itself. A gas expert demonstrated that the gas itself was effective. However, it became evident that the respirators issued to the troops were not effective. The head pieces were effective to protect the eyes so they would be used. However, in addition an ordinary cap comforter would be worn. It was also becoming evident that further operations were not going to go ahead soon so the focus was switching to deep mining under the German trenches around the site of the newly created mine crater. The Division had also received a circular from Haig that bombs [grenades] should now be treated as a standard element in the stocks carried by DACs and subordinate units. With shells in short supply, it is interesting to see the flow of other munitions developing.[4]

Offensive operations were once again postponed by corps headquarters on 9 June. On the following day, after a meeting at IV Corps HQ, it was noted that there "did not seem to be much ammunition about". Indecision at Corps also related to who was going to carry out the attack, 2nd Division had been told to reconnoitre the ground south of the La Bassée Road. This issue had arisen because it was now considered difficult just to attack north of the road. This was because a salient in the German line could enfilade such an attack. One might ask why such a basic consideration had not come up for discussion originally.[5]

The divisional war diary for June contains many more lengthy entries than the norm. Part of a long entry on 10 June offers an unusual contemporaneous insight into the thinking of senior commanders in IV Corps and presumably First Army:

> Last month the German line was gradually eaten right through but losses were heavy amongst practically all the divisions of 1st Army. Fresh troops and plenty of ammunition were required to continue the eating through process, after a pause to allow the gunners to rest. These fresh troops were not at hand but they may be now.[6]

The staggering thing about this entry is that seems to show that First Army, that is Haig, believed that the German lines had been "eaten through" at Aubers Ridge. The similarity between this and Haig's assertions after the first day at Loos is also very striking. Haig's mindset was that he was right as long as there were plenty more troops available to "eat through" the German positions. No doubt the evidence here will be ignored by those historians who dismiss "carefully footnoted arguments"[7] which in other historical disciplines are regarded as indicative of scholarship.

---

3   TNA WO 95/1228: War Diary of the 1st Division, 1-4 June 1915.
4   TNA WO 95/1228: War Diary of the 1st Division, 5-6 June 1915.
5   TNA WO 95/1228: War Diary of the 1st Division, 7-9 June 1915.
6   TNA WO 95/1228: War Diary of the 1st Division, 10 June 1915.
7   See Foreword to Gary Sheffield's *The Chief* (London: Aurum, 2011), p.vi. German General Max Hoffman's judgement, the title of Alan Clark's infamous 1962 volume, needs to be taken with

The continuing difficulties in securing enough shells was evident on 14 June. The divisional artillery's task was to fire in support of 47th Division. It was noted that the guns had been allocated only 20 shells per hour. After two days of unsuccessful attacks by IV Corps, the comment was recorded "the lesson of this last attack seems to be that our men are not sufficiently skilful in front turning and were not properly organised to meet what appears to have been a very well planned bombing counter-attack." Clearly this is easier to record as 1st Division had not been directly involved. As there are numerous references to visits from the Corps Liaison officer it would seem he was the source for this view.

On 18 June, 1st Division was informed that it had been selected to be available to assist the French and therefore arrangements were made to move. At the IV Corps commander's conference the next day, a letter from Haig was read asking I Corps to look at supporting the French. This would be by attacking near them if the French gained the Vimy Plateau. It was clear that earlier plans for offensive action by IV Corps were now off the table. Some French Army pamphlets, translated, were distributed and it was noted that they were very informative. The division remained ready to move. Three days later the GOC wrote what was described as a strong letter regarding the need for a proper supply of grenades. He estimated that they needed 250,000 per week of Mills No 6 and Mills No 7 bombs. This he saw as necessary if German trenches were to be taken and held. The diary records they currently had a 1,000 in total. This point is developed later with reference to the considerable correspondence regarding grenades. The GOC states his preference for the grenadiers to be deployed without rifle and pack but carrying a loaded stick. After some interim moves the division finished the month under Sir Henry Rawlinson, as GOC IV Corps, opposite Vermelles.[8]

July began with a focus on strengthening keeps and dug outs. It was soon decided that it would be necessary to construct a new trench to connect up Bradders Point and Fosse No 3. This work was necessary because if the existing line gave way, it would not be possible to withdraw the artillery in daylight. It was decided to begin work that same night on this vital new trench. On the same day several officers left to take up new appointments. Amongst them was Gerald Boyd who was going to 6th Division as GSO 1. Three years later he would be a Major-General leading 46th Division at the Hindenburg Line with 1st Division covering his right flank. Boyd was replaced as GSO 2 by Captain Dobbies who transferred in from the Second Army HQ.[9]

The staff recorded with an "!" on 9 July that First Army intelligence had passed on information relating to a German attack expected on 7 July. Nonetheless, an additional 3,500 grenades were sent to each of the brigades in the line. Against this static background the normal round of intra-brigade and inter-brigade reliefs took place. Coincidentally one assumes, Bastille Day was illuminated by a shed in Cambrin being hit by a German shell. The resulting fire was fuelled by the 25,000 rounds of SAA stored in the shed.[10]

During the rest of the month, trenches and key points were improved. Much effort also went on repairing the damage caused by enemy action. As was common practise, 1st Division provided

---

    considerable salt inasmuch as Hoffman served on the Eastern Front throughout the war. Nonetheless, the dismissal of contentious scholarship just because it cuts across the official view is redolent of Michael Gove's comment that the country had had enough of experts.
8   TNA WO 95/1228: War Diary of the 1st Division, 10-30 June 1915.
9   TNA WO 95/1229: War Diary of the 1st Division, 1-6 July 1915.
10 TNA WO 95/1229: War Diary of the 1st Division, 7-14 July 1915.

training for some officers from, in this case, 15th Division. Unfortunately, several became casualties on 21 July when the Germans shelled Y3. Three more casualties, to 1st Division, were suffered when the Germans blew up a counter-mine. Lieutenant Mitchell of the Black Watch was killed when a trench mortar burst during a practice session at the Bois de Montagnes. All these incidents help to show how the ever present danger around them placed stress on soldiers in the line. The whole period was described as quiet as there was only limited activity.[11]

The daily grind of holding the line continued into August. Divisional HQ were given a demonstration of a catapult bomb thrower by Mr West who had invented it. No verdict was recorded suggesting the reception of these keen amateurs was polite rather than warm. Continuing the programme from earlier in their stay, work on Water Tower Keep and Lowland Keep in the Vermelles sector was begun on 5 August. On 14 August the OC Divisional Ammunition Column was interviewed by the GOC I Corps Lieutenant-General Gough. Following this he spent the next morning at a meeting with Sir John French. Presumably it related to the supply of munitions. As there were two interviews, presumably Sir John knew he would get evidence to support his case to government.[12]

As part of the changes that stemmed from the decision to form a Guards Division, the 8th Royal Berkshires joined 1 Brigade on 16 August 1915, and a day later the 10th Gloucesters arrived. This facilitated the departure of the two battalions, 1st Coldstream Guards and 1st Scots Guards, who had fought with distinction as part of 1 Brigade since the outbreak of the war, on. It was 23 August 1915, the first anniversary of Mons – so much had changed since. These battalions were to become part of 2 Guards Brigade.[13] Lieutenant- General Gough was there to see them depart. For some, this moment might seem the point at which 1st Division lost its special character, but the whole character of the regular British Army had changed anyway due to the level of casualties in 1914. Therefore the departure of the Guards was more symbolic than might once have been thought.

It is also very important to remember that there was a high level of reservists in August 1914. This fact, acknowledged by scholars, has never been properly integrated into the popular understanding of the BEF in 1914. The BEF is usually described as though its ranks were entirely filled with 'old sweats' taken into action straight from their peacetime barrack squares. The casualties amongst the battalions of Guards were often the heaviest so their character, if not their standards, had already changed. 1st Division evolved from a less homogenous unit than many suppose so the departure of the Guards was a further stage in its evolution, rather than a revolution. The departure of the Guards may however be seen as another way in which 1st Division came to be viewed as yet another ordinary division of the line.

These three months out of the line seem to demonstrate that 1st Division was competent and well led. Key officers had been selected for promotion and it had been used to train other units. If the unofficial "attack division" list had been published, 1st Division might have found itself on the substitutes bench rather than on the main team sheet. Aubers Ridge might have counted against them but that was a general failure. Haig had believed they were in Hulluch but then found that they had not reached any of their objectives. Was it therein that doubts began to rise in the mind of the GOC First Army?

11 TNA WO 95/1229: War Diary of the 1st Division, 15-31 July 1915.
12 TNA WO 95/1229: War Diary of the 1st Division, August 1915.
13 Becke, *Order of Battle of Divisions – Part 1*, pp. 36-37.

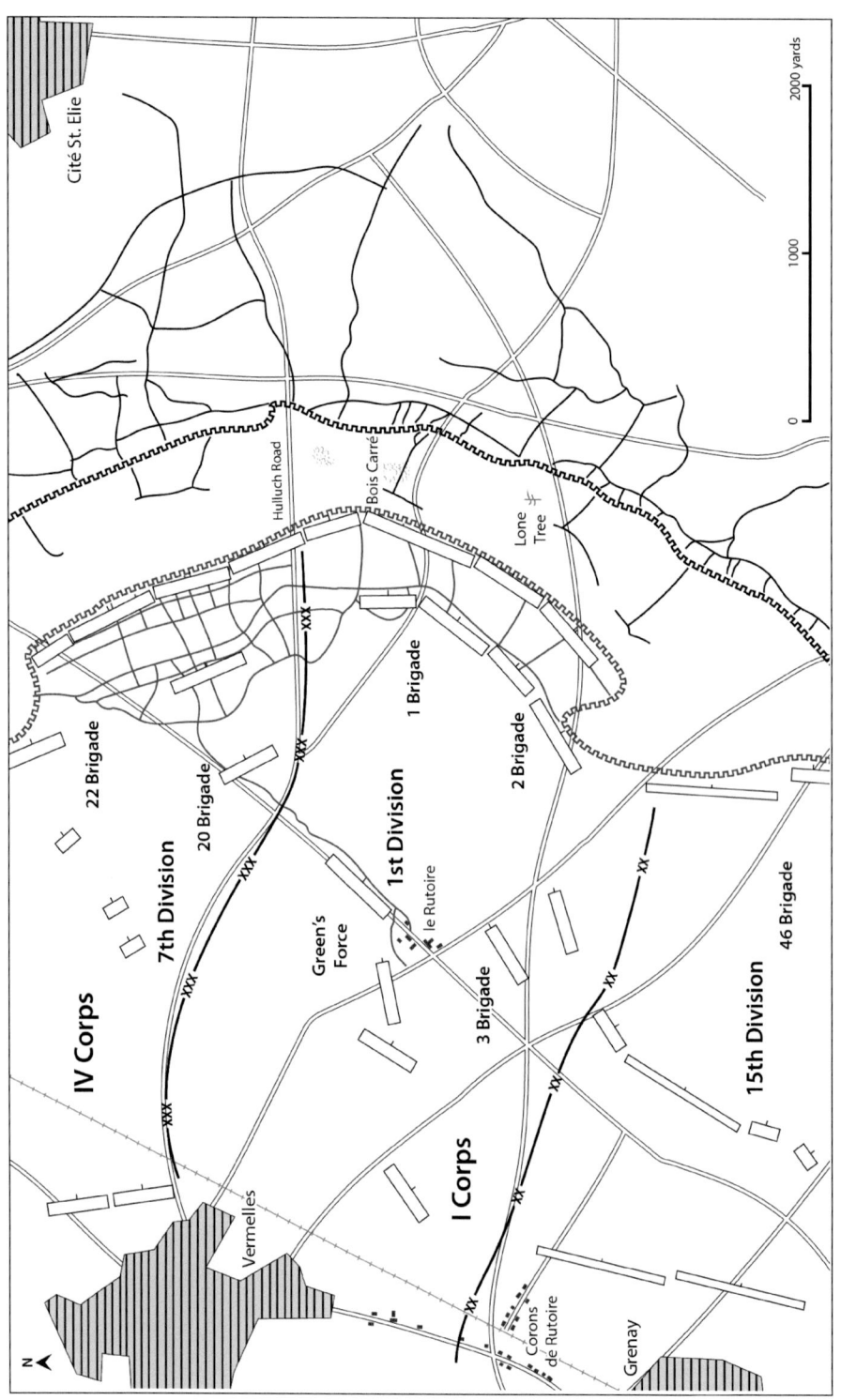

Loos, September–October 1915.

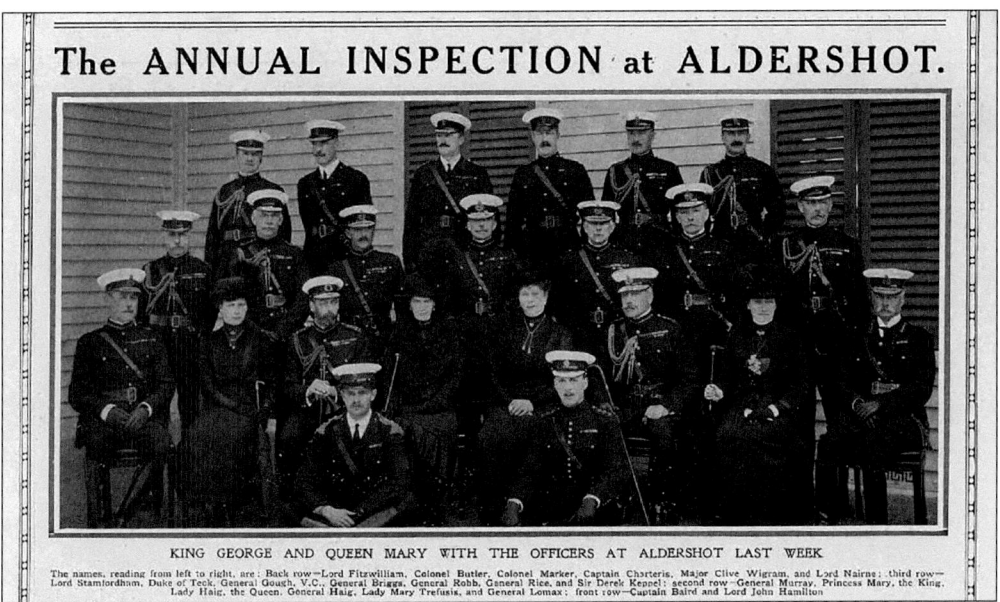

Major General S.H. Lomax (seated far right), King George V, Queen Mary and Lieutenant-General Sir Douglas Haig amongst others at Aldershot. (*The Sphere*, 30 May 1914).

Troyon Spur. Note the steep slope and excellent field of fire. (Sheree Peaple)

Chivy terrain illustrates the difficulties encountered by 1st Division. (Sheree Peaple)

Hooge Chateau. (Private collection)

Major General Sir D. Henderson. (Open source)

Major General Sir R.C.B. Haking. (Open source)

1st Black Watch headquarters, Givenchy May 1915. (Private collection)

Major General A.E.A Holland. (Open source)

IV

The 2nd Royal Munster Fusiliers at Hulluch. (*The Sphere*, 15 July 1916)

Major General E.P. Strickland.
(Open source)

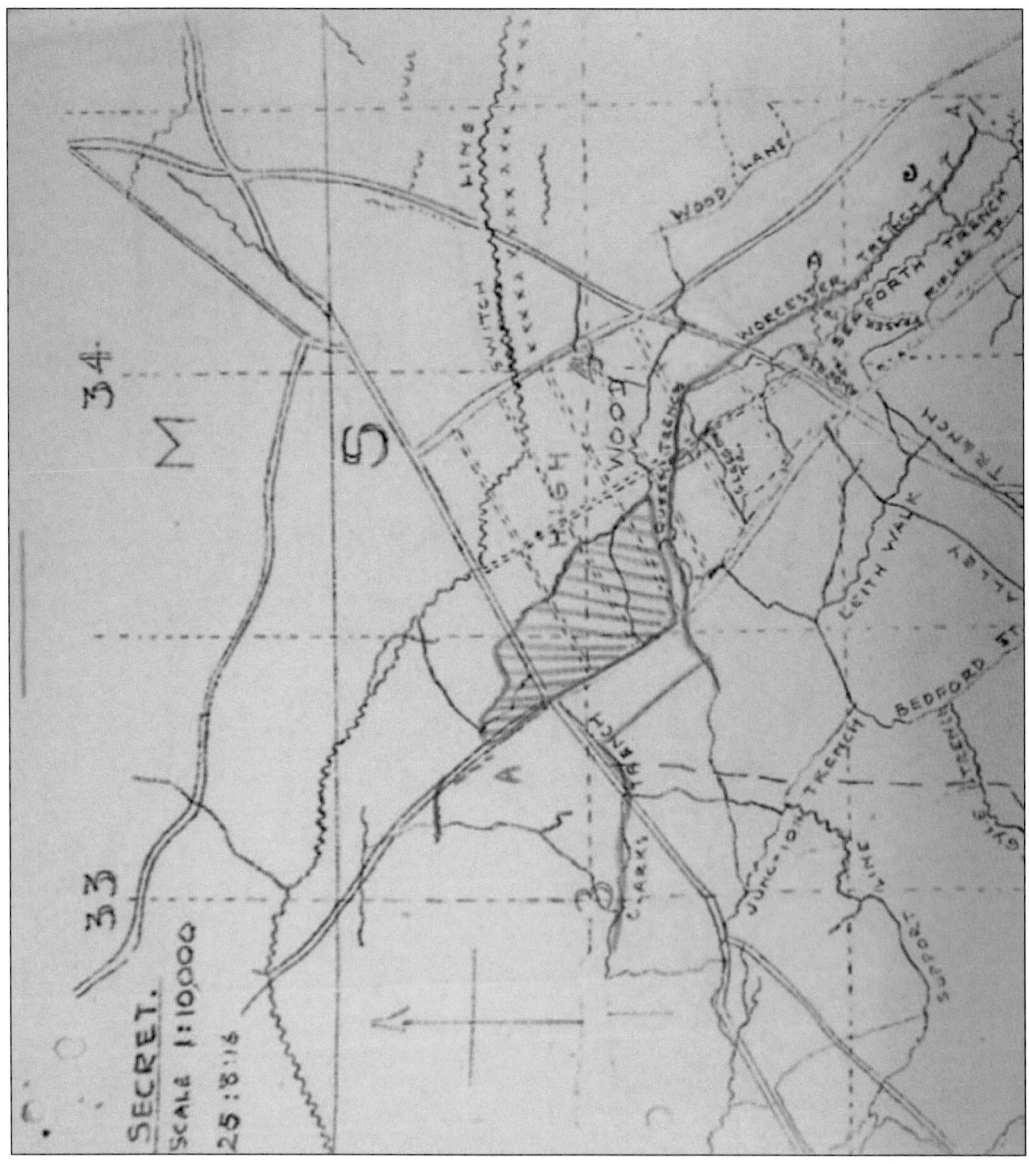

High Wood and vicinity, August 1916. (TNA WO 95/1275: 2 Brigade War Diary)

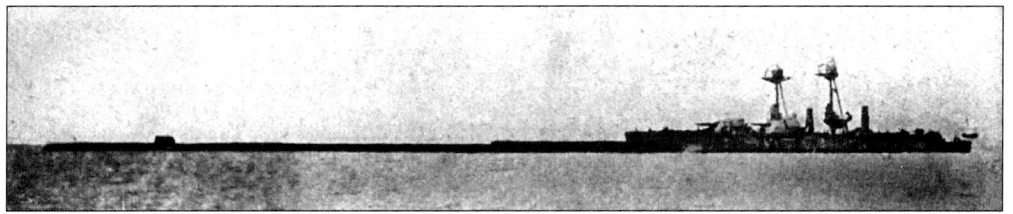

Operation Hush: Assault pier and monitors. (Bacon, *The Dover Patrol*, Vol. I)

Operation Hush: Assault pier interior. (Bacon, *The Dover Patrol*, Vol. I)

Operation Strandfest: 1st Division captive officers and men marching through Brugge, July 1917. (Private collection)

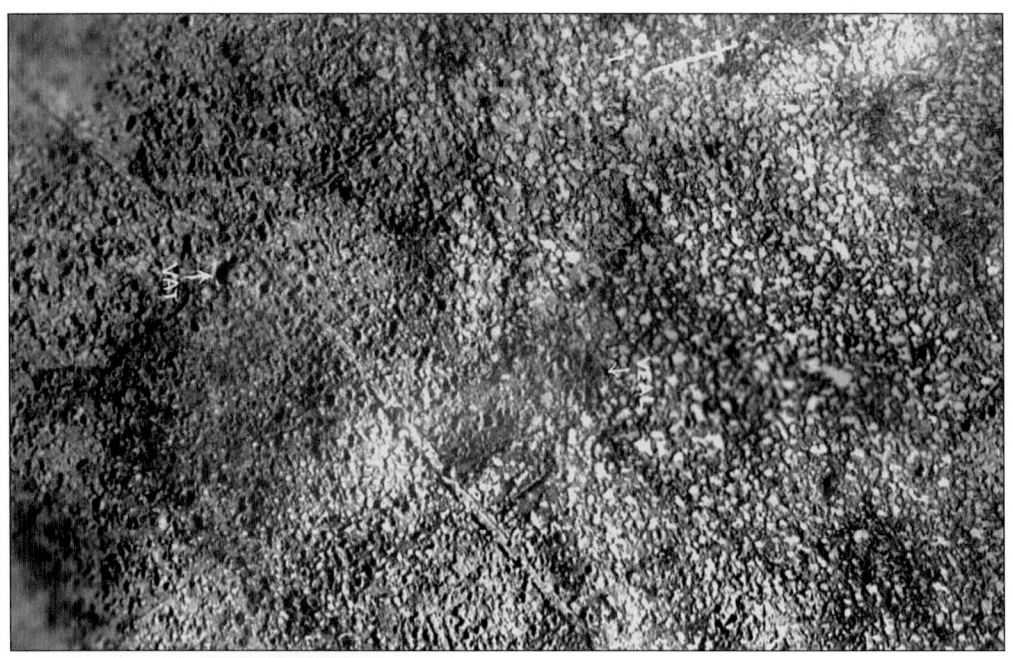

Vat Cottages and vicinity from the air, Passchendaele November 1917. (McMaster University)

Captain A.H.H. Batten-Pooll VC, captured at Passchendaele on 10 November 1917. (Open source)

1st Black Watch roll call, Lapugnoy, 10 April 1918. (Private collection)

Duke of Connaught inspecting 1st Northamptonshire Regiment, 2nd Brigade, Bruay, 1 July 1918.
(Open source)

Lock No. 1, Sambre Canal. (Open source)

Lieutenant Colonel Johnson VC and Runner Sergeant Brown DCM, MM. (Open source)

22

Loos
Preparations for Battle

For the reconstituted 1st Division, the next big test would come at Loos in September.[1] September opened with the division holding the line based at Vaudrincourt. It also began with the departure of 4th Royal Welsh Fusiliers who joined the 47th Division. The 1st Division was providing a lot of working parties. The units in the line were then reorganised. Two and a half battalions were left with 15th Division. These troops were under the command of Lieutenant-Colonel Green DSO of 2nd Sussex. He was clearly a trusted subordinate that could be assigned such a role for Loos. Another man whose role was about to change was Major-General Haking. On 1 September, Haig recommended him for promotion to Lieutenant-General in charge of XI Corps. This was confirmed on 4 September. Therefore, Haking handed over command to Major-General Holland. Holland was a gunner and had been CRA of VII Corps. The next day, Holland held a conference with senior subordinates (including the OC motor machine gun company) regarding future operations. That day Corps postponed the offensive until at least 15 September. Following the conference, brigadier-General Reddie, OC 1 Brigade, sent a long and detailed list of questions to the divisional staff. One question, answered by Lieutenant-Colonel Charteris, on Haig's staff at First Army, was that the maps to be issued would be 1/10,000 and that a special request would have to be submitted for a 1/5,000 map to be supplied. Presumably without warning, the army commander himself, rode over to see Holland but he was out. As was to be typical of his period in command, Holland was out inspecting the trenches and work being done by the working parties.

All the unit commanders had received copies of guiding principles for the attack which had been transmitted from Army to Corps and then to Division. They were marked "Secret" but commanders were to ensure their officers had read them whilst recognising their classification. A lot of the text was devoted to ensuring there was proper organisation of both the assaulting units and those responsible for ancillary tasks. However, some passages dealt with the central issue of guidance in conducting an offensive. It stated that the intention was to break the enemy's line and to stop him reforming. It went on:

---

[1] For a detailed narrative of the battle, see Niall Cherry, *Most Unfavourable Ground* (Solihull: Helion, 2005) and Nick Lloyd, *Loos 1915* (Cheltenham: History Press, 2008).

"once the enemy's line is broken, it is the intention to follow up by such action as will cause a general retirement of a great part of the enemy's line....it is of the highest importance that al commanders should consider carefully the handling of their reserves to maintain the forward movement....under the existing conditions only one definite offensive blow can be expected from one body of infantry." Commanders were therefore to ensure that supporting units followed close on the heels of the assaulting troops and pass through them after the initial objectives had been reached.

Haig's points then became even more specific to the key situation that might well arise for a local commander:

> The attack on the front trenches will probably not be equally successful all along the line." This shows how closely Haking had mirrored Haig's thoughts in his April lecture to the officers of 1st Division. Haig went on to urge them to reinforce success. He added "Where unsuccessful a further attack must be organised from a flank where the line has been broken.

The next passage sought to deal with the common issue of advances stopping when the flank is in the air: "If a certain body of infantry fails to gain its own particular objective, there is no reason why the troops on either flank should be held up." For a man who was famous for being brief, this memorandum was lengthy. Holland backed it up with his own summary on offensive action, restating in three paragraphs Haig's points. On 17 September, Holland personally signed a memo to his Brigadiers regarding the need to stress to company officers the need to push on. He made the point that the unforeseen is what happens in war and that the best response was to act energetically and not wait for orders.[2] These notes provide a very clear insight into Haig's thinking in the late summer of 1915. The reference to the handling of reserves resonates given his impending row with Sir John French.

As well as meeting with his own officers, Holland hosted a visit from the Corps commander which Brigadiers attended. It was on 14 September that Holland attended a demonstration of the new "Stokes gun". It would prove to be a vital close support weapon for the infantry in the future.

Over the next few days, meetings were held with Corps and details of the impending operations were discussed, and a planned date was now stated. One part of the plan had been abandoned. It had been proposed to create a mobile force by combining the mounted divisional troops with those of 15th Division. Major Loekelt of 11th Hussars arrived to take charge of the mobile force but it had been decided the mounted elements of 15th Division would not be available, and so the idea was dropped.[3]

At the time of the re-organisation of 1st Division, a plan for 15th Division to make an assault at Loos had been considered but subsequently abandoned. Instead, 1st Division was brought into the line as part of an assault by I and IV Corps. The 1st Division would form the left flank of IV Corps, and be in touch with 7th Division on the right of I Corps. The section of front extended for 1400 yards from the Northern Sap to the Hulluch-Vermelles Road. The initial

---

2   TNA WO 95/1229: War Diary of the 1st Division, September 1915, Appendix.
3   TNA WO 95/1229: War Diary of the 1st Division, 1- 17 September 1915.

orders sent out on 13 September detailed the forces to be involved as well as the arrangements for rations, medical, veterinary, and other support units. 1 Brigade on the left, and 2 Brigade on the right were to be the assault troops. Each brigade was to contribute a battalion to a force, designated Green Force, under Lieutenant-Colonel Green. This force was to come into being at 6am on the day prior to the assault. Green was to be allowed to select a staff officer from "his own command", so presumably from 2nd Royal Sussex. Green was also to be supported with a signals section. On 16 September it was confirmed that the bomb proof forward HQ of 1st Division at Vermelles would be equipped with wireless, both to send and receive.

The orders stated that the attack would take place after a 4-day bombardment. Each assaulting brigade would be supported by an artillery group. Overall command of the artillery was vested in Lieutenant-Colonel Elton. He had been included in some of the earlier meetings. Elton would have direct control over the 2nd Siege Battery, consisting of 6" howitzers. Under Elton was Lieutenant-Colonel Hinton in command of the Northern group. They were to support 1 Brigade. Hinton had been assigned three field artillery batterys plus a battery of 4.5" howitzers. The southern group, headed by Lieutenant-Colonel Clark had two field batterys and a howitzer battery. They were assigned to supporting 2 Brigade. The whole artillery operation was to be carried out on a budget. Corps circulated a revised allocation signed by Major-General Butler of Haig's staff. Each 18pdr gun was allocated 230 rounds of HE and 682 rounds of shrapnel. The 4.5" Howitzers were allocated rounds of 450HE and 15 rounds of shrapnel whilst their 6" counterparts were to receive 569 HE rounds. The Harrow- educated Butler added, in a tone reminiscent of a schoolmaster dealing with children; that previously there had been a lot of cases of overdrawing and that this must not happen again. He added that the commander, presumably Haig, was going to take severe disciplinary action in future cases. This shows Haig believed there was a shortage of shells before Loos.

The whole assault was to be supported by the use of gas. Over a total of 3 nights, 853 gas cylinders were brought into the line.[4] The divisional engineers were responsible for ensuring that the parapets were flat and the distance from the recess to the parapet was no more than 4'6" so that the pipes would lie flat. There were 12 gas cylinders for each 25 yard bay. In the initial release, the valves on 6 cylinders would be opened. Each cylinder discharged gas for about 3 minutes but 12 minutes were allowed in the timetable before the first batch of smoke candles would be lit. Twenty minutes after the first set of gas cylinders were opened, the second set would be set in motion. A further 12 minutes was allowed before the second set of smoke candles would be lit. These were to be extra thick at the end. The plan finished by stating that after 39 minutes the infantry should leave the trench and move to the assault a minute later. The troops were told that there was evidence to show that the German troops did not possess an effective gas helmet. The troops were also told their own gas helmet gave them complete immunity. The high command also told the men that as the British had not used gas before, its use would be a complete surprise to the Germans.[5]

On a less technological note, the division was told to provide two routes for cavalry to pass through the lines and was promised the assistance of a troop of field cavalry. These men duly arrived and constructed bridges across the trenches. The RE were also told that bridges ready to

4 TNA WO 95/1229: War Diary of the 1st Division, 18-21 September 1915 and Appendix II.
5 TNA WO 95/1229: War Diary of the 1st Division, September 1915.

let cavalry over captured German trenches must be wide enough to take half a section of cavalry. 3rd Cavalry Division were being issued with white screens 4' by 15'. These would be displayed where possible and would indicate the troop was in action about 300 yards ahead. [6]

On 21 September IV Corps headquarters also informed 1st division of the projected infantry reserves being brought forward. It stated that the heads of 21st and 24th Divisions would be moving up to the line Noeux Les Mines – Beuvry and would arrive there on the morning of 25 September. The 21st Division would be marching through the IV Corps area and the order not only described the route (with timings) but explicitly stated that IV Corps must be clear of Marles Les Mines by 6pm. Permission was therefore granted to the DAC to draw extra ammunition on night of 23 September to cover what would normally have been drawn on 24 September. There is a further handwritten note which simply starts by saying the route of 24th Division is uncertain. Then there are a set of orders from Lieutenant-Colonel Longridge, dated 22 September. These detail the movement of some battalions in 1st Division on 24 September. These refer only to numbers of battalions of a particular brigade moving from a place at a certain time.[7] Haig's idea of having the reserves brought up has strength. The reality of its impact on the assaulting divisions on the night before the assault may help to explain the difficulties faced by Haking's Corps on its night march.

The divisional artillery had begun the bombardment of the German lines on 20 September. Gaps in the wire were reported that day. However, on 21 September, Holland went to assess for himself the success of the wire cutting. He was not satisfied with the intensity of the bombardment. Therefore Brigadier-General Budworth was contacted. It must have been an interesting conversation between the two gunners, as Holland secured two more 18pdr batterys and an extra 6" howitzer battery.[8] As shells were rationed per gun, being allocated extra guns got round the difficulty of permitting some batteries to overdraw.

Holland wanted to ensure the wire was properly cut and that the defenders would be fully demoralised. Officer patrols, that same evening, confirmed that the wire had been cut but also reported that the Germans were repairing all the gaps. Therefore, the next morning Holland met with his brigadiers. He issued orders that men and machine guns should be placed in front of the trenches to keep the wire from being repaired. He also gave specific instructions to fire more at night than before. In fairness to the Corps staff, they had made the point that gaps cut would need to be fired on continuously in orders issued as early as 3 September. Unfortunately, Lieutenant- Colonel Longridge had not followed these instructions when he issued the orders to brigades on 10 September. He had specifically referred to maintaining intermittent fire on the gaps made.[9]

On 18 September, Major-General Capper, GOC 7th Division, contacted Holland to say that he intended to keep the key German communication trenches under fire from machine guns up to the moment of the assault. He said there were two trenches of common interest to his division and 1 Brigade. He offered to take care of Hay alley as it was best enfiladed from his area and asked Holland to reciprocate regarding Hulluch Road trench. Holland responded

---

6   TNA WO 95/1229: War Diary of the 1st Division, 21 September 1915, Appendix and TNA WO 95/1245: War Diary of the 1st Division, CRE, 23 September 1915.
7   TNA WO 95/1229: War Diary of the 1st Division, September 1915, Appendix.
8   TNA WO 95/1229: War Diary of the 1st Division, 22 September 1915.
9   TNA WO 95/1229: War Diary of the 1st Division, 22 September 1915, Appendix.

by saying he had issued the necessary orders. Ten more gas cylinders were sent to the division on 23 September. Corps were informed they would be collected at the advanced HQ but it was unlikely they could be got into the trenches on time. Major-General Butler had requested, on 18 September, daily wind reports from divisions at 4.30am, 5.00am and 5.30am with added detail if it had been variable. On 23 September the 1st Division staff noted that the wind, which had been south-easterly in the morning, veered to westerly after a thunderstorm. Such variability on one day was hardly reassuring. By then Corps had said the probable zero hour would be 4.50am, meaning the infantry would attack at 5.30pm.[10]

Edmonds states that to prepare for the assault, jumping off trenches were dug, three to four hundred yards ahead of the British line, close to the crest of the Grenay ridge. He added that, the configuration of the ground dictated that the Germans had needed to run saps forward so it was decided to leave a gap of 600 yards between the frontages of the two divisions to avoid assaulting frontally the machine guns believed to be in the saps. It was believed that once the assaulting waves had passed over, the 15th Division could take the sap in the flank.[11] The detailed records of 1st Division CRE make no mention of such trenches on the divisional front. So, whilst not attacking frontally might be sensible it did mean that 1st Division would have an unsuppressed set of machine guns on its flank. A gap of 600 yards afforded the divisions, on average, no more than 300 yards of space, less than the effective range of a machine gun.

The overall plan for 1st Division was further complicated by the decision to instruct 2 Brigade to attack in a south-easterly direction once they had overrun the 600 yard frontage of main and support lines between the northern sap and Lone Tree. The aim was to bring them in touch with 15th Division at Puits 14 and Bois Hugo. This would cover the gap created in the initial assault. Meanwhile, 1 Brigade would attack due East between Lone Tree and the Hulluch-Vermelles Road. Therefore, a gap would open up between the two brigades. As each brigade had an additional battalion, these battalions, the London Scottish and 1/9th King's Liverpool would advance behind the assaulting battalions and advance to fill the gap. They would come under the command of Lieutenant-Colonel Green of 2nd Royal Sussex, and therefore it became known as Green's Force. Green's Force was to advance to the Redoubt. The assaulting brigades were then to extend towards the Redoubt on their respective flanks and link up with Green's Force.[12]

On 24 September, an exercise was undertaken to try to get the Germans to line their trenches. It is unclear whether they did but the German artillery did retaliate. On the same afternoon, Holland visited the front line trenches of both assault brigades. He then called upon both brigadiers in their HQs. Meanwhile, Lieutenant-Colonel Longridge was at Corps HQ. There, he was again acquainted with the different scenarios Corps had considered if the original plan could not go ahead. These included an attack by 1st Division against limited objectives if gas could not be used and French success made an attack imperative. The senior officers were briefed, in confidence, that a final decision had yet to be made. At 8.05pm, Corps confirmed that the assault would take place on 25 September. However, it said that the final decision on the plan would be communicated later. Corps HQ waited to receive the weather forecast at

---

10   TNA WO 95/1229: War Diary of the 1st Division, 23 September 1915.
11   Edmonds, *OH, 1915*, Vol. 2, p.208-9.
12   Edmonds, *OH, 1915*, Vol. 2, pp.209-10 & TNA WO 95/1229: War Diary of the 1st Division, 18-24 September 1915.

9.45pm before confirming to the assaulting divisions that the operation would go ahead with gas and smoke. They then waited until 3.30am before zero would be at 5.50am. The 1st Loyal North Lancs reported arrival in the trenches at 1.40am and were only advised at 4.30am when zero hour was and to pass this message on to the RE personnel in their area. Half an hour later, Holland and his staff moved to their battle station.[13] Weeks of planning and effort had brought the men of 1st Division to this tense moment. Everyone's watches had been set to "Corps time" so hopefully the whole effort would be synchronised and go like clockwork.

---

13   TNA WO 95/1229: War Diary of the 1st Division, 18-24 September 1915 and WO 95/1266: War Diary of the 1st Battalion Loyal North Lancashire Regiment, 25 October 1915.

23

Loos Battle

On the left flank of the 1st Division's assault was 1 Brigade. Here Brigadier Reddie had decided to attack with 8th Royal Berkshires and 10th Gloucesters in the van. Arguably, these were the less experienced battalions but he may have taken the view that they had been given enough experience in earlier actions. He may also have felt that it would be demoralising for 1st Camerons and 1st Black Watch to be put in first every time. When the gas was turned on, all seemed to go well. The brigade left the trenches on time and advanced towards two copses. The attack by 1st Brigade was led by 10th Gloucesters and 8th Royal Berkshires, both of whom were affected by gas but were able to advance on schedule. Once again, there were significant British casualties from unsuppressed German machine guns.

La Haie was ahead of the Berkshires who pressed forward. The 8th Royal Berkshires had managed an advance of 1200 yards despite some machine gun opposition and partially cut wire. With the close support of 1st Camerons, they were then able to advance together and capture three field guns en route to the Lens road.

Unsuppressed machine guns caused heavy casualties, especially to the Gloucesters attacking Bois Carre on the right. Private Jennings of 10th Gloucesters described exactly the sort of situation Haig and Haking had referred to. The survivors of his section were pinned down by a German machine gun. However, they were able to get forward once other men, who had broken through elsewhere, forced the Germans to surrender.[1] Despite this, 10th Gloucesters overran the German front line and, after a firefight with the defenders of the support line, captured that too but were now reduced to sixty men advancing beyond that point.

Gloucester losses made it difficult to press ahead further after capturing Bois Carre. Therefore, it was decided, in the light of the heavy casualties sustained, not to assault Hulluch village until Green's Force and 2 Brigade had come up to the same line. Brigadier Reddie's report to HQ that his right was stuck was logged at 8.38am. Just under two hours later, Reddie reported that his brigade was in the southern outskirts of Hulluch. He also reported that Hulluch was empty of the enemy. As Holland had a wireless set at HQ, this information could be passed to IV Corps. Reddie was instructed to push on; clearly the many injunctions to do so, as distributed in advance, had not totally influenced Reddie's thinking. The Germans were now beginning to

---

1 Cherry, N., *Most Unfavourable Ground*, p.154.

exploit the gap left by 2 Brigade's difficulties. So Reddie detailed 1st Black Watch to protect the flank of 1 Brigade, rather than to reinforce the advance. In doing so, the leading company sustained heavy casualties. The rest encountered significant delays trying to avoid a similar fate. They listed their casualties as three officers killed and four wounded, of whom one was missing. In addition, 48 men had been killed and 127 wounded as well as 36 who were missing.[2] In his report to Corps, Holland criticised Reddie for creating a defensive flank. Holland argued that commanders were part of larger formations and they should not pay attention to "internal" flanks as they were the responsibility of the higher commander. He was already addressing the issue of 2 Brigade, so Reddie should have pressed on.[3]

During the morning and most of the afternoon, Holland was focused on extricating 2 Brigade from its difficult position. However, by around 6pm IV Corps had informed him that XI Corps were moving forward during the night. Holland therefore gave orders for 1 Brigade to attack Hulluch at 5am after an hour of bombardment. Interestingly, Holland says he told them to stop all work on consolidation. This shows 1 Brigade had effectively halted. Holland also ordered 3 Brigade to be part of the assault and to move up during the night. This would mean that they would be moving into the area that XI Corps would be advancing into. Shortly afterwards, IV Corps contacted Holland to say that XI Corps would be pushing in between Hulluch and Cite St Auguste. Holland therefore despatched a staff officer to XI Corps. It was agreed that XI Corps would relieve 2 Brigade and that 1st and 24th Divisions would attack Hulluch at 11am on 26 September supported by IV Corp's artillery. As Holland noted, this superseded his planned 5 am attack. Given the principle of "pushing-on" was such a key mantra it seems at variance to have further delayed the assault on Hulluch. Worse still, Haig then ordered XI Corps to attack the German second line and so the 1st Division would now be attacking alone, the enemy having been afforded an additional six hours to recover from day 1.

The problems facing Major-General Holland on his right were very different. Everything had started to go wrong even before 2 Brigade could leave their trenches. As detailed above, the canisters were due to empty in about three minutes. Therefore, for the rest of the first ten minutes, the gas cloud began to roll towards the German lines. However, by 6am the wind had veered round. This meant that the cloud of gas came back into the 1st Division's trenches. In addition, gas from 15th Division's front was blown back over them. The waiting assault waves of the 2nd KRRC and 1st Loyal North Lancs therefore took the brunt of the gas meant for the Germans. Approximately 200 men in each battalion were incapacitated. This necessitated a major reorganisation in congested trenches. The second wave were brought forward to replace the first wave. Despite this, the attack started only four minutes behind schedule at 6.34am. However, the release of the gas had confirmed to the Germans that an assault was imminent and therefore the German artillery and machine guns greeted the gallant men coughing their way forwards. Men of *157th Regiment* reinforced their colleagues from positions opposite 15th Division. As noted above, the German machine guns in the northern sap and at Lone Tree had not been suppressed. The losses amongst the Loyal North Lancs included their CO and more than half the officers became casualties. Over 400 of the men became casualties too. To

2   TNA: WO 95/1263: War Diary of the 1st Battalion Black Watch Regiment, 25 September 1915.
3   TNA: WO 95/1229: War Diary of the 1st Division, September 1915, Appendix.

complete the discomfiture of 2nd Brigade, the mist rose about 9am making it even easier for the German defenders to see where to direct their fire. The assault line was increasingly isolated as the supporting troops had been forced back whilst those furthest forward sought to close up to the wire to gain some cover.[4]

It was found that the wire had not been cut. Those brave men who tried to cut the wire were cut down themselves. The fact the wire was not cut is often related to the difficulties of observation. However, as we have seen, the efforts to keep cut wire from being repaired had not been adequate. Heroism in the face of these multiple challenges was recognised in the award of the VC to Rifleman Peachment, of 2nd KRRC; he sacrificed his life trying to save his company commander.

Despite the losses sustained in the initial attack, a second assault was ordered. This took place at 7.30am. It was utterly pointless and simply resulted in severe casualties amongst the men of 2nd Royal Sussex and 1st Northants. It completely contradicted the injunction not to reinforce failure. The heroism of Northants Captain Read in repeatedly trying to lead forward men against the wire and machine guns, was recognised by the award of a posthumous VC. In the fighting, Sergeant Harry Wells, of 2nd Royal Sussex, showed outstanding courage and leadership. With officers having been killed and wounded, he took charge. He led repeated attempts to break through and was eventually killed by machine gun fire. He received a posthumous VC in recognition of his valour. He was a policeman and one of the reservists recalled to the colours. After the losses at Aubers Ridge he had been promoted to Sergeant.[5] To assist 2 Brigade, at Noon, Holland sent four guns from the motor machine gun company forward to the front line to provide covering fire.

Shortly after 9am, Holland ordered Green's Force to assist 2 Brigade. One option for Major-General Holland was try to push his uncommitted forces in to the north and south of the gap in the British advance created by 2nd Brigade being held up. Instead, he decided to launch a further assault on 2nd Brigade's front due to intelligence issued before the battle that this area was weakly held. One would have thought that such intelligence had now been tested and found unreliable. The 3rd Brigade was ordered to support the right of 1st Brigade whilst Green's Force renewed the frontal assault, amidst the remnants of 2nd Brigade. In doing so he breached one of the principles Haig had outlined . Green's Force was delayed in its arrival and was sent forward in a frontal assault either side of Lone Tree which resulted in heavy casualties.

Eventually Holland sent instructions to 2 Brigade to extricate as many men as possible and move to the right. Then use the trenches captured by 15th Division to get behind the Germans opposing his brigade. In doing so he now followed one of the principles Haig had outlined. The support was to be an attack from the flank and the choice of route was assisted by information from 1 Brigade. At the same time, arrangements had been made with the 15th Division to send a strong bombing party up the Southern Sap. 15th Division had now taken their objectives and the plan had included them clearing the saps afterwards. By 2pm, news that Green's Force too was hung up, reached Holland. They too had faced strong opposition from behind uncut wire.

Better news began to arrive at 2.50pm. Major Vivian reported that the German resistance in front of 2 Brigade had broken down. He also said 600-700 prisoners had now been taken.

---

4 Edmonds, *OH, 1915, vol 2*, p.210-12.
5 *West Sussex Past* <http.www.westsussexpast.org.uk> (accessed 28 April, 2023).

The reality behind this was that 2 Brigade had suffered so badly in the morning that only 1st Gloucesters had been able to attempt to follow the orders sent by Holland to 2 Brigade.

Similarly, 3 Brigade's support was to be led by 2nd Royal Munster Fusiliers, who had received few reinforcements and could only bring 250 men to the assault.[6] Two of their companies lost direction and were practically annihilated. The remainder of the battalion did make touch with the advancing troops when it reached Gun trench.

The actual heroes of the hour were Lieutenant Colonel Prothero and the 2nd Welsh. They reached Gun trench by 2pm, having suffered few casualties as they advanced in open order. The 2nd Welsh then advanced on the flank of the Germans resisting 2nd Brigade and captured five officers and 160 men in the support line. They also found a wounded British officer in a German dugout, they reported that he had been treated very well.[7] The breakthrough by the 2nd Welsh, caused the remaining Germans opposing Green's Force to surrender. As evidenced by the Germans surrendering to the 9th King's Liverpool Regiment.

This freed up the survivors of 2nd Brigade to advance but the heavy casualties sustained had blunted and delayed the advance during critical hours. Holland sent orders to both 2 Brigade and Green's Force, as well as 1st Gloucesters (who had been sent forward earlier) to press on to their objectives. Subsequent reports confirmed that 2 Brigade were advancing past Bois Hugo and eventually were in occupation of the Chalk Pit.

Only during the night, was 1st Division able to think it had established a continuous front on its sector. In fact, there was a gap between Green's Force and the left of 2nd Brigade of about 1500 yards. This was partly due to the large number of men, estimated at 1,950, who had become lost or separated when officers became casualties.[8] Some fighting occurred during the night. The South Wales Borderers were engaged. They took some prisoners which they sent back to the rear.[9] Overall control of the assault on Hulluch had been given to Brigadier Davies of 3 Brigade. At 4.45am, Davies reported that 3 Brigade were in position. Holland informed Davies that it was important to push on when the attack went in. They needed to relieve the pressure on 7th Division. The Germans had re-occupied The Quarries overnight. Therefore 7th Division were having to regain The Quarries before going on to attack St Elie. The attack on St Elie had been scheduled originally for 11am to coincide with the assault on Hulluch. Although 1st Division had sent out orders in good time and there was a clear command structure in place, the plans began to unravel.

The 1st Black Watch and 1st South Wales Borderers awaited the whistle in Gun trench. Behind them were 1st Gloucesters and 2nd Munster Fusiliers. Although Davies had been given 1 Brigade and Green's Force in addition to his own 3 Brigade, he told HQ that he would only draw on 2 Brigade if he had to. All four of these battalions were well below strength. The final element in the assault were 2nd Welch who may have mustered 400 men. They were situated on the right. Therefore, they were the ones who saw and reported a German attack on their right. They understood they were to attack anyway at 11am. The barrage opened and they went forward. They suffered heavily from German fire and became confused when the rest of 3 Brigade remained in the trenches.

6   As noted previously, voluntary recruitment in Ireland was drying up.
7   TNA WO 95/1281: War Diary of the 2nd, Battalion The Welsh Regiment, 25 September 1915.
8   Edmonds, *OH, 1915, vol 2*, pp.214-23.
9   TNA WO 95/1229: War Diary of the 1st Division, 26 September 1915.

Due to the interruption of communications, the 2nd Welch had not received the order to delay their attack until Noon. This had been decided in response to their call. The artillery had been called back from the first lift ready for the new zero hour of Noon. As the 7th Division's attempt to retake The Quarries had failed, they were no longer attacking St Elie. Davies had been told to attack without fail at Noon. At Noon the 1st Black Watch and 1st South Wales Borderers attacked alone across 600 yards of open ground with the predictable result that they achieved nothing.[10]

A steady stream of reports during the day had reached 1st Division headquarters. They covered the delays due to the consequences of the movements of 21st and 24th Divisions and, belatedly, the failure of the assaults by its own brigades. The blame game was evident in a message at 3.50pm from 24th Division that their attack had been compromised by the failure of 1st Division.

In the early hours of 27 September 1st Division was informed that it would be relieved and be moving to relieve the 3rd Cavalry Division. Holland conferred with his brigadiers as to the state of their commands, The Brigadiers reported that 1, 2 and 3 Brigades could muster 800, 1400 and 1100 rifles respectively. On that basis, the division could now only muster 3,300 rifles, the equivalent of three full battalions at war strength. It was also noted that this number went up during the day as men were able to get back to their unit.[11] One can also sense the blame game developing further on 27 September when Corps requests numbers from the division. They were asked to say how many Germans were killed and how many machine guns and guns were captured. Holland's staff note that they were a bit busy on 25 September to search the German trenches and now they have been searched by another division. Perhaps naively, they counted the German dead and recorded a figure of 132. It is possible this was accurate but given the proportion of British casualties recorded as missing, they could have finessed the figures. Against this, they reported their own casualties as 145 officers and 3707 men. Corps passed on news that 3rd Cavalry Division had broken through. Therefore, the divisional mounted troops were put on readiness to move at 15 minutes notice. Subsequently, the whole division was ordered to concentrate at Nouex Les Mines. Given all that had occurred, it is unsurprising to find that Holland summoned his brigadiers to meet him. He told them to bring with them all their notes pertaining to the operations.[12]

Normally, these meetings lead to a general gathering of information and some key learning points are identified. The discussion and notes then go into the report required by Corps. We have seen this where Haking sent his detailed comments to Corps after Aubers Ridge and we will see it in other cases later. The unusual aspect of this conference is that subsequently Holland sent a confidential report to his three brigadiers. In the first part of his report he specifically says that Reddie's argument for forming a defensive flank "cannot be considered to carry any weight". Holland goes to the trouble of doing two sketch maps to demonstrate his view. This whole part of the document reads as though it would be reproduced in a report sent to Lieutenant-General Rawlinson as Corps Commander. This would be tough enough for Reddie to read but Holland had shared it with his fellow brigadiers too.

10 TNA WO 95/1229: War Diary of the 1st Division Headquarters, 26 September 1915 and Cherry, op. cit., p.209.
11 TNA WO 95/1229: War Diary of the 1st Division Headquarters, 26/27 September 1915.
12 TNA WO 95/1229: War Diary of the 1st Division Headquarters, 26 -30 September 1915.

In case they read the first part and felt relieved, the other Brigadiers had only to read on. The second point which Holland made related to 2 Brigade but it would also have applied to Green's Force. Here, Holland focused on the qualities needed in a "firefight". He said the troops were no longer those who had been so well trained pre-1914. This was hardly a difficult point to argue given the losses since August 1914. As we have seen, they had just lost Sergeant wells who was part of that reservoir of knowledge. Holland drew the uncontroversial conclusion that more time in training was now be spent inculcating these basic principles. Whilst the brigadiers might feel there was an implied criticism of training to date it was also true that they were having to deal with a very different pool of men.

Holland's third point also related primarily to the troops. However, it also challenged, indirectly, the leadership qualities of his brigadiers and their officers. Holland chose the heading "wastage" for this third section. Holland provided the brigadiers with his figures broken down by battalion. He took the trench strength of the battalion on the morning of 25 September. Then he deducted the casualties incurred over the three days. He then argued that if you took the second figure away from the first then at least that number of men should have been available on 26 September, since some would not have become casualties by then. Holland then compared this number for those who were available with those who actually were available. As the trench strength of battalions and casualties sustained varied considerably, I have inserted a column showing Holland's "wastage" figure as a percentage of the Nett strength he had calculated should have been available.

Battalion	Trench Strength 25/9	Casualties at Loos (3 days)	Nett Strength for Day 2	Actual Strength Day 2	Wastage	% of col 3	Total
Black Watch	760	278	482	330	152	31.5%	
Camerons	690	387	303	150	153	50.4%	
8th Berkshires	790	493	297	200	97	32.6%	
10 Gloucesters	760	459	301	60	241	80.0%	643 46.5%
Northamptons	760	298	462	400	62	13.4%	
King's Royal Rifles	825	460	365	250	115	31.5%	
Loyal North Lancs	785	489	296	220	76	25.6%	
2nd Royal Sussex	790	481	309	140	169	54.7%	422 29.4%
South Wales Borderers	610	121	489	350	139	28.4%	
1st Gloucesters	770	124	646	600	46	7.1%	

2nd Welsh	625	311	414	400	14	3.3%	
2nd Munsters	460	120	340	120	220	64.7%	419 22.1%
London Scottish	610	266	344	220	124	36.0%	
9th Liverpools	650	235	415	80	335	80.7%	459 60.4%

Even if one accepts the "wastage" rates at face value, they provide a very inconsistent picture. One might have expected more issues with units badly hit on day 1, for example. However, the lowest figure is for the Northants. The Munster Fusiliers figure really blots the figures for 3 Brigade. However, it was the only battalion to start at below half-strength. Recruitment in Kerry was clearly not replenishing its ranks. Before the war, there was dire poverty in Ireland and the war had the impact of raising wages. The raising of 16th Division was the focus for those who wanted to follow Redmond's call at Woodenbridge to join the forces of the crown. That division include the 8th (Service) Battalion of the Munster Fusiliers. Holland, having acknowledged some men may have been on working parties, then gave his explanation for the discrepancy:

> The General Officer commanding suggests, and there is some evidence to support the suggestion, that many men got away into the trenches and sat there until the fight was over, leaving their comrades to bear the brunt of the battle.

Ostensibly, this would not explain men not being available for Day 2. However, if men had not gone into the battle and then made themselves less conspicuous it could explain Holland's "there is some evidence". Holland then goes on to say that the brigadiers and battalion commanders will recognise how dangerous this problem is unless it is checked. Holland then goes on to argue that different motives drive different men.

"Some men go forward with "that fierce hunger for battle" that characterises the Japanese soldier. Others go forward because their sense of discipline compels them."

Leaving aside the racial analogy, Holland's point that motivations vary is a fair one, but it only refers to the motivated. He then comes to the nub of his argument. "But our ranks now contain many officers, non-commissioned officers and men in whom the sense of discipline is not deeply engrained". Holland then stressed the vital role of commanders in instilling a deeper sense of discipline. Given that he was a career soldier, Holland was likely to have had a strong sentiment for the pre-war Regular or indeed recalled reservist, whom he had known throughout his career. He may also have been looking to deflect blame from himself. As we have seen, 24th Division were blaming 1st Division. The fact that 24th Division lacked the experienced staff officers it needed was a matter of post-war correspondence. Haig had selected the Corps commander and the divisions so no blame could be laid at their door. They were Kitchener divisions so the Secretary of State for War would not accept they were less than up to the job. The dated copy of the report is 9 October. The tracings attached demonstrate clearly that Reddie was at fault for not advancing into Hulluch on Day 1. Holland had told him to push on and had clearly got plenty to do resolving the issues facing 2 Brigade. By the time 1 Brigade were approaching Hulluch, the success of 15th Division was known to Holland. If Holland had followed the key principles that he had stressed to his subordinates, he would have sent 3 Brigade or Green's Force into Hulluch, thereby isolating the Germans in front of 2 Brigade.

Like his predecessor, Holland did not seek to preserve his own reputation by criticising the army commander. Like Haking too, he would be promoted to Corps command.

Since the 1990s, there has been a discussion of an unofficial British list of "attack divisions". The SHLM group did an analysis of which divisions were used and their success rate. That analysis demonstrated how some divisions just did not make it on to the team sheet. This set of notes probably comes as close to explaining why 1st Division was not on that list. Their commander judged that they were not the division they once were when they had landed with the BEF. The formation of a separate Guards Division had already demoted 1st Division from its place as "senior" division of the British Army. Rank and file were not to blame that their formation was not the same as before, it was just a reality. The would not be selected for a major role again until "Operation Hush" in 1917. The division's selection then only adds to the evidence that the projected amphibious operation never seriously figured in Haig's strategic thinking.

24

Christmas in the Line, 1915-16

One of the key points about service on the Western Front was that much of it revolved around routine. Aside from the Learning Curve, battles, and VCs, much of the war was low tempo. Including these aspects gives a more rounded picture of service on the Western Front. It is particularly important when looking at a division that served throughout the conflict. The 1st Division began a three-month spell in October 1915 predominantly consisting of trench holding.

Following relief on 30 September, the 1st Division was able to rest until 5 October when it relieved 12th Division. The division then received verbal guidance on the plan for the coming week from the BGGS of IV Corps. This was used to draw up a plan of work for 1 and 3 Brigades who were to occupy the front. On 6 October the divisional staff settled into their new headquarters at the Chateau in Mazingarbe. The GOC himself, accompanied by his GSO1 and CRA, attended a conference at Army HQ. This resulted in confirmation of the front to be relieved, and Corps then issued the appropriate orders. The divisional staff then spent the evening drawing up orders to give effect to those received. Their work was completed, and the orders were issued at 11pm which gave the troops approximately 19 hours' notice of the moves next evening. Within two hours, 1 Brigade reported that it could not dig the trench to the point specified in the orders as it was occupied by the Germans. Division responded by saying they were giving the GOC 1 Brigade the discretion as to whether he ejected the enemy.[1]

The Black Watch occupied the old German line at Lone Tree on 7 October. In two days of intermittent shelling, they had lost seven dead and seven wounded, the attritional cost of maintain the Western Front. Four new subalterns arrived, and one was allocated to each company.[2] That same day, the GOC explained to his staff that the division had been tasked with seizing the Lens-La Bassée Road. The aim was to link up with the British trenches where they met the road. To support the assault, gas cylinders had been allocated to the division.

The men began preparations for the assault by preparing the trenches to accommodate gas cylinders. However, on 8 October 1st Division was informed that the attack was to be delayed by two days. On that same day their own trenches were attacked by the Germans. The Germans had approached from the direction of Hill 70. The preparations for the attack had been spotted

---

1   TNA WO 95/1229: War Diary of the 1st Division Headquarters, 30 September-6 October 1915.
2   TNA WO 95/1263: War Diary of the 1st Black Watch, 6-8 October 1915.

by the neighbouring French unit. They informed 1st Division at 10am that the Germans were busy and that this included making gaps in their wire. The divisional staff immediately alerted 3 Brigade of a possible attack. After artillery preparation, the Germans attacked at 3.30pm. The attack was repulsed by 3 Brigade and the French troops alongside them successfully defended their position. 3 Brigade captured one man from the 157th Regiment. Under questioning, he informed his captors that nine battalions had been involved in the attack. He stated that in addition to his own, the 216th Regiment had been involved as well as a "regiment of the Guard". In total 3 Brigade suffered 250 casualties.[3]

Again, on 10 October, the planned assault was delayed so the gas cylinders were not taken up to the trenches. Two days later the cylinders were put in position. The digging necessary required the whole of 2 Brigade so a battalion from 140 Brigade was placed in close support during the night. They returned to their parent brigade before dawn. All these efforts meant that 250 gas cylinders were now in position. The attack was postponed by Corps for a further 24 hours. This was designed to allow 60 more gas cylinders to be brought up. These were to be used to extend the gas field further to the right. On 11 October, 3 Brigade reported sounds of mining under their trenches and an officer of 100th Mining Company was sent to assess the situation. The next day 3 Brigade reported shelling by heavy artillery. The GOC and his staff responded in two ways. First, they requested Corps to direct some heavy artillery on the German batteries. Second, the GOC himself went up to the trenches and visited most of them during the afternoon.

At 11.15am on 13 October, Corps confirmed the attack to go in at 1pm. Within a quarter of an hour, Captain Garden had telephoned to confirm that the wind was favourable. By 2.40pm 1st Brigade reported that it had successfully advanced and taken the German first line opposite, except on the left opposite 1st Camerons. An artillery report suggested that troops had reached right to Hulluch. This was contradicted by 1 Brigade at 3.10pm. The requested artillery fire be directed onto the outskirts of Hulluch as no British troops had got beyond the Lens-La Bassee road. Despite this First Army passed on the information that British troops were in Hulluch. The difficulties in communication were evidenced by an ADC being sent to see Brigadier-General Thuillier. By 6.30pm, Holland had received a revised report that none of the German line had been taken. It was decided to launch a new attack by 2 Brigade as well as 1 Brigade but both brigadiers reported that they could not get their units into position by daybreak. Thuillier had already taken the step of informing his unit commanders not to proceed because they were not able to be ready in time. This forced the hand of Major-General Holland and Corps too accepted that renewal of the attack was not possible.[4]

In his subsequent report, Holland makes clear that the infantry assault went in at 2pm as scheduled. He stressed that headway was initially made under cover of the smoke but that once that cleared the fire from the Germans was too intense and stopped the attack. The Germans were able to enfilade the advance, so the troops received fire from two directions. After detailing the remaining narrative, the report ended by stating that the division had sustained about 1200 casualties. This was presumably designed to ensure that the fighting spirit of 1 Brigade was not questioned.

3   TNA WO 95/1229: War Diary of the 1st Division Headquarters, War Diary & Daily report 8 October 1915.
4   Thuillier, a Royal Engineer, went on to command 15th and 23rd divisions.

On 14 October, orders were received that they were to be relieved by 47th Division. The 1st Division spent the rest of October undertaking training with various units detached on duty at different times. This then continued into November, until 1st Division relieved 47th Division on 13 November.[5] The subject of "Winter work" was discussed at a conference at Army HQ on 8 November so the division would have entered the line aware of the expectations of Haig and his staff. Holland visited the trenches on 13 November and judged them to be in a very bad condition. He felt that a lot of work would need to be done. His attention to detail is evidenced by a further visit to the trenches on 16 November. He was there at 7am and saw bodies unburied from late September. He issued immediate orders for their immediate burial. On 25 November, Holland made another early morning visit; this time to the trenches that had just been taken over from 15th Division. The early morning appearance of a Major-General must have been a challenge to those officers and NCOs who were not on top of their roles.

On 2 December 1915 between 6 p.m. and Midnight, 2nd Brigade relieved 3rd Brigade in the trenches just North of Loos. In preparation for this relief, officers had been sent forward to reconnoitre. "Unfortunately," as the Brigade Major commented, they were seen and shelled, resulting in four men being wounded. Three officers were also wounded Lieutenant Colonel Wakeley and Captain Acton of the Loyal North Lancs and Captain Apperley of the Royal Sussex. Despite this and some German shelling, the brigade relief itself was carried out without further casualties.[6] Two companies of 2 Brigade did delay the relief by getting lost, and this was ascribed to them not trusting the guides provided by 3 Brigade.[7] During their twelve day tour, 2 Brigade suffered a further four other ranks killed and 62 wounded.[8] Although these figures would go unremarked if incurred on the Somme seven months later, they are indicative of the attritional nature of trench warfare where simply holding static positions lead to casualties.

The 2 Brigade moved into divisional reserve, where casualties for the next week fell to three killed and two wounded. However, it found that the large fatigue parties which it was required to furnish interfered with the opportunity to undertake training.[9] This highlights the long term issue of how to deploy the manpower available and the chronic shortage of units to undertake the enormous amount of effort needed to 'maintain a siege' on such a long front. The issue of the poor state of the trenches had been recorded by the Brigade Major of 3 Brigade on 1 December after he had toured them prior to the relief. He concluded that the shelling and the weather had damaged them very badly. Consequently, they needed revetting; He also noted that the Royal Engineers would be supervising troops to undertake work,[10] which accounts for the numerous fatigue parties that would subsequently have to be found by the battalions in divisional reserve.

On 14 December 1915, 1 Brigade relieved 2 Brigade in the front line near Loos and initially deployed the 8th Royal Berks and the 1st Black Watch in the front line with the London Scottish and 10th Gloucesters in support, and 1st Cameron Highlanders in Brigade support. At regular three-day intervals there were internal reliefs conducted to rotate the units.[11]

---

5   TNA WO 95/1229: War Diary of the 1st Division Headquarters, 28 October-13 November 1915.
6   TNA WO 95/1267: War Diary of the 2nd Infantry Brigade, Headquarters, December 1915.
7   TNA WO 95/1275: War Diary of the 3rd Infantry Brigade, Headquarters, 2 December 1915.
8   TNA WO 95/1267: War Diary of the 2nd Infantry Brigade, Headquarters, December 1915.
9   TNA WO 95/1267: War Diary of the 2nd Infantry Brigade, Headquarters, December 1915.
10   TNA WO 95/1275: War Diary of the 3rd Infantry Brigade, Headquarters, December 1915.
11   TNA WO 95/1261: War Diary of the 1st Infantry Brigade, Headquarters, December 1915.

Christmas Day for the 1st Cameron Highlanders in the front line, with French troops to their right, "passed as usual" with artillery activity on both sides. Having relieved the 1st Black Watch in the front line on 23 December, after three days in the support trenches, the Highlanders were able to move to billets on 26 December.[12] Having also spent Christmas Day in the trenches, the men of 8th Royal Berkshires were able to march to their billets in Noeux Les Mines on Boxing Day. It was here that Second Lieutenant Woodford, who had previously been reported wounded, was recorded as having been killed, as his body had been found about 10 yards from the British wire. Second Lieutenant Clarke was transferred back to England whilst 151 other ranks, in two drafts, joined the battalion. The casualties of the battalion during December 1915 were three killed and seventeen wounded.[13] Meanwhile, the Cameron Highlanders remained in their billets at Mazingarbe, though on 30 December they had to stand to for about thirty minutes around 6 p.m., as the Germans had exploded some mines.

The close of the year led the Adjutant of 8th Royal Berkshires to review the prevailing disciplinary situation. He noted that ten men had been tried by Field General Courts Martial during 1915. Of these two men had been found guilty of being drunk in the trenches and been sentenced to 84 days of Field Punishment No 1. Three further men had been tried and sentenced for inflicting wounds on themselves; they had been sentenced to 35, 84 and 84 days of Field Punishment No 1, respectively. Five more men had been found guilty of being asleep on sentry duty. In all their cases, the death sentence had been commuted to between six and twelve months imprisonment with hard labour. The Adjutant then commented that the offences had all occurred during early tours of the trenches and concluded that;

"Evidently the sentences had an excellent deterrent effect on the men."[14] This evidence supports the view that the 1st Division did have discipline problems following the losses in 1914 and subsequent changes. However, this was a New Army battalion so it is perhaps evidence that it was the dilution of the original division that led to an overall drop in standards, which were then addressed. It is hardly surprising that some of those who joined up in the first flush of Kitchener's appeal found the desperate reality nof trench warfare difficult to cope with.

The 8th Berkshires marched back to the trenches on New Year's Day 1916, moving forward at 3 p.m., with 10-minute intervals between companies. They relieved the Northamptons as right support battalion, in 10th Avenue from Hay Alley to Vendin Alley. The Berkshires then remained in the trenches until 1st Division was relieved by 47th London Division on 13 January.[15] Alongside them were the 10th Gloucesters who, unwittingly echoing Remarque, noted that it was a "quiet time" whilst recording several casualties including two killed.[16]

The Cameron Highlanders had also returned to the trenches on New Year's Day, initially relieving the 1st Loyal North Lancs in the support trenches. There, they established two companies in the old German front line and two in the old British front line. The Camerons then

---

12   TNA WO 95/1264: War Diary of the 1st Battalion Queen's Own Cameron Highlanders, December 1915.
13   TNA WO 95/1265: War Diary of the 8th Battalion Royal Berkshire Regiment, December 1915.
14   TNA WO 95/1265: War Diary of the 8th Battalion Royal Berkshire Regiment, December 1915, Appendix 1.
15   TNA WO 95/1265: War Diary of the 8th Battalion Royal Berkshire Regiment, December 1915, 1 and 13 January 1915.
16   TNA WO 95/1265: War Diary of the 10th Battalion Gloucestershire Regiment, January 1916.

relieved the Black Watch in the front line three days later before being themselves relieved by their fellow Scots, in the front line. From there, they moved to billets in Philosophe, where they provided the pool from which various fatigue parties were drawn.[17] The work being undertaken by these fatigue parties can be inferred from the daily Tactical Progress Report being produced by 1st Division, which detailed the work being undertaken on the left where 1st Brigade were positioned[18] as well as on the right. Each report covered a period from noon to noon, reflecting the reality that most of the work would be completed at night.

As 1 Brigade had returned to the trenches and would be there for the first half of January, it seems appropriate to pick the mid-point of their stay as a snapshot of the activity being undertaken to strengthen their position. On the night of 6-7 January 1916, the men of 1 Brigade were busy cleaning and revetting the front line, as well as Merthyr Sap and Seventh Avenue. They also cleaned the Support Line south of Essex Lane and South Street. As well as this they cleaned and deepened 250 yards of trench south of Wings Way towards Devon Lane and commenced work on the fire step. They also deepened a section of the reserve trench. The work on Sap 45 was nearly completed, and the sap was wired; whilst work on Lone Tree Redoubt continued. Regarding Holly Lane it was noted that, following cleaning, it was now passable by day from the support line to the front line. Stone Street, from the support line to the front line, was cleaned and boards laid. The wire to the north of Hay Alley was strengthened. In Devon Lane, which was a defensive flank, thirteen T-heads were completed.

On the same night, the right brigade area saw the work on the fire trenches, including revetting, continue. In addition to this, Vendin Alley was cleaned, and trench boards were laid in it from the fire trench to the support trench. In addition to this, the support trench was extended by 350 yards from Vendin Trench, and in Broadway the traverses were revetted and the fire step was made. Furthermore, the work on the reserve trench and the work to join Strand Alley and Railway Alley continued; as did that on the Keeps. In addition to all this, the wire south of Strand Alley was strengthened.[19] All this illustrates the vast amount of physical labour being undertaken by the British troops between periods of more military activity.

However, despite the time of year and the need to undertake such extensive maintenance, Major General Holland was keen to undertake some offensive military action. He had therefore ordered, in late December, that the GOC 2nd Brigade order the 2nd King's Royal Rifles to prepare to undertake a raid, by eighty officers and men, on the German trenches at Puits 14 Bis. Holland reported to IV Corps that he had intended initially to break into the German line at two points and that the two elements of the raiding party would then have worked towards each other. However, the Germans had then created a new front line so it had been decided to break in at one point, from which the two halves of the raiding group would fan out for a certain time before returning to the entry point. Holland enclosed tracings with his report so that the Corps commander could see what he was referring to. It turned out that it took longer to effect an entry into the chosen sector than anticipated. This therefore significantly reduced the time available to the raiders to explore the German line and do damage. There were no casualties incurred

---

17 TNA WO 95/1264: War Diary of the 1st Battalion Queen's Own Cameron Highlanders, January 1916.
18 TNA WO 95/1230: War Diary of the 1st Division, Headquarters, 30 December 1915.
19 TNA WO 95/1230: War Diary of the 1st Division, Headquarters, 7 January 1916.

amongst the raiders. Holland went on to add that the entry point and route to be covered were chosen because they were not vulnerable to being enfiladed by machine gun fire. [20]

Following relief of the Black Watch, the Camerons were relieved on 13 January by the 15th Highland Light Infantry of 46th Brigade, 15th Division.[21] The relief meant 1st Division moved into Corps reserve.[22] As two different divisions relieved the 1st Division, it is evident that these large moves occasioned the opportunity to adjust major command boundaries.

The normal process of trench familiarisation involved attaching newly arrived units to experienced ones. During January 1916, 1st Brigade had men from the 9th Munsters, and the Royal Irish Rifles attached to them. The attached units experienced rotation with their parent units. It is noteworthy that whereas sometimes stints in the trenches were extended at other times, the bitter days of December and January saw regular three-day rotations for the troops, about half the time spent on an average tour during the bulk of the year.

The opportunity for the men to train in their battalions was matched by the officers in 3 Brigade where the Brigade Major, Major Berkeley, (of 2nd Welsh) went off to attend an advanced staff course at GHQ. In his absence, the role was to be filled by Captain Bosanquet of 1st Gloucesters. The Brigade staff recorded the usual problems of balancing training with the demands to provide substantial working parties. The focus of the initial training was on junior officers and NCOs. This was stated to be in preparation for subsequent training for sections and platoons.[23] On 16 January, the officers of 3 Brigade were visited by Major General Holland who presented ribbons to those officers whose awards had been gazetted on 15 January. On 17 January, the acting-Brigadier visited the Gloucesters and South Wales Borderers during their training, and on 18 January the same battalions were viewed at training, along with the brigade pioneers, by Brigadier Davies who had returned from leave the day before. The Brigadier again reviewed the Gloucesters during training and then went to see the Munsters training.[24] On 1 February, Brigadier Davies of 3 Brigade motored over to First Army training school, to make arrangements for future brigade training.[25]

The period spent between October 1915 and January 1916 illustrates the variety of tasks undertaken by soldiers outside battle. The chronic shortage of available manpower is underlined by the constant need for working parties. This need meant that training was sacrificed to meet current needs. One can see that any unofficial list of "attack divisions" becoming a self-reinforcing circle. Divisions not selected for attacks became more immersed in constant trench routine. They then were more likely to be used for working parties when out of the line and to get very limited opportunities to train. Thus, multiple lanes began to manifest themselves in the BEF's learning curves be. 1st Division was commencing its time in the slow lane.

20 TNA WO 95/1230: War Diary of the 1st Division, Headquarters, Report 12 January 1916.
21 TNA WO 95/1261: War Diary of the 1st Infantry Brigade Headquarters, January 1916.
22 TNA WO 95/1264: War Diary of the 1st Battalion Queen's Own Cameron Highlanders, January 1916.
23 TNA WO 95/1275: War Diary of the 3rd Infantry Brigade, Headquarters, 8 January 1916.
24 TNA WO 95/1275: War Diary of the 3rd Infantry Brigade, Headquarters, January 1916.
25 TNA WO 95/1275: War Diary of the 3rd Infantry Brigade, Headquarters, 1 February 1916.

25

Maintaining the Entente Cordiale

Great Britain's entry into the First World War meant sending a numerically inferior force to assist France whose army was based upon peacetime conscription. The early encounters between Sir John French and General Lanrezac had done nothing to improve relations between the two armies. However, relations had since improved. This was probably partly due to a begrudging and unspoken recognition by the French command that they needed the British. Joffre had dismissed Lanrezac before the Marne in 1914. During the subsequent brutal fighting at Ypres, Joffre's man on the spot was Foch. Foch had a longstanding friendship with General Henry Wilson so relations between the two staffs were bound to improve. During 1915, Joffre, as well as Haig and several British politicians, had continued to voice concerns about Sir John French's performance. The dismissal of French in December 1915, by British Prime Minister Asquith, had therefore opened the door to further improved relations. It is in this context that the French Commander in Chief, Marshal Joffre paid a visit to 1st Division. For Haig, too, it was now an opportunity as CinC of the BEF to return to a division which had served under him in I Corps in 1914.

One can only imagine the joy all ranks felt when Major Fortune issued further orders on 18 January regarding the impending visit of Marshal Joffre. Fortune described Joffre as the "Commander in Chief of the Allied forces". The visit was scheduled for Thursday 20 January at Ferfay Chateau. Joffre was to be met at the chateau by the commanders of First Army, with his Major General General Staff, AA and QMG, and IV Corps. Lieutenant General Rawlinson, was to attend with staff, as well as Major General Holland, who was permitted two staff officers.[1] The dignitaries were to be greeted by a guard of honour consisting of three officers and one hundred men of the Black Watch. The guard's commander was to be told where to position his men inside the grounds by the commandant of the bomb school based at the chateau, which would itself be the first element of the visit. After the planned ten-minute visit to the bomb school, Joffre was to be taken to meet the commander of First Army Engineers and the Major General Royal Artillery, who would join the dignitaries for three demonstrations. Joffre was to be shown trench mortars cutting wire and a demonstration of smoke. Neither seems as tactically

---

[1] Despite Haig's support, Rawlinson had not been given command of First Army. Four days after the parade, Haig informed Rawlinson that he was to have Fourth Army.

interesting as the third, which was the demonstration of a "combined trench mortar, bombing and machine gun attack".[2]

It was planned that Joffre would leave at the end of the forty-minute set of demonstrations and proceed to Chateau Philomel by car. Corps orders had been issued to ensure that the route would be kept clear. Continuing the Scottish theme, presumably to please General Haig, the guard of honour en route as France's top general passed through Burbure would be found by men of 2nd Brigade drawn from the Camerons and London Scottish. Major Fortune was leaving nothing to chance by including instructions that the men should be one yard apart and should present arms as Joffre passed as well as that they should be on both sides of the road facing inwards. The officers were to be on foot and not to carry greatcoats, waterproofs or sticks whilst the men were to be in Field Service Marching Order with their haversack replacing their pack and their waterproof sheet neatly folded under the flap.

Having instructed the officers that the Camerons were to line the road northwards from the church whilst the London Scottish were to line it southwards from the church, Major Fortune left it to them to agree the demarcation point. In Lilliers, men of the Black Watch, 8th Royal Berkshires and the 10th Gloucesters would line the road in the same manner as the troops in Burbure. All these men were to be passed by a procession in which Joffre occupied the first car, but a staff officer from 1st Division would precede the procession. Basic movement orders were included for the units destined for Lilliers as well as the Adjutants of those battalions being summoned to a meeting in the Grand Place in Lilliers at 2.30 p.m. on Wednesday 19 January. The London Scottish were also to mount a guard consisting of three officers and one hundred men at Lilliers Station which was where Joffre would eventually depart from. They were given strict instructions on their movements so that they would not pass Joffre on their way to mount the guard.[3]

Divisional orders were designed to ensure the kind of spontaneous demonstration of approval that the choreographers of the Thatcher and Blair era stop-watch driven "standing ovations" would have approved of. At 8 p.m. on 16 January, Captain Dubbin signed orders for Joffre's visit stating:

> All troops not on parade, or not otherwise on duty, billeted within two miles of the above named villages, including men from the Ammunition Columns, Field Ambulances and Train, shall turn out properly dressed, but not under arms, and will be collected in groups of not more than 30 each, and each under an officer, at convenient points behind the line of troops, and will cheer the Allied Commander-in-Chief as he passes in his car.[4]

This sidelight on life in the British Army out of the line can best be summarised, perhaps appropriately as *plus ça change, plus c'est la même chose*.

At Lilliers, Joffre was due to inspect 2nd Brigade which would be led by Lieutenant Colonel Villers DSO, in the absence of Brigadier Thuillier who was on leave. They had arrived in their billets on Sunday 16 January and had devoted the day to cleaning up. Training had been

---

2 TNA WO 95/1261: War Diary of the 1st Infantry Brigade, January 1916
3 TNA WO 95/1261: War Diary of the 1st Infantry Brigade, January 1916.
4 TNA WO 95/1230: War Diary of the 1st Division, Headquarters, 16 January 1916.

undertaken on the following day whilst the billets of the 1st Northants had been inspected by brigade staff in the afternoon. Training had continued on 18 January, but 19 January was devoted to holding a practice parade. On 20 January, the brigade was drawn up in line of battalions, in order of seniority, with the 23rd Field Company, Royal Engineers on their right. Having the Royal Engineers on the right and therefore first was a nice touch, as Joffre had himself been an engineer until his appointment as France's most senior soldier. On the left of the infantry battalions were the brigaded machine guns. The French Liaison officers and interpreters formed the final group on the left of the parade. Joffre presented the senior officers present, Haig, Rawlinson and Wilson, with decorations and the parade was dismissed at 4.30 p.m.[5]

The route to 1st Division headquarters was lined by men of 3rd Brigade.[6] Apart from its involvement with Joffre's inspection, 1 Brigade spent the second half of January 1916 undertaking training.[7] For the rest of the month, 2 Brigade remained in billets and conducted training each day; however, on 26 January they were put on short notice to move due to increased German activity. On 27 January they were put on three hours' notice, but this did not stop a concert going ahead in the evening or Brigadier Thuillier reconnoitring the 1st Division manoeuvre area on 28 January. Training continued on 29 January whilst the brigadier and his staff received a visit from General Haig at 4 p.m.

On Sunday 30 January there was a Brigade Church Parade, but the rest of the day was designated as a rest.[8] Major General Holland went on leave on 21 January and was replaced temporarily by Brigadier Davies of 3rd Brigade. The next day, the 3rd Brigade Machine Gun Company was formed with Captain Lyttleton and Captain Raikes being assigned to this new unit from 2nd Welsh and 1st South Wales Borderers respectively. They were joined by Lieutenant Hewitt from 2nd Welsh and several subalterns; McCann and Nelder of the Munsters, Cook and Langton from the Gloucesters, Barrett from the Welsh and Geldard from the Borderers.[9] This is an example of the general reorganisation of the BEF in the light of the experience gained in the first 18 months of the conflict.

This period of training provides evidence that 1st Division was trying hard to raise performance, at the micro-level of sections and platoons. as early as January 1916. Leaving aside the disruption caused by visiting VIPs, the primary restriction on training was the need to provide working parties. The available manpower was being used to expand the infantry without providing sufficient labour for them to be freed up to concentrate on improving their performance. This situation provides a key context for the introduction of conscription in January 1916. Major Berkeley's departure reflected GHQ's recognition that the creation of more, larger formations meant expanding the pool of trained staff officers.

5   TNA WO 95/1267: War Diary of the 2nd Infantry Brigade, Headquarters, January 1916.
6   TNA WO 95/1275: War Diary of the 3rd Infantry Brigade, Headquarters, January 1916.
7   TNA WO 95/1261: War Diary of the 1st Infantry Brigade, January 1916.
8   TNA WO 95/1267: War Diary of the 2nd Infantry Brigade, Headquarters, January 1916.
9   TNA WO 95/1275: War Diary of the 3rd Infantry Brigade, Headquarters, January 1916.

Part II

1st Division in the Conscription Era

1916–1919

26

Loos Trenches

Much of the period covered in this chapter involved routine trench holding and necessary rotations. The pressures and problems these created are covered generally in this book. Therefore, this chapter mentions major episodes but also picks out events behind the scenes in a division which had not been selected to take part in the forthcoming offensive on the Somme.

February brought an order for 2 Brigade to "stand down". They had been on two hours' notice to move. However, uncertainty at the front meant it was necessary to initially postpone and then to cancel a divisional exercise planned for 7 February. Instead, they carried out a concentrated march and it was noted that it was very well done with the timings being perfect. As march tables required units to be able to move at an agreed speed it was important that units could achieve the required standard. On 10 February, senior officers visited 47th Division in preparation for relieving them in the line. Two days later, the sickness level was noted to be three officers and 178 men. It was added that 50 Other Ranks had been discharged to jobs other than duty. The following day the Corps Commander gave a lecture to the officers in the theatre at Lillers. Officer training at the Officer School had now started and would continue indefinitely.[1] This reflected the British Army's decision to recruit from the ranks. The Germans, whose officer class was even more exclusive, preferred to delegate more to NCOs than dilute the Officer Corps.

During stormy weather, 2 and then 1 Brigade began to enter the line to relieve 47th Division. Commander Plunkett and a Marine team arrived to be given instruction. Such was the shortage of rifle grenades that 15th Division were ordered to send 200. The reality of returning to trench warfare was brought was brought home by a German attack at 7pm on 19 February. In the fighting around Harts and Harrison Craters, one officer and nineteen men were killed. Eight ORs were posted missing and 74 were wounded, three officers were also wounded. The main unit engaged was the South Wales Borderers. They found some of the trench mortars became unserviceable so 3 Brigade were told to send up replacements and 47th Division left replacements with 3 Brigade. On 26 February, Sir Charles Monro, the newly appointed GOC First Army, visited divisional HQ. This was a period of heavy snow and urgent requests were made for white smocks; less were available than required. Despite the bitter cold only 9 men featured on the "chilled feet" report submitted at the end of the month. Even away from the line, death could

---

1 TNA WO 95/1236: War Diary of the 1st Division Headquarters, 1-14 February 1916.

come suddenly. A shell hit a billet occupied by the Royal Munster Fusiliers, 6 were killed and 13 wounded. This billet in Mazingarbe was then moved.[2]

March opened with more snow before an equally challenging thaw set in. The 1st Division was now designated as part of I Corps and a variety of units were attached for training. Brigadier-General Thuillier was ordered to report for duty at Corps HQ. Thuillier was a Royal Engineer who now spent time on gas warfare. In 1917 he would be promoted to Major-General as GOC 15th Division. Given the experience of the division, it is interesting to note that his replacement came from 20th London Regiment. Hubbach had been the government architect in the Malay Federation before the war. Having been a Lieutenant-Colonel in the Malay States Volunteer Reserve, he was then appointed as a Major in the 19th London Territorials in 1914. He was then promoted in 1915 to Lieutenant-Colonel as OC 20th London Regiment. Moving a territorial officer to command a brigade in a regular division is unusual especially as he had no prior experience in South Africa, for example. At Aubers Ridge, 2 Brigade had struggled to get organised after the first attack, perhaps this explains an outside appointment.

General Monro returned to distribute medals earned during the crater fighting in February. Both the British and the Germans exploded mines on the Double Crassier. Unfortunately, the blast from the British mine caused damage at Fosse 6. This affected the divisional water supply so the staff had to obtain lorries to shift bulk supplies of water whilst repairs were made. Leave had previously been suspended but orders were received that it would re-start on 20 March. The division had been allocated 50.[3]

April started with the Germans shelling divisional HQ at Braquemont. No damage was done. Four days later the Germans shelled Fosse 2, so rapid moves were made to empty the bomb store there. Colonel Berkeley had opened the officer school in March. Their course having been completed; the new officers had been sent out on attachment. The staff were also busy sorting out the billeting area. The boundary between 1st and 16th Divisions had been defined rather vaguely. The HQ was shelled again on 8 April and this time the salvage hut was hit. The sacks of salvaged SAA in the shed ignited. QMS Dorling, the Chief Clerk in the Q Office had been posted to Corps HQ and was replaced by Staff Sergeant Wooster. Major Dobbs, OC Signals, was posted to Fourth Army Signals and Captain Brierley, 2 Brigade Signals was posted to 16th Division. Captain Dobbs was being promoted from GSO2 of 1st Division to GSO2 of VIII Corps. Clearly 1st Division was seen as having experienced people capable of being promoted.[4]

On a very practical note, a collection point for boots was now established at Les Brebis. This was so that boots, that had been repaired, could be tried on by the men before they took them away. The divisional Cyclists were relieved from trench duty so that they could spend time training with 1st Cavalry Division. In their case they would be working with the Northumberland Hussars. The possibility of the cavalry being used to exploit a breakthrough after the Somme seems to have been the context for this training. Lieutenant-Colonel McNaughton RFA was promoted to Brigadier-General on transfer to 15th Division. After being shelled heavily for two days, 1st Division found that it was 16th Division the Germans were actually attacking on 27 April. The next day the Northamptons carried out a raid, they only incurred five casualties. Approximately 30 casualties resulted from a German attack on the Hulluch part of the trenches. The total

2   TNA WO 95/1236: War Diary of the 1st Division Headquarters, 15-29 February 1916.
3   TNA WO 95/1236: War Diary of the 1st Division Headquarters, 1-31 March 1916.
4   TNA WO 95/1236: War Diary of the 1st Division Headquarters, 1-11 April 1916.

number of casualties in April was 625 and 732 men went sick. There were 862 reinforcements which meant the drop in the number of effectives was 495. [5]

On 3 May a raid was carried out. It was notable for having sustained the fewest casualties of any raid since the division had entered the line in February. It was also the day when the army commander presented medal ribbons. It was noted that these included the new Military Medal. The medal had been created to recognise acts of gallantry and devotion to duty under fire by Other Ranks. The awards had been bac dated to 1914. The ever present danger of German shelling was emphasised by new arrangements for the Loos sector. All rations destined for that sector had to go to Maroc first. They were also instructed not to leave Maroc for at least half an hour. On 16 May, 2nd Welsh handed over their sector at Loos to 16th Division. A German raid, during a relief, led to two men being captured. Of wider significance, German gas shells forced the temporary closure of the baths at Les Brebis. Repairing them was made a priority. The Germans had shelled various points on nearly every day of the month. On 26 May German shelling of the Callone sector destroyed a British occupied minework tower. The next day the British succeeded in destroying a gun emplacement at Puits 16. This success drew fire and eight men were killed and twenty were wounded. In another sector a German observer was captured. He talked freely about forthcoming attacks. There was also a German raid. The raiders did not get into the trenches. However, there were 25 casualties. This was due to the shelling and because the German raiding party ran into a British wiring party.[6] The constant tit for tat of siege warfare continued into June. The line along the Double Crassier would remain static until autumn 1918. However, other changes were afoot. On 12 June, Major-General Holland left to become CRA Third Army. His successor was Major-General Peter Strickland.[7]

---

5   TNA WO 95/1236: War Diary of the 1st Division Headquarters, 12-30 April 1916.
6   TNA WO 95/1236: War Diary of the 1st Division Headquarters, 1-31 May 1916.
7   Strickland was to command 1st Division until the end of the war.

27

The Double Crassier

On 6 December 1915, Allied military leaders met to plan how to achieve greater success in 1916. As a result, the forthcoming summer was to result in total victory by denying the Central Powers the benefit of interior lines of communication. The Anglo-French offensive on the Somme, the Western Front contribution the projected Allied offensives, was significantly disrupted by the German assault on Verdun. Despite subordinate pleas, Joffre reduced the French commitment to the planned Somme offensive, as French troops and equipment were despatched along the *via sacré* to the infamous "mincing machine" on the Meuse. The British, led by their new commander General Sir Douglas Haig, therefore continued to prepare for their part in the planned offensive. There was constant pressure from the French High Command to take the weight off their front by forcing the Germans to divert resources away from Verdun.

Strickland's first full day in command was spent at Corps headquarters. The preparations for the Somme offensive involved a series of machine gun, trench mortar and artillery bombardments on the German positions, starting on 25 June, to distract the Germans from preparations elsewhere. It was noted that initially this had drawn no response, but that the Germans had increasingly responded which suggested to the 8th Royal Berkshires that the diversions were working.[1]

One specific diversion was a raid carried out on the night of 25/26 June by 2nd Royal Munster Fusiliers which was temporarily attached to 1 Brigade whilst 10th Gloucesters were temporarily attached to 3 Brigade. D company of the Gloucesters remained out of the line preparing for a raid scheduled for 5 July.[2] The subsequent raid by eight officers and 152 men of the Munsters did not go smoothly and no prisoners were taken. This was despite the wire having been demolished so little cutting was necessary. Brigade requested a report. In responding, Lieutenant Colonel Lyons summarised the reasons, as follows:

> Our parties suffered heavily on entering the gaps. Consequently, our men were in no temper to take prisoners, moreover, the evacuation of our wounded practically occupied the attention of all ranks.[3]

---

1 TNA WO 95/1265: War Diary of the 8th Battalion Royal Berkshire Regiment, 1-2 July 1916
2 TNA WO 95/1265: War Diary of the 10th Battalion Gloucestershire Regiment, 25-28 June 1916.
3 TNA WO 95/1279: War Diary of the 2nd Battalion Royal Munster Fusiliers, June 1916 Appendix 14.

Of the four officers involved, one was killed, two were wounded and the other was posted as Missing presumed killed. Of the men, 1 was recorded as killed, 27 were wounded and 13 posted as missing. This represents nearly a third of the raiders. In the dark and unfamiliar environment of the enemy trenches, casualty evacuation would have been difficult. The first two key objectives laid down in the plan were to bring in at least one prisoner and obtain identifications.[4] The Divisional diary records that both parties encountered stiff resistance. This would explain why the objectives were not met. It is interesting that Lyons does not cite the incapacitation of Lieutenant Batten-Pooll as a reason; perhaps because his VC citation states that he continued directing operations.

The detailed report says that the southern group reacted to temporary wiring in the sap by advancing along the parapets, as planned in case of this eventuality. The report goes on to describe the Germans as having temporarily wired the trench on either side of the gap in the wire. It then explains that all parties had reported that they had come under grenade fire from a position to the rear, even though the aerial photographs showed no trench nearer than the support trench 100 yards further back. The overall impression given is that the Germans had anticipated when the raid was due and prepared accordingly. They had temporarily wired their own trenches. Only the thoroughly cut wire in front of the trenches was visible to the Munsters. The assessment that they would be less vigilant at this point proved to be erroneous.[5] The fire from behind the front trench suggests that some of the defenders had moved to the rear of the trench in a mini version of the tactics adopted later in the war. In this case, the front line trench was effectively abandoned temporarily so that it could become the killing zone. This assessment is further reinforced by the Germans setting off flares as the British troops advanced along the parapets,[6] but there is no record of this leading to a defensive barrage coming down. It would seem therefore that the Germans deliberately avoided using distress flares as they were in the zone that would be barraged.

Faced with these difficulties and dangers, one man's actions were seen to stand out. Lieutenant Henry Batten-Pooll had transferred to 3rd Munsters from the 5th (Royal Irish) Lancers because he wanted to see action. He had then managed to be attached to 2nd Munsters and took a lead part in the raid. The citation read as follows:

> Lieutenant Batten-Pooll was in command of a raiding party when, on entering the enemy's lines he was severely wounded by a bomb which broke and mutilated all the fingers of his right hand. In spite of this he continued to direct operations with unflinching courage. Half an hour later, during the withdrawal, while personally assisting in the rescue of the other wounded men, he received two further wounds, but refusing assistance, he walked to within 100 yards of our own lines when he fainted and was carried in by the covering party.

Lieutenant (Temporary Captain) Dunn, as Adjutant of 3 Brigade, spent 1 July 1916 with the 2nd Welsh. They were laying out practice trenches in the vicinity of Les Brebis, in preparation

---

4   TNA WO 95/1279: War Diary of the 2nd Battalion Royal Munster Fusiliers, June 1916 Appendix 13.
5   TNA WO 95/1279: War Diary of the 2nd Battalion Royal Munster Fusiliers, June 1916 Appendix 13.
6   TNA WO 95/1279: War Diary of the 2nd Battalion Royal Munster Fusiliers, June 1916 Appendix 14.

for a raid,[7] under the eagle-eye of Brigadier Davies. It was noted by Davies staff that attention to detail was important due to the failure of an attack on "the triangle" by 2 Brigade. The raid on "the triangle" had only just taken place on 30 June. In addition to diversionary shelling and barraging of German rear areas, front line positions had been targeted. This included wire cutting as part of the diversionary effort to support the Fourth Army on the Somme.

Of the four desired gaps in the wire in front of "the triangle", two were actual gaps and one was a partial cut through that left a lot of debris. The gaps had then been kept open by machine gun and mortar fire to prevent repairs. This demonstrates one of the great problems for commanders in the First World War. Stopping the wire being repaired was very sensible but the same process had been followed prior to the raid by the Munsters. This would have put the Germans on the alert. In addition, the timescale followed was likely to be similar. The artillery would cut the wire, and the progress would be evaluated in daylight. The raid would then be confirmed for the following night to give time for final preparations. In the meantime, the gaps would be kept open by the machine gun and mortar crews. So, if you were a reasonably alert German you could plot the likely time when you would be attacked. Unless the assaulting force made several extra gaps in the wire and had them all covered by protective fire, then the defenders would also know the target of the attack. That this is not mere supposition is borne out by the details of the raid.

The raid was a 2 Brigade operation, drawing men from 2nd KRRC and 2nd Royal Sussex. The preparations were complete by 6pm and the units had assembled in their positions by 8.30pm ready for zero hour at 9.10pm. Brigadier Hubbach stressed that zero hour had been communicated to those concerned at 3pm under secret covers. Whether consciously or not, he had set zero hour two hours earlier than that of the Munsters. This would be sensible. However, the suppositions laid out earlier may well explain what happened next. At 9pm, the Germans brought down a barrage on the front, support, and communication trenches in front of "the triangle". As explained, it would not need a breach of security to give the Germans the idea that enemy troops would be moving up into these positions on that night.

Despite this setback the attack went ahead. At 9.10 pm, the British barrage opened. It was described by Hubbach as very accurate. Under cover of the barrage, the Bangalore torpedoes were fired. These created the necessary gaps in the British wire and blew the end of the Russian sap. Compared with Aubers Ridge this meant tell-tale removal of British wire was avoided. However, as explained above, the gaps in the German wire were still a giveaway.

Five minutes later four mines were exploded. As at the Somme on 1 July, this was the signal to the Germans that there was now going to be an infantry assault.

The two parties assaulting "the triangle" were drawn from the 2nd KRRC. The left hand column was led by Captain Johnstone. This column met with very heavy rifle and machine gun fire. Nevertheless, it succeeded in blocking off some trenches, or parts thereof, and at least one sap. They then defended their captured area until 3am. During which time, the accompanying members of 173rd Tunnelling Company were able to destroy a German mine. Eventually, the heavy casualties suffered forced them to withdraw.

The right hand column, accompanied by the raid commander Major Barber, was led by Captain Fryer. This group had the initial advantage of attacking point W where one of the

7   TNA WO 95/1281: War Diary of the 2nd Battalion, The Welsh Regiment, 30 June -1July 1916.

mines had done a lot of damage. However, this group too was met with machine gun fire and some rifle fire from the trench itself when it tried to reach the entrances to the German tunnels. The accompanying tunnellers and their escort were unable to reach the enemy mines and were lost in the fighting. The right hand column did secure a small section of trench but were unable to achieve their objectives. Eventually, when the two columns were unable to link up, Major Barber, ordered the column to withdraw.

The third group of raiders, drawn from the Royal Sussex, under Captain MacDonald attacked the Crassier. Here they found the trench full of wire. The Germans had positioned a machine gun so that it could fire along the trench. As with the Munsters, they encountered the same tactics, the Sussex then tried to move along the parapet. However, this was not possible as they were exposed to machine gun fire from the direction of Harrison's crater. The Sussex did succeed in capturing part of an enemy sap and then were involved in a long bombing fight in that sap. Eventually, when it was clear the attack on "the triangle" had not succeeded, the Sussex withdrew.

In his summary, Hubbach stressed that much damage had been done and a large number of casualties had been inflicted. More definitely, he was able to report that 18 prisoners had been captured. His initial estimate was that the casualties suffered by the raiders amounted to 299. This was later revised to 426, including two officers and 44 men killed. A further 14 officers and 285 ORs were wounded and 81 men were posted as missing. Of the 426, 96 were from the Royal Sussex.

That afternoon, the staff of 3 Brigade received first intimations of the attack by Third and Fourth Armies.[8] However, 8th Division had suffered 4,921 casualties on 1 July 1916 and so on the same night it was relieved by 12th Division and, after its artillery had been relieved three nights later, it was transferred to First Army in exchange for 1st Division.[9] This put in train numerous reliefs, as units were initially concentrated behind the front so that the division could make its way to the Somme. On 6 July, 1st Division was placed under II Corps administratively and III Corps tactically. It was then instructed to move forward in "easy stages" before eventually beginning to enter the line on 10 July.[10]

---

8   TNA WO 95/1276: War Diary of the 3rd Infantry Brigade Headquarters, 1 July 1916
9   Edmonds, *OH, 1916*, Vol. 2, p.8,fn.1.
10 TNA WO 95/1236: War Diary of the 1st Division Headquarters, 25 June-12 July 1916 and Appendices.

28

Contalmaison, Mametz Wood and Pozières

The 1st Division relieved 23rd Division in the centre of III Corps sector.¹ On 10 July the Loyal North Lancs, as part of 2 Brigade, moved into the support line in Becourt Wood. The 1 Brigade went into the line to occupy the newly captured Contalmaison village. That left 3 Brigade were in reserve.² The brigade held the line from the north-west corner of Baliff Wood through the front of the village down to where they linked up with 21st Division. The 10th Gloucesters, as support formation of 1 Brigade, were positioned in Albert.³ The brigade spent the date setting up posts based on machine guns and/or trench made, 1 Brigade easily repulsed a small counterattack by one battalion of Germans.

The Loyal North Lancs spent 11 July on half-hour notice to move up in support of 1st Brigade; they commented that the situation was obscure.⁴ The 2nd Welsh were ordered mortars. They sent a patrol down Pearl Alley and established two posts in Pearl Wood. Overnight, with assistance from RE and pioneer personnel, the village was strongly wired. On the following day posts were established in Contalmaison Wood. The former German communication trench was also consolidated into the line. Given all the preparations they had forward to Albert where they were assigned "fairly good billets". During their stay they lost six killed and twenty-one other ranks wounded to a single heavy calibre shell.⁵

On 12 July the Loyal North Lancs understood the situation was clearer because 62nd Brigade held Mametz Wood, the 13 Northumberland Fusiliers having cleared the northern end of the wood and made touch with the right flank of 1st Division.⁶ On 13 July the Loyal North Lancs were taken off 30 minutes notice and therefore further reconnaissance of the line was undertaken.⁷

1   Edmonds, *OH, 1916*, Vol. 2, map opposite p.43.
2   TNA WO 95/1270: War Diary of the 1st Battalion Loyal North Lancashire Regiment, 10 July 1916.
3   TNA WO 95/1265: War Diary of the 10th Battalion Gloucestershire Regiment, 9 July 1916.
4   TNA WO 95/1270: War Diary of the 1st Battalion Loyal North Lancashire Regiment, 11 July 1916 and WO 95/1270: War Diary of the 1st Battalion Loyal North Lancashire Regiment, 1-7 July 1916.
5   TNA WO 95/1281: War Diary of the 2nd Battalion Welsh Regiment, 10-11 July 1916.
6   Edmonds, *OH, 1916*, Vol. 2, p. 54
7   TNA WO 95/1270: War Diary of the 1st Battalion Loyal North Lancashire Regiment, 12-13 July 1916.

Rawlinson had finally prevailed upon Haig to accept the unanimous advice of himself and his relevant senior officers, to launch an attack on 14 July pre-dawn, which relied upon the assembly of the troops during the night. This attack on the German second line was to be carried out by XIII and XV Corps, with the support of one division from III Corps, 1st Division was chosen. In preparation for the renewed assault by Fourth Army. 1st Division was to help secure the left flank by attacking Pearl Alley and Contalmaison Villa and link up with XV Corps at the south-west corner of Bazentin le Petit wood. Therefore, on 13 July 1st Black Watch seized Lower Wood at 10.45 p.m. This feature was at the north-west corner of Mametz Wood. They successfully captured Contalmaison Villa at 3.45 a.m. on 14 July.[8] Shortly afterwards, at 4 a.m., 8th Leicesters, of 110th Brigade, came up on the right of 1st Division.[9] Meanwhile the Loyal North Lancs worked into Bazentin Le Petit wood. Overnight, 3 Brigade relieved 1 Brigade in the line.

The Loyal North Lancs had arrived in their designated positions three hours later, at 7 a.m. on 14 July. They were then instructed to send A and B companies forward to support an attack by 1st Brigade on the German second line system north-west of Bazentin Le Petit wood. In addition, C company was deployed forward to act as a guard for 1st Brigade HQ. The attack by 1st Brigade took place at 2.30 p.m. as planned, but 21st Division did not attack. This exposed the right flank of the battalion's operations. Nevertheless, the Loyal North Lancs went in. They captured and consolidated 300 yards of front line trench from the west edge of Bazentin Le Petit wood and captured one officer and 99 other ranks. They sustained the loss of two officers wounded and fifty other ranks. Meanwhile, at about 5 p.m., C company moved up to support the attack and D company with battalion HQ moved into Mametz Wood.[10]

The heavy fighting in the wood led III Corps to cancel its proposed operations. Despite this, the Loyal North Lancs did see action as the 1st Division's two companies which were to attack westwards. They made slow progress (along with that of the Leicesters and other units of 110th Brigade. During the late afternoon and evening, Brigadier-General Hessey, OC 110th Brigade personally reconnoitred the wood and confirmed it was clear of German troops by 7 p.m. An appraisal of the situation, issued on 14 July by the Brigade Major of the 21st Divisional Artillery, said the Germans still occupied a trench which ran around the north west corner of Bazentin Le Petit wood at a distance of 400 yards. The appraisal also confirmed that the 21st Division had attacked just as prisoners had been taken, and dwells upon the story of the Assistant Provost Marshall using the flat of his sword to persuade a German officer, who claimed he was an aristocrat and cousin of the Kaiser, to walk like the rest of the prisoners.[11]

It was into the attritional fight for Mametz Wood that 1st Division was drawn. On 14 July, the 2nd Welsh received the expected order to move but it was cancelled again at 11 p.m. However, only five hours later the battalion were parading prior to making their way into Mametz Wood. They were to assist the Loyal North Lancs in bombing their way up the German second line trench, just east of Becourt Wood.[12] At 11 a.m., C company were sent to help the Loyal North

---

8   Edmonds, *OH, 1916*, Vol. 2, p.68
9   Edmonds, *OH, 1916*, Vol. 2, p.81
10 TNA WO 95/1270: War Diary of the 1st Battalion Loyal North Lancashire Regiment, Report on Operations 14-15 July 1916.
11 TNA WO 95/2136: War Diary of the 21st Division, Headquarters, Artillery, 14 July 1916.
12 TNA WO 95/1281: War Diary of the 2nd Battalion Welsh Regiment, 14 July 1916.

Lancs and some progress was made, but progress was limited due to machine gun fire. Therefore, at 5 p.m., A and B companies of the Welsh relieved the Loyal North Lancs of this arduous task. Bombing continued to produce results slowly. For this limited progress, the battalion had paid a price of one subaltern killed and another wounded, as well as three other ranks killed and 33 wounded.[13] Meanwhile the 1st Northants were moved up to the support lines before returning to bivouac at 7 p.m.[14]

During the same day, other preparations for the assault on 16 July had been set in motion, as the 25th Brigade RFA were despatched to the vicinity of Acid Drop Copse to take up position preparatory to cutting wire on the morning of 15 July. Later orders were received for the rest of the divisional artillery to move up to the forward areas and to be ready to come into action at any moment. As a result, the 26th and 39th Brigades RFA marched off at 11.15 p.m. to go to Dernancourt, two miles southeast of Albert.[15]

On 15 July at 9 a.m. the Loyal North Lancs attacked the German second – line trenches lying north-westwards of their position. They succeeded in capturing 400 yards of the front line and 200 yards of the support trench.[16] That day too, 25th Brigade RFA, minus D battery which was not in action, cut the wire on the German second line.[17] Meanwhile 1st Northants had relieved the Gloucesters in support. So the Gloucesters had moved into the front line by 12.15am in the positions north of Lozenge Wood on either side of the sunken road from Fricourt to Contalmaison.[18]

At 4 a.m. on 16 July 1916 the 2nd Welsh Regiment launched an ultimately unsuccessful attempt to bomb their way into the German second position along what became known afterwards as Welsh Alley. The reason given for the failure is the machine gun and rifle fire brought to bear by the German defenders.[19] Edmunds ascribes the failure of the assault to the mud and the consequent difficulty in bringing up ammunition for the trench mortars whose fire, when available, had proved effective. The growing use of trench mortars to support local assaults stemmed from the difficulty created by such close fighting. Artillery preparation was essential, but the opposing troops were too close together to permit an accurate field artillery barrage to be used without undue risk to the assaulting British troops.

The battalion of the Welsh was then forced to withdraw to its original positions, having had five junior officers wounded and ten other ranks being killed, whilst a further 44 were wounded. The battalion were then informed that a brigade level assault would take place at midnight. Therefore, the battalion moved into position once again that night; and the assault followed preparatory fire by the artillery. The battalion's assault was made with two companies up and two in support, with B and C companies leading on this occasion. The battalion encountered less resistance than on the previous attempt and ascribed this to the Germans having retired from some of their positions. They also recorded that the whole brigade had overshot the mark

13 TNA WO 95/1281: War Diary of the 2nd Battalion Welsh Regiment, 15 July 1916.
14 TNA WO 95/1271: War Diary of the 1st Battalion Northamptonshire Regiment, 14 July 1916.
15 TNA WO 95/1240: War Diary of the 1st Division, Headquarters, Commander Royal Artillery, 14 July 1916.
16 Edmunds, *OH, 1916*, Vol. 2, p.97.
17 TNA WO 95/1240: War Diary of the 1st Division, Headquarters, Commander Royal Artillery, 14 July 1916.
18 TNA WO 95/1271: War Diary of the 1st Battalion Northamptonshire Regiment, 15 July 1916.
19 TNA WO 95/1281: War Diary of the 2nd Battalion Welsh Regiment, 16 July 1916.

because the trenches were unrecognisable after the bombardment. However, the battalion eventually dug in just behind the original objective, and the recorded casualties are one officer wounded and one man killed.[20] As the men lost were from a bigger pool it is harder to estimate the impact of their loss on the battalion's efficiency, but the loss of six junior officers in one day reflects the constant churn at this level and illustrates one of the reasons why the highest percentage of fatalities were sustained by those holding the rank of Second Lieutenant.

The frontal assault by the rest of 3rd Brigade, ordered for midnight, was very probably another factor in the reduced resistance faced by the Welsh. The artillery had spent the day focusing on wire cutting. The assault was then preceded by an intense 10-minute bombardment and the attacking battalions, the 1st Gloucesters and 2nd Royal Munster Fusiliers, attacked in a north-easterly direction supported by the 2nd Welsh bombing in from the right. The assaulting troops were able to reach 300 yards beyond their objectives but fell back on those objectives at dawn. The Munsters, on the left of the assault, recorded 25 wounded other ranks, of whom thirteen went to hospital, with two killed and two missing on 15/16 July 1916.[21] Most of the casualties were sustained whilst the battalion was taking up position. The Germans shelled them with gas, which suggests the Welsh were right that the Germans had pulled back.

The Munsters had also sent patrols forward which captured a machine gun. The Munsters recorded that they occupied 2 lines of enemy trenches along a stretch of 800 yards.[22] Overall, 3 Brigade succeeded in establishing strong posts in Welsh Alley and Gloucester Alley whilst the 1st South Wales Borderers established a defensive flank in Black Watch Alley.[23] Despite the Welsh attributing success to the Germans retiring, Brigadier Davies, OC 3 Brigade, attributed the success to the "excellent preliminary arrangements of Battalion commanders and the dash and rapidity with which the attack was carried out". The Brigadier also went on to say how well the men had borne the shell fire and that General Haig had visited III Corps Headquarters and asked that his congratulations on their success be passed on to 1st Division, especially 3 Brigade.[24]

Edmonds noted the mud made it difficult to bring trench mortar ammunition forward, but ignores the huge effort wasted in bringing fodder forward for the cavalry divisions. Brigadier Davies's reference to the excellent preparations made by battalion commanders is reflected in the notes written by Lieutenant Colonel Lyons of the Royal Munster Fusiliers. He noted that one company of 1st South Wales Borderers had been put at his disposal to form the flank, and that another company was to reinforce his men once they had seized the trench, by bringing up tools to assist in the consolidation of the captured trenches. Furthermore, two companies of the 6th Welsh, the divisional pioneers, were to dig out Black Watch Alley. The intention behind the latter was to facilitate the evacuation of casualties, but the trench was not completed in time. Therefore, the casualties were evacuated via Contalmaison Villa. From a tactical evolution perspective, it is more interesting to note that close support was to be provided by four machine guns from C company of the Machine Gun Corps.[25] Thus the essential elements of the textbook

---

20 TNA WO 95/1281: War Diary of the 2nd Battalion Welsh Regiment, 16 July 1916.
21 TNA WO 95/1279: War Diary of the 2nd Battalion Munster Fusiliers, Appendix 33.
22 TNA WO 95/1279: War Diary of the 2nd Battalion Munster Fusiliers, 15 July 1916.
23 Chris McCarthy, *The Somme: The Day by Day Account* (London: Cassell, 1993), p.51
24 TNA WO 95/1279: War Diary of the 2nd Battalion Munster Fusiliers, Appendix 27.
25 TNA WO 95/1279: War Diary of the 2nd Battalion Munster Fusiliers, Appendix 25.

success of 46th Division at the Hindenburg Line, 29 September 1918 were present in this assault on 16 July 1916.

Detailed arrangements for the use of artillery are also a common characteristic of the two engagements. The account of the Munsters says that the initial bombardment would be an intense one for ten minutes prior to zero hour and then it would lift to the German second line for five minutes before then moving on to the third or "switch" line.[26]

Moving the infantry into position was complicated by the position of D company, who were to form the left flank of the Munster's assault. They were dug in to individual posts which could not be re-victualled or re-supplied in daylight. As the attack was scheduled for midnight and there would only be a limited period of darkness, much relied on the organisational skills of Major Shildrick. He arranged for the companies to move forward independently to their jump off points approximately 150 yards from the German wire. HQ company moved up first, at about 10.15 p.m. The approach route for most of the men was over un-reconnoitred ground in the dark, it rained heavily and there was sporadic rifle fire and the regular discharge of flares, as well as a German barrage at 10.30 p.m., which inflicted approximately 25 casualties. In these conditions, the Munsters approached their assembly points with the companies in columns of platoons, with ten paces between platoons and twenty paces between companies. The gaps cut in the wire were about 70 yards apart and the two columns had trouble in judging how far they were from the enemy line. Given the conditions, it is likely that the flares that were seen looked further way than they actually were. As a result, after moving forward for approximately ninety minutes in extremely difficult conditions the left-hand column came to a halt approximately thirty yards from the wire. However, the officers in charge of the right-hand column suddenly realised that they had actually reached the gap in the wire, and barely had time to withdraw the men about twenty yards before the barrage started.[27]

D company, which had been in outposts, had only been tasked with seizing a portion of the first German line, but the rest of the battalion headed through to the second line which had been largely obliterated by the artillery. The Germans were seen to withdraw from the first line as the Munsters charged home and it was this momentum that carried them into the second line and, in the case of Second Lieutenant Whelan's platoon, as far as the third line. The shelling had made the landmarks hard to recognise, and the majority of the German defenders were happy to try to escape back into either Pozières or Martinpuinch. The German casualties were estimated at about fifty and those of the Munsters at about ninety, including those suffered in the approach. The work of consolidation took place using the tools abandoned by the Germans. Despite a shortage of tools, the planned arrival of the support troops to assist in consolidation meant that the work was completed in time. The difficulties of that day were replicated, in that attempts to signal brigade by lamp failed, despite two hours of effort.[28] The decision not to send the assaulting troops into action burdened with tools further illustrates how the practice being followed at battalion level was different to that adopted on 1 July, despite barely a fortnight having elapsed.

Having made contact on their right with the Gloucesters, the Munsters eventually met up the South Wales Borderers at 2.45 a.m. when they arrived in Black Watch Alley at 2.45 a.m. The

---

26 TNA WO 95/1279: War Diary of the 2nd Battalion Munster Fusiliers, Appendix 25.
27 TNA WO 95/1279: War Diary of the 2nd Battalion Munster Fusiliers, Appendix 25.
28 TNA WO 95/1279: War Diary of the 2nd Battalion Munster Fusiliers, Appendix 25.

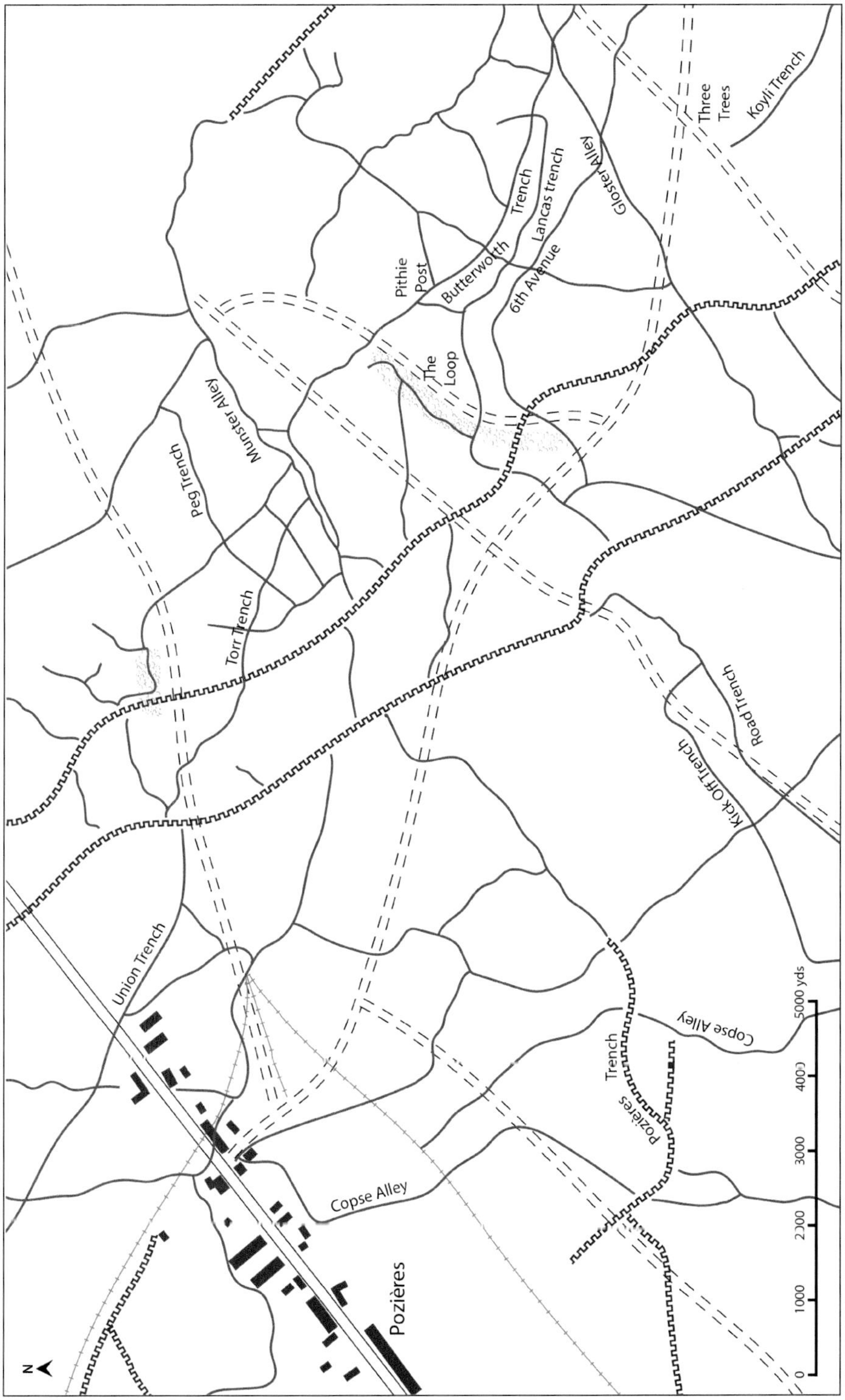

Munster Alley, July–August 1916.

companies had spread to their left, so the Munsters were ordered to close up so as not to leave gaps, and an early morning attempt to recapture the trench by approximately fifty Germans was defeated using small arms fire. The battalion had established outposts and subsequently these were advanced, but eventually had to be pulled back because of the British artillery fire persistently falling short. In his report, the Munsters' CO added that he was "most strongly" of the opinion that troops who had carried out an assault should be relieved by fresh troops as soon as possible; he made this point in the context of the troops being less effective when asked to carry out further action on 18 July.[29] In recommending this approach the future use of leap-frogging units during major assaults is being prefigured.

The Munsters formed the left of the division in the line on 16 July, with 34th Division to their left.[30] On that day, the Brigade Major, Captain Wingate, issued orders for 3 Brigade to move on 18 July with one company of the South Wales Borderers to act under the Assistant Provost Marshal's directions.[31] Therefore, the Munsters remained in line, with the 1st Gloucesters on their right, until they were relieved by the 1st Northamptons of 2 Brigade on 18 July.[32]

During 17 July and 18 July, the Munsters' positions were heavily shelled by the Germans but mostly overshot the battalion. On 17 July, the OC Munsters had put at his disposal two Stokes mortars and machine guns which he deployed to cover his left flank. He reported that they had proved particularly useful. During the day movement by the Germans was seen at the northern end of the positions opposite, but no attack followed, and then the Royal Engineers wired another section of the line. The battalion also received orders for further offensive operations on 18 July, and the officers tried to ensure the men got some rest. The orders were subsequently cancelled[33] but it demonstrates the pressure on the men in the front line which was created by higher Staff In this case, Captain Wingate had sent out the detailed orders for the move to Le Clipon Camp to all the units in 3 Brigade in readiness for the move on 18 July, including a detailed march table, before issuing an "Addendum and Corrigendum" which clarified various points.[34] Such terminology will cause those who studied Latin pre-1980 to recall completing "corrigenda" after homework was returned; and demonstrates the educational background of the Staff officers.

On 18 July, the 2nd Munsters briefly captured the junction of Munster Alley and Old German Support Trench Two, south of Pozières.[35] The 1st Division also established a line of outposts and strong points, "at little cost"[36] running north-west along the crest of Pozières Ridge from Bazentin-le-Petit Wood. These posts were approximately halfway between Old German Support Trench Two and the Switch Line and ran parallel to them. The vulnerability of the troops belies McCarthy's phraseology, as 1st Northants lost Second Lieutenant Knight and twelve other ranks who were killed by German shellfire, as well as a further 25 wounded whilst holding the village line.[37]

---

29 TNA WO 95/1279: War Diary of the 2nd Battalion Munster Fusiliers, Appendix 25.
30 TNA WO 95/1279: War Diary of the 2nd Battalion Munster Fusiliers, 16 July 1916.
31 TNA WO 95/1276: War Diary of the 3rd Infantry Brigade, Headquarters, 14 July 1916.
32 TNA WO 95/1279: War Diary of the 2nd Battalion Munster Fusiliers, 18-23 July 1916.
33 TNA WO 95/1279: War Diary of the 2nd Battalion Munster Fusiliers, Appendix 25.
34 TNA WO 95/1276: War Diary of the 3rd Infantry Brigade, Headquarters, July 1916.
35 McCarthy, *The Somme*, p.53.
36 McCarthy, *The Somme*, p.53.
37 TNA WO 95/1271: War Diary of the 1st Battalion Northamptonshire Regiment, 18 July 1916.

Having moved into support at Lozenge Wood, the Munsters were then relieved by 1st Black Watch of 1 Brigade.[38] The complications for the Munsters and Gloucesters in being relieved from the front line appears to be reflected in the orders for their officer's mess carts, cookers and water carts to march with them. The rest of the infantry in the brigade had their transport marched off in groups, under brigade transport arrangements specifying that 200 yards must be left between companies and units on the road.[39] The Munsters then spent the next three days as divisional reserve in positions around Albert.[40]

On 20 July 1916, the 1st Division was involved in further failed attempts, due to machine gun fire, to take Munster Trench in the vicinity of Bazentin Le Petit.[41] By then the neighbouring division had been relieved. The new left flank was established with 1st Australian Division, who took responsibility for Black watch Alley. On 21 July, 1st Division had established a battle outpost line on the crest of the ridge in front. They had also deployed snipers and were actively patrolling ahead of the trenches.

At 12.30 a.m. on 23 July 1916, the 1st Division were involved in the assault on Pozières Ridge, with 1st Brigade and 2nd Brigade tasked with the assault.[42] The objective for 1st Division was the section of the Switch line which met the Martinpuinch-Pozières Railway. 2 Brigade on the left were to advance on the front up to and including the Contalmaison-Martinpuich road. 2 Brigade were tasked with reaching the re-entrant formed by the German Switch Line and Munster Alley. 2 Brigade were also told that at the left end of its section were the old gun emplacements, and a communication trench. These were seen as very important.

The objective of 1 Brigade was to reach the Switch Line. The right flank meeting the railway was stressed as this would be the junction with 1st Australian Division. The instruction was given that the necessary arrangements be thought out in advance and special parties dedicated to the task. In case they were not sure, the divisional staff said this included filling in at least 50 yards of the Switch Line. To assist 1 Brigade, an agreement had been reached with 19th Division that they could dig an advance jumping off trench. Nonetheless, digging it and manning it in the meantime would be 1 Brigade's responsibility. Each brigade was assigned one RE field company and one company of pioneers to assist them to achieve their flank protection.[43]

The orders for 2 Brigade were then modified. It was told it would now be attacking in three groups. This involved attacking both in a northerly and north-easterly direction. The left-hand group would attack in a northerly direction towards a section of Munster Alley. The time for their attack would be earlier than for the others as they were to co-ordinate with 1st Australian Division. The other two groups would now attack in a north-easterly direction. The objective of the central group was the switch line. The group on the right would aim at a line extending 100 yards either side of the junction of the Switch Line and Munster Alley. The instructions added that if any of the attacks failed, renewed bombardments would be ordered and new assaults made. A further Addendum was later issued. This now said that all the attacks would take place

---

38 TNA WO 95/1279: War Diary of the 2nd Battalion Munster Fusiliers, 18-23 July 1916.
39 TNA WO 95/1276: War Diary of the 3rd Infantry Brigade, Headquarters, July 1916, and TNA WO 95/1279: War Diary of the 2nd Battalion Munster Fusiliers, 18-23 July 1916.
40 TNA WO 95/1279: War Diary of the 2nd Battalion Munster Fusiliers, 18-23 July 1916.
41 McCarthy, *The Somme*, p.54.
42 McCarthy, *The Somme*, p.57
43 TNA WO 95/1231: War Diary of the 1st Division Headquarters, July 1916

simultaneously. It also said that machine guns would be pushed out ahead of the trenches, they were to keep firing until the assaulting waves passed through them. A subsequent order put 2 Brigade's machine guns at the disposal of 3 Brigade. This shows just how much good practise was being developed and applied.

The barrage instructions also show a great deal of thought. It was clearly understood that artillery activity could betray intentions. Therefore, for example, batteries assigned to target Munster Alley were instructed to start firing one shell per minute, from 6pm in the evening. Whilst the rate would be increased for the last five minutes before zero, it was presumably hoped that the change would be less obvious to the sheltering German defenders. At zero the field guns would lift beyond Munster Trench but the howitzers were to switch target to the area beyond the switch line. In a further touch of sophistication, certain assigned batteries would sweep the area up to 50 yards from the German wire during the last 90 minutes before zero. The stated intention was to force the withdrawal of any German patrols or wiring parties.[44]

The 10th Gloucesters and 1st Camerons of 1 Brigade, as well as the 2nd KRRC and 2nd Royal Sussex of 2 Brigade, were stopped by hidden machine gun positions. Even though the battalions had formed up outside the wire and had pressed home the attack with determination, the enemy's machine guns were concealed by the long grass on 1Brigade's front. The 1st Loyal North Lancs also failed to take Munster Alley. Amongst those lost in this action was the commander of the 2nd KRRC, Lieutenant- Colonel HFW Bircham, who was mortally wounded. Bircham had served as Adjutant of the battalion in the Boer War, been Mentioned in Despatches by Lord French, and been gazetted DSO in January 1916. According to Hodgkinson, Bircham had reproved his Adjutant's attempts to get him not to participate in the attack, by saying that the Adjutant should know the place for a colonel of the Rifles when an attack was to be made.[45] His men had entered the trenches of *27th Regiment*,[46] but were too few in number to hold the position they had initially taken. With regard to the performance of 1st Division, it should be noted that the attacks on their flanks also failed.

On 26 July, two companies of 2nd Welsh, who had been left behind by 1st Division when they were relieved by 23rd Division, took part in operations being conducted by X Corps. They attacked the Switch Line at approximately 3 p.m. Initially their attack was successful but they were ejected during a major German counterattack. They did secure a post covering about 70 yards of trench. They did make progress during a second attack conducted in conjunction with Australian troops. The 2nd Welsh managed to bomb their way to gaining another 130 yards of trench.[47] They were subsequently relieved on 27 July.

The casualties sustained by 1st Division during the second half of July amounted to 123 officers and 2,955 other ranks.[48] Whilst many divisions suffered similar or higher levels of casualties during spells in the front line on the Somme. these figures highlight the attritional nature of warfare in Picardy that summer as 1st Division was only being used to replace an

---

44   TNA WO 95/1231: War Diary of the 1st Division Headquarters, July 1916.
45   Peter Hodgkinson, *British Infantry Battalion Commanders in the First World War* (Farnham: Ashgate, 2014), p.160.
46   Edmonds, *OH, 1916*, Vol. 2, p.138
47   TNA WO 95/1231: War Diary of the 1st Division Headquarters, July 1916.
48   TNA WO 95/1231: War Diary of the 1st Division Headquarters, July 1916.

exhausted division and, largely, to carry out local tactical assaults. It therefore demonstrates the reality of a strategy of "wearing out" the enemy.

During its introduction to the Somme battlefield, 1st Division seems to have acquitted itself effectively. A series of small scale operations had been conducted successfully. However, as the month wore on it seemed to fail more often even though the planning at divisional level would appear to have been of good quality. That success was then achieved after they were relieved could have been due to German battle fatigue, X Corps's skill or just luck but 1st Division's reputation would not be enhanced. Nevertheless, the men of 1st Division had earnt the hard way and thoroughly deserved the two days' rest without parades as ordered by Strickland on 28 July.[49]

49 TNA WO 95/1231: War Diary of the 1st Division Headquarters, 28 July 1916.

29

High Wood and Morval

For the first twelve days of August, 1st Division were in Corps reserve. Having given the men two days proper rest after they came out of the line, Strickland upped the tempo considerably. The training was intensive and particular emphasis was given to night operations and contact with aeroplanes. The significance of night operations would have been clear to the men after their recent spell in the line. Each infantry brigade planned two large night schemes. These had to include a short approach march and the formation of an attacking line.

Timings were based upon an attack shortly before dawn. In addition, practically every battalion did a smaller scheme each night. One large scheme involved elements from all the brigades to represent a divisional assault. Strickland had arranged for the assistance of contact planes from the 34th Squadron RFC to take part in some schemes, reporting flares and dropping messages.[1]

On 14-15 August, 1st Division, in its turn, relieved the 34th Division which had suffered 3,000 casualties during the first half of August. This meant that Strickland was responsible for the right hand sector of III Corp's front. Two days later, 1st Brigade took part in a "Chinese attack" to try to deceive the Germans into exposing their positions, but there was little reaction from the enemy. As the "attack" only involved blowing whistles and shouting orders this is perhaps unsurprising.[2] During the Somme campaign considerable effort was devoted to these attacks, but the overall impression given is that they generally did little for the British. The technology of war was very clear to both sides so if the wire had not been cut etc, the British were not going to attack, would have been the conclusion drawn by the German defenders.

Meanwhile the 2nd Royal Sussex, using three companies, and 1st Northamptons, using two companies, had achieved greater success, at 10 p.m. on 16th, by capturing most of a new German trench which ran from High Wood across the Bazentin-Le-Petit road for a distance of about 600 yards. These two battalions, whose attack had been preceded by an intense bombardment which lasted five minutes, were complimented by a captured German officer who said that the British had attacked with resolution and speed. He said this had denied his men the chance to bring their machine guns into action. This ties in with the staff's note that the attack met with stout resistance by the defenders using bombs and their rifles. The captured officer also said the impact of the barrage had been reduced by the high proportion of dud ammunition. This may

---

1   TNA WO 95/1231: War Diary of the 1st Division Headquarters, 1-12 August 1916.
2   Edmonds, *OH, 1916*, Vol. 2, p.188.

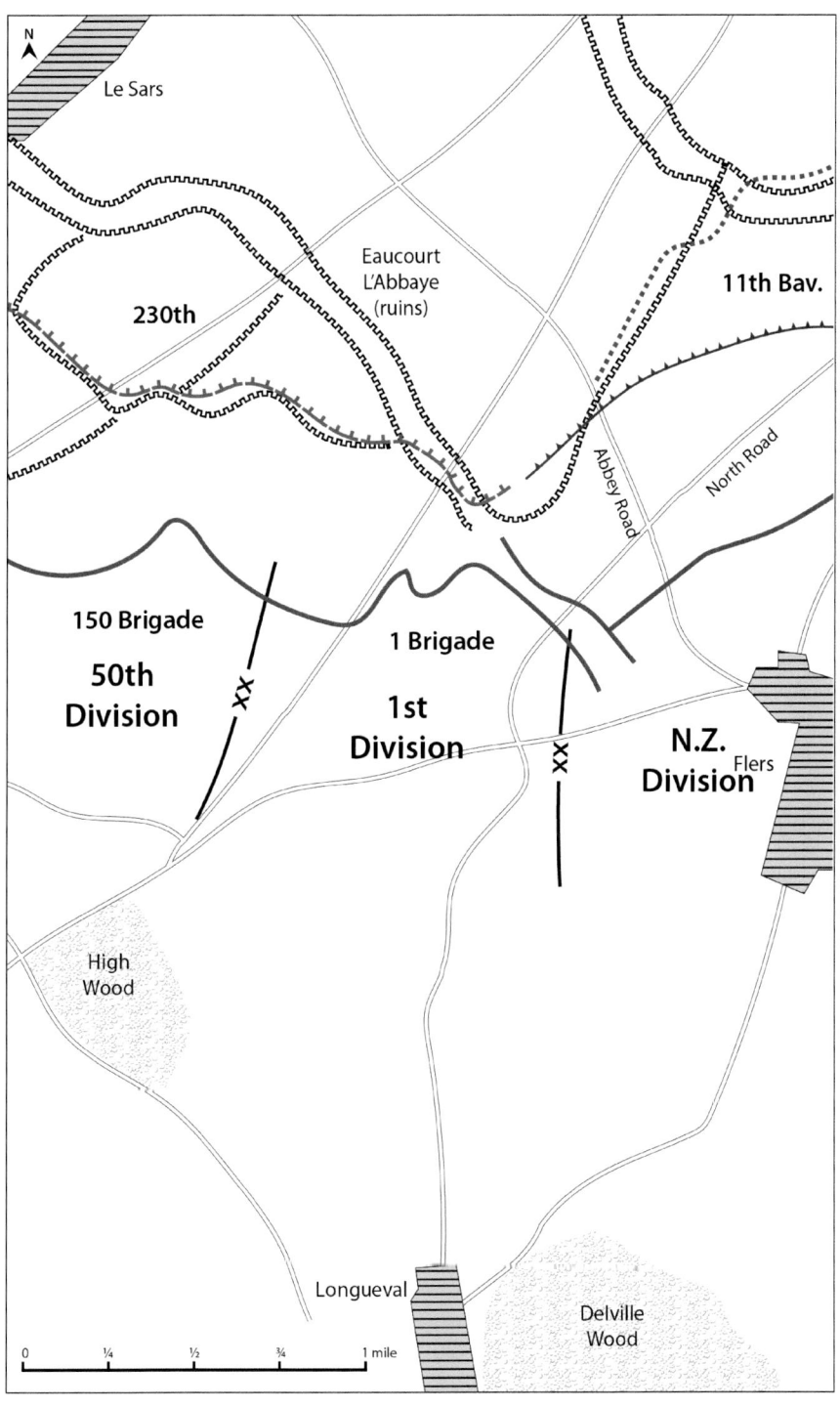

Morval, 25-28 September 1916.

be true but Strickland attributed to a significant number of casualties to his men having caught up with the barrage. An initial German attack was repulsed.[3] Despite barricades having been created at both ends and patrols put out northwards, however, approximately ninety yards of the trench were recaptured by the *181st Regiment* in a counterattack from High wood at 3.15 a.m.[4] Having offered this detail, which is matched by an entry in the divisional diary, Edmonds omits to add that a subsequent British counterattack regained the section of the trench that had originally been recaptured.[5]

That same night, three platoons of the 1st Black Watch (1 Brigade) advanced on Intermediate Trench at 2 a.m. Each platoon had a different role. One platoon was to advance from the portion of Intermediate Trench that was already occupied. Their efforts, to bomb along from the existing block were met with machine gun fire. They could make little progress. One assumes the Germans had anticipated such an attack. Another platoon was designated to make a frontal assault on Intermediate Trench. They too were met with machine gun fire. They also became entangled in a bombing fight with what was presumed to be a strong German patrol. One officer was hit and the other was posted missing. The third platoon were given the objective of attacking the Elbow. This group succeeded in advancing from their assembly position in Lancashire Sap. They managed to kill the garrison and hold the position. Strickland must have been frustrated by the failure of those watching to see the success flares. With no support, this group was eventually forced to retire. The focus then switched to improving the captured sections of trench. The earlier efforts of the Black Watch had borne fruit. At 5pm on 17 August, the Camerons were able to occupy the Elbow which the Germans had not re-occupied. However, they reported that the Germans had established a block about 100 yards down. The staff also noted the success that morning of 15th Division in capturing the Switch Line and Munster alley.[6] It was a mixed set of results across 1 and 2 Brigades but Strickland could probably see the benefits of the recent training programme showing through.

At 2.45 p.m. on 18 August 1st Division assaulted the north-western edge of High Wood. On the left fank of the assault, the 1st Northamptons captured a newly constructed trench on the north-west side of High Wood by bombing forward from the section of the trench that had been captured previously. The Northants then managed to gain touch with the Loyals on their right. Of the two attacking companies of the Loyal North Lancs (2 Brigade), the left hand company was a minute late starting but followed the barrage at the correct pace and made it through to their objective. The right company was practically annihilated after walking into the British barrage (being provided by 15th Division) and suffering from the German defensive barrage. The Loyals were then instructed to make contact on their right with 98 Brigade who were reported to have reached their objectives in High Wood. However, as the right company had lost all its officers and NCOs, this had to be organised by the left company. However, they found that 98 Brigade were no longer there and that the Germans had re-occupied the trenches. Eventually, 2 Brigade were able to consolidate their position almost to the edge of High Wood and create a strongpoint there.[7]

3 TNA WO 95/1231: War Diary of the 1st Division Headquarters, 16 August 1916.
4 Edmonds, *OH, 1916*, Vol. 2, p.188.
5 TNA WO 95/1231: War Diary of the 1st Division Headquarters, 16 August 1916.
6 TNA WO 95/1231: War Diary of the 1st Division Headquarters, 16 August 1916.
7 Edmonds, *OH, 1916*, Vol. 2, p.196

Earlier that morning, at 4.15 a.m., 1st Black Watch had renewed the assault on Intermediate Trench aided by a heavy artillery barrage but had been disorganised by a heavy German artillery response; small parties pushed seventy yards beyond the trench but were eventually forced to withdraw. Their own CRA noted that their objective had been obliterated so 1 Brigade could not occupy it.[8] At the same time as 2 Brigade made their assault, the attack on Intermediate Trench was renewed by the 8th Royal Berkshires of 1 Brigade but this attack failed due to German artillery and machine gun fire breaking the frontal assault. A flank attack, launched from Lancashire Sap was stopped by the planned smoke barrage provided by 15th Division falling short.[9] The division suffered very heavy casualties not only because of the intense fighting but also because the Germans shelled them heavily.

Amongst the casualties in High Wood that day was the senior divisional staff officer, Lieutenant Colonel James Atkinson Longridge CMG. He was there to observe how the operations went. Aged 41 when he was killed, Longridge had been educated at Malvern College before passing out from Sandhurst. He had been commissioned into the West Surrey Regiment in 1895. Having seen active service in China in 1900 as well as Somaliland, he had served in the Indian Army with the 43rd Erinpura Regiment. The award of the CMG had come in 1913 in recognition of his work in the preparation of the war plans and he had initially been retained in Whitehall after August 1914. However, when the Indian Corps was sent to the Western Front, he had volunteered to serve with them in a staff role. He was subsequently transferred to 1st Division as GSO1 on 3 January 1915. In December 1916, his old school's magazine recorded this tribute; "We are authorised by Lieut.-Colonel Sir Maurice Hankey, Secretary of the Committee of Imperial Defence, to observe that in the years preceding the war, Colonel Longridge did invaluable work in connection with the arrangements for the preparation for war. The value of Colonel Longridge's work in this respect was fully recognised by the Prime Minister and the Committee of Imperial Defence, and was rewarded with a C.M.G. Nowhere is Colonel Longridge's death more deeply felt than in the Committee of Imperial Defence and among his colleagues in the Secretariat, who not only placed the highest value on his professional attainments, but were united to him by bonds of intimate friendship."[10] Amongst the less noted casualties sustained by the Black Watch was 27-year-old Archibald Adam from Paisley who had been serving in B company.[11]

There was real initiative shown on 19 August. The day began by consolidating captured trenches and digging a communication trench. Then in the early afternoon it was noticed that the Germans did not seem to be very alert. A four man patrol was sent out and reached the top the ridge 400 yards to the North without being fired at. Immediately two platoons of the Northants were sent forward to establish themselves on the ridge. Two patrols led by officers were sent further forward. One of these patrols was able to reach the Switch Line. Overnight, strong working parties were found to establish a new line and to dig a new communication

---

8 TNA WO 95/1240: War Diary of the 1st Division CRA, 18 August 1916.
9 McCarthy, *The Somme*, pp.75-76
10 *Malvern College Roll of Honour* <http://www.stanwardine.com/cgi-bin/malvernww1> (accessed 26 August 2018)
11 Archibald's name is recorded on Face 10A of the Thiepval Memorial.

trench. The latter was christened "Clarke's Trench". Whilst all this was going on another party of men occupied and garrisoned the Elbow.[12]

Unfortunately, this new outpost line fell to the Germans the next day. The digging had been interrupted by a small-scale German counterattack. Therefore, the trench was only about 2'6" deep. Having failed initially, the Germans massed an estimated 800 men behind the Switch Line and launched an assault heralded by very heavy artillery support. The assembly of their troops was aided by the topography as they could not be seen moving up. They were also assisted by machine gun fire from the protection of High Wood. The commander of the outpost was killed and Strickland was at pains to record that, seeing both his flanks turned, a very young and inexperienced officer gave the order to withdraw. Two companies of 2nd Royal Sussex and two companies of the Northants made a prolonged attempt to seize back the ridge. They were outnumbered and eventually lost what amounted to a hand to hand struggle.[13]

From 21–23 August, the focus switched to consolidating the trenches gained. This was done under constant pressure from very heavy shelling. Not only was the German artillery more active than usual but a great variety of calibres of gun were in use. In an example of what might be termed "aggressive entrenching" a trench was dug from the end of Clarke's trench with a view to making Intermediate Trench untenable.[14]

The 2nd Munster made a further attempt to take Intermediate trench on 24 August but were stopped by small arms fire.[15] Their opponents were the *133rd Regiment* and the preparatory bombardment of the position by trench mortars had failed to do significant damage.[16] Three times the Munsters tried to renew the assault but on each occasion the result was the same. That evening they had to be replaced in the line by the South Wales Borderers. In this case, as in many others during the intermediate engagements on the Somme, two companies were deployed for this assault, one at either end of the trench to be attacked. This constant frittering away of men in penny packets is one of the reasons why the British army bled so profusely in the mud of Picardy. Haig consistently saw it as a wearing-out fight but seems to have lost sight of the limitations on available manpower resources. Many British commentators have pointed to how Ludendorff subsequently said that the old German army was destroyed on the Somme, but it is very important to remember that Ludendorff was keen to deflect the blame from his own time in charge. Many of the same commentators decry Ludendorff's description of the British as "lions led by donkeys"; it is therefore important not to be selective in quoting him. The British were not all lions and their leaders were not all donkeys. Equally many of the problems faced by the German army were there before Ludendorff took over but he made decisions which were critical in bringing about Germany's defeat too.

On 25 August, the South Wales Borderers made a bombing attack along Intermediate Trench from the British section. This was initially successful. Initially, 7 prisoners were taken. However, the 30 yards gained were lost again when the Germans fought back. The officer who led the attack was killed. The attack was repeated the next day after Intermediate Trench had been shelled steadily all afternoon. This time, reinforcements were on hand and twenty men

12 TNA WO 95/1231: War Diary of the 1st Division Headquarters, 19 August 1916.
13 TNA WO 95/1231: War Diary of the 1st Division Headquarters, 20 August 1916.
14 TNA WO 95/1231: War Diary of the 1st Division Headquarters, 21 -23 August 1916.
15 McCarthy, *The Somme*, p.82.
16 Edmonds, *OH, 1916,* Vol. 2, p.202.

were placed in shell holes on either side of the trench to consolidate the gain. The Germans then attempted a frontal assault on the captured trench on 27 August. This was driven off largely by the use of bombs. This was because the very heavy rain had jammed most of the Lewis guns and rifles with mud. Therefore, whilst fresh guns were brought forward all the troops had been issued with more grenades. After the failure of the German assault, some enterprising men pushed forward and seized control of more of Intermediate Trench.[17]

After all this hard fighting, 3 Brigade was relieved by 46 Brigade. In parallel, 1 Brigade relieved 19 Brigade inside High Wood. There, 1 Brigade began digging a new support line. This line was 30 yards to the rear and parallel with the front line. There was also constant work for both 1 and 2 Brigades to maintain the communication trenches, in particular, which were suffering due to regular rain showers. Between 28-31 August, time was also devoted on all three nights to digging a new support trench in High Wood. The Germans were judged to be nervous and there was a lot of shelling. A major attack by III Corps had been planned for 30 August but Corps decided to postpone it for 48 hours.[18]

In agreement with General Foch, the assault was postponed again on 1 September for 48 hours. Given the difficulties being laboured under by 1st Division, the postponement seems to have been very sensible. The German attack on XV Corps on 31 August, the one fine day, demonstrated that the Germans were not exhausted. 1st Division was in one of the two furthest forward points of the British Fourth Army, the other being Delville Wood. This offensive is known as the Battle of Guillemont and was a preparatory action for the assault on Flers-Courcelette. The latter became famous for the introduction of tanks. The attack on Guillemont was to be carried out by XIV and XV corps.

The III Corps formation involved was 1st Division. It was hoped to make tactical gains in High Wood. On 1 September, a German attack on their trenches was repelled by 2 Brigade. About 30 Germans, supported by a machine gun and amply supplied with bombs came forward. The bombs reached nearly to the parapet but the Germans were beaten off. The following day the divisional artillery carried out a "Chinese attack" using smoke. This drew little response from the Germans. 1 Brigade of 1st Division attacked at noon on 3 September, in conformity with the assault by XIV and XV Corps. Their objective was the section of German trench where it entered High Wood. The attack on the left would be led by three companies of the Black Watch with the remaining company in support. They had two companies of the 10th Gloucesters at their disposal. The right of the attack was to be carried out by the Cameron Highlanders. They had two companies of the Royal Berkshires at their disposal.

The left of the attack by the Black Watch were using improvised flame throwers. The This involved cans of oil and a pipe pusher. Very unfortunately, a mortar round fell short and set fire to most of the oil drums in the British trench. Possibly due to the concussion from the mortar round the pipe pusher blew back. Despite this major setback two companies of the Black Watch did advance but made no headway against the now alerted defenders.

To assist the Black Watch, on the right, a mine containing 3,000lbs of ammonal had been tunnelled under the German strongpoint in the east of the wood. This was detonated 30 seconds before the attack. The right company of the Black Watch seized the resulting crater.

---

17 TNA WO 95/1231: War Diary of the 1st Division Headquarters, 21-23 August 1916.
18 TNA WO 95/1231: War Diary of the 1st Division Headquarters, 27-31 August 1916.

Some men acted as a covering party whilst others began to consolidate the position. A further group succeeded in bombing down the trench on their right for 50 yards. A Vickers and three Lewis gun were brought up to stiffen the resistance to the anticipated German counterattack. Unfortunately, all of them were knocked out by German fire from the west of High Wood. This was possible because the eastern lip of the crater was quite low. The Germans then carried out a successful counterattack despite taking heavy casualties. The Black Watch were forced back to their start line. They had taken 27 wounded and 52 unwounded prisoners.[19]

The 1st Camerons were successful in seizing approximately 80 yards of the trench. Even here though there were issues. No 2 Platoon of the Camerons struggled to get forward as the Berkshires were slow out of the trenches after the two minute bombardment ended. The casualties here included the entire team of No. Lewis 1 gun. Nonetheless, the Camerons created a block and mounted a machine gun on it, probably A company's No 2 gun based on the after action report. This was very useful until a German grenade destroyed it.

Meanwhile, the Camerons, with B company's No1 gun and the half company of the Berkshires assigned to bomb down Wood Lane were held back by machine gun fire. A stokes mortar was brought forward. Its fire allowed the assaulting troops to get forward. Having advanced about 100 yards beyond Wood Lane, they then consolidated their positions. They used shell holes to create a defensive position. This was where B company's No 2 gun, and all four belonging to C and D companies, took up position. One of D's should have been in the captured trench but casualties caused it to lose direction. Captain Methuen was in such a shell hole and Lieutenant Boyle in another. The latter was able to command a view of the German line. Boyle saw 2nd Lieutenant Mair shot through the head whilst urging his platoon on, waving his rifle, shouting "Charge the Camerons". Boyle recovered Mair's personal effects but could not get his wedding ring off his finger. The men in Boyle's shell hole were able to pick off one bombing party in the German trench. However, their fire and other men running to their hole attracted the attention of the Germans.

Whilst the right hand half of the left attack was progressing, other parts of the Brigade's plan for the left were going awry. The officer leading a platoon carrying tools was hit. The platoon then strayed too far to the right. The result was the plan to create a strongpoint in the captured trench did not happen. This was made worse by the Vickers and Stokes, destined for the strongpoint, accompanying the lost platoon off course. One Lewis gun did arrive as it came up with a half-company of the Berkshires arriving in support. Boyle and them with him ran to another shell hole which happened to be occupied by the Lewis team of the Berkshires. Most of the team including the sergeant were killed by German snipers. The Lewis gun was salvaged.

As the Black Watch fell back, Boyle was amongst those exposed so he and the men with him conducted a fighting withdrawal to Worcester Trench. In this situation, German counterattacks forced the Camerons on the left back to Worcester Trench. At least one officer reported that Captain Pattison had to point his revolver at some of the Berkshires in Worcester Trench to stiffen their resolve to stay and fight. Having not been able to construct a strongpoint in the captured trench, the right of the Camerons were gradually surrounded, especially once the Black Watch had been forced back. Therefore, at 4.30pm the Camerons were ordered to withdraw.[20]

---

19 TNA WO 95/1231: War Diary of the 1st Division Headquarters, 5 September 1916.
20 TNA WO 95/1231: War Diary of the 1st Division Headquarters, 5 September 1916 and WO 95/1264: War Diary of the 1st Cameron Highlanders, September 1916, Appendix.

It is interesting to note that the machine gun teams of the Camerons suffered severely. 2ndLietenant Drummond reported that 6 out of 8 No 1s and 7 out of 8 No 2s became casualties. The percentage of the carriers was lower, 12 out of 24 or 29 if the reserves are counted. He reported that the re-organisation was straightforward except with A company where the whole team were casualties. Of the eight, three Lewis guns were lost and between them it was estimated that they had fired 16,500 rounds equivalent to 351 magazines. It was stated that this could only be a rough estimate as SAA had been used from numerous sources including that taken from casualties. In total the Camerons took casualties amounting to 9 officers and 275 ORs.[21] It must have been frustrating for Strickland to reflect that margin between success and failure was one short mortar round, the height of the lip of a newly formed crater and, possibly, one unit being slower out of the trenches. From 4 -7 September, the focus reverted to repairing and strengthening the trenches.

On 8 September, to facilitate an attack by 3 Brigade, 2 Brigade took over the trenches. The attack on the German trenches in High wood was carried out by 1st Gloucesters on the left and 2nd Welsh on the right. One company of the South Wales Borderers was attached to 1st Gloucesters whilst the other three were in support. The 9th Black Watch of 15th Division attacked alongside the Gloucesters and therefore were the left flank of the assault. The artillery had been cutting wire for 48 hours. The preliminary steady bombardment had started six hours before zero. With 30 minutes to go this was replaced by an intensive barrage by 2" mortars. At 6 p.m. the 9th Black Watch advanced and captured their objective. In the process they took some prisoners and killed, by their estimate, around sixty Germans.

The 1st Gloucesters were also successful. A few, including the CO, reached their final objective. There they captured the enemy trench after some "brisk" hand to hand fighting. The South Wales Borderers were held up fighting in the wood and therefore failed to reinforce the Gloucesters. The defenders were found, in the wood, to be in wired shell holes which had to be dealt with individually. Unsupported, the Gloucesters decided to retire and the Borderers followed suit. If the Borderers had stayed put and let the Gloucesters fall back on to them the day might have had a better outcome.

The right of 2nd Welsh advanced to the objective but were pinned down by heavy fire to their front. Their left was held up by heavy fire. The Borderers tried to bomb down to join the Welsh but the supply of grenades was exhausted. The carriers could not get through with more so the Borderers fell back. These battalions, along with elements of 15th Division, repelled German counterattacks but were eventually withdrawn, bar one unit. The exception was the survivors of the right company from the 2nd Welsh who were forced to evacuate their positions by 4 a.m. on 9 September. In total, one officer and 47 men had been captured by 1st Division.[22]

A further assault was carried out on Wood Lane and German positions in High wood on 9 September. This time 3 Brigade were on the left attacking the western Eastern edge of High Wood. 2 Brigade were on the right attacking the eastern edge of High Wood. On the left were the 2nd Munsters and 10th Gloucesters. On the right were the 2nd King's Royal Rifles and the 2nd Royal Sussex. The Northamptons also took part, they attacked from the bit of Eastern High Wood that had been captured previously.

---

21 TNA WO 95/1264: War Diary of the 1st Cameron Highlanders, September 1916, Appendix.
22 TNA WO 95/1231: War Diary of the 1st Division Headquarters, 8 September 1916.

On the left flank, the Munsters were met with heavy fire and an almost simultaneous attack by the Germans. They were forced back to their start line. The Gloucesters met with a similar experience but were able to hold on in shell holes 25 yards in advance of their trenches. These holes were afterwards connected up to the British trench. On the right success was partially achieved. The Northamptons seized the crater but were eventually driven out by grenades which destroyed the machine gun posts established. Meanwhile the Sussex and KRRC kept close to their barrage and captured Wood Lane. One machine gun in a shell hole delayed the KRRC. A mortar was fired into the shell hole and then the position was rushed. 2 Brigade immediately set up outposts 100 yards ahead. These outposts were built around Vickers and Lewis guns. As anticipated, the Germans launched a counterattack. With the support of the divisional artillery, the outpost line held and 2 Brigade proceeded to consolidate the position gained.[23] The critical difference here seems to have been twofold. The outpost line was sufficiently far ahead that the artillery could lay down a barrage clear of the British trenches. Unlike the situation faced by the Northamptons at the crater, the Germans could not get within bombing range to negate the power of the machine guns. A total of 55 unwounded prisoners, and some machine guns, were captured from the *II / Fifth Bavarian Regiment.*[24]

On the following night, the New Zealand Division relieved the right of 1st Division as part of the rearrangement of Corps boundaries in preparation for the attack on Flers–Courcelette by Fourth Army. The rest of 1st Division was relieved by 47th Division. With the relief completed, Strickland ordered rest with no parades on 13 September. On the two following days there was rest and training in battalions. During the night of 20 September, the 1st Division completed relief of 47th Division and Strickland once again took charge of the right sector of III Corp's front.[25]

Between 9 and 11pm, 1st Black Watch took part in a bombing attack alongside the 2nd Canterbury's of the New Zealand Division. To achieve surprise there was no preliminary bombardment.[26] Together, they cleared Drop Alley and part of the Flers Line up to the point where there was a cross trench. Drop Alley was consolidated by 1 Brigade who moved into the line. The New Zealand Division consolidated the Flers line which they successfully defended the next day.

Just after dawn on 21 September, aggressive patrols were sent to investigate Starfish Trench. When it was found to be empty, further patrols were sent forward to consolidate it. Further patrols were sent out and one linked up with 50th Division. It was clear that Prue Trench was empty so 1st Division occupied that too, before moving up to secure Prue Copse. A new front line, in front of Drop Alley was completed by 1st Division. This was achieved in just two nights (23 & 24 September).

During the early afternoon of 25 September, the Black Watch, as part of the general assault known as the Battle of Morval (25-28 September), successfully captured part of both the Flers Line and the Flers Support Line. This was despite stiff opposition to their bombing teams. The attack had been timed to coincide with the New Zealand attack on Goose Alley. The Flers Support Line became part of the New Zealand line. In total, 1st Division took ten prisoners.

23 TNA WO 95/1231: War Diary of the 1st Division Headquarters, 9 September 1916.
24 McCarthy, *The Somme*, p.99
25 TNA WO 95/1231: War Diary of the 1st Division Headquarters, 10-20 September 1916.
26 Edmonds, *OH, 1916*, Vol. 2, p.360.

Another joint operation was undertaken at 11pm on 26 September. This time 2 Brigade was working alongside 50th Division. The objective was the new German trenches but they were too strongly held to be taken.

The next day 2 Brigade were more successful. The 2nd Sussex attacked from Prue Trench and were able to break in and bomb along a section. They had been supported by a 20 minute intense bombardment. The same approach was taken for a further attack by the Loyal North Lancs. Their attack was also successful and they occupied approximately 100 yards of the trench. However, neither the Northants who assaulted Flers Trench nor the KRRC who attacked the junction of the new and Flers trenches had any success. That same evening, 47th Division began the relief of 1st Division. Whilst the headlines were grabbed by tanks, the men of 1st Division had played their part in a gruelling slogging match with the German Army that September.

30

Winter, 1916-17

After two months of high-tempo involvement in the bitter fighting around High Wood, 1st Division was withdrawn. III Corps assigned it to Area 7 which was for rest and training. The artillery and RE personnel were left to continue active operations. The rest area afforded the men plenty of room in the billets. The weather was good for the first fortnight but after that it grew colder and rained almost every day. On 28 October, the expected orders came to return to the line. The horsed elements marched but French buses were provided for the infantry. The 8th Royal Berkshires and a company of the 10th Gloucesters had to be left behind. They were put into segregation camps as several cases of German measles had been diagnosed.[1] In total 65 cases were recorded on 28 October and 19 cases were recorded in 8th Royal Berkshires on 29 October. By two days later new cases were in single figures. Despite a few cases amongst the Signals personnel, this group was not held back as a whole.[2] Presumably, it was too central to divisional operations.

The divisional artillery supported other divisions now occupying the line. Initially, one field battery and a howitzer battery were sent forward to support 47th Division. This was then increased to XXV and XXXIX Brigades being wholly deployed as well as half of XXVI Brigade. These units remained in operation when 9th Division relieved 47th Division. The 17 of October saw XXVI Brigade deploy a further battery forward. The recorded losses sustained in the month were Second-Lieutenant D. Scott killed[3] and one officer, Second Lieutenant Jarvis, and three ORs wounded. It was noted later in the month that the horses were becoming very tired taking ammunition forward. The "awful" rain had made the going very heavy.[4] The constant deployment of the artillery certainly helps explain their growing proficiency and the outstanding skills developed by 1918.

For the divisional REs, October meant further work on roads and dugouts. This work was directed by the CRE 47th Division. Their commander was part of the move to the base area. There, one of his key tasks was to spend time locating sources of materials. He also took some leave at this stage. His Adjutant did a tour with the Sanitary Officer, they decided good use had

---

1 TNA WO 95/1231: War Diary of the 1st Division Headquarters, 1-31 October 1916.
2 TNA WO 95/1243: War Diary of the 1st Division ADMS, 28-31 October 1916.
3 Scott lies today in Flat Iron Copse Cemetery, presumably his parents Robert and Emily, from Surbiton, chose the epitaph "I Have fought a Good fight I have kept the faith."
4 TNA WO 95/1240: War Diary of the 1st Division CRA, 1-31 October 1916.

been made of the corrugated iron supplied. The Adjutant also sat on a Board of Inquiry into a fire at the billets of 1st Signal Company. It was decided that the fire had started when flames from the cookhouse set hay in the barn on fire. It was decided that all the proper warnings had been issued so no fault on part of the RE. The CRE also noted that Lieutenant Aldred had been evacuated to England. His injuries resulted from him having been thrown from his horse. The month ended with the CRE being ordered to report to Corps HQ. There he was told to take charge of the road mending in the forward areas in parallel with the 1st Division returning to the line.

November began with 1st Division being used as a pool of labour. The 1st South Wales Borderers, 2nd Welsh and 2nd Munster Fusiliers moved up into Mametz Wood to work on the roads. The other brigades were technically available to continue training. However, they were actually being called upon to provide large working parties. Being based in Albert, 2 Brigade suffered from occasional shelling and enemy aircraft machine gunning the town.[5]

Given the importance of the artillery for defence, the CRA moved to take over from his opposite number on 15 November. The rest of the division gradually moved up into the line. They took over the positions of the right brigade of 50th Division and the left brigade positions of 4th Australian Division. The process was therefore more gradual than in many instances. Strickland only took over responsibility for the line on 22 November. The next day, the artillery carried out a Chinese or mock attack bombardment but there was a limited enemy response. The primary focus was on improving the trenches and installing firesteps. This became more urgent on 25 November when heavy rain led to the collapse of communication trenches, some of which were temporarily impassable. It was noted that there was a lot of sickness in 2 Brigade which was rotated into reserve on 27 November. The staff noted that the men were quite exhausted due to the lack of sleep caused by poor weather and the cold. It was explained that the wet conditions meant that every move by units was exhausting as well as collecting food and stores from the dumps.[6]

The ever present danger on that part of the front was underlined by the orders that all movement by day in front of High Wood should be in parties of ten or less at one hundred yards intervals, whilst movements behind High Wood must be equally spaced out, but could be in groups up to platoon strength.

The detailed orders issued by 1st Brigade reflected the same concerns about trenches expressed a year earlier, but in this case, there was a concerted plan in place. Instead of all the battalions going into support, the 1st Cameron Highlanders were to find the men to form three major working parties. The first group of one hundred men plus NCOs and officers were to act as carrying parties for the 179th Tunnelling Company and were to be based in Turk Lane. One officer and fifty men detailed to work on the two central communication trenches, so they were based in Turk Lane. The third group of one officer, two NCOs and sixty men were detached to live in Longueval where they would be pushing trucks. The orders noted that detachments were to be victualled by their parent unit, so having them all drawn from one battalion meant that battalion's support services had a clear responsibility to cover the dispersed units. The orders

---

5   TNA WO 95/1231: War Diary of the 1st Division Headquarters, 1-14 November 1916.
6   TNA WO 95/1231: War Diary of the 1st Division Headquarters, 15-25 November 1916.

included reference to the brigade's pioneers relieving those of 2 Brigade.[7] On 1 December 1916, 1 Brigade relieved 3 Brigade in the line at Bazentin le Petit and High Wood.[8]

The remainder of the month consisted of battling the weather and taking constant precautions because of the Germans. The divisional records note that there was enemy artillery fire on somewhere within the divisional area on almost every day of the month including Christmas Day. Much of this fire was directed on the back areas. This is why the rules about movement had been stressed to the men. Another threat was posed by German snipers. This threat was greater in the forward areas and required constant vigilance.

The weather was often cold but bright. Any thawing of temperatures tended to cause extra problems due to the mud created. It was noted that less damage was caused after the sides of the trenches had been sloped. Given the bitter conditions the men faced, reliefs were organised around a four-day tour of duty. A lot of effort was denoted to create sufficient shelter for the whole of each support battalion.

One key German position was known as the Maze. The artillery bombarded the Maze on 28 December. The Maze was then raided at 6.02pm by a party of two officers and 25 men of 2nd Munster Fusiliers. This group penetrated as far as the support line but found no Germans. They did note that the German trenches were in a worse state than their own. The group returned almost unscathed; three men had minor wounds. At about 8.30pm, an officer's patrol went out to see if the Germans had since returned to their trenches. This patrol saw some Germans in a shell hole and tried to rush them. Unfortunately, it was a machine gun team and the officer, and another member of the patrol were killed.

Two days later the 50th Division began to relieve 1st Division who doubtless were pleased to be out of such a notorious spot.

---

7   TNA WO 95/1261: War Diary of the 1st Infantry Brigade, Headquarters, November 1916, Appendix 5.
8   TNA WO 95/1261: War Diary of the 1st Infantry Brigade, Headquarters, December 1916.

31

The Daily Grind
January to May 1917

On New Year's Day 1917, For Major General Strickland, GOC 1st Division, it was the day he moved his headquarters to Villa Rocher in Albert. For the next nine days, the men were largely occupied in forming working parties. One of the reasons why the men of the 1st Division were finding so many working parties was that III Corps had issued an order on 5 January 1917 establishing divisional schools for the 8th, 33rd and 40th divisions, and had instructed that they were "not to be disturbed".[1] Of these, only the 33rd would later be used at Arras. Whatever, their pedigree, 1st Division were not seen as part of the cutting edge of the BEF.

There were also a variety of tasks being undertaken daily; for example, one hundred men were assigned to unload ammunition at Meaulte ammunition sidings, whilst 150 worked on the camp at Becourt. One sergeant, a corporal and 25 men were assigned to guard the captured Germans. Another thirty men worked under Captain Robson who bore the title of officer in charge of wood cutting at Becourt. The Sanitary Officer at Albert had 100 men assigned to him to clear mud and 50 wheelbarrows per day were allocated. On Wednesdays and Saturdays, 100 extra men were allocated to this task with an additional 50 wheelbarrows. A further 25 men were assigned to the army workshops, and a hundred men worked under the guidance of 214th army troop company RE laying water pipes. Eighteen other men spent the day acting as the carrying party for 179 Tunnelling Company. Those based at Fricourt camp had to find 830 men per day to unload trains at Bazentin, Fricourt and the quaintly named Contalmaison Circus.[2] The BEF were perennially short of labour, 1st Division were filling an unglamorous role.

On 8 January, the 1st Division HQ was advised of the provisional plan, marked secret, for III Corps to be relieved by I Anzac Corps between 26 January and 3 February. After the battalions shuffled positions on 10 January, the next eleven days saw more working parties absorbing most of the men. On 15 January, 1st Division received specific orders that it would be relieved by 1st Australian Division on 23-24 January and that therefore it would be 1st Division's responsibility to find working parties to work on the roads on 23 January, but thereafter the responsibility

---

1   TNA WO 95/1232: War Diary of the 1st Infantry Division, Headquarters, January 1917- copy of III Corps order.
2   TNA WO 95/1232: War Diary of the 1st Infantry Division, Headquarters, January 1917, Addendum A.

would fall on the Australians. However, 2nd and 3rd Brigades were able to carry out some tactical schemes to assist in training junior officers. This was achieved despite five inches of snow falling on the night of 16 January.

During the night of 23/24 January 1917, the Division started to move to the rear of the Corps area with its headquarters at Bezieux. The artillery of III Corps, and therefore elements of 1st Division, were due to be relieved according to a separate timetable between 28 January and 6 February. Medical units were also allotted their own timetable. Some of the men were to remain with the units to which they had been attached - this applied to those men who constituted the permanent parties attached to 214th and 281st army troop companies of the Royal Engineers. These men would move with their units and not with the division. Two companies of the divisional Pioneers attached to 30th Division would remain with that division.

The importance of the railway siding at Contay was reflected in it being referred to specifically. There the machine guns of 2nd Brigade, devoted to anti-aircraft defence, would be relieved by the Australians under specific arrangements to be made by the two divisions. Once all this was complete, the 1st Division headquarters would close at Bezieux at 11 a.m. on 3 February and re-open at the same time in Mericourt Sur Somme.[3] This movement, in which the British III Corps was to relieve the French XVIII Corps, was to give effect to the British commitment to take over more of the front so that a *mass de manoeuvre* could be created by General Nivelle in preparation for his offensive.

The infantry marched off on 24 January, and initially moved to various camps in the rear area such as Olympe A and Marly B. However, they were to spend only a limited time out of the line, as orders were received to relieve the French 24th Division. Initially 2nd and 3rd Brigade went into the front line. The machine guns were to go into the line twenty-four hours before the rest of the infantry so that there would be an overlap with the French guns before they were withdrawn. This demonstrates, yet again, the growing understanding of the significance of the machine gun in defence; were the Germans to try to take advantage of the handover between the French and the British, they would face a significantly reinforced set of positions. 1st Division was due to take control of the line from the French Chef de Brigade Colonel Odry at 10 a.m. on 8 February. In a further example of the care taken against a surprise attack, the French artillery would only begin to be relieved on the night of 8 February, with the relief spread over two nights, and therefore command of the artillery in the sector only passing to the British at 10 a.m. on 10th February.[4]

Initially, on the night of 6 February 3rd Brigade, with its headquarters in Meudon Quarry, took up position on the left of the new divisional sector, with the 2nd Welsh to the left of 1st Gloucesters in the front line. Behind them were the 1st South Wales Borderers in support, and 2nd Royal Munster Fusiliers in reserve. The next night 2nd Brigade relieved the French in the right-hand sector, positioning the 2nd Royal Sussex on the right and 1st Northants on their left in the front line. Whilst the 1st Loyal North Lancs remained in reserve, the 2nd KRRC occupied the support line.[5] On 8 February, the troops faced a bitter frost. The newly arrived first half of the divisional artillery carried out registration, which led to some German retaliation. The following day saw further registration by the British artillery and another heavy frost as well

3   TNA WO 95/1232: War Diary of the 1st Infantry Division, Headquarters, January 1917.
4   TNA WO 95/1232: War Diary of the 1st Infantry Division, Headquarters, 31 January 1917.
5   TNA WO 95/1232: War Diary of the 1st Infantry Division, Headquarters, 3-7 February 1917.

as a "dangerous wind".[6] Two more freezing cold days followed. It is important to remember how much the men suffered from the poor conditions of the trenches when not in battle.

There was a further adjustment to the divisional front. This involved 2nd Brigade sending 2nd KRRC to take over the left battalion area of French 35th Division. To compensate for this, 1st South Wales Borderers, of 3rd Brigade, took over the positions occupied by 1st Northants, so that each brigade continued to have two battalions in the front line.[7] Meanwhile, orders were issued for 1st Brigade to relieve 2nd Brigade in the right-hand sector on the night of 14-15 February. The routine nature of such reliefs was reflected in the divisional order stating that all the necessary arrangements were to be made between the two brigadiers. The 1st Brigade, acting as reserve to the division, had its HQ at Chuignes, where the 1st Black Watch and 8th Royal Berkshires were also billeted. The 1st Camerons and 10th Gloucesters were based around Chuignolles.

The bitter weather saw the 1st Loyal North Lancs in 2nd Brigade reserve exchange places with the 2nd Royal Sussex in the line two days into the deployment.[8] This is further evidence of how rotations were shortened during very bad weather. Between 14 and 16 January, the troops faced increased hostile artillery fire, including minenwerfers. There was also a thaw which would have meant increased mud in the trenches. As planned, 1st Brigade relieved 2nd Brigade, which meant that the 1st Black Watch entered and occupied the line on the right of 8th Royal Berks, whilst the 1st Camerons were in support and the 10th Gloucesters provided the brigade reserve. The divisional headquarters was relocated to Chuignolles, and intra-brigade reliefs took place in 3rd Brigade, with 1st Gloucesters and 2nd Royal Welsh assuming frontline duties with 2nd Royal Munsters in support and 1st South Wales Borderers being placed in reserve.[9] This period demonstrates what the general experience of troops would have been during periods where they were simply holding the existing line of trenches.

Between 1 February and 1 March, 1st Division completed routine daily progress summaries. The key elements of each summary dealt with sniping, patrolling and work undertaken. They also recorded observations of the Germans at work, for example, where machine gun emplacements were being constructed by the Germans.

Taking the week of 8 to 15 February as a sample, the reports show some interesting detail about what it meant to hold the line during a period when there was no enemy assault or a planned assault by the division itself. Those events or preparations would inevitably distort the type of work undertaken. Regarding sniping, the reports tend to underpin the widely held view that the British were dominant by this stage in the war. Over the week, there were only three days when the German snipers were judged to be active, as against all seven days for the British. However, hits were only claimed by the British on four of those days. The most fruitful day was the 13th-14th when five hits were claimed in three different parts of the divisional sector. However, on the day before two hits were claimed, of which one related to a German sniping post (which may be linked to why no German sniper activity was recorded for the next three days). Therefore, in terms of sniping, the British efforts seemed to have achieved a local superiority.

6 TNA WO 95/1232: War Diary of the 1st Infantry Division, Headquarters, 8-9 February 1917.
7 TNA WO 95/1232: War Diary of the 1st Infantry Division, Headquarters, 10-11 February 1917.
8 TNA WO 95/1232: War Diary of the 1st Infantry Division, Headquarters, 10 -12 February 1917
9 TNA WO 95/1232: War Diary of the 1st Infantry Division, Headquarters, 14-18 February 1917.

On the seven days sampled, the troops were under fire from German artillery or mortars during the afternoon, and on six days in the morning too. Whilst the number of casualties is often very low on the Western Front from programmed area shelling, the psychological strain would be very real. The Germans were observed by the British to be working on their trenches during each 24-hour period, and the British were doing the same. Typically, the Germans were believed to be improving their trenches or wire, but clearly this was informed speculation as they were not directly observed.

The British records provide much more detail on their own activities, so it is possible to glimpse into the daily lives of the ordinary soldiers. At the beginning of this sample week, new latrines were constructed, and old ones filled in, as were sump pits. Baths were also constructed in the rear area on the first day. Work was undertaken on the new divisional headquarters on four successive days. On two days' work was carried out on finishing a bomb store. A new dug out also received two days of effort. Creating a machine gun emplacement took up four days of work. Work was done to deepen and improve the trenches by laying boards. Old trenches were improved by incorporating specific features such as niches in which to store hand grenades.

Reflecting the inevitable result of daily shelling, with a fair proportion of mortars included, three daily reports recorded the need to devote working parties to repairing the damage caused to the trenches. A significant amount of effort, on four different days, was devoted to improving the fire step in various trenches. As the 1st Division had relieved the French, this level of commitment to trench improvement may also reflect the generally held view that the French did not maintain their trenches to the standard that the British saw as appropriate.

Patrolling issues were also covered in these reports. In this sample week, it is recorded that a total of eleven patrols went out from the trenches occupied by 1st Division. Of these, five were recorded as being "officer" patrols. Most of the patrols were initiated by 3rd Brigade, but all three of the patrols sent out by 2nd Brigade on the 13th-14th February were led by officers. Of this latter group, one was led by a German speaking officer who was able to get close enough to the German trenches to hear the occupants arguing over some black rye bread and cheese. His view that they were speaking in the Bavarian patois may have been influenced by overhearing the conversation move on to the topic of what it would be like in Munich after the war.

Most of the other patrols focussed on reporting on the state of the German wire and to what degree the ground had been cut up by shellfire. One officer patrol, initiated within 3rd Brigade on the night of 10th-11th February, seems to have been a response to a non-officer patrol the night before. That patrol had encountered a German wiring party but not engaged it. The officer patrol brought Lewis guns to disperse the Germans found to be continuing wiring and to maintain a fire over that section during the night, to prevent the enemy returning. The reports suggest that units were maintaining a high level of activity. Nevertheless, in assessing these reports, it is important to remember that they are only a snapshot. The requirement to submit daily reports may have been introduced in order to ensure more attention was paid to the work of patrolling and improving the trenches.

On 19 February 1st Division was ordered by III Corps to support the forthcoming attack on La Maisonette by 48th Division. This support included the mounting of two raids, as well as the loan of an army artillery brigade, six medium trench mortars and a heavy trench mortar as well as a machine gun company. Given the introduction of supporting barrages by machine guns during the latter part of the Somme offensive, it is particularly interesting to see the inclusion of the last unit in this list. The unofficial designation of some divisions as "attack divisions" is also implied by the assault being planned; it had been used more extensively than 1st Division on the Somme and was to be used much more extensively during 1917.

By 25 February it was noted that the trenches were improving, and the main communication trench was passable. On the next day orders were received both for support of an attack on 28th February and a postponement of the previously notified attachment of units to 48th Division until 3 March. 1st Division were also informed that the dates of the planned raids should be between 1 and 6 March.

On 27 February, the orders were issued for the demonstration by 1st Division in support of the next day's attack. In consequence, on 28 February, smoke was discharged using approximately eighty of the smoke candles on the left brigade front, but not on the right where the wind was insufficient. 160 smoke candles were issued to the brigade, so it is reasonable to assume half were allocated to each battalion in the front line. The German reaction on the left was to fire up rockets which burst as red stars. However, it was noted that the response of the German artillery on the left was "feeble" and only began 17 minutes after zero hour. At least as much German artillery fire was experienced by those on the right sector, with the addition of trench mortars, so it would seem that the smoke did not add significantly to the level of deception. The divisional artillery batteries were to fire in lifts from the front line to the support line and then back to the front line. The machine gun fire was directed upon the routes by which local reinforcements would be likely to move forward. By this point such feint attacks had been launched many times, and there must have been considerable caution on the part of the Germans, especially when the artillery fire returned to targeting the front line, which it would not do in a real assault unless an infantry attack had already failed. In this case the artillery fire resumed falling on the front line after only five minutes which was much too soon if there had been an actual infantry assault.[10]

March began with a day of heavy shelling by the Germans and, reflecting the level of routine now driving the trench warfare, No. 3 Machine Gun Company relieved No. 2 Machine Gun Company in the right brigade sector. The significance of machine guns for security in defence has already been noted, and it is interesting that, in this case, the relief takes place just two nights before 3rd Brigade relieved 1st Brigade in the same sector. Just as artillery reliefs had become separated chronologically from infantry reliefs to ensure greater security, now those of the heavy machine guns was conducted separately too. On the night in between, 3rd Trench Mortar Company relieved 1st Trench Mortar Battery, so this element too had been divorced from the infantry handover. The security of the sector is also evident, in that the GOC 3rd Brigade only assumed command of the sector from his opposite number in command of 1st Brigade at 10 a.m. on 4 March, that is, after all the reliefs had been completed. The outgoing brigadier remained in charge throughout the relief. 1 Trench Mortar Battery's last day in the trenches had been under heavy fire from German trench mortars. The British artillery retaliated effectively and caused the German weapons to fall silent. On 2 March, the 1st Division had received orders to assist an attack by XV Corps. This involved discharging smoke, barraging the enemy with machine gun fire, and for the artillery to carry out bombardments. However, at 5.15 a.m. on 4 March, the wind did not permit the release of smoke so the machine gunners barraged the routes that local reinforcements would need to use to reach their front line. In this case the

---

10 TNA WO 95/1232: War Diary of the 1st Infantry Division, Headquarters, 19-28 February 1917 including appendices.

artillery bombardment seems to have avoided the errors noted in February, as it started on the German front line with a six-minute period of defensive fire before lifting on to the support line and then slowing to a steady level. Later that day, the divisional command was informed that the proposed attack by III Corp's 48th Division had been postponed indefinitely, and that therefore the troops which had been sent on attachment would be returning to their parent unit. On 3 March, two prisoners, belonging to the *76th Infantry Regiment*, were captured. Thus March began by following the pattern established in February; a mixture of routine reliefs and responding to periodic requests for assistance to neighbouring units. The night after occupying the trenches, 3rd Brigade carried out an intra-brigade relief, which meant that all the troops were familiar with the positions occupied. On 5 March, the divisional artillery, supported by trench mortars, carried out a deliberate bombardment of the German line with a particular focus on wire cutting.[11]

The next day began early for the men of 1st Northants who carried out a major raid at 3.30 a.m. The raid included not only the front line but also the adjacent support line and the sunken road within the sector. The raid was carried out by two parties; the left one of which, led by Second Lieutenant Lenda, was successful in overcoming the resistance it encountered and securing its objectives. This group was faced with a dugout which contained a German troops who refused to come out, so the use of grenades settled the affair. On the Northampton's right the honours went to the Germans, who were ready for them and greeted them with grenades and rifle fire supported by trench mortars. The result was that this party of the Northants were unable to enter the German trenches. Second Lieutenants Hurst and Willoughby were wounded whilst Second Lieutenant Renton, a Londoner, was initially posted as missing, but his grave was subsequently found some distance behind the German lines. The rest of the day saw artillery exchanges with the Germans becoming more active in the afternoon. That night, the Northants were relieved by the 2nd King's Royal Rifles, although it took until 10.30 p.m. due to units becoming lost.[12]

In spring 1917, the German Army shortened its line, and therefore freed up divisions with which to seek a decisive victory against Russia. The Germans had prepared positions to the rear of their line on the Somme, and these positions were known to the British as the Hindenburg Line. The German withdrawal to the Hindenburg Line led to III Corps issuing a warning order on 25 March. This detailed the main points of the line to which Fourth army would advance. III Corps informed its divisions that the Corps cyclists were holding advanced positions, so that divisional staff could reconnoitre advanced ammunition dumps and those for RE stores to facilitate the advance. The recognition that the Germans had withdrawn to strong, previously prepared positions was evident too. Corps instructed divisions to ensure that they brought forward adequate stores to ensure the new line was fully wired. As the Corps advanced, 1st Brigade was put at Corp's disposal to undertake working parties.[13] During the first week in April, the division continued to contribute to building roads, despite the windy, wet weather. The weather improved the following week, although there was heavy snow on 11 April. The South Wales Borderers were working on the road between Brie and Estrees en Chaussee; whilst the rest of 3rd Brigade worked on the railway between Brie and Peronne. An opportunity for

---

11 TNA WO 95/1232: War Diary of the 1st Infantry Division, Headquarters, 1- 5 March 1917.
12 TNA WO 95/1232: War Diary of the 1st Infantry Division, Headquarters, 6 March 1917.
13 TNA WO 95/1232: War Diary of the 1st Infantry Division, Headquarters, March 1917.

training was given to 2nd Brigade; whilst 200 of the gunners, plus the personnel of 3MGC and 3TMB[14], worked on the road from Brie to Villers Carbonnel. Nevertheless, by 16 April 1st Division had moved forward and had moved its divisional headquarters to Mericourt Chateau, with its constituent units appropriately concentrated. For the rest of April, 3rd Brigade were employed on road and railway construction, as well as some men being deployed building the new Fourth Army Headquarters. For the other two brigades, there was an opportunity to spend time on training. However, this was curtailed to some degree by the persistent rain, and days when it snowed.[15]

On 12 May, the divisional artillery began to move to Second Army, under the orders of XIV Corps. Over the next two weeks, the rest of the division followed the artillery into the Second Army area. Here, the 1st Division once again found itself in a support role. 216th MGC were assigned to anti-aircraft work under the direction of X Corps. The 1st Gloucesters and South Wales Borderers were also assigned to X Corps. Their role was to provide carrying parties. To that end, 1st Gloucesters were assigned to work under 41st Division. Half the borderers were assigned to assist 47th division. The other half, and the HQ company, were allocated to the CRE X Corps. Therefore, the history of the 1st Division during the early months of 1917 demonstrates many of the experiences that most soldiers could expect. Much of the work was vital but ancillary to the soldiering that they had trained for. Nevertheless, there is clear evidence that the division was applying techniques both in trench holding and offensive operations that reflected lessons learnt and best practise in early 1917. There is also ample evidence to suggest it was not on GHQ's "list" of attack divisions.

---

14 By this stage in the war each brigade had a component machine gun company and a trench mortar battery designated by the ordinal of the parent brigade.
15 TNA WO 95/1232: War Diary of the 1st Infantry Division, Headquarters, 1-30 April 1917.

32

Operation Hush

Background & Context

There were two key aspects to planned British operations in Flanders. The main offensive known as the Third Battle of Ypres or Passchendaele. The other, which ultimately did not occur, was the projected amphibious landing to turn the enemy flank on the coast. This operation was known as "Operation Hush" for which 1st Division was assigned the crucial role.

The wider significance of Operation Hush was that it reassured the War Cabinet that there was a wider purpose to the proposed offensive in Flanders. The costly Somme campaign had engendered concerns in the War Cabinet especially after further mixed results at Vimy Ridge and Arras. February 1917 had seen the introduction of unrestricted submarine warfare by Germany. It immediately had a massive impact on Great Britain. Ever since Peel had introduced freer trade in the 1840s, Great Britain had relied upon manufacturing to generate the income from which raw materials and food could be purchased. Great Britain was therefore highly reliant upon her trade links. On 27 April 1917, Admiral Jellicoe, the First Sea Lord told the War Cabinet that Britain's policy was based upon command of the sea. He added that "We have not…Disaster is certain to follow, and *our present policy is heading for disaster.*"[1] Critically, Davidson, Haig's Chief of Operations, cites the *Official History* in support of the argument that Haig had to launch the offensive. The Cabinet were influenced to support the offensive because of the loss of over two million tons of shipping between February and June 1917 due to U-boats.[2]

How does Operation Hush fit into this? The stated objective of the offensive in Flanders was Roulers–Thourout. Achieving this objective would have pushed the Germans back from a key lateral railway line. Loss of the railway line would have meant the German supply lines to Oostende and Zeebrugge would have been disrupted. This, in turn, would have meant that an allied landing on the coast would have been possible and denied the use of these ports as U-boat bases. However, one key question that needs to be asked is whether there was any real effort put into *Operation Hush*? It was subsequently cancelled ostensibly due to the lack of progress on the main offensive but had it been fatally compromised by the events of 10th July?

---

1 Hew Strachan *The First World War* (London: Simon & Schuster, 2003), p.244
2 John Davidson, *Haig: Master of the Field*, (Barnsley: Pen & Sword, 2010), p.151

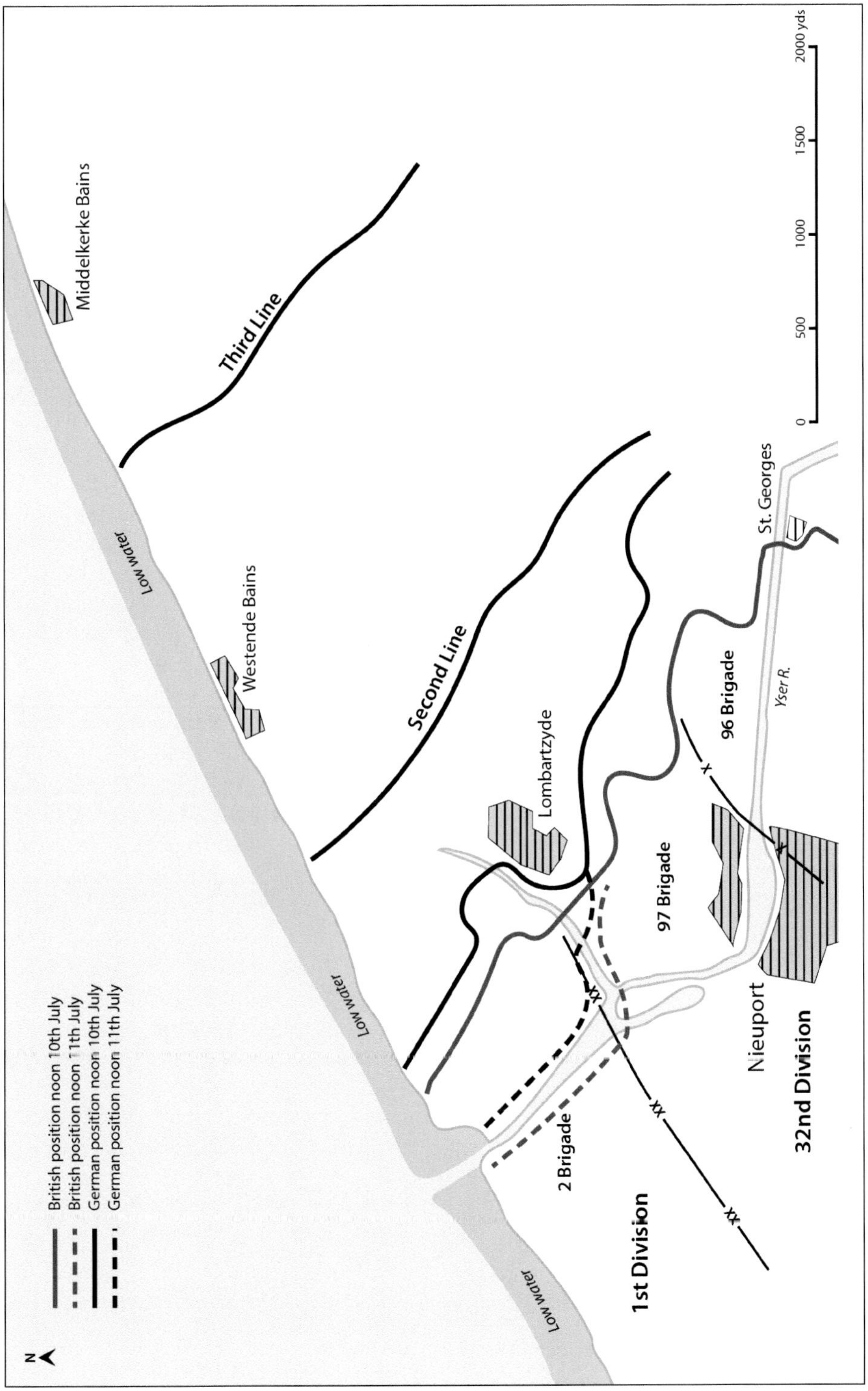

Operation Hush 221

Nieuport, 10-11 July 1917.

General Rawlinson had been disappointed to find that Haig had chosen Gough to head up the offensive in Flanders. Whether the more traditional explanation that Gough was seen as a "thruster" is correct or Sheffield's more sophisticated argument that Rawlinson had not exploited opportunities on the Somme is preferred; it is clear Rawlinson was on the side lines.[3] Not uncharacteristically, Haig had not spoken to Rawlinson before announcing that Gough was to lead and so Davidson (GHQ Chief of Operations) was involved in reassuring Rawlinson that Haig had ideas for employing him and his staff.[4] On 22 May, Haig gave responsibility for "Operation Hush" to Rawlinson who located his XV Corps Headquarters in Malo Les Bains.

The initial concept of Hush lay in a Memorandum by the Operations Staff at GHQ. This was to consist of an attack on the German first line at Nieuport. It was envisaged that the German second line would be attacked at 3am on the following day. The amphibious landing would then be made at the same time as the attack on the second line. This plan envisaged the landing taking place at and south-west of Middlekerke Bains. This would have meant that the landings took place behind the German third line. It would have also meant that the British troops were five miles from Oostende[5] The planners envisaged five divisions of which one was to form the thrust of the landings and two were to carry out the land attack. It was also noted that it would be necessary to discuss the matters with the French as the attack division would need to relieve them but only when the plan was made definite. The planners felt that the whole operation should be under GHQ's direction. They also felt that the trigger for going ahead would be the main offensive reaching Courtemarck.[6]

One change made from the original plan was that the responsibility for the attack on the coast was separated from that of the main offensive. The coastal attack was assigned to General Rawlinson whose command was designated Fourth Army. In accordance with the ideas in the original plan, the force would consist of a single Corps (XV Corps) consisting of five divisions. The 32nd Division was the first to be transferred to Fourth Army. 32nd Division started the relief of the French *XXXVI Corps*. The French *XXXVI Corps* gradually moved across to form part of General Anthoine's French *First Army*. General Anthoine's French First Army.

A total of 189 heavy guns and howitzers were drawn from Second and Third Armies to support the landings. In addition, 306 field guns and 88 howitzers were allocated to XV Corps. The air support for the impending operation was provided by 102 aircraft of IV Brigade RFC and an equivalent force from the Royal Naval Air Service.[7] Rawlinson therefore undertook detailed discussions with the relevant naval and technical specialists regarding the potential for landing units on the coast. One of these options consisted of concrete jetties which would be manoeuvred into place by steamers.[8]

---

3   Prior & Wilson, *Command on the Western Front* (Oxford: Blackwells, 1992), pp. 268-70 and Gary Sheffield, *Somme to Victory*, p.186.
4   Prior & Wilson, *Command on the Western Front*, p.271.
5   Edmonds, *OH, 1917*, Vol. 2, Sketch 9.
6   Terraine, J., *The Road to Passchendaele: A Study in Inevitability* (London: Secker & Warburg, 1984), p.38-9.
7   Edmonds, *OH, 1917*, Vol. 2, p.110-11.
8   Prior & Wilson, *Command on the Western Front*, p.271-73.

However, the success of the Second Army's attack on Messines Ridge had revealed the British strategy to the Germans. Crown Prince Rupprecht commanded the German forces in Flanders. His Chief of Staff, General Kuhl, noted "the axis of the attack ...was known with reasonable certainty".[9] On 19 June, *3rd Marine Infantry Division* captured 11 men of 32nd Division. The conclusion drawn from the examination of the prisoners was that the British were planning an amphibious attack. Armed with this argument, Admiral von Shroder, the German sector commander, sought permission to launch a pre-emptive attack. His request was approved and given the codename "Beach Party" [Strandfest].[10]

Preparations

For 1st Division, June 1917 opened with a mix of training and working parties; the latter being provided by 1st Gloucesters and 6th Welsh, the divisional pioneers. However, on 7 and 8 June, 1st Division was restricted to its billets, as they had been put on stand-by to assist X Corps in its assault on the Messines Ridge. They were not needed, as the attack was successful. On 9 June, the division was informed that they were being transferred from XIV Corps to XV Corps. They were not aware, but this meant they were to be part of Operation Hush. As indicated above, Hush had two elements; the amphibious landing and an advance from the Yser to meet up with those making the landing. Elements of 1st Division were therefore to prepare for each element.

Therefore, on 11 June, most of the division concentrated in the area around Hazebrouck; however, the area was fully cultivated and so training was very restricted. For the next few days, 1st Division had some units still attached to X Corps and some attached to 32nd Division, part of XV Corps. Then 1st Division was ordered to move to the XV Corps sector and began the staged relief of 32nd Division. 1st Brigade began the process by relieving the support battalions of 96th Brigade. By 24 June, responsibility for the left of XV Corps's sector had passed to 1st Division. Under this arrangement, the GOC 2nd Brigade was responsible for the coastal defences from Nieuport-Bains to just west of St Idesbalde. The machine gun battalion of 3rd Brigade were at 2nd Brigade's disposal. Heavy German artillery fire was noted on 29 June but the intra-brigade relief within 1st Brigade was completed as planned. This meant that 1st Camerons and 10th Gloucesters were holding that part of the front.[11] The forward positions occupied consisted of a line of sand dunes approximately 600 yards east of the Yser, the ground being soft in places.[12] The CRE inherited the charges prepared for the demolition of the bridges over the Yser. The key to the boxes of charges was held by the duty Corporal of the Guard of the RE.[13]

Meanwhile, German preparations continued. On 30 June, General von Quast took charge of the land element of Operation Strandfest. For this operation he would have *199th Division* in reserve, whilst the assault would be carried out by 3rd Marine Division. For the assault, the *3rd Marine Division* would be heavily reinforced.[14]

---

9   Sheldon, J., *The German Army at Passchendaele*, (Barnsley: Pen & Sword, 2007), p. 31
10 Sheldon, *The German Army at Passchendaele*, p. 36
11 TNA WO 95/1232: War Diary of the 1st Infantry Division, Headquarters, 1- 30 June 1917.
12 TNA WO 95/1268: Private report contained with War Diary of 2 Infantry Brigade, July 1917.
13 TNA WO 95/1245: War Diary of the 1st Infantry Division, CRE, 24 June 1917.
14 Sheldon, *The German Army at Passchendaele*, p.36.

The plans to blow the bridges in case of an attack fitted into the French plan to abandon the bridgehead if assaulted. However, the bridgehead was essential as a jumping off point for the offensive. The Yser was tidal here and deep, as well as being between 100 and 200 yards wide. Therefore, Lieutenant-General Du Cane, OC XV Corps, ordered it to be held at all costs. This created a real problem for Strickland as the defences beyond the Yser were weak. They only consisted of three lines of raised breastworks.[15]

Daily enemy activity reports show that not only were the Germans being active but that the British noted the creation of camouflage screens etcetera but took no apparent action. The blow when it came should not have been a surprise.[16] For example, on 24/25 June, trains were observed heading towards Ghistelles and large movements were noted but could not be identified. Four days later, three more trains were spotted moving in the same direction. On 29 June the intra-brigade relief within 1st Brigade was completed as planned. This meant that 1st Camerons and 10th Gloucesters were holding that part of the front.[17] The forward positions occupied consisted of a line of sand dunes approximately 600 yards east of the Yser, the ground being soft in places. It was also noted that there was heavy German artillery fire.[18] The Germans had allocated 73 additional batteries to support Strandfest, as well as some super-heavy pieces and three railway guns. The allocation of 300,000 rounds of ammunition demonstrates the importance the Germans attached to this operation.[19] On 1 July and 2 July 1917, 1st Division noted the very active German artillery faced by the forward units who were under bombardment by 5.9" guns firing high explosive, and therefore there was a lot of damage done. It was also noted that the Germans were making use of smoke barrages to conceal the flashes of their guns.[20]

On 1 July a group of Germans were sighted. The report said four were wearing greatcoats and round hats but the fifth was using field glasses whilst wearing a hat with a shiny peak. Although the report did not offer any comment, it did note they were observing the British lines. A more rigorous assessment might have concluded the shiny peak belonged to an officer not normally stationed in the trenches. The report does not refer to any fire being brought to bear to disrupt the Germans in their work.[21]

During 1 and 2 July 1917, 1st Division noted very active German artillery faced by the forward units who were under bombardment by 5.9" guns firing high explosive, and therefore there was a lot of damage done. It was also noted that the Germans were making use of smoke barrages to conceal the flashes of their guns.[22] There was additional German air activity on 2 July. The British struck back during the intervening night through 1st Black Watch who carried out a raid. The raiding party came up from reserve. The successful raid, by one officer and fifteen other ranks, had been supported by artillery and trench mortar barrages. Several Germans were killed, and two prisoners were taken. One died in the German lines and the other only lived long enough to reach the British lines but was identified as belonging to 2nd

15 Edmonds, *OH, 1917, vol 2*, p.117.
16 TNA WO 95/1232: War Diary of the 1st Infantry Division, Headquarters, 24 June -1 July 1917.
17 TNA WO 95/1232: War Diary of the 1st Infantry Division, Headquarters, 1- 30 June 1917.
18 TNA WO 95/1268: Private report contained with War Diary of 2 Infantry Brigade, July 1917.
19 Sheldon, *The German Army at Passchendaele*, p.36
20 TNA WO 95/1232: War Diary of the 1st Infantry Division, Headquarters, 1 July 1917.
21 TNA WO 95/1232: War Diary of the 1st Infantry Division, Headquarters, 1 July 1917.
22 TNA WO 95/1232: War Diary of the 1st Infantry Division, Headquarters, 1 July 1917.

Radfahr-Bataillonen.²³ On the following night another raid, in this case by two officers and twenty men of 8th Royal Berkshires, was unable to reach a German post due to the obstacle posed by the German wire. The following night saw 1st Brigade relieved by 2nd Brigade and the customary morning handover of sector command to the incoming brigadier. It was noted that on the division's right, 32nd Division had carried out a successful raid that captured a member of *3rd Marines*.

On 4 July 1917, 1st Cameron Highlanders were relieved in the line and marched to Coxyde-Bains where they had the opportunity of bathing, as well as taking part in night operations and other battalion level training schemes for the next eleven days.²⁴ This was the training related to the projected landings that were cancelled. The landings were due to take place at around 3am, hence night exercises featuring in the training. This was initially part of 1st Brigade going into reserve, whilst GOC 2nd Brigade took charge of the line and GOC 3rd Brigade took charge of the coastal defences.²⁵ Two days later the battalion arrived at Le Clipon Camp where it would remain for an extensive period of training lasting until late October.²⁶ One question that is posed by these deployments is that the original plan was for a division to be used to carry out the amphibious landing. However, only 1 Brigade was being trained for night operations whilst the other brigades were holding the line.

The Germans were now ready to launch Operation Beach Party their counterattack that would pre-empt Operation Hush. Due to the poor weather the initial artillery preparation continued for several days. From the British side it was noticeable but without awareness of where it was leading. On 5 to 7 July the German artillery was continually active and retaliatory bombardments were organised. Despite the British retaliation, by late on 7 July virtually all the observation posts west of the river had been damaged. The 7 July also saw 23rd Field Company RE replaced by their counterpart from 66th Division, and some companies of units from 3rd Brigade move outside the divisional area. The German targeting of the western positions continued on 8 July, and now virtually all the observation posts west of the river had been destroyed and two of the bridges had been damaged. All this detail was noted but no conclusion seems to have been drawn that the Germans had now "blinded" the elements of 1st Division holding the line. No comment was offered on the fact that the bridges had been damaged and that therefore the forward elements were at risk of being cut off. It does seem that Major-General Strickland was not being analytical.

Presumably driven by the sense of an impending assault, two raids were launched just ten minutes before midnight on 9 July, with the express intent of securing identification of the units opposite. Of the two raids that night, one, carried out by an officer and twenty men of 1st Northants, was driven off by machine gun fire and grenades losing two men killed and six wounded. The other, carried out by an equally sized group from 2nd KRRC did secure identification from a prisoner who died; he was of the 9th Company, 2nd Marine Infantry Regiment, 2nd Naval Division. This raiding party also suffered casualties with one man killed, and its leader and a further eight of his men wounded.²⁷ Considering the effort involved and

---

23 TNA WO 95/1232: War Diary of the 1st Infantry Division, Headquarters, 2-3 July 1917.
24 TNA WO 95/1264: War Diary of the 1st Cameron Highlanders, 4-16 July 1917.
25 TNA WO 95/1232: War Diary of the 1st Infantry Division, Headquarters, 5 July 1917.
26 TNA WO 95/1264: War Diary of the 1st Cameron Highlanders, July- October 1917.
27 TNA WO 95/1232: War Diary of Headquarters 1st Division, 2-9 July 1917.

the casualties sustained, the intelligence gathered was minimal. Especially, given the earlier identification from a live prisoner by 32nd Division.

Assault

The German plans to support their land assault with aircraft were scaled back due to strong, gusting winds from the north-northeast. The plans to use torpedo boats were abandoned for the same reason.[28] At 6.30 a.m. on 10 July, the German bombardment of the front line started at an intense level and continued; it was accompanied by counter-battery fire, and therefore a request was sent to the artillery to conduct counter-preparation fire. According to the German sources this response was limited due to the use of gas against the British artillery.[29]

It was at first thought that the intense bombardment was retaliation against the 2nd KRRC for the raid, but once the shelling was sustained over a period of hours the British troops began to expect an attack. This evidence and the analysis came in a private report written by the Adjutant of 2nd King's Royal Rifles, Captain Humphrey Butler, which he sent to his father, Lieutenant Colonel Lewis Butler.[30] Captain Butler, then 24, was the youngest of Lieutenant Colonel Lewis Butler's three children. The latter went on to write a multi-volume history of the regiment published in the post-war years.

The British artillery began counter-preparation fire at 11.30 a.m. and by 1 p.m. the German fire appeared to slacken, but the British artillery's efforts continued anyway. Amidst all this high-tech weaponry, it was a pigeon (one of a complement of eight with the battalion), due to Fullerphone lines having been cut, that brought news of the beleaguered 2nd King's Royal Rifles who were the left most battalion.

They reported heavy casualties, with some companies being without officers and great difficulty in trying to reinforce their frontline due to the intensity of fire.[31] The reality for the individual companies holding the front line that morning, upon which these reports were based, was described starkly by Captain Humphrey. The right of the battalion's line was held by B company that day, and during the course of the morning 2nd-Lieutenant Heberden was killed in the front line and the company commander, Lieutenant Munro, had been buried by a shell that demolished company HQ. The surviving officer, 2nd-Lieutenant Taylor, who had himself been shot in the hand, was the one who had brought the news to battalion headquarters.

Meantime, the KRRC Intelligence Officer, Lieutenant Gott, volunteered to find out the situation in D company holding the centre of the battalion's position. His report on his return, at about the same time as Taylor had reached battalion HQ, brought similarly depressing news. On the plus side, he reported that Captain Clinton and his officers, Lieutenant Pinnock, and subalterns Chevis, Sheepshanks and Simpson were all alright. However, Gott himself became a casualty when he later set out, during a period of heavy shelling, to try to find out the situation of the left company; he was brought to the dressing station with wounds in his left arm and left leg. The battalion HQ said that it had therefore had no direct communication with the forward units, rear, or the artillery throughout the day. The report added that Lieutenant Colonel Abadie

---

28 Sheldon, *The German Army at Passchendaele*, p.37
29 Sheldon, *The German Army at Passchendaele*, p.37
30 TNA WO 95/1268: Private report contained with War Diary of the 2nd Infantry Brigade, July 1917.
31 TNA WO 95/1232: War Diary of Headquarters 1st Division, 10 July 1917.

kept sending out orders and everyone had great confidence in him.[32] Abadie had originally been commissioned into the regiment but had subsequently served as Brigade Major of 137th Brigade, where he was involved in trying to organise the second attack on the afternoon of 1 July 1916.

The 2nd KRRC also requested relief but expressed concern that the bridges had been blown. The CRE subsequently confirmed that the bridges had been destroyed and that enemy aircraft were keeping the riverbank under heavy machine gun fire.[33] At around 3 p.m., the battalion headquarters was moved because the dugout had already suffered two hits and it was felt it would not take much more. In moving to a tunnel eighty yards to the left, the headquarters staff encountered men of an Australian tunnelling company under the command of a sergeant. They issued the men with a hundred rounds each for their rifles and some rations. Abadie then organised the Australians into four squads of ten and put them under the command of Second Lieutenant Gracia, the battalion signals officer.[34] The battalion had in fact been under periods of intense shellfire for most of the day with the Germans pausing at intervals for ten or fifteen minutes so that when the final assault did come it had been disguised by the previous lulls.

At 6 p.m. the German bombardment again became intense and there was heavy shelling of the west bank of the Yser and the batteries situated in the dunes. At 7.20 p.m., the British artillery responded to rocket signals by laying down an SOS barrage. According to the Germans only one break in the wire was under shrapnel fire.[35] Nevertheless, twenty minutes later the Brigade Observer was reporting that German troops were advancing across the British trenches and that by 8 p.m. the positions east of the river had been lost to the Germans.[36]

To divisional headquarters, there seemed to be continuing resistance around the headquarters of 2nd KRRC and this ties in with Butler's account that three platoons of A company had been left by the old battalion headquarters and that they believed Abadie headed there with the Australians.[37] According to Captain Butler's account, the Germans had already sent a party round to the beach so that the final assault fell upon the 2nd KRRC simultaneously from both the front and the rear. Butler's account says that the Australians remained with Abadie, himself and Captain Smith and Second Lieutenant Richards, the artillery liaison officer, until the German assault and that the first they knew was when German troops threw bombs into the tunnel and used liquid fire.

The German account of the capture of the "regimental staff" is more derogatory. According to Hauptmann Engholm, Viz feldwebel Lez, armed only with a flare pistol, captured them after tossing two hand grenades. According to this account, the Germans were not satisfied when only a single officer, wounded in the hand, emerged. Therefore, the Germans sent the officer back in to fetch his colleagues. The result, they claimed, was the emergence of four senior officers and the capture of valuable files, orders and communications equipment.[38] They believed

---

32 TNA WO 95/1268: Private report contained with War Diary of the 2nd Infantry Brigade, July 1917.
33 TNA WO 95/1232: War Diary of Headquarters 1st Division, 10 July 1917.
34 TNA WO 95/1268: Private report contained with War Diary of the 2nd Infantry Brigade, July 1917.
35 Sheldon, *The German Army at Passchendaele*, p.37.
36 TNA WO 95/1268: Private report contained with War Diary of the 2nd Infantry Brigade, July 1917.
37 TNA WO 95/1232: War Diary of the 1st Division Headquarters, 10 July 1917.
38 Sheldon, *The German Army at Passchendaele*, p.38.

that they had captured the regimental commander. Unless they subsequently shot Abadie, or he was killed by artillery fire after capture, this would suggest they were mistaken.

At the second attempt, according to Butler, Abadie was able to lead the Australians out of the tunnel, revolver in hand. After this, Butler did not see him again and Abadie's body was never subsequently found. This account could be consistent with the German account as they say the senior officers were captured in a dugout which had several entrances. Abadie may have led his men out of another entrance. Butler and his colleagues may have been able to hide because the Germans thought they had captured all the officers. Also, the German account says they subsequently found the officer's mess and availed themselves of all the food they found.[39] Butler and his fellow escapees may have benefitted from the Germans being distracted by the food.

Instructions were now given to the 1st Loyal North Lancs and 2nd Royal Sussex to hold the river line as the new front line. Over the next two hours, four officers and 32 men swam the Yser to regain the British lines. They were subsequently followed by a further four officers and 72 men the following night; these men had managed to remain hidden from the Germans during daylight. Butler says that he and his companions decided to remain in the tunnel and await a counterattack. Later, Second Lieutenant Richards managed to get out and find they were surrounded. The others subsequently confirmed this and identified that it might be possible to reach the beaches in small groups. The officers, fifteen riflemen and twenty survivors from the Australian tunnelling company, began their perilous journey through the Germans, who were digging in, at about 11 p.m. The officers took only their revolvers, as they knew they would have to swim. Having crossed the three hundred yards of open beach to reach the river they then swam across the Yser to reach the headquarters of the support battalion. These four officers of the 2nd KRRC were the only survivors of the twenty with the battalion at the start of the day; and 481 other ranks were lost out of the 520 originally engaged. Whilst the surviving officers concerned would not have been able to turn the tide, the fact that they did not join their commanding officer in leading men out and decided to stay under cover was clearly an uncomfortable comparison. This helps to explain why Captain Butler took advantage of unique circumstances by sending a private report to his father in order to ensure their side of the story was told. Meanwhile the German artillery, in the form of a 6-inch naval gun, had turned its attention to the divisional headquarters at Coxyde Bains. Two further days of shelling eventually forced Major General Strickland to relocate his headquarters to the Grand Hotel des Dunes at St Idesbalde.[40]

Commentary

The subsequent report by Major General Strickland, regarding the fighting on 10 July, focused on the severity of the casualties as the cause of only isolated pockets of resistance occurring. He added that the intensity of fire precluded the organisation of lines of resistance. He also focused on the geography of the area, as precluding the application of the normal approach of using infantry to reinforce the sector under attack. He omitted any reference to the prolonged German preparations which signalled their intentions.

---

39 Sheldon, *The German Army at Passchendaele*, p.38.
40 TNA WO 95/1232: War Diary of the 1st Division Headquarters, 10 July 1917.

Therefore, "Recourse to a purely artillery defence remained possible … The primary cause of our failure to stop the infantry attack was, in the circumstances, the weakness of our artillery defence due directly to the paucity of guns."[41] The failure of the artillery defence, partly due to the observation points having been destroyed, undermines Strickland's opening statement in this assertion. Strickland was distracting Rawlinson from the failure of both himself and Du Cane to read the enemy's intentions and take appropriate action. If these were indeed the lessons they were drawing, then both senior officers were wilfully ignoring all the evidence at their disposal.

Butler's report was subsequently sent on to General Rawlinson, commander of Fourth Army, and he responded by placing the centrality of the argument on the issue of artillery support. Rawlinson dismissed the view that the raid had woken up the Germans. His reason for dismissing the issue of the raid were that the seizure of the eastern bank of the Yser was the key to the German objectives. Rawlinson might also have felt it was important to say nothing that would seem to excuse units from the need to mount raids.

Rawlinson also argued that naval support could never be as accurate as ships were inevitably an unstable gun platform. He very loyally went on to argue that the heavy guns had been retained to support the assaults by Third Army and First Army and that the commander in chief had been correct to do so. Rawlinson also chose to refer to the inability of the army to concrete the positions, due to limited resources, and to reflect positively upon the men not trying to abandon their positions. All this left a warm feeling and was signed "yours ever Rawly".[42] Rawlinson had neatly argued that no one was to blame, as the troops had not tried to run away despite inadequate shelter and artillery protection, and Haig had been correct to withhold the artillery until it could be spared. As President Johnson said, urinating down your trouser leg gives you a warm feeling but does not move you forward; Rawlinson's analysis demonstrates how tight Haig's grip was on his subordinates and the stifling of thought this induced.

Given that the positions lost were beyond the Yser, it would seem more accurate to say that this was yet another illustration of the power of well supplied artillery in 1917. Assuming ample ammunition was available, it was always possible to carry out bite and hold operations, as the Anglo-French armies were about to demonstrate during the Third Ypres offensive and would do so again during the last three months of the war. Widely reported in the contemporary British press, the Germans had successfully snuffed out the Yser bridgehead. They had also upset, albeit temporarily, the strategic element of the forthcoming offensive in Flanders. For his part, Haig duly informed the government through Chief of the Imperial General Staff General Sir William Roberston that the setback was only temporary in a correspondence dated 15 July.[43]

---

41 TNA WO 95/1232: War Diary of the 1st Division Headquarters, 10 July 1917.
42 TNA WO 95/1268: Response from General Rawlinson, War Diary of the 2nd Infantry Brigade, July 1917.
43 See Liddell Hart Centre for Military Archives (LHMCA), Field Marshal Sir William Roberston Papers,7/7/37, Haig to Robertson correspondence, 15 July 1917 and Edmonds, *OH, 1917*, Vol. 2, p.122.

33

BEF Training

The WFA Conference in 2022 focused on the year 1917. In many cases, the discussion centred around transition. As the 1st Division was relieved on 15 July by 66th Division and did not re-enter the battle line until mid-October following two months training. Its experience therefore provides an insight into the focus of the training within the BEF. As 1st Division was an old regular division which had not achieved distinction since December 1914, it may be judged to sit in the mainstream of the BEF.

On 15 July, 66th Division commenced the relief of 1st Division including "what was left of 1st Northants, and 2nd KRRC and No. 2 M.G. Coy." On 20 July, the GOC assembled all his unit commanders and briefed them about what was expected from the next period of training. Reflecting the priorities laid down in Training of Divisions, physical fitness was to be a key element, so units constructed a good obstacle course. Fatefully, the training was interrupted on 31 July by heavy rain.[1] This poor weather continued to disrupt training during August. On 14 August, Haig observed the men training. There was also a break from training on 25 August when the whole division conducted a ceremonial parade under the watchful eye of General Rawlinson.[2] Whatever the theory about training, spit and polish were not to be neglected.

The nature of the training undertaken during September was quite different. The focus switched to movement in open warfare over a variety of terrain. This could have still been part of the requirements for Operation Hush. However, as Hush had been effectively postponed from August, although the possibility of execution continued well into October, circumstances suggest Haig still believed a breakthrough was possible in the salient.

Each brigade conducted field day schemes, with a small force tasked with acting as the enemy. At the end of each exercise, the officers received feedback. The GOC conducted a staff ride for his senior officers. The brigadiers, in turn, conducted a staff ride with their company and platoon commanders. It is interesting to see how far these exercises reached down the chain of command. Apart from a further visit by General Rawlinson, to see a new style of ceremonial parade, the men were able to enjoy many afternoons of sport; rugby, football and tug-o'-war contests took place. The war still impinged; a German plane, part of a raid on Calais, dropped a large bomb on the transport lines. On that moonlit night, five men were killed and nine

1   TNA WO 95/1232: War Diary of the 1st Division Headquarters, 10-30 July 1917.
2   TNA WO 95/1232: War Diary of the 1st Division Headquarters, 1-30 August 1917.

wounded, as well as four horses being killed. For the officers, the month ended with a lecture by Major General Montgomery of the Fourth Army staff on the current military situation.[3] This suggests that although 1st Division was still in training, they had already been earmarked for the Ypres Salient.

Although, 1st Division still had opportunities to train, it was very restricted because the land had now been ploughed and sown. Therefore, during the first half of the month, two shooting competitions were held. The latter attracted over 350 officers to participate in the revolver shooting competition. General Rawlinson visited twice, once for an inspection, and the second time accompanied by American officers. The visitors were provided with a demonstration of modern fighting techniques. In line with modern pedagogical practice, the demonstrations were provided by different units from 1st Brigade.

The three demonstrations were on the use of rifle grenades, rapid wiring, and bombing. The demonstration on how to use rifle grenades was provided by 1st Black Watch and was based upon a tactical scenario where the British and Germans had been holding weak outpost lines approximately 700 yards apart. The scenario then supposed that the Germans had pushed forward an outpost overnight to overlook the British lines, and this had been discovered at dawn when several British soldiers had become casualties. To remove this threat, two rifle grenade sections and two rifle sections had been assigned to dislodge the Germans.

In the narrative of events detailed steps are described, with the British troops coming under fire as soon as they debouched from the outpost line. Then the platoon commander sought to get his grenade sections forward on the flanks by sending out scouts. Once the scouts had identified ways forward and signalled the rifle grenadiers to advance, the rifle sections opened heavy fire to cover the grenadiers' approach. The grenadiers then registered on the German position before providing heavy fire to cover the advance of the rifle sections to within 100 yards of the enemy positions. This reflected that the ground in between the line the rifle sections reached, and the German positions was entirely flat. The final step involved the rifle grenadiers creating a smoke barrage to cover the rifle sections advancing further towards the enemy before actually carrying the position by assault.[4]

This sort of demonstration makes it clear that the British tactics to be adopted in the "100 Days" were already being practised and cascaded well before the March offensive of 1918. This is important as traditionally, the German success in that month is seen as demonstrating to the British how to win. However, they were in fact already moving along "the Learning Curve". This demonstration would have benefitted from the address given to officers on 7 October by two of the divisional staff. They had been on a visit to Second and Fifth Armies to see the modern tactics that were now in use.[5]

The 3rd Brigade bombing area was the venue for a bombing demonstration by 1st Cameron Highlanders. This demonstration, too, was based upon a scenario; in this case a British attack had penetrated a German line to a depth of half a mile, except for a position where a German machine gun had defied the British efforts. The scenario was then built around B company to the right of A coming to A's assistance, by detaching its Lewis gun and bombing sections to attack the German position from the flank. The demonstration then showed how the Lewis guns are

---

3   TNA WO 95/1232: War Diary of the 1st Division Headquarters, 1-30 September 1917.
4   TNA WO 95/1262: War Diary of the 1st Infantry Brigade, Headquarters, October 1917, Appendix.
5   TNA WO 95/1232: War Diary of the 1st Division Headquarters, 1-18 October 1917.

used to provide covering fire to enable the bombing section to bomb their way up to the machine gun emplacement. The emplacement was then to be assaulted with No. 27 Phosphor grenades. An interesting twist in the scenario is that once A company advanced after the machine gun emplacement is destroyed, it had to face a German bombing counterattack from its left, that is on the other side to where B company was. A company had to respond and then bomb its way to clear the trench from which the German counterattack had been launched.[6]

Apart from training troops in how to deal with a variety of challenges, the scenario is very interesting, in that it focuses upon developing responses that could be led by NCOs or very junior officers. The scenario addresses the issue of breakdowns in the chain of command due to casualties. In this scenario, being stopped by machine gun fire, A company might well have already lost several officers. It also addresses the common issue of a unit being held up, by encouraging them to find ways to restore momentum. Therefore, it directly addresses the problems encountered in earlier battles where the failure of a unit on its flank had led to a remorseless tendency to halt by its neighbour. This sort of training would have provided the underpinning necessary for troops to adapt to the semi-open warfare they would experience in between the major assaults that constituted the "100 Days" of 1918.

Outside the camp occupied by the 10th Gloucesters, 8th Royal Berkshires presented a demonstration of rapid wiring. In this case there was an element of competition, as each group were to start to work for twenty minutes when the whistle was blown. Each team had to create fifty yards of wiring in a particular style, with the equipment being stockpiled about thirty yards from the assembly point. In the case of the team producing fifty yards of standard French wire obstacle and the one producing fifty yards of standard double apron fence, one NCO and nine men were in each team. The teams assigned to produce an equal length of low wire entanglement, and a standard belt of double concertinas were assigned only seven men each in addition to their NCO.[7] Whilst it might be felt that wiring would now be a routine task, it has to be remembered that the constant losses meant that there were always new men in need of training as well as the encouragement to existing men to be more productive when assigned to these tasks. The audience of visiting American officers, led by Major General Grebble, would be commanding men who would need to acquire these skills.

The evidence from 1st Division therefore shows that the groundwork for the success of 1918 was being laid in late 1917. The officer training was designed to give junior officers a greater understanding of the larger picture and more confidence with decision making. The scenarios selected for company and platoon actions were realistic and addressed key issues that had limited progress during attacks in earlier years. Therefore, the men had received the training to act the part of lions. Unfortunately, as one of the speakers at the aforementioned WFA Conference stated, the training could not always save them from poor staff work.

6   TNA WO 95/1262: War Diary of the 1st Infantry Brigade, Headquarters, October 1917, Appendix.
7   TNA WO 95/1262: War Diary of the 1st Infantry Brigade, Headquarters, October 1917, Appendix.

34

Third Ypres
Second Battle of Passchendaele

Third Ypres was one of the cornerstones of the "Lions led by donkeys" view of the BEF generals in the Great War. Greater balance is now being achieved. Lloyd's "Passchendaele" sits close to the current consensus. The consensus tends towards the conclusion that at least the last phase, following the Battle of Broodseinde, was unjustified on military grounds because it involved simply extending an already vulnerable salient. The criticism of Haig is balanced by making it clear that Lloyd George too failed to exercise political control of his generals. The latter probably being the driver for the bitterness towards Haig in Lloyd George's memoirs. Lloyd George's inept and maladroit attempt to subordinate Haig to Nivelle in early 1917 carried a cost, in that it weakened Lloyd George's position when Nivelle failed to deliver upon the exaggerated expectations Nivelle himself had created.

By acting as he had done, Lloyd George had helped to unify the British senior officer corps, who distrusted him as well as his politics. Lloyd George, a Liberal, was the head of a Conservative dominated coalition. The extraordinarily strong links between the senior officers and the Opposition prior to 1914 meant that Lloyd George would have to act very cautiously if he were to try to remove Haig.[1] Haig, whilst keeping his own head down, had protected Gough's younger brother during the Curragh Mutiny. Gough was on Haig's side. Bonar Law as Leader of the Opposition had famously proclaimed that he could not see any step opponents to Home Rule could take which the Conservative Party would not support. Therefore, Lloyd George could not expect Opposition support against Haig. It is often omitted from accounts of Lloyd George's success in replacing Robertson with Wilson, that Wilson was a die-hard Unionist.

It was into this futile end game at Passchendaele that the 1st Division was again committed to battle, initially under the command of Fifth Army. On 18 October 1917, the day after the order had arrived for the transfer of the division to XVIII Corps, 3rd Brigade began the move. Three days later, under their new commander, Brigadier-General Grant DSO, 1st Brigade left the camp. Having gradually re-concentrated in the Wormhoudt area, by the end of October 1st

---

1 These links were at odds with the self-proclaimed non-political position of the generals. General officers like Wilson may have dismissively referred to civilians as "the frocks", but they were only dismissive of the ones who did not agree with them.

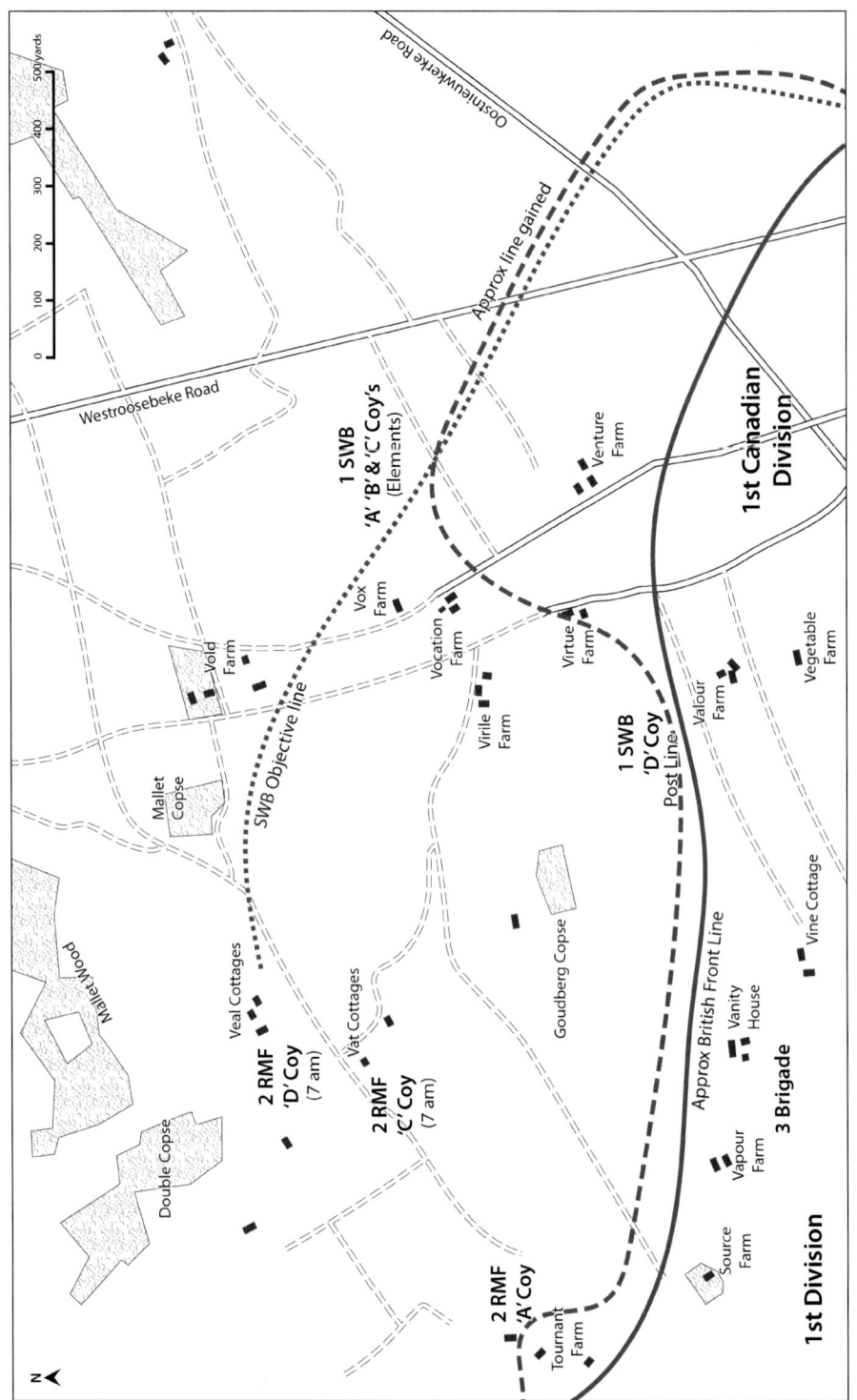

Passchendaele, 10 November 1917.

Division moved up to the canal bank at Ypres. Then II Corps relieved XVIII Corps and the division became part of II Corps. The responsibility for that sector of the front passed to Second Army.[2] 1st Division was tasked with protecting the flank of 1st Canadian Division during what became known as the Second Battle of Passchendaele.[3]

Initially, responsibility for this sector of the line passed to Major General Strickland, whilst the units of 63rd Division remained in place. This was presumably intended to hide the arrival of a fresh division, as the next day, 6 November, orders were received for 1st Division to carry out an assault. 1st Division noted on 6 November that the Canadians had captured and held Passchendaele, Mosselmarkt and Goudberg. The German counterattacks were defeated by artillery and machine gun fire, including that of 1st Division and 188 MGC which was under the orders of Strickland. As a result of the preliminary orders, all the brigades of 1st Division began to move forward. In moving on roads, the units were instructed to leave a hundred yards between companies and five hundred yards between battalions.[4]

The orders issued on 6 November were for an attack designed to capture the spur running from Vocation Farm through Vat and Veal cottages to Tournant Farm. This attack was designed to support the Canadian attack on the ridge between Passchendaele and Vocation Farm. The attack was to be carried out by two battalions of 3rd Brigade with a battalion of 2nd Brigade holding a defensive line west of the Paddebeek. One battalion was to form up around Valour Farm and attack Vocation Farm. The other was to advance from the environs of Vapour Farm towards Vat and Veal cottages, capturing Tournant Farm as it did so.

A key objective for the CRE was to ensure the duckboard tracks were sufficiently advanced to support the assault. He was also arranging for boards with the names of the objectives to be made. These were then to be attached to the buildings when they were captured, so that the contact aeroplanes could report on the progress of the attack. To support the assault, there were to be both artillery and machine-gun barrages. Once again, this is evidence of the facets of successful operations in 1918 being based upon methods adopted in 1917.

Two days later, more detail was added to the orders. One artillery battery was to be put at the disposal of GOC 3rd Brigade. Command of the assault fell to Lieutenant Colonel Pagan of 1st Gloucesters, in the absence of the Brigadier. The main artillery barrage would be 150 yards ahead of the infantry and after three minutes it would start to advance at a pace of one hundred yards every eight minutes.[5] The pace of the barrage (half of the speed adopted as standard in 1918) demonstrates how poor the ground was felt to be and the nature of the objectives.

In the BEF, divisions were rotated between corps as required by the overall strategic plan. Corps staff were fixed and therefore expected to provide incoming divisions with local knowledge as well as overall guidance. In this case, Strickland was answerable to General Jacob, GOC II Corps. Prior and Wilson offer the view that Jacob was complacent at the start of Third Ypres.[6] Here, the Corps staff seem to have expected 1st Division simply to perform the role of flank guard to the Canadians. A better Corps staff would have already been aware of the key terrain

---

2   TNA WO 95/1232: War Diary of the 1st Division Headquarters, 19 October – 2 November 1917.
3   Edmonds, *OH, 1917, vol. 2*, pp. 358-359.
4   TNA WO 95/1232: War Diary of the 1st Division Headquarters, 1 – 6 November 1917.
5   TNA WO 95/1232: War Diary of the 1st Division Headquarters, November 1917, Appendix.
6   Robin Prior & Trevor Wilson, *Passchendaele: The Untold Story* (New Haven, Connecticut: Yale University Press, 2016), p.86.

features and ensured the ground was inspected sooner. The evidence here suggests that Jacob and his staff were ciphers for Army HQ. They were just delegating tasks to incoming divisions without adding value during the planning process.

The quality of the ground was indeed poor. The planning had not involved looking at the ground until 8 November. The Paddebeek stream had marshes on both sides and was found to be impassable. Given the conditions under which the battle of Passchendaele had been fought, it is incredible that the plan had been drawn up without considering the terrain. It was therefore arranged for the Canadians to afford an area on their left to be used for the right of 1st Division's assaulting battalions. This meant that this battalion would now attack in a north-westerly rather than northerly direction. On the positive side, by 9 November 6th Welsh had done a lot of work to improve the Gravenstafel–Mosselmarkt road, and to extend forwards the duckboard tracks, directed by and assisted by RE personnel.

On 9 November, there was less shelling and more aerial activity by the Germans. This suggests that they were expecting further British assaults and wanted to get a clear picture. The 1st Division artillery fired practice barrages at Noon and 1 p.m.[7] The two assaulting battalions were already at Irish Farm. There they were visited by the entire divisional staff, headed by Major General Strickland, "all very cheery and high hopes of success".[8] At 6 p.m. the 1st South Wales Borderers began to make their way towards their jumping-off point, "under large loads"[9] followed an hour later by 2nd Royal Munster Fusiliers. Each battalion was guided on their way by tapes laid during the day. If the German aircraft had spotted the tapes, it would help explain the difficulties faced during the assault.[10]

The assaulting battalions were able to reach their start points, but 2nd RMF, on the left, had the most difficulty due to the state of the ground. The OC 2nd RMF had problems in locating Tournant Farm, only the battalion Intelligence Officer had previously reconnoitred the ground. The assaulting battalions had been assigned three guns each from 3 MGC to go forward with them. However, due to the softness of the ground, the plan to deploy stokes mortars in close support had to be abandoned. Nonetheless, 2nd RMF were successful in capturing their objectives, as they benefited from an accurate and well-defined barrage. They drove in the German outposts and took approximately fifty prisoners. The left company took Tournant Farm and two dugouts north-east of it (not on their maps) but were held up at a third one. The right of the battalion was able to reach Veal and Vat cottages but there was a lot of sniping from all directions. As the left flank was a salient and the right flank was open, the Germans could fire at 2nd RMF from three sides. One statement in the report filed with the battalion records did not make it into the final divisional report. It is easy to see why. Major General Strickland decided not to tell his superiors; "The men were apparently perturbed at not being able to get in touch with the 1st South Wales Borderers on their right and came back". The 2nd RMF had bluntly stated that the main reason for the attack failing was failure of the neighbouring South Wales Borderers.

Problems manifested themselves on the right. 1st South Wales Borderers were attacking with two companies in the lead. B company would be on the left and A company (supported by a

---

7   TNA WO 95/1240: War Diary of the 1st Division Artillery, 10 November 1917.
8   TNA WO 95/1280: War Diary of the 1st South Wales Borderers, 9 November 1917.
9   TNA WO 95/1280: War Diary of the 1st South Wales Borderers, 9 November 1917.
10 TNA WO 95/1232: War Diary of the 1st Division Headquarters, 8-9 November 1917.

platoon of C company) on the right. The remaining three platoons of C company were situated about 200 yards behind the centre of the two leading battalions, as the reserve company. A further 200 yards back was D company, who had been designated as the counter-attack company.[11] Before zero-hour, A company of 1st South Wales Borderers lost nearly all of one platoon. Therefore, the platoons had to be re-organised. When the British barrage started it was described as ragged and hard to follow, leading to the battalion getting caught in it. According to the battalion's view, benefitting from the Canadian barrage, A company did reach their objectives and maintain contact with the Canadians. However, the whole battalion had drifted to the right. Strickland did not include the explanation given by 1st South Wales Borderers. This was that the Canadian barrage was thick and effective, so the battalion followed it. They had not taken Vocation Farm, so there was a dangerous gap between them and 2nd RMF. The first German counterattack against 1st South Wales Borderers came at around 7.15 a.m. but was beaten off by the machine guns of D company.[12] However, around noon, the Germans successfully worked through Goudberg Copse and began to take the post established by HQ company in the flank and forced it back.

The gap was especially dangerous for the 2nd RMF, as their left flank was already exposed, because the operation involved them creating a further salient in the German line. Around 7 a.m., about an hour after the assault commenced, German aircraft flew over the area. Soon afterwards a rolling barrage began. The Munsters complained in their report that they were under enfilade machine gun fire from their left and that they were under a lot of sniper fire. They noted that this was the phase where many officers and NCOs became casualties; presumably, the snipers were looking for them. A company lost its commander and three other officers and B company lost its OC and two more; each of the other companies lost three officers.[13] German troops advanced to retake the ridge captured by the 2nd RMF, under cover of a rolling barrage.

The divisional after-action report explained the retreat by 2nd RMF by reference to the Germans being able to access both their flanks, as well as the fatigue induced by the terrain and rifles being caked in mud. They also reported that the Germans were able to attack from within the protective barrage. This would have partly arisen from the failure of 1st South Wales Borderers. The protective barrage, designed to allow consolidation of captured positions, would have been falling beyond the line of the objectives, so untaken positions were a German base within the barrage. The report was careful to note that only four of the seventeen officers involved in the assault returned, and that total 2nd RMF casualties exceeded 400. One of the notable casualties, posted missing later determined prisoner of war, was Captain Batten-Pooll VC, MC.

The divisional report carefully noted that 1st South Wales Borderers lost ten officers and 374 other ranks. Focusing on casualties was the standard way in which reports deflected unspoken questions about the fighting spirit of the unit concerned. Similarly, the report noted that the officer commanding the machine guns section supporting the 1st South Wales Borderers was killed reconnoitring ahead of his men at Virile Farm. It noted too, that the machine gun section only withdrew once all four guns had been put out of action by shellfire. The section assigned to 2nd RMF also took heavy casualties before zero hour but was able to cover the retirement of the unit. It was then assigned to work with 1st Gloucesters at Inch House, where it helped

---

11 TNA WO 95/1280: War Diary of the 1st South Wales Borderers, 9 November 1917.
12 TNA WO 95/1280: War Diary of the 1st South Wales Borderers, 9 November 1917.
13 TNA WO 95/1279: War Diary of the 2nd Royal Munster Fusiliers, 10 November 1917.

to cover the gap between the two attacking battalions. The report then added that a company of 1st South Wales Borderers were sent to assist the Canadians in securing their flank and that Lieutenant Colonel Pagan was wounded whilst ascertaining the situation on that flank.[14]

The weather was also mentioned as a factor, as it rained overnight on 9/10 November and on 10 November, so the ground became increasingly impossible. The heavy rain was also put forward as reducing the rate of fire of three artillery batteries situated at Wallommolem Cemetery which had been deployed to deepen the barrage. Major General Strickland also observed that rifles and guns kept in their cases functioned on arrival at their objective, but only for a short time as the men and their uniforms were caked in mud. He also argued that for small scale attacks, it was even more necessary to devote effort to counter-battery work, as the enemy could concentrate their firepower on a small area.[15] The divisional artillery noted that the German counter-barrage started about eight minutes after zero-hour.[16] Given the initial three minute standing barrage, and the planned pace of the barrage, that means the leading troops would have only covered about seventy yards before it fell on the supporting troops. The decision to have the machine gun sections move independently, and therefore behind, the leading wave, helps explain how the German barrage caught them.

It would be simple to conclude that this was a largely pointless operation which failed because it was ill conceived, poorly planned and carried out in heavy rain. The difficulty for the reputation of 1st Division was that the Canadians, under the same conditions, had reached most of their objectives. The whole exercise was planned in considerable detail but major issues such as the state of the ground were not addressed. The evidence here is that the staff of II Corps were negligent. Simpson concurs with Prior and Wilson's negative assessment of counter-battery work.[17] This is another instance of where poor counter-battery work made a significant contribution to the failure of an assault. The Canadian success flattered II Corps but the combat reputation of 1st Division would remain indifferent.

Postscript

On the evening of 10 November, one company of the Gloucesters was inserted into the line to help the 1st South Wales Borderers connect up their posts. This proved not to be possible until B company of the Gloucesters were also sent forward on 11 November. That evening the 1st South Wales Borderers and supporting men of the Gloucesters were relieved by 1st Loyal North Lancs.

Strickland's care in editing his subordinates' reports meant that much emphasis had been placed upon the bravery of the individual soldiers. Eighteen days later, the corps commander presented thirty men with the Military Medal, in relation to the operation.[18] There were twelve MMs presented to the men of 2nd RMF, including that to 10099 Private Murphy who was receiving a bar to his previous MM.[19]

14 TNA WO 95/1232: War Diary of the 1st Division Headquarters, November 1917, Appendix.
15 TNA WO 95/1232: War Diary of the 1st Division Headquarters, November 1917, Appendix.
16 TNA WO 95/1240: War Diary of the 1st Division Artillery, 10 November 1917.
17 Simpson, *Directing Operations*, (Stroud: Spellmount, 2006) p.100
18 TNA WO 95/1280: War Diary of the 1st South Wales Borderers, 10-11 & 29 November 1917.
19 TNA WO 95/1279: War Diary of the 2nd Royal Munster Fusiliers, 29 November 1917.

Whatever their shortcomings in the attack, the artillery was credited with completely breaking up an attempted German assault which formed around Vat Cottages on 13 November. A more successful operation was carried out at 5 p.m. on 16 November. This was done by the troops attacking without artillery support and therefore achieving surprise. Strickland noted that army barrages had trained the Germans to expect attacks at dawn. Artillery support was used to help beat off the counterattack. On the left, 8th Berkshires moved the line forward 150 yards beyond Tournant Farm. On the right, 1st Camerons advanced at 5.40 p.m. (due to the light) and encountered stiff opposition around Vocation Farm but succeeded in linking up with the Canadians. The Camerons captured 27 men of *14th Infantry Regiment* and a machine gun. A supporting platoon drawn from 1st Northants had crossed the Paddebeek. They were able to occupy two pillboxes but were caught in the barrage triggered by the Camerons' assault. The result was that they suffered 23 casualties, nearly 50%. This was more than the twenty casualties suffered by the two companies of 8th Berkshires and proportionately more than the 120 suffered by the two companies of Camerons. Nonetheless, these operations supported the view that 1st Division had a good fighting spirit.

The remainder of the month involved patrols, and the routine of holding the line; with regular brigade and battalion reliefs taking place. On 24 November 32nd Division relieved 1st Division. On 26 November, the GSO1, Lieutenant Colonel Dobbie, led a group of staff officers on a visit to the French *2nd Division*. The meeting was to begin to prepare to relive the French in the sector south-west of the Houlthulst Forest from Kortebeek to Liaison Farm. In due course, the relief was completed, and Strickland became responsible for the sector at 10 a.m. on 5 December.[20]

The first half of December passed in the usual round of trench reliefs. An active patrol policy kept the division appraised of the enemy on its front. German artillery activity increased as the month continued. A number of patrols identified Ops and other headquarters which enabled the artillery to destroy some of the positions. For the men out of the line on Christmas Day, arrangements had been made for the "usual celebrations". The German supply route known as Ferret Junction was fired on from 5.15 p.m. until 11.20 p.m. by the machine guns of 2 MGC. They delivered 7000 rounds during that time.[21] For those in the frontline, patrols had to be undertaken. The latter were however, limited by it being noticeably light. They did report that the Germans were singing. Boxing Day saw the start of the American General Bundy's attachment to the division. The final week of the year followed the pattern for December, though there was less shelling.[22] Whilst popular mythology continues to cast an aura over Christmas 1914, there was no cessation of hostilities for Christmas 1917.

---

20 TNA WO 95/1232: War Diary of the 1st Division Headquarters, November 1917, Appendix B.
21 TNA WO 95/1273: War Diary of the 2nd Machine Gun Company, 25 December 1917.
22 TNA WO 95/1232: War Diary of the 1st Division Headquarters, December 1917.

35

Lull Before the Storm

After the bloody events officially designated Third Ypres, the British Army faced its fourth winter of the war increasingly short of manpower. The disagreements between the leading politicians and their generals are well known. Lloyd George moved to replace Haig's ally Robertson as CIGS with Wilson, the political general par excellence. Whilst these issues were being hammered out in London the Western Front remained static. However, momentous changes were taking place to the East.

The second Russian revolution of November 1917 had brought the Bolsheviks to power. V.I. Lenin's support in the key cities relied heavily on his slogan "Bread, Peace and Land". To achieve the opportunity to consolidate power, Lenin had agreed to an Armistice with Germany in December 1917 and then begun peace negotiations. This fulfilled the hopes of the German General Staff who permitted Lenin and colleagues to cross Germany from Zurich in a "sealed train". The first revolution in Russia had led to the creation of a Provisional Government which pledged to continue the war with Germany. This was deeply unpopular and so the German decision to let Lenin travel back to Russia proved immensely clever. In the knowledge that Germany would be able to transport many of its forces from the Eastern to the Western Fronts the Allies had decided to stand on the defensive.

To defend the Western Front, the BEF decided to adopt two measures that reflected their dilemma of how to confront an increased number of Germans despite being short of men. The first was tactical and led to the adoption of defence in depth. The creation of a forward zone, a battle zone and a rear zone would mean lots of digging. The second measure was the decision to reduce brigades from four battalions to three. This would allow battalions to be made up to full strength but obviously each battalion would have to do more work, for example, hold a longer length of line.

Against this background, 1918 opened with 1st Division holding the line as part of XIX Corps. For the men, the rotational existence - moving from rear to support then front line before starting again - continued. On the left, their neighbours were the Belgian army, and on their right flank, the 18th Division. On 18 January, the overall shortage of men, and the plan to withdraw from the salient, bought so dearly the previous autumn, manifested themselves. Corps ordered two battalions to be made available for work on the Army Line. One had to be found from a frontline brigade and one from support. This necessitated holding the front line more thinly and therefore adjusting battalion boundaries. The two battalions selected were 10th Gloucesters and 1st Loyal North Lancs. On 25 January, 32nd Division commenced the relief of

1st Division, which was being transferred to II Corps. The relief began with 3rd Brigade, who were in support, and was finally completed at 10 a.m. on 30 January. The intervening period had afforded the officers of 32nd Division the opportunity to reconnoitre the forward areas.[1]

In the case of 1st Division, 10th Gloucesters were to be disbanded. On their final tour of duty 10th Gloucesters had demonstrated some ingenuity. They held the line with just two companies. This enabled the other two companies to focus on wiring and general improvements to the line. They also situated their cooks in the Café de Londres, about a mile behind the line. From there the support companies had the duty of taking hot tea and soup to the two companies holding the line.[2] However, in 1st Brigade, they were serving alongside two regular battalions from famous regiments, 1st Black Watch and 1st Cameron Highlanders. Therefore, it was the two service battalions who were moved / disbanded. The 10th Gloucesters became the 13th Entrenching battalion and the 8th Royal Berkshires were transferred to 53 Brigade of 18th Division. By taking both service battalions out of 1 Brigade, it was possible to slim 2 Brigade down by transferring 1st Loyal North Lancs to 1 Brigade.

The final piece in the jigsaw was the transfer of 2nd RMF to the 16th (Irish) Division. Major General Strickland visited each battalion prior to its departure; the 2nd RMF, who had been with the division since mobilisation, were accorded the honour of marching off, led by the divisional band.[3]

On 8 February 2nd Brigade began the process of relieving the right section of 35th Division. The relief was completed the next day, with 1st Brigade in support and 3rd Brigade in reserve. Divisional headquarters and 1st Brigade HQ were on the canal bank in Ypres. Amidst the normal routine, the 2nd KRRC occupying a forward post, were attacked at 5.45 a.m. on 17 February by two parties of Germans, who cut through the wire. Initially, the Germans captured a Lewis gun but, despite each of their parties having a light MG, a firefight developed. The 2nd KRRC captured one of the German MGs and recovered their own. Three days later, 1st Brigade relieved 2nd Brigade in what was now described as the "forward system". The rest of the month passed in a routine manner.[4]

The new idea of a "battle zone" was reflected in the note, that Brigadier-General Kemp DSO was wounded whilst visiting it. He was replaced as GOC 2nd Brigade by Brigadier-General Sir W A I Kay DSO, 6th Baronet, who had been an officer of the KRRC. The changing ideas on defence were illustrated when two companies of the support brigade and fourteen machine guns were deployed in localities in the "Support System of the Forward Zone". The front occupied was extended to allow a division to be withdrawn from the line. To reflect this, 1st Division deployed its two brigades in different ways. The right-hand brigade had two battalions in the line and two in support. The left brigade was deployed with one battalion in line, one in support and one as reserve. In mid-March 2nd Brigade was the reserve brigade, but it had been assigned to Corps reserve. On 18 March, the Germans raided Requette Farm at 4 a.m. but were driven off. Another raid fifteen minutes later, on another section, resulted in three men being captured. This led Brigadier-General Sir W A I Kay DSO to reconnoitre the front line, where he was wounded. Two days later, the Germans raided Meunier Farm and Helles House but

1   TNA WO 95/1233: War Diary of the 1st Division Headquarters, January 1918.
2   TNA WO 95/1265: War Diary of the 10th Gloucestershire Regiment, 21 January 1918.
3   TNA WO 95/1233: War Diary of the 1st Division Headquarters, 1-5 February 1918.
4   TNA WO 95/1233: War Diary of the 1st Division Headquarters, 6-28 February 1918.

were driven off, with the loss of four members of the "Assault Detachment" of 12th Company, 103rd Reserve Infantry Regiment. On 22 March 1st Northants carried out a "silent raid" and captured a soldier of 94th Infantry Regiment. The rest of the month saw routine reliefs and a lot of patrolling to identify enemy positions.[5]

Thus, it is possible to see that the re-organisation of the BEF did not impact hugely on the daily lives of most of the men serving in 1st Division. The references to the new dispositions do suggest that the concept of forward and battle zones were recognised but not yet completely clearly understood. The German High Command's decision to back Lenin had helped create an opportunity for them to launch a potentially decisive offensive in the West. After their offensive failed, the spectre of a communist revolution in Germany, emulating that in Russia, would come back to haunt them.[6]

---

5 TNA WO 95/1233: War Diary of the 1st Division Headquarters, March 1918.
6 Amongst numerous others, a demobilised Austrian corporal would be employed to spy on potential revolutionaries; by this route, Hitler would get into politics.

36

A Successful Defence

April 1918 began with the army commander providing an appraisal of the situation on the Somme Front, at a meeting of divisional commanders with brigadiers in attendance. This followed the opening of the German offensive there on 21 March. The German offensive had led to a retreat by Fifth Army. The 1st Division received a warning order that it might be transferred to another army (minus the divisional artillery). This was confirmed on 3 April, and the following day 1st Division learnt it was to be relieved by 30th and 36th Divisions. Both divisions had suffered heavy casualties in the Somme fighting. On 5 April 2nd Brigade were entrained but no machine guns went with them. Given the situation on the Somme front, they were likely to be thrown into a defensive battle, so this shows poor thought on the part of the Corps staff. By 8 April, the rest of the division was able to entrain in preparation for moving to First Army.[1]

Due to the success of the latest German attack, units of 1st Division were soon in action. The German assault on the Lys sector had been delivered against the Portuguese divisions, which broke. The situation would have been even graver, were it not for the gallant defence put up by 55th Division on the southern side of the breakthrough. The German success in entering Givenchy meant I Corps put 1st Brigade on one hour's notice and ordered 3rd Brigade to stand to. Two companies of 1st Gloucesters led the way, moving forward to Le Preol. Then the rest of the battalion went forward to hold Vauxhall and Westminster Bridges. A machine gun company was sent forward to reinforce 166th Brigade. Late that evening, 1st South Wales Borderers were sent forward to guard the bridges over the La Bassée Canal between Le Preol, and Bethune. 1st Division noted the excellent work of 164th Brigade in regaining Givenchy, and the success of 165th Brigade on 164th Brigade's other flank.[2]

On 10 April 1st Division received orders to prepare to relieve 11th Division. Therefore 3rd Brigade sent a reconnaissance group to visit the line. 1st Camerons relieved 1st South Wales Borderers in the role of guarding the bridges. On the next day, 1st Division relieved 11th Division in the Cambrin sector but 11th Division remained in the Hohenzollern sector. News that German troops were dribbling through the British line led 1st Camerons to be moved forward to cover some bridges further east, pending the arrival of 3rd Division. Following a

---

1 TNA WO 95/1233: War Diary of the 1st Division Headquarters, 1-8 April 1918.
2 TNA WO 95/1233: War Diary of the 1st Division Headquarters, 9 April 1918.

reconnaissance of the Le Quesnoy area, new defensive localities were taped out and the divisional pioneers, 6th Welsh, began preparing them. On 12 April 1st Brigade was re-deployed to support 55th Division, as 3rd Division had now arrived in their designated sector. On the following day, Strickland attended a conference at Corps HQ regarding 1st Division relieving 55th Division. Strickland held a conference with his senior officers when he returned at 6 p.m. The fighting qualities of C company 1 MGC were recognised in the commendations received from GOC 55th Division and the brigadiers under whom they had served, whilst on attachment.[3]

The carefully undertaken relief of 55th Division began on 15 April when 3rd Brigade relieved 165th Brigade in the Festubert sector. 1st South Wales Borderers occupied the frontage from Tuning Fork East Keep to the Loisne defences (both inclusive), with its HQ in the Loisne Chateau. To ensure the security of the line, 3rd Brigade came under the orders of 55th Division temporarily. Subsequently, 1st Division HQ moved to Fouquieres. However, this proved to be a temporary move as, under orders from First Army, two 12" guns were placed at the end of the garden. It was therefore decided to move the divisional headquarters to Chateau de Charmeux at Gosnay. The chateau had previously been used for a I Corps school. The next day, 1st Brigade relieved 164th Brigade in the Givenchy sector. 1st Black Watch were deployed in the left sub-sector with HQ in Southmoor House. They had D company on the left with two platoons in the Le Plantin South position and two in Grenadier Road. Their centre was formed by C company in Ware Road and New Cut. B company occupied the system of Keeps; with one platoon in Herts Keep and another in Moat farm. Strongpoints were often named as 'keeps'. The remaining two platoons were in Givenchy Keep and Givenchy Tunnel. A company was responsible for the trenches on the right up to Berkley Street. Provision was made for initiating a local counterattack by placing a platoon under Second Lieutenant P W Mackay in the Givenchy tunnels (the "Bunny Hutch") where they were joined by the local reserves of A and C companies. This trench system had exits into Piccadilly and Caledonian Road plus a further battle exit.[4]

The 1st Loyal North Lancs completed the relief of the 2/5th Lancashire Fusiliers at 3.55 p.m. on 17 April. They occupied the trenches north of the La Bassée Canal, with three companies in the line and D company in support.[5] News of enemy intentions was gleaned by 1st Gloucesters who captured prisoners on 16 and 17 April. The first said the attack at Givenchy would be renewed. The second, under questioning at I Corps, said that the attack was scheduled for 9 a.m. on 18 April, and that it would be preceded by a four-hour bombardment. Therefore, warnings were issued.[6]

In fact, the German artillery began a general bombardment of the British lines between Loisne and the La Bassée Canal at 1 a.m. The bombardment intensified at 4 a.m., to a level consistent with a preparatory one. Three hours later, the bombardment was extended south of the canal. All the elements of the new standard offensive methodology, demonstrated in March, were present. A mixture of varied calibres of artillery and trench mortars were used to bombard

---

3   TNA WO 95/1233: War Diary of the 1st Division Headquarters, 10-14 April 1918.
4   TNA WO 95/1263: War Diary of the 1st Black Watch, 16 April 1918.
5   TNA WO 95/1263: War Diary of the 1st Loyal North Lancs, 17 April 1918.
6   TNA WO 95/1233: War Diary of the 1st Division Headquarters, 15 – 17 April 1918.

the front and support areas. In addition, reserve and battery areas were targeted with gas. The 2nd Welsh were forced to wear their respirators for two-and-a-half hours.[7]

The artillery fire reduced the garrison of Route A Keep, held by 1st South Wales Borderers, from seventy to twenty, and destroyed two Vickers guns and three Lewis guns. The Germans were able to occupy it, and therefore there was a gap on the right flank of the South Wales Borderers. This led 1st South Wales Borderers to call on their support battalion, 2nd Welsh. They despatched B company under Captain Morgan, who worked through the German barrage and took up position on the right of 1st South Wales Borderers, as requested. However, the Germans were unable to dislodge the 1st South Wales Borderers from Loise Keep, the Switch line or the Tuning Fork Keep, even when some Germans used an old trench to get closer to the British positions.[8] Part of the blocking force was led by CSM Biddle of D company, 1st Gloucesters. Some of the Germans, baulked at the Tuning Fork line, had begun to filter around D company of the Gloucesters. CSM Biddle, a signals specialist, managed to report to battalion HQ and was given a party of twelve; "all that could be spared". He then led this group to block the German incursion on the west side of Festubert. His party was made up of Signals Sergeant Coles, orderlies, and cooks. Biddle's leadership and courage led to him receiving a second bar to his DCM.

At least some of the German infantry were successfully using infiltration tactics. Making use of the topography, the Germans, coming from the north, were able to occupy the main line of resistance of the 1st Loyal North Lancs before the Loyals could react. This meant that the attack fell on A and B companies. After fierce counterattacks by C and D companies, most of the positions were regained, but some of the outposts were held by the Germans. The initial German infantry assault made some headway and, some say, reached Windy Corner.

According to the obvious self-exculpatory account of 1st Black Watch, the success of the Germans was due to three factors that made it different to when 55th Division successfully resisted the Germans on 9 April. The first factor given is that there was no mist, whereas the 1st Camerons' report specifically refers to the mist and smoke from the barrage making the situation difficult to determine. The other factors put forward by the Black Watch are that the Germans did not launch a frontal assault, and that they had marked out the exits from the "Bunny Hutch".[9] The leading German infantry arrived whilst the bombardment was still intense and secured the front line. This meant the "Bunny Hutch" was captured after the Piccadilly end had been blown in; the prisoners taken accounted for a majority of the 258 Black Watch posted missing after that day. This group consisted of the local reserves of A and C companies plus the counter-attack platoon.

Meanwhile, the Germans attacked Givenchy Keep from both the east and the north. The Black Watch put up a desperate defence. During the first assault Captain Cooke and Lieutenant Kilgour were killed.[10] The garrison of two officers and forty other ranks was reduced to one NCO and eight other ranks, but they held on. Eventually, Lieutenant Addison DCM and six other ranks reached them as reinforcements. According to the Camerons, it was this fight by

---

7 TNA WO 95/1281: War Diary of the 2nd Welsh, 18 April 1918.
8 TNA WO 95/1280: War Diary of the 1st South Wales Borderers and WO 95/1281: War Diary of the 2nd Welsh, 18 April 1918.
9 TNA WO 95/1263: War Diary of the 1st Black Watch, 18 April 1918.
10 Their remains lie in Windy Corner Cemetery.

the Black Watch that prevented the Germans reaching Windy Corner. The old trenches close to Windy Corner were the initial assembly point for the blocking group tasked with preventing a breakthrough. Senior battalion staff of the Camerons and 1st Loyal North Lancs began burning maps in case the Germans reached the shared HQ at Windy Corner. The HQ details of both battalions helped the main body of 1st Camerons to line the trenches. Two platoons of C company, who had been brought forward from the canal bank, and one platoon of A company who had come forward from Pont Fixé, were sent forward to Lone Farm. The purpose in sending them was so that they could protect the left flank of the 1st Camerons if the Germans got past the flank of the Gloucesters.[11]

The garrison of Moat farm, led by Lieutenant Burton, were also facing a furious assault by troops that had kept close to their creeping barrage. Here, the Germans only got to within about forty yards of the defences. On the left of the battalion, Captain Robertson led the defence which relied upon intense rifle and Lewis gun fire. Amongst the many casualties was Second Lieutenant Balmain MM.[12]

Two platoons of D company, 1st Camerons, were sent forward to support 1st Black Watch. Initially they occupied the communication trench behind the left company of 1st Black Watch before moving forward to the Keeps. The 1st Camerons were assisted by the 1st Northants moving forward to the bridges, without waiting for the additional support battalion (5th Notts & Derby of 46th Division) to move forward. By 10.20 a.m., it was clear that 1st South Wales Borderers were holding out on the division's left, but that the Germans were filtering around them.

The Festubert East Keep's garrison was reduced to eight by enemy artillery fire; of those eight, two were killed later in the day. The problems for 1st Gloucesters also developed in a patrolled area (so not garrisoned) extending across eighty yards either side of Willow Road. The intense artillery fire widened this gap to about 200 yards, and therefore enabled the Germans to assault A company. The machine gunners of B and D companies of 1st Gloucesters, to the right of 1st South Wales Borderers, were key to the defence of Givenchy. They were assisted by seven Vickers guns. The Germans suffered heavy casualties in the face of machine guns, often firing at ranges of between 500 yards down to less than a hundred yards. The approach offered the Germans no cover. One platoon of B company, with a Lewis gun, started with 175 rounds per man and got through eight more boxes of SAA, a further 8000 rounds.

The importance of the role of junior officers once battle commenced is underlined by the actions of Second Lieutenant Hall of A company. He was on one side of the gap with two platoons, whilst his company commander was on the other side. Second Lieutenant Hall also had a platoon of C company with him, so he used one platoon to form a protective flank. The remainder of his command and Captain Handford then used A company's firepower to cut off further German troops getting through. This denied support to the advanced troops that had got through to Le Plantin. A Company achieved this despite the Germans bringing up field artillery to provide close support. At around 4 p.m., another junior officer, Lieutenant Gosling, was sent forward with a reserve platoon. They cleared the Germans out of Le Plantin and rushed a crater full of Germans and bombed them out of it.[13]

---

11 TNA WO 95/1264: War Diary of the 1st Camerons, 18 April 1918.
12 TNA WO 95/1263: War Diary of the 1st Black Watch, 18 April 1918.
13 TNA WO 95/1278: War Diary of the 1st Gloucestershire, 18 April 1918.

This stubborn defence, and the prompt arrival of 1st Camerons to plug the gap between 1st Gloucesters and 1st Black Watch blunted the German advance. At 12.40 p.m., two platoons of B company, 1st Camerons were sent forward to Le Plantin. They were able to confirm that there was no gap between 1st Gloucesters and 1st Black Watch, so they returned. In many ways, albeit on a small scale, this action exemplifies the theory behind zonal defence. Given the weight of artillery that could be brought to bear on a target area, a breakthrough was inevitable; but being able to plug it was key to a successful defence. The focused activity of 1st Camerons was vital here, as the two platoons of B company were sent back to Le Plantin again around 2 p.m. This time they went to the north of Le Plantin. There they found a gap between two companies of 1st Gloucesters, so they filled it until relieved by elements of 2nd Welsh.

During the early afternoon, 1st South Wales Borderers began carrying out local counterattacks in front of their lines. They were able to destroy machine gun posts set up by the Germans during the assault which were only about 250 yards from the British positions. Some Germans were captured during these operations. 1st Camerons focused on clearing the Germans out of Festubert South but East Keep and Route A remained in German hands. A counterattack by a company of 2nd Welsh meant that, by 3.30 p.m., nearly all the original line had been restored, except New Cut, Ware Road, Scottish Trench and Piccadilly. In addition, the Germans held posts around a line of craters as well as East Keep and Route A. All the units involved called forward the details that had been left behind at the outset. Despite further efforts, including that of No 8 Platoon of 1st Black Watch led by Lieutenant Smith, the tunnelled system known as the Bunny Hutch remained in German hands. A small bombing attack by a platoon of D company and a platoon of C company 1st Camerons, scheduled for around 8 p.m., never developed due to a lack of artillery support. Second Lieutenant Burns, the leader of the platoon of C company, was wounded when they tried to start their attack. The 1st Division seized 34 prisoners including an officer. Although the fighting had died down by 7 p.m., the Germans maintained steady artillery fire to protect their hold on Route A.[14]

Despite this fire, Lieutenant Ainsworth led six platoons in regaining possession of Route A and the Keep during the early hours of 19 April. In doing so, they captured 19 Germans as well as a machine gun. 1st Brigade had brought forward two companies of 1st Loyal North Lancs across the canal to carry out a counterattack. They succeeded in regaining the Bunny Hutch, New Cut, Piccadilly, Scottish Trench and Ware Road. They took twelve prisoners in the process. The two days of fighting had cost the 1st Division 59 officers and 1530 other ranks, with 1st Loyal North Lancs and 1st Black Watch having hundreds of men captured. The other casualties of the Black Watch included 35 killed and 7 who died of their wounds, as well as 66 others wounded. Amongst their officers, six were killed and one wounded. Another officer was posted as wounded and missing, whilst one was wounded and eight recorded as missing. The gallantry shown by some was recognised in the award of the MM to five men, whilst Sergeant Sharp and Corporal Yarley each received the DCM.

The 1st Loyal North Lancs recorded their casualties at the end of their trench tour on 23 April. In total, two officers and 16 men had been killed. A further five officers had been wounded, along with 105 of their men. Reflecting the success of the Germans in surprising

---

14 TNA WO 95/1233: War Diary of the 1st Division Headquarters, 18 April 1918.

A and B companies, five officers and 189 men were posted as missing.[15] The 1st South Wales Borderers recorded the praise received, for their determined resistance, from their Brigadier and from General Horne, GOC First Army. Their officer casualties amounted to one killed, four evacuated wounded and three wounded but remaining on duty. A total of 146 casualties had been sustained amongst the other ranks. The 2nd Welsh had one officer and seven men killed, as well as 32 other ranks wounded.[16] The Gloucesters had three officers killed and four wounded, whilst 53 other ranks were killed or missing and a further 123 were wounded. The gallant defence meant that there were numerous decorations awarded to the battalion. Their commander Lieutenant Colonel Tweedie was awarded a bar to his DSO, and CSM Biddle DCM, MM was awarded a bar to his DCM. Sergeant Coles DCM might have been decorated too, but he was killed during the action. Second Lieutenant Hall and Lieutenant Gosling were awarded the MC, alongside Captain Seldon and Second Lieutenant Dobson. CSM Reece was awarded a bar to his DCM, whilst Sergeant Corbett MM and Private Mitcham received the DCM. A further 24 men received the Military Medal.[17]

The day after the battle, 166th Brigade was attached to 1st Division. On 22 April, the Germans seized Route A Keep from 1/5 Royal Lancs Regt., who were unable to retake it. On 28 April, C company of 1st Black Watch paraded prior to going into the trenches. A single shell exploded behind them causing 59 casualties, including six dead.[18] In general, the month ended with activity around the craters held by the Germans after 18 April. 55th Division could not retake them, and the neighbouring line was withdrawn sufficiently to minimise casualties from sniping. Route A Keep was retaken by 46th Division on 29 April so the sector effectively stabilised around the positions held in the middle of the month.[19]

Throughout the first week in May, the defences of the right battalion of the Hohenzollern sector were altered. This reflected orders from I Corps to reduce casualties from mortar fire by holding the line in greater depth, and therefore fewer troops at the front. Therefore, platoon posts were constructed between the reserve and village lines. On 8 May, information from I Corps led to special preparations to resist a German attack, but it did not materialise. Major discharges of gas using projectors were made against the Germans on several occasions in May. Much of the rest of the month passed quietly, with regular reliefs being carried out. Field Marshal Haig visiting divisional HQ on 14 May and a successful raid by 2nd KRRC on 23 May were the highlights.[20] Haig's diary for 14 May focuses on his discussions with Horne, GOC First Army, about Maxse.[21]

The raid on 23 May by the 2nd KRRC had been planned before the battalion had gone into the line. The four officers and 110 other ranks had been drawn from D Company and were led by Captain Fryer. This aspect, ensuring the men knew each other, appears to have been copied by the Black Watch for their raid in July.[22] The men involved had been held back from trench

---

15 TNA WO 95/1263: War Diary of the 1st Loyal North Lancs, 23 April 1918.
16 TNA WO 95/1280: War Diary of the 1st South Wales Borderers, and TNA WO 95/1281: War Diary of the 2nd Battalion, Welsh regiment, 18 April 1918.
17 TNA WO 95/1263: War Diary of 1st Gloucestershire, 18 April 1918.
18 TNA WO 95/1278: War Diary of 1st Black Watch, 18 April 1918.
19 TNA WO 95/1233: War Diary of the 1st Division Headquarters, 21-30 April 1918
20 TNA WO 95/1233: War Diary of the 1st Division Headquarters, 1 – 31 May 1918.
21 Sheffield & Bourne (eds.), *Douglas Haig*, p.412
22 See account in following chapter.

duty to prepare for the raid. They were accompanied by eight members of the Royal Engineers. A dummy gas projection and box artillery barrage supported the raiders. In addition, the stokes mortar sections fired on specified targets. In this case, the machine guns were not asked to fire a barrage but concentrated upon vulnerable areas of the German line.

The raid achieved all its objectives including the destruction of dugouts using P-bombs and explosive charges. After some debate, only the latter were to be used by the RE personnel. As well as killing Germans, the raiders captured four enemy soldiers and a light machine gun. The captured troops were from the 4th Company, 209th Reserve Regiment belonging to the 207th Division. The prisoners were handed over to Sergeant Brooksbank, who had been assigned to this role. His other role was to ensure the returning raiders took the correct route via raid HQ on their return. To help the raiders orientate themselves, a bonfire was lit to aid their return. Sergeant Brown was detailed to check the men in, using the discs that they had been assigned for the raid.[23]

Overall, the units of 1st Division performed very well in the difficult fighting in April 1918. The 55th Division had set a very high standard to match. The performance was not flawless as the fate of the men in the "Bunny Hutch" illustrated. Nonetheless, the defence was tenacious in the main. Company and Platoon commanders as well as experienced NCOs demonstrated leadership and skill. In doing so, they demonstrated the efficacy of zonal defence against determined assault.

---

23   TNA WO 95/1273: War Diary of 2nd KRRC, May 1918.

37

Aggressive Defence

Following the failure of the German March Offensive and the subsequent operations, which had also failed to deliver victory, the Germans had lost the strategic initiative. The German armies were now faced by the Allied armies, under the overall direction of Marechal Ferdinand Foch. As Greenhalgh's research has demonstrated, he had a clear vision that victory could be obtained by a rolling series of limited offensives.[1] Therefore, the key to success was to use the material resources of the Allies to conduct successive "bite and hold" offensives. The success of these operations had been clearly demonstrated by Plumer's army in 1917 in recovering Messines Ridge, but it had not been possible before to move resources quickly enough to new fronts to maintain the pressure. As Foch could direct the various armies to develop schemes, he was able to keep the Germans off balance.

As the 1st Division is a British unit, this account inevitably fits within the Anglo-centric narrative of the "100 Days" but there will be opportunities taken in the text to indicate what was happening on the fronts where French and American troops were engaged. This is not to deny the important role played by the British Army, but to offer a proper context to its operations in this decisive period.

On 1 June 1918, First Army was covering the Western Front from south-west of Hazebrouck to south-west of Arras.[2] The 1st Division headquarters, as part of I Corps, was situated near Barlin with the troops occupying trenches in Cambrin. Barlin was then a coal mining town and is situated seven miles from Bethune and approximately thirty miles south-west of Lille. The next two days saw the British being subjected to German artillery using yellow cross shells and a large number of German aircraft overflying the area. The yellow cross contained mustard gas. This gas had been used in March 1918, and at other times, to create flank protection for an assault. The gas residue would be dangerous for German soldiers to advance into these areas; therefore, it was an area denial weapon. The use of mustard gas would have pointed to an impending assault against a neighbouring area. It was therefore imperative to gain further intelligence about the enemy's intentions and so a major raid was conducted on 4 June.

The raid was executed by 1st Gloucesters at 9.50 p.m., supported not only by their own divisional artillery but with the co-operation of artillery from the 11th and 55th divisions. The

---

1   Greenhalgh, *Foch in Command*, passim esp. pp.263-508.
2   *OH, 1918*, Vol. 3, pp.25, 93.

importance of the raid was also shown by the inclusion of barrages by machine guns, trench mortars and mortars firing smoke shells. Unfortunately, the latter may have contributed to the left half of the second wave losing direction, due to the amount of smoke drifting across the area. However, the first wave and the right half of the second wave were successful in reaching their objectives. A mine shaft with two entrances was found and bombed. The attached troops from 26th Field Company Royal Engineers then blew in the shaft using the charges they had brought forward. Astutely, given the importance of capturing prisoners for intelligence gathering, the raid had been planned to include the German second line. It was in this line that two prisoners from the *9th company* of the *209th Reserve Infantry Regiment*, part of *207th Division* were taken.

The raid commander, Captain Claude Templer, was killed as the party was withdrawing; two other men were killed, and one officer was wounded, but remained at duty, whilst seven of the men were wounded. Templer had been Mentioned in Despatches. He had a most unusual set of wartime experiences. He had been captured on 22 December 1914 and subsequently sought to escape. Having succeeded at the seventeenth attempt, he was subsequently granted an audience with King George VI before returning to front line service.[3]

The two German prisoners were examined on 5 June and told their captors that preparations for a large-scale attack in their sector were almost complete. They supported their statements by saying that a large stock of trench mortar ammunition had been brought up and stockpiled ready for use by 6 June. The immediate response to this was to strengthen Mountain Keep, by placing an extra machine gun there, and ordering C Company of 1st battalion MGC to move up from Barlin to Noeux Les Mines where they would be in closer support to the units in the line. The infantry brigadiers were summoned to a conference with the GOC at Chateau des Pres at Sailly Labourse. The planned relief of 2nd Brigade by 3rd Brigade in the Cambrin sector was allowed to proceed.

As was now standard practise, the sector was only to pass under the control of GOC 3 Brigade once the whole relief was complete. The movement of formed bodies of troops was always a concern. West of the Beuvry – Noyelles Road, troops were to keep one hundred yards between platoons before 9 p.m., but after that they only had to have one hundred yards between companies. East of that road, the troops were more vulnerable and were told to keep two hundred yards between platoons before 9 p.m. and to still move in platoons after that time but were allowed to reduce the interval to one hundred yards. Regardless of where they were, transport was to move with one hundred-yard intervals between each group of four vehicles. These precautions proved necessary. The German artillery was active between 6 p.m. and midnight dropping approximately 160 gas shells of various types, on to this sector. A further 250 gas shells fell on the following night.

The Germans had shelled the British observation posts in the Cambrin sector during the day. In the evening it suffered further heavy shelling by 5.9s. However, the Germans did receive some retaliation when one hundred drums of gas were projected on to their lines from the Cambrin sector. The British also noted what they took to be registration fire by German guns on targets south of the canal. On the night of 7 / 8 June, a small patrol mounted by 1st Loyal North Lancs, consisting of an officer and three men, encountered a German listening post. This led to

---

3   TNA WO 95 /1232: War Diary of the 1st Infantry Division, Headquarters, 1-5 June 1918. Templer and Private Albert Hobbs, also killed during the raid, are both commemorated on the Loos Memorial.

a bombing fight in which two of the British soldiers were wounded and the other was missing when the patrol returned. The evening of 8 June saw a major bombardment of the positions held by 1st Division and 55th Division to the south, including both artillery and trench mortars.[4] On 9 June, a patrol found the enemy to be very alert, and, as the missing man had not been found, the GOC cancelled a projected raid in that sector.[5] Therefore the rumoured offensive had not yet been launched but clearly both sides were very much on the alert.

Three days later, the men of 1 Brigade were relieved by those in 3 Brigade without incident, whilst the 55th Division carried out a successful raid in which two prisoners, belonging to the 94th Infantry Regiment, were captured. Amongst the men of 3 Infantry Brigade there was a great deal of sickness. It what was described as an outbreak of a new type of trench fever. It was also noted that a high number of officers were suffering the standard symptoms of a high fever and generally feeling weak. Nevertheless, routine reliefs continued. Divisional Headquarters noted, on 18 June, that the 11th Division had captured seven prisoners in a raid but that they had given away little information. These prisoners from 2nd Bavarian Reserve Regiment, were, like the others captured by 1st and 55th divisions described as "normal,". This indicated that there had been no change in the units opposite the British in this sector. The attritional nature of trench warfare was further underlined on 18 June when the 2nd Welsh in Annequin, having been previously relieved and moved back into support, suffered twenty casualties when their new positions were targeted with mustard gas. The constant search for intelligence was underlined on 19 June when it was recorded that the initial raid by 55th Division in the early hours had failed to capture anyone and that therefore a further raid had been carried out which did lead to the capture of a member of 5th Company, 94th Infantry Regiment of 38th Division but that he had not been able to provide them with any useful information.[6] It is interesting that, according to 1st Division's own records, neighbouring divisions were more active than they in conducting raids.

Sickness amongst the men continued. Due to the levels of sickness amongst the personnel of 3rd Trench Mortar Battery, their colleagues in 2nd Trench Mortar Battery had to remain in the trenches, as they could not be relieved as planned. However, the relief of 2 Infantry Brigade by 1 Infantry Brigade was completed on 21 June. Two days later, the GOC held a conference at Chateau des Pres, where the discussion centred on changing the methods used to hold tunnel entrances and outposts across the divisional sector. In addition to the infantry brigadiers, the meeting included the CRE and the officer in charge of the 170th Tunnelling Company. The decisions reached at the conference reflect a growing sense on the British side that fewer men should be occupying the front line. From now on, small posts containing one section only would be posted in the front line as observation posts only. The rest of the garrison would be in the reserve line at the tunnel entrances, and the reserve line was now to be referred to as "The Outpost Line of Resistance". It was explicitly stated that the new divisional defence scheme was to be based on not requiring the men to hold the front line, to the last, but to withdraw to a line of resistance further back. This reflects what the Germans had concluded at Passchendaele after suffering from well executed bite and hold assaults at Messines Ridge. The attempt to establish defence in depth in March 1918 had taught the British further lessons. Apart from noting some

---

4   TNA WO 95/1232: War Diary of the 1st Infantry Division, Headquarters, 5-8 June 1918.
5   TNA WO 95/1232: War Diary of the 1st Infantry Division, Headquarters, 8-10 June 1918.
6   TNA WO 95/1232: War Diary of the 1st Infantry Division, Headquarters, 11-19 June 1918.

successful counter-battery shoots and the activity of enemy aircraft, the staff at 1st Division Headquarters saw the remainder of the month as quiet.[7]

In contrast with the normal pattern of trench life, 1 July 1918 found the men of 2nd Brigade on parade for a visit by His Royal Highness the Duke of Connaught. The troops marched past after the duke had presented medal ribbons to ten selected recipients and addressed the men. The Duke of Connaught was Queen Victoria's third son and therefore an uncle of the then King George V. A visit to a camp the previous month was recorded by Pathé news.[8] Whilst this photograph cannot be said to be that of 2 Brigade it is illustrative of the Duke of Connaught being marched past. As was accepted form, he sent his congratulations on the soldierly bearing of the men of 2nd Brigade to I Corps.

The men of 2nd Brigade would probably have been in good spirits, as the brigade records show it had only suffered three casualties during the previous month, of which one was due to accidental wounding.[9] The men had been taken in motor lorries to the parade near Drury, where they had formed a hollow square. These ranks were those that the Duke of Connaught passed amongst. The Duke of Connaught had concluded his speech by leading three cheers for the king before the march past concluded the parade.[10]

The following day saw a return to reality for the men of 2 Brigade as they took over the line in the Hohenzollern sector from 3 Brigade. The brigade HQ was established at Chateau des Prés near Sailly Labourse whilst 2nd King's Royal Rifles on the left and 2nd Royal Sussex on the right occupied the front line, with 1st Northants in support.[11] The two pages that make up the war diary of 1st Northamptonshire for July 1918 make no mention of any casualties and describe the period 8 – 16 July as quiet with normal trench warfare.

The divisional records include references to three patrols that sought to reconnoitre enemy positions on the night of 2 July, and therefore offer an insight into the nature of static trench warfare in this period.

The prodigious requirements for ammunition of the BEF by mid-1918 are further underlined by the notes on the expenditure of ammunition between 6 p.m. on 30 June and 6 p.m. on 1 July by 1st Division in an ostensibly static sector. In addition to the field artillery shelling the German rear areas heavily during the afternoon, the trench mortars were also active. In the equivalent of counter-battery fire, the 9.45" heavy trench mortars fired 25 rounds at the German mortars, whilst the medium trench mortars delivered 55 rounds against enemy mortars in Audit and Cross trenches. Meanwhile the stokes mortars loosed off 190 bombs on "the usual trench targets".

What is also noticeable, in comparison to trench warfare in 1915, is the amount of harassing fire being undertaken by the British forces. The machine guns expended, in one 24 hour period, 7,100 rounds against specific areas where German troops were likely to be on the move. The

---

7 TNA WO 95 /1232: War Diary of the 1st Infantry Division, Headquarters, 23-30 June 1918.
8 For what is possibly the only surviving footage of the division see <https://www.britishpathe.com/video/duke-of-connaught-in-army-camp> (accessed 20 March 2019).
9 TNA WO 95 /1267: War Diary of 2nd Brigade Headquarters
10 Typical of the close relations between royalty of Great Britain and Imperial Germany, the Duke of Connaught was married to Princess Louise Margaret of Prussia; so, whilst he was the Colonel in Chief of the 6th Duke of Connaught's Own Rifles, a Canadian regiment, she had been made Colonel in Chief of the 64th Brandenburg Infantry Regiment in 1885.
11 TNA WO 95 /1267: War Diary of 2nd Brigade Headquarters, 1 July 1918.

diary records, two days later, that, in addition to selective artillery fire, the 6" trench mortars fired 30 rounds against specific targets in the German trenches as well as 41 rounds designed to cut wire. The Stokes mortars fired thirty and 31 rounds respectively at Fosse Trench and Franks Keep with a further 200 rounds being dropped on the German positions. This was accompanied by the machine gunners firing 8000 rounds on the roads behind the German positions and using 1600 rounds to ward off the unwanted attention of low flying German aircraft.[12] This also meant that the soldiers faced greater strain, since there was no quiet on the Western Front. The expenditure of such quantities of ammunition in a quiet sector on a succession of nights during a quiet period reflects the enormous difference made by the mechanization of warfare by 1918. Without the enormous efforts to ensure the industrial mobilisation of the Home Front, it would not have been possible to allocate such resources to a single division distant from the crux of the current fighting.

The intelligence summary noted the positive news that the Australians had retaken Hamel and that there had been successful attacks by the Belgians and the French.[13] The British focus on the period after Amiens has neglected these earlier smaller actions that proved to be the first signs that the tide had turned. Such was the static nature of 1st Division's sector that on 3 July, a meeting of relevant officers took place at Barlin to plan the divisional horse show which had been scheduled for a date in August.[14]

The following day's summary also noted Australian success and recorded less fire on the enemy lines, as well as noting three further patrols that had entered or got close to German front line positions. These patrols reinforce the picture of the Germans holding their front line very thinly. Patrols tended to report that the German wire was in good condition and that some of it had been recently renewed, which may explain why, on 4 July (whilst no fewer than seven patrols were out in No Man's Land) the trench mortars again expended considerable amounts of ammunition on wire cutting. The machine guns again expended 8000 rounds on interdictory tasks[15], demonstrating once again the abundance of small arms ammunition.

On 7 July, 1st Black Watch carried out a successful raid in which six prisoners from the 369th Regiment of 10th Ersatz Division were captured. This raid was carried out by no fewer than four officers and 120 men. The senior officer was Captain Robertson MC; he was supported by three subalterns, Clarke, Smith DCM (therefore an ex-ranker) and Buchanan (who was on attachment). It is interesting that the raid was assigned to D company with the support of the Lewis gun sections from C company, so all the men involved would have known each other very well. The raiders began moving forward to their initial assembly points at 6 p.m. and were served their tea at 7.30 p.m. Having had an hour for tea, the men then proceeded to their forward assembly positions between 8.30 p.m. and 9.15 p.m. At the latter time they received their rum ration. Considerable emphasis was laid upon the need to avoid detection, and C company was given the task of removing any necessary barriers or obstacles that would impede exiting the trenches. The artillery scheme, again reflecting what was to come in the "100 Days", was very detailed and delivered over a wider area, southwards, than that covered by the raid itself. The initial barrage on the German line would last only three minutes before lengthening

---

12   TNA WO 95 /1234: War Diary of 1st Division Headquarters, 2 July 1918.
13   TNA WO 95 /1234: War Diary of 1st Division Headquarters, 2 July 1918.
14   TNA WO 95 /1237: War Diary of 1st Division, A & Q Branch, 3 July 1918.
15   TNA WO 95 /1234: War Diary of 1st Division Headquarters, 4 July 1918.

to a line 100 yards further ahead for the next four minutes. Then the artillery would fire on the German reserve line for a further four minutes. Presumably reflecting the results of the patrols regarding how lightly the Germans were holding the line, the infantry were only to enter the German trenches in this third phase; that is, eleven minutes after the barrage commenced. The raiding parties then had 24 minutes to conduct their operations before the protective barrage was brought back to the German reserve line. After forty minutes the guns would cease-fire, so the raiding parties were being afforded five minutes to return to the British lines. Under cover of the field gun barrage, the howitzers and 6" mortars would direct fire against specific targets.[16] This would disguise the extent of intelligence gained from the other patrols carried out over the preceding days. Much was made by generals of the importance of raids in maintaining fighting techniques and preventing a "live and let live" atmosphere taking hold. However, in the context of the "100 Days" it may be more important to see the supporting barrages as also providing the training and preparation necessary for the artillery. This experience enabled the artillery to achieve the standards required to enable the intricate barrage tables of late 1918, to be translated into the lifts, and curtains of fire that enabled the infantry to occupy their assigned objectives.

The detailed planning was reflected in D company being made responsible for the transfer of all prisoners that were secured. The HQ for the attack was to be Robertson's tunnel, and a line was laid to it from brigade headquarters. Interestingly, watches were to be synchronised, but the assaulting troops were to take their time from the start of the barrage; this ensured they knew exactly how much time they had once they started. The barrage began promptly and was reported by the Black Watch to have been accurate and effective. The assaulting troops were assisted by attacking in good light as they could see the barrage, but the smoke from the bursting high explosive shells obscured them from the Germans. The troops were able to get within forty yards of the barrage and No 13 Platoon seized their first line objectives, assisted by the platoons designated to reach the reserve line. This suggests they were not truly operating a leapfrog system as was to characterise later assaults, but knowing the Germans were only holding lightly their front line meant this would probably not be needed. The difficulty of taking prisoners was illustrated by three being captured after some others were killed. The difficulty was emphasised when six Germans were seen to take cover in a dugout and then greeted the Black Watch with rifle fire on the stairs. The Scots then tried to talk them out, using one of the captured men as the interpreter but after initially hesitating then starting to come out, the Germans decided to stay in the dugout. This was them bombed using grenades as there were no KJ bombs or mobile charges available. The troops who reached the reserve line did have mobile charges and used them to blow in the empty dugouts they found.

The troops who entered the southern communication trench secured two further prisoners, whilst one more was captured on the left of the position. As usual, the butcher's bill was estimated to be higher for the Germans with 25 dead and six captured, compared to that of the Black Watch with one wounded officer and 23 other ranks wounded, of which one remained at duty. Nonetheless, the raid report said many of the wounded were described as only slight. Apart from detailing the alert lights fired by the Germans, the report noted that not only was the German defensive barrage directed at the British rear lines and observation points; but that it also extended to the south of the raid due to the feint barrage. In addition to the light, the

---

16   TNA WO 95/ 1278: War Diary of 1st Black Watch, July 1918.

ability to keep direction was ascribed to the training undertaken. The report also ascribed some of the casualties to the troops having closed up too far to the barrage due to the accuracy of the original barrage. A more credible explanation is that one battery, on the right, was believed to have been firing shrapnel which was high and short. The opinion was also given that the barrage had probably exploded some gas cylinders. Gas was encountered by the troops but there was no sign of projectors, so it had not been fired in response to the attack. It was also noted that the barrage did not prevent the Germans from putting up resistance. The Germans had responded with their bayonets; but the Black Watch judged their skills to be inferior as no bayonet wounds had been reported. Given the success of the raid it was unsurprising that the battalion received a strong commendation from their divisional commander. Doubtless, Strickland was conscious of the greater success of other divisions in carrying out raids so this was one to reassure Corps that he was succeeding in his role.

Captain Robertson MC and Second Lieutenant Smith DCM found themselves selected for a quite different duty on 10 July. They were to be amongst six officers and 220 men detailed to form part of a composite battalion, supported by the band of the 2nd Battalion Irish Guards, which was to represent the British Army at the Bastille Day Parade in Paris. In addition to the company from the Black Watch, the battalion was comprised of one company found by 4th Guards Brigade, a company drawn from the Royal West Surreys, and men drawn from the white overseas troops of the Empire. This last company included a platoon from each of Australia, Canada, New Zealand, and South Africa. The men entrained for Paris, having had Strickland deliver a typical speech about the honour being shown and the need to maintain it. They were inspected on the Bois de Boulogne at 6.45 a.m. on 14 July by President Poincare and General Joffre. The subsequent two-and-a-half-hour march was witnessed by thronging crowds and the Black Watch were reportedly singled out for particular applause. It was only on 16 July that the men entrained to leave Paris, so they had enjoyed a bit of bonus leave.[17] Three days later, the battalion re-entered the trenches for a five-day tour of duty.

During the week covered by this excursion, the division received a total of six new officers and over 500 men previously destined for many different duties, including being part of the heavy railway company. The new arrivals were inspected by Brigadier Lewin on 16 July, as Strickland was then on leave.[18] Since the number of casualties during the week was less than fifteen, these reinforcements represented a genuine accretion of strength, and suggest that the combing out of those not serving or previously wounded was effective.

On 10 July, Strickland conducted a staff ride and exercise for officers of 3 Brigade and, according to the records of his own divisional staff, offered important points of advice at the end. For this exercise they were joined by the Corps Commander, who also made invaluable comments.[19] Despite not being used in many major assaults since 1915, 1st Division was used to help others train. On 12 July, Major Clerck of the South African forces was attached to the A & Q office to gain experience of staff work. Training was taking place at a higher level on 17 July when the staff and officers of 1st Brigade took part in a tactical exercise. A similar exercise was

---

17 TNA WO 95/1278: War Diary of 1st Black Watch, July 1918.
18 TNA WO 95/1237: War Diary of 1st Division, A & Q Branch, 10- 16 July 1918.
19 TNA WO 95/1234: War Diary of 1st Division, Headquarters, 10 July 1918.

undertaken by the staff and officers of 2 Brigade five days later. At a more basic level, units of 176th Brigade were attached to 1st Division for trench instruction between 20 July and 22 July.[20]

A further tactical development is evident in 1 Brigade adapting to a system where platoons were left in the front posts and tunnel entrances were made into observation posts, which meant that the bulk of the troops were in the reserve line. When the brigade was relieved by 3 Brigade it adopted the same system, confirming that this was an agreed new scheme. Since we know that significant reinforcements were in the process of being absorbed, this suggests that the need to hold the front line thinly was now the accepted tactical doctrine, rather than simply expedient.

Throughout this period, another raid had been carried out on 20 July, this time by the 2nd Royal Sussex. The raid had been assisted by feint barrages fired by artillery of 11th and 55th Divisions. The failure to obtain any identification was put down to the enemy running away. The raiders included engineers who had brought mobile charges. These were used to destroy two dugouts, of which one was believed to be occupied. Two captured machine guns were brought back, at a cost of one OR killed, one officer and one man missing believed dead, and sixteen further men wounded including three of the engineers. Having not captured any prisoners, the raiders brought back notice boards from the German dugouts.

On the following night, the alternative was tried; the 1st South Wales Borderers carried out a raid on two posts, which was conducted without artillery and relying upon stealth. Artillery support was used for the approach to a third post.[21] Part of this support came from the third trench mortar battery, and during the registration Lance-Sergeant William James Hodges MM, of Abertillery in Monmouthshire, was killed. He was serving with the battery on attachment from the 1st South Wales Borderers. A court of enquiry was held three days later at Brigade HQ, attended by Second Lieutenant Clarke. It was concluded that the yoke had become separated causing the shell to hit the front of the parapet. Therefore, no one was to blame for the accident.[22]

However, all the posts raided were empty, so the same battalion mounted another raid on the following night. On 22 July, the first two posts were again found to be unoccupied but the third was strongly garrisoned.[23] This led to casualties being sustained including the raid commander, Second Lieutenant Treloar, being wounded. After the battalion was subsequently relieved and moved into the support lines, it was employed in finding carrying parties at night, whilst wiring classes were held during the day. Another successful raid took place on 27 July, this time by 55th Division, whose prisoners were from 18th Reserve Division, proving that the 1st Guards Reserve Division had been relieved.[24]

On 28 July, the men of the 1st Loyal North Lancs received a new commanding officer, in the form of Major Forsyth-Forrest from their fellow 2nd Brigade unit, the 1st Northamptonshire. Forsyth-Forrest had originally been a Lieutenant in the 2nd KRRC so he was a much travelled survivor of 2 Brigade. The officers of the 1st Northamptonshire welcomed Major Gould of the Durham Light Infantry as their new second in command. Three days later, after Major

---

20 TNA WO 95/1237: War Diary of 1st Division, A & Q Branch, July 1918.
21 TNA WO 95/1234: War Diary of 1st Division, Headquarters, 20 July 1918.
22 TNA WO 95/1251: War Diary of 3rd Trench Mortar Battery, 20-23 July 1918.
23 TNA WO 95/1234: Diary of 1st Division, Headquarters, 22 July 1918.
24 TNA WO 95/1280: War Diary of the 1st Battalion South Wales Borderers, 23-28 July 1918 and of 1st Division, Headquarters, WO 95/1234: 27 July 1918.

General Strickland had returned from leave and resumed command; Brigadier Lewin went on attachment to I Corps Heavy Artillery. This meant that Lieutenant Colonel Scarlett DSO of 25th Brigade RFA continued to act as divisional CRA.[25]

The month concluded with a German raid supported by artillery and machine gun fire after an initial approach, described as an attempt at a "silent raid," was detected and repulsed. This larger raid was also defeated with the use of rifles and machine guns. Even with support, only six men reached the British wire, and no British casualties were sustained. The daily intelligence summary recognised the static nature of the sector when it noted that the wire in front of the old German front line was thin and cut, in places, but that behind it there were thick belts of new concertina wire. A patrol, of six men working in two groups of three, inspected various shell holes and posts before discovering one that was clearly occupied. Entering by the one spot possible under the wire was considered but the Germans, coming from their own front line, then entered and the patrol leader decided to withdraw even though it would have been possible to bomb the Germans.[26]

These two months of constant activity demonstrate that the British Army was developing its techniques even amongst units away from the major battles. It is natural and appropriate that much scholarly attention has been devoted to March 1918 and the "100 Days". Nevertheless, this account gives depth to an understanding of the experience brought by the BEF to the "100 Days". When there were limited numbers of British offensives, GHQ could operate its informal "attack division" list. Now that Foch's strategy would call for a series of rolling offensives, it would be crucial that the standard of the average was high enough to beat the average of the Germans facing them.

---

25   TNA WO 95 /1271: War Diary of 1st Battalion Northamptonshire Regiment, 28 July 1918 and of 1st Division, Headquarters, WO 95 /1234: 30 July 1918.
26   TNA WO 95 /1234: War Diary of 1st Division, Headquarters, 30-31 July 1918.

38

Training Under Maxse

The concept of the learning curve within the BEF is now well understood. It had been developed and refined. Formations/units progressed along the learning curve at different rates at different times. The pace at which a unit progressed along the learning curve might depend upon exposure to key influencers. Lieutenant General Sir Ivor Maxse is seen as one of these key influencers. Having already been afforded extensive training time in 1917, 1st Division were now to come within Maxse's orbit.

The 2nd Welsh war illustrates the issues faced by dedicated trainers like Maxse. The battalion had been relieved in the line on 31 July and had returned to occupy billets in Noeux Les Mines. The diary records that there was no training on 1 August. The next day they marched to the training ground at Bois D' Olhain but returned to billets due to the rain. They then recorded that the next day was a "day off" from training. The following day was Sunday, so in lieu of training there was the opportunity to attended the divisional horse show. On 5 August the battalion noted it "continued" training; an interesting choice of adverb since this would have been the first day any training was done. The next day it was recorded that they were "training as usual" whilst the officers went on a tactical exercise under the Brigadier. Two more days of training at Bois D' Olhain were followed by a final day when the CO and the company commanders were absent reconnoitring ready for returning to the line.[1] In reality, much of the day would have been devoted to preparing the battalion for returning to the line.

Meanwhile, on 3 August, a fortnight prior to the meeting with Maxse, Holland had conducted a staff ride, with no troops, for 3 Brigade. This was attended by the Brigadier, his staff and "unit commanders". The record states that all the attendees were mounted. The subject of the exercise was a fighting withdrawal. Holland reviewed the situation at various stages. At the end both Holland and the Corps Commander offered useful criticism.[2] This event was not recorded in the 3Brigade HQ diary but participation in the next day's commemorative service was recorded.[3] It may have been cascaded down when the brigadier took officers on a field exercise three days later.[4]

---

1 TNA WO 95/1281: War Diary of 2nd Battalion Welsh Regiment, 31 July-9 August 1918.
2 TNA WO 95/1234: War Diary of 1st Division, Headquarters, 3 August 1918.
3 TNA WO 95/1277: War Diary of 3rd Brigade, Headquarters, 3-4 August 1918.
4 TNA WO 95/1281: War Diary of 2nd Battalion Welsh Regiment, 6 August 1918.

The first manifestations of a new assignment came on 15 August, when the division received verbal notification that it was to be relieved by 16th Division, with a provisional date of 22 August. The next day, a large number of officers met with Lieutenant General Maxse at Hesdigneul aerodrome, where he spoke to them about training; and they were then able to watch a series of demonstrations.[5] This was very much in line with Maxse's own assessment of his new role as "we do not command but we expect to stimulate those who do".[6] As Baynes goes on to illustrate, some officers resisted the idea that all platoon commanders were ready to be instructing their platoons. Whilst this objection might be based on a reluctance to devolve authority; the wider objection that large parts of platoons were constantly needed for other duties when out of the line, has considerable basis in fact.[7]

The divisional relief began on 19 August with 1st Brigade being relieved in the Hohenzollern Sector by 47th Brigade. Quiet prevailed on 20 August, until the evening, but the night was disturbed by air raids. Nevertheless, the I Corps Horse Show took place at Bois des Dames. The divisional artillery remained in the line and formal responsibility for the line passed to 16th Division on the morning of 22 August.

On 19 August, 1st Brigade had issued orders that the period of time for training was to be assumed to be three weeks and that there were two key objectives: to improve the standard of all units in <u>open warfare</u> (emphasis in the original) and, to make the men as fit as possible. To this end, battalion commanders were enjoined to arrange short active periods of training in the morning and well organised recreation in the afternoons. The dates for the subsequent tactical exercises were given in the order, and the broad outline was for the first phase of the training to be focused on platoons, the second on companies and the third on battalions, and on brigades using the lessons drawn from the tactical exercises. In addition, it was stated that during the first phase of the training Major General Strickland would meet with each of the Brigadiers and their battalion, company and platoon commanders.[8] This suggests a move towards the philosophy advocated by Maxse.

The training schedule recorded by 1 Brigade to reflect the orders issued by division reflects some of the ideas Maxse was promoting. Platoon commanders were to train their platoons themselves. However, there was the caveat "under supervision, as far as it is necessary". The afternoon would be devoted to officer training which would presumably leave the men free to undertake recreational sport. However, the morning should begin with the company commander instructing the company "in the preliminary movements and dispositions for open warfare". Although this was designed to accustom the platoons to working together it was stated that no schemes were necessary.

The next phase of the training was to be focused on the companies. Given that the war had been going on for four years, it is disturbing to see that the same caveat was applied to company commanders as to platoon leaders. Platoons might be headed by newly commissioned officers, but company commanders should have been experienced officers with significant combat experience. The instructions also stated that half-an-hour every other day should be devoted to drill. The focus of the company training was stated clearly to be on the movements and tactics

---

5   TNA WO 95/1261: War Diary of the 1st Infantry Division, Headquarters, 16 August 1918.
6   Baynes, J., *Far from a Donkey* (London, Brassey's, 1995) p.210
7   Baynes, *Far From a Donkey*, p.213.
8   TNA WO 95/1262: War Diary of 1st Brigade, Headquarters, August 1918, Appendix 20.

of open warfare. Seven key areas were highlighted. Protection on the march and assembly under cover would have drawn quite heavily on previous experience. The next two headings of protection after assault and during consolidation were also similar to previous set-piece assaults as was re-organisation after an assault. The last two areas would be put under more stress in open warfare. The first was communication between platoons and companies. The last area was the tactical handling of Lewis guns. The army never went forward without looking over its shoulder and so it was also stressed that the last 400 yards of any return to base should involve marching "to attention".[9]

Some of the training was focused at a higher level. On 26 August, the commander, and staff of 1st Brigade plus the unit commanders took part in a staff exercise without troops led by the GOC. Two different positions were outlined and reviewed appropriately during the ride, with comments being made by Major General Strickland, despite the heavy rain impinging upon the morning's activities. Three days later, the staff exercise was again undertaken by the staff and unit commanders of 1st Brigade but this time with troops, as a demonstration. The efforts of 1st Brigade were made under the gaze of not only the Corps commander and his GSO2, but also their peers from 2nd Brigade and 3rd Brigade. None of the participating units record the nature of the exercise but presumably it involved movement in open warfare. The Corps Commander expressed great satisfaction regarding the exercise.

The next day a warning order was received that 1st Division were to be transferred from I Corps to the Canadian Corps near Arras.[10] This move effectively put an end to the third phase of the training programme outlined above, which was due to start on 30 August. The 1st Division had been in the thick of the fighting on the Aisne when trench warfare had been born in September 1914; now it was to play a part in the return to semi-open warfare that would become known as "the 100 Days". It would go into the campaign having been introduced to the principles of fighting in open warfare but only up to company level. The officers had been introduced to the demands of brigade management of battalions but two-thirds had been non-participatory observers. The perennial problem of not having a guaranteed period of time had cut short the programme that had been envisaged. The case of 1st Division adds to the evidence in favour of the view that Maxse did not have enough time to shape the way the BEF performed during late 1918.

---

9   TNA WO 95/1262: War Diary of 1st Brigade, Headquarters, August 1918, Appendix 20.
10 TNA WO 95/1234: War Diary 1st Division, headquarters, 18 - 30 August 1918.

39

Semi-Open Warfare

Following a month focused on training, on 1 September, 1st Division was concentrating in the Wancourt–Guemappe area ready to return to offensive combat operations. By that evening, 1 Brigade and 3 Brigade were in position approximately 100 yards to the rear of 4th Canadian Division. The latter formed the right wing of the Canadian Corps. The Canadian Corps were about to attack the high ground to the east of the Canal du Nord. 1st Division were tasked with holding the ground gained by the Canadians or being prepared to carry out a further forward bound to exploit the success of the Canadians. The advanced divisional headquarters was established at Wancourt, which suggests the division was more focused on consolidation. To advance in a second bound would have required them being closer to the headquarters of 4th Canadian Division. However, as at the Hohenzollern, 1st Division was subject to enemy air attack and the signal company of 2 Brigade, in support to the leading brigades, suffered casualties that evening.[1]

On the following day, the Canadians succeeded in breaking the Drocourt – Queant Line behind what 1st Division recorded as an "excellent creeping barrage". The early reports of Canadian success meant that at 10 a.m. the 1st Division received orders to move forward, and both the leading brigades were underway by 10.45 a.m. It is interesting to note that 2nd KRRC went into artillery formation by platoons in anticipation of joining the assault.[2] The reality that 4th Canadian Division was still engaged in fighting around Dury meant that by noon, elements of 1 Brigade and 2 Brigade were joining in the fighting. However, this was only two platoons of 1st Camerons and one platoon of 1st Loyal North Lancs, so it was hardly a decisive intervention. The limited liaison between the divisional staffs was evident in a dispute that arose over the siting of the advanced divisional headquarters. At 2 p.m., the 1st Division staff established their new advanced headquarters in a set of dugouts, only to have to move out by 6 p.m. as the 4th Canadian staff had selected the same position. The 1st Division record states that the Canadians had previously said they would not use this position, but the whole episode suggests that neither side was without blame.[3]

---

1 TNA WO 95/1234: War Diary 1st Division, headquarters, 1 September 1918.
2 TNA WO 95/1273: War Diary of 2nd King's Royal Rifles, 2 September 1918.
3 TNA WO 95/1234: War Diary 1st Division, headquarters, 2 September 1918.

The following day, 1st Division were given warning orders to relieve 4th Division, who were in line on the left flank of the Canadian Corps. This required 1st Division to move up to the sector south from the River Sensee. Strickland was briefed at a conference with the Corps Commander. Strickland then two meetings with his own brigadiers, at 11 a.m., followed by another one at Noon. During these meetings it was decided that 1 Brigade would occupy the right sector of their new position, with 2 Brigade to their left. This enabled 3 Brigade to be withdrawn into reserve. Subsequently, the infantry moved forward to relieve the 4th Division, and once the infantry relief was complete, Major General Strickland assumed command of the sector just after Midnight. It is interesting that the transfer of authority now came immediately rather than on the morning after, as had become the norm during the last phase of static warfare. The extent of the success achieved by the Canadians is evident in the fact that the 1st Loyal North Lancs occupying the first two lines of trenches of the Drocourt-Queant Line were 1Brigade's reserve. Ahead of them the 1st Black Watch, reinforced by a company of the Camerons, occupied the new British frontline with the rest of the Camerons in support. Alongside the Black Watch, 2 Brigade had placed the 2nd KRRC with 2nd Sussex in support and 1st Northamptons in reserve.[4] The position of the 2nd Sussex was, in their own view, less of a support role, as there was a gap between 1st Division and 11th Division astride the Sensee river, and therefore they were actually in the frontline with only the river between them and the Germans.[5] The division now formed part of XXII Corps under the command of Lieutenant General Godley, whose reputation for being coldly aloof had apparently been confirmed by his insistence on pushing forward during Third Ypres, despite the heavy casualties suffered by the men under his command.[6] Godley's subsequent post-war promotion to full General and command of the British Army of the Rhine certainly suggests that a reputation for being indifferent to casualties did not handicap one's career in the senior echelons of the British Army.

Strickland visited his brigadiers on 4 September in their new positions. However, the 2nd KRRC had to move the men, of B Company and two platoons of D company, out of L'Ecuse, to higher ground to the south-west during the next morning as they were saturated with gas in certain trenches, leading to 200 casualties. The position had been heavily shelled with yellow cross gas during the night, and the water seeping into the shell holes had been absorbing the gas. Once the sun rose, it vapourised the gas and the high level of casualties presumably reflects the fact that, whilst the men might have been wearing respirators during the bombardment, they would have removed them when there was no apparent threat. It only emphasises the element luck played in war that, in contrast, 2nd Royal Sussex recorded that their casualties for this short spell in the line were two men killed and three wounded. Even as the 2nd KRRC were sorting themselves out, parties from 168th Brigade, 56th Division, arrived to reconnoitre the positions preparatory to relieving 2nd Brigade. 1st Division's period under Lieutenant General Godley's command was to last only two days.

On 5 September 1918 General Rawlinson, in command of 4th Army, was concerned that he needed to rest the Australians and so he requested fresh troops to be released by GHQ.

4   TNA WO 95/1234: War Diary of 1st Division Headquarters, 3 September 1918.
5   TNA WO 95/1269: War Diary of 2nd Royal Sussex, 3 September 1918.
6   TNA WO 95/1232: War Diary of 1st Division Headquarters, 3 September 1918.

Rawlinson then noted that his chief anxiety was to get the railways "through on time".[7] Given the use of the Australians throughout 1918 it was obviously sensible to rest them.

Although Rawlinson commented on 8 September that he had "got nothing out of him", Haig had told Rawlinson that IX Corps would be found about 12 September with General Braithwaite to command it.[8] Orders had in fact been received by 1st Division that they were to be relieved by 56th Division and transferred to Fourth Army on the same day as Rawlinson had met Haig.[9] Two days later, Rawlinson expressed his frustration that he could not "remain one and a quarter-hours by motor from my Corps Commanders," but that his new headquarters should be ready by the end of that week. This anxiety reflected the 1918 focus on maintaining momentum by not losing the opportunity to push the forward elements on.

On 7 September 1918 2 Brigade assembled on the Cambrai-Arras road west of the factory at St Rohart, as the division prepared to join Fourth Army. The Brigade was embussed without incident and travelled to billets in the Hermanville Area, eight miles north-west of Arras. In common with other units, they were permitted to time their journey to suit their readiness once the relief was complete and could make use of whatever route they chose, except they could not use the roads through Arras. The divisional pioneers were transported to Hauteville, eight miles west of Arras. The machine gunners of A Company, who had been deployed in the right sector, were also withdrawn to the rear of the divisional area. The following day, amidst wind and rain, 3 Brigade moved from Blangy to Noyelle-Vion where they were billeted. Meanwhile, the remaining units in the line had carried out a number of patrols led by officers, reporting on which bridges were still intact and which had been destroyed. The patrols also contributed to the intelligence summary that it was possible to advance to the edges of local lakes and on to some of the causeways in-between but not beyond, as the Germans were holding the posts there. The divisional artillery was engaged in putting down harassing fire.

That evening, 169th Brigade relieved 1 Brigade, the latter handing over responsibility at midnight. During this final period 1 Brigade had sustained losses of nineteen men killed and 106 wounded, including two officers as well as three men posted as missing. Nevertheless, it proceeded to its new posting with the Camerons having forty officers and the other battalions 42 each, and the Camerons having 960 other ranks whilst the Lancs had 874 and the Black Watch 842. These numbers suggest that the move to smaller brigades and the combing out of men not in front line service had succeeded in filling the depleted ranks of the infantry, despite the losses sustained during the first half of 1918. 1 Brigade then followed the route of 2 Brigade and embussed on the Cambrai-Arras road west of the factory at Saint Rohart, from whence they were conveyed to the huts at Etrun. In Etrun too, were No.1 Field Ambulance, as well as the headquarters company and A and D companies of 1st battalion MGC. The official handover to 56th Division was at 10 a.m., when the 1st Division headquarters closed.[10]

Divisional headquarters was opened at Bayonvillers, five miles east of Villers-Brettoneux, with two notable absentees. One staff officer had been left to superintend the entraining of the division. The other absentee was Major General Strickland, who was temporarily in command of IX Corps pending the arrival of Lieutenant General Braithwaite. Therefore Strickland was

---

7   Churchill College Cambridge (CCC), Sir Henry Rawlinson's War Journal.
8   CCC, Sir Henry Rawlinson's War Journal.
9   TNA WO 95/1234: War Diary of 1st Division Headquarters, 5 September 1918.
10   TNA WO 95/1234: War Diary of 1st Division Headquarters, 7-8 September 1918.

occupied in establishing the new Corps headquarters at Villers-Carbonnel. The trains, bearing the infantry and associated support units, began to arrive on the next afternoon; each train had an "OC Train" who had been designated by the Rail Transport Officer. The "OC Train" was responsible for the mounting of Lewis guns on the train as defence against attack by enemy aircraft. Upon arrival, the brigades were dispersed, with 3 Brigade going to Villers-Brettoneux, 1 Brigade to Morcourt and 2 Brigade to Proyart.

The brigadier and unit commanders of 3 Brigade spent 11 September reconnoitring forward, in the wind and the rain, preparatory to relieving a brigade of 32nd Division in the line. This was to be part of the much bigger operation for IX Corps to relieve the Australian Corps, in fulfilment of Haig's acceptance of Rawlinson's request. The IX Corps, comprised of 1st, 6th and 32nd Divisions, was to move into line and become the southernmost corps in Fourth Army.

Initially, 1st Division was to enter the line between 4th Australian Division on its left and 32nd Division on its right. The schedule then involved 6th Division relieving 32nd Division two days later, on the night of 13/14 September. As this was a period in which offensive operations predominated, 32nd Division was operating with one brigade forward and 3 Brigade would be relieving this "advance guard". Therefore, 3 Brigade was to relieve 96 Brigade which was, according to the intelligence report, then engaged with enemy rearguards from the *79th Reserve Division* and elements of *119th Division*. As it entered the combat zone, 3 Brigade was to be supported by a brigade of field artillery, C company of the machine gun battalion, a section drawn from 26th Field Company RE and the bearer unit of 141st Field Ambulance. They would be backed up by 1 Brigade in support, with 2 Brigade in reserve.[11]

The different nature of the fighting during this period of semi-open warfare is illustrated by the planned operations of 1st Gloucesters, who had relieved the 16th Lancashire Fusiliers in Villeveque on 13 September. That the war in 1918, to a degree, resembled some of the actions of 1914 is implied by the fact that the Gloucesters deployed with D company in front, supported by C company, who occupied Martville's cemetery, and B company in a sunken road behind the cemetery. The Gloucesters' intention was to push forward their right flank up to a road, to dislodge the Germans in front of them. If their advance stalled, they were to send the codeword "Maxim," and this would be forwarded by Brigade HQ to the artillery and machine guns in support. Receipt of this codeword would lead to 298th Brigade RFA laying down a barrage, which would then lift and creep forward at a rate of one hundred yards every two minutes until it reached a pre-determined final line. The field artillery would also arrange for an agreed heavy artillery element to the bombardment. Meanwhile the machine guns would also barrage the enemy positions. If the Gloucesters were successful, they would send the codeword "Vickers".

The Gloucesters were successful in pushing forward and capturing the Maissemy Ridge, and the South Wales Borderers also came up on their left. The Borderers lost Lieutenant David killed and around twenty other ranks in this assault.[12] It was noted that the German resistance was stronger in the afternoon, and that some German guns had not been located. During the afternoon, the British trenches had come under heavy shrapnel fire and from 4.2" howitzers. The strong level of resistance was reflected later, when the Germans counter-attacked in bombing parties, causing two notable casualties amongst the Gloucesters. These were Captain

---

11   TNA WO 95/1234: War Diary of 1st Division Headquarters, 11 September 1918.
12   TNA WO 95/1280: War Diary of 1st South Wales Borderers, 13 September 1918.

Seldon MC and Company Sergeant Major Biddle, DCM & 2 Bars, MM & Bar, who were both severely wounded.[13]

Before being relieved by 1st Loyal North Lancs, on the night of 15 September, the Gloucesters went on to seize more high ground and receive the commendation for their success from Lieutenant General Braithwaite.[14] This involved an advance north of the River Omignon and meant that the troops now occupied securely the old British second line trenches. Therefore, the Germans had now lost nearly all their gains from the March offensive in this particular sector. However, in the hours before their relief, they suffered heavily from enemy sniper fire, which underlines that it was not just machine gunners opposing the British advance during the '100 Days'. The South Wales Borderers also took all their objectives, capturing three machine guns and approximately twenty prisoners from the *79th Reserve Division*, but at a cost of ninety casualties. Stiff resistance in the village of Maissemy itself meant that it was not completely occupied until the late afternoon.[15] As with the campaign in North-West Europe in the next war, the advance was only achieved at the cost of significant casualties.

The Camerons then replaced their Welsh comrades in the front line. Regular reliefs were important given the continuous strain of semi-mobile engagement. These operations were designed to keep 1st Division moving forward, and this is why Braithwaite was so positive. As 3 Brigade advanced, 1 Brigade and 2 Brigade were immediately pushed forward so that there would be no loss of momentum. 1st Division also now saw the return of the divisional artillery. The advance was achieved whilst broadening the divisional front by relieving an Australian battalion.

The fighting on 16 September reflected the context of a fighting retreat by the Germans. Having carried out local advances with artillery support, 3 Brigade had run into stiff resistance, and its patrols on the flanks were unable to cause the Germans to retire further. Therefore, we can see here a mini version of "bite and hold" and now was the moment to pause and regroup. 1st Division took the opportunity to alter its configuration. The divisional frontage was expanded, by using both of the other brigades to relieve 3 Brigade. With the Maissemy – Berthancourt road as the inter-brigade boundary, 2 Brigade were put in to the right and 1 Brigade were on the left. 3 Brigade were withdrawn to the area around Caulaincourt. The divisional staff were then preparing an advanced to be sited at Caulaincourt. In contrast to the static period, advanced divisional headquarters was being co-located with the reserve brigade. At the storming of the Hindenburg Line, Major General Boyd would insist on his brigade HQs being beside his own - but that did not involve holding them back, but rather pushing his forward. This suggests that 1st Division staff were recognising the changes they needed to make, albeit gradually.

As 1st Division prepared for the next assault, 17 September saw 6th Division and the neighbouring French troops carry out a preparatory attack designed to improve the jumping off positions, but the results were minimal. It was evident that the Germans were prepared to offer stiff resistance. The 1st Loyal North Lancs also carried a small attack to straighten out the jumping off line by taking some high ground.[16] The divisional view stated in the operational

---

13   The latter is considered to be the Gloucestershire Regiment's most decorated soldier. He was later to receive the MC personally from King George V in 1920.
14   TNA WO 95/1278: War Diary of 1st Gloucesters, 11-15 September 1918.
15   TNA WO 95/1280: War Diary of 1st South Wales Borderers, 15 September 1918.
16   TNA WO 95/1266: War Diary of 1st Loyal North Lancs, 17 September 1918.

orders for 18 September was that this stiffening resistance reflected the fact that the battle line was approaching the Hindenburg Line. The intelligence appraisal continued by saying that in front of 1st Division, on the front Fresnoy & Gricourt to Berthacourt & Pontruet (inclusive), were all three regiments of *179th Reserve Division,* whilst north of the Omignon, they were opposed by *46th Reserve Infantry Regiment* of *119th Division.* The strategic objective of the assault by Fourth Army and its French neighbour was to place those armies in a position of observation of the Hindenburg Line. Each brigade was to assault on a two-battalion front, and the second objective was to be treated as the main line of resistance for the division if there were counterattacks. It is interesting to note that the brigades were specifically entrusted with ensuring that their machine guns provided defence in depth and safeguarded the flanks of the division. Such precautions would provide against both counterattacks and the problems that would be created by the failure of neighbouring divisions. Thus, there was to be no excuse for not getting forward due to the failure of others. To this end, each infantry brigade was to be supported by one company of machine guns A and B, with 1Brigade and 2 Brigade, respectively. The OC of the machine gun battalion was also to organise another company into two sub-groups of eight guns each, which would assemble 2500 yards behind the jump-off line. Each group, one per brigade, would then advance three and a half hours later to establish positions from which they could support the defence of the second objective and put down harassing fire, if required, beyond it.

The third objective, along the line of exploitation, would be assaulted only after a two-hour pause, during which time there would be heavy artillery bombardments of Forgans and Fausille Trenches as well as the villages of St Helene and Pontruet. It is noteworthy that for the final part of the advance, beyond the second objective, the infantry were to liaise directly with the assigned batteries from the divisional artillery. The artillery which had not been assigned to assist the infantry would be under the orders of the divisional CRA. He was tasked with ensuring they were ready to defend the line gained at the second objective. The ground gained beyond this was to be held with outposts, and only lightly manned. This applies the idea of zonal defence to an attack. If the Germans made strong counterattacks, they might regain the nearest ground they had lost, but would quickly come up against a line of resistance amply supplied with machine guns and supported by artillery firing on pre-determined lines. The divisional headquarters was still situated at Mereaucourt, but the day of the attack would see the opening of the new advanced headquarters at Caulaincourt. That it did not open earlier underlines that the divisional staff were adapting gradually to the new style of operations. However, the orders did require the leadership of the divisional artillery and engineers, to be based at the advanced headquarters.[17]

Fourth Army had insisted on a single straight line for the assault, and so on both flanks 1st Division pulled back its troops to behind the agreed jumping-off line. However, in the middle, it was necessary to advance the start line by 600 yards. The troops here had to wait for the creeping barrage to catch up with them before the two brigades could all advance together. Grappling with the difficulties of achieving flexibility as well as success, the Corps CRA retained all the artillery under his command and delegated control to Brigadier Lewin of only the six artillery brigades operating on the divisional front; his own 25th and 39th Field Artillery Brigades,

---

17   TNA WO 95/1234War Diary of 1st Division Headquarters, Ops Order 295, September 1918.

168th RFA Brigade (attached from 32nd Division), 298th Army Brigade RFA and two horse artillery brigades, the 5th and 16th. In addition, Lewin had direct call on 14th Brigade of the Royal Garrison Artillery who could provide him with the support of 3" and 6" howitzers. All the artillery had been positioned in order to be able to fire up to the second objective without moving. Once the second line was reached, the 25th and 39th Field Artillery Brigades would advance.

The 18- pounder barrage itself was to start 200 yards ahead of the infantry forming up line, whilst the howitzer barrage would be 400 yards ahead of the infantry. The barrage itself was designed to allow for little variation in pace by the infantry; the first lift would come after three minutes and the second after five minutes, in each case the lift would be 100 yards. The third to eleventh lifts would occur at three-minute intervals. Thereafter, the 100-yard lifts would occur every four minutes.[18] As the level of resistance generally rose during an advance, slowing the expectations in the later stages was realistic. To help ensure that the commanders knew how the attacks were going, the troops were told that a contact aeroplane would fly over them half an hour after they were due to reach the Red Line sounding a klaxon. This was to be responded to by the flashing of discs. If the red line had been reached, commanding officers were to order a signal in the form of three rifle grenade flares – white over white over white. To assist in warning of counterattacks, aeroplanes would fly over and drop a white parachute flare in the direction from which the Germans were approaching.[19]

In retrospect, the attack was judged, by Strickland, to have started too early as visibility was poor; it opened at 5.30 a.m., fifty-seven minutes before sunrise. In a lame opening to the operations report, Strickland stated that the performance of his division reflected that of the neighbouring divisions. Whilst this was accurate it hardly reflected credit on the level of battle-worthiness to which he had raised his division. He started by saying that his right-hand battalion, the Loyal North Lancs, lost direction and was diverted towards Fresnoy. The 6th Division had failed to storm Fresnoy. The village was strongly held and 6th Division, had their own difficulties when forming up.

By contrast, 2nd Royal Sussex on the left flank of 2 Brigade benefitted from the way in which 4th Australian Division was successful in reaching all its objectives, defeating *119th Division* who surrendered "freely". The overall result of the operations was an advance forming a rough triangle in relation to the jumping-off line. On the 1st Division's left, 2nd Royal Sussex, despite being slow to exploit their early success, managed to advance beyond the red line but did not reach the blue line. However, the 4th Australians did reach the trenches which were a prolongation of those assigned to the Sussex. To the right of the Sussex, the 2nd KRRC managed to reach the red line but had to offer a refused flank on their right where they joined up with the Camerons. The Camerons had got through the Blue Line but had to refuse their right flank in turn, because the Loyal North Lancs had only just about reached the blue line. The Loyal North Lancs also organised a refused flank back to 6th Division, whose left battalion had only got halfway to the blue line. By relating his division's performance to those divisions around him, Strickland definitely creates the impression that 1st Division was not a crack division in 1918 and deserved its place on the unofficial list of non-attack divisions.

18 TNA WO 95/1234: War Diary of 1st Division Headquarters, Ops Order 295, September 1918.
19 TNA WO 95/1268: War Diary of 2nd Brigade Headquarters, 17 September 1918.

The attack by 2 Brigade involved advancing on both sides of the River Omignon; the 2nd Sussex were on the left, that is north of the river, whilst the 2nd KRRC were on the right to the south of the river. As has already been alluded to, 2nd Sussex had elements of 12 Australian Brigade to their left. On the left, the line of exploitation would take the 2nd Sussex to the St Helene ridge. Brigadier Kelly had stationed his reserve, 1st Northants, north of the river. He stated that the reason for this was that there was less space south of the river, and so the 2nd KRRC would be able to deploy in sufficient depth with only one battalion. The Northamptons were to advance behind the Sussex, as the latter advanced, and occupy the positions taken. He also kept eight guns of B company 1st MGC in brigade reserve whilst allocating one section each to the two assault battalions. The battalions each had two guns attached from the 2nd Light Trench Mortar Battery which was under the command of Captain Barfoot. Brigadier Kelly's plan was to send the reserve machine guns forward in bounds, behind the Sussex, as the Sussex advanced, in order to be able to consolidate the ground gained (as the Northants would do).

The ground over which the battalions had to advance was marshy and intersected by a series of re-entrants, which were also marshy at the edges of the spurs running down to the river. The brigade also anticipated that the villages of Vadencourt, Pontruet and Berthacourt would offer points of resistance. However, the brigade had entered the line on the night of 16/17 September and had used the time not only to reconnoitre the terrain but also to observe the source of enemy machine gun fire that harassed the likely assembly positions. It was arranged for these German machine guns to be suppressed by artillery fire during the assembly period prior to the attack. This reveals a very detailed level of planning by Brigadier Kelly. The result was that the brigade assembled unhindered except by heavy rain and the pitch darkness.[20] According to the Sussex they were in position by 4.30 a.m. They were deployed in artillery formation on a front of 1100 yards with a depth of 400 yards.[21]

The Sussex left flank, formed by A Company (led by Captain Mason MC), deployed in two lines of platoons, was less obstructed by the terrain than its right, formed by D Company, also deployed in two lines of platoons. Formed up one hundred yards behind A Company, and also deployed in two lines of platoons, was B company (led by Captain Jaques MC). Level with the rear of B company was the left leading platoon of C company, under the command of Lieutenant Lane MC, who were the battalion reserve. This leading left platoon was to follow the left platoon of D company and turn back into Vaudencourt to help mop it up.[22] Thus, the weight of the battalion was on the side where the terrain was most favourable. Therefore, the battalion was able to advance successfully and capture the trench system situated a thousand yards east of Vaudencourt which represented the Green Line. The left company met with little resistance. The progress by the right company was achieved in the face of the resistance put up by the Germans occupying Vadencourt and on the Green Line, as well as additional machine guns sited on the path of the right company. Brigadier Kelly singled out the qualities of the right front commander but did not name him in the summary section of his report. It was in fact Captain Dolleymore, leading D Company; the only company commander in the battalion without the Military Cross. He is specifically commended by Lieutenant Colonel Johnson in

20   TNA WO 95/1268: War Diary of 2nd Brigade Headquarters, 19 September 1918.
21   TNA WO 95/1269: War Diary of 2nd Royal Sussex, 19 September 1918.
22   TNA WO 95/1269: War Diary of 2nd Royal Sussex, 19 September 1918.

the battalion narrative of operations. Johnson reported that, despite the men losing the barrage due to the stiff resistance, thanks to Dolleymore the right of the brigade reached the green line thirty minutes before the creeping barrage was due to re-start. C company were then ordered to place two platoons in support of D company. Captain Jaques was ordered to extend the depth of two of his platoons in case it was necessary to call them into reserve.

After the appropriate pause and the renewal of the creeping barrage, the Sussex progressed to the red line, represented by the high ground and slopes overlooking Pontruet. Johnson reported that at this stage, many Germans tried to run away but that his men were too quick for them and took a lot of prisoners. The prisoners were mainly captured around the quarry and in the defences centred on Tumulus Trench. The slopes were swept by machine gun fire from Pontruet. So, having consolidated the new position in depth, Johnson set Lewis and Vickers guns the task of supressing the German fire. At each stage, the Northamptons followed up and maintained touch with the Sussex. However, the difficulty in subsequently exploiting the success forward to the blue line was blamed by Kelly fairly and squarely on higher command. Kelly said that the neighbouring Australians were not told to delay before going forward, whereas 2 Brigade had been told to wait for a further fixed period.

Kelly argued that this delay meant that his men faced German troops who had had time to recover in Pontruet and Formi Trench. He added that his men could not advance down forward slopes in the face of the machine guns in Pontruet in particular. Johnson's account supports this, in that he says C company sent forward two platoons that entered Formi Trench despite hostile fire but were counter-attacked on their right flank. The counterattack was beaten back but Johnson then ordered C company to create a string of outposts. The village of Pontruet was subsequently taken in a night attack by 138 Brigade of 46th Division during which Lieutenant Barratt won the Victoria Cross. Kelly's decision to blame division probably accounts for Strickland's lack of praise for Kelly.

The Australians commenced their assault on the St Helene Ridge at 11 p.m. Johnson stated that 2nd Sussex were ordered to conform to this by attacking at midnight. This required hasty preparations with a tired battalion. Nevertheless, the battalion organised a further attack at midnight, which succeeded in capturing Formi Trench and establishing posts just south of Entrepot Trench. In doing so, the Sussex were able to make touch with the Australians, but Kelly says distance made liaison difficult as the Australians were also organising operations that night to continue in the line of exploitation. Liaison across Corps boundaries was never easy and perhaps this explains Kelly's reference to distance. Kelly's report on this further attack by the Sussex referred to the fact that they suffered considerable casualties particularly due to machine gun fire from Pontruet and goes on to complement them for doing well despite being very tired.[23] According to Strickland, knowledge of the ground explained why the Northants were not used instead. Johnson took account of the day's actions and brought B and C companies to carry out the attack, with D assigned to providing the flank cover. Both companies were organised into three lines of platoons for the assault, with two platoons in the front line. On the left, C company made good progress and the leading platoons reached the sunken road north of St Helene with the rest of the company in support behind. However, on the right, B company were unable to advance from Formi Trench because of heavy machine gun fire from Pontruet and St Helene.

---

23   TNA WO 95/1268: War Diary of 2nd Brigade Headquarters, 19 September 1918.

Therefore, the Sussex finalised connections on the left in touch with the Australians and on the right through a refused flank back to the 2nd KRRC, the right of 2 Brigade. The diary of the Sussex records its lost officers as Lieutenant Ormrod and four subalterns: Little, White, Gordon and Earl. Nineteen-year-old Second Lieutenant Gordon from Cambridge was on attachment from 3rd b Royal Sussex. All five were platoon commanders; two company commanders, Jaques and Dolleymore, were wounded along with two more platoon commanders, subalterns Vaughan and Bush, DCM.[24] The Northamptons then relieved the Sussex after their night attack.

As described above, 2nd KRRC were formed up in front of Maissemy and had to await the arrival of the creeping barrage which had started further back. As expected, the battalion faced resistance from machine guns in the marshy margins and on the green line. Kelly cited the support provided by the machine guns attached to the left battalion assisting the right battalion in knocking out an enemy machine gun south of the river, as an example of the success of this integration of units created.

The 2nd KRRC, like the Sussex, were formed up by 4.30 a.m. on 18 September, but they were attacking on a frontage of 800 yards. This narrowed gradually to 500 yards by the time it reached the line marked as the final objective. Their first objective was a line of high ground approximately half-way to Berthaucourt. They advanced led by A company under Captain Barnes MC. Behind them was B company led by Second Lieutenant Cunningham MM on the right and C company under Captain Cook MC on the left. The battalion reserve was D company under Second Lieutenant Cotter. The prevailing thick mist meant their commanding officer had no idea what was happening, and so he went forward to speak to his company commanders. He found that the battalion was held up on both flanks by machine guns. He therefore ordered A company to hold the enemy to the front whilst the flanks were turned. C company was detailed to turn the position to the left; in which, as noted above, they were assisted by the Sussex tackling German defenders on their right by firing across the river. On the right, B company and the left flank elements of 1st Camerons (1 Brigade) were led by Second Lieutenant Cunningham MM, whose leadership is described as the key to the success achieved. Inevitably, these operations took time and the battalion therefore lost touch with the barrage. Nevertheless, the battalion was determined to make progress. It advanced up to the green line with the leading three companies in line, C on the left, A in the centre and B on the right. D company was described as still at full strength and advancing in reserve. Captain Barnes had been seriously wounded so A was now under the leadership of Second Lieutenant Nugent-Head.

As with the Sussex, the 2nd KRRC paused on the green line and then advanced successfully taking Berthaucourt, where there was stiff resistance, and reached the red line. They established a line of outposts just beyond the village and battalion headquarters was established in a half dug trench just short of the village from which there was particularly good observation of the ground ahead. This meant that the battalion was approximately 500 yards from the outskirts of the village of Pontruet.

Kelly observed that both battalions made good use of the attached trench mortars, given the available amount of ammunition. The 2nd KRRC then linked to 1 Brigade by throwing back its flank towards Villemay Trench and joining up in the vicinity of the local quarry. The 2nd KRRC repaid the Sussex for their earlier support by spotting a German counterattack

---

24 TNA WO 95/1269: War Diary of 2nd Royal Sussex, 19 September 1918.

aimed at the Sussex. They used a telephone line, which they had laid as they advanced. The 2nd KRRC then alerted Kelly. Brigadier Kelly was able to ensure that the counterattack was immediately stopped by artillery fire and shrapnel. This bears out his statement that liaison between the infantry and the artillery was entirely satisfactory. The 2nd KRRC had to beat off a serious bombing attack on 19 September. This cost the life of Second Lieutenant Cunningham MM, who hailed from Fife, and who died of his wounds. The attack came along Gallichet Trench towards Berthaucourt and initially succeeded in driving in the outposts. The situation was restored by a determined counter-attack by Stokes mortars and the 6" Newton. The latter reflects well on the decision to deploy the light mortars as attachments to the infantry. As soon as Kelly knew the Green Line was taken, he moved his own headquarters and that of the 39th RFA to Maissemy, whilst the latter's batteries advanced to just behind that village. His actions in moving forward immediately offer a contrast with those of the divisional staff described above.

Kelly argued that it would not have been wise to attack Pontruet directly, as he would have had one flank open due to 1 Brigade not being able to achieve its objectives. He pointed out that it was only supposed to be attacked once it could be overlooked on both sides. His view was that the brigade had been successful, but he said that many of the prisoners taken were used by the RAMC as bearers, and so found their way into other divisional areas. The cost to the 2nd Sussex was five dead officers and 22 dead men, plus four officers wounded alongside 107 other ranks, with eighteen posted as missing.[25] The supporting Northamptons lost seven men killed and four officers wounded, along with 77 wounded other ranks. The 2nd KRRC lost similar numbers to the Sussex; three officers killed, and one missing, with four wounded. Amongst the other ranks, 39 were killed and 115 wounded with a further four missing. Kelly concluded his report by saying that his officers had led their men well and very effectively.[26]

The day's operations had not proceeded as well on 1 Brigade's front. Attacking on the right of 2nd KRRC were 1st Cameron Highlanders, with 1st Loyal North Lancs on the right and 1st Black Watch in support. The Camerons were advancing with C and D companies in the lead, with A and B in support. The first objective for the Camerons was Villemay Trench, 1300 yards ahead of their jumping off position, meaning they had to travel further than some other battalions.[27] The attack started in the same mist that faced 2 Brigade. The left of 1st Camerons, C company, were able to push on towards the second objective, Ledue Trench, 400 yards northeast of Berthaucourt, and were supported by B company. However, the Camerons right company, D, found a thick belt of wire in front of Villemay Trench. There was stout resistance based upon machine guns to be overcome. Therefore at 8.15 a.m., two platoons of A company were sent forward to assist D company. Once C had achieved its objectives, men from B company were re-tasked to assist D company. Eventually, the Camerons prevailed. by 9.50 a.m., D company reported that it was consolidating a position in front of Villemay Trench. Inevitably the attack was now behind schedule. The two platoons of A company were deployed to form a defensive flank and the battalion recorded that the situation was seen as very precarious. According to Strickland's own report, the Black Watch, 1st Brigade's reserve battalion had not been brought up quickly enough.

25 Private Tolley and Private Chapple now lie in Brie British Cemetery.
26 TNA WO 95/1268: War Diary of 2nd Brigade Headquarters, 19 September 1918.
27 TNA WO 95/1264: War Diary of 1st Cameron Highlanders, 18 September 1918.

At noon, the Germans took the opportunity to debouch from Arbousiers Wood and counterattack down Essling Alley, where the flank of the Cameron Highlanders should have been protected by the advancing 1st Loyal North Lancs. Unlike their colleagues, 1st Loyal North Lancs lost direction. The German attack was frustrated by the machine guns deployed by A company and artillery support. The arrival of two companies of the Black Watch further stiffened the line. By 2.45 p.m. the line had stabilised; with C company 1st Camerons in touch with 2nd KRRC of 2nd Brigade on the left and extended along the sunken road to the quarry. There A company began the refused flank that was then extended by B company down to the junction with 1st Loyal North Lancs.[28] It was noted that the German artillery fire was relatively light, and most of the casualties were caused by machine guns and snipers. Nonetheless, the brigade believed it had captured eighty prisoners along with seventeen machine guns of mixed type. The Brigade also laid claim to capturing one 77cm gun, two 8" mortars and two 3" mortars; the mortars had now been used to attack the Germans.[29]

At a conference, held at about 8 p.m. and chaired by Brigadier Thornton, plans were made to gain the objectives that had not been taken so far. The Black Watch were tasked with attacking Fourmoy and Essling Alley. In total three companies were to attack two trench systems with D company being attached to 1st Camerons. The latter would be given verbal orders by the OC Camerons, whereas the others would receive verbal orders from their own commanding officer.[30] The decision to send forward small numbers of men against prepared positions suggests that some senior officers had learnt little from the later stages of the Somme offensive.

Therefore, at 6 a.m. on 19 September, B and C companies of the Black Watch, followed by the battalion headquarters, headed north-eastwards along the sunken road through the village of Maissemy. Once they reached Fourmoy Alley, they established the battalion headquarters in conjunction with those of 1st Camerons. The two assaulting companies formed up in Fourmoy Alley. Lieutenant Colonel Anderson then went forward with Captain Colquhoun MC, who was in command of B company to show him the ground and the objectives. Lieutenant Colonel Anderson then went back to see Captain Duncan in charge of C company for the same purpose. However, Anderson was then told Captain Colquhoun MC had been shot through the head by a German sniper. Consequently, Anderson gave command of B company to Lieutenant Galbraith, and so it was under his leadership that the advance from the sunken road resumed at 9 a.m., supported by a strong artillery barrage. The battalion's report states that they had been told there would be little or no resistance, but in fact were met with strong resistance in the form of a German counterattack from Muguet Copse and up the sunken road.

This operation put B company at a serious disadvantage, as the trench they occupied was seven to eight feet deep with no fire-step. Fortunately, the Lewis guns of C company came into action and saved the day. Their fire enabled B company to withdraw, but initially six wounded men including Lieutenant Galbraith were left behind, that is, beyond the sunken road. In order to rescue these men, 23-year-old Second Lieutenant Smith immediately organised a party to retrieve the wounded and they successfully did so, but the effort cost him his life as he was killed

---

28 TNA WO 95/1264: War Diary of 1st Cameron Highlanders, 18 September 1918.
29 TNA WO 95/1262: War Diary of 1st Brigade Headquarters, 18-19 September 1918.
30 TNA WO 95/1263: War Diary of 1st Black Watch, 18 September 1918.

by a grenade.[31] He was one of approximately fifty casualties suffered by the Black Watch that day.[32]

Meantime, D company had successfully bombed its way down Essling Alley. In the light of the resistance encountered, the battalion was told to cease trying to advance and to establish a bombing block. Due to the results achieved, it was decided by a conference at divisional headquarters that units would not be sent to attack strong positions on the high ground. That night the Black Watch established a series of forward posts. On the night of 20 September, the Black Watch extended their line to facilitate the withdrawal of 1st Loyal North Lancs from the line. During the period of 21 – 23 September, the Black Watch recorded heavy artillery fire on potential assembly positions and at around dawn and attributed this to the Germans being nervous about another attack.

A key feature of the 100 Days was the maintenance of constant pressure. Thus 2 Brigade would soon be recalled to the fight. Having been relieved by 8th Notts & Derbys of 139 Brigade on 20 September, the Sussex spent 21 September resting and re-organising.[33] Further assistance was given to 46th Division on 22 September by 1st Loyal North Lancs. They deployed their machine guns and rifle fire to enfilade a counterattack on positions held by 1/5th Notts & Derbys in Gallichet Trench.[34]

On 22 September, the 2nd Sussex were told to prepare for a divisional assault on the high ground around 1000 yards north of Gricourt, which was intended to deny the Germans observation of the back areas of a division preparing an assault. Strickland stated in the introduction to his narrative of operations that a further advance was judged to be not necessary, as it would only create a salient that would have to be held until the assault on the Hindenburg Line took place. He also said that capturing Gricourt itself was not thought to be necessary either, but it was taken following a decision on the spot by the brigade. In Strickland's opinion, Fresnoy represented such a strong position that trying to capture it according to a timetable was liable to fail. Part of the strength of the position lay in the machine guns sited in Marronniers Wood. It was therefore decided that these positions, and those in Cornouillers Wood, would have to be neutralised by fire whilst the initial attack towards Fresnoy took place and then mopped up afterwards.[35] In many ways, the concept of this attack resembles the German infiltration tactics of March 1918 as it seeks to bypass strongpoints, rather than adopting an attritional approach like that of late 1916, where the woods would have been attacked first.

Strickland described his planned operations as consisting of three attacks, of which two were eastwards in direction. The first of these was to be on his right where one battalion of 3 Brigade would assault eastwards, south of Fresnoy, alongside 6th Division. Its final objective would be Argonne Trench, and it would extend leftwards as it advanced to take in Bugeaud Alley. Also attacking eastwards, in this case from south of Berthaucourt, would be two battalions of 2 Brigade. Both assaults were planned to commence five minutes after zero under a creeping barrage, which would lift one hundred yards every four minutes. The battalion assigned to the left of 3 Brigade would be the final piece of the plan. Here, the battalion would advance

---

31 Second Lieutenant Smith is now commemorated on the Vis-en-Artois Memorial.
32 TNA WO 95/1263: War Diary of 1st Black Watch, 17-21 September 1918.
33 TNA WO 95/1269: War Diary of 2nd Royal Sussex, 21 September 1918.
34 TNA WO 95/1266: War Diary of 1st Loyal North Lancs, 22 September 1918.
35 TNA WO 95/1266: War Diary of 1st Loyal North Lancs, 24 September 1918.

north-eastwards through Fresnoy itself. Accordingly, the barrage ahead of this battalion would lift one hundred yards every five minutes, to make allowance for the likely resistance. Behind the right battalion of 3 Brigade, four Mark V tanks would assemble (two male, one female and one composite). The tanks' objectives were Fresnoy Cemetery, Cornouillers Wood and Marronniers Wood. Sending tanks to attack woods seems to suggest Strickland had not followed tactical developments closely since September 1916. Tanks were best used in open territory. A further eight tanks (five male, one female and two composite) were also deployed; six to support the main attack and two to assist in mopping up Arbousiers Wood and the valley up to Cornouillers Wood.

The deployment of aircraft was agreed with Army Wing and the use of machine guns seems very detailed and reflective of operational difficulties. After the way in which the Germans had used Muguet Wood on 19 September, it had been arranged for the RAF to bomb it and the sunken road to the west of it. This is a further example of the way in which aircraft were being integrated into the interdictory role at a tactical level, by blocking the path of German reinforcements. The RAF were also tasked with bombing Sambon, Chevillard and David trenches. They were also asked to neutralise the "Three Savages" (East of Gricourt, Gloutons trench in the vicinity of Galopins Alley) by dropping smoke bombs. They were also to use smoke to neutralise Blainoy Trench and the high ground just east of it. Given the terrain, the RAF were to play a key role in denying the Germans the observational advantage of holding the higher ground to facilitate the infantry assault. The final task of the RAF was to machine gun the positions on the ridge, which constituted the final objective of 2 Brigade.

The plan also provided for the deployment of heavy machine guns on the ground. Each infantry brigade was assigned one company of the divisional machine gun battalion to support them. In addition to this, 32 machine guns took part in the barrage to assist the assault. Eight of these guns were then to go forward and fill the positions vacated by the guns that had gone forward with the assaulting infantry. This was designed to enable them to assist in providing a machine gun barrage to protect the ground won by the infantry, and to stiffen the line of resistance in the case of a German counterattack. All this planning suggests that the best way to exploit the value of machine guns was now grasped pretty clearly.

Pursuant to these wider objectives Lieutenant Colonel Johnson, of 2nd Sussex, took his company commanders and surviving platoon commanders forward on a reconnaissance, as they were part of the planned attack by 2 Brigade. The battalion moved forward to the quarry east of Vermand on the evening of 23 September. Here they received a meal and were issued with stores. The Sussex departed at 11 p.m., moving cross country, to avoid the German shellfire falling on the crossroads at Maissemy. Five hours later, the battalion had formed up, in a north-south line, based on Fourmoy and Villemay trenches. On the right, occupying a 200-yard frontage, was A company led by Captain Roberts. They were deployed in two lines of platoons with a depth of 100 yards. Their right rested on the junction of Villemay and Essling Trenches. This deployment was matched by C company on their left, who were now under the command of Lieutenant Sunderland. Neither officer is listed in the detailed list of those taking part in the operations on 18 / 19 September. Captain Mason had replaced the wounded Captain Dolleymore in command of D company. D company was now organised as three platoons due to the casualties it had sustained. One platoon was attached to A company, specifically to assist in mopping up, whilst another was to act in support, the third was deployed in support to C company. B company was to act as the battalion reserve; its commander, Lieutenant Gardner was also not listed in those taking part on 18 / 19 September. To support the battalion in reaching the high ground north of Gricourt, two tanks, two trench mortars and a section of B company of the 1st MGC were deployed. This time the Sussex were to be the link between the Northamptons on their right and 3 Brigade on their left.[36]

Captured German orders show that the Germans had told their troops to deal with tanks using hand grenades and heavy machine guns. The grenades were to be tied in bundles and strewn around as an improvised minefield. The heavy machine guns were to be echeloned and supplied with armour piercing bullets. The same orders included an operational appraisal that the standard method being employed by the British was to attack with tank support after a short artillery barrage just before dawn. The official comment on this was that therefore it was extremely hard to predict exactly where the blow would fall.[37]

As 2nd Brigade formed up, at 4 a.m. the Black Watch were withdrawn, but the outposts remained occupied for thirty minutes longer. The outposts would have acted as a screen against a German counterattack during the final deployment. By 9.30 a.m., the whole battalion of the Black Watch had collected at Vermand. Again, B company suffered; this time twelve men were hit when the Germans shelled the back areas. In total over the period 17 – 24 September 1st Black Watch suffered casualties amongst the other ranks of fourteen dead and five that died of their wounds, as well as 113 wounded and fifteen posted as missing. Officer losses were comparatively light with two dead and two wounded.[38]

Initially, the attack started well at 5 a.m., with the Sussex advancing with the creeping barrage. Despite the German resistance, the advance continued and prisoners were captured. However, Lieutenant Colonel Johnson reported that problems then arose because of the failure of 46th Division to take Pontruet. He said that this failure led the leading companies of the Northants to fall back, which in turn exposed the flank of his own C company. That company then came under heavy artillery and machine gun fire, and therefore fell back to Sampson's trench. This left A company of the Sussex exposed on the forward objective, but this was also partly due to the failure of 3 Brigade to reach its objectives. Johnson then deployed one platoon of his reserve company to form a defensive flank, linking up A company who were 200 yards ahead of Sampson's Trench with the Northamptons in that trench. Johnson felt his troops were disorganised by the assault, so he put two more platoons from B company in Chevillard Trench and his last reserve platoon in Leduc Trench.

Approximately 400 Germans advanced at 11.25 a.m. to attack A company, who were about eighty strong. According to Johnson, the Germans began to waver at approximately 50 yards due to the rifle from A company. That was when Captain Roberts ordered his men to fix bayonets and charge. The result was the capture of forty Germans. Many of their comrades died from being caught in the British SOS Barrage as they ran back towards their own trenches. Johnson added with pride that it was a very fine example of how to use infantry weapons and "the value of the dash and fighting spirit shown by all ranks". He then went on to say that Haig cited the action in his despatches and that congratulatory messages arrived from all levels of command and former officers of the regiment. Strickland came in person to offer his congratulations.[39]

36   TNA WO 95/1269: War Diary of 2nd Royal Sussex, 21 September 1918.
37   TNA WO 95/1269: War Diary of 2nd Royal Sussex, September 1918.
38   TNA WO 95/1263: War Diary of 1st Black Watch, 24 September 1918.
39   TNA WO 95/1269: War Diary of 2nd Royal Sussex, 23 September 1918.

The Sussex consolidated the position by creating a line of outposts, with the aid of the divisional pioneers and men of the Royal Engineers. The battalion's deployed B company to hold the outpost line. D, C and A companies were organised as a composite company under Captain Mason in support. On 26 September, Captain Mason took temporary command of the battalion when Johnson went to take temporary command of 2 Brigade. On 28 September, the Sussex were relieved by 1st Gloucesters. 2 Brigade were now the divisional reserve. During the next two days the Sussex rested and were reorganised into three companies due to the casualties sustained on 23–24 September.[40] It is important to remember the great strain on British battalions when reflecting on the decision of the higher command to agree to an armistice in November.

This strain was reflected in the casualty list. Of the other ranks, 18 had been killed, 117 wounded and 39 were listed as missing. This meant that in the two main actions fought during a week, 40 men had been killed, 224 had been wounded and 57 were unaccounted for. Compared with the famous tallies for 1 July 1916 this may seem modest, but the constant drain was going to be a factor during the armistice negotiations. Amongst the officers, following the pattern of the first engagement, the second saw the deaths of four officers, of whom three were platoon commanders. The fourth was the 28-year-old Intelligence Officer, Second Lieutenant Fowler. The deceased platoon commanders included Lieutenant Basil Wright MC, and 29-year-old Second Lieutenant Arthur Garton. Much younger was 19-year-old, Sir John Shiffner, 6th Baronet Coombe, from Lewes in Sussex.[41] The other two officer casualties, initially posted as missing, were Captain Sunderland, a company commander from Chislehurst, and thirty-four-year-old 2nd-Lieutenant Adkin MM from Reading, another of the platoon commanders.

The strain on the Germans is also evident. Prisoners were captured from 261st, 262nd and 263rd Reserve Infantry Regiments as well as the 12th and 63rd Reserve Artillery Regiments, 7th Jaegars and the 10th Bavarian Bearer Company and members of the "12th" Machine Gunners. Such a diverse bag demonstrates how successful the Sussex had been in penetrating the German positions.

The 2nd KRRC were also successful on 24 September. They had gone forward well from the outset. They succeeded in mopping up Arbousiers Wood and worked their way down to Cornouillers Wood. The main difficulty they faced had been a party of approximately 200 Germans, who held out until dusk when they were finally mopped up. Strickland referred to the 2nd KRRC as the reserve battalion of the brigade and that the resistance was why they were unavailable until later than planned.[42] 3 Brigade were planning to capture Gricourt. Strickland informed 3 them that their first responsibility was to free up 2nd KRRC from the Cornouillers Wood area. This does beg the question why the plan did not provide for a battalion of 1 Brigade to be held in readiness to be the reserve, rather than a battalion that was already committed to action. Eventually, this decision was made and 1st Camerons were put at the disposal of 2 Brigade.

That evening the KRRC, freed up from Cornouillers Wood, took over Chevillard Trench and part of Sampson Trench from the Sussex. Strickland says that they waited until dusk and

---

40 TNA WO 95/1269: War Diary of 2nd Royal Sussex, 23 September 1918.
41 Fowler and Garton left widows. One of Shiffner's ancestors had been killed under Wellington in the Peninsula and his brother would be killed during the Second World War.
42 TNA WO 95/1266: War Diary of 1st Loyal North Lancs, 24 September 1918 Narrative of Operations.

then arranged a local barrage which put the Germans to flight and enabled the 2nd KRRC to occupy the high ground that marked the final objective.

Strickland's summary of the day's operations was positive, as not only had the objectives been gained but 3r Brigade had materially improved the overall position by capturing Gricourt. Strickland was full of praise for the way in which Brigadier Kay had assessed the situation and not only freed the 2nd KRRC for other duties but also captured Gricourt. Strickland was also keen to praise Brigadier Kelly for the way in which the tired, and much depleted, battalions of 2 Brigade were made aware of the overall situation, and their agreement to free 1st Camerons and hold the ground unaided. Their GOC recognised that the men of 2 Brigade realised that they were likely to be counter-attacked but undertook the task anyway, holding all the ground gained when they were attacked on 25 September. Strickland deserves some credit too. He had planned to move up companies of pioneers and engineers and therefore, they had been available to prepare and wire the new positions. Strickland observed that this commitment from 2 Brigade meant that he had a relatively fresh 1 Brigade to use in the operations that followed as Fourth Army continued its offensive.

Enemy material captured amounted to four 77mm guns, four heavy trench mortars and nine light ones, as well as two anti-tank rifles and an unenumerated number of machine guns. Strickland restricted his criticisms to 46th Division for its failure to gain Pontruet, leaving his men open to annihilating machine gun fire on exposed positions. This can be seen in the balance within the overall casualties incurred by the division; twelve officers and 83 men were killed (with 64 posted as missing) but no fewer than 35 officers and 430 men were wounded. The success of the division was also evaluated in the capture of three wounded officers and 132 wounded other ranks, as well as 21 officers and 943 men unscathed. In that sense, the 1st Division had contributed positively to the "wearing out fight". Importantly, Strickland and the men of his division had proved they were now up to the task of tackling the Germans. Taking the 2nd KRRC, for example, their performance showed how far they had restored the battalion's reputation since the debacle on the Yser. In April 1918, 1st Division had shown skill and determination in defence. Now it was demonstrating that it could bite and hold too.

40

The Hindenburg Line

The orders for the assault on the Hindenburg Line were issued by Rawlinson, on 22 September, to IX Corps under the command of Lieutenant- General Sir Walter Braithwaite. The approach to the Hindenburg Line represented the semi-open nature of the "100 Days," whereas the next step was a reversion to the kind of operation that the BEF had faced during the Somme and at Passchendaele campaigns. The original ideas envisaged the key role being played by the Australians and Americans. However, Braithwaite now had 46th Division instead of the Australians, as Rawlinson had decided to rest his very valued colonial troops.[1] As the official historian noted, tactical surprise was all that could be achieved, as the nature of the positions forming the Hindenburg Line meant the strategic objective was very clear.[2] The degree to which Fourth Army had achieved a level of proficiency was reflected in its ability to make a last minute adjustment to 1st Division's front, without detracting from the success of the assault. The central role for 1st Division was to advance and detach some troops on its left to support the right flank of 46th Division as the former advanced over the canal.[3]

The Official Historian summarises 1st Division's attack in less than a paragraph, with the summary that they advanced with little difficulty for approximately 1200 yards up to the St-Quentin–Bellecourt Road but were prevented from continuing their advance by heavy enfilade fire from the south. 1Brigade were assisted by 46th Division's stunning success on their left, but 3 Brigade suffered from the decision not to include 6th Division to in the active part of the assault. 6th Division were only ordered to keep in touch with the enemy through patrols if the Germans retired. This seems to be a good example of how the British Army had yet to learn some of the lessons of the Somme. Clearly, one division had to be the last in action but in such a small area, the inactivity of one division allowed problems to develop. If 46th Division had not exceeded expectations, there could have been a different end of war outcome.

To facilitate the assault by 46th Division, 1st Division had side-slipped into the line on the night of the 26th / 27th September. 1 Brigade had been brought from divisional reserve to relieve 46th Division's right-hand brigade. 3Brigade had initially gone in to divisional reserve after being relieved by elements of 6th Division but was switched to relieve 2 Brigade on the

---

1 Edmonds, *OH, 1918*, Vol. 5, Appendix VI.
2 Edmonds, *OH, 1918*, Vol. 5, p.99.
3 Edmonds, *OH, 1918*, Vol. 5, p.101.

night of the early morning assault.⁴ The role of 1st Division was therefore a supporting one in this instance, and this role had two elements. The first part involved supporting the right flank of 46th Division's advance and forming a defensive flank between Pontruet and Bellenglise whilst 46th Division crossed the canal. The 1st Division was therefore also tasked with engaging the enemy who occupied the high ground south of the canal and east of Pontruet. To help them achieve this, 1 Brigade were to assign some troops to go forward under the right of the creeping barrage provided to support 46th Division's advance. By advancing under the same creeping barrage, the adjoining troops of the two divisions would be co-ordinated, which shows that considerable thought was being given to the problem of attacks breaking down along the lines of major unit boundaries. The 1st Division was also required to assist the corps attack by assaulting the Thorigny and Talana Hill Ridge.⁵ This latter part of the operations was due to take place at the same time as 32nd Division leapfrogged through 46th Division.

For this assault, 2 Brigade would be held in reserve, as it was described as "very weak and tired".⁶ As it had been one of the leading brigades in the advance to the Hindenburg Line, this is understandable. As we have seen, it had suffered heavily. Therefore 1 Brigade, under the command of Brigadier-General Wheatley, advanced with "A" company of 1st MGC in support whilst 3rd Brigade, under the command of Brigadier-General Kay, had "C" company in support. Each brigade had the support of a section of Royal Engineers. In addition to 25th and 39th Brigades RFA from the divisional artillery, under the command of Brigadier-General Lewin, the advance was to be supported by 5th Army Brigade RHA and 298th Army brigade RFA.⁷

The supporting artillery were to include a proportion of smoke shells during the bombardment, but as the supply was insufficient to last for more than two and a half hours, two of the artillery brigades, one in each group,⁸ were to revert to only firing HE after that point. The men of 1 Brigade were to be supported, in particular, by "if possible" eight machine guns laying down a barrage on Flute Trench. Brigadier Wheatley was also informed that at zero plus two hours and thirty minutes there would be a brigade of field artillery available support to support him.⁹

The greater level of co-ordination associated with the British Army by late 1918 is evident in the instruction to 3 Brigade regarding liaising with the Royal Engineers Special Company, who were responsible for laying down a smoke barrage to screen 46th Division from the high ground in front of 3 Brigade. They were to have at their headquarters an officer from the engineers who

---

4   TNA WO 95/1264: War Diary of the 1st Battalion Cameron Highlanders, Narrative of Operations 29 September-3 October 1918.
5   TNA WO 95/1264: War Diary of the 1st Battalion Cameron Highlanders, Narrative of Operations 29 September-3 October 1918.
6   TNA WO 95/1264: War Diary of the 1st Battalion Cameron Highlanders, Narrative of Operations 29 September-3 October 1918.
7   TNA WO 95/1264: War Diary of the 1st Battalion Cameron Highlanders, Narrative of Operations 29 September-3 October 1918.
8   TNA WO 95/1266: War Diary of the 1st Infantry Brigade Trench Mortar Battery, Narrative of Operations 29 September-3 October 1918.
9   TNA WO 95/1264: War Diary of the 1st Battalion Cameron Highlanders, Narrative of Operations 29 September-3 October 1918.

could stop the smoke barrage when they were in position to take the high ground.[10] The fate of 3 Brigade's assault may lie in the initial orders. According to these orders, 3 Brigade was initially to send forward patrols and, if the Germans had not retired, engage in a sufficient fire fight with rifles and machine guns in order to keep the units opposite them occupied. Greater sophistication is evident in the rest of the orders, which say that once news is received of 46th Division having crossed the canal 3 Brigade should gradually increase the pressure and that at zero plus two hours and thirty minutes there would be artillery support available.[11] Divisional orders gave the Brigadier discretion over when and how far to push his brigade forward whilst establishing a refused flank, and it was explicit that progress would be dependent upon the advance of 1 Brigade.[12]

The Cameron Highlanders narrative starts with the observation that the assault by 1 Brigade took place at 5.50 a.m. and that it was greatly assisted by a thick mist, which amounted to a fog, which did not lift until 9 a.m.[13] The 1st Loyal North Lancs advanced on the left under the extremity of the 46th Division barrage and captured some forty to fifty prisoners. Their role was to create a defensive flank for 46th Division by seizing the bank and dugouts, and therefore were accompanied by machine guns. The mist did make it difficult to maintain cohesion, but the German positions west of the canal were cleared up to the St Helene – Bellenglise Road.[14] To their right they had the Black Watch who advanced to clear the trenches north-east of Pontruet. The Black Watch then had to fight their way due east on the south bank of the canal. This meant that the Loyal North Lancs were squeezed out of the line and dropped back into reserve.[15]

For 3 Brigade the task proved to be tougher, as the 1st Gloucesters found the Germans holding the trenches on the ridge of the spur just west of Sycamores Wood, south-east of Pontruet. As noted above, the plans for 3 Brigade did not involve the launching of a strong frontal assault and so these trenches were not taken until after nightfall.[16] This summary is borne out by the detail available in the Gloucester's own records. The overall orders are reflected by their recording that their right remained stationary and that the battalion pivoted on that point. At 5.45 a.m., patrols reported that the enemy trenches were strongly held by machine guns. As planned, the barrage to support the assault came down on time at 9 a.m., but the battalion failed to advance due to the thick mist, and the noise of the German shelling making it difficult to know if the British barrage was being fired.[17]

10   TNA WO 95/1264: War Diary of the 1st Battalion Cameron Highlanders, Narrative of Operations 29 September–3 October 1918.
11   TNA WO 95/1264: War Diary of the 1st Battalion Cameron Highlanders, Narrative of Operations 29 September–3 October 1918.
12   TNA WO 95/1264: War Diary of the 1st Battalion Cameron Highlanders, Narrative of Operations 29 September–3 October 1918.
13   TNA WO 95/1264: War Diary of the 1st Battalion Cameron Highlanders, Narrative of Operations 29 September–3 October 1918.
14   TNA WO 95/1266: War Diary of the 1st Brigade Trench Mortar Battery, Narrative of Operations 29 September–3 October 1918.
15   TNA WO 95/1264: War Diary of the 1st Battalion Cameron Highlanders, Narrative of Operations 29 September–3 October 1918.
16   TNA WO 95/1264: War Diary of the 1st Battalion Cameron Highlanders, Narrative of Operations 29 September–3 October 1918.
17   TNA WO 95/1278: War Diary of the 1st Battalion Gloucestershire Regiment, 29 September 1918.

The situation was still difficult by 11.40 a.m. when the smoke barrage on the battalion's left ceased and bright sunshine prevailed.[18] This is presumably a reference to the end of the smoke barrage designed to protect the advance of the 46th Division from being enfiladed from the high ground, as detailed in the divisional orders. The diary also states that the South Wales Borderers had orders not to advance until the Gloucesters had captured their first objective. Therefore, at this stage the advance of 3 Brigade was in danger of stalling. However, a creeping barrage commenced at 11.40 a.m. and two companies of the Gloucesters began to assault the German positions. With B company in support, A company under the command of Captain Merrick MC tried to advance, with C company under Captain Chaney to its left. However, they encountered heavy artillery and machine gun fire. The leading companies were still pinned down 250 yards short of Faucille Trench by 3 p.m.. This had been designated as their first objective. The improved tactics being adopted by 1918 can be seen in that the situation was partially resolved by Lieutenant Forbes of B company. He took a platoon around the left flank of C company and was reported to be in occupation of Faucille Trench by 5.30 p.m.[19]

In capturing Faucille Trench, the Gloucesters were materially assisted by the South Wales Borderers. The Borderers decided to attack despite their orders to await the Gloucesters capture of Faucille Trench. B company of the South Wales Borderers was their left assault element, and they advanced 850 yards at zero hour and captured the section of Faucille Trench that represented their first objective. They noted that a certain amount of opposition from machine guns was encountered but it was dealt with.[20] As a result of the initiative of Forbes and the South Wales Borderers, the Gloucesters had succeeded in achieving their initial objectives.

However, there was still a machine gun nest at the top of the ridge, so the Gloucesters under Forbes now bombed their way up the trench to knock it out. The Germans then withdrew using Forestier Trench and Fortaits Trench. The Germans using the latter found it occupied by the South Wales Borderers and consequently had to surrender.[21] According to the plan of attack, the South Wales Borderers were supposed to await the capture of Faucille trench before advancing to their second objective of Fortraits Trench, but the commander of B company, seeing that the Gloucesters were held up by machine gun fire, also showed initiative and assaulted it anyway "making excellent use of the cover which the ground afforded".[22]

B company of the South Wales Borderers established themselves in Foreats [sic] Trench whilst C company formed up ready to carry out the assault to reach the third objective, Thorigny village and Talana Hill. The barrage opened at 6 p.m. as planned, but the battalion now encountered very heavy machine gun fire and C company was only able to advance approximately 500 yards where it dug in as night fell, with D and A companies in support.[23]

Meantime, the Gloucesters had been able, by the time darkness fell, to occupy their second and third objectives and therefore the battalion occupied the line comprising Glu Trench, Forestier Trench and Fumiates Alley. In reaching their objectives, their casualties amounted to

18 TNA WO 95/1278: War Diary of the 1st Battalion Gloucestershire Regiment, 29 September 1918.
19 TNA WO 95/1278: War Diary of the 1st Battalion Gloucestershire Regiment, 29 September 1918.
20 TNA WO 95/1280: War Diary of the 1st Battalion South Wales Borderers, 29 September 1918.
21 TNA WO 95/1278: War Diary of the 1st Battalion Gloucestershire Regiment, 29 September 1918.
22 TNA WO 95/1280: War Diary of the 1st Battalion South Wales Borderers, 29 September 1918.
23 TNA WO 95/1280: War Diary of the 1st Battalion South Wales Borderers, 29 September 1918.

8 killed and 47 wounded, having taken 23 prisoners including an officer.[24] To those accustomed to the major battles of 1916 and 1917 these casualties may seem limited, but two days later the strength of the battalion is given as 618 Other Ranks, so 55 casualties represents 8.1% of the battalion's strength on 29 September and, as D company had not been engaged, more than that in relation to the rifle strength engaged. With the battalion operating at under 70% of nominal strength it is easy to see why there were those in mid-1918 who had begun to feel that waiting for the United States Expeditionary Force to reach full strength would be a sensible strategy.

The subsequent capture of the ridge was due to the South Wales Borderers gradually extending round to the left flank, after which they occupied Rood Wood. The Black Watch of worked round to their right and secured the line of the St Quentin – Bellenglise Road.[25] On 1 October 1918, the enterprising B company returned to its support role by occupying Faucille Trench whilst D, A and C companies occupied the line from right to left respectively.[26] The Gloucesters' diary also lists the officers with the battalion on 1 October 1918, under the command of Lieutenant Colonel Tweedie DSO, as Major Guild, Captains Mackenzie, Merrick MC, Mallett MC, Morris MC, Hodges MC, Chaney and Jarvis (who was the Adjutant). They were supported by Lieutenants Ford, Stotesbury, Forbes and Greene with Second Lieutenants Dobson MC, Barnard, South and Calvert-Fisher. With 17 officers, the proportion of officers to men was roughly that of a full-strength battalion. On the same day, the battalion moved to an area south of the canal opposite Lehaucourt.[27]

Whilst the Gloucesters remained in their newly captured positions on 30 September, the South Wales Borderers had been completing the task left unfinished on 29 September. Their attack on their third objective was carried out on 30 September in a manner which demonstrates how far the British Army had progressed along a learning curve since the Western Front had formed. At 8 a.m., A company engaged the German machine gun post which had held sway in the darkness during the previous evening's fighting. Meanwhile C and D companies worked around the north of the slope and captured the German post, and the machine guns therein, from behind. This enabled C company to advance and occupy the village of Thorigny, and Talana Hill. Next, D company was given the task of garrisoning Thorigny, whilst A company formed a defensive flank facing south and linked to the Gloucesters. That they would be congratulated on their success would be unsurprising but the haul of three field guns, four trench mortars and 36 machine guns made it a certainty. The price paid was four other ranks killed and 31 wounded, as well as the deaths of Second Lieutenants Martin, King and Parker.[28] In contrast, 3 Brigade's remaining battalion, 2nd Welsh (which was in reserve) recorded only three men being wounded over the two days, before moving forward to relieve the Black Watch in the line east of Lehaucourt. The Adjutant, Captain Dunn, recorded their strength as 24 officers and 709 other ranks - roughly the strength of the other battalions prior to the battle.[29]

24   TNA WO 95/1278: War Diary of the 1st Battalion Gloucestershire Regiment, 29 September 1918.
25   TNA WO 95/1266: War Diary of the 1st Brigade Trench Mortar Battery, Narrative of Operations 29 September-3 October 1918.
26   TNA WO 95/1278: War Diary of the 1st Battalion Gloucestershire Regiment, 30 September 1918.
27   TNA WO 95/1278: War Diary of the 1st Battalion Gloucestershire Regiment, 1 October 1918.
28   TNA WO 95/1280: War Diary of the 1st Battalion South Wales Borderers, 30 September 1918.
29   TNA WO 95/1281: War Diary of the 2nd Battalion The Welsh Regiment, 29-30 September 1918.

On 4 October, having spent the previous day in the village of Joncourt, the Gloucesters came under the temporary command of Brigadier Campbell VC's 137 Brigade when they entered the Beaurevoir-Fonsomme line in front of Preselles. The Adjutant then records the death from shellfire of their own brigade commander, Brigadier-General Sir William Kay CMG DSO, 6th Baronet, and of the Brigade Major, and the consequent temporary role as officer commanding 3 Brigade being assigned to Lieutenant Colonel Tweedie DSO.[30]

---

30 TNA WO 95/1278: War Diary of the 1st Battalion Gloucestershire Regiment, 3-4 October 1918.

41

Final Push

As IX Corps advanced 1st Division and 46th Division brigades and battalions rotated to maintain maximum momentum. Brigadier Kay's funeral on 6 October saw the senior officers of the division joined by the corps commander. His successor was appointed that day; Lieutenant Colonel E. St G Aubyn, who had been CO of 2nd KRRC. The Fourth Army's advance continued, as 46th Division had captured Bellenglise. Units of 1st Division moved up to occupy the positions at Bellenglise, and by 10 October the HQ of 1st Division was located in the old German Hindenburg Line.

According to reports received, a new German division had dug a shallow trench west of Mennevret. As the staff of 1st Division continued the preparations for an assault on 17 October, they were visited by Field Marshal Haig. Strickland took the opportunity to introduce his brigadiers to the commander-in-chief. The following day saw Lieutenant General Braithwaite, GOC IX Corps, visit divisional HQ. They were preparing for opening a combined advanced HQ next morning, to be shared by 1st Division and 2nd Brigade. This is another example of how Major General Boyle's dispositions for 46th Division on 29 September were being mirrored by 1st Division. Ironically, Boyd had recreated Haking's arrangements for 1st Division at Aubers Ridge in 1915.

BEF ability to adapt to semi-mobile warfare is evidenced in the instructions issued on 16 October. In preparation for operations around Andigny. Corps were organising for artillery to be brought forward. The artillery were to support the infantry, as they moved beyond the dotted Red Line towards the objectives designated as the Green Line. It was noted that the artillery would therefore be firing from hastily arranged positions. Therefore, the artillery would deliver an area shoot rather than the normal creeping barrage. The front of the area shoot would advance like a creeping barrage at 100 yards every three minutes and would therefore appear like a normal barrage on maps. However, the infantry units were warned that this element of the barrage would be more ragged than usual. Therefore, they should not try to follow it too closely.[1]

The reason for the separate barrages was that 1st Division was to leapfrog through 46th Division and 6th Division, who were to take the red line. 1st Division was tasked with taking the green line and exploiting up to the Canal de La Sambre. The attack was to be undertaken by

1   TNA WO 95/1234: War Diary of the 1st Infantry Division, Headquarters, October 1918, Appendices.

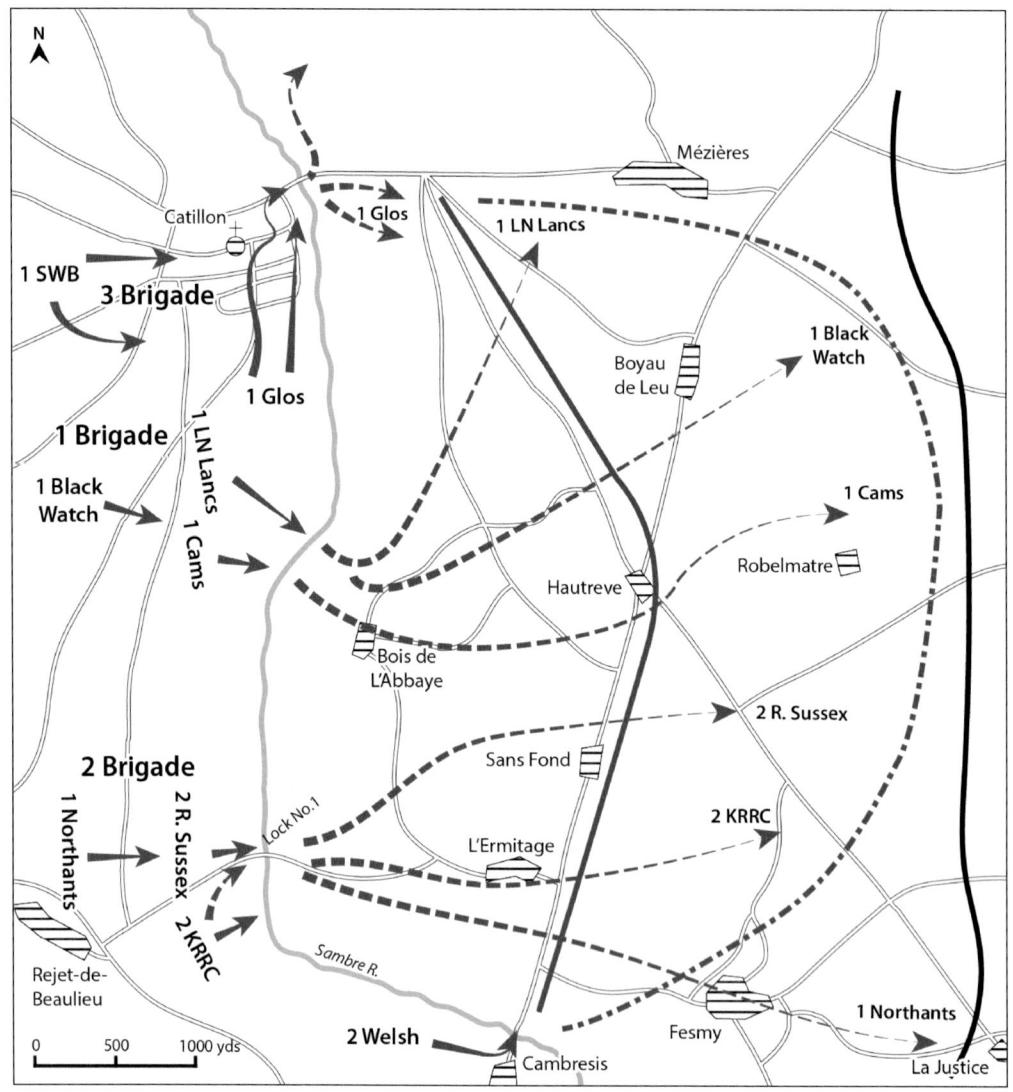

Sambre–-Oise, November 1918.

2 Brigade and 1 Brigade. From left to right, 2nd KRRC, 1st Northants, 1st Camerons and 1st Loyal North Lancs were leading the assault. Each brigade had their third battalion supporting their assaulting units. At midnight on 17 October, the two brigades set off and were in position, close behind the units of 6th Division, by zero hour.

Thick fog, which persisted until about 10 a.m., caused significant difficulties for both brigades. They were unable to find the tracks that had been reconnoitred, therefore they were forced to proceed through Vaux Andigny. The Germans had anticipated such an advance and brought heavy artillery fire down on the village. Nevertheless, 1st Division's assaulting battalions kept in touch with each other and the tail of 6th Division. Whilst 46th Division succeeded in reaching the dotted red line, 6th Division only partially reached their objectives. Furthermore, 6th Division had missed a lot of machine gun positions due to the fog, and so 1st Division found itself engaging with the enemy about 2,000 yards earlier than planned. The battalions had therefore lost the barrage. Having reached the dotted red line, they fought forward for about 1000 yards, which took the 1st Camerons and 1st Loyal North Lancs up to the divisional redline. It was then decided that it was not sensible for the infantry to fight forward with only local artillery support organised by officers on the spot. However, its value had been shown when the HQ of 1st Camerons became surrounded. One platoon was sent out and got behind the enemy to retrieve the situation. The battalion was also helped by a section of 18 pdrs; and it was decided to organise a further barrage for 5.15 p.m. However, this proved to give the artillery too little notice given that communications were slow, with many batteries having moved location. The problems were increased by the Germans dropping gas shells into the British front. Nevertheless, 1st Northamptons did re-take La Vallee Mulatre, from which they had been forced out by the gas shells. They continued forward until they were close to Bellevue. German resistance there was stiffened by a lot of machine guns and so the advance ceased. The division had captured twelve officers and 255 men from four different divisions including *29th Division*, which had been brought up from reserve. It was then decided to organise a further attack late on 18 October as there needed to be time, in daylight, to determine exactly where the British line had reached. The important role that machine guns continued to play in the German defence helps to explain their specific inclusion in the terms of the armistice in November 1918.

Strickland had ordered forward 3 Brigade, and at 6.30 a.m. on 18 October he settled on the details of the attack to be launched at 11.30 a.m. On the 1 Brigade front, the attack was to be carried out by the brigade reserve, 1st Black Watch. They succeeded in capturing Wassigny, with the assistance of 48 guns of 1st MGC, who laid down barrages to support the assault. By nightfall they had gained touch with the French to their right. They were aided in doing so by an attached squadron of the Royal Scots Greys. In addition, 2nd Welsh and 1st South Wales Borderers advanced the line by capturing the Wassigny to Ribeauville road. This then enabled the 1st Gloucesters to be sent forward into Ribeauville, where they met opposition only from hostile artillery fire.

On 19 October, 1st Black Watch moved forward again and met up with the French at Oisy before being relieved by 2nd Welsh. It is an interesting feature that, despite the changing nature of operations, care was taken to relieve brigades. 1 and 2 Brigade led on 17th, 3 Brigade and 1 Brigade led on 18th and at the end of 19th, 1 Brigade became divisional reserve, leaving 2 and 3 Brigade in front. One of the added strains of mobile warfare related to the state of the horses. A divisional order had to be issued forbidding hay to be taken from barns to use as bedding. A number of animals had been put in barns with old material. They had then become sick after eating gassed forage. The animals of both 23rd Co RE and 26th Co RE were noted to be in poor condition so barns could only be used once approved by veterinary officers.[2]

By 20 October, when Strickland received a visit from General Rawlinson, the division had reached a position close to the west bank of the Sambre Canal. The Germans were still holding it. Nevertheless, the possibility of a future operation to cross the canal was recognised, and so the accumulation of maps, bridging materials and reconnaissance by engineers began straight away.[3] Three days later, 1st Division were on the extreme right of an operation involving the whole of XIII Corps as well as 6th Division and themselves. Their local objective was some high ground that would enable them to reach the line of the canal itself.

This time the assault was to be led by (from left to right) 2nd Royal Sussex, 2nd Welsh and 1st Northamptons. Before the attack, some troops in the most forward positions were withdrawn so that a straight line could be used for the opening of the artillery barrage. Despite a German barrage falling on the front line almost immediately after the British barrage opened, all the units managed to reach their objectives and by mid-day posts had been established along, or close to, the canal on a 4000-yard front. This represented a move forward for the division of approximately 2000 yards. Patrols, including engineers, were sent forward, to reconnoitre the approaches to the canal bank.[4]

On 24 October, patrols were pushed out towards Catillon and outposts were established around the western edge of that village. Three days later, Strickland held a conference with his senior officers to discuss possible future operations. At this meeting, it was decided to select two sites to be bridged, one at the lock and a second at a bend in the canal. The lock site had the benefit of being narrower and having solidly constructed ground on each bank. The canal bend had muddy ground on either side and was estimated to be over forty feet wide with a masonry wall on each side. The assessments were checked against aerial photographs and proved to be perfectly accurate. It was felt best that no construction work was needed.

Therefore, on 28 October, a demonstration was given and the types of bridge to be used were decided. For the crossing at the bend, a light bridge, with wheels, supported by Gorman steel floats was selected. The materials were available, the shape of the floats made them easier to move in muddy conditions and overall, the bridge would be as light as possible. Each bridge, whose sections were hinged, was fitted with a lever to release the extension so that there need not be anyone on the far bank to receive it. This was the same system as was used for contemporary fire escapes. There was also a ladder at the end so that the first man could scale up the far side to secure the bridge. The bridge was designed to carry between four and six men at a time. Nevertheless, it was felt that the bridges would mean that the infantry would get across more quickly than by using Berthon boats. At the lock, similar bridges would be used, but here stones would have to be dislodged in order to anchor the bridges. There was no lever release mechanism used there as there was only half the distance to cross. All the supplementary bridges for the infantry were constructed from barrels, and other readily available material as floats. At the lock, a bridge was designed to take tanks. As these bridges were too heavy to move completed, they went forward in two halves. To minimise difficulties, they were designed to be put together

---

2   TNA WO 95/1247: War Diary of the 1st Infantry Division, Ordnance, November 1918.
3   TNA WO 95/1246: War Diary of the 1st Infantry Division, CRE, November 1918.
4   For an account of the overall operations involved in the crossing of the Sambre see the excellent Clayton, D., *Decisive Victory: The Battle of the Sambre, 4 November 1918* (Warwick: Helion, 2018)

using only joists and members, so that a large party of men could be supervised more easily. In this case, the men were to be drawn from 1st Australian Tunnelling Company. The transport bridges were effectively constructed by laying two infantry bridges beside each other without the central elements. The complexity of operations at the lock meant that 26 Co RE would be assisted by 409 Co RE whilst 23 Coy. RE would have sole responsibility for the canal bend.[5]

That hard fighting remained to be done was evident during an operation by 1 Brigade on 29 October. A minor operation to reach the canal bank was blocked by a German strongpoint. It required a further attack, in the afternoon, to capture it. Over succeeding days, the Germans made attacks on outpost lines, some of which were successful. This necessitated local operations by 1st Division to regain their outpost lines. On 1 November, 1st Gloucesters were attacked by a party of 200 Germans under cover of both artillery and trench mortar fire. The attack was beaten off. Meanwhile the GOC was holding a conference with all his senior officers. They were discussing the attack being planned to force the Oise-Sambre Canal. The attack involved IX Corps (of Fourth Army) attacking with 1st and 32nd Divisions. 1st Division was on the right of its Corps front, with the French 66th Division, of XV Corps, on its right. The need to reflect the varying objectives of the divisions on their flanks, meant that 1st Division artillery were given lengthy instructions about areas into which fire should not be directed. The British artillery had been organised into three groups; of which 1st Division's artillery were in Group 3, under the command of Lieutenant Colonel Scarlett DSO, 7th Baron Abinger.

The next day, 1st Camerons and 23rd Company RE practised the arrangements for bridging during the forthcoming assault. The GOC watched their preparations and on 3 November he visited all his brigadiers in their HQs. That day saw 1 and 2nd Brigades advance to their assembly positions; their leading battalions began relieving 3 Brigade in their positions on the canal, opposite the points of attack. In a miniature way, this reflected the way that the arrival of the Canadians had been screened at Amiens in August. By 5.25 a.m. on 4 November, the assault troops were in position. All the officers in the assaulting battalions had benefitted from studying aerial photographs. These photographs helped identify streams that could not be identified by patrols. All the briefings to officers were then passed on to the NCOs and men. The British barrage was designed to deliver three minutes of intense fire on the German positions on the canal before lifting for four minutes to the general line of the canal on the eastern side. 1st MGC were also barraging the German front, two sections of 'C' company supported the 2nd Royal Sussex at the lock.

The 1 Brigade assault was planned to be in two parts. The first involved 1st Camerons and 1st Loyal North Lancs reaching the first set of objectives across the canal including Hautreve. For this first phase, the Camerons had decided C and D companies would lead, with A and B in support, and that the responsibilities would reverse in phase two. It was planned to halt on the first objective for one-and-a half hours. Then 1st Black Watch would leapfrog through the right of 1st Loyal North Lancs to assist 1st Camerons in the second phase. Phase 2 had Mézières and Fesmy amongst its objectives. Meanwhile, 1st Gloucesters would assist the left flank by establishing bridgeheads on the eastern side of Catillon.

5   TNA WO 95/1234: War Diary of the 1st Infantry Division, Headquarters & CRE, October 1918, Appendices.

The 1st Camerons and 1st Loyal North Lancs took up positions behind a row of parallel hedges which were between 300 and 800 yards from the canal. The battalions shared a headquarters in a sunken road. Under camouflage, the bridges were in the orchard to the rear of the hedges. The assault by 1 Brigade, supported by 1st TMB, went according to plan with the bridges in place ten minutes after zero, and the infantry across ten minutes later. Second Lieutenant Bryson MC led his platoon from D company forward as the covering party for the sappers. Another platoon from B company carried ropes and lifebelts to assist the engineers. Here the German barrage fell behind the leading battalions. 1 Brigade felt that the fog assisted them by obscuring their position. Bryson was the first across the canal. The battalion moved forward to the village of Bois de L'Abbaye. The success of the Camerons in taking this village and capturing a lot of the defenders was assisted by the artillery. There was a pre-planned pause in the movement of the creeping barrage. The barrage rested on the village for twenty minutes. This is another example of the increasing sophistication of British Army operational methods by the final months of the war. 1st Camerons advanced to the dotted-blue line, by 8.30 a.m., still shrouded in mist, capturing many Germans en-route.

Advancing in support, 1st Black Watch encountered some organised resistance. In one case, a formal assault had to be made against a building. Lieutenant Wilson DCM was wounded in this assault. Once captured, the building disgorged its garrison of three officers and fifty men. One German machine gun on the west bank tried to resist, but was silenced by a Sergeant of 23rd RE. Others, on the east bank, were eliminated by the leading platoons of 1st Loyal North Lancs. Their left company linked up with 1st Gloucesters east of Catillon. This operation demonstrates the more sophisticated approach of 1918. Previously, the attack methodology would have included the village in the initial assault and probably would have led to failure due to difficulties in the village. Here it is being treated like a large strongpoint that needs to be by-passed. Therefore 3 Brigade was tasked with capturing it, in an operation separate from crossing the canal.

The capture of Catillon is an excellent example of the standard operational method applied to a specific action. There was a dedicated barrage by 298th Brigade RFA and A company of 1st MGC. As well as the 3rd TMB, the infantry had the support of a section of tanks from A company 10th battalion of Tank Corps. The latter proved particularly useful in eliminating the persistent resistance of machine gunners situated in houses near the church. With this support, 1st Gloucesters, advancing from the south, and 1st South Wales Borderers advancing from the west, were able to end all German resistance. They found that the Germans had bound up a large mass of farm machinery in barbed wire. Then it had been pushed into the river. The tangled mess was cleared.

The subsidiary element of the main assault by 2 Brigade went well. The bridgehead on the canal near Cambresis was secured by 2 Platoon of C company, 2nd Welsh, led by Lieutenant Roberts. They captured two machine guns and took 23 prisoners, at the cost of six wounded. The battalion then held its position and provided fire support to 2nd Royal Sussex during their assault. On the right, a swampy stream added to the difficulties, faced by 2 Brigade, in capturing the lock. Presumably, the German artillery had pre-registered on this feature, as this is where the heaviest and most accurate artillery fire fell upon the advancing British troops. The British artillery noted that this sector saw the greatest fire from German 15cm howitzers. It was the most obvious place to attempt a crossing so the Germans were prepared.

The 2nd Royal Sussex, led by No. 11 Platoon of C company and No.5 Platoon of B company, advanced with sappers and men of 1st MGC. However, the bridge sections were too short, and, just as some men managed to scramble across, the first German shells landed. Officers then took charge of re-organising the leading troops to get the bridges into place. Naturally, this meant delays. More German salvoes fell amongst the troops, causing casualties amongst both the infantry and the sappers. This shelling caused the succeeding waves to become bunched up with the assault wave. The German shelling had broken up the attack, but the CO of 2nd Royal Sussex took charge. According to his VC citation:

> The position was strong and the assaulting and bridging parties were halted on arrival at the waterway 100 yards from the canal by a heavy barrage. At this point Lieutenant Colonel Johnson arrived and personally led an assault but heavy fire again broke up the attack. He reorganized the assaulting and bridging parties and this time effected a crossing but the success of this dangerous operation was entirely due to his splendid leadership.[6]

As the plan had allowed the infantry four minutes to effect a crossing, it is clear how difficult the situation was, that Johnson had now retrieved. The bridge intended for reaching the lock was put into place over the stream, by a mixed group of sappers and infantry. Johnson's leadership was reflected in his men. Once across the stream to the canal bank, they immediately engaged the defenders of the lock houses. The Germans had sited numerous machine guns in these buildings. It was noted that Lewis gunners stood up, firing from the hip, traversing their weapons. They were assisted in doing so by the eight mortars of 2nd TMB, who fired 600 rounds. They were in close support because it was felt that the artillery could not fire on the buildings, as the assaulting troops would be too close. The next bridge, across the lock, was placed in position under the personal supervision of Major Findlay MC, of 409 Co RE, assisted by Lieutenant Mansfield and 28 men of 1st Northants brought forward from support. Due to the congestion and confusion, A company of 2nd KRRC had difficulty carrying out the plan for it to cross by a subsidiary bridge, a hundred yards south of the lock.

Once the main bridge was laid out, the 2nd Royal Sussex crossed in force, and the 2nd KRRC passed over too. The leading units of the latter overlapped with the tail of 2nd Royal Sussex, but despite this the units moved on to reach their first objectives on schedule. In the ranks of 2nd KRRC were fourteen men who had just joined the battalion on the evening it marched forward.

By 9:17a.m., reports had reached Strickland that all six of his assaulting battalions were across the canal. Fifteen minutes later, the barrage started that was to trigger the second phase of the advance. On the left, 1st Loyal North Lancs advanced and secured the Catillon-Mézières road. Mézières was the ultimate objective for 1st Black Watch, their assault being led by B, C and D companies. 1st Camerons continued their advance, the fog now having cleared. Some German resistance to A and B companies occurred around the village of Robelmetre, but D company of 1st Camerons moved to the flank and reached its second objective. Further German resistance at La Gambotte brought 1 Brigade's advance to a halt. The 1st Loyal North Lancs encountered stiff opposition at La Galop Farm. When it was finally captured, they noted that eleven of the

---

6 *The London Gazette (Supplement)*, 3 January 1919.

prisoners were holders of the Iron Cross. The 1st Black Watch also took part in this assault and laid claim to the capture of three 77mm guns. This battalion also noted that the Germans retreated to a prepared position, and that even the supporting trench mortars could not dislodge them from it. Around Mézières, 1st Black Watch's B company surprised some German gunners and captured about fifty men and a dozen horses. Two German officers who tried to ride off were shot dead, as were the horse teams of two limbers. Meanwhile Second Lieutenant Grant, C company, was wounded in the arm and leg whilst carrying a white flag offering to allow some other German gunners to surrender. He was one of the three officers of 1st Black Watch that were wounded that day. Of the men, four were killed and thirty were wounded.

Once the fog cleared it was evident to the 2nd Royal Sussex that the enemy resistance would revolve around isolated machine guns. To help suppress these, they had the help of elements of 2nd TMB, who advanced in support. The battalion report said that as the battalion was evenly spread, and facing light opposition, they were able to advance after the planned halt, in conformity with the Camerons, whilst pivoting to create a defensive flank. On the right, 2nd KRRC also advanced using three companies echeloned in depth, against "slight" opposition and were able to form a defensive flank for 2nd Royal Sussex. Throughout 2 Brigade's assault, 1st Northamptons had been in close support. They then went forward at 2 p.m. to assault Fesmy where the Germans were putting up resistance. The stiffest resistance was found at the eastern end of the village, and the support of 2nd TMB was instrumental in eliminating almost all the pockets of resistance by 4.30p.m. when it was getting dark. The 1st Northamptons had difficulty in the darkness making touch with the French, on their right. By 5 a.m. next morning this junction had been achieved at the crossroads in La Justice.

During the morning, two sections of 26 Co RE arrived to assist. Bridges to allow tanks and pack transport across were put in place with their help, despite periodic barrages by the Germans. The day had proved to be one of great success for 1st Division; twenty artillery pieces, 1698 prisoners and 20,000 square yards were captured. In addition to forcing the canal crossing, the division had liberated Catillon, Mézières and Fesmy as well as seven hamlets. Due mainly to the initial phase, 2nd Royal Sussex lost one officer and eight men killed, with four missing. They also had seven officers and 86 men wounded. The battalion had entered the action with twelve subalterns; of these Second Lieutenant Loader was killed and five more were wounded. They listed material captured as two field guns, seven trench mortars (including four heavy ones) and fifty machine guns. In addition, they took 200 prisoners. Johnson's VC was announced later but the battalion recorded five awards of the MC to officers, and four receiving a Bar to their MC. Eight men were awarded the DCM and fourteen the MM. The accompanying 2nd KRRC lost two officers and ten men killed, with one officer and 59 men wounded and three missing. The 1st Camerons claimed to have bagged approximately 500 prisoners as well as 25 machine guns, four field guns and six trench mortars. The 1st Loyal North Lancs recorded seven dead, four missing and 41 wounded in achieving a haul of approximately 400 prisoners, five field guns and six trench mortars as well as 82 machine guns, of which 36 were heavy. The haul of 1st Black Watch was put at five 77mm guns, eleven horses and 133 prisoners, of which five were officers.

A 3 p.m. conference determined that 1st Division would now be relieved by 46th Division. Over the next three days of pouring rain, 1st Division was gradually squeezed out of the line by brigades of 46th Division. There was a notable departure on 8 November when the A-A & QMG, Lieutenant Colonel Spender-Clay, left for London. An old Etonian, and former officer in the Life Guards, he had served in the Boer War. Spender-Clay was the Conservative MP for

Tunbridge and was returning to Parliament after fifteen months with 1st Division. As armistice negotiations were already underway, his departure must have confirmed to his colleagues that the end was in sight.[7]

The troops trained on 9 November and Strickland held a church parade on the penultimate day of the fighting. It was attended by representatives of all units in the division. Meanwhile, the "pursuit" of the Germans was being undertaken by the cavalry, armoured cars, and cyclists. On the following morning, 1st Division troops were continuing training as the news came of the cessation of hostilities. The First Division had served continuously on the Western Front throughout the war. Of those who had served in its ranks, 16,000 had been killed. Many corners of many fields would be forever Irish, Welsh, Scottish, or English; made so by their sacrifice. Many too had been wounded; for the disabled and mentally scarred there would be more, often lonely, battles to come.

---

7   TNA WO 95/1234: War Diary of the 1st Infantry Division, Headquarters, 5-8 November 1918.

42

Occupation of Germany

On 12 November 1918, the 1st Division Headquarters received preliminary orders for a move forward to the Rhine. On the following day, the divisional headquarters and each of the brigades were embussed and advanced towards the Rhine. On 14 November Fifth Army's Brigade of RHA joined 1st Division and came under the orders of the CRA. A further accession of strength came the following day when a platoon of IX Corps cyclists was attached to the division. On 16 November 1 Brigade, in the lead, advanced to Hestrud. It was at Hestrud that they recorded meeting many escaped prisoners of war. The former prisoners were processed and sent to the rear.[1] This suggests that the retreating German army may have quickly released prisoners that they held, as the Allied blockade of Germany remained in operation and therefore prisoners of war would constitute an additional burden on an already overstretched food supply.

The primary concern of the German High Command was to bring the army home to avoid a Bolshevik-style revolution. As the Kaiser departed, General Groener telephoned Ebert, the leader of the Socialists who had declared a republic in Berlin. Groener offered Ebert the support of the army in return for Ebert confirming the authority of the officers over the army. Thus, there would be no repeat of the Russian army's phase of electing its officers and a potential coup by the Independent Socialists (USPD) would be blocked. Releasing POWs was a small price to pay to achieve these larger aims.

At 2 p.m. on 17 November, Major General Strickland held a conference of his senior officers to discuss the future movement of the division. The advance proceeded with 2nd Cavalry Division in the lead as a screen, and 1st Black Watch close behind on 1st Division's front, to protect the road repairing parties made up from the 6th Welsh (Pioneers) and 23rd Field Company RE. On the following day, the advance continued with Strickland being given a civic welcome when he moved his headquarters forward to Barbencon Chateau. In this advance, 1st Division was the left of IX Corp's advance, with 66th Division on their right and the French 36th Corps to their left. 1st Division advanced at 8.30 a.m. with 1st Brigade leading and the other brigades following. The advance continued for the next three days.[2] The advance was to be carried out with caution; divisional orders stated that any units not covered by the advanced guard (that is,

---

1 TNA WO 95/1234: War Diary of the 1st Infantry Division, Headquarters, 12-16 November 1918.
2 TNA WO 95/1234: War Diary of the 1st Infantry Division, Headquarters, 17-21 November 1918.

on different roads) should provide their own advance guard and fifty yards should be maintained between groups.³

General Sir Henry Rawlinson, GOC Fourth Army, visited Strickland's headquarters, which had now moved forward to Castillon. Thus there was an opportunity for the divisional band to play on the village green to which the local inhabitants responded by dancing to the waltzes. Another divisional conference was held at Bouvignes on 25 November, which was followed by the GOC and his staff joining the Burgomaster for drinks at his invitation. The town had seen 20 houses burnt and 31 civilians shot by the German *178th Regiment* as they advanced in 1914. The divisional staff was also experiencing change, as Lieutenant Colonel Barnard DSO assumed his new duties as GSO1, replacing Lieutenant Colonel Tandy DSO, who had been appointed as Brigadier-General General Staff of XIX Corps. The latter was not destined to be part of the force occupying the Rhine. The ongoing importance of good staff work was underlined by the decision to cancel the advance on 26 November, due to the difficulties in maintaining logistical support to the advancing troops.⁴

An intelligence report dated 25 November includes an assessment of the state of returning British prisoners of war. It observed that the majority were malnourished, that they had often had only one bath since capture, and that some had received a change of underwear that was made from paper. An example of such garments can be found in the Royal Welsh Fusilier's Museum.⁵ The report detailed that the prisoners had suffered being struck by their guards, and that the worst periods had been during the British advance in 1918. The men had generally been used to carry out heavy manual lifting tasks and were most bitter about the way the German female clerks had spat in their faces.⁶

At midnight on 28 November, IX Corps became part of Second Army. Brigadier-General Lewin assumed temporary command the next day, whilst Strickland went off on leave to England. However, a greater sense of urgency is evident in the orders received on 30 November to resume the advance and to be across the Meuse by 4 December.⁷

The 1st Division responded by beginning to cross the Meuse on 1 December and several elements had crossed by the following day. The reserve element of the division crossed on 3 December, with the forward elements remaining stationary so that it became more concentrated. Brigadier-General Lewin as officer commanding, and the divisional staff, were entertained to dinner by the owner of Rochefort Chateau. This hospitality was reciprocated by Divisional HQ, who gave a dance, which was enjoyed by the local inhabitants at the Hotel de Ville at 8 p.m. on 4 December. On the following night, a dance was given at the same venue by the other ranks of the divisional headquarters, and this was attended by a much wider number of local inhabitants.⁸ Thus a good relationship was established, with due regard to social protocol. As the division was now advancing through recovered territory attention had to be given to

---

3 TNA WO 95/1234: War Diary of the 1st Infantry Division, Headquarters, order dated 17 November 1918.
4 TNA WO 95/1234: War Diary of the 1st Infantry Division, Headquarters, 22-25 November 1918.
5 This can be found at <http://1914-1918.invisionzone.com/forums/topic/17636-paper-undies/>; accessed 30/09/17.
6 TNA WO 95/1234: War Diary of the 1st Infantry Division, Headquarters, intelligence report dated 25 November.
7 TNA WO 95/1234: War Diary of the 1st Infantry Division, Headquarters, 22-30 November 1918.
8 TNA WO 95/1234: War Diary of the 1st Infantry Division, Headquarters, 1-5 December 1918.

how billeting was managed. Where possible municipal buildings were to be used. If billeting was to be organised in private dwellings, then billeting certificates had to be issued even if the inhabitants were absent. In the latter case, the billeting certificates should be issued to the local Maire. Orders were also issued to remind troops that "messes were not a public expense". It was stated that the normal daily rate was 1 Franc for the mess and 50 centimes for the kitchen. No one could accuse the army hierarchy of being slow to spot this potential cost issue, the relevant circular had been issued on 13 November.[9]

Meanwhile, the band of the Northamptonshire regiment was sent to Tournai to entrain for Germany. The first three miles took over fifteen hours due to the obsession of French and Belgian officials with regulations, according to Lieutenant Timpson. However, once the train began to make progress it was still possible for the men to get off, secure fuel and get back on again. The fuel was needed for the braziers constructed in each carriage from petrol tins or buckets. To afford these constructions sufficient draughts of air, the men would swing them out of the train. One corporal in the Royal Engineers, who had served since Mons, confirmed his reputation for being adept in more ways than one. Not only did he acquire a proper stove, but he also contrived to hide the pipe with a waterproof sheet so that the smoke issued out of the slightly open door.[10]

On 6 December, orders were received that the march to the Rhine was to be postponed until 9 December, and the nature of this advance was reflected in the arrival of the colours of the units from Britain (though the Adjutant, according to the usage of the time, refers to England). The groups in which the division had been advancing were amended so that the artillery would now move with the main body; the only exception to this was that Fifth Army Brigade RHA would remain with the advanced group. On 7 December, Major General Strickland returned from leave and resumed command. Two days later, the march to the Rhine resumed, and 1st Division proceeded in four groups - Advanced, Support, Reserve and HQ, in that order. On 12 December, Strickland visited all four groups, before the advance partially resumed on 13 December when only the advanced group moved forward. On that day too, the Fifth Army Brigade RHA received the probably welcome orders that they had been transferred to the HQ group and should therefore remain in their billets until the HQ group caught up with them.[11]

The advance continued and the first climactic moment was reached on 16 December when 1st Division crossed into Germany just east of Beho. There the unit colours were unfurled, and Strickland took the salute. On the following day, the support group crossed the German border with the same attendant ceremonial. Meanwhile the advance group was moving five miles forward uphill across a barren area, to reach a level 1800 yards above sea level. On 18 December, amidst periodic blizzards, the reserve group began crossing the border with Strickland taking the salute, but his role in the proceedings was omitted due to the "continued inclemency of the weather" when the remainder of the division crossed on 19 December. Strickland could go back overnight to the houses erected for the director and engineers of the munitions factory just east of Allmuthen. These had been taken over by the divisional staff on 18 December. Having made

---

9 TNA WO 95/1238: War Diary of the 1st Infantry Division, Headquarters, AA& QMG, 4 December 1918.
10 R.V. Emden, *1918; The Decisive Year in the Soldiers' Own Words and Photographs*, (Barnsley: Pen & Sword, 2018), pp.332-333.
11 TNA WO 95/1234: War Diary of the 1st Infantry Division, Headquarters, 6-13 December 1918.

some progress in the bad conditions, and following overnight snowfalls, the whole division was allowed to rest on 20 December.[12]

When the march was resumed on 21 December, the men had to cope with the wet conditions created by a partial thaw. On 23 December, the advanced group reached their final areas and divisional HQ transferred from Allmuthen to Rheinbach. This was the point at which the march groups began to be dissolved, and the brigades returned to operating as brigades. This process continued on Christmas Eve, as the support and reserve groups reached their final areas. All three brigade HQs were visited that day by Strickland. This meant that on Christmas Day, heavy snow having fallen overnight, the division could remain at rest and that "The officers and OR of all units of Div. HQ had excellent Xmas dinners, all having turkeys and plum puddings."[13]

By 28 December 1918, all the units were in final positions. The 1st Division was disposed as follows;

1st Infantry Brigade with HQ at Bornheim	1st Black Watch – Roisdorf, 1st Loyal North Lancs – Bornheim, 1st Camerons – Dersdorf No 1 Field Ambulance - Hemmerich
2nd Infantry Brigade with HQ at Medinghoven	2nd Royal Sussex at Witterschlick, 1st Northants at Duisdorf, 2nd KRRC moving to Alfter, (on 30th) No 2 Field Ambulance moving to Volmershoven
3rd Infantry Brigade with HQ at Burg Ringsheim	1st SW Borderers at Kircheim, 1st Gloucesters at Palmersheim, 2nd Welsh at Flamersheim, No 141 Field Ambulance at Odendorf
Divisional Artillery with HQ at Burg Kriegshoven	25th Bgd RFA at Morehoven, 39th Brigade RFA at Miel, 5th Brigade RHA at Heimerzheim, 1st DAC at Metternich, 5th BAC at Dunstrkoven
1st Bn MGC at Flerzheim and Luftelberg	
1/6 Welsh (Pioneers) at Ersdorf	
Div Eng HQ plus 23rd, 26th and 409th Fd Co RE at Ober and Nieder Drees	
Reception Camp at Euskirchen	

On 30 December, a conference regarding education was held, chaired by Strickland; this was attended by all brigadiers, unit commanders, and the education officers of each unit. On the following day, 1 January 1919, the divisional staff and the staff of 3rd Brigade went off shooting at

---

12   TNA WO 95/1234: War Diary of the 1st Infantry Division, Headquarters, 14-20 December 1918.
13   TNA WO 95/1234: War Diary of the 1st Infantry Division, Headquarters, 21-25 December 1918.

Arensbergche, but noted that there was little sport.[14] More importantly, for 56 men of 1st Loyal North Lancs, New Year's Day was the day they were demobilised.[15] Better news for 2nd Brigade came on 2 January 1919 during a divisional conference on equipment and organisation; IX Corps confirmed that Lieutenant Colonel Johnson of the South Wales Borderers, in command of 2nd Royal Sussex, had been awarded the Victoria Cross for his bravery on 4 November 1918 during the assault crossing of the Sambre Canal.[16]

The BEF was now in possession of some of the key Rhine crossings. For the moment it would be the 1st Division and their colleagues in the Army of Occupation who would be maintaining the "Wacht am Rhein". The negotiations regarding the future of these strategic points would be discussed at the forthcoming Versailles Conference.

---

14 TNA WO 95/1234: War Diary of the 1st Infantry Division, Headquarters, 28 December 1918-1 January 1919.
15 TNA WO 95/1266: War Diary of the 1st Loyal North Lancs, 1 January 1919.
16 TNA WO 95/1234: War Diary of the 1st Infantry Division, Headquarters, 28 December 1918-2 January 1919.

43

The Post-War British Officer Corps

On 4 January 1919, the future of the senior officers was given attention as Strickland held a conference on the future organisation of the army. General Plumer subsequently arrived and was introduced to and interviewed each brigadier individually.[1] The context for these conversations is evident in Sir Henry Wilson's diaries. In January 1919, he had two great concerns. The first was the loss of discipline in the BEF due to the pressure from the men for rapid demobilisation. The day before Plumer's arrival, 10,000 men had refused to re-embark at Folkstone to return to France. The second was the need to secure enough men to cover the needs of the army going forward. He noted that Ireland had already requested reinforcements and that the Army of the Rhine was to be composed of ten infantry divisions plus two cavalry divisions. There was the need to garrison India as well as numerous other strategic posts.[2] Whilst enlisting the press's help to secure favourable coverage on how to retain manpower, thought had also to be given to those who were to be given commands.

Of the three, Brigadier-General Wheatley (1876-1954) of 1st Brigade (Argyll and Sutherland Highlanders), was the son of a Lieutenant Colonel in the Royal Artillery. Wheatley held the substantive rank of Major with a Brevet as a Lieutenant Colonel, and the Temporary rank of Brigadier-General. Having joined the army in 1896 and won the DSO for his part in the defence of Chakdarra Fort in 1898, he had also served on the staff of the army in India. Wheatley had spent a month in early March 1917 commanding 1st Battalion Royal Scots Fusiliers and had been appointed to the command of 1st Brigade on 22 September 1918. He was therefore a 42-year-old career soldier, who had married a year earlier and who would later become a member of the Corps of Gentlemen at Arms.[3] Holding only the substantive rank of Major, he returned to duty with the Argyll & Sutherland Highlanders in 1919. He subsequently served as a senior officer with the Territorial Army during the Second World War.

Wheatley's colleague, Brigadier Kelly of 2nd Brigade, had first assumed command of the brigade on 23 March 1918, a fortnight after Brigadier-General Sir W Kay Bt. was wounded.

---

1 TNA WO 95/1234: War Diary of the 1st Infantry Division, Headquarters, 4 January 1919.
2 Callwell, C, *Field Marshal Sir Henry Wilson*, Vol. 2, (London: Cassell, 1927) pp 160-78
3 See *Prabrook* <http://prabook.com/web/person-view.html?profileId=735415> and *Online Library* <http://www.ebooksread.com/authors-eng/arthur-charles-fox-davies/armorial-families--a-directory-of-gentlemen-of-coat-armour-volume-2-dxo/page-253-armorial-families--a-directory-of-gentlemen-of-all> (accessed 9 October 2017).

Kelly himself became the seventh commander of 2nd Brigade to be wounded. Having been wounded on 26 September 1918, he returned to command ten days after the armistice. Like Kay, Kelly had been commissioned into the King's Royal Rifle Corps. He had seen early service as a subaltern in Somaliland in a mounted infantry force. In January 1915 he was mentioned in despatches by Sir John French.[4]

The commander of 3rd Brigade was Brigadier-General E St G Aubyn (1880-1960), the son of Colonel Edward St Aubyn. Like his colleagues, St Aubyn was of relatively recent vintage as a brigadier as he had only been appointed on 6 October 1918, after Brigadier-General Sir W Kay Baronet, who, had been killed on 4 October whilst commanding 3rd Brigade. St Aubyn was the son of a barrister. He had been educated at Eton and Cambridge. He would go on to be awarded the DSO and the Croix de Guerre in 1919. His only post-war command, following demobilisation, was 128 Brigade in the years 1928 to 1932. This was a territorial brigade drawn from units related to Hampshire. St Aubyn was also Deputy Lieutenant of Hampshire. Therefore, his role with the Territorial Army did not really constitute an extension of his wartime career.

Strickland, himself, was transferred to command 6th Division in Ireland in 1919. Strickland was GOC Cork at the time Cork was burned by the Auxiliaries. He was then placed in charge of the military inquiry by Lloyd-George. Strickland subsequently attended a Cabinet meeting at which it was agreed not to publish the report as it would undermine British policy in Ireland.[5] Having proved his loyalty to the state, Strickland's own failures were overlooked. After the creation of the Irish Free State in 1922, Strickland moved to command 2nd Division. After several years as GOC British Forces in Egypt, Strickland retired in 1931 having attained the rank of General.

It was clear that the British Army would be reduced in size from its wartime expansion and therefore Plumer was assessing which officers might be continuing and to what extent their acting rank rather than their substantive rank would be reflected in their future careers. Strickland's career would continue alongside new highflyers like Gerald Boyd. Boyd had been appointed to command the unfancied 46th Division. Their triumph at the Hindenburg Line propelled Boyd into senior staff roles working directly for the CIGS.

4　See *KRRC Association* <http://www.krrcassociation.com/index.php/history/13-first-world-war/35-the-first-world-war?start=3> (accessed 9 October 2017).
5　Younger, C., *Ireland's Civil War* (London: Fontana, 1979, pp.129-30.

44

A Last Hurrah

On 15 January 1919, the strain of demobilisation was sufficiently strong for an application to be made to set a minimum threshold for units in order that they could function effectively.[1] For 1st Loyal North Lancs, who had only one of their old team left, the impact of demobilisation offered a partial explanation for the 5-2 defeat in the football match against 1st Camerons. However, the subsequent 3-1 defeat suffered at the hands of 1st Black Watch was ascribed to a less good performance. At a lower level, the inter-platoon football competition within the battalion culminated in the triumph of No. 13 Platoon in the final where they defeated No.1 Platoon.[2]

The team representing 1st Camerons went on to win the divisional competition,[3] so putting up a good show against them was creditable, with hindsight. On 16 January, Strickland and the brigadiers of 2 and 3 Brigades and several officers went shooting. The class divides in sport at home were fully reflected in those during military service.

As noted above, Field Marshal Wilson was worried about retaining the men needed to meet Britain's strategic commitments. Bound up in class attitudes, he failed to recognise that the other ranks were not likely to appreciate all the pseudo-education being imposed on them. On the positive side, 7 January, saw Captain Ozanne of the "Intelligence Corps (Propaganda)" give lectures on the housing scheme. These were well attended and appreciated, according to the official source.[4] The attendance at evening training lectures was around 50-70 men of the Loyal North Lancs. This number represents less than 10 per cent of those still serving. As the promised "Homes Fit for Heroes" were later slashed under the Geddes Axe, the absentees missed little.

Of less benefit in retaining the men's interest in soldiering, Reverend Gay arrived on 14 January and delivered two lectures on "dramatic recitals". A week later the men received Gough's prebendary lecture on the subject of "Democracy and citizenship". Given the government's failure to include soldiers in the "Khaki Election" of 1918, lecturing them on democracy is

---

1 TNA WO 95/1234: War Diary of the 1st Infantry Division, Headquarters, 14-15 January 1919.
2 TNA WO 95/1266: War Diary of the 1st Loyal North Lancs, 15-22 January 1919.
3 TNA WO 95/1266: War Diary of the 1st Cameron Highlanders, February 1919.
4 TNA WO 95/1234: War Diary of the 1st Infantry Division, Headquarters, 7 January 1919.

loaded with irony. Of greater moment than the lectures for 1 Brigade was that they finally had showers and were issued with their first change of underwear since the armistice.[5]

Another visitor was Brigadier-General Guggisberg DSO from the training department at GHQ. A Canadian-born, Royal Engineer officer, Guggisberg would by the end of 1919 have swapped the cold weather on the Rhine for the warmth of the Gold Coast, of which he had been made governor.[6] GHQ was providing little except jobs for the boys and opportunities for busybodies. The men also had to listen to a lecture on Canada by Lieutenant Somers. Viscount Broome's lecture on the role of the Royal Navy in relation to minesweeping must have seemed especially relevant. As the weather was generally cold, the attraction of these events may be explained by them being indoors! With such entertainment to keep them going, the remaining 36 officers and 824 men of the 1st Loyal North Lancs were unlikely to share the CIGS desire to slow demobilisation.[7]

Some sport did more to divert men's attention from pending demobilisation. In February, 1st Camerons won not only the divisional football title but also were divisional champions in the light-weight and catch-weight tug of war competitions.[8] The end of February saw the triumphant 1st Camerons and 1st Loyal North Lancs receive orders to proceed to England. The boxing championships saw fewer Scottish successes, as the featherweight title went to Lance Corporal Ward of 1st Black Watch but the bantam division was won by Gunner Iredale of the RHA. Welsh successes came in the light and welter weights; won by Drummer Cotton of 2nd Welsh, and Lance Corporal Philips of 1/6th Welsh respectively. Private Buckler of 1st MGC won the middleweight title, and the unit had double cause for celebration when Private Bradley took the heavyweight title.

The sporting day concluded with a dinner at which 118 officers sat down. Major General Strickland proposed a toast to the First Division. In his speech he referred to their many engagements. He also referred to Captain Robinson, Quartermaster of 2nd KRRC, who was the only officer to have served with the division from its arrival in France through to the end without a break.

On 2 January 1919 during a divisional conference on equipment and organisation; IX Corps had confirmed that Lieutenant Colonel Johnson of the South Wales Borderers, in command of 2nd Royal Sussex, had been awarded the Victoria Cross for his bravery on 4 November 1918 during the assault crossing of the Sambre Canal.[9] News of awards relating to the final phase of the war continued to flow in; the 1st Loyal North Lancs were delighted that Captain Bare DSO, MC, Lieutenant (acting Captain) Roberts and Lance Corporal O'Brien had been gazetted as Mentioned in Despatches on 27 December 1918.[10] The New Year's Honours included an MC for Captain Robertson of 1st Camerons alongside a DCM for CSM Ford and an MSM for each of Sergeants Pearson and Eagleson.[11]

---

5   TNA WO 95/1266: War Diary of the 1st Loyal North Lancs, 7-10 January 1919.
6   As detailed at *British Empire.co.uk* <http://www.britishempire.co.uk/biography/guggisberg.htm> (accessed 11 October 2017).
7   TNA WO 95/1266: War Diary of the 1st Loyal North Lancs, 31 January 1919.
8   TNA WO 95/1266: War Diary of the 1st Cameron Highlanders, February 1919.
9   TNA WO 95/1234: War Diary of the 1st Infantry Division, Headquarters, 28 December 1918, 2 January 1919.
10 TNA WO 95/1266: War Diary of the 1st Loyal North Lancs, 6 January 1919.
11 TNA WO 95/1266: War Diary of the 1st Cameron Highlanders, February 1919.

Early March saw the departure of the regular battalions as they were replaced by units such as 51st Cheshires, some of which were seriously under strength. There was also fear of riots in Bonn; 2nd Brigade were tasked with covering the Rhine bridges if 32nd Division had to deal with riots. By 12 March, it was noted that the division was changing its spots and that de-mobilisation fever was easing, as most of those eligible had gone home.

Nevertheless, one final triumph for 1st Division lay ahead. Two days later, 1st Camerons beat 1st Leicesters (of 6th Division) with the army commander amongst the crowd. Their triumphant progress continued, on 17 March when they beat the Corps RE, by two goals to one, to become the Corps champions. The divisional command noted that their inability to shoot meant the victory was narrower than it might have been. Despite a continued weakness in taking too long to shoot, 1st Camerons beat the X Corps champions and the II Corps champions on the way to the final of the Army Commander's Cup. The final saw 3000 men entrained from 1st Division to watch it. They were not disappointed, as 1st Camerons scored after only ten minutes. Their opponents, 8th Black Watch, did equalise, during a goalmouth scramble, with ten minutes to go. However, with five minutes left, the 8th Black Watch's goalkeeper fell over in the snowy conditions. Taking advantage of the situation, 1st Camerons scored again. General Plumer presented the cup; it was effectively the last triumph for 1st Division. It had been re-designated as the Western Division of the Army of Occupation on 15 March. Thus the distinguished service of 1st Division closed after four years and nearly eight months of continuous service on the Western Front.

Appendix I

Planning a War

In 1914, the British government despatched an expeditionary force to Europe. The decision to support France in a war against Germany represented continuity with the policy of "maintaining the balance of power in Europe". Great Britain had followed this policy at least since the 17th Century, but arguably even from before that. Cromwell had allied with France against the Dutch who were Britain's commercial rivals. Subsequently, Britain had been a key partner in the coalition that blunted French ambitions in the period of Louis XIV of France. Later Britain allied with Prussia against Louis XV and subsequently the two were allied again at Waterloo in 1815 to bring about the defeat of Napoleon. Britain then supported Prussia's aggrandisement at the Congress of Vienna to balance the vast strength of Russia. Prussia was to help balance France by maintaining the "Wacht am Rhein". Prussia was granted the Rhenish provinces to ensure she would be a strong power on France's eastern border. Lord Castlereagh preferred to see Prussia grow rather than see the already powerful Russian Empire gain a permanent presence on the Rhine. However, the Congress system led to the creation of a much stronger Prussia than he anticipated. The newly Prussian Rhineland was in a good position to benefit from the industrial revolution whereas the old eastern lands of the Hohenzollern kings included much less productive agricultural land. The reforms by Stein and Hardenberg, including the adoption of a single currency for the whole state, meant that Prussia would grow stronger economically, especially after she created the single customs area, known as the Zollverein in 1834. Thus, it was, that Britain inadvertently created a future opponent in Germany whilst attempting to limit French ambitions. However, it also took further developments in Prussia itself before she became powerful enough to challenge Britain. Prussia's economic growth had continued but in 1848 it faced a constitutional crisis as the revolutionary tide spread across Europe. Initially the Prussian monarchy seemed to accept liberal reform but having weathered the storm, it sought to reassert its unfettered authority.

Externally, Prussia's first attempt to assert leadership in Germany failed. Prussia was forced to recognise continued Austrian leadership of the German Confederation under the Punctuation of Olmutz in 1851. A subsequent attempt by the Prussian monarchy to build up the armed forces met with liberal opposition to new taxes. The liberals wanted to see Prussia develop along the English model. In 1863, Bismarck, whom King Wilhelm I of Prussia had reluctantly appointed Chancellor in September 1862, declared that there was a "Gap Crisis". The "gap" he referred to was in the interpretation of the Prussian Constitution of 1848. Conservatives, like Bismarck, argued that taxes to cover military expenditure could be collected without parliamentary consent. He then proceeded to collect the taxes and create new regiments whose flags were consecrated in the KaiserKirke at Potsdam. Creating new regiments gave General Von Moltke, head of the Prussian General Staff the tools he needed. Bismarck dealt with the political and diplomatic situation whilst Moltke provided military skill. Working together they succeeded in fighting three wars which unified Germany under Prussian leadership.

The Danes were defeated in 1864, with the assistance of Austria, and then Austria was defeated in 1866 to place Prussia at the head of the North German Confederation. This represented a victory for the *kleinedeutsch* view of German nationalism which excluded Austria and its non-German empire. Despite British monarchical links to Hanover, Britain had accepted Prussian aggrandisement and had not intervened. The war came as Britain was experiencing political instability during the debates over further parliamentary reform. In addition, Queen Victoria was strongly pro-Prussian and anti-Danish. Queen Victoria's daughter, Victoria, was married to the heir to the Prussian throne.

In 1870, Bismarck engineered a war with France. The constitution of the North German Confederation gave Prussia leadership over the Confederation and allied states such as Bavaria, in time of war. As Moltke achieved victory in battle, Bismarck conducted the negotiations which led to the proclamation of the German Empire at Versailles in February 1871. The British government was now faced with a significant change in the balance of power in Europe but did not immediately feel threatened. Germany was a land-based power whilst Britain had a largely informal empire stretching across the globe and the largest navy in the world to protect the empire and the trade which it fostered. The first steps towards formalising the British empire took place after an assassination attempt on the German Emperor. This had raised the possibility of Queen Victoria's daughter, Victoria, becoming an Empress and outranking her mother at royal gatherings. Therefore, Queen Victoria raised the issue of being made an Empress with the minister in attendance. When the request was repeated the government acted and subsequently passed the Royal Titles Act in 1876 making Queen Victoria Empress of India.[1]

Bismarck's foreign policy was designed to prevent France being able to launch a war of revenge to recover Alsace-Lorraine which Germany had gained under the Treaty of Frankfurt in 1871. Therefore, he followed a policy of isolating France through uniting the Eastern powers and causing distrust between Britain and France. The creation of the Drei Kaiser Bund meant that Germany was allied with both Russia and Austria-Hungary and could therefore reduce the likelihood of conflict between them. Especially aware of Austro-Russian rivalry in the Balkans, Bismarck declared that the Balkans were not worth a Pomeranian Grenadier's life. In 1871, he had reassured Britain through its ambassador in Berlin that "Germany's geographical position did not necessitate her development into a first-class maritime power".[2] In 1884, at the Berlin Conference on West Africa, Bismarck created the concept of "effective occupation". This concept required colonial powers to actually occupy territory rather than operate less defined "spheres of influence". This meant that British and French colonial rivalry would intensify. The effectiveness of this policy, from a German perspective, was evident in 1898 when Britain mobilised her fleet in a stand-off with France over control of the headwaters of the Nile. However, in 1888,

---

1   I regard it as an enormous honour to have trained under Professor John Vincent who edited the Stanley Diaries from which these details are drawn.
2   Hamerow, T, (ed.) *The Age of Bismarck*, quoted in Williamson D., *Bismarck and Germany 1862-1890* (Harlow: Longman, 1986) p.119.

the liberal Kaiser Frederick died from throat cancer after a brief reign of a few months. Kaiser Wilhelm II ascended the Imperial German throne and by 1890 he had parted with Bismarck. Bismarck's fall coincided with the lapsing of the "Re-insurance Treaty" with Russia. The pressure for this split partly lay in the influence of the socially exalted, but increasingly cash-strapped Junkers who struggled to compete with Russian horse breeders. Needing to raise money to fund industrialisation, Russia was not permitted to use the German money markets and so turned to the Bourse in Paris. Archetypal republican France and the ultimate autocrat in Russia decided to work together, so France was no longer isolated. Britain was apparently content in her "Splendid Isolation", however, events in Germany began to change this view of European affairs.

In 1897, Wilhelm II decided to make several new ministerial appointments and these changes all pointed to the opposite approach to Bismarck's regarding relations with Great Britain. The new foreign minister, Bulow, articulated the idea of Germany having a *weltpolitik* (world policy) which posed a threat to Britain. This threat was made explicit by the appointment of Admiral Tirpitz as head of the Imperial Navy Cabinet. Tirpitz and the Kaiser had read Admiral Mahon's book on the importance of sea power and began to build up the German navy starting with a new naval law in 1898. This and subsequent naval laws were effectively appropriation bills authorising expenditure on new vessels. As each law was presented to the Reichstag they were closely scrutinised by foreign powers.

British Admiral Jackie Fisher decided it would be more important to deal with the threat from Germany and so he began to re-orientate naval policy towards co-operation with France. This agreement would pave the way for war in 1914. Fisher concentrated his new dreadnoughts in the North Sea and France covered the Mediterranean. The Anglo-Japanese alliance of 1902 enabled Fisher to reduce naval commitments in the Far East. Therefore, even before the famous dreadnought naval race began there was growing tension between Germany and Britain.

This growing rivalry with Germany provides a key context for the forging of the Entente Cordiale between Britain and France in 1904. The alignment moved closer with the authorisation in 1905, by the Foreign Secretary Lord Lansdowne, of talks between the naval staffs of the two countries. The "alliance" was reinforced by the first Moroccan Crisis which led to the Conference at Algeciras in 1906. France was desperate to maintain her commercial preponderance in Morocco despite growing pressure from Germany. Britain did not want Germany gaining a naval base in the Western Mediterranean to offset Gibraltar. The Conference left Germany isolated with only Austrian support. However, such discussions were restricted to the naval staffs whilst the military talks took place through an intermediary. However, in early 1906 the military talks were put on a direct basis. By then, Lord Grey, the Liberal Foreign Secretary, had replaced Lansdowne when the Conservative government resigned in December 1905. Grey was a "liberal imperialist", on the wing of his party that supported the Empire. Grey had a clear view of Germany as a threat. Grey recorded in a letter to Sir Francis Bertie who was the British Ambassador to France from 1905 to 1918: "I told M. Cambon to-day [sic] that I had communicated to the Prime Minister my account of his conversation with me on the 10th instant. ..., with regard to the communications between the French Military Attache and the War Office, I understood from him that these had taken place through an intermediary. I had therefore taken the opportunity of speaking to Mr Haldane... and he had authorized me to say that these communications might proceed between the French Military Attache and General Grierson direct;".³

These military conversations were supplemented by long conversations between Wilson and Foch during their tenures as commandants of their respective staff colleges. Wilson was a great admirer of the French and spoke the language fluently.

Bourne's view that Wilson was not a significant factor in the decision to go to war is based upon Wilson's role during the Curragh Mutiny.⁴ However, Fanning's *Fatal Path* argues that Asquith was never really committed to imposing Home Rule on all 32 counties of Ireland.⁵ Therefore Wilson need not necessarily have been persona non-grata with Asquith. Asquith chaired the meeting where Wilson presented his case regarding despatching a British expeditionary force to the continent in the event of war. Therefore, the deployment of a British expeditionary force so was adopted with Asquith's assent. The meeting took place, on 23 August 1911, against the background of the Second Moroccan Crisis. Three years later, the BEF, including 1st Division, engaged the Germans at Mons. As Wilson recorded, in 1911, Asquith was accompanied by his cabinet colleagues, Lloyd George, Haldane, McKenna, Churchill and Grey. The invasion of Belgium was not the key to the decision taken in 1911 and merely a convenient fig leaf in 1914.

The key issue for the BEF in 1914 was that the British realignment had been fully reflected in naval planning but not in the army's. Despite the plan being to despatch a BEF based on Aldershot command; the units there were not maintained at full strength. The emphasis remained upon keeping the battalions in India at full strength and those in Ireland at a higher level than those in India. It has become the norm for the British politicians to be blamed for committing the country to war. However, this failing has been used to sidestep the army's failure to re-prioritise the available manpower.

When Great Britain was faced with the possibility of war in 1914, it only had one fully prepared plan; to send the British Expeditionary Force to Belgium to fight with France against Germany. Therefore, that is what the Cabinet decided to do, as Wilson and Grey had intended. Grey had acted to localise the war to the Balkans in 1912-1913. Grey also told Cambon that Britain had no commitment to France because the crisis involved Russia about whose alliance with France he had not been informed.⁶ This was legally true, but the Franco-Russian Alliance had been signed in 1892-93 (the formal signature by Russia was delayed) and had inspired the creation of the Schlieffen Plan.

Grey's offer to remain neutral if Germany did not attack in the West shows that he was fully cognisant of the basic German war plan as otherwise a German attack on France would not have been relevant to a crisis in the East. Britain remaining neutral would have left France to her fate. Equally it would have meant abandoning Britain's traditional policy of maintaining the balance of power in Europe.

In 1866, Britain had stood aside and allowed Austria to be defeated and thus lost Hanover. In 1870, Britain had stood aside once more, and Germany had emerged as an even stronger

---

3   Viscount Grey of Fallondon, *Twenty-Five Years 1892-1916* (London: Hodder & Stoughton, 1925) vol. 1, p.76
4   John Bourne, *Who's Who in World War One* (London: Routledge, 2001) p.306
5   Ronan Fanning, *The Fatal Path, British Government and Irish Revolution 1910-1922* (London: Faber & Faber, 2013), passim.
6   Searle G.R., *A New England?* (Oxford: OUP, 2004) p.521

challenge to Britain. That was under the leadership of Gladstone who believed in a "moral foreign policy". By 1914, the Liberal Imperialists so outweighed the Gladstonian Liberals, in the Cabinet, that only Burns and Morley, resigned from the Cabinet. Using the German invasion of Belgium, to assuage the consciences of others, Asquith and Grey led the Liberal Party and the empire into a war from which neither the empire nor the Liberal Party would ever fully recover.

Appendix II

Who ordered the counter-attack that restored the British position at Gheluvelt, 31 October 1914?

According to John Giles,[1] with whom Sheffield and Bourne concur, the order for the attack by the Worcesters was given by Brigadier-General Fitzclarence VC.[2] However, in his addenda to "How the Worcesters Saved the Day", Major EWS Balfour DSO, quotes the diary of 2nd Division to argue that Colonel Pereria was responsible for sending the Worcesters to aid 1st Division.[3] The ambiguity may have arisen from an entry in the 2nd Division diary. The diary provides the details of the mortally wounding of General Lomax:

> A staff officer 2nd Division had an interview with GOC 1st Brigade and Colonel Pereria whose troops were in touch with 1st Brigade when it was reported that the position held by the 1st Brigade N of Gheluvelt was secure. The 2nd Worcesters had been sent by Colonel Pereria to assist the right of 1st Brigade and supported by the fire of 41st Bgd RFA succeeded in driving the enemy from the northern outskirts of the village of Gheluvelt by 3 p.m.[4]

This would strongly suggest that the attack was the offspring of several fathers. Such a conclusion is supported by a correspondence found in the 1st Division headquarters file dated 4 June 1922. The letter's author states he is unable to confirm who gave specific orders and that Fitzclarence may have asked for the Scots to be assisted if required.[5] This statement made in 1922 seems very strange, however, as there exists in 1st Division's records, a statement by Lieutenant–Colonel Hankey, dated 15 August 1915.

Hankey confirmed that he was in command of 2nd Worcesters on 31 October 1914, and that he was summoned to see Fitzclarence. He states that Fitzclarence gave him the explicit order to attack, including indicating the line to take. For good measure, Hankey added that he believed Fitzclarence had saved the day. Given Haig's and Fitzclarence's connections to Court

---

1 John Giles, *The Ypres Salient, Flanders Then and Now* (London: Leo Cooper, 1970), p.17. I had the privilege of making a tour of the Ypres salient with John as guide in 1981.
2 Sheffield and Bourne, *Douglas Haig*, p.76
3 TNA WO 95/1251: War Diary of the 2nd Battalion Worcestershire Regiment, October 1914.
4 TNA WO 95/1283: War Diary of the 2nd Division, Headquarters, 31 October 1914.
5 TNA WO 95/1261: War Diary of the 1st Division, Headquarters, October 1914.

circles, Haig may have initially accepted the idea of Fitzclarence's role uncritically. However, it seems that a considerable effort was gone to subsequently. Hankey's statement was signed as a true copy by Major General PEF Hobbs, DA & QMG of 1st Army, which was under Haig's command.[6]

The day before, Hobbs took a statement from Brigadier-General Corkran on the same subject. Corkran had been Brigade-Major of 1st (Guards) Brigade on 31 October 1914. His account confirms that Fitzclarence gave the orders to Hankey. His testimony does, however, differ in two respects. The first is that he remembers, which Hankey had not, that the officer Fitzclarence assigned to guide Hankey was Captain Thorne. The second difference is that Corkran said that Fitzclarence had thrown in his own last reserves and had gone back to report to 1st Division. Corkran then says that on returning to his brigade, Fitzclarence found the 2nd Worcesters had been sent up. Therefore, the question arises about the identity of the officer who had sent the Worcesters to the key position at this vital moment in the battle. However, Corkran reinforces the idea of Fitzclarence's decisive intervention by saying that initially Hankey said he was in reserve to 2nd Division and could only spare a company. This part of Corkran's narrative is borne out by Captain Thorne. Thorne says that earlier in the morning, one company of the Worcesters, who were in reserve to 2nd Division, had been borrowed and done effective work. According to Corkran, Fitzclarence showed Hankey that this was the decisive moment and persuaded him to use his whole battalion.[7]

When it comes to the critical situation arising from the problems on the flank of the Scots Guards; Fitzclarence is seen to act decisively. He sent Thorne to persuade the reluctant Hankey to commit his whole battalion to the counterattack. The difficulty arising from studying the three accounts is that Hankey says he was given direct orders by Fitzclarence, whereas Thorne is the messenger in his own account but Hankey himself cannot remember Thorne.[8] Taken at face value, all three accounts assign the key role to Fitzclarence, so the decision in 1922 to say there is no clear evidence available could only arise from three causes.

The first reason could be ignorance of the files, but the three documents, created in 1915, had been filed with the A&QMG records for October 1914 so they have been "hidden in plain sight". The second explanation might be that the two accounts by staff officers suggest Hankey was reluctant initially, which might upset Hankey and cause him to alter his view from that stated in his 1915 interview. A third, and perhaps more compelling answer, is that Lomax had been arranging the attack, since his discussions with Colonel Whigham at 11 a.m. Hence the significance of Lieutenant Colonel Pereira's role as intermediary. However, it suited Edmonds to give the dramatic credit to Fitzclarence VC, in favour of whom Haig had assembled the evidence, in 1915. Therefore, Edmonds follows Corkran's detail, but omits Hankey's hesitancy, whilst leaving enough evidence in the narrative to show that Lomax had masterminded the move. In the tradition of Wolfe and Moore, Lomax was to fall on the field which had witnessed his skills as a general. It was his finest hour.

---

6 TNA WO 95/1235: War Diary of the 1st Division, A&QMG, 14 August 1915.
7 TNA WO 95/1235: War Diary of the 1st Division, A&QMG, 18 August 1915
8 TNA WO 95/1235: War Diary of the 1st Division, A&QMG, 14 August 1915.

Appendix III

BEF Divisional Command – 1st Division as a Snapshot

The mortal wounds suffered by Major-General Lomax necessitated the first change amongst senior commanders in the 1st Division. He was initially replaced on a temporary basis by Brigadier-General Landon. From December 1914 onwards, four more men came to command the division through to the Armistice. Taking their rank on appointment, they were Major-Generals Henderson, Haking, Holland and Strickland.

Landon and Henderson came from mercantile families, whilst Haking was the son of a clergymen. Only Holland came from a military background, his father being Major-General Butcher. Only Landon was educated at one of the "Great Public Schools" covered by the Clarendon Commission; in his case, Harrow. However, Strickland attended Warwick School. In keeping with the times, only Henderson had experience of higher education. He had studied engineering at Glasgow University. However, Henderson did not graduate before moving to Sandhurst. Holland was commissioned into the Royal Artillery after completing his training at Woolwich. Henderson and Haking were both graduates of the Staff College at Camberley. Haking was subsequently appointed to the teaching staff there.

Of the six, Lomax had the least pre-war combat experience; only seeing action as a subaltern in the conflicts with the Zulus in 1877-78. Landon and Strickland both served as junior officers at the Battle of Omdurman. Henderson gained experience as a company officer on the Nile Expedition. Haking had taken part in operations in Burma. With the exceptions being Strickland and Lomax, the majority gained experience in South Africa during the Boer War. Landon led his battalion, the 2nd Royal Warwickshires, for eight months. Haking and Henderson both fulfilled staff appointments in the conflict with the Boers. In terms of regimental background, the two artillerymen and Henderson were anomalies. The career infantry officers were drawn from the Scottish Rifles, Norfolks, the Royal Warwickshires and the Hampshires. All good regiments but not socially elite. Ironically, Henderson was originally commissioned into the more illustrious Argyle and Sutherland Highlanders.

The reasons for departure were very varied. Lomax was mortally wounded and was the only one to become a casualty whilst commanding 1st Division. Landon returned to England after a meeting with Haig. Landon told Haig that 1st Division was a spent force in need of rest and reorganisation. Haig seems to have decided that was a more accurate description of Landon. Landon subsequently returned to divisional command. However, his appointment to command

9th Scottish Division was terminated by Haig on the grounds of continuing problems due to Landon suffering from lumbago. Subsequent divisional commands were of less prestigious units.

Henderson's appointment and rapid recall seems to reflect Kitchener's nickname; K is for chaos. There was no obvious reason to appoint Henderson as an infantry commander. Holland was a career artillery officer so his appointment to command an infantry division does not really fit. His appointment seems to reinforce the view that by late 1915, if not earlier, command of 1st Division was not a plum appointment.

By contrast, the appointment of Haking was far more appropriate. Haking had shown considerable enterprise in leading 5 Brigade at the Aisne. He was wounded in the head on 14 September and returned home to convalesce. He was part of Haig's circle so he would have been both an appropriate and welcome appointment as GOC 1st Division.[1] There are very significant debates regarding Haking's subsequent career. Therefore, Haking's subsequent appointment to command XI Corps may owe more to his closeness to Haig. Certainly, his retention of Corps command until the Armistice probably owed a lot to his support of Haig against Sir John French in the controversy over Loos.

Haig's subsequent attempts to have Haking made an army commander would support this view. Nonetheless, his appointment to command 1st Division should not be judged according to later events. Like Haking, Holland subsequently progressed to be a Corps Commander.

Strickland, too, was promoted to command 1st Division after holding more junior commands. Strickland began the war commanding the 1st Battalion of the Manchester Regiment. He was subsequently promoted to command the Jullundur Brigade in the Indian Division.

---

1   Senior, M., *Haking, a Dutiful Soldier* (Barnsley: Pen & Sword, 2012), p.36.

Appendix IV

Availability of Artillery Ammunition During First Ypres

As is clear from much of the relevant literature, Great Britain was not prepared for the military commitments it had made. One of the issues was the availability of artillery ammunition. Although this issue would assume enormous prominence in 1915, it was manifesting itself in 1914.

The simple reality was that peacetime production levels were based on preferred manufacturers. With Lord Kitchener as Minister for War, the focus was placed on recruiting the men for the mass armies he envisaged commanding. Neither the bureaucrats in the War Office nor the leaders of the highly skilled engineering workers were yet ready to embrace the changes needed to supply a massed army in the field. How did these issues manifest themselves in reality?

The shortage of ammunition faced by the British artillery during First Ypres, is discussed by Beckett.[1] Hutton also asserts that on 30 October, the field artillery of 1st Division was restricted to nine rounds per gun.[2] As 1st Division was central to operations at Ypres, it provides an opportunity to assess these views.

From 25 October to 2 November the divisional ammunition column was based at Dickebusch, thereafter it moved to Poperinghe. Each day, its task was to take ammunition up to the artillery brigades, as well as to the infantry.[3] The Divisional Ammunition Column (DAC) fed the Brigade Ammunition Column (BAC), who were responsible for taking shells up to the gun batteries in their brigade.

Alongside the daily casualty returns, the artillery records refer to "ammunition" which therefore, in context, appears to be expenditure, and reflects stated activity levels. These figures[4] are shown in the table below and averaged out by the official complement of 76 guns for the division. In reality the number of guns in action would have been less on any given day, for example two guns were captured on 2 November. Therefore, these figures understate the number of rounds available to those guns that were in action.

---

1 Beckett, *Ypres*, pp.88-89.
2 Hutton, *The Gunners of August 1914*, p.203.
3 TNA WO 95/1251: War Diary of the 1st Divisional Ammunition column, 2 November 1914.
4 TNA WO 95/1239: War Diary of the 1st Division, Royal Artillery, October-November 1914.

Oct 26th – 287 Avr 3.77	Oct 27th – 1178 Avr 15.5	Oct 28th – 2150 Avr 28.3	Oct 29th – 4227 Avr 55.6	Oct 30th – 1342 Avr 17.6	Oct 31st – 4136 Avr 54.4
Nov 1st – 2913 Avr 38.3	Nov 2nd –3071 Avr 40.4	Nov 3rd – 890 Avr 11.7	Nov 4th – 1090 Avr 14.3	Nov 5th – 620 Avr 8.1	Nov 6th – 1950 Avr 25.6
Nov 7th – 2240 Avr 29.5	Nov 8th – 3800 Avr 50.0	Nov 9th – 898 Avr 11.8	Nov 10th – Not recorded	Nov 11th –2417 Avr 31.8	Nov 12th – 930 Avr 12.2
Nov 13th – 1171 Avr 15.4	Nov 14th – 2096 Avr 27.6	Nov 15th – 1940 Avr 25.5	Nov 16th – 1032 Avr 13.6	Nov 17th – Not recorded	Nov 18th – 1302 Avr 17.1

These figures challenge the assertions made by Beckett and Hutton, especially as they are based on all 76 guns being in action. On the days of fiercest engagement at the end of October, the guns were being replenished with at least 50 rounds each. This was not ideal as doubtless batteries would have preferred a continuous unlimited supply. However, given the limitations of supply and wartime conditions of service, the situation was not as bad as has been suggested.

Inevitably, there were hiatuses. On 19 November, the DAC reported that there was no lyddite available at the ammunition park.[5] On 26 October, the XXXIX Brigade ammunition column supplied its guns with 387 rounds for the 18 pdrs. On the following day, this dropped to 52 rounds, linked to a need to move their base. The following day there was no movement, but the total supplied only reached 298; but on 29 October they delivered 1244 rounds. On 30 October this fell again to 211. Despite moving under orders from a staff officer, on 31 October, they were able to supply the guns with 1766 rounds for the 18 pdrs. However, this left them empty by 4 p.m.; but they were able to indent for 1090 rounds and refill completely by 8 p.m., from the Divisional Ammunition Column.[6]

XXVI Brigade Ammunition Column did not record its deliveries in such detail. Nevertheless, after the bitter fighting of 29 October, XXVI Brigade RFA recorded receiving a divisional order to economise on ammunition on 30 October. Nevertheless, it recorded that both 116 and 117 batteries, fired steadily that morning at their designated targets. Their targets were German artillery positions. They also recorded that 118 battery could not be manned because of very heavy German artillery fire on their position, which led to eleven men being wounded.[7] So it was the level of enemy fire rather than shortage of ammunition that kept 118 Battery out of the fray.

On 27 October, the howitzers of XXXXIII Brigade RFA expended 72 shrapnel and 48 lyddite shells at the German batteries they were targeting. The following day this rose to 189 and 103 respectively. The German attack on 29 October led to a sharp increase in the ammunition expended, 294 shrapnel and 162 lyddite. The quieter 30 October saw the firing drop to 73 and 96 respectively. On 31 October, the batteries were forced to move due to the German success, and so the expenditure, of 272 and 181 respectively, rose but not to the levels seen on 29 October.[8]

5 TNA WO 95/1239: War Diary of the 1st Division, Royal Artillery, 19 November 1914.
6 TNA WO 95/1250: War Diary of the XXXIX Brigade RFA, October-November 1914.
7 TNA WO 95/1250: War Diary of the XXVI Brigade RFA, 30 October 1914.
8 TNA WO 95/1250: War Diary of the XXXIII Brigade RFA, 27 -31 October 1914.

A "shortage" of ammunition provided a ready stick for the military to beat "the frocks" with, to borrow a term from General Wilson. Later developments only demonstrated how unready Britain was for the reality of war in 1914. Therefore, it was easy to overstate the situation. However, the British Army was never as short of ammunition as Hutton states. Ironically, both the generals and their bete noire, Lloyd-George shared an interest here. For the generals, ammunition shortages helped explain the casualties suffered by the BEF and therefore to hide command shortcomings from French downwards. For Lloyd-George, it only served to emphasise the extent of the miracle his wizardry would bring about when he was Minister for Munitions. Haig and Lloyd-George would both advance their careers at the expense of those who appeared to let things drift in the conditions of 1914-15.

Select Bibliography

Primary Sources
Churchill College Cambridge, General Sir Henry Rawlinson journal.
The National Archives of the United Kingdom (TNA WO 95) War Diary series. Sub-classifications vary. See footnote citation nomenclature for particulars:
1st Cavalry Division
4th Royal Irish Dragoon Guards
3rd Hussars
1st Infantry Division
2nd Infantry Division
3rd Infantry Division
7th Infantry Division
21st Infantry Division
1st Infantry Division CRA
1st Infantry Division, RE
1st Infantry Division, A&QMG
1st Division Signals
1st Infantry Brigade
2nd Infantry Brigade
3rd Infantry Brigade
XXV Brigade RFA
XXVI Brigade RFA
XXXIX Brigade RFA
XLIII Brigade Royal Field Artillery
1st Battalion Coldstream Guards
1st Battalion Scots Guards
1st Battalion Cameron Highlanders
1st Battalion Black Watch
2nd Battalion of the Royal Munster Fusiliers
1st Queens Royal West Surrey
2nd Battalion of the Welsh Regiment
1st Battalion Gloucestershire Regiment
1st Battalion South Wales Borderers
1st Battalion Loyal North Lancashire Regiment
2nd Battalion King's Royal Rifle Corps
1st Battalion Northamptonshire Regiment

2nd Battalion Royal Sussex Regiment
2nd Machine Gun Company
1st Infantry Brigade Trench Mortar Battery
3rd Trench Mortar Battery
2nd Battalion Worcestershire Regiment
1st Battalion of King's Royal Rifle Corps
1st Battalion Royal Berkshire Regiment
1st Battalion of the Royal Scots Fusiliers
9th Battalion King's Liverpool Regiment
8th Battalion Royal Berkshire Regiment
10th Battalion Gloucestershire Regiment
46th Battery, RFA
54th Battery, RFA
113th battery, RFA
1st Division Ammunition column
XXXIX Brigade Ammunition Column
2nd Brigade Trench Mortar Battery

Published Sources

Bacon, Admiral Sir Reginald, *The Dover Patrol 1915-1918, Vol. I* (London: Hutchison & Company, 1919).
Becke, A.F., *Order of Battle of Divisions – Part 1* (Uckfield: Naval & Military Press, 2007).
Beckett, Ian, *Ypres: The First Battle 1914* (Harlow: Longman, 2004).
Bourne, John M., *Who's Who in World War One* (London: Routledge, 2001).
Brackenbury, H., *The River Column* (Uckfield: Naval & Military, 2005).
Bucholz, Arden, *Moltke, Schlieffen and Prussian War Planning* (Oxford: Berg, 1991).
Carnock, Lord, *The History of the 15th (the King's). Hussars 1914-1922* (London: Naval & Military Press reprint of 1932 edition).
Clayton, Derek, *Decisive Victory: The Battle of the Sambre, 4 November 1918* (Warwick: Helion, 2018).
Craster, Michael, *Fifteen Rounds a Minute* (Barnsley: Pen & Sword, 1976).
Cooksey, Jon and Murland, Jerry, *The Retreat from Mons 1914: South: The Western Front by car, by bike and on foot* (Barnsley: Pen & Sword, 2014).
Davies, F. & Maddocks, G., *Bloody Red Tabs: General Officer Casualties of the Great War 1914-1918* (London: Leo Cooper, 1995).
Drumm, Alan, *Kerry and the Royal Munster Fusiliers* (Dublin: The History Press, 2010).
Dunn, J.C., *The War the Infantry Knew 1914-1919* (London: Sphere, 1987).
Edmonds, Brigadier General Sir James (ed.), *Military Operations in France and Belgium 1914, 1915, 1916, 1917, 1918* (London: Macmillan/HMSO, 1922-48).
Emden, Richard Van, *1918: The Decisive Year in the Soldiers' Own Words and Photographs* (Barnsley: Pen & Sword, 2018).
Eyre, Giles, *Somme Harvest: Memories of the P.B.I. in the Summer of 1916* (Uckfield: Naval & Military Press, 2009).
French, Field Marshal Sir John, *The Graphic Special No. 1: Sir John French's Despatches* (London: The Graphic, 1914).

Giles, John, *The Ypres Salient: Flanders Then and Now* (London: Leo Cooper, 1970).
Greenhalgh, E., *Foch in Command* (Cambridge: Cambridge University Press, 2011).
Hammerson, Michael (ed.)., *No Easy Hopes or Lies: The WWI Letters of Arthur Preston White* (London: London Stamp Exchange, 1991).
Herwig, Holger, *The Marne 1914* (New York: Random House, 2009).
Hodgkinson, Peter, *British Infantry Battalion Commanders in the First World War* (Farnham: Ashgate, 2014.).
Hutton, John, *The Gunners of August 1914: Baptism of Fire* (Barnsley: Pen & Sword, 2014).
Jacobs, Kristof, *Nieuwpoort Sector 1917: The Battle of the Dunes* (London: Unicorn, 2018).
Jervis, H.S., *The 2nd Munsters in France* (London: Naval & Military Press, orig. 1922).
Joffre, *Memoires Du Marechal Joffre* (Paris: Librarie Plon, 1932).
Jones, Spencer (ed.)., *Stemming the Tide; Officers and Leadership in the British Expeditionary Force 1914* (Solihull: Helion, 2013).
Kipling, Rudyard, *The Irish Guards in the Great War, Vol. 1* (Staplehurst: Spellmount, 1997).
Lloyd, Nick, *Passchendaele: A New History* (London: Penguin, 2017).
McCarthy, Chris, *The Somme: The Day by Day Account* (London: Cassell, 1993).
Macdonald, Lyn, *1914* (London: Penguin, 1987).
Peaple, Simon, *Mud, Blood and Determination* (Solihull: Helion, 2015).,
Petre, F. Loraine, et al, *The Scots Guards in the Great War 1914-1918* (Uckfield: Naval & Military Press reprint, John Murray, 1925).
Prior, Robin & Wilson, Trevor, *Command on the Western Front* (Oxford: Blackwell, 1992).
---------- *Passchendaele: The Untold Story* (New York: Yale University Press, 2016).
Senior, Michael, *Haking: A Dutiful Soldier* (Barnsley: Pen & Sword, 2012).
Sheffield, Gary, *Douglas Haig: From the Somme to Victory* (London: Aurum, 2016).
Sheffield, Gary & Bourne, John, *Douglas Haig: War Diaries and Letters 1914-1918* (London: Weidenfeld & Nicholson, 2005).
Simkins, Peter, *Kitchener's Army: The Raising of the New Armies, 1914-16* (Manchester: Manchester University Press, 1988).
Terraine, John, *The Road to Passchendaele: A Study in Inevitability* (London: Leo Cooper, 1977).
Wylly, H.C., *The Loyal North Lancashire Regiment 1914-1919* (Uckfield: Naval & Military Press, 2007).

Index

People

Abadie, Lieutenant Colonel R.N., 227–28

Beckwith-Smith, Second Lieutenant M., 67–68
Bulfin, Brigadier-General E.S., 45–46, 48–51, 56, 58–59, 61, 64–66, 75–77, 81, 86, 88, 91–92, 94, 99, 102, 105

Cavan, Brigadier-General Lord, 92, 105, 117, 119, 125, 127–28, 130, 135
Charrier, Major P.A., 23, 26, 28–29
Cunliffe-Owen, Acting Brigadier/Lieutenant-Colonel C., 122-24, 126

Davies, Brigadier-General H.R., 166, 176, 179, 188, 193

Fanshawe, Brigadier-General E.A, 144–45

Fitzclarence VC, Brigadier-General C., 63, 68, 74, 76, 81, 84–87, 89, 99, 103, 109–11, 122–26, 125–27

Gough, General Sir H., 10, 34, 39–40, 56–57, 108, 126, 222, 233

Haig, Field Marshal Sir D., 10, 29, 34, 36, 46, 56–57, 66–67, 79, 99, 102, 104–5, 139–40, 150–51, 153–55, 157–60, 177, 222, 229–30, 233, 311–13
Haking, Major-General R.C.B., 56, 131, 134–39, 142, 144–46, 148–52, 157–58, 163, 167, 170, 312–13, 319
Holland, Major-General A.E.A., 5, 157–58, 160–70, 172–73, 175–76, 259, 312–13
Horne, Brigadier-General H., 19, 46

Joffre, Marshal J., 32, 69–70, 140, 177–79, 186, 319

Kay, Brigadier-General Sir W.A.I., 278, 285
Kelly, Brigadier-General G.C., 269, 272, 299
Kitchener, Field Marshal Lord H.H., 20, 31–32, 140

Landon, Major-General H.S., 37, 44-45, 55, 58, 61-62, 66, 77, 79, 87-88, 93, 100, 104
Lewin, Brigadier-General E., 256, 258, 267, 280, 295
Lloyd-George, David, 10, 300, 316
Lomax, Major-General S.H., 20–21, 23, 39, 41, 49, 56, 61, 64, 66, 76, 79–80, 83–88, 99–100
Lovett, Acting-Brigadier/Lieutenant Colonel A.C., 114, 116
Lowther, Brigadier-General H.C., 134–35, 148

Maxse, Brigadier-General I., 21, 25, 48, 61, 63
Morland, Major-General T.L.N., 96–98

Rawlinson, General Sir H., 10, 126, 177, 179, 191, 222, 229-31, 263-64, 279, 288

Strickland, Major-General E.P., 185–86, 199–200, 202, 207–8, 213, 228–29, 235–36, 238–39, 241, 244, 256, 261, 263–64, 268, 270, 274–78, 287–88, 293–97, 299–302

Thuillier, Brigadier-General H.F., 172, 178-79. 184

Wheatley, Brigadier-General L.L., 280, 299

Places

Aisne, 3, 31, 33–39, 41–45, 56, 66, 113, 131, 261, 313
Albert, 190, 192, 197, 211, 213
Arras, 213, 220, 250, 261, 264
Aubers Ridge, 3, 6, 140–53, 155, 165, 167, 184, 188, 285

Barlin, 250–51, 254
Bazentin, 191, 197, 212–13
Bergues, 23–26, 29–30
Berthaucourt, 271–72, 274

Cambrin, 243, 251
Caulaincourt, 266–67
Cerney, 46, 48, 51–52, 58
Chateau Wood, 124–27
Chemin des Dames, 3, 6, 42–43, 45–47, 49, 51, 53–55, 58, 60, 132
Chivy, 60–61
Cornouillers Wood, 274–75, 277

Double Crassier, 3, 184–87, 189

Etreux, 3, 6, 19–31

Faucille Trench, 282
Fesmy, 21, 23, 25–27, 289, 292
Flers Support Line, 208
Formi Trench, 270
Fresnoy, 268, 274–75

Gallichet Trench, 272, 274
Gheluvelt, 3–4, 6, 80, 83–103, 105, 107, 310–11
Givenchy, 5, 133–34, 151, 243–44, 246

High Wood, 200, 202–7, 210–12
Hindenburg Line, 4, 11, 154, 194, 218, 266–67, 274, 279–81, 283, 300
Hooge, 79, 84, 99–100, 106, 112–14, 116, 118, 121, 124, 126, 128
Hulluch, 5, 155, 163–64, 166, 170, 172

Koekuit, 71–74, 78

La Bassée Canal, 3, 133, 135, 137, 139, 243–44
Langemarck, 71–74, 76, 78
Lizerne, 75–76
Loos, 3, 6, 11, 153, 156–69, 173, 185, 313

Mametz Wood, 190–91, 211
Menin Road, 79–81, 85–88, 92–94, 98, 100, 106–7, 109, 111, 114, 117, 119, 124
Mézières, 289, 291–92
Morval, 4, 6, 200–209
Munster Alley, 6, 195–98, 202
Munster Trench, 197–98

Oisy, 20–21, 26, 287

Paissy, 44–45, 49, 51, 53–54, 59
Passchendaele, 4–6, 10, 220, 222–24, 226–28, 233–37, 239, 252, 319
Plantin, 136, 246–47
Plessis, 33–34
Poelcappelle, 71–72
Poezelhoek, 80, 86–87
Polygon Wood, 80–81, 87, 92, 102, 111, 122–26
Poperinghe, 70–71, 77, 314
Pozières, 4, 190–99
Prue Trench, 208–9

Quarries, 166–67

Rhine, 8, 11, 263, 294–96, 299, 302, 305

Sambre, 6, 10–11, 285–86, 288, 318
Somme, 10–11, 183–84, 186, 188–89, 193, 196–98, 203–4, 208, 214, 217–18, 222, 279
Switch Line, 197, 202

Triangle, the, 188–89
Troyon, 45, 48, 52, 57

Veldhoek, 80, 84, 91–92, 98, 102, 105, 109, 111, 117, 122
Vendresse, 45–46, 51–53, 57, 63
Verbeek Farm, 120–22, 125, 127
Villemay Trench, 271–72
Villers-Brettoneux, 264–65
Vocation Farm, 235, 237, 239

Windy Corner, 138, 143, 246

Ypres, 11, 52, 63, 66, 69, 79–80, 83, 85, 96, 98, 102, 120–22, 231
Yser, 70–71, 223–24, 227–29, 278

Zandvoorde, 81, 87, 91
Zillebeke, 79–80

Formations & Units
Armies
British Expeditionary Force (BEF), 4, 7, 15, 16, 18, 20, 28, 32, 42, 43, 46, 65, 66, 70, 76, 90, 103, 104, 131, 140, 145, 155, 170, 176, 177, 179, 213, 230, 231, 233, 235, 240, 242, 253, 258, 259, 261, 279, 285, 298, 299
First Army, 136, 137, 153–55, 157, 172, 176, 177, 183, 189, 229, 243, 244, 248, 250
Second Army, 51, 154, 219, 223, 235, 295
Third Army, 185, 229
Fourth Army, 177, 184, 188, 191, 205, 208, 218, 219, 222, 229, 231, 264, 265, 267, 278, 279, 285, 289, 295
Army of Occupation, 298, 303

Corps
I Corps, 15, 19, 21, 29, 31, 37, 42, 43, 44, 46, 62, 63, 64, 66, 69, 70, 71, 72, 77, 78, 94, 99, 100, 102, 112, 114, 118, 120, 121, 122, 123, 124, 125, 128, 129, 130, 131, 133, 134, 135, 136, 137, 138, 140, 145, 148, 149, 150, 151, 152, 154, 155, 158, 159, 167, 177, 184, 186, 243, 244, 248, 250, 253, 258, 260, 261
II Corps, 15, 20, 31, 42, 189, 235, 238, 241, 303
III Corps, 189, 190, 191, 193, 205, 210, 213, 214, 216, 218
IV Corps, 73, 149, 153, 154, 158, 160, 163, 164, 171-72, 175, 177
VII Corps, 157
IX Corps, 264, 265, 279, 285, 289, 294-95, 298, 302
X Corps, 198, 199, 219, 223, 303
XI Corps, 157, 164, 264, 313
XIII Corps, 191, 288
XIV Corps, 205, 223
XV Corps, 191, 205, 217, 222-24
XVIII Corps, 233, 235
XIX Corps, 240, 295
XXII Corps, 263
Indian Corps, 136-37, 146, 148, 152, 203
I Anzac Corps, 213
Canadian Corps, 261-63

Divisions
Guards Division, 117, 170.
1st Cavalry Division, 46, 49, 58, 184.
3rd Cavalry Division, 124, 160, 164.
1st Division, 11-13, 16, 19-21, 24, 29-31, 33, 37, 40, 42, 44-46, 50, 54-58, 61-66, 70-72, 75, 79-80, 83, 88, 91-96, 99, 102-11, 113-15, 117-37, 139-40, 144-45, 148-154, 156, 158-64, 166-67, 169-79, 184, 189-91, 193, 196-200, 202-3, 205, 207-12, 214, 216-17, 219-20, 223-24, 230-33, 235-36, 238-44, 247-250, 252-54, 256-57, 259, 261-70, 278-80, 285, 287-9, 292-4, 296-8, 302-3, 308, 310-12
2nd Division, 19-23, 31, 33, 35, 41-42, 45-46, 49-50, 55, 57, 61-63, 66, 71, 80-81, 83, 99, 102, 115, 123, 125, 127, 130, 134, 136, 148-149, 151, 300, 310-11
3rd Division, 122, 128-9, 243-44
4th Division, 42, 263
6th Division, 60, 154, 265-66, 268, 274, 279, 285, 287-88, 300, 303
7th Division, 80, 83, 87-88, 91, 93-94, 99, 102, 105, 110, 112, 158, 160, 166-67.
8th Division, 189, 213
9th (Scottish) Division, 210
11th (Northern) Division, 243, 250, 252, 257, 263
12th (Eastern) Division, 171, 189.
15th (Scottish) Division, 155-56, 158, 161, 163-65, 170, 173, 176, 183-84, 202-3, 207
16th (Irish) Division, 17, 169, 184-85, 241, 260
18th (Eastern) Division, 30, 240-41
19th (Western) Division, 197
21st Division, 17, 61, 160, 167, 190-91
23rd Division, 190, 198
24th Division, 160, 163, 167, 169.
25th Division, 61
30th Division, 106, 214
32nd Division, 222-23, 225-26, 239-41, 265, 268, 280, 289, 303
33rd Division, 213, 243
34th Division, 196, 200.
35th (Bantam) Division, 241
36th (Ulster) Division, 17, 243
40th (Bantam) Division, 213
41st Division, 219
46th (North Midland) Division, 11, 154, 194, 245, 248, 270, 274, 276, 278-82, 285, 287, 292, 300
47th (London) Division, 145, 152-154, 156, 173-4, 183, 208-10, 219
48th (South Midland) Division, 216-18
50th (Northumbrian) Division, 209, 211-12
55th (West Lancashire) Division, 243-45, 248-50, 252, 257
56th (London) Division, 263-64
63rd (Royal Naval) Division, 235
66th Division, 225, 230, 294
1st Australian Division, 197, 213
4th Australian Division. 265, 268.
1st Canadian Division, 235
4th Canadian Division, 262
Lahore Division, 133
Meerut Division, 133, 146
New Zealand Division, 208

Brigades
1st Cavalry Brigade, 43
2nd Cavalry Brigade, 48
3rd Cavalry Brigade, 91
6th Cavalry Brigade, 81, 114
7th Cavalry Brigade, 114-15, 124
16th Cavalry Brigade, 113
1 Brigade, 17, 20-21, 23-4, 29, 31-35, 44-46, 49, 51-52, 55, 57, 59, 63-67, 70-71, 73-78, 80, 83-84, 87. 89, 91, 94, 99, 100, 102-3, 105, 107, 110, 116-18, 121-22, 124-26, 131, 133-36, 138, 145, 148-50, 152, 155, 157, 160-7, 170-76, 183, 186, 190-91, 197-98, 200, 202-3, 205, 208, 211-12, 215, 217-18, 223-25, 231, 233, 241, 243-44, 247, 252, 256-57, 260-67, 271-72,

277-81, 287, 289-91, 294, 297, 299, 302, 310-11
2 Brigade, 16, 17, 21, 24, 26, 31, 36, 42-46, 48, 51, 54, 57-8, 60-61, 64-66, 70-1, 75-7, 81, 84, 86, 91-2, 94, 99-100, 105, 112-14, 116-19, 121, 123, 130, 133-6, 142-145, 148-51, 155, 159, 161, 163-68, 170, 172, 173, 175-76, 178-9, 183-84, 188, 190, 196-8, 202-3, 205, 207-9, 211-12, 214-16, 219, 223, 241, 243, 251-53, 257, 261-80, 285, 287, 289-90, 292, 297-99, 301, 303
3 Brigade, 19, 21, 24, 35, 37, 39-40, 44, 49, 54-6, 58, 61-2, 64-65, 71-73, 75, 81, 83-84, 86-92, 96, 98, 102-4, 106, 109-12, 114-16, 118-20, 130, 133-36, 138, 142, 148-50, 152, 165-67, 169-173, 179, 183, 186, 189-91, 193, 196, 198, 205, 207, 212, 214-9, 225, 231, 233, 235, 241, 243-44, 251-53, 256-57, 259, 261-66, 274-83, 287, 289-90, 297, 300-1
4 Brigade, 33, 57, 80, 85-87, 92, 115, 118-19, 125, 127, 136, 256
5 Brigade, 56, 72, 83, 86, 92, 122, 125-26, 135, 313
6 Brigade, 49, 60-1, 76, 83, 128, 134
8 Brigade, 123, 135
9 Brigade, 18, 122-24, 128-29.
17 Brigade, 60
18 Brigade, 60
20 Brigade, 80, 84, 87-88, 92
22 Brigade, 86, 92, 94, 115-16
25 Brigade, 138
29 Brigade, 63
39 Brigade, 138
46 Brigade, 176, 205
47 Brigade, 260
53 Brigade, 241
62 Brigade, 190
96 Brigade, 223, 265
98 Brigade, 202
110 Brigade, 191
137 Brigade, 227, 284
138 Brigade, 270
139 Brigade, 274
140 Brigade, 172
164 Brigade, 243-44.
165 Brigade, 243-44
166 Brigade, 243, 248
168 Brigade, 263
169 Brigade, 264
176 Brigade, 257
12th Australian Brigade, 269
Ferozpore, 133
Jullunder, 313
Sirhind, 133

Regiments/Battalions
9th Bhopal Rifles, 133
1st Black Watch, 16-18, 23-24, 27-28, 31, 33-35, 51-3, 59, 64, 68, 73-76, 81-82, 84-85, 87-89, 91, 94, 97, 107, 111, 113, 117-20, 122-27, 129, 135, 149-50, 155, 163-64, 166-68, 171, 173, 175-8, 197, 202-3, 205-6, 208, 224, 231, 241, 244-48, 254-56, 263-64, 272-74, 276, 281, 283, 287, 290-92, 294, 297, 301-2
8th Black Watch, 303
9th Black Watch, 207
1st Cameron Highlanders, 31-32, 34, 51-53, 59, 61, 64, 73-76, 81, 94, 113, 120-23, 125, 127, 129, 133, 135, 149-50, 163, 168, 172-74, 176, 178, 198, 202, 205-7, 211, 215, 224, 231, 239, 241, 243, 246-47, 262, 264, 266, 271-73, 281, 287, 289-90, 292, 297, 301-3
1st Coldstream Guards, 18, 19, 23-24, 27-28, 30, 32-33, 35-36, 44, 46, 48, 51-53, 59, 64, 66-68, 70, 74, 77-8, 80-82, 84-85, 87-89, 94, 106-8, 112-13, 117, 128, 135, 143, 155
2nd Coldstream Guards, 113, 136
1st Dragoon Guards, 94
4th Dragoon Guards, 57
1st Gloucestershire Regiment, 40-41, 55, 58-59, 71-74, 76-78, 82-88, 90, 96-99, 103-4, 106, 109-113, 115-16, 121-27, 129-30, 166, 168, 176, 193, 196, 207, 214-15, 219, 223, 237-38, 243, 245-48, 250, 265-66, 277, 281-83, 287, 289-90, 297
10th Gloucestershire Regiment, 155, 163, 168, 173-4, 178, 186, 190, 198, 205, 207-8, 210, 224, 232, 240-41
2nd Gordon Highlanders, 91-92, 105
1st Grenadier Guards, 57, 124-25, 127
2nd Grenadier Guards, 105, 112, 119, 121, 125-26
4th Hussars, 26
10th Hussars, 112
15th Hussars, 18-20, 23, 25-26, 29, 31, 33, 75, 81, 123, 125, 136, 138
1st Irish Guards, 63, 114-15, 124-26, 129, 136
9th King's Liverpool Regiment, 16, 142, 144, 148, 151, 166, 169
1st King's Royal Rifle Corps, 105-8, 113, 142
2nd King's Royal Rifle Corps, 16-17, 43-4, 48-50, 57-59, 61, 76-77, 88, 92-93, 95-96, 106-119, 121, 127-28, 130, 134-35, 147, 164-5, 175, 188-89, 198, 207-9, 214-5, 218, 225-228, 230, 241, 248, 253, 257, 263, 268-69, 271-72, 277-8, 285, 287, 291-92, 297, 302
16th Lancashire Fusiliers, 265
9th Lancers, 48
1st Leicestershire Regiment, 303
8th Leicestershire Regiment, 191

1st Life Guards, 124, 126
London Scottish, 117-18, 134, 161, 169, 178
1st Loyal North Lancashire Regiment, 49, 65, 88-9, 91-3, 96, 106, 109, 111, 113-9, 122, 124-5, 128-9, 131, 144, 149, 152, 162, 164, 168, 173-74, 190-92, 202, 214-15, 228, 238, 240-41, 244-5, 247, 251, 262-64, 266, 268, 272-74, 281, 287, 289, 290-91, 297, 301-2
1st Northamptonshire Regiment, 48, 58-61, 65, 75-76, 92, 94, 105, 112-14, 116,118, 122-27, 129, 135, 140, 142-44, 146-47, 165, 168-69, 184, 192, 196, 200, 202-4, 207-8, 214-15, 218, 225, 230, 242, 246, 253, 257, 269-70, 272, 276, 287-8, 291-92, 296-97
1st Northumberland Fusiliers, 129
13th Northumberland Fusiliers, 190
1/5th Notts & Derby Regiment, 274
1/8th Notts & Derby Regiment, 274
2nd Oxfordshire & Buckinghamshire Light Infantry, 105, 112, 123, 125, 127
1st Queen's Royal West Surrey Regiment, 36, 44, 54, 57-59, 62, 64, 71-75, 77, 81, 83, 86-88, 91-93, 95-96, 100, 113, 115, 118, 131
2nd Queen's Royal West Surrey Regiment, 86-87, 95
1st Royal Berkshire Regiment, 102, 106-7, 111, 113-16
8th Royal Berkshire Regiment, 155, 163, 168, 173-74, 178, 186, 203, 206, 210, 215, 225, 232, 239, 241
2nd Royal Munster Fusiliers, 20-1, 23-29, 65-66, 68, 118-19, 125, 128, 131, 133, 138, 142, 146, 166, 169, 176, 184, 186-7, 193-4, 196-97, 204, 207, 211-12, 214, 236-37, 241
9th Royal Munster Fusiliers, 176
2nd Royal Sussex Regiment, 43, 48-50, 61, 65, 76, 91-92, 94-95, 105, 112-18, 122-29, 135, 138-39, 142-44, 146-47, 157, 159, 161, 165, 168, 173, 188-89, 198, 200, 204, 207-9, 214-15, 228, 253, 263, 268-9, 271-2, 274-77, 288-89, 291-92, 297-98
1/5th Royal Sussex Regiment, 138, 143-44, 147-50
4th Royal Welsh Fusiliers, 157
5th Royal Welsh Fusiliers, 142
1st Scots Guards, 33-35, 37, 41, 51, 57, 59, 61, 64, 68, 70, 73-77, 80, 84-88, 94, 97-98, 100, 117, 120-21, 133-34, 155
2nd Scots Guards, 87-88
1st South Staffordshire Regiment, 91-92
2nd South Staffordshire Regiment, 76
1st South Wales Borderers, 16-17, 35-37, 41, 44, 55-56, 60-62, 64, 72-73, 75, 83, 87-88, 94, 97, 103, 106, 112, 114, 118-19, 127, 129, 134, 142, 166-68, 176, 193-94, 196, 204, 207, 211, 214-15, 218-19, 236-38, 244-48, 257, 265-66, 282-83, 287, 290, 297-98
2nd South Wales Borderers, 135
1st Welsh Regiment, 97
2nd Welsh Regiment, 17, 21, 40-41, 54-56, 58, 60, 62, 64, 71-73, 76-78, 81, 84, 86-88, 94-95, 97-99, 102, 109-11, 113, 115, 118-9, 124, 128, 134-35, 142, 166-67, 169, 176, 185, 190-93, 198, 207, 211, 214-15, 245, 247-8, 252, 259, 283, 287-8, 290, 297
1/6th Welsh Regiment, 193, 223, 236, 294, 297, 302
2nd Worcestershire Regiment, 99, 102, 310-11